THE THEATERMANIA GUIDE TO MUSICAL THEATER RECORDINGS

Michael Portantiere

BACK STAGE BOOKS / NEW YORK

This book is dedicated to the memory of Fred Ebb.

Acquiring Editor, Mark Glubke
Project Editor, Robbie Capp
Interior Design, Leah Lococo
Graphic Production, Ellen Greene
Text set in Garamond 3

First published in 2004
by Back Stage Books, an imprint of
Watson-Guptill Publications,
a division of VNU Business Media, Inc.
770 Broadway, New York, NY 10003
www.wgpub.com

Library of Congress Control Number   2004111478
ISBN: 0-8230-8435-3

Printed in the United States of America

First printing, 2004

1 2 3 4 5 6 7 8 9 / 12 11 10 9 8 7 6 5 4

Contents

Foreword

Cast albums, thank God, are everlasting. The joy of being able to listen to the fifty-years' worth of musical theater recordings that I own is one of my greatest pleasures. These recordings are of utmost importance to me because there is really no film of the stage productions; only the cast albums will tell future generations what *Out of This World* was or what *Milk and Honey* was. I'm sure that Bock and Harnick and Kander and Ebb and Strouse and Adams would say the same thing: It's the recordings that outlast everything else. Most of us can't quote dialogue from *Finian's Rainbow,* but we can sing "How Are Things in Glocca Morra?" exactly as it was performed in 1947. I have memories of what the earliest shows that I saw looked like, but they are decades-old memories and they're pretty vague. What's crystal clear is the cast album of *A Tree Grows in Brooklyn.*

Movie musicals of Broadway shows usually miss the mark, but even when a film version of a stage musical is done well, it's still not the show. I think the film of *Chicago* is a masterpiece, but that's not the point: To get a sense of the original show, it's best to hear it performed by Gwen Verdon and Chita Rivera. I grew up listening to Gertrude Lawrence singing songs from *Nymph Errant* and *Lady in the Dark.* I don't know what those shows looked like because they were before my time, but my imagination goes wild when I hear the albums. And when you combine the actual recordings with good liner notes and photos, it's as close to seeing a show as you can possibly get without actually having been there.

When I was a boy, we lived in Jersey City, New Jersey, which is almost like living in Manhattan. Every Friday night, my parents took me to see a Broadway musical. If I saw a show that I loved, I would buy the album as soon as I had enough money scraped together, or I might receive it as a present for Christmas or a birthday. I remember wearing out *Call Me Mister—* now, that's going way back! I still have my collection and it's awesome. I love to listen to *Paint Your Wagon, Destry Rides Again, Bloomer Girl, Out of This World,* and other wonderful shows that I grew up with.

Just what makes a great cast album? Well, for one thing, I have never listened more than twice to any recording with a lot of dialogue, so that was something I insisted on for the albums of my shows. If a line or two was necessary, fine. On the *Mame* album, for example, Bea Arthur says, "It's about this lady astronomer . . ." to explain the odd song she's about to sing. But what I enjoy most is listening to a great overture and hearing a show unfold musically.

I was always there for the recording sessions of my cast albums, running around from the oboe player to the conductor to the performers. There's a lot of me in those recordings! What I would try to do with Don Pippin, my musical director, was to make the performance sound live—as if the singers were unaware of the microphones. Some cast albums sound severe and antiseptic, but I tried to make mine real. The "Hello, Dolly!" number is a perfect example. And, even today, listening to the orchestral section of the "Mame" number makes me picture Onna White's whirling dancers because it's played and conducted with such fervor.

I can't really pick favorites among the cast albums of my shows because each one accomplished what I wanted it to. I felt that the recording of *La Cage* should begin with an air of mystery because the whole purpose of the opening number was to slowly reveal the secret that we had onstage—so it starts quietly with "We are what we are," then it grows in excitement until it absolutely knocks my socks off. But on the *Mame* album, "It's Today" really bursts forward with Angela Lansbury's first entrance because it's just a big, celebratory number.

For me, one of the great joys of cast albums is that they've captured the performances of so many artists who are not with us anymore. That I can still hear Gertrude Lawrence and Mary Martin is a joy. Ethel Waters singing "Taking a Chance on Love" puts a smile on my face. Cast albums keep these great artists alive—and they also keep shows alive. *Mack & Mabel* and *Dear World* were not hits, but I think they contain some of my best work; without the cast albums, they would be forgotten. Because they were recorded, they at least have cult audiences who dote on every lyric and every note. From a historical viewpoint, the cast albums of shows that did not run very long are even more important than the hits.

I'm very happy that this book is being published, because I think we need to continually celebrate a great American art form. That's why I'm all in favor of revivals and why I love cast albums. Our musical theater creations should not be disposable—and it's the recordings that make them permanent.

Introduction: The Sound of Musicals

Michael Portantiere

While perusing the excellent *Metropolitan Opera Guide to Recorded Opera* some years ago, I found myself wondering: Why hasn't anyone done a book of this sort devoted to musical theater recordings? When I finally decided to undertake the editing of just such a volume, it became clear to me why a comprehensive guide to recordings of the great scores of Jerome Kern, Irving Berlin, the Gershwins, Rodgers with Hart, then with Hammerstein, Lerner and Loewe, Stephen Sondheim, Jerry Herman, and so many other luminaries hadn't already been published: Literally thousands of cast albums and soundtrack albums of shows exist, so this compilation has proven to be extremely challenging.

My initial concept of the book was to have it include reviews of every English-language recording of every musical ever written for the stage, film, or television. That idea lasted about ten minutes. Even though more than a dozen writers were eventually hired to contribute reviews (in addition to my own), it soon became clear that the scope of the project had to be limited in some way. At first, I thought we might focus on Broadway scores only—but that would have left out Off-Broadway gems from *The Fantasticks* to *Hedwig and the Angry Inch.* Then I thought we would eschew reviews of film-soundtrack recordings, but some of those are arguably better representations of certain scores than the original Broadway cast albums. Maybe we could have avoided non-American musicals? But, like it or not, such shows as *Cats, The Phantom of the Opera,* and *Les Misérables* dominated the art form during the 1980s and 1990s. So, what do to?

To keep the size of this book manageable, we opted with a few exceptions to skip recordings of scores that haven't been heard in professional New York productions. Among the excluded shows are those launched in London that have not yet been seen on Broadway and/or failed to yield a cast album on this side of the pond. We have tried to be comprehensive in our reviews of London cast recordings of American musicals, although many are out of print. The book admittedly is light on reviews of Australian cast recordings, often for lack of availability. Finally, we did not have space for foreign-language cast albums of American (or British or Australian) musicals, many of which are excellent; the only non-English language show reviewed in these pages is *Rugantino,* an Italian musical that was performed in Italian on Broadway.

A few notes about terminology. Although many people consider the word "album" obsolete in this context, we've retained it as a valuable alternative to "record" and "recording." One dictionary definition of "album" is "a recording of different musical pieces," so please think of it in those terms. Also bear in mind that "album" originally referred to those bulky sets of 78-rpm records stored together in jackets under one binding. In that sense, a CD isn't any less an "album" than is a single-LP.

The book is organized alphabetically by show title, and any title starting with "A" or "The" is alphabetized under the second word in the title: For instance, you'll find *A Chorus Line* in the "C" group, *The Band Wagon* under "B." However, titles beginning with a foreign article (*La, Les, Das*) alphabetize under that letter (e.g., *La Cage aux Folles* is under "L."). Each review heading includes the date of the recording's release, followed (in parentheses) by the recording label(s). Where more than one recording of a score is reviewed, they are arranged in chronological order. Identifying the recording label is often tricky, what with releases, rereleases, and re-rereleases in various formats. To make things as simple as possible, we've tried to list the label on which each recording first appeared (in whatever format), followed by a slash, followed by the label of the most recent CD edition (where applicable). Then there is a star rating:

★ ★ ★ ★ ★ Superlative; outstanding
★ ★ ★ ★ Highly recommended
★ ★ ★ Recommended
★ ★ Recommended with reservations
★ Recommended with major reservations
Not recommended

Our reviews cover the scores themselves as well as their various recordings. Of course, opinions vary widely from one writer to another. For example, many readers will be surprised to note that the Claude-Michel Schönberg-Alain Boublil musical *Miss Saigon,* a long-running hit in London, on Broadway, and on tour, receives an extremely negative review from me, while the same team's far less successful *Martin Guerre* is rated highly by David Barbour. Such differences point up a fact that can never be overstated: When it comes to musical theater, as with anything else in life, what's "great" and what's "awful" comes down to a matter of personal opinion. (I've even met a few people who don't like *South Pacific*!) To make the point further, we asked a number of theater notables to name their ten favorite stage musicals of all time. Two dozen such lists are scattered through these pages and they show just how diverse such choices can be.

About 95.5 percent of our reviews were written expressly for this project; the rest are revisions of earlier reviews posted on TheaterMania.com. The contributors worked largely from their own personal collections of recordings, with a good deal of lending and borrowing among them. Copies of discs that weren't in any of our collections were generously provided by Decca Broadway (thanks to Brian Drutman) and JAY (thanks to John Yap). I'd also like to acknowledge the staffs of Footlight Records and the Rodgers and Hammerstein Archives of Recorded Sound at the New York Public Library for the Performing Arts at Lincoln Center for research assistance. The online database www.castalbumdb.com has proven to be an invaluable reference resource. Finally, a special thank you to my TheaterMania colleague Matthew Murray, who went above and beyond the call of duty as assistant editor of this volume.

For decades, people have been saying that the musical theater is moribund. The deathwatch has been especially grim over the past twenty-five years or so, but things have improved with the advent of such great shows as *Ragtime, Hairspray* and *The Last Five Years.* Those scores have an honored place in this book alongside the classics—*Show Boat, Oklahoma!, My Fair Lady, Fiddler on the Roof, Company,* and so on. We hope you will find *The TheaterMania Guide to Musical Theater Recordings* an important reference and that you will forgive us for any omissions—which we will attempt to rectify in future editions.

ABOUT THE CONTRIBUTING WRITERS

Gerard Alessandrini has written and directed every edition of *Forbidden Broadway* and *Forbidden Hollywood* in cities around the world. The recipient of an OBIE Award, an Outer Critics Circle Award, a Lucille Lortel Award, and four Drama Desk Awards, Alessandrini was honored in 1998 with the Drama League Award for Lifetime Achievement in Musical Theater.

David Barbour, a past president of the Drama Desk, is the editor-in-chief of *Lighting&Sound America,* a monthly publication covering technology for live performance. He was previously editor of *Entertainment Design* and *Lighting Dimensions* magazines, and was managing editor of *TheaterWeek.* He has contributed articles on theater to *Stagebill, InTheater,* and *Playbill.*

Richard Barrios, writer, musician, and historian, is the author of *Screened Out: Playing Gay in Hollywood From Edison to Stonewall* and the award-winning *A Song in the Dark: The Birth of the Musical Film.* He has lectured on film history and has written articles for *The New York Times* and other publications. His television credits include narration and onscreen commentary for the TMC production *Busby Berkeley: Going Through the Roof.*

Ken Bloom is the author of *American Song, Hollywood Song; Tin Pan Alley; Broadway: An Encyclopedia; Jerry Herman: The Lyrics;* and *Broadway Musicals: The 101 Greatest Shows.* On radio, he has worked with *All Things Considered* and *Morning Edition.* His theater credits include many years with New Playwrights Theatre of Washington.

Seth Christenfeld, a member of the BMI Lehman Engel Musical Theater Workshop, has worked as a production assistant (read: unpaid gofer) on such shows as *Avenue Q* and *Harmony.* Among his current projects is the rock musical *Blue Flame,* which he is slowly writing with Christie Baugher. Seth is also a freelance script consultant and theatrical archivist.

Jeffrey Dunn has directed musicals in the United States and abroad, including a three-year European tour of *West Side Story.* As an instructor of musical theater performance and history, he has worked at Marymount Manhattan College, Syracuse University, New York University, Weist-Barron, and, currently, at the American Musical and Dramatic Academy.

Peter Filichia is a theater critic for the *Newark Star-Ledger,* TV News 12 New Jersey, and a regular columnist for TheaterMania.com. The author of *Let's Put on a Musical!* Filichia wrote/emceed the Drama Desk Awards for four years, serving as its president and chairman of the nominating committee during that period. He has also been a member of the nominating committee for the Lucille Lortel Awards and is host of the Theatre World Awards.

David Finkle is a journalist covering theater, music, dance, movies, and books. A regular contributor to TheaterMania.com, *Back Stage, The Trenton Times,* and the *Philadelphia Inquirer,* he has also contributed articles to *The New York Times, The New Yorker, Newsday, Publishers Weekly, Mirabella,* and other publications. He has taught journalism at Fordham University and has written/performed with the award-winning cabaret trio Weeden, Finkle and Fay.

Marc Miller, deputy copy chief at *BusinessWeek,* has written for TheaterMania.com, *InTheater, Stages, Stagebill,* and other publications, and contributed a chapter on movie musicals to the book *Film Genre 2000.* Notes for musical theater CDs are also among his credits. He is also a lyricist whose songs have been performed at the American Music Theatre Festival in Philadelphia, and other venues. Miller is a member of the Drama Desk, Outer Critics Circle, and ASCAP.

Matthew Murray graduated from Western Washington University with a major in play-writing and participated in regional theater before moving to New York in 2000. Now an associate editor at TheaterMania.com, his writings on the New York theater scene also appear on broadwaystars.com, where he is a regular contributor, and on talkinbroadway.com. A member of the Drama Desk, Murray also serves on the nominating board for the Theatre World Awards.

Brooke Pierce is a former associate editor of TheaterMania.com. As a freelance writer, she has contributed reviews to *Show Business Weekly, New England Entertainment Digest,* and *Washington Square News.* Staged readings of her plays have been held at Louisville's Stage One Theater and other venues. A member of the Dramatists Guild and the Drama Desk, Pierce has been a judge at the New York International Fringe Festival for the past three years.

Michael Portantiere is the editor-in-chief of TheaterMania.com. He previously served as managing editor of *InTheater* magazine and regional editor for *Back Stage.* He has contributed freelance articles to *Playbill* and *Stagebill* and has written notes for recordings of *Little Me, The Most Happy Fella,* and the New York Philharmonic's *Sweeney Todd* with George Hearn and Patti LuPone. He holds a master's degree in theater education from New York University.

Robert Sandla was the editor-in-chief of *Stagebill* for many years; prior to that, he was co-founding editor of *TheaterWeek.* He has also been a contributing editor at *Dance Magazine, Opera News,* and *Lighting Dimensions;* has written for *Interview, InTheater, BBC Music Magazine,* and *Playbill;* and has provided notes for many musical theater recordings. He has worked with the New York State Council on the Arts, the New York Philharmonic, and the Drama Desk.

Morgan Sills, a graduate of Wake Forest University with majors in theater and English, is a writer, actor, and singer. Nominated for a MAC award for *The Roger Edens Songbook,* Sills wrote and performed that show in New York and around the country; he has also written for TheaterMania.com. As a performer, Sills toured nationally in *Forever Plaid* and has appeared in regional stagings of *A Tree Grows in Brooklyn, Flora the Red Menace,* and *Wish You Were Here.*

David Wolf won an Emmy Award for one of his *Unicorn Tales* scripts, a series of musicals for children that aired on NBC-TV. He has also written theater criticism and taught musical theater history. Highlights of his early career included working for Harold Prince as stage manager of *Fiddler on the Roof* (in the last years of its run) and *A Little Night Music.* Wolf holds a master's degree in musical theater from New York University.

Charles Wright, a reviewer of books for TheaterMania.com, has written program notes for the York Theatre Company's biannual series of "Musicals in Mufti." As an executive at A&E, Wright has been involved in the commissioning/production of numerous documentaries, including *The Farm: Angola, USA,* which received the 1998 Grand Jury Prize at Sundance and an Academy Award nomination for Best Documentary Feature.

THE ACT
Original Broadway Cast, 1978 (DRG) ★★

The last word in star vehicles, *The Act* centers on Liza Minnelli as "Hollywood's own Michelle Craig," performing in Las Vegas. Between the numbers are scenes (by George Furth) from her troubled life. With Liza basically playing herself, singing nonbook tunes tailored for her by John Kander and Fred Ebb, this is essentially an album of special material designed to capitalize on her celebrity as the free-loving, club-hopping "It" Girl of the 1970s. The numbers take in a high-camp, sardonic New York tribute ("City Lights"), an enraged torch song ("The Money Tree"), losers in a Midwestern bar ("Bobo's"), the joys of sex with hustlers ("Arthur in the Afternoon"), and the corrosive effects of a permissive society ("Hot Enough for You?"). The oh-so-'70s lyrics include references to TM, EST, waterbeds—and, of course, there's a ballad titled "My Own Space." (Then there's "Turning," a funked-up version of a Shaker hymn; those always go over big on the Strip!) Throughout, Ralph Burns' arrangements have a propulsive energy. Minnelli's mannerisms are vividly on display; the disc features some of the most unrestrained belting ever heard in a Broadway show. You'll either love it or run screaming from the room, but its pleasures aren't really those of a cast album.   —DAVID BARBOUR

AFTER THE FAIR
Original Off-Broadway Cast, 1999
(Varèse Sarabande) ★★

It's the very model of a modern chamber musical: a four-character, four-musician adaptation of a Thomas Hardy short story, here brought to life by Matthew Ward (music) and Stephen Cole (book and lyrics) in a faithful, loving recording produced by Bruce Kimmel. The slight plot—about a bored, unhappy, provincial couple (Michele Pawk and David Staller) and the wife's Cyranoesque adventures in helping her maid (Jennifer Piech) conduct a romance with a London barrister (James Ludwig)—comes through clearly and affectingly. Cole's lyrical craftsmanship is striking ("With each passing missive, you grew more passive") and Ward's music, aside from some dreary recitative, isn't afraid of tunefulness or smart melodic development when the occasion demands. Diligent as the authors are, though, the score's a bit studied: It sounds like a Sondheim disciple's thesis for a graduate degree in musical theater. And the unvarying parade of duets,

ALL-TIME FAVORITES
OF COMPOSER-LYRICIST

Jerry Herman

1. A Tree Grows in Brooklyn
2. Carousel
3. Gypsy
4. She Loves Me
5. Cabaret
6. Kiss Me, Kate
7. Show Boat
8. The King and I
9. Guys and Dolls
10. My Fair Lady

quartets, and genteel accompaniment adds up to a rather limited musical palette. (Maybe it worked better onstage.) The cast is variable: Pawk is excellent, Ludwig is sturdy, but you could drive a lorry through Staller's hammy, reedy vibrato. And Piech's cartoon-Brit accent simply won't do; who was her dialect coach, Dick Van Dyke?   —MARC MILLER

AIDA
Studio Cast, 1999 (PolyGram) ★★

Before the Broadway launch of *Aida,* composer Elton John recorded this studio set with a host of pop stars, including Sting, Tina Turner, Janet Jackson, Shania Twain, and James Taylor. The songs are out of their show order and no synopsis is included; yet, perversely, this is a more entertaining disc than the Broadway cast album. That's because, swathed in elaborate pop arrangements, the songs are advantageously displayed as the middle-of-the-road standards that they really are. The stars are well showcased—The Spice Girls, for example, lend some genuine oomph to "My Strongest Suit." Elton John himself partners effectively with Heather Headley and Sherie René Scott in the trio "A Step Too Far," and Headley solos on "Elaborate Lives." John and Lulu also perform "The Messenger," which is not to be found on the Broadway album. The set concludes with a bombastic "Orchestral Finale," produced by Phil Ramone, that sounds like the perfect background music for an Olympic ice-skating competition.

Original Broadway Cast, 2000 (Buena Vista) ★

The show's a smash hit, so somebody must love it. On disc, however, shorn of spectacle and the leads' good looks, *Aida* comes across as an extremely morose collection of Elton John power ballads. Amazingly, it took three writers—Linda Woolverton, Robert Falls (who also directed), and David Henry Hwang—to come up with the libretto, adapted from the classic opera. In their version, it's a teen triangle with vague political overtones: Adam Pascal is Radames, captain of the Egyptian army, engaged to the air-headed clotheshorse Princess Amneris (Sherie René Scott). After subduing the nation of Nubia, Radames brings back the Princess Aida (Heather Headley), with whom he promptly falls in love. The three of them proceed to scream their heads off for two acts—lamenting cruel fate, etc., etc. There are a couple of catchy pop hooks in "The Gods Love Nubia" and "Written in the Stars," but Tim Rice's bone-headed lyrics drag everything down, as in the clunky "Elaborate Lives." All three leads provide vocal thrills in abundance, especially Headley, whose intensely dramatic singing made her an instant star. Pascal does solid work throughout and Scott manages to keep her dignity even while performing the bizarre "My Strongest Suit," in which Amneris exposes her extreme dedication to fashion. Still, this is one of the dullest entries in the pop-opera genre.   —DAVID BARBOUR

AIN'T MISBEHAVIN'
Original Broadway Cast, 1978 (RCA, 2CDs) ★★★

Manhattan Theatre Club presented *Ain't Misbehavin'* to rave reviews before its hugely successful transfer to Broadway. What this show had that other composer songbook revues lacked was personality, theatricality, and a cast of unknowns that rocked the theater: Nell Carter, Armelia McQueen, Ken Page, André De Shields, and Charlaine Woodard. These were not the pretty, white-bread, very bland sort of performers featured in revues that make one think of cruise ships and amusement parks. Under Richard Maltby, Jr.'s adroit direction and unsung hero Murray Horowitz's concept, this show featured (gasp) fat performers, skinny performers, and not-especially-good-looking performers—but boy, could they sing, act, and sock Fats

Waller's songs into the rafters! With arranger extraordinaire Luther Henderson traversing the stage on a rolling piano, *Ain't Misbehavin'* was the first—and last—of the great Broadway songwriter revues. — KEN BLOOM

AIN'T SUPPOSED TO DIE A NATURAL DEATH
Original Broadway Cast, 1971 (A&R, 2LPs/no CD) ★★

Onstage, this piece by Melvin Van Peebles was intensely theatrical; I was actually frightened when cast member Minnie Gentry looked straight at me and vowed to "Put a Curse on You." On record, it's a less powerful experience—an interesting assemblage of jazz-based songs, dramatic monologues, and narratives. Much of it is written in what might be called a "street poetry" style, if that phrase is not too pretentious. *Ain't Supposed to Die a Natural Death* is skillfully constructed; the songs and the very attractive underscoring enhance the monologues as they move into, out of, and around them. I can't say that this is a record I listen to every day but, if you can find a copy, it certainly won't bore you. — DAVID WOLF

ALADDIN
Original Television Cast, 1958 (Columbia/Sony) ★★★

The later-in-life work of most great musical theater writers isn't up to the quality of their more youthful forays; but with the exception of his score for the film *Les Girls,* Cole Porter ended his career at something close to his own high standard. *Aladdin* was an original television musical, a popular entertainment form at the time. Major teams such as Rodgers and Hammerstein, Bock and Harnick, and other great composers contributed to the genre, with mixed results. But Porter's *Aladdin,* with a libretto by S.J. Perelman, was among the best of the bunch, produced at the end of a wonderful era wherein most entertainment suitable for children was equally enjoyable for adults. Apart from its tuneful and witty score, it had a dream cast: stage veterans Dennis King and Cyril Ritchard; film favorites Una Merkel and Basil Rathbone; and newcomers Anna Maria Alberghetti and Sal Mineo. All of them brought their unique talents to the project. A highlight of the score is "Come to the Supermarket (in Old Peking)."

Original London Cast, 1960 (DRG) ★

Cole Porter's *Aladdin* was never adapted for presentation on Broadway, but the London stage production—tarted up as a Christmas pantomime—yielded this unfortunate recording. It includes a few songs interpolated from other Porter shows, none of which fit the spirit and tone of the original; they're too jazzy and out-of-period. Doretta Morrow has a wonderful voice but it's, shall we say, too mature for the character of the Princess (she does offer a first-class rendition of "I Am Loved," interpolated from *Out of This World*). Cyril Ritchard is sorely missed on this recording, as is the maturity and authority of Dennis King. Where the original TV production had great Robert Russell Bennett orchestrations, this one features more "mod" arrangements that haven't withstood the test of time. — KEN BLOOM

ALL AMERICAN
Original Broadway Cast, 1962 (Columbia/Sony) ★★★★

How many Joshua Logan flops can a person do in one year? Anita Gillette managed two in 1962, soubretting through *Mr. President* and this misbegotten provincial-college satire—with a book by Mel Brooks, no less. (That sure sounds like Brooks in the opening number, exclaiming "Look at him, the Lone Ranger!") Columbia gave both shows the deluxe treatment, but this

Charles Strouse-Lee Adams score is by far the more felicitous. Robert Ginzler's orchestrations are among the best Broadway has ever heard; listen to the brass well up halfway through "If I Were You" and try not to smile. Star Ray Bolger is a little short on vocal equipment—and, more surprisingly, on star quality—but his vis-à-vis, Eileen Herlie, is wonderful, particularly when helping him introduce "Once Upon a Time." Sturdy-voiced juvenile Ron Husmann gets an even better ballad, "I've Just Seen Her," and Gillette smolders through "Night Life." Some of the rest is by the numbers—the patriotic salute, the football rally fight song—but some quirkiness seeps through. Fritz Weaver, as a Madison Avenue sharpie, even gets a merciless send-up of "Climb Ev'ry Mountain." Pretty gutsy in 1962. — MARC MILLER

ALLEGRO
Original Broadway Cast, 1947 (RCA) ★★★

Of all the musicals that desperately need a new and complete recording, here is the most urgent case. All we have of Rodgers and Hammerstein's third collaboration is this repackaging of a five-disc set—which sounds impressive, until you realize that the discs were 78-rpms made shortly after the show's 1947 premiere. So there's less than thirty-four minutes' worth of music here, with six songs and two dances excluded entirely. Granted, we're not talking about a score that's up to the level achieved by the masters in their previous two shows, *Oklahoma!* and *Carousel.* Still, this is accomplished work, even if the recording sounds antique. The story takes Joseph Taylor, Jr. from birth to middle age, so we witness the lad's first steps ("One Foot, Other Foot") and early courtship (the now sexist-sounding "A Fellow Needs a Girl" and the pulsating "You Are Never Away"). "Money Isn't Everything" is a nifty waltz and "The Gentleman Is a Dope" a stirring complaint, each displaying Oscar Hammerstein in a rare cynical mood. Richard Rodgers' biggest missteps occur at the end of each act. First comes a wedding ceremony wherein the composer sets the famous vow "to have and to hold from this day forward" to a solemn melody instead of a joyous one that just might have become a standard at real-life nuptials. Similarly, at the end of the show, the music for "Come Home" (a command that Joe obeys) is so dreary that it seems to mark a defeat for the hero. Ironically, the title song of the musical defines the term "allegro" as "brisk, lively, merry, and bright"—but those two numbers certainly don't fit that description. — PETER FILICHIA

ALL IN LOVE
Original Off-Broadway Cast, 1961 (Mercury/no CD) ★★★★

This LP is reason enough to buy a turntable. The show is an all-but-forgotten Off-Broadway musical from an era when adapting classic plays to the small musical stage was in vogue; here, the source material was Richard Brinsley Sheridan's *The Rivals.* As was the case with many of these adaptations, the musical didn't outshine the original, but there are pleasures to be had in the score by composer Jacques Urbont and lyricist Bruce Geller. "Why Wives?" has a felicitous melody, as does "I Found Him," and David Atkinson sings three nice ballads. The then-unknown Dom De Luise has the score's poorest song ("Odds") but he's a good straight man in one of its best numbers ("Honour"). And while Geller didn't do a terribly good job with Mrs. Malaprop's "A More Than Ordinary Glorious Vocabulary," Urbont's music again compensates. The album features a larger orchestra than was heard in most Off-Broadway shows of the day (and, might we add, some Broadway shows of today), playing uncredited orchestrations by a just-starting-out Jonathan Tunick. Note the heavenly ride-out that he provided for the equally heavenly "What Can It Be?" You can hear that this guy was going places. — PETER FILICHIA

ALWAYS . . . PATSY CLINE
Original Nashville Cast, 1994 (Decca) ★★

She was talented and popular; she died suddenly and young; her recordings have sold steadily ever since. So it was only a matter of time until Patsy Cline's story inspired a stage musical. *Always . . .* takes a somewhat novel approach: Instead of offering a straight bio or a "This Is Elvis!"-style career overview, it is based on the true story of Cline's friendship with Louise, a working-class Texan who reminisces while a faux Patsy sings "Crazy," "Sweet Dreams," and many other songs. The through-a-fan's-eyes concept works well as written by Ted Swindley; the show enjoyed an Off-Broadway run, plus numerous regional productions. The cast recording was made live at the Ryman Auditorium, former home of the Grand Ole Opry. Mandy Barnett nails all of the star's inflections and tonal colorings with razor precision; her vocal resemblance to Cline is as eerie as it was no doubt intended to be. Of course, as is always the case in these clone/tribute shows, the untouchable charisma and talent of the evoked legend goes missing. Just listen to Barnett's perfectly adequate rendition of "Faded Love," then play Cline's far more wrenching original, and you'll see what I mean. (Beverly D'Angelo, who played Cline in the movie *Coal Miner's Daughter,* came closest to duplicating her sound and aura.) As Louise, who narrates and sings along with her idol on a couple of songs, Tere Myers is alternately engaging and annoying. The Opry audience is audibly pleased with the performance, and those who enjoyed the show will certainly be happy with this recording. Nevertheless, all of Cline's oeuvre is available on CD, so why would anyone accept even a creditable substitute? —RICHARD BARRIOS

AMBASSADOR
Original London Cast, 1971 (RCA/no CD) ★★

The original London cast album of this Henry James adaptation is also the de facto original Broadway cast album, since the West End production's two leads, Howard Keel and Danielle Darrieux, reprised their roles in New York not long after the show's quick demise in London, and they are assigned the bulk of the musical program. James' favorite theme, the clash of American ingenuousness and European worldliness, gets a thorough working-over in this story of New England milquetoast Lambert dispatched to Paris by a dominating widow to retrieve her philandering son; instead, Lambert falls under the spell of Paree and, more specifically, of a fascinating countess (Darrieux). The globetrotting narrative was simplified for the stage, which the score reflects. Don Gohman's melodies are attractive, if a bit derivative, and Hal Hackady's lyrics strive manfully to pull James' ideas together into a cohesive package. Some terrible comedy songs—e.g.,"What Can You Do With a Nude?"—were mercifully left behind in London but made it onto the LP. Andrea Marcovicci, who introduced the affecting "Love Finds the Lonely" in her Broadway debut, isn't heard here; her London counterpart, Isobel Stuart, is capable, but Marcovicci must have been heartbreaking. Keel is hardworking but miscast as a milquetoast. Darrieux has very little voice; she tries to compensate with charm and succeeds only halfway. The most vivid performance here comes from Margaret Courtenay as the horrifying harpy who sets the plot in motion; she's no singer, but it's a great character part and she has every vocal nuance firmly under her tight corset. Some fine theater songs are scattered about—"Tell Her," "The Right Time/"The Right Place"— yet they fail to convince us that a Henry James musical is a good idea. While one admires the team's ambition to write a soufflé that's also serious, the results sound more like *Gigi* with a hangover. —MARC MILLER

AMOUR
Original Broadway Cast, 2003 (Sh-K-Boom) ★★★★

The English version of Michel Legrand's French smash hit *Le passe-muraille,* based on Marcel Aymé's short story about a man who gains the ability to walk through walls, lasted all of seventeen performances on Broadway, but the cast recording proves that the length of a show's run is not necessarily a good indication of its quality. Legrand's songs—nearly thirty of them—linger in the ear and heart, revealing his gift for bouncy melody, his talent for setting soaring emotions to music, and his fine sense of humor. The lyrics, adapted by Jeremy Sams from Didier van Cauwelaert's French originals, are not quite the equal of the music but do have their share of clever rhymes and evocative imagery. All of this is put over by a top-notch cast led by Malcolm Gets and the incandescent Melissa Errico, with her shimmering soprano. The supporting performers—Lewis Cleale, John Cunningham, Christopher Fitzgerald, Norm Lewis, Sarah Litzsinger, Nora Mae Lyng, and Bill Nolte—are dynamic in voice and character, the epitome of a tight Broadway ensemble. Their work and that of musical director Todd Ellison, together with Legrand's modest yet ideal orchestrations, keep the energy level high and the atmosphere magical from beginning to end. Clocking in at about an hour and fifteen minutes, the recording omits some musical material but includes a bonus track of Legrand accompanying himself on one of the show's songs. Even on audio disc, *Amour* is an enchanting, romantic fairy tale for adults.
                                                                                    —MATTHEW MURRAY

A . . . MY NAME WILL ALWAYS BE ALICE
Great Barrington Cast, 1995 (Original Cast Records) ★★★

In the beginning, there was *A . . . My Name Is Alice,* a 1984 Off-Broadway revue that took a look at women's issues, rights, fears, and joys. Twenty-eight writers contributed material and, under the codirection of Joan Micklin Silver and Julianne Boyd, created a show that ran a year. Eight years later, under the same directors, twenty-six writers begat a semi-sequel that wasn't so successful. Alas, neither show yielded a cast album; so, in 1995, when Silver and Boyd staged *A . . . My Name Will Always Be Alice* regionally, they made sure that their cast recorded the twelve best songs from the first show and the five best from the second. The disc features material by David Zippel (*City of Angels, The Goodbye Girl*) and the team of David Crane and Marta Kauffman (TV's *Friends*), plus contributions by lesser-known writers. The highlight is Crane-Kauffman's "Welcome to Kindergarten, Mrs. Johnson" in which a self-assured mother (Barbara Walsh) is challenged by a teacher (Heather MacRae) with old-world views. There's also composer Glen Roven and lyricist June Siegel's haunting "At My Age," in which a widow and a teenager separately wait for their dates to arrive (sensitively performed by MacRae and Marguerite MacIntyre). And while "The French Song" by Don Tucker (nicely rendered by Walsh) doesn't have any inherent attachment to a feminist issue, it's a hilarious parody of Gallic songs that includes every cliché in the Berlitz book. Even if *Alice* doesn't rate an "A," it's an enjoyable disc.   —PETER FILICHIA

AND THE WORLD GOES 'ROUND
Original Off-Broadway Cast, 1991 (RCA) ★★★★

The songs of John Kander and Fred Ebb, never lacking in heart, entertainment value, or theatricality, were a natural for the revue showcase format. This is a sparkling recording of a show for which the creative team—director Scott Ellis, choreographer Susan Stroman, "conceiver" David Thompson, and musical director and arranger David Loud—mined nearly every possibility from the team's catalog. There are traditional renditions of familiar material ("My Coloring

Book"), radical new interpretations of standards (the theme from *New York, New York* is sung in multiple languages as an international tribute to The City That Doesn't Sleep), and interesting combinations of unrelated numbers ("I Don't Remember You," from *The Happy Time,* and "Sometimes a Day Goes By," from *Woman of the Year*). Only a few of the album's eighteen tracks fall flat, most notably an arrangement of the title song from *Cabaret,* which has some almost-scatted lyrics and a synthetic smoothness befitting a parody of a modern-day cabaret standard. It's no surprise that almost all of the powerhouse performers (Robert Cuccioli, Karen Mason, Brenda Pressley, Jim Walton, and Karen Ziemba) and the creative team went on to bigger things in bigger shows; the musical, dramatic, and comedic colors they find in this material help Kander and Ebb's songs seem as vibrant and relevant as ever.　　—MATTHEW MURRAY

ANKLES AWEIGH
Original Broadway Cast, 1955 (Decca) Not recommended.
This is a four-alarm disgrace—even worse than its title implies. A tip-off is the description of the Guy Bolton-Eddie Davis libretto and the Sammy Fain-Dan Shapiro score on the back cover: "Things happen so fast in *Ankles Aweigh*—plot, music, and lyrics are so rapidly paced and so tightly integrated—that a synopsis is difficult." So is the score: dull for the first four cuts, then turns really bad with "Headin' for the Bottom Blues" and "Here's to Dear Old Us." If you can make it past these losers, you'll groan through "La Festa," a terrible tarantella, followed by the pseudo-exciting casino number "Ready Cash." Then comes "Nothing Can Replace a Man," which insists that "Throughout the world of science, no one's found a new appliance that ever can replace a man." (Oh, really? Check out any "adult entertainment" store.) "Honeymoon" is possibly the first show tune to encourage premarital sex, but that's not to say that this musical was ahead of its time. It was *way* behind it.　　—PETER FILICHIA

ANNIE
Original Broadway Cast, 1977 (Columbia/Sony) ★★★
Ironically, Charles Strouse's biggest hit is one of his less interesting efforts. Thomas Meehan's book capably adapts the adventures of comic-strip icon Little Orphan Annie to the stage, focusing on how she got together with billionaire Daddy Warbucks. The music by Strouse and lyrics by Martin Charnin (who also directed) sometimes have a slightly by-the-numbers quality; still, it's a landmark show, boasting the preternatural belting of thirteen-year-old Andrea McArdle as Annie and the hilarious Dorothy Loudon as the vengeful, alcoholic orphanage keeper, Miss Hannigan. Loudon's rendition of "Little Girls" ("Some day I'll step on their freckles / Some night I'll straighten their curls!") is a classic. Reid Shelton and Sandy Faison are pleasant as Daddy Warbucks and his assistant, Grace, while Robert Fitch is amusingly sleazy as Rooster, Miss Hannigan's ex-con brother. The bouncy production number "NYC" features the late Laurie Beechman, whose astonishing belt made her a legend among Broadway insiders. Generally, the more sophisticated numbers are the best. They include "We'd Like to Thank You, Herbert Hoover," sung by a gang of sardonic Depression bums; "Easy Street," in which Miss Hannigan and cohorts scheme to defraud Daddy Warbucks; and "You're Never Fully Dressed Without a Smile," a charming parody sung by a radio crooner, then reprised by Annie's orphan friends. There are many uninspired items, too, especially "Something Was Missing," "You Won't Be an Orphan for Long," and "I Don't Need Anything but You," all of which suffer from plodding melodies and obvious lyrics. But Philip J. Lang's orchestrations give every number extra sparkle; if you can still listen to "Tomorrow" without wanting to blow your

brains out, McArdle's rendition is tops. The latest reissue features cuts from an early backers' audition with Charnin and Strouse performing seven numbers written for the show, of which only "Tomorrow" survived. The others are lame and, in one case, appalling; even Charnin admits in the CD booklet notes that they were on the wrong track.

Film Soundtrack, 1982 (Columbia/Sony) Not recommended.
For those of you who never miss a John Huston musical, this disaster is a must; everyone else should stay away. In the time-honored tradition of hack Hollywood adaptations, several numbers from the show score were dropped for the film (including "We'd Like to Thank You, Herbert Hoover"). Even the weakest item from the original is better than the mediocre new entries, which include "Sandy," a love song for Annie to her favorite dog, and "Let's Go to the Movies," a contrivance to get Annie, Daddy Warbucks, and Grace Farrell to Radio City Music Hall. Carol Burnett is an amusingly glum Miss Hannigan, but Albert Finney is a dull Daddy Warbucks. Tim Curry and Bernadette Peters are wasted as Rooster and Lily, and Ann Reinking is miscast as Grace. Although Aileen Quinn is perfectly fine in the title role, even hard-core Annie fans will be bemused by this lackluster disc.

London Studio Cast, 1998 (JAY) ★★
Since the original Broadway cast recording of *Annie* has never been out of print, a studio cast album hardly seems necessary. Still, this accomplished edition offers a slightly expanded version of the score, including reprises of "Little Girls" and "Easy Street." The cast includes Ruthie Henshall as an excellent Grace and Ron Raines as a stentorian Daddy Warbucks. Kim Criswell channels the spirit of Dorothy Loudon as Miss Hannigan and Sarah French is an acceptable Annie. Overall, the recording suffers from slow tempi and a lack of personality.

Television Film Soundtrack, 1999 (Sony) ★★★
"We'd Like to Thank You, Herbert Hoover" is once again missing in action, along with a couple of lesser numbers, but what's left is beautifully served by an all-star cast in this Disney television adaptation. Alicia Morton is the best Annie since Andrea McArdle and is well matched by Victor Garber's warmer-than-usual Daddy Warbucks. As Grace, Rooster, and Lily (respectively), Audra McDonald, Alan Cumming, and Kristin Chenoweth are almost laughably overqualified, and they all deliver commensurately. Kathy Bates is a blunt, funny Miss Hannigan with a surprisingly effective singing voice. As a bonus, Andrea McArdle appears in "NYC," taking Laurie Beechman's original role. In what may be a Hollywood first, Martin Erskine's ebullient orchestrations rival and, in some cases, surpass Philip J. Lang's Broadway originals. — D A V I D   B A R B O U R

ANNIE GET YOUR GUN
Original Broadway Cast, 1946 (Decca) ★★
When this album was made, cast recordings were still very much in a developmental stage. The classic Irving Berlin score is presented here as a collection of songs from the show with no attempt to recreate the theatrical experience. There is no overture and no "Colonel Buffalo Bill." Most unhappily, the great anthem "There's No Business Like Show Business" is not sung by the great Ethel Merman as Annie Oakley, with others, as it was onstage; instead, the song is given a bland choral rendition. On the plus side, Ray Middleton is a full-voiced Frank Butler. Unsatisfying as it is overall, the album served its purpose until better recordings of the score came along.

Original London Cast, 1947 (World Records/various CD labels) ★

This production made a star of Dolores Gray; as recorded here, her unique voice marks her as someone destined for greatness. Gray's interpretation of Annie Oakley is very different from Ethel Merman's, but it's wonderful to hear her sing Berlin's tuneful songs so smoothly—especially "I Got Lost in His Arms" and other ballads. As Frank Butler, Bill Johnson sounds equally terrific. Issued in four large 78-rpm platters, these recordings are very quaint-sounding, much more so than American cast albums of the same period. Although it's fun to hear Gray and Johnson, the selections are so brief and the sound quality so fuzzy that this set will only be of interest to historians.

Film Soundtrack, 1950 (MGM/Rhino-Turner) ★★★★

When MGM prepared to film *Annie Get Your Gun,* the studio pulled out all the stops. The soundtrack recording exemplifies the high standards set for the movie, which raised the bar for screen versions of stage musicals. Great care was taken in expanding the show's orchestrations and choral parts. Howard Keel was cast as Frank Butler; he had just come to Hollywood via the Broadway and London stages and was still fresh, theatrical, and gorgeous—with a big, bright, melodic baritone to boot. The really questionable aspect of this recording is the performance of Betty Hutton as Annie Oakley. Although she was a huge star in her day, beloved for her rowdy comic style, Hutton never had the vocal range of an Ethel Merman. Annie's great songs, particularly the ballads, are shortchanged here. But wait! Included as bonus tracks are the songs as sung by the great Judy Garland, who was to have starred in the film. (The reasons for her dismissal are detailed by George Feltenstein, producer of the CD, in his notes on the release.) Garland's renditions of "They Say It's Wonderful" (with Keel) and the reprise of "There's No Business Like Show Business" are spine-tingling. Her comic timing and wit come through sharp and clear in "Doin' What Comes Natur'lly" and "I Got the Sun in the Morning," putting Hutton's over-the-top performances to shame. It's a safe guess that this generally excellent stage-to-screen transfer would have been one of the best movie musicals of all time if Garland had completed the film. Note that the disc includes both Hutton's and Garland's renditions of "Let's Go West Again," a song that was apparently written by Irving Berlin for *Annie* in 1946 but was cut before the show opened; the number was to be reinstated for the film but never made it.

Studio Cast, 1957 (Capitol/Angel) ★★

Mary Martin and John Raitt were acclaimed for their performances in *Annie Get Your Gun,* but this recording fails to capture the excitement, personality, or vocal artistry of their interpretations. It's less a cast album than a recording of songs from the show with 1950s pop orchestrations that bear little or no resemblance to the originals and are quite untheatrical—a very strange artistic choice, considering that this score contains the anthem "There's No Business Like Show Buisness." Martin and Raitt starred in a fine television production of the musical around the time of this recording, and it's a shame that Capitol Records didn't produce a true TV cast album. In the surviving kinescope of the broadcast, the stars are as vibrant and thrilling as any other Annie Oakley or Frank Butler—but the Capitol recording is flat, dry, and altogether forgettable.

Studio Cast, 1963 (Columbia/no CD) Not recommended.

This is one of the most disappointing studio cast recordings of any Broadway score. It's conducted by the great Franz Allers and was produced by Columbia Records, the company responsible for many of the classiest cast albums ever issued. But almost every choice made here was misguided and the result is embarrassing. Doris Day should have been terrific in this role (as she was in the film *Calamity Jane*) but her performances of Annie Oakley's songs are sleepy and tepid. As Frank Butler, Robert Goulet probably seemed perfect in theory, but what might have been dream casting is sabotaged by his Vegas-like renditions of songs that require a robust, legit sound. To compound this misuse of talent, there are pallid new orchestrations by the usually reliable Phil Lang. It's a shame that Day, Goulet, and Allers didn't offer a more straightforward reading of Irving Berlin's greatest score.

Music Theater of Lincoln Center Cast, 1966 (RCA) ★★★★★

Here's the gem—the most enjoyable recording of *Annie Get Your Gun.* Even though it was made years after the original Decca album, it's a more accurate representation of the score as a theatrical experience—and Ethel Merman, two decades after creating the role on Broadway, never sounded fresher. Her vibrato is tight, her pitch perfect, her acting and comic timing impeccable. By 1966, stereophonic sound was at its peak, and the spacious, crisp sound of the recording makes you feel as if you've got a front-row seat for the performance. Supporting Merman is Bruce Yarnell, who possessed one of the most thrilling musical theater voices ever. His big baritone is melodic and hearty, and he delivers every wonderful Berlin lyric with absolutely clarity. Also in the cast is Jerry Orbach in the character role of Charlie Davenport; his performance leaps out of the speakers when he performs the opening number "Colonel Buffalo Bill" and leads "There's No Business Like Show Business." This Music Theater of Lincoln Center production was also notable for introducing "An Old-Fashioned Wedding"; the last new Irving Berlin song to be performed on Broadway, it's a terrific contrapuntal duet between Annie and Frank. Also, the recording was the first to include all of the verses to "You Can't Get a Man With a Gun." Masterfully performed by Merman, the number is a laugh-out-loud exercise in lyrical perfection; it's Berlin at his most witty and playful, and it doesn't get any better than this. The score is conducted to perfection by the great Franz Allers.

Studio Cast, 1990 (EMI) ★★

John McGlinn, the masterful conductor who created complete digital recordings of such classic shows as *Show Boat* and *Brigadoon,* does the same here for *Annie Get Your Gun,* but much less successfully. The album suffers from less-than-perfect casting and from the decision to use the original score and orchestrations with none of the improvements, cuts, and additions that were made since the show premiered in 1946. ("An Old-Fashioned Wedding" is included as an addendum.) As Annie Oakley, Kim Criswell displays a stunning belt voice, but there's something about her personality that doesn't quite mesh with the role; she's sassy but she's not the equal of Ethel Merman, Mary Martin, Judy Garland, Judy Kaye, or even (can you believe it?) Betty Hutton. Although Thomas Hampson has the big baritone bravura required for Frank Butler, he is too operatically trained to pull off the laid-back, cowboy crooner aspects of the part and he lacks the comic ability to interact effectively with Annie in "Anything You Can Do." Jason Graae and Rebecca Luker are fine as Tommy and Winnie, but this recording makes it clear why these roles are usually eliminated from the show in revival; their songs are somewhat interesting from a historical standpoint but otherwise negligible. As Charlie Davenport and Colonel Buffalo Bill, respectively, David Garrison and David Healy are well cast but don't do much to help this album sound particularly theatrical or exciting.

Studio Cast, 1995 (JAY, 2CDs) ★★★★★

This is an excellent, complete recording of the show as revised for the 1966 Lincoln Center production, with its superior orchestrations and the added showstopper "An Old-Fashioned Wedding." Annie Oakley is played by Judy Kaye at her best. Her voice is melodic and rich, her characterization full of wit and bite; in fact, Kaye is the best Annie on record next to Merman. Barry Bostwick is also well cast as Frank Butler, totally believable as a bragging, hunky cowboy. Robert Russell Bennett's fine orchestrations are remarkably well conducted by John Owen Edwards; his tempi are interesting and fresh, and it's all the more enjoyable to hear every note of the score in full, clear, digital stereo.

Broadway Cast, 1999 (Angel) ★★★

By 1999, much of *Annie Get Your Gun* seemed politically incorrect, so this great show was edited and reinvented. Therefore, this cast recording is not a true interpretation of the show as originally written. It's a fresh, crisp, new version of the musical, showcasing Bernadette Peters—a star who, in her own way, is as vibrant and beloved as Merman. Some contemporary listeners may find this interpretation of the classic score more palatable than what's heard on earlier recordings, but the orchestrations and some of the vocal performances leave a lot to be desired. Still, the great Irving Berlin songs and the dynamic star performances compensate for any shortcomings. Peters has great range; she handles the comedic lyrics (edited here) hilariously and delivers the ballads heartbreakingly. Tom Wopat is always an appealing leading man and his attractive baritone gets a chance to shine here in "The Girl That I Marry" and "My Defenses Are Down." On the whole, this album is perhaps more successful than the 1999 revival itself; without the drab scenery and questionable book revisions to distract us, the brilliant score is allowed to shine. —GERARD ALESSANDRINI

ANNIE WARBUCKS
Original Off-Broadway Cast, 1993 (Angel) ★★★

Everyone's favorite redheaded orphan sparkles once more in this Off-Broadway sequel to the Broadway mega-smash *Annie*. After a prolonged gestation period, *Annie Warbucks* emerged as neither a second golden egg nor a turkey. The cast recording has its share of appealing moments, thanks to capable Broadway pros Donna McKechnie and Harve Presnell and a full-sounding orchestra effectively delivering the Charles Strouse-Martin Charnin score. Things get off to a zippy start with "Annie Ain't Just Annie Anymore" and "Above the Law." The orphans are still livin' la vida hard-knock and they have such spunky numbers as "The Other Woman" and "I Got Me." Presnell displays his luxurious baritone in "A Younger Man" and "When You Smile." A standout is the ballad "It Would Have Been Wonderful," sung by Marguerite MacIntyre as Grace Farrell. One of the disc's major assets is the plucky, high-belting Annie of Kathryn Zaremba. She anchors the recording with "Changes," "I Always Knew," and other bang-it-out songs. The single CD is housed in a double-disc case to accommodate the opulent, forty-eight-page color comic booklet that explains the story. Also included is a text-only synopsis for grownups and all of the show's lyrics. —MORGAN SILLS

ANYA
Original Broadway Cast, 1965 (United Artists/no CD) ★★★

What Robert Wright and George Forrest had previously done successfully with Grieg and Borodin, they did with Rachmaninoff in creating a musical based on the play *Anastasia*. The

Russian composer's music was well suited to a piece that takes place shortly after the Russian Revolution; while classical music aficionados might find this adaptation hard to take, it's a lush, beautifully sung, latter-day operetta. Onstage, the show was plodding, but the recording is very entertaining. Constance Towers and Michael Kermoyan are excellent in all of their songs, particularly in "My Kind of Love" (the melody had previously served as the basis for the popular hit "Full Moon and Empty Arms") and the dramatic "Six Palaces" (in which Anya is drilled on the facts of her "life"). Irra Petina, the grande dame of the floperetta genre, is a joy in the comic "Leben Sie Wohl" and "On That Day," and she also leads the haunting "Homeward." For camp value, there is Lillian Gish as the Grand Duchess, "reciting" lyrics to a vocalise sung by Anya. The show—billed as "The Musical Musical"—was one of the late-career flops of director George Abbott, who also collaborated on the book with Guy Bolton. (This was Bolton's final Broadway credit.) The album notes detail which Rachmaninoff pieces have been adapted for each song. There are also two songs listed on the back of the jacket that are not actually on the album; they were cut from the show during previews and, from all reports, weren't recorded. With such great vocal work and so many wonderful Rachmaninoff "tunes," *Anya* would be welcome on CD.

The Anastasia Affaire/Anastasia: The Musical, Studio Casts, 1992–98 (Bay Cities/Original Cast Records) ★★

These recordings are not just *Anya* with two pianos. When it became clear that the Wright-Forrest musical was going to close on Broadway after sixteen performances, director and co-librettist George Abbott graciously ceded all of the rights to Wright and Forrest. This allowed the team to revisit the story of the woman who claimed to be Anastasia, the only surviving member of the Romanov-family assassination. The musical was revised and produced regionally as *A Song for Anastasia* and *The Anastasia Game.* A recording titled *The Anastasia Affaire,* based on a production at the Merrimack Theatre in Massachusetts, was released in 1992 and quickly went out of print. In 1998, with the title now changed to *Anastasia: The Musical,* the CD was reissued with bonus tracks of six "premiere recordings" of Wright and Forrest songs from other shows. The majority of Rachmaninoff melodies utilized for Anya were used again in the revisions, but most of them were given new lyrics and made to serve different dramatic functions. While the Broadway score leaned heavily toward "nouveau operetta," the final version is definitely a chamber musical with two-piano accompaniment (well handled by Albin Konopka and Seth Rudetsky). The principal singers on the CD are Judy Kaye, Regina Resnik, Len Cariou, Steve Barton, George Lee Andrews, Walter Willison, and David Green; all are in top form. The story of Anastasia is more clearly discerned from the songs in the new version; still, the original Broadway cast album, with its grand orchestrations and operatic singing, is a more enjoyable listen.   —JEFFREY DUNN

ANYONE CAN WHISTLE
Original Broadway Cast, 1964 (Columbia/Sony) ★★★★★

The show was a flop but virtually every number is a winner, and so is this disc. Broadway audiences were bored by Arthur Laurents' bizarre, satirical fable in which corrupt, small-town politicians fake a miracle by pumping water out of a rock, thus creating a new Lourdes with its attendant tourist trade. But what a cast! Angela Lansbury launched her musical theater career as Cora Hoover Hooper, the scheming mayor. Her costars were Lee Remick as Fay Apple, head nurse in the local nuthouse (named The Cookie Jar!), and Harry Guardino as

J. Bowden Hapgood, a phony psychiatrist who stirs up trouble. And what a score! Stephen Sondheim's wildly inventive songs include a lengthy musical-dramatic sequence, "Simple," and a campy ballet, "The Cookie Chase." Lansbury's opener, "Me and My Town," is a riotous spoof of nightclub-diva dramatics. Remick gets the achingly beautiful title tune and Guardino delivers the biting, driving "Everybody Says Don't." The final duet for Hapgood and Fay, "With So Little to Be Sure Of," is one of Sondheim's finest, most adult love songs. Don Walker's orchestrations are brassy and delightful. Recorded the day after the show closed, the disc has a raw quality—Lansbury, for one, evidences some vocal strain—that, paradoxically, makes it seem fresher than many albums that are more polished. (One of Remick's numbers, "There Won't Be Trumpets," was cut before the show opened and left off the LP but has been restored for the CD.) This kind of failure is far more interesting than lots of long-running hits. Note: Look for the version of the disc marked "Deluxe Expanded Edition." It includes bonus tracks of Sondheim singing demo versions of, among other things, the cut number "The Lame, the Halt, and the Blind" and an alternate version of "With So Little to Be Sure Of."

Carnegie Hall Concert Cast, 1995 (Columbia/Sony) Not recommended.

This live recording of a starry concert version of *Anyone Can Whistle,* produced as a benefit for Gay Men's Health Crisis, preserves more of the score than is heard on the original cast album. It includes "There Won't Be Trumpets" as well as "There's Always a Woman," an unpleasant bitch-fest between Cora and Fay. But, thirty years on, nobody can muster much conviction for Laurents' talky satire. As Cora, Fay, and Hapgood, Madeline Kahn, Bernadette Peters, and Scott Bakula offer tentative, vocally wobbly performances, while Angela Lansbury narrates. Peters manages a lovely version of the title tune, but lacks Remick's vulnerability; she's really at a loss in the scenes where Fay impersonates a sexy French temptress. Kahn is the biggest disappointment here, giving a performance that lacks bite or energy. And Bakula doesn't possess Guardino's rough authority. What's especially missing is the urgency of the original album. As sometimes happens in live recordings, the balance between singers and the orchestra is not ideal; even Don Walker's orchestrations, supervised by Jonathan Tunick, lose some edge. This album is of archival importance, but the original is the one to own.   —DAVID BARBOUR

ANYTHING GOES
Recordings by Original New York and London Cast Members, 1934 (various labels/Prism) ★★★

While it wasn't Cole Porter's first success or biggest hit, *Anything Goes* has always seemed the quintessential Porter musical. Its screwballs-at-sea plot and score filled with standards still exude a vintage 1934 smartness even as revivals fool around with the book and pad the score with other Porter tunes. Ethel Merman, indelibly cast as evangelist-turned-chanteuse Reno Sweeney, recorded a couple of the songs and the first London cast laid down several tracks. The results, as collected here, are intriguing and mixed. Merman, of course, is swell in "You're the Top" and "I Get a Kick Out of You." The disc also includes an extremely rare live cut by William Gaxton, the original Billy and a key Broadway leading man of the time. Meanwhile, the 1935 London production of *Anything Goes* was quite a different show. American brashness was traded in for a somewhat more decorous cheekiness and Jack Whiting is a much more juvenile Billy than the wiseacre Gaxton. As for Reno Sweeney, what is about as far from Merman as it's possible to get? Try a light soprano, add a French accent, *et voilà:* You have the London

Reno, Jeanne Aubert. She's certainly spirited as she trills "Blow Gabriel Blow," but whether or not she fits the role is another matter. As this disc also features Porter's own recordings of three songs from the score plus extras, it's a good bargain all around.

Film Soundtrack, 1956 (Decca) Not recommended.

Anything Goes did not fare well in its transfer to other media. A 1936 film version with Merman and Bing Crosby was truncated and compromised; so were two 1950s TV productions, one with Merman and the other with Martha Raye. Worst of all was the mess that Paramount made of the property in 1956, again with Crosby. There are a few Porter songs and a boat in the movie, but that's about as faithful to the original show as it gets. The soundtrack album tells the tale: It features dispirited renditions of the songs by Crosby, Donald O'Connor, Jeanmaire, and Mitzi Gaynor, plus some woeful new efforts by Sammy Cahn and James Van Heusen (sample: "Ya Gotta Give the People Hoke").

Off-Broadway Cast, 1962 (Epic) ★★★

This revival managed to respect the show even as it tinkered with it, adding several Porter songs and souped-up arrangements. The album is sprightly and enjoyable. Eileen Rodgers is fine in a sort of girlish-Merman way, and Hal Linden—years before his Broadway and TV fame—is one of the best Billys ever, brash in the Gaxton manner yet able to sustain a romantic vocal line with panache. Barbara Lang and Mickey Deems are fine as Hope and Moonface Martin, and as Bonnie, chirpy-voiced Margery Grey has fun with a little-known Porter interpolation: "The Heaven Hop." And also added to the score are "It's De-Lovely" (from Porter's *Red, Hot and Blue*) and "Friendship" (from his *DuBarry Was a Lady*). Best of all, there seems to be a concerted effort to evoke the original spirit of *Anything Goes* without camping up the material or playing down to it.

London Cast, 1969 (Decca/TER) ★

This version of *Anything Goes* had still more alterations—so extensive that the name of Guy Bolton, who cowrote and revised the original book, was nowhere credited. The production was an instant flop; in fact, it was such a disaster that the cast album was packaged but remained unissued for a long time. (Years later, one vagrant copy sold for £1,000.) When it was finally released, everyone yawned. Some of the new orchestrations sound cheesy, but they're a good match for Marian Montgomery, whose Reno is pathetically unworthy of over-the-title billing. She's toneless, humorless, and graceless in the role; Britney Spears as Magnolia in *Show Boat* would be better casting. The recording can't survive such a major liability, but it should be mentioned that James Kenney is almost as good a Billy as Linden was and Valerie Verdon's Hope is charming.

Broadway Cast, 1987 (RCA) ★★★

Renewed interest in *Anything Goes,* after its absence from Broadway for more than fifty years, brought the show back in this Lincoln Center Theater production. There was again some tinkering with the score—"Friendship" and "It's De-Lovely" were interpolated once more, as was "Easy to Love"—and the evening began with Porter's own voice in that ancient recording of the title tune. The show once again held up under all the changes, making for one of the happier Broadway events of its time. As for casting, Howard McGillin's Billy, with his attractive light tenor and earnest manner, worked somewhat better onstage than it does on records. Opposite him in the role of Reno Sweeney, Patti LuPone seems to be zapped in from a different galaxy;

her portrayal is both magnetic and quite controversial. As always, her authority and commitment are never in doubt, but her vocal style will annoy some listeners even as it enraptures others. The rest of the cast is less formidable, with the Tony-winning Bill McCutcheon a particularly sweet Public Enemy 13. As always, this score seems to inspire an enthusiastic performance from all forces involved.

Studio Cast, 1988 (EMI) ★★★

While the 1987 Lincoln Center production was still packing them in, the first full recording of the *Anything Goes* score as it was originally heard on Broadway was put together by the team responsible for the magnificent 1988 *Show Boat.* Once again, conductor John McGlinn leads a cast of musical theater and opera singers—but while that blend worked fine for the epic *Show Boat,* here it's a different story. The wonderful mezzo Frederica von Stade, so great as Kern's Magnolia, seems too substantial an ingenue for *Anything Goes,* overpowering the role of Hope. Tenor Cris Groenendaal is a light, acceptable Billy but is poorly matched with his Reno, the soubrette-belter Kim Criswell. Only Jack Gilford, his endearingly scratchy nonsinging just right for Moonface, seems perfectly cast.

London Cast, 1989 (First Night) ★★★

The success of the New York revival of *Anything Goes* generated a London production, and Howard McGillin crossed the Atlantic to play Billy opposite Elaine Page. He sings the role with more authority here than he did on the earlier disc. Veteran character actor Bernard Cribbins is another good Moonface and Ashleigh Sendin is an attractive Hope. But, even more so than in New York, this production was obviously intended as The Reno Sweeney Show. Paige is more vocally reliable than LuPone, though she occasionally sounds a bit too enraptured with her own divadom. Still, a performer's self-confidence never did *Anything Goes* any harm (Marian Montgomery excepted), and a good time is had by all, including the listener.

Studio Cast, 1995 (JAY) ★

The world was not holding its breath for another studio recording of *Anything Goes* in 1995, but that didn't stop JAY Records from assembling a group of singing actors who had replaced Paige, McGillin, and Cribbins in the 1989 London stage production. Unlike other JAY albums, this one was based strictly on the '87/'89 revival version, with new orchestrations by Michael Gibson and the same tune stack. Comparisons with the cast albums of those productions are inevitable; this disc lacks the excitement and theatrical luster of its rivals. Gregg Edelman conveys some of Billy's brashness but Louise Gold lacks LuPone's charisma and Paige's tower of vocal strength. No one else is either offensive or magnetic in this unnecessary recording.

London Cast, 2003 (First Night) ★★★

The British fascination with *Anything Goes* continued in 2003 with a National Theatre revival of the late-'80s version. Directed by Trevor Nunn, this production strayed a bit further from the original than its predecessors but did so with high style and energy. Nunn treats the show as an ensemble piece rather than a star vehicle, so there's no Merman/LuPone/Paige sort of dominance. But if Sally Ann Triplett is a dainty Reno, she can simulate a belt when she needs to. John Barrowman is a light Billy with lots of juvenile charm. The supporting cast is spirited, the chorus is strong, the orchestra is having a great time, and "Blow, Gabriel, Blow" raises the roof.   —RICHARD BARRIOS

APPLAUSE
Original Broadway Cast, 1970 (ABC/Decca) ★★★

When librettists, composers, and lyricists take on a masterpiece, they rarely improve it. Such is the case with this musical version of *All About Eve.* Though *Applause* was a hit, it has dimmed in the public's consciousness and the Charles Strouse-Lee Adams score can best be described as one that has its moments. Lauren Bacall is Margo Channing in the disco era, and though her opening song "But Alive" could be better, "Who's That Girl?"—in which Margo sees herself on TV in a movie she made many moons ago—comes across as extra-special material. The title song is sometimes known as The Actor's Anthem, although many performers may relate more readily to the acerbic "Welcome to the Theater." There are laid-back charms in "Good Friends" and "One of a Kind," the latter a pleasant jazz waltz, but the rest of the score seems little more than filler. The CD offers four fascinating bonus tracks taken from demos that Strouse played and sang during the show's creation. One is the title song but the other three numbers were dropped; they indicate that the show was more ambitious in the planning stages. "'Smashing!'—New York Times" is a smart idea set to a haunting tune. — PETER FILICHIA

THE APPLE TREE
Original Broadway Cast, 1966 (Columbia/Sony) ★★★★

What could Jerry Bock and Sheldon Harnick do to follow *Fiddler on the Roof?* The team answered that question with an unconventional evening of three one-act musicals, each only tangentially connected to the others. It was a concept that would show off the versatility of the performers as well as the writers. The first act, "The Diary of Adam and Eve" (adapted from a Mark Twain short story), is written in standard musical theater form; the second act, "The Lady or the Tiger" (based on a Frank R. Stockton story), has a pop-operetta writing style; and the third act, "Passionella" (based on the Jules Feiffer fantasy book), is cartoonish with a mid-'60s flavor. *The Apple Tree* is primarily remembered for the tour-de-force performance(s) of Barbara Harris as Eve, Barbara, and Passionella (plus Ella). Listening to this recording, one can fully understand why Harris won the Tony Award for Best Actress in a Musical over Mary Martin in *I Do! I Do!* and Lotte Lenya in *Cabaret.* After using a light, dry voice for Eve's innocent exploration of her first feelings and singing the lullaby "Go to Sleep, Whatever You Are," the star then rises to a sexy combination of breathlessness and belting for the almost-striptease number "I've Got What You Want." She employs a wonderfully realized, barely-on-pitch sound for the determined dreamer Ella and then, finally, her voice rises to a full-throated Broadway belt for Passionella. Equally versatile, if not quite as dazzling, is Alan Alda: He morphs from a simply acted and sung Adam to a pseudo-legit Captain Sanjar and then to a rock 'n'roll star turn before a surprise reconciliation with Ella. The recording works hard to give you enough of each segment so that you can almost follow the stories; this is aided by the presence of Larry Blyden as The Snake, The Balladeer/Lion Keeper, and The Narrator. If one laments that even more music and dialogue (especially from Act I) was not recorded, the cuts were very well thought out; those who want a more complete document of the score should seek out the hard-to-find two-CD Takarazuka recording in Japanese. — JEFFREY DUNN

ARCHY AND MEHITABEL
Original Concept Album, 1954 (Columbia/DRG) ★★★

Based on the 1920s newspaper columns of Don Marquis, *archy and mehitabel* stars a cockroach. Ostensibly, the columns were the work of said cockroach, named archy, who wrote them for

Marquis in exchange for some apple peels left in the trash. The roach handled the mechanics of writing by hurling himself head first at the typewriter keys; everything was in lower case because he couldn't reach the shift key. This recording is sort of a grab-bag suite taken from different archy pieces, with scenes and narration by Joe Darion (lyricist of *Man of La Mancha*) underscored by George Kleinsinger (composer of *Tubby the Tuba*). The underscoring provides a real New York atmosphere and it occasionally explodes into whimsical songs and entrancing melodic fragments. The text is made up of archy's thoughts (e.g., "people may think they amount to a great deal, but to a mosquito, they're just a meal") and stories of the odd characters he runs into. Most of his stories are about mehitabel (Carol Channing), the alley cat whom he loves unrequitedly. She takes up with a disreputable tomcat that leaves her with a litter of kittens saved by archy (Eddie Bracken) from drowning in a rainstorm. She "studies acting" with a disreputable old theater cat, then reluctantly gives in and takes a job as a house cat—but, unable to stand domesticity, she returns to the alley. In 1957, the piece was adapted for the stage as *Shinbone Alley,* with a full Kleinsinger-Darion score and a book by Mel Brooks. Eddie Bracken repeated his role and Eartha Kitt played mehitabel. Three years after the Broadway failure, it turned up in a two-hour TV adaptation with Bracken and Tammy Grimes. Finally, in 1970, it became an animated cartoon with Bracken and Channing. Pirated recordings exist of the TV show and there's also a complete, live, two-CD pirate of the Broadway cast. —DAVID WOLF

ARMS AND THE GIRL
Original Broadway Cast, 1948 (Decca) ★★★

The Theatre Guild was riding the success of *Oklahoma!* and *Carousel* when Armina Marshall Langner suggested that *The Pursuit of Happiness,* a play she had written with Lawrence Langner, would make a good musical. Rouben Mamoulian, who had directed the Guild's earlier successes, was brought in to direct *Arms and the Girl.* Morton Gould and Dorothy Fields wrote the score—their only Broadway collaboration. The show is distinguished primarily by its three leading performers: Georges Guetary (a French musical theater star), Nanette Fabray, and Pearl Bailey. For Fabray, this show was another unsuccessful vehicle that would keep her from achieving major Broadway stardom on a par with Ethel Merman or Mary Martin. Still, her work here is colorful and exciting in "Girl With a Flame" and "That's My Fella." She's great in her duets with Guetary, who also does very well with the charming if corny "A Cow and a Plough and a Frau." But the big news of the show was Pearl Bailey in a scene-stealing role. She played a slave who changes her name according to where she is geographically—so, as "Connecticut," she sings the bawdily humorous "There Must Be Something Better Than Love" and the lesser "Nothin' for Nothin'." The CD also includes cast recordings of *Up in Central Park;* both albums have been meticulously remastered and sound as good as any recordings of the period could be expected to. The disc filled an important gap in the cast album catalogue, so we should all be grateful to Decca Broadway for its release. —JEFFREY DUNN

ASPECTS OF LOVE
Original Cast, 1989 (Polydor) ★

Beyond being one of Andrew Lloyd Webber's most inscrutable shows, *Aspects of Love* is also one of his most ridiculous—more soap opera than pop opera. Though the show's story doesn't diverge much from the 1955 David Garnett novella on which it's based, you may wish it did when listening to this almost complete recording (only a few bits are missing). The endlessly foolish romantic machinations of the characters are not made more palatable by the leads, Ann

Crumb and Michael Ball; they serve the score well but can't do much to make their sex-obsessed characters ingratiating or sympathetic. Kevin Colson, Kathleen Rowe Martin, and Diana Morrison, who have supporting roles in this game of musical beds, come across better. With lyrics by Don Black and Charles Hart, some of the score is attractive and musical director Michael Reed gets rich results from the orchestra, but the performers' emoting is so over-wrought that suffering through the whole thing for the sake of a few good songs is exhausting. The recording is worthwhile for "Love Changes Everything," "Seeing Is Believing," "The First Man You Remember," and "Anything but Lonely" but not for the sort of plot twists and relationship games that even daytime television might reject. —MATTHEW MURRAY

ASSASSINS
Original Off-Broadway Cast, 1991 (RCA) ★★
There's no doubt that Stephen Sondheim's scores are brilliant. His lyrics are innovative; he's the master of intellectual argument in rhyme. His best melodies, though often overshadowed by acclaim for his superb wordsmithery, are slyly inventive. Yet when the messages in his musicals are examined, they often turn out to be less than the sum of the sung parts. Perhaps the most callow of his enterprises, with librettist John Weidman as collaborator, is this revue, which trots out a bevy of men and women who shot at, and in some instances killed, U.S. presidents. Sondheim and Weidman suggest that, for many unfortunate citizens, the American Dream is a nightmare. Accordingly, they set forth a series of ditties—some portentous, some ironically lighthearted—to show how a sense of disenfranchisement can lead to assassination. Sondheim's score, frequently in folk-song mode, is jaunty but instantly forgettable. Worse are Weidman's sketches, which aren't included here in their entirety. There is, however, the attenuated Lee Harvey Oswald skit, wherein John Kennedy's murderer is visited in his Texas Book Depository hideout by the spirits of assassins past and future. (The idea is that Oswald acted as a representative of a continuing, perhaps inevitable tradition.) The cast assembled to play this group of history's outcasts includes some of the best musical theater performers of the time, although only Victor Garber as John Wilkes Booth really gets to shine. Among the others warbling and emoting to little avail are Annie Golden, Jonathan Hadary, Patrick Cassidy, Eddie Korbich, William Parry, Terrence Mann, Lee Wilkof, and Debra Monk.

Broadway Cast, 2004 (PS Classics) ★★★★
It's likely that there will never be a better production of this revue about bumping off presidents as a viable pastime for disgruntled citizens with irrational gripes. From start to finish, the Roundabout Theatre Company staging was a honey. Tony Awards were handed to the production, director Joe Mantello, and supporting actor Michael Cerveris, who infused the plum role of John Wilkes Booth with great fervor. The same kind of care has been given to the recording, on which Becky Ann Baker, James Barbour, Mario Cantone, Mary Catherine Garrison, Alexander Gemignani, Neil Patrick Harris, Marc Kudisch, Jeffrey Kuhn, Denis O'Hare, and Cerveris raise their voices in disturbing song. Sondheim's Americana pastiches, with big and brassy and plangent arrangements by Michael Starobin, fully demonstrate the composer-lyricist's mastery. Much of the dialogue by John Weidman is retained on the CD, including the penultimate scene in which Lee Harvey Oswald's predecessors come out of the shadows on the sixth floor of the Texas Book Depository and cajole their hesitant boy into firing. This is bold if not always convincing material, polished to near perfection. —DAVID FINKLE

AS THOUSANDS CHEER
Off-Broadway Cast, 1998 (Varèse Sarabande) ★★★★

At a time when large-scale revues were part of the standard traffic on Broadway, Irving Berlin's *As Thousands Cheer* (1933) was a Bentley. It had great stars, terrific songs, and clever sketches, all with a specific focus: The show was a Sunday newspaper come to life, its varied components commenting on or illustrating topical stories, Hollywood gossip, comic strips, and even the weather report ("Heat Wave"). If anyone wonders about that "rotogravure" line in "Easter Parade," this show provides an explanation. Original cast members Clifton Webb and Ethel Waters left recorded souvenirs of the show and nothing will ever top Waters' performances of "Harlem on My Mind" and "Heat Wave." (She did not record the devastating "Supper Time" until years later.) The show itself remained an irretrievable legend until 1998, when a scrappy and inventive "revival" was produced Off-Broadway by the Drama Dept. Wisely, there was no attempt to reproduce the show as it was or to have modern performers pretend to be Marilyn Miller or Ethel Waters. Instead, the production put Berlin's songs and some of the show's original sketches into one zippy act performed by a talented cast of six who constantly shifted roles; the accompaniment was piano and bass. The charm of the stage production is communicated by this "world premiere cast recording," as it is labeled, which reverts to the original order of the songs and generously reinstates "Easter Parade" (not heard in the actual revival). Howard McGillin, Judy Kuhn, B.D. Wong, Mary Beth Peil, Kevin Chamberlin, and Paula Newsome sing and cavort with skill and enthusiasm—and if Newsome's "Supper Time" can't touch the Waters version, neither can anyone else's. There's even an unknown Berlin gem here: "Through a Keyhole," a moody evocation of a Walter Winchellesque gossip reporter. The show may sound more like "As Dozens Cheer" in this version, but at least the cheers are heartfelt.　　—RICHARD BARRIOS

THE ATHENIAN TOUCH
Original Off-Broadway Cast, 1964 (Broadway East/AEI) Not recommended.

I remember the day in the 1980s when several boxes of the long out-of-print LP of *The Athenian Touch* turned up in a store in midtown Manhattan. Musical theater enthusiasts swarmed the place and the shop was depleted in an afternoon. Then people got home and actually played the thing. This record is as bad as cast albums get. In most musicals, the music is usually the "safest" component; even if the book and lyrics are poor, there are usually at least a couple of tunes with some appeal. That's not the case here. These songs not only have useless lyrics by David Eddy, the tunes by Willard Straight are ugly to listen to. And the book, a love story between Aristophanes and some whore, is simply not a professional effort. Camp followers may be interested in the album because it stars Butterfly McQueen and Marion Marlowe, the Arthur Godfrey TV show favorite who also played Elsa in the original Broadway production of *The Sound of Music,* but there's no other reason to purchase it.　　—DAVID WOLF

AT HOME ABROAD
Recordings by the Original Broadway Cast, 1935 (Smithsonian/no CD) ★★★

Always welcome on Broadway during the Depression was a star-packed musical revue. *At Home Abroad,* which is billed as "A Musical Holiday," bolstered its thin and engaging overall theme—travel—with a fine score by Arthur Schwartz and Howard Dietz and a cast headed by Beatrice Lillie, Ethel Waters, and Eleanor Powell. The show was designed and staged by a gifted newcomer, Vincente Minnelli; all was escapism and dazzle. While the production's 198-performance run was something of a disappointment, there were a number of recordings made by the cast members, including Waters' insinuating "Thief in the Night" and two definitive Bea Lillie numbers, "Paree" and "Get Yourself a Geisha" (with its insistent refrain, "It's better with your shoes off"). As part of its ongoing attempt to reconstruct lost musical shows, the Smithsonian Institution collected these old discs and added a few numbers recorded later by Karen Morrow, Nancy Dussault, and other performers. If the score lacks the classic stature of Schwartz and Dietz's earlier *The Band Wagon,* there's still a lot to treasure here, including Eleanor Powell's extended tap breaks in "What a Wonderful World" and "Got a Bran' New Suit." As always with Smithsonian releases, the notes are nearly as good as the recordings they detail with such erudition and enthusiasm.

Live and Studio Recordings by the Original Broadway Cast, 1935 (AEI) ★★★
The Smithsonian collection might have seemed the last word on *At Home Abroad,* but guess again. There also exists a set of decrepit discs containing large portions of the show in performance. Whether it was a radio broadcast is unclear; although the sound quality gives new meaning to "low fidelity," the material was skillfully transferred to CD by the intrepid folks at AEI. Studio recordings by Lillie, Waters, and Powell are also included, and the patient listener will be rewarded with a very good sense of how this big and bouncy show operated. AEI obviously poured great care into the project, going so far as to splice parts of Bea Lillie's studio version of "Dinner Napkins" into an otherwise live recording so as to get better overall sound quality. Also to be enjoyed here are Waters' live performances of "Loading Time" and "Got a Bran' New Suit," which she did not record elsewhere. Unfortunately, the notes are inadequate—a chronic failing with AEI. And it's really too bad that the original recording technology sounds as if it relied heavily on tin cans and strings. —RICHARD BARRIOS

AT THE DROP OF A HAT
Original Cast, 1959 (Angel) ★★★★
Alexander Cohen had the good sense to bring a host of newcomers to Broadway from England, among them the two raconteurs of *At the Drop of a Hat,* Michael Flanders and Donald Swann. These two wonderful satirists-songwriters-performers included the audience in their nightly party at the Golden Theatre. Their humor was a little naughty and sometimes political, silly and sophisticated by turns, with lots of allusions that belied the songs' supposed simplicity. Intellectuals and average theatergoers could find equal amusement in the evening, albeit with different depths of understanding. Wisely, the original cast album was recorded in London before a live audience, which makes all the difference. Not only are we cued as to where the laughs are but we also feel part of the inside group that's enjoying these masters of song and monologue. This is one comedy record that can never be overplayed; the music and lyrics sound just as fresh the fiftieth time as the first, unlike many such albums. The songs are in the grand satirical and political tradition of the late 1950s-early 1960s. (Seven years later, Broadway saw the sequel, *At the Drop of Another Hat.*) —KEN BLOOM

AVENUE Q
Original Broadway Cast, 2003 (RCA) ★★★★★
What a devilishly clever parody of *Sesame Street* this Tony Award-winning musical is! Robert Lopez and Jeff Marx's songs are mostly upbeat and catchy ("Everyone's a Little Bit Racist") yet tender when called for ("Fantasies Come True"). The guys have come up with everything from a fast, funky waltz ("My Girlfriend Who Lives in Canada") to upbeat rock ("Purpose") to soul

("You Can Be as Loud as the Hell You Want," which Natalie Venetia Belcon growls perfectly). But there's also a fine, fine melody line in "There's a Fine, Fine Line." The Lopez-Marx lyrics are often monosyllabically simple, which they should be for a kid's-show spoof, yet they can also be wildly funny and raunchy. Talent-wise, along with librettist Jeff Whitty, are Lopez and Marx the real turtle soup (or merely the mock)? To quote their own creation, Lucy T. Slut: "Yeah, they're real." By the time you reach "Mix Tape"—a masterstroke of a song in which one puppet infers that another likes her from the songs that he's selected and recorded on a cassette for her—you'll realize that you don't want a mix tape of songs from different shows. You just want the *Avenue Q* CD, which showcases the superbly talented ensemble cast of John Tartaglia, Stephanie D'Abruzzo, Rick Lyon, Jennifer Barnhart, Ann Harada, and Jordan Gelber along with the aforementioned Belcon.   —PETER FILICHIA

AVENUE X
World Premiere Recording, 1997 (RCA) ★★★★

Avenue X shows how some folks in the racially divided America of the early 1960s tried to achieve social harmony through rock 'n' roll. Though the theme is similar to that of *Hairspray,* here the locale is Brooklyn rather than Baltimore, and the show ends in tragedy rather than joy. The unique feature of this musical is that all the songs are sung a cappella; they are persuasively performed on this recording by an excellent cast. There are only eight singers—Colette Hawley, Cheryl Alexander, Ted Brunetti, John Leone, John-Martin Green, Jerry Dixon, Chuck Cooper, and Wilbur Pauley—yet their vocal harmonies are so lush that they sound like twice that many people. (Dixon is the music director.) Indeed, the wall of sound heard in the arresting "Prologue" may convince you that you're hearing an orchestra playing along. Rather than advancing the plot or establishing the characters, the songs of Ray Leslee (music) and John Jiler (lyrics) are performance numbers that skillfully conjure the style of the period. Highlights include the ensemble number "A Thousand Summer Nights," Hawley's "Woman of the World," and the two songs that end the show: "Go There," in which Alexander laments "There are dreams that die before they ever live," and the touching "Where Is Love" (not to be confused with the song of the same title from *Oliver!*). The CD booklet tells us that, following "an extended run Off-Broadway at Playwrights Horizons, [*Avenue X*] played in roughly two dozen cities, winning 'Best Musical' awards and nominations virtually everywhere it has gone." This recording is a winner, too.   —MICHAEL PORTANTIERE

BABES IN ARMS

Studio Cast, 1951 (Columbia/no CD) ★★

Richard Rodgers and Lorenz Hart's 1937 classic, the father of all those hey-kids-let's-put-on-a-show movies with Mickey and Judy, has an expendable book and a gold-plated score: The opening number on this recording is "Where or When" and only a few tracks away are "I Wish I Were in Love Again," "My Funny Valentine," "Way Out West," and "The Lady Is a Tramp." While *Babes in Arms* was a good show to inaugurate Lehman Engel's studio cast series, this thirty-six-minute sampler LP plays more like "Mary Martin and Friends Sing the Best of Rodgers and Hart." Miss M. commandeers most of the hit songs and overworks her adorableness, yet she delivers a spectacular "The Lady Is a Tramp." Engel's orchestrations reflect the originals but they're heavy on strings and include some obvious effects—whistles in "Johnny One Note," clip-clops in "Way Out West." Jack Cassidy brings intensity to "You Are So Fair," but doesn't get to do the whole number. And Mardi Bayne, rather than singing both great verses of "I Wish I Were in Love Again," does the first one twice! How nuts is that?

Studio Cast, 1989 (New World) ★★★★

Now, this is more like it: a nearly complete recording with restored Hans Spialek orchestrations, all the ballet music (*Babes in Arms* was a George Balanchine show), and Evans Haile energetically conducting the New Jersey Symphony Orchestra. All that's missing is the now-unacceptable "All Dark People," written by R&H as a specialty for the Nicholas Brothers. Although the ballet music isn't all that interesting, the orchestrations are terrific, from the pearly celesta in "My Funny Valentine" to the twangs and woodwinds in "Way Out West." There's also some spiffy close-harmony work from the guy group JQ and the Bandits. While the casting is vocally deluxe, Judy Blazer, Gregg Edelman, Judy Kaye, and Jason Graae aren't convincing age-wise as the needy teen offspring of down-on-their-luck vaudevillians. But it would be hard to top Blazer's reading of "My Funny Valentine," Kaye's sarcasm in "Imagine," or the sheer joy of the title song. It makes you want to go paint a barn, wheel the piano in, and start the auditions!

Encores! Concert Cast, 1999 (DRG) ★★★★

This is a welcome addition to the musicals-in-concert canon. Surprisingly, it doesn't surpass the 1989 studio version in terms of theatricality; the lead-in dialogue to

ALL-TIME FAVORITES

OF PERFORMER

Carol Channing

1. Sugar Babies
2. Hello, Dolly!
3. My Fair Lady
4. Fiddler on the Roof
5. Cabin in the Sky
6. The King and I
7. Peter Pan
8. Chauve Souris
9. Porgy and Bess
10. As Thousands Cheer

the songs merely betrays what a wispy book *Babes in Arms* has. Rob Fisher's conducting isn't as vibrant as that of Evans Haile, but the orchestrations come through with more clarity here. Melissa Rain Anderson is no vocal match for Judy Kaye, nor can Erin Dilly wring nuances from a ballad as Judy Blazer can. But David Campbell is more ingratiating than Gregg Edelman and, in general, this cast is more age-appropriate than the other. The New World album has more ballet music, but this one has "All Dark People"—although it's listed as "Light on Their Feet" and only the verse lyrics are included. Which of the two recordings to buy? The New World, ten minutes longer, is for the archivists; the DRG has a less expert but more persuasively up-and-coming cast. As listening experiences, both are just dandy. —MARC MILLER

BABY
Original Broadway Cast, 1983 (Polydor/JAY) ★★★★★

The first ten minutes or so are a bumpy ride, with a too-busy opening number that includes some smarmy humor about having babies. Then Liz Callaway sings to Todd Graff, "Picture a flailing spermatozoan / Not even knowin' where he is goin'"—and the sun breaks out, never to leave. The David Shire-Richard Maltby, Jr. score is easily one of the best of the decade, thoroughly contemporary yet melodic and as clever and hilarious as it is heartfelt. When Callaway lets loose with the soaring "The Story Goes On" or when Graff offers the beautiful ballad "I Chose Right," you could weep at the bad career luck of Maltby and Shire. Other highlights: the strong women's trio "I Want It All"; the joyous "Fatherhood Blues"; James Congdon's funny-sad "Easier to Love"; and Beth Fowler's "Patterns." (That last-named song was cut from the Broadway production but is generously included here.) Martin Vidnovic and Catherine Cox are wonderful as an infertile Yuppie couple, and a belting Kim Criswell figures prominently in the chorus (she's the country singer in "The Ladies Singing Their Song"). Jonathan Tunick's orchestrations make a great score sound even better, as does Peter Howard's conducting. Although this musical couldn't find its audience in its overproduced Broadway mounting, it has done well in community and regional theaters. Thanks to Polydor for having given the score such a complete recording; just zip past the first two tracks and bliss out. —MARC MILLER

BAJOUR
Original Broadway Cast, 1964 (Columbia/Sony) Not recommended.

Some ethnic groups have all the luck and some don't. The same year that *Fiddler on the Roof* so beautifully celebrated the joys and sorrows of Jewish life, *Bajour* featured Nancy Dussault as an NYU anthropology major who latches onto a tribe of gypsies led by Herschel Bernardi. Top-billed Chita Rivera plays the daughter of a rival tribe, doing her trademark spitfire thing and belting out cheesy numbers like "Mean." Ernest Kinoy's libretto and Walter Marks' score (astonishingly, inspired by *New Yorker* stories by Joseph Mitchell) are a mishmash of gypsy intrigue that's enough to induce a heart attack in the politically correct. The disc starts off with a dynamic overture orchestrated by Mort Lindsey and Dussault's amusing "Where Is the Tribe for Me?" But too often, *Bajour* is merely desperate and loud. The second-act show-stopper, "Honest Man," with Bernardi and rival gypsy king Herbert Edelman trying to con each other, is pretty embarrassing. Give it one ★ if you're a Chita fan. —DAVID BARBOUR

BAKER STREET
Original Broadway Cast, 1965 (MGM/no CD) ★★

One of the last in the cycle of *My Fair Lady* wannabes, *Baker Street* is complete with handsome

Victorian settings, a misogynistic hero (Sherlock Holmes), and a Cockney chorus high-kicking all over London. The problem was that songwriters Marian Grudeff and Raymond Jessel emphatically were not Lerner and Loewe, not even with Bock and Harnick ghostwriting three numbers ("I'm in London Again," "Cold Clear World," and "I Shall Miss You") during the troubled tryout period. The melodic lines are facile, the lyrics occasionally intricate—as in the ironically named "It's So Simple"—yet it's all on the surface. As Holmes, Fritz Weaver is fine, but doesn't make anything memorable of the material. His leading lady, Inga Swenson—by all accounts impressive onstage—doesn't come across on this recording. Even the old-fashioned, three-part, would-be showstopper "Letters" lands with a thud. Martin Gabel as Moriarty, Peter Sallis as Watson, and Teddy Green as a leading Baker Street Irregular round out the cast; they all work hard, but in vain. Although the album is well designed, with color photos and a verbose synopsis, it never convinces you that this was "The hottest musical of 1965." It's worth noting that an even shorter-lived show from that year (*Drat! The Cat!*) had one throwaway number in it ("Holmes and Watson") that encapsulated what was special about the duo better than this entire score.

—MARC MILLER

THE BAKER'S WIFE
Original Cast, 1976 (Take Home Tunes) ★★★★★

This wonderful cast album continues to mystify listeners as to why *The Baker's Wife* was a huge flop. Based on the play and subsequent film *La femme du boulanger* by Marcel Pagnol and Jean Giono, the musical's book is by Joseph Stein, with music and lyrics by Stephen Schwartz. The fable is set in long-ago provincial France, where a middle-aged baker's young wife leaves him for a torrid affair with a handsome young villager. The show closed on the road to Broadway; most of the cast and creative-team members were replaced during its lengthy tryout tour. When it finally shuttered in Washington, the leads were Paul Sorvino, whose semioperatic voice sounds great in the songs of Aimable, the baker; Patti LuPone as his wife, Genevieve, belting to high heaven when she has to but wonderfully warm in the more lyrical passages of the score; Kurt Peterson, appropriately sexy as her young lover, Dominique; and Teri Ralston as Denise, a village woman who gets to sing the beautiful "Chanson" in her silvery soprano. All ten songs sung by the principals are superb, from character-establishing numbers like "Merci, Madame" to ravishing ballads like "Endless Delights." Other highlights include "Gifts of Love," a gorgeous and poignant piece in which Genevieve resigns herself to a marriage that's based on companionship rather than passion; "Meadowlark," the magnificent story-song that the baker's wife belts out when deciding to go off with her young stud; and "Proud Lady," sung by the strutting peacock Dominique. Schwartz's score differs impressively from the style of his monster hits *Godspell* and *Pippin*, and the recording boasts lovely orchestrations.

Original London Cast, 1990 (JAY, 2CDs) ★

Even while applauding the high-profile London production of *The Baker's Wife* that yielded this recording, we must lament that the results are unpersuasive in terms of text and performance. Directed by Trevor Nunn, this version has some new Stephen Schwartz songs along with several restorations, but these discs will disconcert fans of the original cast album. As performed here, the songs carried over from the earlier recording have many unfamiliar lyrics. Schwartz is famous for tinkering with his own work when his shows are revived but it's hard to justify such revisions when the new lyrics don't represent an improvement over the originals. In "Chanson," for example, we now hear gulls cry rather than sheep bleat. Was this change necessary? Sadly, the new and new/old songs aren't very interesting; many involve the villagers gossiping about the Aimable-Genevieve-Dominique affair (the young man's name is here spelled Dominic). As for the leading players, Alun Armstrong's attempt to compensate for his substandard singing with fine acting is noble but unsuccessful; he sings the baker's songs in much lower keys than Paul Sorvino's and the results are dispiriting. The plum role of Genevieve is filled by Sharon Lee Hill, who is no Patti LuPone. As Dominic, Drue Williams sings poorly and sounds effeminate, which certainly doesn't work for this character. Jill Martin displays the best voice of all the London principals in Denise's "Chanson" but, here again, the song is performed in a considerably lower key than on the American cast album and is therefore considerably less exciting.

—MICHAEL PORTANTIERE

BALLAD FOR BIMSHIRE
Original Off-Broadway Cast, 1963 (London/no CD) ★
This Off-Broadway oddity probably got produced because of the reputation of its composer, Irving Burgie—also known as Lord Burgess. Having written several major songs popularized by Harry Belafonte, Burgie was one of the most prominent calypso writers of the period. Here, the show is more well meaning than well crafted; the writers and production team all had limited musical theater experience and they produced a piece that, judging from the album, doesn't seem to know what it wants to do or how to do it. *Ballad for Bimshire* clearly had a book—coproducer-costar Ossie Davis, a driving force behind the production, narrates the story—but it's not compelling and more than a little amorphous. The lyrics are negligible, which leaves only the tunes. They're frequently appealing but, because they're on their own, dramatically unrewarding.

—DAVID WOLF

BALLROOM
Original Broadway Cast, 1978 (Columbia/Sony) ★
Michael Bennett's big post-*Chorus Line* flop is beloved by those who saw it but, sadly, the show's special qualities are not retained on disc. Jerome Kass' libretto is based on his television film *Queen of the Stardust Ballroom.* Dorothy Loudon stars as Bea, a lonely Bronx widow who finds glamour and romance at the local dance palace. Fans remember Loudon's performance and Bennett's magical staging but the score by Billy Goldenberg and Alan and Marilyn Bergman contains only a handful of book numbers; everything else is a dance sequence featuring faux-pop hits covered by the ballroom's house singers. These tunes are very pleasant in a Steve-and-Eydie kind of way, especially in Jonathan Tunick's jazzy orchestrations, but they don't convey a sense of the show's story. Given a chance, Loudon scores big—especially with her nervy, volatile delivery of the scorching eleven-o'clock number, "Fifty Percent," in which Bea chooses to accept the love of a married man (Vincent Gardenia). Overall, the album is a disappointment; but if you want to understand what made Loudon one of the most distinct theatrical personalities of her time, it's worth a listen.

—DAVID BARBOUR

THE BAND WAGON
Studio Cast, 1950 (Columbia/Sony) ★
Yet another of the great 1930s Broadway revues, *The Band Wagon* (1931) was graced with a terrific Arthur Schwartz-Howard Dietz score (including "Dancing in the Dark" and "I Love Louisa") and a fine cast. It contained too good a collection of songs to pass away when some-

thing as temporal as a revue had closed. There was a mangled, sort-of-musical film version in 1949, titled *Dancing in the Dark*—and then, of course, the 1953 Fred Astaire-Cyd Charisse classic. Coming between them, at the dawn of the LP era, was a recording by Mary Martin. This can in no way be termed a re-creation of the original score; instead, it offers a big star singing the show's best numbers. Martin is in great voice—but don't expect any probing vocal drama here or, indeed, anything other than perfunctory commitment. This is simply a group of fine songs performed in a resoundingly professional manner but with no theatrical flavor.

Film Soundtrack, 1953 (MGM/Rhino-Turner) ★★★★

Fans of this film may not be aware that Fred Astaire starred in *The Band Wagon* on Broadway in 1931 as well. The movie adds Schwartz-Dietz songs from other shows, and a new gem written for the movie—the evergreen showbiz hymn "That's Entertainment!" The plot has little or nothing to do with *The Band Wagon* as it existed on stage. Astaire is in fine company here: Jack Buchanan, Oscar Levant, and the effervescent Nanette Fabray in her only good film role. Cyd Charisse, one of Astaire's finest dance partners, is dubbed by India Adams—a good singer, but this is not the best of such match-ups. Fabray's "Got a Bran' New Suit," originally from *At Home Abroad* is a special treat, as is Adams' rendition of "Two-Faced Woman." Although this soundtrack CD is obviously not a memento of the show as performed on Broadway, it's crammed with musical pleasures.

— RICHARD BARRIOS

BAR MITZVAH BOY

Original London Cast, 1978 (Columbia/Sony) ★★★

The notes for the CD edition of this recording quote an ad from the theater program, predicting that "the show will be onstage a long time—the album will be on your turntable even longer." But *Bar Mitzvah Boy* closed quickly in London. Jack Rosenthal based his book for the musical on his successful British teleplay about a London family planning a bar mitzvah; the title character, Eliot Green, disapppears in the midst of the service. This little-known, under-appreciated music by Jule Styne has lyrics by Don Black. With Styne returning to his roots (he was born in London), the score is one of the better efforts of his late career. Highlights include Eliot's initial discussion with his rabbi about the meaning of a bar mitzvah, "Why?" / "If Only a Little Bit Sticks"; "The Bar Mitzvah of Eliot Green," which deals with the tumult of preparing for the event; the parents' love song, "We've Done All Right"; Eliot's sister's ballad of reassurance, "You Wouldn't Be You"; and "Rita's Request," a hilarious number for the mother. The score has a unique, Judeo/British, 1970s sound; it's solid, impressive work even if it's not in the same league as Styne's *Gypsy* or *Funny Girl.* Directed by Martin Charnin, the strong cast includes many West End theater veterans. As of this writing, the show's only production in New York was Off-Off-Broadway, but the hard-to-find CD is filled with nuggets of pleasure—and Eliot's final, conciliatory song, "I've Just Begun," is guaranteed to warm the heart of even the most jaded listener.

— JEFFREY DUNN

BARNUM

Original Broadway Cast, 1980 (Columbia/Sony) ★

This Jim Dale vehicle has a book by Mark Bramble, music by Cy Coleman, and lyrics by Michael Stewart. A fictionalized biography of the showman P.T. Barnum, it's really a series of production numbers looking for a musical. There is a sort-of plot about Barnum's up-and-down marriage to the disapproving Charity (a young, chipper Glenn Close), but the real drawing cards were Joe

Layton's inventive staging, Dale's inexhaustible energy, and the manically cheerful score. Coleman and Stewart's work is thoroughly professional, especially the witty "There Is a Sucker Born Every Minute" and the catchy "Thank God I'm Old" (sung by Terri White as one of Barnum's attractions, allegedly the oldest woman in the world). And just try to get the Act II opening march "Come Follow the Band" out of your head. But the score could use a dose of Ritalin; even the ballads are extroverted and Hershy Kay's orchestrations add to the forced cheerfulness. Despite the surface cleverness, it all adds up tohumbug. —DAVID BARBOUR

BAT BOY
Original Cast, 2001 (RCA) ★★

Ever since *Little Shop of Horrors*, Off-Broadway has spawned lots of campy musical sci-fi spoofs. *Bat Boy* is one of the better ones, though that's not saying much. Keythe Farley and Brian Flemming's book about the discovery of an alleged "bat child" is a convoluted tale of small-town viciousness, family secrets, and incest, all played for marginal laughs. Still, the wildly uneven score by newcomer Laurence O'Keefe is worth your attention. Oddly enough, the most ambitious passages are the most successful. The comic "Show You a Thing or Two" is a mini-masterpiece in which the bat boy, renamed Edgar, is transformed into an Anglophile whiz kid; anyone who can work Ruby Ridge, Cole Porter, and *The Remains of the Day* into a lyric is OK by me. Also nifty is the first-act closer, "Comfort and Joy," which advances the plot with speed and wit. And the ballad "Let Me Walk Among You" weds a touching melody to hilariously deadpan lyrics. So how can O'Keefe have also written junky numbers like "Another Dead Cow" (in which the townspeople wonder who killed their livestock) or the tasteless "Children, Children" (an interspecies sex orgy)? Similarly, the orchestrations by O'Keefe and Alex Lacamoire range from clever to crass. In the title role, Deven May has a powerful voice and a light comic touch. There's also skillful work from Kaitlin Hopkins as Edgar's adoptive mother (her "Three-Bedroom House" brings down the house) and from Kerry Butler as his innocent love interest. Steel yourself for the worst of the score and prepare to enjoy the best. —DAVID BARBOUR

THE BEAUTIFUL GAME
Original Cast, 2000 (Telstar Records) ★★★

Those who enjoy typing Andrew Lloyd Webber as a purveyor of spun-sugar poperettas won't know what to make of this tragic love story set against a background of social strife in Northern Ireland. Although the score lacks emotional variety, with too many sweet melodies, and Ben Elton's frequently profane lyrics are hardly cliché-free, it's a sincere attempt at something different and challenging from a composer who could certainly have rested on his lucrative laurels. Josie Walker and David Shannon sing attractively as Mary and John, the young couple whose lives are destroyed by the escalating violence between Catholics and Protestants. Walker partners beautifully with Dianne Pilkington as a Protestant girl in the unsettling "God's Own Country" and makes something wrenching out of "If This Is What We're Fighting For," a bitter denunciation of the self-righteousness behind the violence. The title number has a harsh, celebratory vigor that one rarely associates with Lloyd Webber, who did the orchestrations with David Cullen. If the score is far from a total success, the CD is definitely worth a listen. —DAVID BARBOUR

BEAUTY AND THE BEAST
Film Soundtrack, 1991 (Walt Disney Records) ★★★

This recording of songs from the animated film makes it clear why the material was destined for stage adaptation. Paige O'Hara, with her vibrant Broadway belt, is full of warmth as Belle; Jerry Orbach is a delightful Lumière in "Be Our Guest"; and Angela Lansbury as Mrs. Potts is perfect in the title song. Richard White is a grand Gaston and Robby Benson is just wonderful as the beast. The six Alan Menken-Howard Ashman numbers are orchestrated by Danny Troob with a true Broadway sound. While subsequent stage cast albums include additional songs (with music by Menken and lyrics by Tim Rice), this CD is fun to hear as a reminder of how it all began.

Original Broadway Cast, 1994 (Walt Disney Records) ★★★★

This disc demonstrates how a solid Broadway score was created by adding terrific new songs to the film version's song stack, and it also serves as a document of many fine performances. Susan Egan is a strong-voiced Belle, Terrence Mann an excellent Beast, and Burke Moses the definitive Gaston. Giving fine support are Tom Bosley as Belle's father in the new song "No Matter What"; Gary Beach, who performs Lumière's "Be Our Guest" and his part of "Human Again" with great éclat; and Beth Fowler, using her ravishing tones to burnish the title tune. David Ogden Stiers is the "Voice of Narration"; Barbara Marineau plays Madame de la Grande Bouche; Stacey Logan as Babette and Kenny Raskin as Lefou round out the laudable cast. Alan Menken and Tim Rice were perceptive about how to give the film score the additional depth it needed to serve as the score for a full-length stage musical, and the cast album also boasts orchestrations by Danny Troob. It is now difficult to conceive of *Beauty and the Beast* without Belle's "Home," the Beast's "If I Can't Love Her," and Gaston's "Me." This "tale as old as time" is destined for a long life onstage and on CD as it introduces youngsters all over the world to the joy of musicals.

Original Australian Cast, 1995 (Walt Disney Records) ★★★

Here, Hugh Jackman played Gaston, making this cast album of *Beauty and the Beast* worthy of attention if only for that reason. But the recording as a whole has great energy. Rachael Peck as Belle is strong in the opening ensemble number, saucy and audibly amused by Gaston in "Me," and her alternately sweet and powerful voice really opens up in "Home." As the Beast, baritone Michael Cormick is heart-wrenching in "How Long Can This Go On?" and "If I Can't Love Her." Jackman's delivery of "Me" makes this comic gem his own. In "Gaston," he is exultant and genuinely funny, assisted by Zachary McKay's zany Lefou; in later numbers, when his character turns from amusing to evil, Jackman delivers totally. Robyn Arthur is not in her best voice for the title song but is nevertheless compelling. The rest of the supporting cast is solid without being distinctive.

Original London Cast, 1997 (Walt Disney Records) ★★

The content of this album is virtually the same as the Broadway disc (both were produced by Bruce Botnick and Alan Menken), although there is a small cut in "Home" here. But this performance differs in style; it has a gentler quality and lacks a certain magic. Julie-Alanah Brighten is a light-voiced, very proper Belle with little spunk or fire. Alasdair Harvey is a well-mannered, sweet-voiced Beast; he misses the surface gruffness that's needed for the role, but he's moving in the reprise of "If I Can't Love Her." Burke Moses plays Gaston and he lifts the proceedings with "Me" and "Gaston," supported in the latter by Richard Gauntlett's cockney Lefou. Mary Millar is delightful as Mrs. Potts, finding some interesting nuances in the title song and making this track a highlight of the CD. The opening narration by Barry James, who plays Cogsworth, sets the subdued tone for this pleasant if unexceptional recording. —JEFFREY DUNN

BED AND SOFA
Original Off-Broadway Cast, 1996 (Varèse Sarabande) ★★★★

A stylized, three-character "silent movie opera" by composer Polly Pen and playwright Laurence Klavan, *Bed and Sofa* premiered just over a decade after Pen's avant-garde *Goblin Market*. Like that show, it was presented Off-Broadway by New York's Vineyard Theatre, was directed by André Ernotte, and was showered with awards and nominations. Based on the 1927 Soviet film *Tretya meshchanskaya* by Abram Room and Victor Shklovsky, the play centers on a married couple that invites the husband's homeless army buddy to crash indefinitely on the sofa in their tiny flat. When the husband leaves town on business, his wife and friend embark on a passionate affair. Returning to find himself displaced in the bed, the husband winds up on the sofa. For a time, the resulting ménage à trois works pretty well—but then it's beset by conflicts such as how to deal with the wife's pregnancy and the mystery of which guy is the sire. The wife discovers that her new man is as flawed as the old one and she departs, leaving both sofa and bed to the males. Pen is often accused of lacking a flair for melody, but here she delivers a stirring score with dulcet arias that owe a debt to Mussorgsky, Prokofiev, and Russian folk tunes. With supervision by musical director Alan Johnson and record producer Bruce Kimmel, Terri Klausner gives the wife earthiness and vigor; Michael X. Martin as her spouse and Jason Workman as the interloper complete an ideally balanced ensemble. —CHARLES WRIGHT

BELLS ARE RINGING
Original Broadway Cast, 1956 (Columbia/Sony) ★★★★★

There was only one Judy Holliday—a comic genius who could make you laugh, then break your heart a split second later. Her good friends Betty Comden and Adolph Green provided her with a loving showcase in *Bells Are Ringing* and this essential disc preserves one of the great Broadway performances. Holliday stars as Ella Peterson, a lonely operator for the Susanswerphone answering service, who meddles in the lives of her clients. Breaking all the rules, she helps Jeff Moss (Sydney Chaplin), a boozing, self-doubting Broadway playwright, get his career back in order—without revealing her identity. There's more trouble brewing when another client, Sandor, posing as the head of a classical record company, uses Susanswerphone as the front for a betting ring. This less-than-magisterial plot is fitted out with the most delightful score to come from the long-running partnership of Comden, Green, and Jule Styne. Holliday is given free rein in "It's a Perfect Relationship," her fantasy about Jeff; in "Is It a Crime?" (her defense of meddling), in which she says that if she'd been around in the days of Romeo and Juliet, "Those two kids would be alive today!"; and in the number to end all eleven-o'clock numbers, "I'm Going Back." "Drop That Name," sung by the chic guests at an Upper East Side party, is a dazzling catalogue of celebrities circa 1956, and "The Midas Touch" is a typical Comden and Green spoof of nightclub shows. The story's melancholy undertone comes through in the moving "Long Before I Knew You" and in that ultimate song of resignation, "The Party's Over." As Jeff, Sydney Chaplin's masculine manner and boyish enthusiasm are real assets, and he partners delightfully with Holliday in the lovely "Just in Time." Eddie Lawrence is an amusing Sandor—especially when seducing Jean Stapleton as Sue, Ella's boss and cousin, in the comic waltz "Salzburg." Peter Gennaro is Holliday's playmate in the Latin dance spoof "Mu-Cha-Cha." Robert Russell Bennett's orchestrations are jaunty and witty. Bonus tracks on the CD include Jule Styne performing "It's a Perfect Relationship," "Just in Time," and the cut song "Boogie, Woogie, Shoogie, Baby."

Film Soundtrack, 1960 (Capitol/DRG) ★★

The *Bells Are Ringing* film is essential viewing for Holliday's performance, but the soundtrack album is less interesting. Most of the numbers highlighting Comden and Green's oddball humor have been cut, including "Is It a Crime?" and "Mu-Cha-Cha." Much more mysteriously, "Long Before I Knew You" has been eliminated as well. But one addition is a jazzy, percussive gem: "Better Than a Dream," sung by Ella and Jeff at their first meeting. Dean Martin's crooning as Jeff is a plus and the two stars sound like they're having fun in "Just in Time." If anything, Holliday's reading of "The Party's Over" is even more affecting here than on the original recording, and she provides another zesty performance of "I'm Going Back." Still, it's not the full score, so stick with the Broadway album. (Note: A very young Hal Linden, who had understudied and replaced Sydney Chaplin on Broadway, turns up in "The Midas Touch.")

Broadway Cast, 2001 (Fynsworth Alley) ★

Faith Prince was at sea in this misbegotten revival, which lacked both hilarity and heart. The disc is much the same; gone are Holliday's marvelously offhand humor and compelling sadness. Prince projects a tough professionalism that's at odds with the role of Ella, and her accomplished vocals further rob the character of any vulnerability. However, she does offer a lovely rendition of "The Party's Over." Marc Kudisch works much too hard as Jeff and the strain shows. In the hands of David Garrison and Beth Fowler, the Sandor/Sue subplot falls flat, and Don Sebesky's brassy, reduced orchestrations pale in comparison to the originals. —DAVID BARBOUR

BEN BAGLEY'S SHOESTRING REVUE
Original Off-Broadway Cast, 1955 (Offbeat/Painted Smiles) ★★★

Ever wonder what bookwriter Michael Stewart and composer Charles Strouse were doing before they collaborated on *Bye Bye Birdie*? They were writing songs together for the *Shoestring Revue*. (Future *Birdie* lyricist Lee Adams collaborated with Stewart on a *Shoestring* sketch, too.) You may know that Sheldon Harnick wrote revue material before he linked up with Jerry Bock, but if you've never actually heard a young Beatrice Arthur sing Harnick's hilarious torch song "Garbage" ("You called me garbage!") and if you've never experienced the deranged whimsy of Dody Goodman complaining that "Someone Is Sending Me Flowers" ("Sometimes they're thrown through my window / Or down through the chimney they fall / Sometimes at night, when I've turned out my light / They come through a crack in the wall")—well, you've been culturally deprived. Of course, not all of the material holds up fifty years later. But this album shows the astonishing amount of talent that was just waiting to be plucked by people like Ben Bagley, who produced this show when he was twenty-one years old. In the 1950s, New York was flooded with determined young writers from around the country, many of them represented here: Bud McCreery, Arthur Siegel, June Carroll, G. Wood, Ronny Graham, and Ken Welch. As for the performers, compare the eccentrics in this cast (Arthur, Goodman, Jane Connell, and Dorothy Greener) with the talented but often indistinguishable cabaret singers you hear these days. —DAVID WOLF

BEN BAGLEY'S SHOESTRING '57
Original Off-Broadway Cast, 1957 (Offbeat/Painted Smiles) ★★★

Beatrice Arthur, Dorothy Greener, and Dody Goodman were back for more in this even more successful *Shoestring Revue* sequel, joined by Fay de Witt and *Shoestring* veterans John Bartis, Bill McCutcheon, and G. Wood. There was no Sheldon Harnick material this time, but Charles Strouse wrote a song with Lee Adams; Claibe Richardson composed several pieces with Paul Rosner; Tom Jones and Harvey Schmidt contributed one song; Carolyn Leigh and Philip Springer another; and Michael Stewart was back with an opening number and some special sketch material for Greener, the show's most unique talent. It's more fun listening to the first album: Arthur and Goodman don't have quite the musical showcases here that they had in the first edition, but Goodman does have a very amusing sketch called "The Trouble With Miss Manderson." This recording has more sketches, including a bizarre little item called "Coffee" (by Herbert Hartig and Lois Balk) that could have been written yesterday. Basically, this edition is a little less crazy than the first *Shoestring Revue,* and not as startling. Still, there's fun to be had with a song about how "Fifth Avenue buses never go out alone" and with another in which Mrs. Hemingway, Mrs. Porter, and Mrs. Eliot bemoan the fact that their sons Ernest, Cole, and T. S. work in "the arts"; the moms envy Mrs. Luciano ("Lucky Mrs. Luciano," they call her) because her son is not an artist. My favorite track is one of the items added to the CD: a live performance by Sheldon Harnick (with Charles Strouse on piano) of "The Sea Is All Around Us," which was actually in the first *Shoestring Revue.* This was recorded at a 1991 Bagley benefit to raise money to get his oeuvre transferred to CD. The song is a delightful example of Harnick's extraordinary cleverness, wit, and skill, and the performance couldn't be warmer or more charming.
— DAVID WOLF

BEN BAGLEY'S THE DECLINE AND FALL OF THE ENTIRE WORLD AS SEEN THROUGH THE EYES OF COLE PORTER
Original Cast, 1965 (Painted Smiles) ★★★

This charming disc offers two kinds of nostalgia: for Cole Porter's chic world of cocktails and heartbreak, and for the revues that thrived decades later featuring elegantly dressed singers sitting on stools and making risqué remarks between ballads. Be warned, however: The CD transfer of this album is problematic. The first thirteen tracks, from the original cast LP, are a collection of Porter rarities done to perfection by an accomplished cast led by Kaye Ballard, Harold Lang, and William Hickey. Ballard offers wicked imitations of Sophie Tucker ("Tomorrow") and Mabel Mercer (introduced as "New York's most incurable diseuse" singing "Down in the Depths"). Lang is urbanity itself in the name-dropping "I Introduced" and the stunning anthem "I Happen to Like New York," while Hickey is perfect for the indescribable "I'm a Gigolo." Elmarie Wendel is the spirit of naughtiness in "Give Him the Oo-La-La," and Carmen Alvarez, with both men in tow, gives a jaunty spin to "What Shall I Do?" If nothing else, this disc is a testament to Porter's ability to stock his lyrics with dirty jokes. Listeners may ponder these lines from "Farming," which purports to detail the rural enthusiasms of celebrities: "Now don't inquire why Georgie Raft's / Handsome bull has never calfed / Georgie's bull is beautiful / But he's gay!" The CD contains an additional twelve tracks, many from later versions of the show and featuring Tammy Grimes, Dody Goodman, and Bobby Short in performances recorded live—but, unfortunately, the sound quality is so execrable that they amount to a waste of time. Still, if you don't mind getting half a disc for your money, there's delicious fun to be had here.
— DAVID BARBOUR

BEN FRANKLIN IN PARIS
Original Broadway Cast, 1964 (Capitol/DRG) ★★★★

Timing is everything, and this lush show about the life and loves of Benjamin Franklin is an excellent example of the right musical at the wrong time. With its melodic score and literate lyrics, it's a winsome foray into the mind of Franklin if he had been a musical comedy star as well as a great statesman. But the show is only remembered as a precursor to the more successful *1776*, produced a mere five years later. If *Ben Franklin* had arrived on Broadway a decade earlier, it might be remembered as an old favorite. At any rate, the cast album represents a gem of a lost Broadway musical. It stars Robert Preston, fresh from his stage and screen triumphs in *The Music Man*; his performance leaps off of the recording and into your lap. The album also features charismatic singing by the Swedish musical theater star Ulla Sallert and the ingenue favorite Susan Watson. Many of the songs by Sidney Michaels and Mark Sandrich, Jr. are top-notch and appropriate to the subject and time period; two numbers, "To Be Alone With You" and "You're in Paris," were ghostwritten by the talented young Jerry Herman. Others lapse into a tired operetta genre but, on the whole, this album is a joy to hear and a prime example of showmanship from Broadway's golden era. — GERARD ALESSANDRINI

BERLIN TO BROADWAY WITH KURT WEILL
Original Off-Broadway Cast, 1972 (Paramount/no CD) ★★★

This sampler of Weill's theater songs played Off-Broadway at the Theatre de Lys (now the Lucille Lortel), where Marc Blitzstein's version of *The Threepenny Opera* enjoyed a stunning success in the 1950s. It's a brisk run-through of the composer's career, with extended medleys from *Threepenny* as well as *Happy End, The Rise and Fall of the City of Mahagonny, Marie Galante, Johnny Johnson, Knickerbocker Holiday, Lady in the Dark, One Touch of Venus, Love Life, Street Scene,* and *Lost in the Stars.* (Oddly, there's not a trace here of Weill's *The Firebrand of Florence,* which, like *Lady in the Dark,* has lyrics by Ira Gershwin). The narration, written by Gene Lerner, is overblown at times but allows us to hear how Weill's music evolved over the course of his career. The cast members—Jerry Lanning, Judy Landers, Margery Cohen, Hal Watters—capture the peculiar blend of romance and bitterness that was the composer's hallmark. Ken Kercheval narrates. The album is not available on CD and, now that so many more of Weill's shows have been recorded, it may not be as essential as it once was. But it's an excellent introduction to the work of this singular talent. — DAVID BARBOUR

BEST FOOT FORWARD
Film Soundtrack, 1943 (Rhino-Turner) ★★★★

Good News was the college musical par excellence in the 1920s and *Best Foot Forward* did the same for high schools soon after it opened in 1941. The rousing "Buckle Down Winsocki" became an instant classic, and the show's young and gifted creators, Hugh Martin and Ralph Blane, promptly moved to Hollywood. Much of the *Best Foot Forward* cast went with them for the unusually faithful movie version, headlined by Lucille Ball (vocals dubbed by Gloria Grafton) and the Harry James orchestra. Among the surprises here are an overture that's not heard in the film and the added-then-cut "Who Do You Think I Am?" If the James orchestra is decidedly upscale for Winsocki High—"Two O'Clock Jump" is sensational—there is abundant energy in the air as a talented cast of youthful pros rips through Martin and Blane's funny and spirited score. Possibly best of all is the young Nancy Walker, who, with June Allyson and Gloria de Haven, makes "The

Three B's" one of the film's highlights. Tommy Dix, short of stature and big of voice, had a supporting role in the Broadway show but was upgraded to male lead in the movie; his "Buckle Down Winsocki," moved to the eleven-o'clock spot, is a stirring conclusion to a fine film.

Off-Broadway Cast, 1963 (CAD/DRG) ★★★
When *Best Foot Forward* was revived in 1963, Martin and Blane added a sort-of-new song, "You Are for Loving," originally written for a television production of *Meet Me in St. Louis*. The interpolation was deemed necessary for a headline-grabber in a supporting role: Liza Minnelli made her New York stage debut at the age of seventeen in a well-received production with a spirited cast. When lead Paula Wayne left the show, she was replaced in the role of the washed-up movie star by a real-life washed-up movie star, Veronica Lake. The company also included a pair of brothers named Glenn and Christopher Walken. Judging from this recording, the production had just the kind of enthusiasm needed for *Best Foot Forward*. Wayne is particularly attractive in the rueful "Hollywood Story," and "The Three B's" is almost as much of a showstopper as it is in the movie. In the secondary role of Ethel, Liza throws off the show's balance somewhat, but no complaints can be made over her youthful glow or her integration into the ensemble numbers. With its modest piano accompaniment, this performance has the appropriate air of a high-school musical done by an unusually gifted group of students.   —RICHARD BARRIOS

THE BEST LITTLE WHOREHOUSE GOES PUBLIC
Original Broadway Cast, 1994 (Varèse Sarabande) ★★★
Those looking for a guilty treat can seek out this cast album of a show that ran for fifteen performances on Broadway in 1994. The sequel to the long-running smash *The Best Little Whorehouse in Texas* (below) reunited that show's creators: songwriter Carol Hall, director-choreographer Tommy Tune, and bookwriters Larry L. King and Peter Masterson. Whatever problems the show may have had onstage, the well-produced recording is brassy, occasionally campy, and full of enjoyable music. Hall's score alternates between country-style melodies and a lush Vegas sound. The dialogue swatches on the CD and the notes in the accompanying booklet convey an idea of the plot's complexities. If you think you'd enjoy hearing a Broadway chorus chanting "Keep It Up for A. Harry Hardast," this album belongs on your shelf. The opening number, "Let the Devil Take Us," bursts with old-time Broadway vitality. The performers sound like they're having fun even if they collectively press the gas pedal all the way to the floor in an effort to make the show work. The wink-nudge jokes and showbiz tricks pile up, but by the time the disc ends with a patriotic flourish and a medley-style curtain call, only the most stone-hearted will not be at least partially won over. Dee Hoty sings "Picture Show" with a smile in her voice, puts over "I'm Leavin' Texas" well, effectively superintends the phone-sex number "Call Me," and has a charming duet with Scott Holmes, "It's Been a While." Peter Matz (orchestrations) and Wally Harper (vocal and dance arrangements) do powerful teamwork. Just listen to the "Bankity-Bank" section of "I'm Leavin' Texas," and you'll hear how the creativity of these two men gives the music a slick, easygoing sheen.   —MORGAN SILLS

THE BEST LITTLE WHOREHOUSE IN TEXAS
Original Broadway Cast, 1978 (MCA) ★★★★
On the off chance that you've never seen or heard this show, don't be put off by its title. Yes, it's about a house of prostitution and its central character is the brothel's madam, Miss Mona. But here's a musical that is smart, funny, and sexy rather than stupid and smarmy—in contrast

to its flop Broadway sequel (described above). With a book by Larry L. King and Peter Masterson, the based-in-fact story tells about the fallout that occurs when a self-righteous TV personality "exposes" the existence of the Chicken Ranch, a whorehouse that's been in operation for decades. Carol Hall's tuneful songs are amusing, heartfelt, and rousing by turns. Among the highlights are the expository songs "20 Fans" and "A Lil' Ole Bitty Pissant Country Place"; the "Aggie Song," in which a bunch of horny football players plan their victory celebration at the whorehouse; and "Hard Candy Christmas," sung by the Chicken Ranch girls when they learn that the place will soon close. Miss Mona is played by Carlin Glynn, the wife of Peter Masterson, who also codirected the show with Tommy Tune. Glynn does a bang-up job with such numbers as "Girl, You're a Woman," "No Lies" (a sassy duet with Delores Hall), and "The Bus From Amarillo." There are amusing turns by Clint Allmon as TV snoop Melvin P. Thorpe and Jay Garner as the slick Governor of Texas. Henderson Forsythe as Sheriff Ed Earl delivers the solid country ballad "Good Old Girl." Hot damn, this is a terrific album!

Film Soundtrack, 1982 (MCA) ★★

Country-music superstar Dolly Parton was an excellent choice to play Miss Mona in the movie version of *Whorehouse.* Opposite her is Burt Reynolds, for whom the role of Sheriff Ed Earl was transformed into a younger, more self-involved character. The soundtrack orchestrations are fuller than the stage originals, although not too Hollywoodized. The huge mistake made here was the excision of several of Carol Hall's great songs in favor of items written by Parton. Apparently, the star wrote several new songs for the flick but only the lame Parton-Reynolds duet "Sneakin' Around" made the final cut; another Parton addition, "I Will Always Love You," had been written earlier. The great Theresa Merritt, who plays Jewel in the movie, is heard here singing a few lines of "A Lil' Ole Bitty Pissant Country Place." Fortunately, "Texas Has a Whorehouse in It" was retained—it's sung by Dom DeLuise as Melvyn P. Thorpe—and the governor's number, "The Sidestep," is done to perfection by Charles Durning.

National Tour Cast, 2001 (Fynsworth Alley) ★★

This recording of a national tour production of *Whorehouse* is disappointing at first; the CD has neither the spontaneity of the original Broadway album nor the polish of the film soundtrack. But repeated listening reveals that it's successful on its own terms, mostly due to the presence of Ann-Margret as Miss Mona. A-M's work in the tour engendered strong opinions, many of them negative; the star's live performances had hitherto been limited to Vegas acts and arena concerts, and she reportedly seemed unsure of herself in a book show. This album gives credence to the charge of tentativeness that was leveled at her. She never really lets go and belts any high notes, which is a problem in songs like "A L'il Ole Bitty Pissant Country Place," "No Lies," and "The Bus From Amarillo." Still, Ann-Margret works well within her limitations, sounding just fine in the lower-lying sections of the role and adopting her sexy, breathy head voice for the higher parts—so even if her overall vocal performance lacks theatrical energy, it has its own sort of charm. As for the rest of the cast: Gary Sandy is appealing in the one song, "Good Old Girl," which he sings as the sheriff; Rob Donohue is a stitch in Melvin P. Thorpe's big number, "Texas Has a Whorehouse in It"; Roxie Lucas acts her way through "Doatsy Mae" with persuasive results; and Avery Sommers has a high old time as Jewel. "A Friend to Me," a pretty new ballad by Carol Hall, is well rendered by Ann-Margret and by Hall herself in a bonus track.   —MICHAEL PORTANTIERE

BIG
Original Broadway Cast, 1996 (Universal/Decca) ★

Onstage, *Big* was a textbook example of how a top creative team with all the right intentions could destroy the charm of a beloved film. On disc, the score by Richard Maltby, Jr. and David Shire provides sporadic enjoyment, even if it's somewhat overbearing. John Weidman's book closely follows Gary Ross and Anne Spielberg's screenplay: Josh (Patrick Levis) is a frustrated twelve-year-old who wakes up one morning in the body of an adult (Daniel Jenkins); he runs off to New York, becomes a successful toy executive, and falls in love with a colleague named Susan (Crista Moore). The overture starts things off on an exciting note and the opening number, "Can't Wait," sets the right tone of generation-gap exasperation. But the songs tend to dwell on the characters' feelings when they're not straining for exuberance; this is especially true of "Fun," in which Josh kicks up a ruckus in F.A.O. Schwartz with the toy magnate MacMillan (John Cypher). The quieter tunes work best—especially "Stop, Time," sung by Josh's mother (Barbara Walsh), and "I Want to Know," sung by Josh when he realizes that he's going to spend the night with Susan. There's also a catchy chorus number, "Cross the Line," performed at a toy-company party. But too much of the score, especially as arranged by Doug Besterman, is bombastic and full of false high spirits. —DAVID BARBOUR

BIG CITY RHYTHM
Original Off-Broadway Cast, 1996 (Original Cast Records) ★★★

The heyday of the intimate revue may have been decades ago, but some good ones have surfaced more recently. Consider Barry Kleinbort's winning song cycle *Big City Rhythm,* blessed with Christopher Denny's tasteful piano arrangements and a high-powered cast. As a composer-lyricist, Kleinbort has lots of range and is willing to serve up old-fashioned melody or new-fashioned lack thereof as suits the material. Some inside jokes may be lost on some listeners—like the salute to Broadway leading ladies who can't sing—but those in the know will love them. Lots of accessible stuff is here, too, such as an extended medley of proposed theme songs for unlikely movies ("Psycho, Are You Lonely Tonight?"). Marcia Lewis is adorable as a peripatetic sophisticate in "I Get Around," Lewis Cleale and Eric Michael Gillett are stalwart leading men, and Melanie Vaughan is exceedingly funny as a difficult chanteuse just out of the Betty Ford Clinic. Some of the strongest numbers are from Kleinbort's proposed musical version of Garson Kanin's *The Rat Race;* they'll make you eager to hear more. —MARC MILLER

BIG RIVER
Original Broadway Cast, 1985 (MCA) ★★★

Country-music songwriter Roger Miller furnished the score for this musical version of the Mark Twain classic *Huckleberry Finn* and the result is a twangy Broadway sound that's just right for the beloved tale. The rollicking "Muddy Water" and the more serene "River in the Rain" represent Miller at his country best, while quirky comic numbers such as "Hand for the Hog" (Tom Sawyer's tribute to his porcine pals) illustrate why Miller is also well known as a novelty songwriter. His skill as a tunesmith is unimpeachable here—but his lyrics, though frequently quite clever, are sometimes too simplistic or repetitive for a Broadway book musical. "Waitin' for the Light to Shine," for instance, may be the show's most melodically beautiful number, but there is little to distinguish it from any other gospel song. As far as good show-tune writing is concerned, Miller does prove himself with the lively opener "Do Ya Wanna Go to Heaven?" and the affecting "Leavin's Not the Only Way to Go." The finest performances on this disc are by

Daniel Jenkins as Huck and Tony Award-winner Ron Richardson as his best friend, the runaway slave Jim. And a pre-*Roseanne* John Goodman does a memorable turn as Huck's crazy father, Pap, railing comically against the "Guv'ment." —BROOKE PIERCE

BILLION DOLLAR BABY
World Premiere Recording, 2000 (Original Cast Records) ★

Betty Comden and Adolph Green followed *On the Town* with this disappointment, a scathing satire of the 1920s. Except for a dance sequence that appeared in *Jerome Robbins' Broadway,* the 1945 show was largely forgotten until a concert performance at the York Theatre led to this disc. In the title role, Kristin Chenoweth chisels her way to the top, going from failed beauty-contest entrant to gangster's moll and landing a billionaire just as the stock market crashes. Among her victims are Debbie Gravitte as a Texas Guinan-like nightclub owner, Marc Kudisch as a mob figure, and Richard B. Shull as the bank account of her dreams. In general, Morton Gould's score lacks distinction, and the many dance interludes have been condensed in James Bassi's four-piece orchestrations. The celebrated Comden and Green wit isn't always in evidence, but Gravitte gets the best numbers—"Broadway Blossom" and "Havin' a Time"—and Kudisch delivers a jazzy item called "Bad Timing." Considering that she has the title role, Chenoweth has relatively little to do (the part was written for dancer Joan McCracken), and her numbers—including "Dreams Come True" and "Faithless"—are forgettable. Still, even if this show is no lost classic, fans of the cast members and of Comden and Green will want to give the CD a spin. —DAVID BARBOUR

BILLY NONAME
Original Off-Broadway Cast, 1970 (Roulette/Original Cast Records) ★★

An interesting autobiography of a fictional black playwright who is frequently angry and sometimes simply yearning, this musical covers his life from conception (in a street rape), through World War II, the civil rights movement, and the death of Martin Luther King (the final song is "Burn, Baby, Burn!"). The playwright ponders his role in the struggles of his era, but the ending of the show offers no answers. Of course, it's impossible to know from the cast album how detailed and skillful William Wellington Mackey's script is. The songs, by Johnny Brandon, travel confidently through the story's thirty years, moving easily along with swing, rhythm and blues, early rock, and the sounds of the late 1960s. Although there's not a lot of dramatic musical writing here, the tunes are mostly vibrant and rhythmic and it's certainly easy to accept them as the language of these characters. The title role is uncommonly well sung by Donny Burks, and there are fine supporting performances by Alan Weeks, Hattie Winston, and Urylee Leonardos. —DAVID WOLF

BIRDS OF PARADISE
Original Off-Broadway Cast, 1987 (JAY) ★★★★

On hearing this recording, listeners are bound to wonder why the show was not more successful. The score is filled with intricate, catchy melodies by David Evans and intelligent, witty lyrics by Winnie Holtzman. From start to finish, the cast sings and acts as if they have discovered a pot of gold. The opening number, "Too Many Nights," cleverly introduces actors in a community theater awaiting the arrival of someone who's coming to direct them in a new musical. Two other highlights are Todd Graff's duet with Crista Moore in the exciting "Coming True" and Donna Murphy, Mary Beth Piel, and Barbara Walsh joining their powerhouse voices in the title song. When Graff and Piel confront each other in "After Opening Night," it's engrossing and moving. Some of the comedic numbers may not work very well outside the play's context, but John Cunningham's "Somebody," J. K. Simmons' "She's Out There," and Piel's "You're Mine" are among the other fine songs in this top-notch score. Also worthy of note is the lovely ballad "Imagining You." The show was directed by Arthur Laurents and it seems clear that he encouraged the writers to spread their wings. This album is altogether necessary for discriminating enthusiasts.

—JEFFREY DUNN

BITTER SWEET
Studio Cast, 1962 (Angel/no CD) ★

It seemed a radical idea in 1929: an operetta with believable characters, literate dialogue, first-rate lyrics, and a minimum of the coyness associated with the form. With Noël Coward providing all of the above, plus the music, a classic was born—a sentimental love story with grace, intelligence, wit, and irony. Alas, the recording industry has yet to do the show justice. Aside from a few tracks featuring the original New York cast (including Peggy Wood, whose "Zigeuner" sounds like a madwoman's hysterics), *Bitter Sweet* has rated only a couple of studio cast recordings; none of them has been transferred to CD thus far and all are difficult to track down. The first one that pops up in used-record shops or online is this atrocity, issued in overemphatic early stereo and clocking in at a modest but by no means brisk forty minutes. Are the singers at fault? Not really: Vanessa Lee's Sarah has spirit and excellent top notes while Roberto Cardinali's sturdy tenor lends romantic presence in the role of Carl. On the other hand, Julie Dawn's Manon—who sings "If Love Were All" and "Kiss Me"—is a sexy French kitten, not the world-weary chanteuse so superbly embodied by Ivy St. Helier in the original. But don't blame Dawn or even Michael Collins' turgid conducting; blame the orchestrations, by Brian Fahey and Ray Terry. Overwhelmed by screaming violins, they spread a thick, maple-sugar glaze over Coward's delicate story.

Studio Cast, 1969 (EMI/no CD) ★★

If the preceding album represents operetta performance at its most clueless, this entry isn't far behind. Johnny Douglas' orchestrations are a step above the primordial soup of the earlier set, but they proceed from the same premise: Disguise an operetta's age by pretending it's a 1960s musical, loading it up with too many strings, too many brass flourishes, and even jazz-combo drums (at the end of "Ladies of the Town"). The conducting is glacial, especially in the waltzes: "Kiss Me" is a dirge. But this disc does have a superior set of singers. The great Australian operetta soprano June Bronhill sings quite lusciously, trilling an audacious high C at the end of "What Is Love?" Opposite her, Neville Jason has more personality than most Carls. Julia D'Alba's Manon is another purring feline, but her throaty alto is pleasant to hear. The meaningless finale, which miraculously brings Carl back from the dead to duet with Sarah on "I'll See You Again," is a miscalculation. Nevertheless, some of Coward's material shines through the mishandling on this well-engineered album, like the sun through a British cloud cover.

Sadler's Wells Cast, 1988 (JAY, 2CDs) ★★★

Now, this is more like it. The excellent Sadler's Wells light opera company aimed for a complete *Bitter Sweet,* true to the spirit of Coward and definitive in its musical presentation. This is by far the most complete recording of the score: It lacks only an overture, a couple of incidental songs, and some underscoring. Finally, we get to hear all of Coward's unflinching lyrics to "Green Carnation" and "Alas, the Time Is Past." There's also an entrancing, instrumental-only "Bitter Sweet Waltz"; its flatted thirds show Coward to be a more adventurous composer at age twenty-nine than many fans realized. But *Bitter Sweet* needs inspired casting to catch fire, and this is merely a pretty good operetta ensemble. Valerie Masterson is a no-nonsense Sarah, vocally secure and suitably warm, yet the character is supposed to metamorphose from a will-ful romantic to a wise grande dame, and the singer doesn't differentiate much between the two. As Carl, Martin Smith has scant personality and not enough voice. Rosemary Ashe is a capable Manon, up to the demands of "If Love Were All" and the saucy "Bonne Nuit, Merci," but she's not distinctive. The orchestrations aren't the originals and there's a blandness to them, as there is to Michael Reed's conducting. Transitional dialogue is included in over-perky line readings that never convey how much smarter *Bitter Sweet* is than the average operetta. The lavish, dual-CD packaging promises something special—but what's really special about the album is Sir Noël's material, not this hit-or-miss rendition of it.   —MARC MILLER

BLACK AND BLUE
Original Broadway Cast, 1989 (DRG) ★★★★

The title of this show, taken from a Fats Waller song, pretty much announces what it will be: Another revue-style look at African-American entertainment in the first half of the twen-tieth century, this time emphasizing the music of such great blues women as Bessie Smith and Ma Rainey. Interestingly, the show was created by Argentineans (Claudio Segovia and Héctor Orezzoli) living in France, reminding us that some aspects of American culture are more appreciated by so-called outsiders. It's not easy to feel the shape of the show from this disc and it's a pity that the three leads had to share the stage and recording studio with less charismatic performers. Still, most of the songs are delivered by a powerful star trio. In the opening number, Ruth Brown, Linda Hopkins, and Carrie Smith announce, "I'm a Woman." The Tony Award-winning Brown has the roughest voice and rawest style. Smith lends a smoother tone to such standards as "Am I Blue?" and Hopkins channels her enormous voice compellingly. While there is no clear-cut winner among the three, Brown's wry double-entendres in "If I Can't Sell It, I'll Keep Sittin' on It" rate special mention. As long as this recording focuses on the stars and their first-rate instrumental support, it's boisterous, funny, and frequently moving.   —RICHARD BARRIOS

BLACKBIRDS OF 1928
Original Broadway Cast Members, 1928 (Columbia/no CD) ★★★

All-black shows became the Broadway rage in 1920 with the long-running *Shuffle Along*. Eight years later, an even bigger smash matched a talented black cast with a white creative team. *Blackbirds of 1928*—the very title would be a flashpoint today—successfully launched the song-writing team of Dorothy Fields and Jimmy McHugh and gave the world "I Can't Give You Anything but Love," not to mention "Diga Diga Do" and other songs. The artists, so often con-fined to segregated vaudeville houses, were clearly thrilled to be on Broadway and they perform with irresistible panache. Bill "Bojangles" Robinson had but one number in the show, "Doin' the New Lowdown," but it's a winner. Strangely enough, Adelaide Hall did not record "I Can't Give You Anything but Love" or "Diga Diga Do" for this set; she was, however, given the chance to revive a good song cut from the original production, "Baby!" Ethel Waters is won-derful in a dramatic choral version of "St. Louis Blues" and the Duke Ellington orchestra plays spectacularly. If the whole thing isn't quite a cohesive cast album, it's a zingy evocation of a bygone era and a memorable show. Odd footnote: "I Can't Give You Anything but Love" was originally written in tribute to Charles Lindbergh, and only when "Baby!" was substituted for "Lindy" did the song go anywhere!

—RICHARD BARRIOS

BLOOD BROTHERS

Original London Cast, 1983 (Castle) ★

This is the story of Mrs. Johnstone, a lower-class Liverpudlian whose husband deserts her, even though she's pregnant and already has seven children. Having determined that she can afford to care for only one more child, Mrs. J. is devastated to learn that she's to have twins. In desperation, she agrees to let her rich employer, Mrs. Lyons, take one of the babies to raise as her own. At age seven, the two nonidentical twin boys—Mrs. J's Mickey and Mrs. L's Eddie—meet and become fast friends, unaware that they are siblings. Years later, this melodramatic situation leads to tragedy, explicated in ominous tones by a Narrator. It's easy to make fun of *Blood Brothers* (and, indeed, the show inspired a hilarious *Forbidden Broadway* spoof). With book, music, and lyrics by Willy Russell, the show leaves much to be desired in terms of professional polish, yet it has sincerity. Some of the lyrics don't quite fit the music and there are some false rhymes ("chap/chat") along with some neat ones ("soldier/told yer"). Near-constant allusions to a certain screen goddess are annoying. In the first version of a song titled "Marilyn Monroe," references to the star are apt and clever but they become strained to the point of ridiculousness in subsequent numbers. On the whole, Russell's music is better than his lyrics; the melodies of "Sunday Afternoon," "Easy Terms," and "Tell Me It's Not True" are haunting, while "Bright New Day" is joyous. Some melodies recur with added impact, as when the tune of "My Child," sung by the two mothers, is later used for "My Friend," the two boys' declaration of their bond with each other. The strong cast is led by Barbara Dickson as Mrs. J., George Costigan as Mickey, Andrew C. Wadsworth as Eddie, and Andrew Schofield as the Narrator, but the score's virtues are undermined by keyboard-and-synthesizer-heavy arrangements.

London Cast, 1988 (RCA) ★★★

This recording is superior to its predecessor, offering better arrangements and more music—about fifteen added minutes. Oddly, the song originally called "The Devil's Got Your Number" is now called "Shoes Upon the Table"; other titles have changed as well. Kiki Dee is strong as Mrs. Johnstone and so are Con O'Neill as Mickey, Robert Locke as Eddie, and Warwick Evans as the Narrator.

"The International Recording," 1995 (First Night) ★★★★

Three starry leads and the Royal Philharmonic Orchestra will make this the preferred *Blood Brothers* recording for many listeners. At over an hour, it's also the longest of the recordings under review. The singers and the huge orchestra are recorded in a weighty, reverberant acoustic that, depending on one's taste, makes the score seem lush and important or annoyingly pretentious. The soaring overture is a far cry from the synthesized sound of the first *Blood Brothers* album and the famous lead singers are excellent. Petula Clark, a onetime pop star with impressive stage and film credits, has a compelling, soulful voice that's perfect for Mrs. Johnstone. The American teenybopper idols David and Sean Cassidy, half-brothers in real life, sing very well as Mickey and Eddie—and their Brit accents are quite convincing. The Narrator here is Willy Russell, who wrote the show's book, music, and lyrics.

London Cast, 1995 (First Night) ★★★

This recording is worth tracking down for the performance of Stephanie Lawrence, who played Mrs. Johnstone in *Blood Brothers* on Broadway in 1993. Heading a fine cast that includes Warwick Evans, David Hitchen, Mark Hutchinson, and Joe Young, Lawrence is in a class by herself as Mrs. J. The fact that she died at age fifty in 2000 makes the disc valuable as a memento of her deeply committed, heartbreaking characterization.　　　　　　—MICHAEL PORTANTIERE

BLOOMER GIRL
Original Broadway Cast, 1944 (Decca) ★★★

Though the show is seldom revived and threw off no enduring hit songs, the cast album of this Harold Arlen-E.Y. Harburg wartime hit has rarely been out of print. Inspired by the life of feminist/industrialist Dolly Bloomer (though the bloomer girl of the title is her fictional niece Evelina) and set during the Civil War, its score has long melodic lines and blues-tinged harmonies, subtle satire, and loads of Harburgian wordplay. As he often did, the master lyricist pokes fun at the battle of the sexes, skewers moral hypocrisy (Evelina lives in a community so staid that "Even the rabbits / Inhibit their habits"), and argues stirringly for the cause of freedom in the stunning song "The Eagle and Me." (It's one of the fifty songs that Stephen Sondheim says he wishes he'd written, and you'll understand why.) *Bloomer Girl* was one of the first post-*Oklahoma!* Americana musicals and it borrowed that show's personnel liberally—not just choreographer Agnes De Mille, but also soubrettes Joan McCracken and Celeste Holm, the latter promoted to leading lady. Truth to tell, Holm is vocally underpowered for Evelina, falling back on scoops, head voice, and other tricks to make it through such rangy Arlen melodies as "Right As the Rain." McCracken is even worse, so overplaying her comedy songs that she nearly spoils such choice couplets as "Utopia, Utopia / Don't be a dope, ya dope, ya!" The men aren't vocal godsends, either: David Brooks' "Evelina" and Dooley Wilson's "The Eagle and Me" lack flavor. The most powerful singer on the album is probably Arlen himself, making an impressive cameo appearance in "Man for Sale." As to the album's various issues and reissues, this Decca CD is the keeper; a simulated stereo LP edition made everyone sound like they were singing at the bottom of a well. This version is sonically improved and it has some dandy extras, such as a longer, funnier version of "Sunday in Cicero Falls" and a clearer take of "I Got a Song."　　　　　　—MARC MILLER

BLUES IN THE NIGHT
London Cast, 1987 (First Night) ★★★★

This live recording of the revue *Blues in the Night* is a real gem. Arrangements that split the difference between jazz and theater combine with fetching performances of familiar and less-well-known material by a variety of composers and lyricists to tell the story of three women (Carol Woods, Maria Friedman, and Debbie Bishop) who are in love with the same rotten guy (Clarke Peters). A rowdy, appreciative audience adds to the atmosphere and fun. Each of these gifted ladies gets a shining personality number: Woods does "Take Me for a Buggy Ride," Friedman nails "Taking a Chance on Love," and Bishop describes her "Rough and Ready Man." Peters is most enjoyable in "Baby Doll." The ladies make a sassy trio in "Take It Right Back," and the ballads are also done full justice: Woods' well-acted "Lover Man," Friedman's thoughtful "Willow Weep for Me," and the group's sweet "It Makes My Love Come Down." In fact, several of the group numbers are home runs, among them haunting renditions of "Blues in the Night" and "Nobody Knows You When You're Down and Out." Within the theatrical sub-genre of 1980s and 1990s revues crafted along similar lines (*Sophisticated Ladies, Five Guys Named Moe, Black and Blue*) this is my personal favorite. (Note: A previous version of the show played briefly in New York in 1982 with Jean Du Shon, Debbie Shapiro (Gravitte), Leslie Uggams, and Charles Coleman in the cast, but that production yielded no cast album.)   —MORGAN SILLS

BOMBAY DREAMS
Original London Cast, 2002 (Sony) ★★★

This is the world's first pop-rock, English-Hindi-Punjabi stage musical—but it isn't as exotic as it sounds. Andrew Lloyd Webber produced the show, "based on an idea" that he and Shekar Kapur devised about a naif finding fame in the hyperactive Bombay film industry known as Bollywood. Like most Lloyd Webber shows, *Bombay Dreams* is big on spectacle (the saris! the fountains!) but short on logic; it exists mainly as a showcase for a popular young composer, in this case, A. R. Rahman, who has written the scores to some fifty Bollywood films. Rahman is a real talent with a lively gift for melody and a wide palette of styles. The recording opens with quiet mystery: Chords waft in as chantlike singing creates an atmosphere of suspense. Then you can practically hear the smoke clearing as the slums of Bombay (now called Mumbai) awaken. The pace picks up and a beguiling tune kicks in, along with Don Black's leaden lyrics, as the ambitious hero Akaash (Raza Jaffrey) dreams of stardom: "Like an eagle was born to fly, ride across the open sky / I was born to be seen on a screen in Bollywood." And then the show plows through the expected: good guys versus bad, concerned families, broad humor, splashy musical numbers. It all adds up to a boy-meets-girl, boy-loses-girl, eunuch-sings-about-love musical. With breathy voices given digital treatments à la Cher, the album has a trendy pop sound that's impossible to resist. The lyrics of "Shakalaka Baby" are silly, yet the song is infectious and lots of fun. (Note: A revised version of *Bombay Dreams,* with a book adapted by Thomas Meehan and some new songs, opened on Broadway in 2004.)   —ROBERT SANDLA

BOUNCE
Original Cast, 2004 (Nonesuch) ★★

Stephen Sondheim's first new musical in nearly a decade, *Bounce* was highly anticipated when it played Chicago and Washington in 2003. Though this disc benefits from the lack of John Weidman's book, the score doesn't sound appreciably better here than it did onstage, despite a good orchestra conducted by David Caddick and a top-notch cast including Howard McGillin, Richard Kind, Michele Pawk, Gavin Creel, Herndon Lackey, and Jane Powell. What's missing is a sense of vivid inspiration, although there are a few nice selections. The title song, sung by McGillin and Kind, is catchy; McGillin and Pawk have an attractive duet in "The Best Thing That Ever Has Happened"; and "Addison's City" and "Boca Raton" make up an entertaining musical scene that chronicles the Florida land boom. Otherwise, the music has uncomfortable echoes of Sondheim's superior work in such shows as *Sweeney Todd* (a vamp in the title song recalls "By the Sea") and *Merrily We Roll Along* (Jonathan Tunick's orchestrations could have been lifted from there). There's much here to appreciate but little to love; Sondheim's previous scores set the bar so high that a middling effort like this one never seems quite good enough.   —MATTHEW MURRAY

THE BOY FRIEND

Original London Cast, 1954 (HMV/no CD) ★★★

A pastiche of 1920s tuners with an absurd but dear book and a Sandy Wilson score packed with wonderful tunes, *The Boy Friend* presented here is a recording of the show's first full production. As such, this is the most "authentic" of the musical's various albums, but others are more complete, more fully orchestrated, and boast better singers. Many of the show's songs were edited down for this recording, and "Safety in Numbers" and "The 'You-Don't-Want-to-Play-With-Me' Blues" are missing entirely. The performers set the tone for those who followed. Anne Rogers is Polly, the finishing-school student who falls in love with a messenger who turns out to be the son of a lord. Denise Hurst is Maisie, in love with wealthy Bobby Van Dusen, and Maria Charles is Dulcie, who has a flirtation with Lord Brockhurst. The plot comes to what is described as an ending "in which everybody is successfully paired off in a matter of minutes."

Original Broadway Cast, 1954 (RCA) ★★★★

When top-flight Broadway producers Cy Feuer and Ernest Martin got the American rights to *The Boy Friend,* they agreed to bring author Sandy Wilson and director Vida Hope to New York to ensure that the U.S. edition would be faithful to the London original. But the plan soon soured. According to Feuer's autobiography, Wilson and Hope insisted on adding a new scene and song, which the producers vetoed. According to Wilson's book, Feuer and Martin cut a song, switched actors from one role to another, and fired others. Wilson claims they even tried to get rid of star Julie Andrews; Feuer writes that he knew she was a genius all along. From all reports, the New York production was faster, louder, and broader than the original. In the only change that Wilson approved, the music was reorchestrated (by Ted Royal and Charles L. Cooke) and more musicians were added. The Broadway cast performs with punch and precision, and the score sounds great on this recording—especially the snazzy new overture, which rides to a dazzling conclusion.

Broadway Cast, 1970 (Decca/no CD) ★★★★

The Boy Friend ran 485 performances on Broadway, beginning in 1954. Three years later, it was revived Off-Broadway and ran nearly twice as long. In 1970, it was revived on Broadway again and, although unsuccessful, it produced a cast album that includes the Act II finale and other previously unrecorded numbers. Judy Carne, then a star of TV's *Laugh-In,* got above-the-title solo billing but proved uninteresting onstage; though she sings well enough as Polly, she can't compare with Julie Andrews or Anne Rogers. People who remember this production always refer to it as "the Sandy Duncan *Boy Friend*": Duncan was adorable in the secondary role of Maisie and got all the reviews (with her charming partner, Harvey Evans), but on the recording, she has trouble with "Safety in Numbers." Leon Shaw as Percy Browne sings his part of "Fancy Forgetting" poorly; Barbara Andres as Hortense speaks "It's Nicer in Nice" rather than sings it; and the orchestra performs without the glorious abandon of the players on the first Broadway album.

Film Soundtrack, 1971 (MGM/no CD) ★

MGM had long owned the rights to *The Boy Friend* but did nothing with them until the studio took the lunatic step of handing the property to director Ken Russell. His screenplay has a repertory troupe visited by a Hollywood director who turns *The Boy Friend* into a lavish movie musical. The film is filled with striking images, yet it's campy and witless. We're left with the charming performances of Twiggy and a young Tommy Tune. The score, with too-cute orchestrations by Peter Maxwell Davies, has little feel of the '20s. Two songs, "The 'You-Don't-Want-to-Play-With-Me' Blues" and "It's Nicer in Nice," were cut from the film but are on the soundtrack album; two vintage non-Sandy Wilson numbers, "You Are My Lucky Star" and "All I Do Is Dream of You," have been added. Their interpolation can only be described as unnecessary, which is also a good word for this recording.   —DAVID WOLF

THE BOY FROM OZ
Original Australian Cast, 1998 (EMI) ★★★

Peter Allen wrote only one musical—the inane *Legs Diamond,* still prized by connoisseurs of flops—but his life story plays itself out in this glossy show. *The Boy From Oz* is a fast-paced biography and the first home-grown Australian musical hit. It traces Allen's life from his tap-dancing, piano-playing youth through his career as pop songwriter, showman, and celebrity gadabout. His meteoric rise to fame ended in his death from AIDS in 1992. The musical covers Allen's work with Judy Garland, his marriage to Liza Minnelli, and—to no one's surprise but his own—his belated realization that he was gay. Nick Enright's flimsy book shoehorns Allen's songs into dramatic contexts with varying success. "When I Get My Name in Lights" (from *Legs Diamond*) works well for the young Peter (Mathew Waters). Todd McKenney is charming and engaged as the adult Allen, with a reedy tenor that sails through the anthemic "I Still Call Australia Home." Chrissie Amphlett makes an interesting Garland—she and McKenney have great rapport in "Only an Older Woman"—while Angela Toohey's Liza is a dizzy whirlwind. Bits of script heard on the recording, such as a news flash about the Stonewall Riots, give context to Allen's growing self-knowledge. Although the album has an earnest, unpretentious feel, Allen's original renditions of his songs are catchier than these, and nothing can beat Olivia Newton John's version of "I Honestly Love You" for syrupy bathos. Still, this is a fun album—hokey but warm-hearted.

Original Broadway Cast, 2004 (Decca) ★★★

The Broadway cast album of *The Boy From Oz* is like the Australian album on steroids: It boasts punchier orchestrations, stronger voices, and, most crucially, Hugh Jackman in the title role. All of this plus superior sound gives this recording lots of presence and oomph—just what Peter Allen was all about. Even the CD packaging is more luxurious, with crisp graphics, complete lyrics, and colorful production shots. The Broadway version retains the structure of the Australian original, but some songs have been assigned to different characters or scenes and the show now opens with the ruminative "The Lives of Me." None of this disguises the fact that the musical is insubstantial and Jackman is its sole reason for being. His strong, flexible voice is full of energy, easy confidence, and star power. While his thrilling stage performance does not translate fully to the CD, he is still an engaging leading man; his "Bi-coastal" and "Everything Is New Again" shine with showbiz know-how. Isabel Keating's Judy Garland is febrile and funny, delivered with a belt. Stephanie J. Block rises to the challenge of the dramatic range that the Liza character gets in this version; she seems to grow in her songs, climaxing with a frenetic "She Loves to Hear the Music." Jarrod Emick does what he can with the treacly "I Honestly Love You," and Beth Fowler, as Allen's mother, is a quiet powerhouse in "Don't Cry Out Loud." Of the two recordings of the show, this is the one to get.   —ROBERT SANDLA

BOY MEETS BOY
Original Off-Broadway Cast, 1974 (Records & Publishing/AEI) ★★

No, this is not the "reality" TV show of the same title that caused tongues to wag in 2003. This *Boy Meets Boy* is from an earlier time and its heart lies more with *The Boy Friend* than with *The Boys in the Band.* The creators took one of those cheerfully asinine 1930s musical comedy plots (globe-trotting reporter meets incognito aristocrat) and gave it a gay spin. There's no post-Stonewall anger here, no *Suddenly, Last Summer* angst and self-loathing; this show is a fizzy, good-hearted romp. The missing ingredient is a true sense of style. Composer-lyricist Bill Solly came up with some competent wordplay and nice melodies, but the score is more '70s-generic than '30s satiny chic. That problem is exacerbated on this recording by the tinny noises of synthesized accompaniments. Still, the small cast performs enthusiastically; if this is not a masterful confection, it is a tasty cupcake at the very least. As heard from today's perspective, *Boy Meets Boy* seems a period piece twice over, a giddy bauble that appeared just before a very dark time in gay history began. Even nostalgia can wield a double-edged sword.

Original Minneapolis Cast, 1979 (Private Editions/no CD) ★★★

Boy Meets Boy was sufficiently successful in its initial New York and Los Angeles runs to become a hot item on the burgeoning gay-regional-theater circuit of the late 1970s. (Some playgoers will recall those halcyon days of generous grants from the National Endowment for the Arts!) One company in particular, the Out & About Theatre of Minneapolis, gave Bill Solly's show a comparatively lavish production. A special boon for the home listener is that the cast album boasts a small but bona fide orchestra to supplant the nattering synthesizer heard on the original recording; the intrepid orchestrator Brad Callahan worked with Solly to expand the score somewhat, and the added resources give the show more of a faux-Deco sheen. A new overture, extended dance music, and an ingratiating group of performers add to the fun. Calling something "the Original Minneapolis Cast Recording" may sound as camp as anything in the show itself, but this disc demonstrates how a good budget and a thoughtful presentation can benefit a little musical.

—RICHARD BARRIOS

THE BOYS FROM SYRACUSE
Studio Cast, 1953 (Columbia/Sony) ★★★

Rodgers and Hart's 1938 adaptation of *The Comedy of Errors* is one of their most sublime achievements. The score, melodically and harmonically unsurpassed and lyrically ingenious, has ensured frequent revivals of the show, so it's no surprise that there are many recordings. The surprise is that they're all at least pretty good. The first, an early entry in Lehman Engel's series of then-unrecorded musicals, is well cast and gratifyingly complete; it even includes the entire Act II ballet. Casting Jack Cassidy as both Antipholuses is a little less fun than hiring two actors, but he's at his vocal peak and a persuasively sensuous balladeer; when Cassidy sings "You Have Cast Your Shadow on the Sea," you know he's not talking about refracted light. Portia Nelson delivers the goods in "Falling in Love With Love," Bibi Osterwald lands all of her comic songs and Engel conducts at quite a clip. The orchestrations aren't quite the Hans Spialek originals but are modeled upon them. (The one exception: a bizarre, jazz-combo-backed version of "This Can't Be Love" that Rodgers himself was on record as loathing.) Columbia's subsequent studio cast albums became mired in star casting and '50s orchestral bloat; this one is closer to the real thing, with the correct spirit of silliness and a knockout of an overture.

Off-Broadway Cast, 1963 (Capitol/Angel) ★★★★

Like other recordings of scaled-down versions of *Boys*, this one approximates the original Spialek charts; by Off-Broadway standards, the orchestra is quite large. The cover art is that great Al Hirschfeld drawing of Jimmy Savo and Teddy Hart in the 1938 original, and what's on the disc is pretty delectable, too. Karen Morrow's brazen voice richly mines the comedy songs while Clifford David and Stuart Damon split the ballads ably and Ellen Hanley breaks your heart with "Falling in Love With Love." Also on hand are Danny Carroll, Julienne Marie, and Cathryn Damon. The Encores! album (below) may be the gold-standard recording of this score, but this one is more persuasively about hot-blooded young folks jumping into the wrong beds.

Original London Cast, 1963 (Decca) ★★★

Apparently, when *The Boys From Syracuse* made its belated London debut, the elements didn't quite jell: A three-month run was all that the show could muster in the West End. But the album has good ensemble work from a big-name British cast headed by Bob Monkhouse, Denis Quilley, and Maggie Fitzgibbon. The production is a bit boisterous; all that hearty chorus laughter at Hart's jokes tells us that the director (Christopher Hewett) didn't trust the audience to identify the funny bits. Still, this is an above-average recording of a fabulous score. The CD reissue boasts an excellent essay on the show, including a scholarly mini-course in Richard Rodgers and Lorenz Hart appreciation by John Hollander. Six vintage tracks by Frances Langford and Rudy Vallee are included on the CD as bonuses, but they're soporifics.

Encores! Concert Cast, 1997 (DRG) ★★★★★

A treat under any circumstances, the score of *The Boys From Syracuse* never sounded better than on this City Center Encores! CD. First and foremost, it restores Hans Spialek's original orchestrations, and that alone is like scraping several coats of paint off an antique that never should have been tampered with. Exquisite details emerge, like the stilled drums in "This Can't Be Love" when Sarah Uriarte Berry complains that her heart "skipped a beat." Also, this is the most complete rendition of the score ever, featuring the seldom-heard "Big Brother" and the premiere recording of "Let Antipholus In!" The casting, while not uniformly inspired, is perfectly sensible. If Debbie Gravitte as Luce never produces an unexpected inflection, she's well partnered by Mario Cantone's Dromio; their mutual disgust in "What Can You Do With a Man?" is palpable. The strong Antipholuses are Davis Gaines and Malcom Gets; Rebecca Luker as Adriana is all that you want her to be; Patrick Quinn invests "Come With Me" with mock-Romberg testosterone; and the underutilized Michael McGrath taps directly into the show's spirit. He also delivers one of my favorite Hart couplets: "Come on, crystal, act like ya know me / Come on, crystal, show me Dromie!"   —MARC MILLER

BRAVO GIOVANNI
Original Broadway Cast, 1962 (Columbia/DRG) ★★★

This is a swell listen with a game cast, a lively Ronny Graham-Milton Schafer score, and the sort of floppola production numbers that are more fun than higher-reaching material in worthier musicals. A contrived tale of dueling restaurateurs in Rome, *Bravo Giovanni* also takes in a May-September romance (September didn't look too bad in the person of Metropolitan basso Cesare Siepi), a teenage Michele Lee belting power ballads with intensity, and a manic Maria Karnilova flogging something called "The Kangaroo." Siepi is strong and authoritative, especially in the winning "If I Were the Man," and such sundry talents as George S. Irving and

David Opatoshu work hard selling their substandard songs. There's even a hit faux-Italiano ballad, "Ah! Camminare," delivered by the reliable Broadway tenor Gene Varrone. The CD reissue has a bonus-track enticement: Lee in a rock-beat version of "Steady, Steady." Like *Bravo Giovanni* itself, it's cheesy fun.

—MARC MILLER

BREAKFAST AT TIFFANY'S

World Premiere Cast, 2000 (Original Cast Records, 2CDs) ★

This is possibly the strangest cast album ever. The show *Breakfast at Tiffany's,* a notorious flop of the 1960s, underwent tryout traumas and then flamed out after a couple of New York previews. Nobody involved knew how to adapt Truman Capote's novella about the adventures of winsome Holly Golightly. Philadelphia audiences expecting the fey charm of the Audrey Hepburn film instead got a leering sex comedy by Abe Burrows with brassy songs by Bob Merrill. In an act of desperation, producer David Merrick replaced Burrows with Edward Albee, whose weird new concept—Holly as a fictional character romancing the writer who invents her—was quickly dismissed. As the changes kept coming, Merrill kept churning out songs. This two-disc studio album, actually recorded in 1995, has thirty-three tracks, including the overture, entr'acte, and exit music. The notes provide synopses of both Burrows' and Albee's libretti, allowing you to program different versions of the score on your CD player. (There are also several alternate numbers that were written on the road.) It's a pity that all this effort wasn't expended on a better show. The Burrows version has its moments, but even so, Holly is stripped of her charm and made into a pushy gold digger. The Albee version isn't as crass, but is humorless, with much weaker songs. There are a few nice items, including the swingy "Holly Golightly" and "Traveling." But too many numbers, such as "Lament for Ten Men," "The Home for Wayward Girls," and "The Wittiest Fellow in Pittsburgh," are simply tasteless. (Ralph Burns' orchestrations underline every joke, in case you're not paying attention.) The studio cast features Faith Prince singing her heart out as Holly, with strong contributions by John Schneider as the writer who loves her from afar, Hal Linden as her hayseed first husband, Ron Raines as her Mafia confidant, and, from the Broadway cast, Sally Kellerman as Holly's friendly competitor (whose big solo, "My Nice Ways," has a certain dirty allure). Hardcore show fans will want to give these CDs a spin at least once, but don't expect a lost masterpiece.

—DAVID BARBOUR

BRIGADOON

Original Broadway Cast, 1947 (RCA) ★★★★★

This may be the most exciting cast album of the pre-LP era. It was RCA's first stab at Broadway, and although the mono sound is antique by today's standards, it's crisp for its day. The orchestra seems augmented for the recording and Franz Allers' conducting is often rousing. David Brooks plays Tommy, a world-weary romantic who stumbles upon a mythical Scottish village. He falls in love with the lass Fiona, played by Marion Bell. The two leads combine legitimate vocal training and a full-bodied Broadway sound with believable acting and unaffected diction. They soar through the magnificent Alan Jay Lerner-Frederick Loewe songs "Heather on the Hill" and the showstopper "Almost Like Being in Love." Lee Sullivan as Charlie delivers impeccable renditions of "I'll Go Home With Bonnie Jean" and the wistful ballad "Come to Me, Bend to Me." Since these recordings were originally released as a 78-rpm set, the score is truncated, but cuts were made so carefully that the album doesn't sound incomplete; even some of the ballet music is included. The few songs that are missing include the hilariously naughty

"The Love of My Life." Still, this wonderful cast album offers a vibrant reading of a great score that has all the freshness of a new Broadway smash by two songwriters who went on to more than fulfill their promise.

Studio Cast, 1957 (Columbia/no CD) ★★★★

This is one of the best studio cast albums of the 1950s, conducted by the great Lehman Engel. The orchestral and choral work is excellent for the most part and the cast nearly perfect. Shirley Jones is the embodiment of Fiona, but the most thrilling bit of casting is Susan Johnson as Meg. Since the LPs of the time had room for more music than the 78-rpm records of earlier decades, both of Meg's great comic turns—"My Mother's Wedding Day" and "The Love of My Life"—are here in their raunchy entirety, and Johnson's delivery of Lerner's witty lyrics is brassy and brilliant. As for the male leads, Jack Cassidy doesn't have quite the right sort of legit Broadway voice to play such a romantic role; and Frank Poretta as Charlie, although a fine tenor, sounds too mature for this boyish part.

Film Soundtrack, 1954 (MGM/Rhino-Turner) ★★

MGM's screen version of *Brigadoon* was misguided in many ways. Lerner and Loewe's great score is all but unrecognizable here; the orchestrations sound transparent and timid. Casting Gene Kelly and Cyd Charisse in what were difficult singing roles therefore transformed them into dancing roles, causing many beautiful ballads to be discarded. (So were both of Meg's comic songs, because they were considered too risqué for 1954 movie audiences.) However, bits and pieces of the score remain intact and are robustly performed. Some of the dance music might entertain fans of "The MGM Musical Sound," and if you're a big Gene Kelly fan, you might enjoy Rhino's expanded CD, which includes "There but for You Go I," "Come to Me, Bend to Me," and "From This Day On." But this isn't *Brigadoon* as we all know and love it.

Studio Cast, 1992 (Angel) ★★★★

If you're looking for a complete recording of *Brigadoon* in contemporary digital sound, here it is. The London Sinfonietta lovingly performs every bar of the score and the cast is top-notch. Conductor John McGlinn presents the songs in a most lyrical, lush setting, achieving the perfection of a fine classical music recording. As Tommy, Brent Barrett sounds gorgeous. Rebecca Luker is just as well cast; she glides through Fiona's numbers blissfully, her standout performance being "Waitin' for My Dearie." John Mark Ainsley is first-rate as Charlie, and Judy Kaye is a terrific Meg, giving her character's comedy songs just the right amount of sassiness. Most of the ensemble work is excellent (although some of the chorus members sound a bit too operatic in their solo lines) and McGlinn's conducting is impeccable.   — GERARD ALESSANDRINI

BRING BACK BIRDIE

Original Broadway Cast, 1980 (Varèse Sarabande) Not recommended.

What were they thinking? Clearly unaware that Elvis had left the building, the creators of *Bye Bye Birdie* reunited in 1980 for this misbegotten sequel, which trashed everything that was charming about the original. The cast album proves that even Charles Strouse and Lee Adams are capable of writing a lousy score. In Michael Stewart's barely coherent story line, Albert and Rose, happily married for twenty years, search for the vanished Birdie to have him appear on a Grammy Awards telecast. They wind up in Bent River Junction, Arizona, where an overweight Birdie is the mayor and Albert's mother, Mae, is a bartender. Meanwhile, daughter

Jenny takes up with the religious cult "The Sunnies," and son Albert, Jr. joins a band called Filth (they perform on toilets). Presiding over the mishmash is Chita Rivera—who, amazingly, never condescends to the material. For her efforts, she gets the score's two most pleasant items, "Twenty Happy Years" and "Well, I'm Not!" Donald O'Connor does what he can with several numbers that make Albert out to be a selfish dope. Other hard workers include Maurice Hines as a private eye and Maria Karnilova as Mae; she gets the eleven-o'clock number, a pointless Charleston titled "I Love 'Em All." As Birdie, Elvis impersonator Marcel Forestieri is amusing in "You Can Never Go Back"—words that the show's creators might have heeded. With this as an example of what can happen when you try to make lighting strike twice, how did Strouse ever get involved with *Annie 2*? —DAVID BARBOUR

BRING IN 'DA NOISE, BRING IN 'DA FUNK
Original Broadway Cast, 1996 (RCA) ★★★★

The songs aren't the point of this brilliant revue, which uses dance to chart the history of black men in America. The hip, hip-hop survey stretches from the days of slavery, when people were brought to this country in chains, to the "freedom" of today, when hailing a taxi to Harlem is still a challenge. It makes cogent stops at cotton fields, factories, soundstages, and prisons. Savion Glover, the musical's driving force, astounded audiences with his groundbreaking approach to tap dancing. He calls what he does "hitting" and, in an endless series of lightning-fast, bravura movements, he changed the face (the foot?) of an ever-adaptable art form. Considering that dance was the impetus for *Bring in 'Da Noise, Bring in 'Da Funk*, which was skillfully directed by George C. Wolfe, it might seem that the cast recording would suffer. Not so: Glover and Wolfe knew that rhythm was the underpinning of the show, and the album features lots of recorded footwork. A rock contingent headed by pianist Zane Mark provides the metaphorical floor on which Glover and fellow dancers Baakari Wilder, Jimmy Tate, and Vincent Bingham do their forceful, fanciful stuff. The music is by Mark, Daryl Waters, and Ann Duquesnay. Reg E. Gaines contributed the book, which covers some fantastical and brutal territory, and some of the lyrics, which do the same. Jeffrey Wright speaks most of the narration and Duquesnay, who boasts a great growl, sings most of the songs, some of the time hurling lyrics that she herself came up with. Accompanying the CD is a booklet in which each segment is helpfully described. When musical theater historians look back on the 1990s, they will agree that this innovative show was one of the decade's true triumphs. —DAVID FINKLE

BROWNSTONE
Studio Cast, 2002 (Original Cast Records) ★★★

Five city dwellers share a brownstone for a year but only occasionally interact with one another in this show by Josh Rubins, Andrew Cadiff, and Peter Larson. *Brownstone* feels more like a song cycle than a full-blown musical, which may explain why it disappeared after two brief Off-Broadway runs in the mid-1980s. This studio album, recorded after a well-received revival at the Berkshire Theatre Festival, makes a strong case for the score. Liz Callaway is Claudia, who is getting over a recent breakup; Brian d'Arcy James is Howard, a struggling novelist; and Rebecca Luker is Mary, his wife, who wants their future to include children. Debbie Gravitte plays Joan, a high-powered lawyer with a boyfriend in Maine. Kevin Reed is Stuart, the new guy, who's eager to find excitement and romance in the big city. Song by song, there's much to enjoy here. Highlights include the scene-setting "Someone's Moving In"; "Fiction Writer," in which Howard fantasizes grinding out a best-selling thriller; "Not Today," Joan's dream of another life; and the achingly beautiful "Since You Stayed Here," in which Claudia reviews the changes in her life after her break with her lover. The problem with the show is cumulative: Practically nothing happens, and the single note of wistful longing mixed with ambivalence is stretched extremely thin. Then again, with a first-class cast and a range of material that runs from not bad to very, very good, what's not to like? Plus, there are nice orchestrations by Harold Wheeler throughout.   —DAVID BARBOUR

BUBBLING BROWN SUGAR

Original Broadway Cast, 1976 (Amherst) Not recommended.
This is arguably the least-necessary Broadway album ever. Yes, the show was a hit (766 performances) and it served as the template for many black music revues to come, but this musical tour of Harlem in its Renaissance days is the rough equivalent of one of those compilation albums hawked on cable TV. Jazz fans, who already own many versions of these songs, won't be interested in over-theatricalized renditions of such standards as "Sophisticated Lady," "Sweet Georgia Brown," and "God Bless the Child," while show-music fans will be puzzled by the occasional original number—one of which keeps reminding us that "Bubbling Brown Sugar is the stimulating Harlem treat!" This is one A train you don't have to take.   —DAVID BARBOUR

BYE BYE BIRDIE

Original Broadway Cast, 1960 (Columbia/Sony) ★★★★★
Here is pure pleasure. *Bye Bye Birdie* (book by Michael Stewart) managed to satirize the Elvis Presley craze, *The Ed Sullivan Show,* racial prejudice, the generation gap, Mom-ism, the Shriners, and so on, while retaining a thoroughly plausible air of innocence. The cast is ideal: Dick Van Dyke has an easy charm and faultless timing as pop songwriter Albert, who faces disaster when his meal ticket, the hip-swiveling teen idol Conrad Birdie (Dick Gautier), is drafted. Chita Rivera is sensational as Albert's exasperated assistant/girlfriend Rosie. As Kim, the winsome teenager chosen to kiss Birdie in a televised farewell, Susan Watson shows why she was a top Broadway ingenue in her day. As Kim's harried father, Paul Lynde is the least likely husband and father imaginable but is hilarious nonetheless. *Birdie* was the making of composer Charles Strouse and lyricist Lee Adams, for good reason. This is the rare Broadway score in which the comedy numbers retain their humor. Among the comedic highlights of the score are "The Telephone Hour," in which a horde of teenagers gossip about the budding romance in their midst; "Healthy, Normal American Boy," in which Albert and Rosie feed outrageous lies about Conrad to the press; "Hymn for a Sunday Evening," complete with Lynde's priceless reading of the line, "Ed, I love you!"; "Kids," the parents' *cri-de-coeur;* and "Spanish Rose," in which Rivera is a campy delight ("I'll be more Español than Abbe Lane!"). Add such standards as "Put On a Happy Face," "A Lot of Livin' to Do," and "One Boy," and what more do you need? Robert Ginzler's orchestrations keep the tone light and bright throughout. This recording is essential to any Broadway collection. (A CD bonus track features Strouse discussing the show and singing "Put On a Happy Face.")

Original London Cast, 1961 (Philips/Decca) Not recommended.
Birdie did not thrive in the West End, and this recording is inferior to the Broadway album in every way. Rivera is still on hand, but Peter Marshall, as Albert, tends to overwhelm the numbers—although he does nicely with "Baby, Talk to Me." Sylvia Tysick's chirping as Kim is a trial, and Robert Nichols' straightforward approach (emphasis on the "straight") to Mr.

MacAfee results in no laughs whatever. Marty Wilde, a British pop star at the time, is a persuasive Birdie; but director Alyn Ainsworth's slower tempi undermine the score's humor and brio, especially in "The Telephone Hour," which is further marred by the cast's pitch problems and shaky American accents.

Film Soundtrack, 1963 (RCA) ★

Irving Brecher's screenplay alters the show's plot to the point of terminal silliness, adding such complications as a troupe of snooty Russian dancers and a super-effective pep pill. But Strouse and Adams did come up with a kicky new title tune, delivered with gusto by Ann-Margret's Kim, played as a voluptuous teenager. Van Dyke is still charming and Lynde is still a riot, but a game Janet Leigh isn't an acceptable substitute for Rivera. The role has lost much of its humor along with the cutting of "An English Teacher," "Healthy, Normal American Boy," and "Spanish Rose." This recording doesn't replace the Broadway album but it's fun if you're an Ann-Margret fan. The most recent CD edition features three previously unreleased tracks.

Television Film Soundtrack, 1995 (RCA Victor) ★

The television film that yielded this recording is more faithful to the Broadway production than was the 1963 big-screen version. The CD benefits from the charmingly sung Kim of Chynna Phillips and the amusingly over-the-top Birdie of Marc Kudisch. George Wendt offers a refreshing take on Mr. MacAfee but, as Albert, Jason Alexander pushes too hard for his laughs; thirty seconds into "Put On a Happy Face," you'll be yearning for Dick Van Dyke. Vanessa Williams is a vocally confident Rosie, yet her performance lacks fire; even outfitted with clever new lyrics, "Spanish Rose" isn't really her thing. Two numbers have been added: "A Mother Doesn't Matter Anymore," sung by Tyne Daly as Albert's castrating mom, makes an obvious point obviously; and "Let's Settle Down," a ballad for Williams, sounds jarringly like one of the singer's pop hits.   —DAVID BARBOUR

BY JEEVES
London Cast, 1996 (Polydor) ★★★

Andrew Lloyd Webber and Alan Ayckbourn cleverly reworked their 1975 megaflop *Jeeves* into this chamber-size musical comedy chronicling the misadventures of the hapless, rich-and-spoiled-but-lovable Bertie Wooster and his invaluable manservant. In size and style, it's not that different from the musical comedies that the characters' creator, P. G. Wodehouse, wrote with Guy Bolton and Jerome Kern. Lloyd Webber, after many years of creating supersized neo-operettas with awful lyrics, downscaled his ambitions and found his most sympathetic wordsmith yet: The distinguished playwright Ayckbourn turns out to be a deft lyrical craftsman with a gift for light verse. The modestly orchestrated songs are slight but ingratiating, and this London cast recording sets them up quite brilliantly with a running commentary by Jeeves and Wooster that untangles the convoluted plot with precision and aplomb. Malcolm Sinclair is an ideal gentleman's gentleman, Steven Pacey a dexterous Wooster. Unfortunately, Lucy Tregear as Honoria Glossop and Cathy Sara as Stiffy Byng grate their way through such good songs as "Half a Moment" and "That Was Nearly Us." Also, pleasant though the proceedings generally are, they're a little forced: You can almost hear the creative team in the sound booth, yelling "More charm! More charm!" (Note: Polydor's 1996 Scarborough cast recording, unavailable in the U.S., merely substitutes "Code of the Woosters" for the subsequent opening number, "Wooster Will Entertain You.")

American Premiere Recording, 2001 (Decca) ★★

In New York, *By Jeeves* honorably attempted to inject some Wodehousian fun into the very tense post-9/11 Broadway atmosphere; the show struggled for about two months, shuttering the night before New Year's Eve. The selling points of this cast album are mainly on the distaff side. Donna Lynne Champlin's Honoria Glossop is more vocally assured than Lucy Tregear's on the London recording—but Champlin, too, goes overboard, hamming through "That Was Nearly Us." Emily Loesser's Stiffy Bing has it all over Cathy Sara's turn in London. Becky Watson's Madeline Bassett is charming in "When Love Arrives" and "It's a Pig!" As Bertie Wooster and Bingo Little, respectively, John Scherer and Don Stephenson sing well. But the CD is poorly packaged with only a few thumbnail photos and no lyrics or plot synopsis. And while the London cast album has all that smart verbal interplay between Jeeves and Wooster, this edition gives us just the songs. Martin Jarvis' Jeeves is on hand for a few tracks and then slips discreetly away—very Jeevesian of him but, plot-wise, it leaves us hanging.   —MARC MILLER

BY JUPITER
Off-Broadway Cast, 1967 (RCA/no CD) ★★★

While this production did not achieve great success onstage, it did yield a cast album to be reckoned with. Most important, this is the only complete recording of one of the longest-running musicals by Richard Rodgers and Lorenz Hart; but the original 1941 cast never made it into a recording studio. The score contains some of the team's catchiest up-tempo numbers ("Ev'rything I've Got," "Jupiter Forbid") and loveliest ballads ("Wait Till You See Her," "Nobody's Heart," "Careless Rhapsody"), all performed with gusto. Bob Dishy is very suitable as Sapiens, the reluctant groom to the Amazon Queen Hippolyta, whose numbers are sensationally belted out by Jackie Alloway. Meanwhile, the songs of the secondary romantic couple are beautifully delivered by Sheila Sullivan and Robert R. Kaye. (Note: During the Richard Rodgers centennial year, it was announced that this recording would be issued on CD, but, alas, it never happened.)   —JEFFREY DUNN

BY THE BEAUTIFUL SEA
Original Broadway Cast, 1954 (Capitol/DRG) Not recommended.

Shirley Booth never had much luck with her musicals. Witness this elegant piece of hackwork—which, at eight months, ran longer than most of her shows. Here, she's cast as vaudeville star Lottie Gibson, who, with her father, owns a boarding house on Coney Island. (Herbert and Dorothy Fields' libretto is set in 1907.) The plot consists of some thoroughly manufactured romantic mix-ups and the score, by Arthur Schwartz and Dorothy Fields, is overburdened with interchangeable production numbers that could have been authorized by the Coney Island Chamber of Commerce. (The weirdest of them is "Hooray for George the Third.") Booth has one dryly amusing solo, "I'd Rather Wake Up By Myself," in which she recalls her many exes, and Mae Barnes, as Lottie's black housekeeper, sasses up a couple of tunes ("Happy Habit," "Hang Up"). As Booth's love interest, a Shakespearean actor, Wilbur Evans is suitably stentorian. Robert Russell Bennett's orchestrations add a bit of zing. Minutes after this disc is finished, however, you'll have forgotten that you ever listened to it.   —DAVID BARBOUR

CABARET

Original Broadway Cast, 1966 (Columbia/Sony) ★★★★★

Christopher Isherwood's *I Am a Camera,* set in Berlin during the rise of Hitler, had been a notable stage success, but the property entered a new sphere with this musicalization. The John Kander-Fred Ebb score is rich in songs that move the plot. Directed by Harold Prince, the show darted effortlessly between the Isherwood narrative and the Kit Kat Club scenes dominated by Joel Grey, whose Master of Ceremonies—insidious, humorous, and peerlessly decadent—was unlike anything ever seen on Broadway. This performance ignites the cast album from the first notes of "Willkommen," but the show also featured another great casting choice. Who, after all, could bring more authority to a story set in this time and place—and one presented very much in the Brecht-Weill style—than Lotte Lenya? In "So What?" Lenya as Fraulein Schneider growls out decades of cynicism and hope in the same haggard/grand style that she brought to "Pirate Jenny" and the rest of her Weill repertoire. Opposite her is Jack Gilford as the sweet, doomed Herr Schultz; his "Meeskite" is at once amusing and grotesque. Sally Bowles, played by Jill Haworth, is also central to the story. A big point of the role is that Sally's not a good singer and her show-biz ambitions are among the greatest of her many delusions. Capturing that on a recording isn't easy, and Haworth's vocalism would be helped by more style; when Sally sings "Cabaret," the song needs to matter more than it does here. As Cliff, Bert Convy is a comforting presence. All in all, this album is essential.

Original London Cast, 1968 (CBS/Sony) ★★★★

It's not surprising that the first London production of *Cabaret* kept close to the Broadway original, since Hal Prince was again in charge. But the cast differed, and in the case of Sally Bowles, this was particularly heartening. Judi Dench was no more of a singer than Jill Haworth had been and possibly not even as good; her cracked tones sometimes suggest Bette Davis on a dark night. But who needs vocal polish when your acting is this good and you're playing an untalented fraud? Seldom has Sally's mercurial nature been so evident: Dench is pushy, touchy, and insecure as she croaks out the title song. Fraulein Schneider fares well, too: Lila Kedrova brings a layer of fragile appeal to the role. Kevin Colson is a good Cliff and Peter Sallis is an

> ALL-TIME FAVORITES OF
> COMPOSER-LYRICIST
>
> ## Jason Robert Brown
>
> 1. West Side Story
> 2. Sweeney Todd
> 3. Sunday in the Park With George
> 4. Once on This Island
> 5. Floyd Collins
> 6. Merrily We Roll Along
> 7. Candide
> 8. The Fantasticks
> 9. Anything Goes
> 10. She Loves Me

adequate Schultz. As the Master of Ceremonies, Barry Dennen performs with distinction. The overall reading of the score is less glossy than the original, its rough edges entirely appropriate to the show and a harbinger of productions to come.

Film Soundtrack, 1972 (MCA) ★★★★★

This is not *Cabaret* as seen onstage. In the hands of Bob Fosse, the film version is a true reimagining of the show and it was a major sensation upon release. Gone are the plot songs and the relationship of Fraulein Schneider and Herr Schultz; with the exception of "Tomorrow Belongs to Me" and a brief rendition of "Married" as heard on a phonograph, all of the songs are confined to the Kit Kat Club. They comment on the action in brilliant fashion. The Kander-Ebb score went through many other changes as well. "Don't Tell Mama" was replaced with "Mein Herr," "The Money Song" became the wicked "Money, Money," and the new Sally Bowles—Liza Minnelli—got her own torch song, "Maybe This Time" (written years earlier and performed by Minnelli on her first solo album in 1964). Some critics took issue with the gifted Minnelli playing the amateurish Sally, but such objections seem pointless. Simply put, this is a terrific recording. Minnelli and Joel Grey are in top form in their Oscar-winning roles, and Ralph Burns' orchestrations have a more intimate period élan than those of the original show.

London Cast, 1986 (First Night) ★

The *Cabaret* movie threw a long shadow over subsequent revivals, which have taken place in many different lands and languages. This first English-language recording after the soundtrack shows the film's influence: "Mein Herr" and "Money, Money" replace their stage counterparts and "Maybe This Time" is included as well. Also, the Master of Ceremonies has become the star of the show in both billing and emphasis. It's not clear why anyone thought that creating the role of Mr. Mistoffelees in *Cats* qualified Wayne Sleep for the star treatment he receives here. His mincing, cutesy Emcee displays no style or charm, let alone menace or danger. Kelly Hunter is an indifferent Sally, while Vivienne Martin is a dead ringer for Lenya. The other players are adequate—at least in comparison with the show's over-hyped, underachieving star. The best feature of this disc is the musical direction of Gareth Valentine; this is one of the most authentic-sounding *Cabaret* bands ever.

Studio Cast, 1994 (JAY, 2 CDs) ★★★

With the rise of the compact disc, longer recording times became possible. Spreading *Cabaret* over two CDs allowed the inclusion of all the music from the original version plus the movie variants and songs added for the 1987 Broadway revival. But since this is a familiar and popular score, the interest shifted to some fascinating casting: Judi Dench moving from Sally in the 1960s to Schneider in the 1990s, Jonathan Pryce as the Master of Ceremonies, and lyricist Fred Ebb as Schultz. Dench is most successful; her throaty tones fit the saturnine character, yet she doesn't hit us over the head with faux-Lenya posturing. Ebb, for his part, sings well and lacks only the last degree of Gilfordesque skill needed for this endearing role. Pryce approaches the emcee with intelligence, striving for something free of the influence of Joel Grey (and *Miss Saigon*); but without the visual element, the performance comes off as rather mousy and tentative. Gregg Edelman does his usual adequate job as Cliff, a role he played on Broadway in 1987, and Maria Friedman's Sally is terrific. The recorded sound gives the orchestra a bit of a synthesized sheen, but it's nice to have all the music for this fine show in one place.

Studio Cast, 1997 (Carlton) Not recommended.

In 1997, the world wasn't exactly holding its breath for another *Cabaret* recording—especially not a badly performed, half-hour rundown of the movie songs alone. But, evidently, British record companies abhor a vacuum. The result is this silly mess, with just two singers and a cutdown band. The notes tell us that Toyah Willcox and Nigel Planer are big stars and great performers; it's good to have these statements in writing, because nothing that's heard of them would clue us in. There's no need to spend much time detailing how ghastly this disc is, but if you're just dying for an instrumental version of "Two Ladies" or for a "Willkommen" without a chorus, here you go.

Broadway Cast, 1998 (RCA) ★★★★

Few were prepared for what Sam Mendes wrought with this revival. (His interpretation of the show opened in London in 1993 and moved to Broadway five years later.) Not everyone was comfortable with this darker *Cabaret,* its overt sexuality and actual cabaret-style audience seating, but the imagination and theatricality of Mendes and codirector-choreographer Rob Marshall's vision could not be denied. The cast album, riveting and unsettling, evokes the production as accurately as possible without the visual element of S.S. grunge/chic. Alan Cumming makes the Master of Ceremonies more athletic and nasty than ever, dripping with sleazy sexuality. His success in the role proves that this show is good enough to hold up to widely varying interpretations. Natasha Richardson is in the Judi Dench mold: She has enough musicality to carry the tunes, and her acting ability takes care of the rest. Her "Cabaret" is as far as it could be from Liza Minnelli's force-of-nature defiance, yet both versions work. Mary Louise Wilson and Ron Rifkin are touching as Schneider and Schultz even if their accents are shaky. Everyone else works hard and well, and the atmosphere of the production is powerfully conveyed on disc.

—RICHARD BARRIOS

CABIN IN THE SKY
Film Soundtrack, 1943 (Rhino-Turner) ★★★★★

It may not have been *Porgy and Bess,* but *Cabin in the Sky* was, in 1940, a new type of all-black Broadway show. Its tale of a heaven-and-hell struggle for one man's soul had the dignity of *Porgy* combined with the jazziness of some earlier black revues. Composer Vernon Duke, lyricist John Latouche, and director-choreographer George Balanchine propelled the efforts of a superb cast: Ethel Waters, Dooley Wilson, Katherine Dunham and her dancers, Todd Duncan, and Rex Ingram. The result was an overwhelming artistic (if not financial) success. Waters made records of four of the show's songs and MGM had the good sense to buy the property for the movies. Only Waters and Ingram remained from Broadway, but few could complain about the new cast members: Eddie "Rochester" Anderson, Lena Horne, Louis Armstrong, Butterfly McQueen, and Duke Ellington and his orchestra. With director Vincente Minnelli in charge, the film adhered closely to the stage original. This soundtrack disc is an absolute joy, a rare example of a movie adding a new song that's fully equal to anything in the original score: the sublime Harold Arlen-E. Y. Harburg ballad "Happiness Is Just a Thing Called Joe," sung by Waters. Occasionally, the trademark sighing strings of the MGM orchestra threaten to make the score droop, but then another great performer comes along and things are set right. As icing on the cake, this disc gives us two performances—both cut from the film—of Arlen's nifty "Ain't It the Truth": One is a big-scale production number headlining Armstrong, the other is a creamy purr from Horne.

Off-Broadway Cast, 1964 (Capitol/Angel) Not recommended.

After many years, a legendary score finally gets a full recording—and no one in the cast can sing! OK, that's an overstatement, but it's close enough. *Cabin in the Sky* was revived Off-Broadway in 1963 and composer Vernon Duke declared he was pleased with the result. But, as heard on this Capitol album, the show was little short of a disaster. Whose idea was it, for instance, to cast the fine, nonsinging character actress Rosetta LeNoire in a role created by Ethel Waters, one of the greatest singers in the history of American music? In the Dunham/Horne role of Georgia Brown, Ketty Lester fares only marginally better; her "Honey in the Honeycomb" is frightening from a vocal standpoint and about as seductive as a speech at a beekeeper's convention. The men are not quite as bad but, overall, the only value of this recording is that it gives us the show's full program of songs (excluding the dance music) plus some new/old additions by Duke, including the jaunty "Living It Up" with Duke-penned lyrics. Still, it could be argued that *Cabin in the Sky* would have been better served had this album not been made at all. —RICHARD BARRIOS

CALL ME MADAM
Dinah Shore With Original Broadway Cast, 1950 (RCA/Flare) ★

After the smash-hit *Annie Get Your Gun,* an Ethel Merman-Irving Berlin rematch was inevitable. In *Call Me Madam,* once again, a real-life character inspired a musical fantasy: Mrs. Perle Mesta, an American widow known for her financial largess and lavish parties, had been a major supporter of Harry Truman and, as a reward, was appointed ambassador to Luxembourg. In the show, she became Sally Adams, ambassador to Lichtenburg; Truman remained Truman, and the Howard Lindsay-Russel Crouse script contained any number of jokes about the President's detractors and his singing daughter Margaret. Berlin's score is good, not great; the standout number is the bouncy duet-in-counterpoint "You're Just in Love," which was added late in previews. RCA backed the hit show and owned the recording rights; Merman was under contract to the rival Decca label, so two albums emerged. RCA made theirs with Dinah Shore instead of Merman, whose Decca set is reviewed below. Neither recording is very successful. RCA gives a fuller sense of the show, with overture, choruses, and a strong supporting studio cast—plus some lame narration to explain the plot to home audiences. Shore sings with her trademark smoothness and verve but with no theatricality; even something as sly as "The Washington Square Dance" sounds like a generic pop tune when she delivers it. As for Paul Lukas, with just enough singing voice to get by, he makes as suavely Continental an impression here as he did in his movie roles. Russell Nype is an ideal juvenile, neither too light-voiced and callow nor heavy-handed, and Galina Talva does very well opposite him. The recording would be a worthy memento of the show were it not for the utterly miscast star at its center.

Ethel Merman With Studio Cast, 1950 (Decca/MCA) ★

Star quality is present in spades on this album, but the Broadway aura is gone. Neither the recording acoustic nor the arrangements add up to a worthy equivalent of a "cast album." Even Merman sounds a tad dispirited (for her), which is understandable under the circumstances; how could theatrical magic have been created when her cohort is the bland Dick Haymes? The rest of the support is equally uninspiring and shows just how much of a make-do effort this was. In theory, the recording is essential; in reality, it's for completists and Mermanites only.

Original London Cast, 1952 (Columbia/Sepia, on *Irving Berlin in London*) ★★

Call Me Madam is so quintessentially American—one of its songs, after all, is "They Like Ike," later retooled by Berlin to serve as Eisenhower's campaign song—that a successful overseas transfer might not have seemed to be in the cards. But with a cast of mixed nationalities and no Merman in sight, the show was a hit in London. British affection for Berlin certainly helped, and so did the star. Billie Worth was a second-rank player in America, understudying Mary Martin and appearing in flops; as the London Sally Adams, she's a delightful leading lady. If Merman's voice suggested a trumpet, Worth's is more like a muted cornet. Her singing is firm, her top notes ringing, her diction crisp, her mien enthusiastic. In the ballad "Marrying for Love," her softer-grained tone is very appealing, and she holds up her end of "You're Just in Love" nicely. Speaking of adventurous casting, Worth's vis-à-vis is a real curio: Anton Walbrook, best known as the domineering impresario in *The Red Shoes,* is a suave Cosmo who does everything he can to sing as little as possible. Jeff Trent, another Yank, is nearly as good as Russell Nype; he's partnered by the teenage Shani Wallis who, in her West End debut, sings with lovely ingenue tone and a bizarre heart-of-Transylvania accent. It's also odd to hear "They Like Ike" with British accents. Still, on the whole, this is a worthy recording.

Film Soundtrack, 1953 (Decca/Hallmark) ★★★

Depite the usual deletions and toning-downs that mark stage-to-silver screen transfers, *Call Me Madam* and its star worked well on film. In fact, the soundtrack is a far better representation of Merman in the show than the earlier Decca set, with added vitality and Oscar-winning musical arrangements by Alfred Newman. Donald O'Connor is a splendid sidekick; his "You're Just in Love" is a career highlight. George Sanders is the best singer of all the Continental actors who ever played Cosmo, and Carole Richards (dubbing for Vera-Ellen) is an acceptable Maria. The recording consists mostly of tracks by Merman, in top form. "The Washington Square Dance" is gone and "Something to Dance About" has been shifted to the O'Connor/Richards team, but compensation comes with a 1913 Berlin interpolation, "International Rag," that's as well suited to the star as anything else in the show. (A new Cold War lyric was added for the occasion.) Some people felt that Merman was too big for the movies, but the fit was just right here.

Encores! Concert Cast, 1995 (DRG) ★★

A great thing about the New York theater is that the sheer number of producing groups and available artists allows for both new musicals and revivals of all sorts. Some resources are devoted to bringing back older properties and none has done so more dynamically than City Center Encores! Having said that, the series' presentation of *Call Me Madam* was not one of its best efforts. Sally Adams was played by Tyne Daly, who sounds oddly at sea on this recording. An intelligent and incisive actress, she tries too hard to "characterize" Sally with frontier inflections and a self-consciously hearty manner. Without the compensation of fine singing, this quickly becomes tiring. Rob Fisher and his Coffee Club Orchestra play the score with a good deal of spirit, but while the remainder of the cast is adequate, no one makes a great impression; even Melissa Errico, whose later performance in *One Touch of Venus* was an Encores! high point, sounds correct rather than distinctive.

—RICHARD BARRIOS

CALL ME MISTER
Original Broadway Cast, 1946 (Decca) ★★★★

The well-produced CD transfer of this cast album, which features a rediscovered, extended version of composer-lyricist Harold Rome's aristocratic ballad "When We Meet Again," proves that *Call Me Mister* had more of an emotional arc than most revues. It starts thrillingly with a racially integrated chorus (rare in 1946) led by the excellent baritone Lawrence Winters in "Going Home Train." The number is a multi-part rondo, a Rome specialty ("Did our share for liberty / Fought the guys who would destroy it / Now we're goin' back to enjoy it"), and an unusual instance of postwar patriotism that's neither mawkish nor overbearing. The same happy-returning-G.I. motif resurfaces in the title song ("Just call me Mister from now on"), which is still a roof-raiser. But the score isn't all flag-waving: "Military Life" presents the funny flip side of army conditioning. A moving tribute to F.D.R., "The Face on the Dime," is sung by Winters, and the show had some rising-star power in the person of Betty Garrett, whose spirited rendition of "South America, Take It Away" swept the country. Also appealing are Garrett's wistfully comic "Little Surplus Me" and confidently satirical "Yuletide, Park Avenue." At thirty minutes, the *Call Me Mister* portion of this CD (which also includes selections from *This Is the Army and Winged Victory*) must be missing loads of material that was performed in the show itself; but what's here, as they used to say, is cherce.　　　　　　　　　　　　　—MARC MILLER

CAMELOT
Original Broadway Cast, 1960 (Columbia/Sony) ★★★★★

Composition, performance, and audio technology all came together to make this a first-rate cast recording. Although *Camelot* is not as highly regarded as Lerner and Loewe's masterpiece *My Fair Lady,* this album makes it sound like one of the best Broadway musicals of all time. Richard Burton in the role of King Arthur is at his absolute peak as a great stage actor, bringing extra substance to the character with his classical training. Surprisingly, Burton's singing voice is rich and clear; he easily sails through the score, serving the Frederick Loewe melodies beautifully and delivering the witty and romantic Alan Jay Lerner lyrics as if they were the immortal words of the Bard himself. As if that weren't enough, Julie Andrews is Guenevere; "The Simple Joys of Maidenhood" and "I Loved You Once in Silence" are as good as anything she has ever recorded. To round out the perfect casting, Robert Goulet is Lancelot; when he introduced the great love song "If Ever I Would Leave You," Goulet had one of the finest baritone voices ever heard on Broadway. Roddy McDowell and Robert Coote are also on hand for some star-power fun. The book of *Camelot,* based on the massive novel *The Once and Future King,* by T. H. White, has often been called unwieldy; but with the score isolated, the album is a gem. The songs are ambitious, intricate, and operatic. Meticulously conducted by Franz Allers, the orchestrations are a fine example of those written during the golden age of Broadway musicals. By 1960, stereophonic recording on magnetic tape had been perfected and, even by today's digital standards, this glorious score sounds magnificent here. Avid collectors may want to seek out the original vinyl LP edition; look for a laminated, blue-and-gold, double-fold album loaded with stunning color photos that give it a lavish storybook quality. Not only that, you may find that a copy of the LP in good condition sounds more expansive and warmer than subsequent compact discs editions of the recording. It's a grand memento of the glamorous Kennedy era and a time when Broadway shows were the ultimate in entertainment.

Original London Cast, 1964 (First Night/no CD) ★★

This London rendition of the Broadway hit lacks the fine musicality of the original recording. As King Arthur, Laurence Harvey has a resonant voice, and his classical training and romantic appeal are evident on the recording. What's missing is a melodic lilt to his voice and, unlike Richard Burton, he cannot sustain notes; the tempi of many of his songs are too fast, presumably in deference to his vocal limitations. As Guenevere, Elizabeth Larner displays a beautiful voice and delivers her songs very appealingly. But in her case and in Barry Kent's as Lancelot, listeners may feel they're hearing stand-bys for the absent stars, Julie Andrews and Robert Goulet. The album does include a recording of "The Joust," which is not on the Broadway album. If only for that reason, it may be of interest to collectors.

Film Soundtrack, 1967 (Warner Bros) ★★★

Wonderful orchestrations almost elevate this Hollywood version of the enduring Broadway hit into the category of great recorded music—but not quite. Conductor Alfred Newman and his team of Ken Darby (choral arrangements) and Edward Powell (orchestrations) gave the Lerner-Loewe songs the royal treatment, but the uneven vocal performances keep this disc from equaling the Broadway album as a definitive recording of the score. Although Vanessa Redgrave does a fine acting job in the film as Guenevere, her singing is barely adequate. She does her best to "act" her way through songs written for the voice of Julie Andrews, but seems to be trying too hard for effect. As a result, she sounds campy in many of her musical moments. Richard Harris is a better singer with a greater range, but his acting is overwrought and forced in the role of King Arthur. Gene Merlino, dubbing Lancelot's songs for Franco Nero, fares better. Fans of this durable score may delight in the magnificent arrangements of the overture and choral selections such as "Follow Me." If Warner ever decides to issue a more complete version of the soundtrack album, including the Korngold-like treatment of Loewe's background score, that would be a must-have disc. As it is, this edition is disappointing.

London Cast, 1982 (Varèse Sarabande) ★

Richard Harris, who starred as King Arthur in the movie version of *Camelot,* toured extensively in the role. By the time he recorded this London cast album, his performance was as petrified as aged wood and anything that was good about his characterization in the film had been obliterated. The concept of the Lerner-Loewe musical was to portray King Arthur as a young, vibrant leader, not a stodgy old monarch. When Harris made the film, he was an attractive, sexually viable young actor; when he returned to the part on tour as a considerably more mature man, it completely subverted the story. In this recording, Harris rasps his way through the jaunty title song and delivers an over-the-top performance more appropriate to the dusty old Shakespearean actor in *The Fantasticks.* By the end of the album, he is indulging in vocal histrionics that are ludicrous. Fiona Fullerton as Guenevere sounds quite lovely, but Robert Meadmore as Lancelot is no baritone; rather, his voice has a bleating, high-tenor timbre that's jarring. This disc is of no value to collectors except as one of the most unintentionally comedic show albums of all time. Ultimately, Harris himself chisels its epitaph when, at the end, he screams insanely: "R-U-U-U-N-N-N, BOY, R-U-U-U-N-N-N!"
—GERARD ALESSANDRINI

CAN-CAN
Original Broadway Cast, 1953 (Capitol/Angel) ★★★★★

Although Gwen Verdon was catapulted to stardom in this pizzazz-y, Broadway-Gallic concoction, the true star of this show is Cole Porter. The great composer-lyricist wrote many songs dedicated to the "oo-la-la" aspects of the Paris he adored, and *Can-Can* is his most melodic excursion into Parisian love, sex, and nightlife. The lyrics are as witty and lusty as the infectious music. The score includes the much-loved standards "It's All Right With Me," "I Love Paris," and "C'est Magnifique." The cast album captures the exuberance of a live Broadway show. Its clear, high-fidelity monophonic sound and crisp performances combine to make it an excellent example of 1950s showbiz chutzpah. Lilo, the lead chanteuse, belts out her numbers with tremendous joie de vivre. Her most effective song is the naughty, defiant "Live and Let Live." Her authentic French accent adds to the fun, although it may take some doing to decipher all of Porter's clever uses of the word "can" when Lilo tongue-twists her way through the title song. Verdon is heard only briefly on the recording, since she was the dancing star of the show, but her comedy numbers with the inimitable Hans Conried are fun throwaway songs. Peter Cookson is the stalwart baritone who beautifully, if stiffly, renders great lines like "It's the wrong time and the wrong place." His best number, "I Am in Love," is a little-known Porter masterpiece, a choice line being, "Should I order cyanide or order champagne?" You should definitely order champagne while listening to this gem.

Film Soundtrack, 1960 (Capitol) ★★
Frank Sinatra, Shirley MacLaine, Maurice Chevalier, and Louis Jourdan were huge stars when this soundtrack for the film version of *Can-Can* was recorded. With all those famous names over the title, the flick was a hit, but an avalanche of Hollywood kitsch suffocated almost all of the charm and wit of Cole Porter's Broadway show. Musical director Nelson Riddle provided overblown, frantic orchestrations. This isn't music to drink French champagne by; it calls for several glasses of scotch in the leopard-skin lounge of a Pasadena golf course. However, Porter's songs are so durable that even their saloon interpretations by Sinatra and MacLaine are somewhat appealing. The French costars fare better: Chevalier's devil-may-care performance of "Just One of Those Things" (added to the score) has its own charm, while Jourdan's rendition of "You Do Something to Me" is surprisingly well sung; indeed, it may be one of the most enchanting versions of the song ever recorded. But too much of the show score has been eliminated or altered. Although the title song is heard as an instrumental, MacLaine never gets to sing those witty Porter lyrics. Some of the better ballads, such as "Allez Vous En," are missing altogether. And "I Love Paris" is bizarrely performed as a romantic duet between Chevalier and Sinatra!   —GERARD ALESSANDRINI

CANDIDE
Original Broadway Cast, 1956 (Columbia/Sony) ★★★★★
This recording starts with the most exciting overture in Broadway history and just keeps getting better after that. Leonard Bernstein's gilded score for this adaptation of Voltaire's classic is one of the great glories of the American musical theater. Unfortunately, Lillian Hellman's libretto failed to please and the show had a pitifully short run. (Happily, numerous "revisals" have kept the work alive.) Bernstein's peerless melodies and piercingly witty lyrics by a trio of poets—Richard Wilbur, John Latouche, and Dorothy Parker—are performed by a first-rate cast. Robert Rounseville plays the title role of the naive youth whose optimism sees him through a series of disasters; he's especially touching in the ballad "It Must Be So." Max Adrian is delightful as Dr. Pangloss, whose boundless optimism infects his young charges; in "The Best of All Possible Worlds," he gets things off to a jaunty start. Other standouts are William Olvis

as a gleefully corrupt governor (his wooing ways made explicit in "My Love") and Irra Petina as the Old Lady (she leads the showstopping "I Am Easily Assimilated"). Best of all is young Barbara Cook as Cunegonde, Candide's compromised love. She's ravishingly innocent in the duet "Oh Happy We" and then, a few tracks later, riotously cynical and corrupt in the stupendous aria "Glitter and Be Gay." (Her rendition of this number is one of the essential recorded performances in Broadway history.) Among the album's other highlights are "What's the Use?" performed by a quartet of connivers, and the stunning choral finale "Make Our Garden Grow." The entire score is wrapped in the brilliant orchestrations of Bernstein and Hershy Kay. This recording is a permanent pleasure and a must for every musical theater collection.

Broadway Cast, 1974 (Columbia, 2LPs/no CD) ★

For this production, Harold Prince gave *Candide* a new book by Hugh Wheeler and additional lyrics by Stephen Sondheim. Prince's staging, with plenty of sight gags and sex jokes, enjoyed a good run. This album, however, is the least of the show's many versions on disc. It includes most of the book, so you must endure long stretches of obvious humor to get to the songs. You also have to deal with Hershy Kay's reduced orchestrations and the capable but unexciting voices of Mark Baker as Candide and Maureen Brennan as Cunegonde. June Gable makes an amusing Old Lady, but Lewis J. Stadlen, playing Voltaire (who narrates), Dr. Pangloss, the Governor, and others, offers a performance that consists mainly of trick voices. The song list includes the "Auto Da Fe" sequence (it's not on the original disc), plus "Candide's Lament," a moving ballad. But the fine "El Dorado," "What's the Use?" and "Venice Gavotte" are gone; "Sheep Song," a too-cute entry, more or less replaces "El Dorado." A very nice innovation is having "Life Is Happiness Indeed" introduce the lead characters. Another is having the Governor sing "My Love" not to Cunegonde but to Maximilian, her foppish brother. Paradoxically, the most successful production of *Candide* yielded this least interesting recording, which is not available on CD.

Opera House Version, 1982 (New World Records, 2CDs) ★★

Harold Prince created yet another version of *Candide* for the New York City Opera, combining elements of the previous two productions. This two-disc set has its moments, but these opera singers don't make the most of the brilliant lyrics and, at times they seem overwhelmed by the orchestra. The more serious songs come off best, including a superb "Make Our Garden Grow." Erie Mills' Cunegonde was much admired and her "Glitter and Be Gay" is certainly adept. David Eisler and Joyce Castle are capable as Candide and the Old Lady, as is John Lankston as Voltaire, Pangloss, and others. Pangloss has a new number, "Dear Boy," and Candide has a "Ballad of the New World." The first act "Quartet Finale" is back; so are the trio "Quiet" and "What's the Use."

Final Revised Edition, 1989 (Deutsche Grammophon, 2CDs) ★★★★★

This welcome entry is titled *Bernstein Conducts Candide.* The great composer-conductor, who had little to do with the two Harold Prince productions, finally decided to compile everything for an all-conclusive, final revised edition of the score. Eschewing the labored gags of the previous two versions, this one restores the somber undertone that is central to the composer's original conception. Additions include the opening "Westphalia Chorale"; the frequently heard refrain "Universal Good"; "Words, Words, Words," written for Martin, the alter ego of Pangloss; "We Are Women," a duet for Cunegonde and the Old Lady; and "The King's Barcarolle," in which five deposed monarchs yearn for the simple life. Restored are "El Dorado" and "Venice Gavotte." Best of all is "Nothing More Than This," an anguished solo for Candide that functions as a kind of eleven-o'clock number. Bernstein's conducting is nothing less than thrilling; on no other disc does the orchestra make such an impression. The high-profile cast is led by Jerry Hadley (Candide), June Anderson (Cunegonde), Christa Ludwig (the Old Lady), and Nicolai Gedda (the Governor, among other roles). Although opera singers aren't always at home with such challenging lyrics, this cast is fine in that regard, Ludwig and Gedda being the standouts. Leave it to Adolph Green, of all people, to shine in such company, showing off his clear diction and comic gusto in the dual role of Pangloss/Martin. This recording is a must for fans of the score, thanks to Bernstein's conducting and the sheer mass of material.

Scottish Opera Cast, 1991 (JAY) ★★★

This disc has a song stack that's a close match to the original Broadway cast album. It's also one of the more sparkling renditions of the score, with a cast of full-bodied opera singers. Nickolas Grace's impeccable diction and comic sense make him a fine Pangloss; Mark Beudert offers an exceptionally well-sung Candide; Ann Howard is a vivacious Old Lady. As Cunegonde, Marilyn Hill Smith delivers a memorable "Glitter and Be Gay" with a fine sense of high comedy. The orchestra, conducted by Justin Brown, tends to favor brass over strings, but Brown's tempi are energetic throughout.

Broadway Cast, 1997 (RCA) ★★★

Although this fussy, over-elaborate production quickly closed, the cast recording has its points of interest, beginning with Jim Dale's urbanely witty performance as Voltaire, Pangloss, and others. The show's book was retooled yet again, this time to give Andrea Martin more to do as the Old Lady, and she is a riotous presence; her rendition of "I Am Easily Assimilated" is a gem. As Candide, Jason Danieley's golden voice and innocent manner are right on, in contrast to Harolyn Blackwell's well-sung but occasionally too knowing Cunegonde. Brent Barrett is very strong as Maximilian, and turning up here and there are Borscht Belt clowns Arte Johnson and Mal Z. Lawrence. While not on a par with the best *Candide* recordings, this disc does offer acceptable performances of the score's highlights.

Royal National Theatre Cast, 1999 (First Night) ★★★★

According to the disc's notes, this production featured Hugh Wheeler's book "in a new version by John Caird," who also directed. Actually, it's a blend of many previous editions. Bruce Coughlin's orchestrations are not as sparkling as the Berstein-Kay originals, but they have a pleasing intimacy, and music director Mark W. Dorrell takes the score to a rapid clip. Innovations include a slightly different opening sequence, "Life Is Happiness Unending"; a new version of "Universal Good"; new lyrics for "Nothing More Than This" and the "Quartet Finale"; and a totally new version of "What's the Use." Simon Russell Beale displays savoir faire and a fine voice as Voltaire/Pangloss; he's particularly amusing in "Dear Boy," rationalizing syphilis as a gift of the New World ("Without the little spirochete / We'd have no chocolate to eat!"). The cast also includes distinguished artists Denis Quilley (the Baron/Martin) and Clive Rowe (the Drill Sargeant/Cacambo). In the latter role, Rowe sings "El Dorado" as a duet with the fine Candide of Daniel Evans. Alex Kelly is the best Cunegonde since Cook, delivering a grand "Glitter and Be Gay," and Beverly Klein is a lively Old Woman. The entire company blends superb diction with fine musical values, skills that are particularly noticeable in the most exciting rendition ever of "Auto da Fe." Not everything here works—the new version of "What's the Use" disappoints, for example—but this recording represents what is surely the definitive modern playing edition of *Candide*.　　　　　—DAVID BARBOUR

CANTERBURY TALES
Original London Cast, 1968 (Decca/no CD) Not recommended.
After a long period during which London produced few musicals of consequence, things picked up in the sixties. Some even called it the Golden Age of British musicals. One of the London hits of that period, perhaps because it was "racy," was *Canterbury Tales*—a loud, tuneless bleat of a musical that adapted the Chaucer stories without knowing how to do so. Martin Starkie, working with Professor Neville Coghill's translation, dramatized the tales just as two young composers, Richard Hill and John Hawkins, were writing a suite based on the work. When an LP called *The Canterbury Pilgrims,* narrated by Starkie, proved successful, a full musicalization evolved with book by Starkie and Coghill, lyrics by Coghill, and music by Hill and Hawkins (none of whom had ever written a musical). The disc reveals no characters and no sense of plot, just a series of short, formless pieces couched in a weird, ugly combination of medieval harmonies and trashy rock music. The songs announce themselves but don't develop; for example, a number called "Darling, Let Me Teach You How to Kiss" just keeps repeating that phrase. This is the kind of show that thinks using the word "cock" for "rooster" is pretty hot stuff—ergo the "joke" behind the song "I Have a Noble Cock."

Original Broadway Cast, 1969 (Capitol/Angel) ★
It isn't just chauvinism that makes me prefer this recording of the failed New York production of *Canterbury Tales* to the successful British original, and it isn't just stubbornness that makes me tell you it's still no good. But it is much better. For one thing, the cast is superior, almost without exception. Sandy Duncan, Ed Evanko, Ed Steffe, Martyn Green, Hermione Baddeley, and George Rose perform the mostly dreary material as if it were *My Fair Lady.* Rose, who brought great style and humor to a number of unfortunate musicals, performs a remarkable bit of alchemy with "If She Has Never Loved Before" in a recording so different from the original that it almost sounds like a new song; here, it's alive and even funny, a kind of joyous calypso number. Of course, that's partly thanks to musical director Oscar Kosarin, who really knows how to drive this shaky score while managing to downplay the ugly rock noises heard on the London cast album. This remains a show about a group of English travelers passing the time by telling each other stories; one of the stories, "The Priest's Tale," was cut for the American production along with five songs. Three new songs were added and one of the originals, "What Do Women Most Desire?" was rewritten totally as "What Do Women Want?" But the improvements are largely negligible.　　　　　—DAVID WOLF

CARMELINA
Original Broadway Cast Members, 1980 (Original Cast Records) ★★★
Picture *Mamma Mia!* leavened with wit, charm, and soaring melody, and you'll have some notion of this two-week 1979 flop based on the same source material as *MM*—the 1968 film *Buona Sera, Mrs. Campbell* (though the creators of both shows denied any connection to it). With music by Burton Lane, lyrics by Alan Jay Lerner, and a book by Lerner and Joseph Stein, *Carmelina* was critically excoriated as "old-fashioned," which is sort of like complaining that snowfalls and Courvoisier are old-fashioned. There's plenty wrong with this not-quite-cast

album, assembled well after the show's closing: Leading man Paul Sorvino, filling in for Broadway lead Cesare Siepi, is vocally and temperamentally miscast; Hershy Kay's original orchestrations have been replaced with thin, new charts by Philip J. Lang; and Virginia Martin is missing, as is her amusing reprise of "The Image of Me." Even the vocal balances in the show-stopping male trio "One More Walk Around the Garden" are off, robbing the listener of one of Lane's most gorgeous melodies. But this remains a rich, romantic score in the classic tradition, with a wonderful title-role turn by Georgia Brown. Convincingly Italian and Anna Magnani-earthy, Brown brilliantly navigates the plot exposition and character-conniving of "Someone in April," commits wholeheartedly to "Why Him?" and "Love Before Breakfast," and growls entertainingly through "I'm a Woman." Note how ingeniously the score tells this offbeat story and compare it with the enormously successful but brainless ABBA-thon that is *Mamma Mia!* There is no justice.

—MARC MILLER

CARMEN JONES
Original Broadway Cast, 1943 (Decca) ★★★★

It's easy to understand why *Carmen Jones* was such a hit on Broadway in 1943. Not only was it a novelty—an Americanized opera with an all-black cast—it was also valid on its own terms. In writing the book and lyrics, Oscar Hammerstein adhered quite closely to Georges Bizet's opera. This was no jazzing-down of the score, but there were some bright vernacular equivalents: a factory that makes parachutes (it was 1943, remember) instead of cigarettes, a prize-fighter (Joe) in place of a toreador (Don José), and so on. The opera's arias, ensembles, and choruses were adapted with great skill; for example, the famous quintet lost none of its spirit and dash in being revamped as "Whizzin' Away Along de Track." The show had spoken dialogue rather than recitatives, and what might now seem dated or even jarring to some ears—"dats" and "doses," for example—was seen as candid at the time. (There's a fun bonus track: Kitty Carlisle's "Beat Out Dat Rhythm on a Drum.") As heard here, some cast members show the strain of singing this demanding material several times a week; others seem intent on proving that this is *too* an opera! But, overall, the album is excellent. Reportedly a knockout onstage, Muriel Smith would be a good Carmen under any circumstances; she sings with fire and conviction. The rest of the company is pretty much up to her standards, with Luther Saxon offering a beautifully sung "Dis Flower." The commitment level of the performance in general more than makes up for the recording's minor flaws.

Film Soundtrack, 1954 (RCA/no CD) ★★★★

Otto Preminger's film version of *Carmen Jones* was daring on numerous fronts: a filmed opera (albeit with spoken dialogue), an all-black cast, and a forward look at sexuality. It was a huge success. For movie purposes, a smaller-scale vocal approach than would be heard in an opera house or on Broadway was deemed necessary; but, like the film itself, this recording works very well on its own terms. Setting the tone as Carmen is the twenty-year-old Marilyn Horne, billed in the credits as "Marilynn." In voice and style, Horne is closer here to Dorothy Dandridge—the on-screen Carmen and a pop singer of some merit—than to the later Horne, who was to become one of the greatest divas of the twentieth century with her rich, low notes and electrifying Rossini roulades. Most of the remainder of the movie cast was dubbed as well, including two other pop singers, Harry Belafonte (by LeVern Hutcherson) and Diahann Carroll (by Bernice Peterson). As Cindy Lou, Olga James sings with warmth and sincerity even if she ducks a high note in her big aria, "My Joe." Pearl Bailey avoids any such problem by singing "Beat

Out Dat Rhythm on a Drum" down in her own range; aided by no less than Max Roach on drums, she makes it a piece for the ages. Herschel Burke Gilbert's musical arrangements are superb, and even though Dandridge's scorching Carmen needs to be seen, this aural record of the movie is a winner. (Technical note: Although the score was recorded in stereo and may be heard that way on DVD, the soundtrack LP was never issued in true stereo.)

Studio Cast, 1967 (WRC/DRG) ★★

Another opera diva, Grace Bumbry, built a sizable part of her career on Bizet's *Carmen* and turned to the gypsy's American sister in the recording studio. The result, if not theatrical, sounds beautiful. Bumbry had one of opera's most luscious voices and she could be a compelling dramatic performer as well. As Ms. Jones, her tone is plush, but the fire is there only intermittently. Since this recording is very much a "Diva Gets Down" kind of event, the supporting cast takes a back seat; in the case of Joe, that's just as well, for George Webb is a milquetoast in voice and manner. Bumbry demolishes him in the last scene without so much as chipping her nail polish. The others fare better and it's worth noting that the veteran Elisabeth Welch gets to do "Beat Out Dat Rhythm," which is again transposed down; she's good, but Pearl Bailey still wins the prize. This is an acceptable *Carmen Jones* in true stereo, but a few minutes of either previous recording will show you what's missing.

Original London Cast, 1991 (EMI) ★

It took nearly fifty years for *Carmen Jones* to cross the Atlantic, and she picked up some baggage for her trip to the Old Vic. The show in its original version was felt to be old-hat, even offensive to some, resulting in this glossy production by Simon Callow with reduced orchestrations and a jazzed-up overture. There were rapturous reviews, numerous awards, and the production had a long run—but, apparently, it was an experience far better suited to live viewing than home listening. At least two factors disqualify this recording from the *Carmen Jones* pantheon: drastically cut-down orchestrations and back-and-forth switching between the lead singers. Wilhelmenia Fernandez and Damon Evans sing Carmen and Joe in Acts I and IV, while Sharon Benson and Michael Austin do so in II and III. All are committed to the task at hand, but some fall a bit short. Fernandez has a warm tone but faulty diction; even more unfortunate, Benson makes "De Cards Don't Lie" sound nice, light, and even-tempered. (Yes, that's the number in which the cards foretell Carmen's death!) Evans is a slightly more substantial Joe than the reedy Austin, whose "Dis Flower" is a trial. Karen Parks gets through "My Joe," and Gregg Baker, another genuine opera singer, is a decent Husky.   —RICHARD BARRIOS

CARNIVAL

Original Broadway Cast, 1961 (MGM/Polydor) ★★★

Is there an odder Broadway musical than *Carnival*? Even with an all-American creative team, its sensibility—alternately sentimental, stark, and raucous—is distinctively French. In Michael Stewart's book for the musical, based on the film *Lili* (from a Paul Gallico novella), Anna Maria Alberghetti is the waifish heroine who joins a traveling carnival after the death of her father. She's dazzled by the philandering magician Marco the Magnificent (James Mitchell) but real love is waiting in the form of Paul (Jerry Orbach), a disabled war vet who has given up dancing to become a puppeteer. Paul can only express his feelings for Lili through his puppets— and the fact that this conceit doesn't make you scream is a testament to the authors' skills. Bob Merrill's melodic score blends whimsical music-box melodies, big dramatic arias, and comedy numbers into a surprisingly persuasive whole. He effectively dramatizes Lili's vulnerability ("Mira") and wonderment at the marvels of the carnival ("Yes, My Heart") as well as Paul's inner torment ("Everybody Likes You," "Her Face") while also making room for broadly farcical songs like "Humming" and "Always, Always You" for Mitchell and Kaye Ballard as his jealous, way-ward girlfriend. The show's one standard, "Love Makes the World Go Round," is a haunting lit-tle tune. Merrill, who spent much of his career working on flops or serving as Jule Styne's lyri-cist, was an underrated talent as this unique, often wrenching piece reveals. A large set of CD bonus tracks includes the composer delivering demo versions of five numbers plus four pop cov-ers by, among others, Richard Chamberlain and Mel Tormé. —DAVID BARBOUR

CAROLINE, OR CHANGE
Original Broadway Cast, 2004 (Hollywood Records, 2CDs) ★★★
Tony Kushner writing the book and lyrics for a musical full of inanimate objects? If you did not see *Caroline, or Change* onstage, you may have difficulty getting past the novelty of a singing washing machine, dryer, radio, bus, and moon—but once you do, this show is revealed to be an attractive and often emotionally explosive folk opera. Jeanine Tesori supplies intriguing and highly listenable music, heavily steeped in the styles of the show's 1963 setting, for this tale about the relationship between a black woman named Caroline Thibodeaux and the southern Jewish family that employs her as a maid. Tonya Pinkins gives an earth-shaking, all-encom-passing performance as Caroline, making the emotionally and musically difficult score sound easy, reaching stratospheric heights in her monumental, five-minute-long eleven-o'clock num-ber "Lot's Wife." She receives solid support from such Broadway notables as Veanne Cox, Chuck Cooper, and Alice Playten, while Tony Award-winner Anika Noni Rose is impressive as Caroline's daughter. Although there are a handful of striking individual songs—including the youthfully catchy first-act finale "Roosevelt Petrucius Coleslaw" and "The Chanukah Party," with its already immortal lyric "Chanukah, oh Chanukah / Oh Dreydl and Menorah! / We cel-ebrate it even though / It isn't in the Torah!"—this recording is best experienced straight through from beginning to end. —MATTHEW MURRAY

CAROUSEL
Original Broadway Cast, 1945 (Decca) ★★★★
This landmark musical is not the most popular of the Rodgers and Hammerstein canon, but it may well be the most beloved and respected. A dramatic musical fantasy that ponders the power of love lasting beyond death, the show is said to have been the favorite of its composer, Richard Rodgers; indeed, this is one of the most melodic and dramatic scores ever created for the musical theater, and even opera; Oscar Hammerstein's lyrics are equally rich. Therefore, any competent recording of *Carousel* reaches the stratosphere of musical delight. The original Broadway cast album was released on 78-rpm records and is heavily truncated; it's also an antique in many ways as compared with subsequent efforts that capture the beauty and pas-sion of the musical far more successfully. What this album does contain is the powerful, spine-tingling vocal performances of the very first Billy Bigelow and Julie Jordan: John Raitt and Jan Clayton. Although Raitt's later recording (below) has advantages over this one, his origi-nal performance is definitive. Some of the other singers sound a bit arch and some tempi rushed. Still, this is an invaluable time capsule and a worthy addition to any Broadway show album collection.

Original London Cast, 1950 (Columbia/various CD labels) ★

These recordings add up to only about sixteen minutes of music from *Carousel* as performed in the original London production. Billy Bigelow is sung by Stephen Douglass, who went on to a successful career on Broadway, starring in *Damn Yankees* and other shows; he sounds wonderful here, as does Iva Withers as Julie Jordan. Although both are a bit mannered in style, their beautiful voices lend much to these great Rodgers and Hammerstein songs. Too bad that more of the score wasn't recorded in these London sessions.

Studio Cast, 1956 (RCA/no CD) ★★★

This recording contains much more music than the original cast album of *Carousel,* and it captures Don Walker's orchestrations in hi-fi glory. Conductor Lehman Engel does a fine job of coaxing theatrical performances from his operatic leads, Robert Merrill and Patrice Munsel, and the young Florence Henderson is in her element as Carrie. The album was quite satisfactory in its day but was superseded by subsequent releases. Today, it's almost forgotten, but it's still a joy to listen to in its own right.

Film Soundtrack, 1956 (Angel Records) ★★★★★

This magnificent recording achieves the impossible: Can you think of any other Hollywood film soundtrack album that is the definitive version of a great Broadway show score? The *Carousel* album features inspired, brilliantly expanded orchestrations by Edmund Powell and the 20th Century Fox scoring department under the supervision of Alfred Newman. The stereophonic sound heard on the remastered CD edition is mostly outstanding. Perfectly cast as the lovers, Gordon MacRae and Shirley Jones deliver Rodgers and Hammerstein's songs with artistry and unpretentious acting. As in the film soundtrack of *Oklahoma!* they offer stellar examples of how to execute American musical theater songs. Their singing is melodic and strong, yet it sounds like a natural extension of their speaking voices. Among the film's supporting cast, Robert Rounseville as Mr. Snow and Claramae Turner as Nettie are vocal powerhouses. Barbara Ruick as Carrie and Cameron Mitchell as Jigger are possessed of less "legitimate" voices, but they give character performances loaded with personality. This recording also contains the best recording of the "Carousel Waltz." Under Newman's direction, it's a thrilling performance of an arrangement that at once elaborates upon, yet remains faithful to, the original. The expanded soundtrack CD includes the songs recorded for the film but not used in the finished release ("Blow High, Blow Low" and "You're a Queer One, Julie Jordan") as well as all of the ballet music and the spectacular main title cut, an artfully edited version of the "Carousel Waltz." If you had to choose only one recording of this magnificent musical to own, this would be it.

Studio Cast, 1962 (Command/no CD) ★★

What makes this disc notable is the cast. Alfred Drake was the original Curly in *Oklahoma!* and here proves what a natural he was for the part of Billy Bigelow. Listening to him sing these songs, you might think that he had created the role. Roberta Peters is vocally if not dramatically well suited to Julie Jordan, and none other than Claramae Turner is Nettie, recreating her performance from the movie. The gorgeous-voiced Lee Venora is a fine Carrie. Its sturdy casting aside, this is a reorchestrated version of the score that stresses stereo effects over musicality; the added xylophones and other excessive percussion seem silly and annoying by today's standards, and the sound quality of the recording is extremely bright. On the whole, this is sort of a Muzak version of the score and, therefore, a collector's curiosity.

Music Theater of Lincoln Center Cast, 1965 (RCA) ★★★★

This first stereophonic stage cast album of *Carousel,* though skillfully recorded and mixed, lacks the theatricality that an album drawn from a stage production should exhibit. Richard Rodgers himself was the revival's producer, and we can assume his preferences are reflected in the recording. Impeccably conducted by Franz Allers, the score sounds glorious, and the performances are solid: Eileen Christy as an appealing Julie; Susan Watson as a soubrettish Carrie; Reid Shelton as a charming Mr. Snow; and the always impressive Jerry Orbach as a colorful Jigger. Rounding out the fine cast is Katherine Hilgenburg as Nettie. But what gives this album importance is the fact that is offers "Living Stereo" recordings of Billy Bigelow's songs by the original Billy, John Raitt. Here, the timbre of Raitt's voice is different from what is heard on the 1945 album—not better or worse, just different. He sounds more like a tenor, less like a baritone. Some may prefer this interpretation, but the operatic thrill of the original is missing. Still, this is a lovely recording overall.

Studio Cast, 1987 (MCA) ★★★

In this fairly complete but oddly lackluster recording, Barbara Cook's phrasing and acting as Julie Jordan are superb, but her rich, mature voice lacks the vulnerability that only a young ingenue can bring to the role. Opera star Samuel Ramey is a full-bodied Billy Bigelow, yet his "legit" sound plays against the more impetuous, youthful facets of the character. Sarah Brightman is quite charming as Carrie. The disc includes the rarely recorded "Geraniums in the Winder" along with a complete version of "If I Loved You." "June Is Bustin' Out All Over" and "You'll Never Walk Alone" are powerfully sung by Maureen Forrester. Yet, overall, the recording is unexciting. Perhaps that's partly because the new orchestrations lack theatrical drive, although they are conducted by Broadway veteran Paul Gemignani with professionalism and precision.

London Cast, 1993 (First Night) ★★★

Director Nicholas Hytner's imaginative production of *Carousel* for the Royal National Theatre yielded this cast album. On it, Michael Hayden sounds pretty much the same in the role of Billy Bigelow as he does on the recording of the subsequent Lincoln Center Theater production, also directed by Hytner but with an otherwise different cast. Here, Hayden's colleagues include Joanna Riding, Meg Johnson, Katrina Murphy, and Clive Rowe. Martin Yates conducts the score with feeling and this is an enjoyable reading of the score, but many listeners will feel that the 1994 disc reviewed below has superseded it if only through greater star power in some of the supporting roles.

Broadway Cast, 1994 (Angel) ★★★★

This is a stirring aural document of the Lincoln Center production of *Carousel,* directed by Nicholas Hytner. As he did in London, Hytner proved here that the piece was much more than a quaint folk musical. Audra McDonald was thrust into Tony Award-winning stardom with her performance as Carrie; every nuance of her excellent interpretation is captured here. Sally Murphy makes a fine Julie Jordan, Eddie Korbich is delightful as Mr. Snow, and opera star Shirley Verrett is outstanding as Nettie Fowler. The newish orchestrations are excellent if not as large as the originals, and all of the choral numbers sound glorious in digital stereo. The star of the show in London and New York was Michael Hayden, who brought solid acting and vibrant sexuality to the role of Billy Bigelow. Unfortunately, most of that doesn't translate to the recording, and Hayden's vocal limitations overshadow his charisma. For that reason alone, this cannot be considered the definitive cast album of *Carousel*. Still, if you want a memento of a great production and a fairly complete recording of the score in digital sound, it should be added to your collection. —GERARD ALESSANDRINI

CATS
Original London Cast, 1981 (Geffen) ★★★★

Before it was a joke and before it became one of the longest-running musicals in history, *Cats* was a true phenomenon. While Trevor Nunn's direction placed spectacle above emotion and story, the show has a better score than it's usually given credit for. T. S. Eliot's *Old Possum's Book of Practical Cats* may not have been a natural choice for musicalization; still, Andrew Lloyd Webber found some remarkably creative ways to get Eliot's feline characters to sing, whether in the style of straight-out pop ("The Rum Tum Tugger"), mock-operetta ("Growltiger's Last Stand"), or a host of others. The magical (and highly electronic) overture, the rapidly shifting strains of the lengthy first-act Jellicle Ball, and the lush finale "The Ad-Dressing of Cats" all help to make this a musical theater score full of variety and invention. Even the now standard "Memory" works within the weird universe created by the half-posthumous collaboration of Eliot and Lloyd Webber. Here, that song is delivered beautifully by West End diva Elaine Paige in the role of Grizabella the Glamour Cat, the figure who ties together the show's story about junkyard strays meeting to decide which of them will be reborn into a new, presumably better life. Paul Nicholas' Rum Tum Tugger, Brian Blessed's Old Deuteronomy (and Bustopher Jones), and Kenn Wells' Skimbleshanks also provide lots of fun. This recording of *Cats* captures the ineffably English tone of the piece and is a highly entertaining listen.

Original Broadway Cast, 1983 (Geffen) ★★★★

As *Cats* is the most inherently British of all the mega-musicals, the unconvincing Brit accents and American vocal mannerisms of the original Broadway company do not lend this recording much authenticity. Still, with a cast this good, it barely matters. Betty Buckley is a worthy successor to Elaine Paige as Grizabella, and her "Memory" is one of the most powerful on record. Ken Page is particularly charming as Old Deuteronomy; future stars Terrence Mann and Harry Groener do very good work as the Rum Tum Tugger and Munkustrap; and Timothy Scott and Anna McNeely as Mr. Mistoffelees and Jennyanydots are delightful. Of special note is Stephen Hanan, whose hilarious Bustopher Jones, heartbreaking Gus, and dynamic Growltiger make him a standout. As with the London cast recording, this one is missing a certain amount of material, including some dance music and "The Awful Battle of the Pekes and the Pollicles." But the superb cast and knockout orchestra, under the musical direction of Stanley Lebowsky, make it sound fresher and more vibrant than its predecessor. —MATTHEW MURRAY

CELEBRATION
Original Broadway Cast, 1969 (Capitol/Angel) ★

The hero and heroine are called Orphan and Angel; the villain is a bloated millionaire named Edgar Allen Rich; the production was designed to resemble a workshop—but the result is nothing to celebrate. Indeed, this is one of Tom Jones and Harvey Schmidt's less successful experiments. Taking its structure "from an ancient Sumerian ritual play" and with an underlying theme of the passing of the seasons, *Celebration* is a flower-power fable pitting youth and goodness against wealth and experience. As reviewer Walter Kerr put it, "I'm surprised the over-50s in the house didn't retire as a group to the lobby and shoot themselves." Michael Glenn-Smith is Orphan, who wants the grasping Mr. Rich (Ted Thurston) to give him a garden. Rich manufactures all things artificial—flowers, fruit, foundation garments—and is only interested in having his way with the winsome Angel (a somewhat earthier-than-usual Susan Watson). The show starts off strongly with the percussive title number, sung by master-of-ceremonies Keith Charles, and Glenn-Smith scores with his first number, "Orphan in the Storm." Jim Tyler's orchestrations are fairly inventive throughout. But Jones' narrative is too predictable and the songs quickly wear out their welcome. This recording belongs in a time capsule. —DAVID BARBOUR

CHARLOTTE SWEET
Original Off-Broadway Cast, 1983 (John Hammond Records/DRG) ★★

I find librettist Michael Colby to be extremely talented, with more natural gifts as a lyricist (his shows are through-sung). Set to music by Gerald Jay Markoe, Colby's lyrics are clever, carefully rhymed, and properly accented—but, invariably, twenty minutes into each of his shows, I want to wring his neck. The plotting of his musicals is always silly and goes too far, leaving amusement behind. In effect, his cleverness calls repeated attention to itself, which becomes tiresome. *Charlotte Sweet* is a musical about a young woman whose mother, "a chronic shiverer," has smothered under the many "Layers of Underwear" (song title) that it took to try to warm her up. Paying for all that underwear has put the family in debt to the unbelievably evil Barnaby Bugaboo, who loves Charlotte and who runs a music-hall show filled with singing schizophrenics and lunatics. Charlotte has a freakishly high voice and Barnaby agrees to cancel the family's debt if she will join his Circus of Voices. She does so. Eventually, Barnaby destroys her voice and then addicts her to balloons filled with helium so that she can still hit the high notes. All kinds of people dress up as other people and, at the end, just about all the characters are killed before it's revealed that they weren't really (killed, that is). Clever isn't enough for this kind of writing; you have to be actually funny, which is a very different thing and which, I'm afraid, Colby isn't. —DAVID WOLF

CHESS
Studio Cast, 1984 (RCA, 2CDs) ★★★★★

Dramatically incoherent but musically thrilling, *Chess* concerns the fierce rivalry between a Russian chess champion (Murray Head) and his American opponent (Tommy Körberg), a rivalry complicated by nasty Cold War politics and because both men become romantically involved with a Hungarian woman named Florence (Elaine Paige). The music is by Benny Andersson and Björn Ulvaeus, who wrote the songs for their mega-famous pop group ABBA; the lyrics are by Tim Rice, the most talented of Andrew Lloyd Webber's writing partners. Rice's work here is occasionally ungrammatical ("We wish, no must, make our disgust") but there are also many wonderful turns of phrase ("I see my present partner in the imperfect tense.") Frankly, the music is so great that even if the lyrics were less good than Rice's, *Chess* would probably still have gained a huge following. In a score that's exciting, moving, and witty by turns, highlights include the Russian's "Where I Want to Be" and passionate "Anthem"; the American's searing "Pity the Child"; and Florence's angry "Nobody's Side" and wistful "Heaven Help My Heart." Also check out the extended "Mountain Duet," during which Florence and the Russian fall in love, and "I Know Him So Well," in which Florence and the Russian's wife, Svetlana (Barbara Dickson), commiserate. The performances of Körberg and Paige have never been surpassed, and if Head tends to scream more than sing at the top of his range, that's not inappropriate to the character he portrays. The other two soloists on the recording are Denis Quilley (a round-toned Molokov) and Björn Skiffs (a sexy Arbiter). As conducted by Anders Eljas, who also provides terrific orchestrations, the London Symphony Orchestra and The Ambrosian Singers sound magnificent; but note that the recording level of this two-disc set is unusually low, so crank up the volume of your sound system for an exciting aural experience.

Original Broadway Cast, 1988 (RCA) ★★★

It's generally agreed that *Chess* flopped on Broadway because of the awful book that Richard Nelson wrote around the score in a vain attempt to make dramatic sense of it all. Tim Rice reworked his lyrics extensively, but the revisions aren't really improvements. Some songs were added, the most notable being the hauntingly beautiful "Someone Else's Story." As performed by Judy Kuhn, playing Florence, that number alone would justify the purchase of this recording, but there is much more to recommend it. Philip Casnoff as the American chess champ (now named Freddie) is superb; in his amazing "Pity the Child," he maintains full vocal control while not stinting on the song's outsized emotions. (Casnoff is also the only Freddie who sounds American, which matters in terms of the plot.) The late David Carroll brought a major voice to the role of the Russian champ (now named Anatoly), sung with an excellent accent but with a voice that has a nasal quality that may not appeal to all listeners. And don't let the CD packaging fool you; this single disc of highlights from the score is contained in a thick, two-disc jewel case.

Danish Touring Cast, 2001 (Scanbox, 2CDs) ★★★★

The performance captured here is so fine that this set would be worth buying even it were less complete. In the role of Anatoly, Stig Rossen sounds a lot like the original Tommy Körberg—and that's meant as a compliment. As Florence, Emma Kershaw may not have quite the voice of her predecessors; still, she's impressive, especially in the more lyrical sections of the score. Note that the lovely "Someone Else's Story" is sung here by the character Svetlana, played persuasively by Gunilla Backman. The best news is that this set includes just about every scrap of music ever written for *Chess;* the not-so-great news is that the songs are sequenced in questionable order. The rage-filled "Pity the Child," beautifully sung by Zubin Varla, occurs toward the end of Act I rather than the middle of Act II, thereby making the songs that follow it seem anticlimactic—even Rossen's heartfelt rendition of "Anthem." On the plus side, the recording boasts a large orchestra and choir conducted by Mikkel Rønnow, and the sound quality is the best of all the offerings reviewed here.
— MICHAEL PORTANTIERE

CHICAGO
Original Broadway Cast, 1975 (Arista) ★★★★★

Not fully appreciated during its initial run of only two years in the mid-1970s, the John Kander-Fred Ebb-Bob Fosse musical *Chicago* is now recognized as a model Broadway show of its kind, thanks to the terrific reincarnations described below. The central role of Roxie Hart would have been a perfect fit for Gwen Verdon in her prime; indeed, Verdon and her frequent collaborator/sometime husband Fosse had been trying to get a *Chicago* musical off the ground for years before it finally happened. By that time, Verdon was really too old for the role and, as a second strike against her, was having vocal problems that eventually caused her to take a hiatus from the show. (She was replaced, spectacularly, by Liza Minnelli.) Still, despite these handicaps, Verdon brings her notable brand of charisma (which earned her four Tony Awards over an extraordinary career) to Roxie, as heard on this original cast recording. Her partner, Chita Rivera, will always remain the definitive Velma Kelly in the minds of many theatergoers. Jerry Orbach is ideally cast as Billy Flynn—smooth in "All I Care About," sexy in "Razzle Dazzle," and hilarious in "We Both Reached for the Gun." M. O'Haughey is a riot as Mary Sunshine and has all of the required high notes, while Barney Martin's Amos Hart stands up well in comparison with such later, terrific exponents of the role as Joel Grey, Nigel Planer, and John C. Reilly.

Broadway Cast, 1996 (RCA) ★★

Here's a cast album that does a disservice to the production it represents. Inspired by a rapturously greeted City Center Encores! concert version of *Chicago,* the 1996 Broadway revival of *Chicago* was thrilling, largely due to Ann Reinking's hot-hot-hot choreography in the style of her mentor Bob Fosse. But listening to the performers without seeing them reveals that three of the principals are very weak in their singing. Never famous as a chanteuse, Reinking is in terrible vocal health here, sounding so raspy throughout that it almost hurts to hear her. On top of that, her weird mannerisms of pronunciation are distracting; her spoken line "Nobody walks out on me!" sounds like "Nobody walks out on Mae!" and "I gotta pee!" sounds like "I gotta pay!" Though the timbre of James Naughton's voice is perfect for Billy Flynn, he has pitch problems. And though David Sabella sounds fine in most of Mary Sunshine's "Little Bit of Good" aria, his high notes are horribly screechy. On the positive side, Bebe Neuwirth is a vocally strong if rather cold Velma Kelly; Marcia Lewis is sassy as Mama Morton; Joel Grey is felicitously cast as Amos Hart; and the band really swings under Rob Fisher.

London Cast, 1998 (RCA) ★★★★

This audio memento of the London edition of the City Center/Broadway *Chicago* revival is markedly superior to the album reviewed immediately above. In terms of vocal strength, Ruthie Henshall is the most impressive Roxie Hart on records. Many will find the performance of the Roxie-Velma duet "My Own Best Friend" on this album to be the best ever recorded. (Verdon's delivery of the song on the original album is tremulous, and the number had to be transposed downward for Reinking to get through it at all in the New York revival.) While Henshall and Ute Lemper (as Velma Kelly) are terrific singers, both leading ladies sound stilted in their spoken lines, probably because they were working to tone down their thick accents— Henshall's British and Lemper's German. Henry Goodman is suavity personified as Billy Flynn and also sports a decent American accent, as do Meg Johnson (Mama Morton) and Nigel Planer (Amos Hart). C. Shirvell fakes some of the high notes in "A Little Bit of Good" but then really knocks one over the wall in the final phrase of the song. The recording is conducted by Gareth Valentine with much more style than British conductors normally bring to American musicals, perhaps because he worked under the supervision of Rob Fisher.

Film Soundtrack, 2002 (Epic) ★★★★

This soundtrack CD, like the *Chicago* movie itself, is almost too good to be true. Renée Zellweger, who apparently had no real training or experience as a singer (or dancer!) prior to being cast by director Rob Marshall, is perfect as Roxie; her sexy, kewpie-doll voice can rise to an impressive belt when she needs it to do so, as at the end of "Funny Honey" and elsewhere. Catherine Zeta-Jones was a musical theater performer in London before becoming a movie star and is therefore in her element as Velma. Richard Gere, who did a couple of stage musicals early in his career, sings with charming artlessness as Billy. John C. Reilly is a fully sympathetic Amos, while Queen Latifah is so perfectly cast as Mama Morton that the role might as well have been written for her. The excision of some of the stage musical's songs—most notably, "My Own Best Friend"—is regrettable, but what's here is choice. And the album does include the Zeta-Jones/Latifah duet "Class," cut from theatrical release prints of the movie. On top of everything else, Doug Besterman and Larry Blank did a superb job of adapting Ralph Burns' original orchestrations for the soundtrack.   —MICHAEL PORTANTIERE

CHILDREN OF EDEN
American Premiere Recording, 1998 (RCA, 2CDs) ★★★★

Because of its biblical subject and the style of Stephen Schwartz's music and lyrics, *Children of Eden* might be thought of as an oratorio rather than a musical, but it does have quite a bit of dialogue. (The book is by John Caird.) This complete recording of the score is the cast album of a staging at the Paper Mill Playhouse in New Jersey. Act I tells the story of Adam and Eve, Cain and Abel, in the Garden of Eden; Act II is about Noah and family before, during, and after the Ark. Both tales are given a postmodern psychological spin, showing how patterns of family dysfunction are repeated down through the ages. Highlights of the score include the magnificent opening chorale, "Let There Be"; Eve's "The Spark of Creation"; the lovely title song; and Cain's soulful "Lost in the Wilderness." The strong cast is headed by William Solo as Father (i.e., God), Adrian Zmed as Adam/Noah, Stephanie Mills as Eve/Mama Noah, Darius de Haas as Cain/Japheth, Hunter Foster as Abel/Ham, Vincent D'Elia as Seth/Shem, and Kelli Rabke as Yonah. Rabke does a fine job with "Stranger to the Rain" and duets persuasively with deHaas in another beautiful song, "In Whatever Time We Have." As of this writing, *Children of Eden* has not had a commercial New York staging, but it was given a fine concert performance at Riverside Church in 2003.   —MICHAEL PORTANTIERE

A CHORUS LINE
Original Broadway Cast, 1975 (Columbia/Sony) ★★★★★

When *A Chorus Line* was in the midst of its record-smashing Broadway run, buses in New York bore ads proclaiming: "A Chorus Line. The Best Musical. Ever." For anyone who was not around then, it's worth pointing out that the show was indeed, as the song says, one singular sensation: a monstrous box-office hit that ran on Broadway for fifteen years, spun out endless companies, inspired two generations of performers, and launched a million teary renditions of "What I Did for Love." Conceived, choreographed, and directed by Michael Bennett, with a book by James Kirkwood and Nicholas Dante, music by Marvin Hamlisch, and lyrics by Edward Kleban, *A Chorus Line* had its genesis when Bennett rounded up a bunch of dancers to talk about their lives. Together, they shaped the material into a searing look at an audition for an unnamed musical. Following a wildly successful debut at Joseph Papp's Public Theater, the show opened on Broadway in 1975, eventually sweeping the Tony Awards and picking up the 1976 Pulitzer Prize for drama. Thirty years later, how does the original cast recording hold up? It's terrific: fresh, bold, achingly sad, and funny as hell. Each character is vividly etched and the competitive edge of the audition-as-horse-race is palpable. Anyone's who's worked in the theater will get palpitations from the excitement of the opening number: a perfunctory piano bangs along, a choreographer's voice counts out a grueling repetition of steps, and then, five, six, seven, eight . . . BANG comes the full orchestra! In the yearning, heartbreaking "At the Ballet," Kleban's thoughtful lyrics merge beautifully with Hamlisch's melodies. The wry

"Nothing"—about a mean acting coach—is hilariously nailed by Priscilla Lopez, who also delivers the anthemic "What I Did for Love." The "Music and the Mirror" track captures the narcissism of the stellar performer if not Donna McKechnie's goddesslike dancing, and the arrangement is exhilarating. If *A Chorus Line* isn't truly the best musical ever, this recording proves that it's right up there.

Film Soundtrack, 1985 (Casablanca) ★

To paraphrase a lyric from the show's opening number, "God, they really blew it!" when they made the movie of *A Chorus Line*. For some reason, producers Cy Feuer and Ernest Martin hired Richard Attenborough—the man who gave the world *Gandhi*—to direct the film version of the ultimate backstage musical. It's true that there were endless complications over the rights for the material, many concerning Michael Bennett, but . . . Richard Attenborough? He had directed the anti-war revue *Oh! What a Lovely War* but then turned out such hummable cinema funfests as *A Bridge Too Far* and *Young Winston*. Jeffrey Hornaday was tapped to choreograph the *Chorus Line* film, which made commercial sense; he had struck gold with the tacky/fabulous *Flashdance* in 1983. But the movie is a joyless, plodding dud and the soundtrack album is mainly of interest as a historical oddity. Arranger-conductor Ralph Burns beefed up some of the orchestrations in disco style that sounds surprisingly dated compared with the pit-band showbiz orchestrations of the Broadway production. Several members of the movie's cast had performed in the show onstage and their personalities emerge with energy and spirit. As Morales, Yamil Borges is perkier than Priscilla Lopez in "Nothing" and sounds more convincingly like a Latina from the Bronx. But alas, poor Borges, "What I Did for Love" went to Alyson Reed as Cassie. A case can be made for the switch: Cassie is the most mature character and the story's romantic interest, so the song gains metaphoric heft when she sings it. Reed brings sophistication and sheen to her numbers, although the introspective "Music and the Mirror" is replaced here by the shallow "Let Me Dance for You," a new Marvin Hamlisch tune with reworked bits of Edward Kleban's lyrics. A better addition is "Surprise, Surprise," a snappy number about sexual discovery that's given a slam-bang reading by Gregg Burge. Unfortunately, such pleasures are few and far between. The film version of *A Chorus Line* effectively killed the movie musical genre until the success of *Chicago* seventeen years later. —ROBERT SANDLA

CHRISTINE
Original Broadway Cast, 1960 (Columbia/DRG) Not recommended.

Maureen O'Hara, in her only musical, is Christine FitzSimmons—an Irishwoman who journeys to India and falls in love with her son-in-law, an earnest doctor named Rashil Singh (her daughter is, thankfully, dead), only to realize that they are from Different Worlds. With lyrics like "Why, Shiva, do you desert me?" this dreary soap operetta is like an amateur theatrical staged by the U.N. Security Council. There's even a "UNICEF Song," in which a pack of cute Indian tykes sing about the joys of vaccination. The luckless librettists were Pearl S. Buck and Charles K. Peck, Jr. The lyrics by Paul Francis Webster are given to such meditations as "Where is the medicine for sorrow?" and Sammy Fain's music sounds like the score of an unreleased Douglas Sirk film. Broadway wisecrackers Nancy Andrews and Phil Leeds, inexplicably cast as Indians, sing a couple of comedy relief numbers about the differences between East and West, and then there's the indescribable "The Lovely Girls of Akbarabad." O'Hara's singing is unexpectedly lovely and one or two melodies are quite nice, but the rest of it is pure curried corn. —DAVID BARBOUR

A CHRISTMAS CAROL
Original Cast, 1993 (Columbia/Sony) ★★★

The Alan Menken-Lynn Ahrens musical version of *A Christmas Carol* lit up Madison Square Garden for ten seasons, and though the production's spectacle played a vital role in its success, this recording documents the fact that an enjoyable score may also have had something to do with it. The adaptation is very straightforward; Menken and Ahrens' took few chances with Charles Dickens' classic story. There are the requisite numbers for Scrooge's feelings about Christmas (as compared with those of his neighbors), his visits with the ghosts of Christmases past, present, and future, and his eventual change of heart. The score is unremarkable, but that's OK; songs like "The Lights of Long Ago" and "Christmas Together" are pleasant enough, "Mr. Fezziwig's Annual Christmas Ball" is an attractive toe-tapper, and "A Place Called Home" is a charming, tuneful duet for the young-adult Scrooge and his ladylove. Walter Charles is nothing short of ideal as Scrooge, acting and singing with all the necessary crotchety conviction. He leads a cast that includes such once-and-future Broadway stars as Christopher Sieber, Bill Nolte, Robert Westenberg, Ken Jennings, and Emily Skinner. This CD makes for an enjoyable, if not quite essential, listen during the holidays or at any other time of the year. — MATTHEW MURRAY

CHU CHIN CHOW
Studio Cast Recordings from the 1960s (Angel) ★★★★

Chu Chin Chow was a huge success on the London stage from 1916 to 1921; a Broadway production, with a shorter run, opened in 1917. Billed as a "Musical Tale of the East," it was an extravaganza with an ensemble of sixty-four, plus eight children! This was "the show to see" for British soldiers on their way to fight in The Great War. The CD combines cuts from two LPs (EMI and World Record Club) that were issued in the 1960s. EMI gave most of the male vocals to the excellent bass-baritone Inia Te Wiata, and there were new orchestrations by Brian Fahey; World assigned the songs per the show and used the original arrangements. Frederic Norton's music is lush and melodic in a quasi-Oriental style; Oscar Ashe's lyrics are less inventive for the most part. Basically the story of "Ali Baba and the Forty Thieves," with numerous additional plots and characters, the book is rather delicious nonsense. From the stately opening "Here Be Oysters," the riches keep coming: the elegiac "Cleopatra's Nile," the comedic "When a Pullet Is Plump," the martial "We Are the Robbers of the Woods," the comedic "Mahbubah," the heart-rending "I Long for the Sun," and the exuberant "I'll Sing and Dance," among others. This CD wafts us back to a bygone theatrical era the likes of which we may never see or hear again. As a bonus, there are five tracks from the original 1916 production and three songs from the 1934 revival. — JEFFREY DUNN

CINDERELLA
Original Television Cast, 1957 (Columbia) ★★★★★

In the age of television's big-cast, major-hoopla "spectaculars," one program stood out as a truly gala event: "Rodgers and Hammerstein's *Cinderella* Starring Julie Andrews." Forget the Fairy Godmother; here, the magic lay in the score and the star. Broadcast on March 31, 1957, *Cinderella* still stands as one of the most-watched programs in television history. Those were the days of live television (the show survives in a kinescope) and also the days of quick turnover for cast albums; the LP was in stores six days prior to the telecast! R&H's *Cinderella* may not be their greatest achievement, but the team produced a fine score that is romantic and funny by turns, and the album is wonderful. Naturally, Andrews dominates. Wistful singing "In My

Own Little Corner," rapturous in "A Lovely Night," this great star is utterly believable as a fairy tale heroine. Nearly everyone else in the cast is up to Andrews' level, with only Jon Cypher as the Prince seeming a tad out of his league. Kaye Ballard and Alice Ghostley are darling step-sisters—not hateful, just buffoonish in an endearing way. Dorothy Stickney and Howard Lindsay are sweet as the King and Queen, and Edith (Edie) Adams is a Fairy Godmother almost as young and charming as her cinder-smudged charge. Listening to this souvenir of a long-vanished era of TV entertainment, you think: "It really hasn't gotten better, has it?"

Original London Cast, 1958 (Decca/Bayview) ★★

Although it was written for television, *Cinderella* soon found its way onto the stage in productions that were usually fleshed-out with additional material, as in this recording. Rodgers and Hammerstein normally kept close tabs on major foreign productions of their work, but in this exceptional case, the property was sold outright for a Christmas pantomime at the London Palladium. A beloved British tradition, the "panto" format was pretty much set in stone—a star comic, special music-hall material, comic drag—and the show had to conform. Oddly enough, a version of the Cinderella story had been presented at the Palladium some years earlier, with the title role played by—Julie Andrews! (That was before she became famous as Eliza Doolittle.) But here, the star was the young Tommy Steele in a role that R&H never dreamed of: Buttons, a servant with a thick Cockney accent. The added songs are English-music-hall pop. The heroine's role is diminished by all of this, but still fares pretty well as performed by Yana, a British pop singer and TV personality of the time. As the prince, Bruce Trent is given an additional R&H gem, "No Other Love." There are other changes here and there but, fortunately, the drag stepsisters are not as campy as might have been feared. All in all, the recording is a curiosity at least and sometimes more.

Television Cast, 1965 (Columbia) ★

The 1957 *Cinderella* telecast was an instant classic, but since it wasn't preserved on videotape, it quickly passed into legend. Eight years later, it was ripe for remake—albeit without Julie Andrews, who was by then a big Hollywood star. Hammerstein had died and the new production very much reflected the Rodgers-alone aesthetic: painfully "sincere," no sly winks at the story, the whole of it done with solemnity. Changes such as turning "A Lovely Night" from a quartet into a solo were not improvements, and the interpolated "Loneliness of Evening" (cut from *South Pacific*) makes the show seem all the more funereal. As Cinderella, teenager Lesley Ann Warren tries to fill some very large glass slippers. While she displays a certain charm, her singing is thin and uncertain, and she is not yet the assured performer she would later become. Stuart Damon's prince is well sung but stodgy, and Celeste Holm is a synthetic Fairy Godmother. Only Pat Carroll and Barbara Ruick escape the gloom, but they have far less opportunity to shine than did Ballard and Ghostley. Despite its inadequacies, the show was rerun numerous times. (In 1997, another TV version aired, starring singer Brandy with Paolo Montalban, Bernadette Peters, Whitney Houston, Jason Alexander, Victor Garber, and Whoopi Goldberg. That production was released only on video, not on CD.) —RICHARD BARRIOS

CINDY

Original Off-Broadway Cast, 1964 (ABC-Paramount/no CD) ★★

This little Off-Broadway musical with a perky score by Johnny Brandon placed the Cinderella story in contemporary Manhattan. It concerns the fortunes of Cindy Kreller (Jacqueline

Mayro) and her friend Lucky (Johnny Harmon), based on Buttons, a character who shows up importantly in British versions of the Cinderella story but is absent from most American versions. Cindy is from the poor Lower East Side; David (the Prince Charming character, played by Joseph Masiell) is from the rich Upper East Side. A trio of storytellers help to move the plot forward, and the score is nicely split up among the principals and secondary characters. Mayro does fine with her "Genuine Feminine Girl" solo and delightfully duets with Harmon in "Let's Pretend" and the big melodic ballad "If It's Love." The comedy numbers, "Papa, Let's Do It Again" for Cindy's parents and "Think Mink!" for her stepsisters, can be described as guilty pleasures. The score only disappoints when it attempts to get serious or "pop-rockish." *Cindy* was not available for long on LP and is unlikely for CD release, but it is good-natured and worth a listen.   —JEFFREY DUNN

CITY OF ANGELS
Original Broadway Cast, 1990 (Columbia/Sony) ★★★★
Cy Coleman's blending of 1940s musical styles—swing, blues, *film noir* soundtrack, and more—with David Zippel's deft and witty lyrics helped make *City of Angels* one of the best musicals of the 1980s. The excellent cast recording preserves Billy Byers' hot orchestrations and the performances of an almost ideal cast. Gregg Edelman's rich, rangy baritone is exciting in the songs written for author/screenwriter Stine; René Auberjonois finds plenty of oily comedy in the role of Buddy Fidler, flim-flam film producer extraordinaire; and Scott Waara's smooth tones are ideal for radio crooner Jimmy Powers. Rachel York and Dee Hoty both give dynamic performances, but Hoty is hampered by the exclusion from the recording of one of her big numbers. The major standouts are the show's Tony winners: James Naughton's easygoing manner and voice are just right for film detective Stone; and Randy Graff, playing two "Girl Friday"-type secretaries, walks away with the show's brashest and funniest number, the one-woman duet "You Can Always Count on Me." The Naughton-Edelman duet "You're Nothing Without Me" is another highlight. Only Kay McClelland, playing both Stine's wife and Stone's longtime flame, is just adequate, although her two songs—"It Needs Work" and the torchy "With Every Breath I Take"—are well written. The recording's most significant flaw is the omission of much material that would have balanced the characters and illuminated the show's razor-sharp humor. Still, this is an essential recording of a top-notch Coleman score. Don't stop the CD until "Double Talk Walk"—some of Broadway's best-ever exit music—has finished playing.

Original London Cast, 1993 (RCA) ★★
With almost every important musical moment of *City of Angels* captured and enough of Larry Gelbart's incisive dialogue included to set the scenes, this is the kind of recording that should have been made of the original Broadway production. Unfortunately, the performances here leave much to be desired, with most of the cast overemoting in both speech and song; Henry Goodman, superb as Buddy, makes this work only because his character is so far over-the-top to begin with. The style feels far less organic to the other performances, with Roger Allam a particularly uncomfortable Stone and Susannah Fellows (Alaura), Fiona Hendley (Gabbi/Bobbi), and Haydn Gwynne (Oolie/Donna) doing little better. Martin Smith keeps his Stine grounded, but his eleven-o'clock number, "Funny," is a restrained disappointment here. Even if the cast's problems with American accents and 1940s speech patterns come through, this disc's more thorough documentation of the score makes it useful as a companion, if not a substitute, for the otherwise superior Broadway recording.   —MATTHEW MURRAY

THE CIVIL WAR
Concept Recording, 1998 (Atlantic, 2CDs) ★★★

Composer Frank Wildhorn's third show to reach Broadway (following *Jekyll & Hyde* and *The Scarlet Pimpernel*), *The Civil War* was the most ambitious; it's also the weakest and the only one without a Broadway cast recording. With lyrics by Jack Murphy, the show's structure falls somewhere between a song cycle and a cantata. This two-disc concept album features a few of the Broadway cast members: leads Michael Lanning, Gene Miller, Michel Bell, and Cheryl Freeman plus choristers Dave Clemmons and Royal Reed. They are joined by Betty Buckley (in the affecting "Five Boys"), Carl Anderson, Linda Eder, and, in a few chorus numbers, "the Broadway All Stars"—a group that includes Brian d'Arcy James, Raymond Jaramillo McLeod, and Rob Evan. However, most of the score is sung by country-western musicians who may have an affinity for the down-home rhythms of this music, but lack theatricality in their delivery. "Freedom's Child" (sung terrifically by Darius Rucker) and Trace Adkins's "Old Gray Coat" (a song dropped for Broadway) are notable exceptions. Tracy Lawrence's "I'll Never Pass This Way Again" isn't bad, but what made the number so wonderful onstage was its simplicity: one man and his guitar. Here, it's one man, four backup singers, an eighteen-piece band, and a thirty-three-piece orchestra. My advice: Focus on the numbers performed by the stage actors, mostly doing songs they would later sing on Broadway.　　　　—SETH CHRISTENFELD

A CLASS ACT
Original Off-Broadway Cast, 2001 (RCA) ★★★

Although *A Class Act* represents an important bit of modern musical theater history, this recording of the Manhattan Theatre Club production is little more than an intriguing artifact, documenting the original, intimate show that was abandoned when a move to Broadway necessitated bigger laughs, bigger emotions, and bigger orchestrations. The show is a warm-hearted tribute to composer-lyricist Edward Kleban, who died in 1987. For those who know his work only from *A Chorus Line,* the fine handle on composition that Kleban displays here may come as a surprise. The songs assembled for *A Class Act*—orchestrated by Larry Hochman under Todd Ellison's musical direction—show Kleban's impressive talents in dealing with a variety of subjects, ranging from music and musicals ("One More Beautiful Song," "Charm Song") to the City of Lights ("Paris Through the Window") to the complexities of human relationships ("Under Separate Cover," "Self Portrait"). There are also some traditional, all-out showstoppers ("Gauguin's Shoes," "Better"). A fine, laid-back band and an eight-person cast led by director Lonny Price (as Kleban) and Carolee Carmello give all of the songs wonderful performances, but Tony-winner Randy Graff steals the show and listeners' hearts with her emotional renditions of the score's most sensitive numbers, including one true classic: "The Next Best Thing to Love."　　　　—MATTHEW MURRAY

CLOSER THAN EVER
Original Off-Broadway Cast, 1989 (RCA, 2CDs) ★★★★

To one set of critics, this four-person revue of songs by composer David Shire and lyricist Richard Maltby, Jr. was a long-overdue outpouring of material from a gifted, underappreciated team; to another, it was largely an evening of self-involved, spoiled yuppies whining in song. Both viewpoints are correct. The two dozen numbers on this double CD, representing the entire show, are impeccably crafted, with music and lyrics that are melodic, intelligent, humorous, and reflective. But many of the characters that sing them are unappealing: urban, well-off thirtysomethings yammering yards of pentameter about health crazes, Muzak, and personal discovery. So while there's some first-rate stuff here—"Miss Byrd," "One of the Good Guys," "The Bear, the Tiger, the Hamster, and the Mole," each the equivalent of a self-contained one-act play—there are also such odes to emotional self-indulgence as "Next Time," "I Wouldn't Go Back," and "Like a Baby." Uneven as the musical program is, there's a saving grace: This is one of the best-sung cast albums of the decade. Brent Barrett, at the peak of his powers, puts over even the second-tier songs with assurance and thrilling high notes. Sally Mayes' natural warmth and comedic skill shine in "You Want to Be My Friend?" and "Back on Base." The prodigiously talented Lynne Wintersteller's "Life Story" is one of the most affecting show-tune tracks of the '80s. Even Richard Muenz, normally a ham, keeps his preening in check until the heavy-breathing "If I Sing." The cast is also splendid collectively—listen to how gorgeously they harmonize in "She Loves Me Not"—and the album's arrangements, augmented from the stage to include a swinging combo, lend color. *Closer Than Ever* may have lacked the sense of discovery that marked the earlier Maltby-Shire revue *Starting Here, Starting Now,* but as an album, it's consistently better sung.   —MARC MILLER

COCO
Original Broadway Cast, 1969 (ABC-Paramount/MCA) ★

It's terrible, fascinating, and possibly the most unreviewable disc in this book. Alan Jay Lerner cooked up this musical bio of Coco Chanel and somehow got Katharine Hepburn to star. The result is a camp hoot as viewed from many different angles. Hepburn's singing makes Lauren Bacall sound like Joan Sutherland; she ends up in a statistical dead heat with Bette Davis for the title of least vocally qualified star in Broadway musical history. Just listen to her gamely navigate Lerner's tongue-twisting lyrics ("Should I drive myself to drink / For some ruffians who think / That chic is someone riding on a camel?") while a drumbeat struggles to keep her in some kind of rhythm. Furthermore, the show is a museum of dated social attitudes: Lerner constantly raps Chanel on the knuckles for putting a career before love, and much of the action focuses on Coco's pathetic attraction to a young model, Noelle, whom she views as a surrogate daughter. (As Noelle's boyfriend points out, "To me this emporium / Is sex in memoriam / Where feelings are frozen / And face lotion flows in your veins.") Furthermore, Chanel's nemesis is Sebastian (René Auberjonois), a screaming queen of a dress designer described in the original liner notes as "almost male, almost female, almost human." His number "Fiasco," in which he hyperventilates in triumph over Coco's flop showing, is best described as grisly. And yet—André Previn's music is jazzy, impudent, and often gorgeously romantic in the style of his years at MGM; Lerner's lyrics have much of his old urbanity; and Hepburn's star power burns through everything. You've got to hear this album once, even if you never want to hear it again.   —DAVID BARBOUR

COLETTE/COLETTE COLLAGE
Original Off-Broadway Cast, 1970 (MIO International/no CD) ★★★

This version of *Colette* is a charming play written by Elinor Jones (then married to lyricist Tom Jones). Colette is played by Zoe Caldwell, who attacks the role boldly. Ruth Nelson plays Colette's mother vividly. The other actors—Keith Charles, Holland Taylor, Louis Turenne, and Tom Aldredge—are fine but, on the record anyway, they're just props. The only person Caldwell ever really shares the spotlight with is composer Harvey Schmidt. He and Tom Jones contributed three numbers that begin the recording; all of them are odd and delightful, and one of them ("Earthly Paradise") is as lovely as anything the team ever wrote. Schmidt's under-scoring of a long montage sequence is stunning—it plays almost like a small comic ballet—and his gorgeous, dramatic music fills the record. The composer was onstage throughout the play, in period costume, accompanying the action on piano. Apparently, the music was impro-vised every night during the run. When Schmidt got sick, performances had to be canceled because he'd never written any of the music down, so no one else could play it!

Members of the Off-Broadway Cast, 1994 (Varèse Sarabande) ★★

A production of the full-length musical *Colette* starred Diana Rigg and was intended for Broadway but closed on the road in 1982. Authors Tom Jones and Harvey Schmidt revised the show in '83 and again in '91; along the way, it was retitled *Colette Collage.* Act I of the final ver-sion concentrates on the French novelist's first marriage to Willy, a writer who thinks nothing of printing work by others—including his wife—under his own name. Her books, which everyone thinks are his books, become hugely successful, and she finally leaves him. Act II cov-ers Colette's later years of fame and her long relationship with a younger man, Maurice. The music is lovely, amusing, and evocative, but nothing here is as beautiful as Schmidt's best work. Colette is played by Judy Blazer in the first act, Judy Kaye in the second. Both sing gloriously and they are matched by George Lee Andrews as Willy, Rita Gardner as Colette's mother, and Jason Graae as Maurice. The only piece retained from the Elinor Jones play is Schmidt's thrilling musical-hall tour montage, cut down and fitted out with lyrics by Jones. Un-fortunately, it's less effective here. —DAVID WOLF

COMPANY
Original Broadway Cast, 1970 (Columbia/Sony) ★★★★

A shocking musical when it first opened and still an insightful if somewhat dyspeptic view of modern romantic relationships, *Company* explores the games, angst, loneliness, and badinage of love and marriage in an alternately brittle and heartfelt manner. In a sense, it's a revuesical—a string of nonlinear scenes built around a single theme. When it first burst into view, the show was revolutionary: no chorus, no legs (save Donna McKechnie's in "Tick Tock"), no salve for the tired businessman. Instead, the show boasted one of Stephen Sondheim's most brilliant scores, Jonathan Tunick's metallic orchestrations, Boris Aronson's architectural sets, George Furth's sharp book, and Hal Prince's sparse, savvy staging. The original cast album, produced by Thomas Z. Shepard, is a marvel of clean, no-nonsense theatricality, an exemplary souvenir of a momentous turn in the history of musical theater. (*Company* unfortunately led to numerous sec-ond-rate imitations by Sondheim wannabes.) The highlight of the recording is "The Ladies Who Lunch," exclaimed by Elaine Stritch in career-capping fashion. Other standouts in the cast are Pamela Myers, Beth Howland, and Teri Ralston. The album preserves the performance of central character Bobby's songs by Dean Jones, who left the cast shortly after the show's open-ing. (Larry Kert took over for Jones; his wonderful performance can be heard on the "Original London Cast" recording of *Company.* Since that cast was identical to the Broadway cast, sans Dean Jones, all the label did was take out Jones' vocals and slap in Kert's. If you can find the album, listen closely and you'll hear ghosts of Jones' vocals. Spooky!)

Broadway Cast, 1995 (Angel) ★★

The cast members here are not up to their counterparts in the original company. Somehow, they aren't as cynical or pointed, and that definitely includes Boyd Gaines as Bobby. Debra Monk is an exception: She isn't quite as hard-bitten a Joanne as Elaine Stritch, but she comes close. *Company* is a hard show to revive because it was so much of its time and we're still close enough to that era to know when a production doesn't capture the right flavor. That's the major flaw of this recording.

London Cast, 1996 (RCA) ★★

Face it: Americans don't do Shakespeare all that well and the English can't get American musical theater quite right. They're fine with falling chandeliers and helicopters, but less well versed in American attitudes, accents, and performance style. This *Company* is rather subdued, and none of the cast members sound really comfortable in their roles; they all seem too concerned with impersonating Americans rather than inhabiting their characters. Although Bobby is the focal point of the show, he is not the most interesting character—but at the end, he's got the bang-up number "Being Alive," in which he has to be really honest with himself and the audience. Adrian Lester just doesn't make it; he's more of a cipher who substitutes technique for honest emotion at his big moment. — KEN BLOOM

A CONNECTICUT YANKEE
Broadway Cast, 1943 (Decca) ★★★★

This Rodgers and Hart treasure is now available on CD in beautifully restored, remarkably clear sound. The wonderful 1927 show benefits greatly from the new songs written by the team to augment the original score. Included here are some of the last lyrics ever penned by Hart, who died shortly after the 1943 revival of *A Connecticut Yankee* opened. Among the numbers retained from the 1927 score are the standards "My Heart Stood Still" and "Thou Swell," charmingly performed by Dick Foran and Julie Warren. It's fun to hear the actual singing voice of Vera-Ellen, who was always dubbed in Hollywood films; her quirky sound is ideal for this soubrette role. "On a Desert Island With Thee" and "I Feel At Home With You"—her duets with Chester Stratton as the stalwart Sir Galahad—are punchy and humorous. Furthermore, this recording offers Vivienne Segal as Morgan Le Fey, a role that was beefed up for this revival. Her extended version of "To Keep My Love Alive," one of the new songs, makes it clear why Segal was an acclaimed leading lady of her era. The two other "new for the revival" songs are Segal's "Can't You Do a Friend a Favor?"—a duet with Foran—and "You Always Love the Same Girl" (a lusty duet sung by Foran and Robert Chisholm as King Arthur). This CD also includes "It Never Entered My Mind" and three other songs from Rodgers and Hart's *Higher and Higher,* performed by Shirley Ross. As if that weren't enough, The Incomparable Hildegarde's album of four songs from *By Jupiter* was added, making this revival CD an indispensable Richard Rodgers and Lorenz Hart compendium. That said, it's regrettable that Decca chose not to record the one other notable new song written for the 1943 revival of *Connecticut Yankee,* Segal's "This Is My Night to Howl."

Television Soundtrack, 1955 (AEI) ★

This version of *A Connecticut Yankee* was one of a series of 1950s television presentations of Broadway musicals. Based on the 1943 Broadway revival, the TV book was adapted by William Friedberg, Neil Simon, Will Glickman, and Al Schwartz. Included are several songs written for the revival, such as the elusive "This Is My Night to Howl" and "Ye Lunchtime Follies." The sound quality of the CD is rather poor, but leads Eddie Albert and Janet Blair sing well, although "My Heart Stood Still" is painfully slow. The tempo is also off for the comedy song

"On a Desert Island With Thee," which seems to have been mistaken for a ballad. Several choruses of "To Keep My Love Alive" have been cut but are not missed, given Gale Sherwood's humorless performance. On the other hand, this disc provides a rare opportunity to hear Boris Karloff singing (not too well) as he joins Albert in "You Always Love the Same Girl." There is a bonus track of Jessie Matthews performing "My Heart Stood Still" from the British revue *One Dam Thing After Another.*   —JEFFREY DUNN

COWGIRLS
Original Off-Broadway Cast, 1996 (Varèse Sarabande) ★★
This cute little show with music and lyrics by Mary Murfitt and a book by Betsy Howie had a decent run in 1996. The song titles alone—"From Chopin to Country," "Love's Sorrow," "Don't Call Me Trailer Trash," "Saddle Tramp Blues," "They're All Cowgirls to Me"—give you an idea of what sort of entertainment we're talking about. The material is slight but lots of fun, and the charming cast consists of coauthors Murfitt and Howie, plus Rhonda Coullet, Mary Ehlinger, Lori Fischer, and Jackie Sanders. They all give their all, and the CD is a pleasant diversion.   —MICHAEL PORTANTIERE

THE CRADLE WILL ROCK
Original Broadway Cast, 1938 (Musicraft/Pearl) ★★★
The Cradle Will Rock, produced by John Houseman and directed by Orson Welles, was created under the auspices of the WPA's Federal Theatre Project. What was to have been its opening performance at the Maxine Elliott Theatre was blocked by guards who were ordered to close down the controversial show. The company and audience then marched to the Venice Theatre on 59th Street, where the premiere took place with the actors performing from the house as composer-lyricist-librettist Marc Blitzstein played a lone piano on a bare stage. For two weeks, performances continued without sets and costumes and with solo piano accompaniment. When the show reopened six months later for a Broadway run, it was recorded; this may be the first original Broadway cast album ever. It includes narration and accompaniment by Blitzstein, and the score sounds like no other. Influenced by Brecht-Weill work, Blitzstein turned his classical training toward creating an agitprop piece about the Great Depression. It offers musical theater songs, protest songs, pastiche numbers, recitative—whatever would engender audience response to the unpleasant truths being revealed. The performances on this vivid recording are full of passion. Olive Stanton is vulnerable in the historic "Moll's Song" and later grabs you with "Nickel Under the Foot." As Larry Foreman, Howard Da Silva delivers a powerful "Leaflets," leading into the title song with an effective mixture of humor and outrage. As Ella Hammer, Blanche Collins sings "Joe Worker" with appropriate defeat in her voice. Other highlights are "Honolulu," a spoof of tropical songs; the satirical "Art for Art's Sake"; and the sarcastic "The Freedom of the Press." Documents of great historic value, these recordings are available on CD in the two-disc Pearl set *Marc Blitzstein—Musical Theatre Premieres,* which includes the 1941 cast album of *No for an Answer* (featuring a young Carol Channing) and *The "Airborne" Symphony,* conducted by Leonard Bernstein.

Off-Broadway Cast, 1964 (MGM, 2LPs/no CD) ★★★
Two notable aspects of this revival were its superb direction by Howard Da Silva and the contribution of Leonard Bernstein as musical consultant. Gershon Kingsley's piano playing and musical direction are crisp and driving. Nancy Andrews, who dominates the first half as Mrs.

Mister, rips into her material with gusto and great pipes. In the second half, Jerry Orbach as Larry Foreman sings with power and outrage, especially in the title song. Also impressive are Gordon B. Clarke, Joe Bova, and Rita Gardner.

Original London Cast, 1985 (Polygram/JAY, 2CDs) ★★★

This production reawakened interest in *The Cradle Will Rock* when The Acting Company presented it Off-Broadway and then took it to London. Again directed by Howard Da Silva, each performance began with John Houseman recounting the saga of the show's cancellation in 1937; that twelve-minute prologue is recorded here. At the piano is musical director Michael Barrett, a Bernstein protégé. Randle Mell is a powerful Larry Foreman and Michele-Denise Woods as Ella Hammer stops the show with "Joe Worker." Patti LuPone's rendition of Moll's "Nickel Under the Foot" is one of her finest performances on disc, searingly honest and faultlessly nuanced. Other standouts are David Schramm, Casey Biggs, and Leslie Geraci. This is an often exciting, concise recording of the piece, priced as a single CD. (The first disc of the set consists entirely of Houseman's narration.) It should be your first stop in getting acquainted with this groundbreaking musical.

Film Soundtrack, 1999 (RCA) ★

Tim Robbins' film *Cradle Will Rock* (no "The") tells the story of the original production intermingled with other plots concerning art and censorship. About half of this CD is devoted to songs from the original show; the other half is new music composed for the film by David Robbins. "Moll's Song" (sung by Emily Watson), "Croon Spoon" (Eddie Vetter and Susan Sarandon), "Honolulu" (Erin Hill, Dan Jenkins, Vicki Clark, Tim Jerome), "Reverend Salvation" (Vicki Clark and Chris McKinney), "The Freedom of the Press" (Henry Stram and Tim Jerome), and "Art for Art's Sake" are all here in unedited form—plus Audra McDonald's compelling rendition of "Joe Worker." (Other songs in the film are not on the CD.) In the notes for the recording, David Robbins writes, "The arrangements you hear are, for the most part, Blitzstein's original orchestrations." This may be technically true but, because the orchestra here consists of only twelve instruments with a single violin, the score has more of a Brecht-Weill sound than the operatic heft that Blitzstein intended. The disc begins with an awful rendition of "Nickel Under the Foot," heard in the film over the end titles, but don't let this one disgraceful track keep you from exploring the pleasures of this recording. —JEFFREY DUNN

CRAZY FOR YOU
Original Broadway Cast, 1992 (Angel) ★★

This is a faux revival cloned from the DNA of a vintage musical, with a score drawn from the Gershwin songbook. Ken Ludwig's *Crazy for You* book is sort of based on the 1930 Gershwin hit *Girl Crazy,* transferring a standard, let's-put-on-a-show plot to the Wild West. It's hard to get excited about the disc, which is really only a collection of Gershwin standards with a few rarities tossed in, but William D. Brohn's orchestrations have real zing and the cast is fun. As a New York millionaire who dreams of Broadway stardom and ends up putting on a show in Deadrock, Nevada, Harry Groener is a model of period style, tossing off "I Can't Be Bothered Now" and "Nice Work If You Can Get It" with delightful ease. Jodi Benson plays his feisty cowgirl love interest with intensity, and her heartfelt vibrato is put to good use in "Someone to Watch Over Me" and "But Not for Me." There are amusing contributions from Bruce Adler as a Yiddish-accented producer and Michele Pawk as Groener's overbearing fiancée. The show's heart is in its production numbers, such as "Slap That Bass" and "I Got Rhythm," during which Brohn's vivacious arrangements build to a state of ecstasy. It's always more fun to hear a new score in a new show but, of its kind, *Crazy for You* is about as good as it gets. —DAVID BARBOUR

CRY FOR US ALL
Original Broadway Cast, 1970 (Project 3/no CD) ★★★

This was composer Mitch Leigh's follow-up to *Man of La Mancha*—and it was a long way from Spain to Brooklyn. The show was in trouble out of town (there was a temporary title change to *Who to Love?*) and it lasted only nine performances on Broadway. However, the score, with lyrics by William Alfred and Phyllis Robinson, often lives up to what this musical was trying to be: a semi-operatic version of *Hogan's Goat,* William Alfred's Pulitzer Prize-winning play about love and betrayal in the world of 1890s Brooklyn politics. Although the source material might have been better served by a completely sung-through approach, many of the songs are effective and the performers handle them well. Joan Diener does a beautiful job with "Verandah Waltz," "How Are Ya Since?" and "Who to Love?" There is strong legit singing from Steve Arlen in "The End of My Race" and Robert Weede in "The Mayor's Chair." Tommy Rall and Helen Gallagher do their best with some mediocre material, and the three urchins who narrate the story are entertaining in "The Broken Heart or the Wages of Sin" and "The Cruelty Man." A few important songs are missing from this album and others are heard in abridged form. Leigh has been quoted as saying that he wants to re-explore *Cry for Us All* and give it a full operatic treatment. That sounds like a great idea. —JEFFREY DUNN

CYRANO
Original Broadway Cast, 1974 (A&M, 2LPs/no CD) ★★★★

This musical, based on Edmond Rostand's *Cyrano de Bergerac,* boasts a wonderful translation and adaptation by Anthony Burgess; the exquisitely poetic lyrics by Burgess hew closely to his translation of the classic play. Also outstanding is the music of Michael J. Lewis—melodic, stirring, and well suited to the story even if the orchestrations and arrangements fall short. Christopher Plummer gave one of his greatest performances as Cyrano, but the beautiful score is not well served by his singing. Leigh Berry, however, is an excellent vocalist; her "You Have Made Me Love" is, in fact, one of the finest renditions of a musical theater ballad ever recorded. (This gorgeous, relatively unknown song is a gem as worthy of fame as "Some Enchanted Evening," for it's just as romantic and stirring.) Mixed like a 1960s pop album, the recording has a tinny sound quality and lacks the vibrancy of the stage performance. But the double-LP includes much of the show's dialogue, magnificently acted by Plummer, who justly won a Tony Award for his performance. One can only hope that *Cyrano* will someday be revived with an actor of Plummer's caliber in the leading role. —GERARD ALESSANDRINI

DAMES AT SEA

Original Off-Broadway Cast, 1968 (Columbia/Sony) ★★★★★

Jim Wise, George Haimsohn, and Robin Miller's ingenious salute to the Busby Berkeley movie musicals of the early '30s never hits a false note. The show's spoofing is so expert and affectionate that its first production in a Greenwich Village café soon made its way to the Bouwerie Lane and then to the Theatre de Lys, where it ran and ran. This album replaces the show's two-piano accompaniment with wonderful arrangements by Jonathan Tunick, an orchestrator as talented as the hopefuls onstage. The central joke of the original production was staging huge production numbers in a tiny space with a cast of six. Of those original players, only Bernadette Peters went on to stardom but, while she's an adorable Ruby, the others are just as expert and lovable: Tamara Long's temperamental star; Sally Stark's best-buddy blonde; Steve Elmore as the producer and sea captain; and David Christmas as Dick, a songwriting sailor ("Why, I can see it now! As if it were happening on this very stage!"). Only Joseph R. Sicari's Lucky doesn't quite fit in—still, he partners Stark nimbly in "Choo-Choo Honeymoon" and is ingratiating in "Singapore Sue." A nod to the CD booklet's evocative production stills and to Marc Kirkeby's smart notes.

London Cast, 1989 (JAY) ★★★

It's hard to top the original cast album of *Dames at Sea,* and though this recording has its pleasures, it offers no real competition. However, it does contain more dialogue—lines that are so grin-inducing, you'll wish the original had more. Josephine Blake is a terrific Mona Kent, a larger-than-life cartoon of the Temperamental Star with a snarling delivery and a versatile voice. Paul Robinson is appealing as Dick and the other men are fine, too. But Tina Doyle's Ruby lacks individuality, and Sandra Dickinson's squeaky-voiced Joan lacks color. Jonathan Tunick's orchestrations have been reduced and synthesized; the results have so little to do with a '30s sound that going back to the original two-piano arrangement would have been smarter. Two chorus people have been added to the cast of six, and in a musical with a postage-stamp quality as the soul of its wit, that feels like cheating.   —MARC MILLER

ALL-TIME FAVORITES

OF COMPOSER

Stephen Flaherty

1. Porgy and Bess

2. Sweeney Todd

3. West Side Story

4. Guys and Dolls

5. Gypsy

6. Carousel

7. Ragtime

8. Show Boat

9. Once on This Island

10. Sunday in the Park With George

DAMN YANKEES

Original Broadway Cast, 1955 (RCA) ★★★★

For many musical theater buffs, *Damn Yankees* defines 1950s Broadway style: all-American in subject matter and treatment, songs by the hot new team of Richard Adler and Jerry Ross (whose hit *Pajama Game* opened the year before), direction by old-pro George Abbott. Baseball may be the show's surface theme, but it also deals with questions of aging and disappointment as refracted through a modern retelling of the Faust legend with a number of fantasy elements at play: a natty but nasty devil, a suddenly young hero, and a sassy temptress. Also, the show teases audiences with a sort of April-November romance between the young man and the wife of his former, older self. That's not to say this is a dark musical in sum; its serious notions never become grim and, midway through the first act, it's galvanized by the brassy allure of Lola, the devil's choice glamour girl. Gwen Verdon created the role in 1955, and *Damn Yankees* has been under her flame-haired spell ever since. While the original cast album can't give us her legendary dance moves, it does present her fetching vocalism in its freshest form. "Whatever Lola Wants" is essential for the archives and "A Little Brains, a Little Talent" is not far behind. Fortunately, the rest of the cast doesn't fade by comparison. Stephen Douglass was one of the best Broadway baritones of his time, and he's teamed with the appealingly homespun Meg of Shannon Bolin. Russ Brown expertly growls "Heart," Rae Allen is up to the belting of "Shoeless Joe," and Ray Walston reminisces amusingly in the devilish "Those Were the Good Old Days." This first recording of *Damn Yankees* is an apt souvenir of a show and an era.

Film Soundtrack, 1958 (RCA) ★★

Codirected by George Abbott and cinema pro Stanley Donen, *Damn Yankees* didn't fare as well onscreen as the other Adler-Ross transfer, *Pajama Game*. But most of the Broadway leads recreated their roles in the film, and movie star Tab Hunter makes a perfectly acceptable Joe Hardy; Hunter sounds OK here, partly because the role's more challenging songs ("A Man Doesn't Know" and "Near to You") were eliminated. A feeble new tune, "There's Something About an Empty Chair," is sung as a solo by Shannon Bolin. Vocally, Hunter teams well with Verdon on "Two Lost Souls." Again in blissful form, Verdon is partnered in "Who's Got the Pain?" by future husband Bob Fosse, who choreographed *Yankees* (and *Pajama Game*) for stage and screen. Walston is an even more snide Satan, Brown sings "Heart" with brio, and Jean Stapleton's distinctive soprano wails in a supporting role. The soundtrack benefits from expanded orchestrations by Ray Heindorf; an instrumental cut of "Whatever Lola Wants," used as background scoring, is especially lush. But it should be noted that the early-stereo-era sound is shallow and glassily reverberant. This, along with that dull "Chair" song, puts this enjoyable recording a notch or two below the original.

Broadway Cast, 1994 (Mercury) ★★

Perhaps *Damn Yankees* is too light a musical to merit a full-scale, reimagined revival à la *Cabaret* or *Carousel*. Still, one might have wished for something more than the entertaining but uninspired treatment given the show in this revival. In the role of Lola, Bebe Neuwirth is tireless, fun, and pert, but not great. Victor Garber makes an adequate devil without adding any new dimensions to the role. The one arresting new performer is Tony-winner Jarrod Emick, whose Young Joe winningly manages to combine Stephen Douglass' vocal authority with Tab Hunter's boyish charm. However, Linda Stephens is a far more youthful-sounding Meg than Shannon Bolin, so some of the poignancy of the Meg/Young Joe relationship is missing here. Vicki Lewis and seasoned pro Dick Latessa do very well with their big numbers. This is the fullest recording of *Damn Yankees,* with a longer overture and the trial scene. But reassigning the male vocal part in "Two Lost Souls" to Applegate makes no sense, and the numerous dialogue scenes included here do not add to the listening experience. —RICHARD BARRIOS

DANCE A LITTLE CLOSER
Original Broadway Cast, 1987 (TER) ★★

Alan Jay Lerner's sad farewell to Broadway was this 1983 one-nighter, loosely based on Robert E. Sherwood's 1936 drama *Idiot's Delight,* and updated to Cold War days. Len Cariou stars as entertainer Harry Aikens, working in a posh hotel in the Austrian Alps with his backup trio, The Delights. He encounters the girl who got away (Liz Robertson), now passing as British and sleeping with a Kissinger-like diplomat (George Rose); they play romantic cat-and-mouse games as Europe mobilizes for World War III. Broadway audiences definitely weren't interested in Lerner's musings about geopolitical conflict ("We may be headin' / For Armageddon" goes one notorious couplet). The Act II opener, "Homesick," is a low point as The Delights wax poetic about Three Mile Island, Love Canal, and the San Andreas Fault. There's an excruciating subplot involving two gay guys who want an Anglican bishop to marry them, leading to a group theological debate ("I Don't Know"). But when the score by Lerner and Charles Strouse sticks to a mood of romantic disenchantment, it has a glamorous sheen; and even when the songs are ridiculous, Strouse's music is alluring. Harry's lament, "There's Always One You Can't Forget," is a great number, and Cynthia's gold-digging ways are laid out in three sleek items: "No Man Is Worth It," "Another Life," and "On Top of the World." Best of all is the title tune, with its downbeat melody and live-for-the-moment lyric. Jonathan Tunick's orchestrations are beautifully world-weary throughout. —DAVID BARBOUR

DARLING OF THE DAY
Original Broadway Cast, 1968 (RCA) ★★★★

This luckless show suffered from constant turnover on the creative team, arriving in New York without a credited librettist and closing after thirty-one performances. But *Darling of the Day,* as preserved on this disc, has one of Jule Styne's most beguiling scores. The book, based on Arnold Bennett's *Married Alive,* presents the dilemma of Priam Farll (Vincent Price), a Gauguin-like painter who returns to his loathed England after many years in the South Seas. Appalled by society and the art world, he assumes the identity of his deceased butler, even appropriating the latter's feisty, marriage-minded pen pal (Patricia Routledge). Everything is perfect until some of Farll's newer paintings make their way to market, igniting a scandal. Styne's music is warmly inviting and well matched to E. Y. Harburg's wonderful, eccentric lyrics. (A sample: "It's so utterly, ghastly beastly / When your life's all famine without the feastly / And you live so nunnerly and so priestly.") There's a sweet quality to the waltz "Let's See What Happens" and the deeply felt ballad "That Something Extra Special." Price's talk-singing can be a trial, but the album approaches greatness every time Routledge lets loose; she's touching in the quieter numbers and absolutely blissful in such music-hall inspired fare as "It's Enough to Make a Lady Fall in Love." Her second-act showstopper "Not on Your Nellie," a rowdy defense of middle-class life, practically leaps off the disc as Routledge makes sounds that are like nothing you've ever heard before. (Routledge won a Tony for her performance.) This is a delightful score that more people should know about. —DAVID BARBOUR

DAS BARBECÜ
Original Off-Broadway Cast, 1994 (Fynsworth Alley) ★★★

This is a country-western musical takeoff on Richard Wagner's *Der Ring des Nibelungen,* set in Texas. It's one of those cases where the show stands on its own but, to be honest, you're likely to enjoy it more if you're familiar with the source material. *Das Barbecü* is filled with clever songs by composer Scott Warender and lyricist Jim Luigs. The tone is firmly established by the toe-tapping opening number, "A Ring of Gold in Texas." Other titles— "Hog-Tie Your Man," "Rodeo Romeo," "Slide a Little Closer"—are clues to what the listener is in for. The score also includes some nice ballads, such as "County Fair," "River of Fire," and "Wanderin' Man." Making this recording highly listenable are the first-rate singing actors Julie Johnson, J. K. Simmons, Jerry McGarity, Sally Mayes, and Carolee Carmello, all of whom play multiple roles including Wotan, Siegfried, Fricka, Brunnhilde, Gutrune, and Alberich. —MICHAEL PORTANTIERE

A DAY IN HOLLYWOOD/A NIGHT IN THE UKRAINE
Original Broadway Cast, 1980 (DRG) ★★

Can so trite and scattershot a revue about the joys of moviegoing really have charmed Broadway audiences for 588 performances? Apparently, thanks to a bright young cast (including David Garrison and a Tony-winning Priscilla Lopez) and some clever staging by Tommy Tune. But the first half, on disc at least, is dreary indeed: a salute to Richard Whiting here, a tap-danced Production Code number there, some middling additional songs by Jerry Herman (Lopez does shine in "The Best in the World"), and only Wally Harper's piano arrangements to spice up the Dick Vosburgh-Frank Lazarus score. Things perk up greatly in Act II, a version of Chekhov's *The Bear* as it might have been filmed with the Marx Brothers. Garrison is a super Groucho, Peggy Hewett a model Margaret Dumont, and "Samovar the Lawyer" ("I'm wise to all the loopholes / I haven't any scroop-holes") a piece of special material so funny that Groucho himself might have pounced on it. But the ingenuousness is overpeddled—young lovers Kate Draper and Stephen James are actively annoying—and, throughout, the movie-satire points are excruciatingly obvious. Still, the recording does have some nice moments, mostly from Lopez and Garrison. —MARC MILLER

DEAREST ENEMY
Studio Cast, 1981 (Beginners Records/Bayview) ★★★★

A minor milestone in the history of American musical theater, *Dearest Enemy* (1925) was the first book show with a score entirely by Richard Rodgers and Lorenz Hart. It was a big success despite its seemingly killjoy subject matter, the American Revolution. Of course, even though George Washington was on hand as one of the characters, the show didn't really focus on war: Its leading characters are a spunky American girl and a British officer whose romance has a happy ending. Poised engagingly somewhere between operetta and musical comedy, this "baby-grand opera" was notably more clever than most '20s shows, with a cheeky and witty book by Herbert Fields and a score that belies its age. "Here in My Arms" and, perhaps, "Bye and Bye" are the only items that gained any lasting popularity, in part because the remainder of the songs are worked so gracefully into the action; there's just a hint of period pastiche in numbers like "Heigh-ho, Lackaday" and "Where the Hudson River Flows." This London studio cast recording of the score is flawed only in that the singers are accompanied just by piano and the overture is omitted. The cast boasts no star names (one supporting player named Jane Powell is obviously not *the* Jane Powell). But everyone is quite on top of the material. In particular, Michelle Summers as Betsy Burke manages to combine modern and archaic vocal styles with effortless charm. Yes, it would be wonderful to have a full-scale recording of *Dearest Enemy* with full orchestrations, and it's fun to think about the high-powered performers who could take on these roles; still, this lovely show gets much of its due here.   —RICHARD BARRIOS

DEAR WORLD
Original Broadway Cast, 1969 (Columbia/Sony) ★★

Jerry Herman would seem to be the least likely composer to musicalize Jean Giraudoux's *The Madwoman of Chaillot,* but he took on the challenge. The result, *Dear World,* was a four-month Broadway flop in 1969, although Angela Lansbury won her second Tony Award for her starring role. The cast recording reveals a score that, while schizophrenic, is far from unappealing; Herman's songs are tuneful, buoyant, and often evoke France, even if they seldom capture the atmosphere that infused Giraudoux's original play. There's a rousing curtain raiser ("The Spring of Next Year"), a comic list number ("Garbage"), an infectious title song, and a curtain-call medley—all staples of Herman's musical comedy oeuvre but all out of place here. (Pamela Hall's lovely ballad "I've Never Said I Love You" is also out of place, yet her winning performance makes it forgivable.) Some of the other songs are more successful, particularly Lansbury's emotionally surging "I Don't Want to Know" and the hilarious overlapping trio of numbers sung by Lansbury, Jane Connell, and Carmen Mathews in the second act's mad tea party. Every song, regardless of appropriateness, benefits from conductor Don Pippin's vocal arrangements and Philip J. Lang's orchestrations; still, "Mame meets Madwoman" was a gambit never destined for success onstage or on disc.   —MATTHEW MURRAY

DEBBIE DOES DALLAS
Original Off-Broadway Cast, 2003 (Sh-K-Boom) ★★

The stage production of *Debbie Does Dallas* was conceived by Susan L. Schwartz and adapted by Erica Schmidt from the porno flick about a high-school girl's attempts to fulfill her dream of becoming a Dallas Cowgirl. The show was most appealing for its dialogue, much of which was taken from the movie; the songs by Andrew Sherman, Tom Kitt, and Jonathan Callicutt are secondary in quality, not as funny as the dialogue, and uninteresting musically. The score is little more than an intentionally hokey collection of character numbers plus a couple of barely comic plot songs, with musical underscoring that pays homage to the soundtracks of the source film's genre. Luckily, a good deal of dialogue is heard on the CD, and a fine cast—led by Sherie René Scott in the title role—makes listening to this recording an experience that's almost enjoyable in a sort of sick way. Bonus tracks include karaoke mixes of a few of the songs and an "Orgasm Medley" in which select cast members give their all for the microphones. This is a cast album unlike any other.   —MATTHEW MURRAY

THE DESERT SONG
Original London Cast, 1927 (Columbia/Gemm) ★★★

Hot-blooded insurgents battling the Foreign Legion, a hero masquerading as both a milquetoast and the dashing Red Shadow, a prim but passionate heroine, and the lure of the desert. Could this be anything other than operetta? It is, in fact, one of the central works of the genre: a huge hit for Sigmund Romberg in 1926, the first filmed Broadway musical, and a perennial of light opera companies to this day. Romberg's score is a stunner with one great number after another: "One Alone," "Romance," "The Riff Song," and more. Although there is no note-complete recording of *The Desert Song,* the original London cast recorded eight sides at the Drury Lane Theatre. The sound is clear and immediate, if somewhat scratchy, and the recording is a superb time capsule of 1920s British operetta style. As Margot, Edith Day displays a clarion-toned voice that soars above the chorus in the "Marching Song." Her Pierre/Red Shadow, Harry Welchman, is idiomatic and enthusiastic even when sounding like the hammiest member of a shabby touring operetta company. Also enthusiastic is the ace Drury Lane chorus. These eight cuts go by all too fast.

Studio Cast, 1945 (Decca) ★★
When Decca almost single-handedly willed the cast album into existence in the 1940s, it employed a stable of contract artists to go through the repertoire. Preeminent on the label's list of singers was Kitty Carlisle, then in the second decade of a remarkable and varied career that would extend into the twenty-first century. She was cast as Margot for Decca's *Desert Song,* with a firm and big-voiced Wilbur Evans as her two-faced paramour. Some people are still surprised to discover that Carlisle was a good singer; they remember her as a TV panelist and an arts advocate rather than a recording artist or the singing star of *A Night at the Opera* and other movies. Her light, fluttery voice makes her an ideal Margot, although her "Sabre Song" lacks passion and high notes. The recording includes some enjoyably overwrought dialogue snatches; just listen to the "I can't kill you . . . I love you!" finale to Act I.

Studio Cast, 1962 (Angel/excerpts on EMI's *Music of Sigmund Romberg* CD) ★★
Although Gordon MacRae is mostly remembered as the lead in the film versions of *Oklahoma!* and *Carousel,* his ringing baritone was ideal for operetta. Cast as the star of Warner's third filming of *The Desert Song,* MacRae also recorded the score twice: in the early 1950s with Lucille Norman and, stereophonically, a decade later opposite Dorothy Kirsten. On the second recording, his voice is as powerful as it ever was, but the enthusiasm that made his singing so appealing in his youth is beginning to diminish a bit. Kirsten was a rare diva who was equally at home singing Romberg or Puccini, and she's a very appealing Margot. Her tone sounds especially fresh for a lyric soprano in her fifties, and her moments of diva grandness are few and entirely appropriate. The major drawback of this recording is the glitzy sound of the "enhanced" orchestrations: Romberg doesn't need this kind of sweetening, and his melodies are far less dated than the overblown style in which they are presented here.　　　—RICHARD BARRIOS

DESTRY RIDES AGAIN
Original Broadway Cast, 1958 (Decca) ★★★★
One of the happiest CD reissues was the Decca recording of Harold Rome's whip-cracking western musical, complete with good guys, bad guys, saloon girls, respectable prostitutes, and gun fights. This atmospheric album stars Andy Griffith in his only Broadway musical role and Dolores Grey as saloon singer Frenchy, the latter belting up such a storm that it's a wonder she managed to get through eight performances a week. On CD, from the first notes of the rousing overture, there's an added crispness that was always lacking on the LP. This only adds to the pleasure of hearing Griffith's "Tomorrow Morning" (with some great sound effects) and his comedic, double-talking "Only Time Will Tell." But the album is dominated by Grey's songs, most notably the sinuous "I Know Your Kind," the soul-searching ballad "I Say Hello," and one of the more thrilling examples of this singer's style: "Fair Warning." The two leads duet

effectively in "Anyone Would Love You" and the plot-motivated reprise of "Once Knew a Fella." The production number "Are You Ready, Gyp Watson?" is effective even without its brilliant Michael Kidd choreography; "Respectability" is a charming musicalization of what it means to work in a bordello; and "That Ring on the Finger" gives Grey, Rosetta LeNoire (as her spunky maid), and the "working girls" a chance to let go joyously at the prospect of Frenchy getting married. Almost every song on this lively disc is a winner.

Original London Cast, 1982 (JAY) Not recommended.

It took *Destry Rides Again* almost a quarter-century to get from Broadway to London. In the interim, the musical theater of both countries had changed greatly. So it's not surprising that what used to be a show with lots of dancing girls, prostitutes, and cowboys was downsized. The London cast of nineteen had only three women, which meant the deletion of "Respectability. " Almost all cast members doubled as the show's band; the orchestration is reduced to what sounds mainly like guitars and violins with a bass, harmonica, trombone, and a barely audible piano. This approach has a calamitous effect on the score, and musical director Chris Walker must take at least some of the blame for it. Alfred Molina is low-keyed and ineffective as Destry. Jill Gascoine sounds pained as Frenchy; her singing grates on the ear and she only partly compensates with her acting. Harold Rome wrote a wonderfully tuneful score for *Destry Rides Again,* but this recording manages to disguise that fact.   —JEFFREY DUNN

DIVORCE ME, DARLING
Original London Cast, 1964 (Must Close Saturday) ★★★★

If you saw *The Boy Friend* and wondered what happened to its characters ten years later, Sandy Wilson answered that question with this delightful "1930s musical" sequel. It starts with the four "perfect young ladies" exclaiming, "Here We Are in Nice Again"; all the other characters turn up in various disguises. Along the way, both stage and film musicals of the '30s are affectionately spoofed with catchy pastiche songs. The original London cast is perfection, but it should be noted that Patricia Michael (playing Polly) was "indisposed" during the recording session; two of her numbers are sung by Jenny Wren, who does a fine job. The only original *Boy Friend* cast member in this show was Geoffrey Hibbert as Lord Brocklehurst, who delivers the hilarious "On the Loose." Other highlights: the title song, performed by almost the entire cast; the mysterious Madame Kay (Joan Heal) in the sultry "Blondes for Danger"; Polly's lament, "What Ever Happened to Love?"; Bobby's sly seduction of Polly, "No Harm Done" (Cy Young); and the rhapsodic/comedic "Back Where We Started."

Chichester Festival Cast, 1997 (JAY) ★★★

Composer-lyricist Sandy Wilson writes in his notes for this recording that he was not happy with the original West End production of this show but now, thirty-two years later, "I have seen *Divorce Me, Darling* come to life." In the interim, Wilson had rewritten the book for a small production in 1979; that version is recorded here and is now the standard performing edition. Endlessly inventive, this production features several musical theater stalwarts, among them Liliane Montevecchi as Mme. Dubonnet, Ruthie Henshall as Polly, Tim Flavin as Bobby, Linzi Hately as Hortense (the maid from the Villa Caprice, where the "perfect young ladies" were "finished"), Kevin Colson as Percival, and Marti Webb as Hannah—Bobby's sister, a new character. The disc has the same tune stack as the original London cast recording with the addition of "Back to Nature." Many of the songs have revised lyrics, additional dance music, and lead-in dialogue. Wilson wrote an excellent 1930s pastiche score and this recording does it justice. If I have a slight preference for the original recording, I wouldn't want to be without either.　　　　　　　　　　　　　　　　　　　　　　　　—JEFFREY DUNN

DO BLACK PATENT LEATHER SHOES REALLY REFLECT UP?

Original Broadway Cast Members, 1985 (Bay Cities/Sony) Not recommended.
No matter how "informed" the writer of a review is, the critique is largely a matter of opinion. Or as Cole Porter put it, "I like Offenbach, you do not / So what? So what? So what?" Which is my way of explaining that I greatly dislike *Patent Leather Shoes,* even though I know the show has been hugely successful in stagings around the country and is, in fact, the longest-running musical ever to play Chicago. It's certainly possible that I would respond more favorably to it if I had attended parochial school or were a Catholic—or if, like the show's main character, I'd fallen in love with a girl in the fifth grade, watched as she became a nun and then, years later, reunited with her after she left the convent. Not having had those experiences, I view this musical as unevocative nostalgia without the slightest bit of insight or wit. For the record, the music and lyrics are by Alaric Jans and James Quinn, the book by John R. Powers.　　　　　　　　　　　　　　　　　　　—DAVID WOLF

DO I HEAR A WALTZ?

Original Broadway Cast, 1965 (Columbia/Sony) ★★★★
Stephen Sondheim has often bad-mouthed *Do I Hear a Waltz?*—perhaps because it can't compare to his trail-blazing hits. While Arthur Laurents' book is a bit of a confused bore, the score—with music by Richard Rodgers and lyrics by Sondheim—is really good. The musical is an adaptation of Laurents' *The Time of the Cuckoo,* in which spinster Leona Samish (Elizabeth Allen) travels to Venice and meets attractive Renato Di Rossi (Sergio Franchi) but isn't trusting enough to fall in love with him. The show starts briskly with "Someone Woke Up," Leona's claim that she's ready for anything. It continues well with "This Week, Americans," in which the *pensione* owner (Carol Bruce) charms her guests. "What Do We Do? We Fly," a sharply humorous group number about transatlantic air travel, follows. Rodgers gets in his bolt-of-lightning ballads with "Someone Like You" and "Take the Moment," as well as the lovely title song—a waltz, natch. Also enjoyable is "Bargaining," in which Renato teaches Leona the ins and outs of shopping in Venice. Only "We're Gonna Be All Right" seems like filler, but there's a reason for that: See below.

Pasadena Playhouse Cast, 2001 (Fynsworth Alley) ★★★★
On this recording, Steve Orich's brisker musical direction helps make *Do I Hear a Waltz?* sound like a hit. Alyson Reed and Anthony Crivello have more personality than their Broadway counterparts, and what fun it is to hear Carol Lawrence on a cast album after too long an absence, playing the landlady of the *pensione.* Only Tina Gasparra, as her maid, disappoints as she tries much too hard to sound comic. There is one significant, unfortunate cut: "Bargaining" was a charming song and an important one because it made us like Renato, so it's a shame to lose it. On the other hand, there's a nifty reprise of "This Week, Americans" and other additions; most notably, the previously excised lyrics of "We're Gonna Be All Right" make an incisive and sophisticated song out of what had just been a pleasant throwaway number. If these lyrics are an indication of what Sondheim was forced to eliminate at Rodgers' insistence, we can begin to understand why the guy can't stand this show.　　　　　　　　　　　　—PETER FILICHIA

A DOLL'S LIFE

**Original Broadway Cast, 1982 (Original Cast Records/
Bay Cities) ★★★**

A Doll's Life is about what happened to Henrik Ibsen's Nora after she slammed the door at the end of *A Doll's House.* Betty Comden and Adolph Green wrote the book and lyrics, Larry Grossman wrote the music, and Harold Prince directed the production. The show opened on Broadway to terrible reviews and closed after five performances—but fortunately, it was recorded. There's a lot that's wrong with the score but also a lot that's very right with it, as this recording reveals. Most outstanding is Betsy Joslyn in the enormously taxing central role. Nora's songs range from low belt through mid-range mix to high soprano. The character's progression from frightened doll-wife through many bedrooms and boardrooms to successful business woman before she finally returns home to confront her husband is charted with dramatic and musical complexity, and Joslyn is more than up to the role's challenges. She's expressive in her heartfelt "Letter to the Children," probing in "Learn to Be Lonely," sensual in "No More Mornings," triumphant in "Power," and urgent in "Can You Hear Me Now?" These excellent solo pieces alone would make this recording worthwhile, but there are also fine performances by Peter Gallagher, who is particularly effective in "Stay With Me, Nora," and George Hearn, who lends his authoritative baritone to "You Interest Me." Most of the score has an operatic flavor— it even includes a mini-opera called "Loki and Baldur"—so it's not surprising that the supporting cast members have strong, legit voices. So what's wrong with *A Doll's Life?* Well, a few numbers don't work at all and may even cause a groan or two. Of course, you can skip around at will on a recording—and this recording is definitely worthy of a try.   —JEFFREY DUNN

DONNYBROOK!

Original Broadway Cast, 1961 (Kapp/no CD) ★★★★

This musical based on the movie *The Quiet Man* was a spirited but unsuccessful show. *Donnybrook!* did boast an excellent cast that included Susan Johnson, Eddie Foy Jr., and Art Lund, plus a wonderful score by Johnny Burke, who achieved fame by penning terrific lyrics to the music of Jimmy Van Heusen and others in dozens of Hollywood musicals. The songs are tuneful, funny, and romantic. "I Wouldn't Bet One Penny," "Ellen Roe," "A Quiet Life," "Dee-lightful Is the Word," "The Loveable Irish," "Sez I," and "He Makes Me Feel I'm Lovely" may not be household titles, but they are excellent examples of Broadway songwriting at its best. Joan Fagan brings great spirit to the Burke ballads. Johnson, one of the theater's top belters, also shows warmth and vulnerability here; she and Foy have a wonderfully charming comic rapport. And Lund sings with feeling if not quite the requisite amount of theatricality. The album, which has not been transferred to CD as of this writing, sounds clear and immediate; *Donnybrook!* was recorded in the heyday of the stereo-separation craze, so everyone sings left or right of center. Make an effort to find the LP and get acquainted with its many charms.   —KEN BLOOM

DON'T BOTHER ME, I CAN'T COPE

Original Broadway Cast, 1972 (Polydor/no CD) ★★

This is the sort of show that's much more effective onstage than on record. It was easy to get caught up in a live performance of this revue, which sometimes seemed like a revival meeting. As recorded, though, *Don't Bother Me, I Can't Cope* emerges as little more than a collection of R&B numbers, all presented with the same intensity. There's a tremendous sameness to the material. Micki Grant, who won great acclaim for her songs (and who later wrote some of the best material in *Working*), heads the cast, which also includes Alex Bradford, Hope Clarke, Bobby Hill, and Arnold Wilkerson. —DAVID WOLF

DON'T PLAY US CHEAP
Original Broadway Cast, 1972 (Stax, 2LPs/no CD) ★

This Melvin Van Peebles musical is as different from his earlier *Ain't Supposed to Die a Natural Death* as it could be. Though plotless, the earlier show is dramatic and intensely theatrical, whereas *Don't Play Us Cheap* tells a friendly, comical story of two imps who give their souls to the devil. Before they can qualify as full-fledged demons, they must prove their skills by wrecking a party; so they crash a Harlem affair, but their efforts to create mayhem are complicated when one imp falls in love with a young woman who's throwing the party. The numbers embrace jazz, blues, gospel, pop, and R&B. This two-LP set contains the entire score, including seven instrumental selections. Unfortunately, the songs don't function dramatically and the piece is too loosely constructed to have any real impact. Cast as the imps are Joe Hughes, Jr. and the legendary Avon Long, the latter charming as ever in his only solo, "The Phoney Game." The women giving the party are played by Esther Rolle and Rhetta Hughes. —DAVID WOLF

DOONESBURY
Original Broadway Cast, 1983 (MCA/no CD) ★★

For the stage version of his political-satire comic strip, Garry Trudeau fashioned his own book and lyrics, proving himself to be a surprisingly adept lyricist. He elicits honest laughs with "Another Memorable Meal" (about Mike Doonesbury's pathetic culinary attempts) and "Complicated Man" (Honey and Boopsie torching about their difficult boyfriends). Nor does Trudeau leave out the satire, scoring anti-Reagan-era points in "Real Estate" and "It's the Right Time to Be Rich." Unfortunately, these savories are wedded to the shapeless, tuneless rock meanderings of Elizabeth Swados, who also did the clattering orchestrations. And though this is nominally a book musical, there's very little narrative or character development in it; as a result, the ballads bob around on the surface, sounding like nothing more than Lite-FM selections. As rock musicals go, this one has more vocal power than most: Laura Dean's Boopsie is a standout (especially in "I Can Have It All") and Ralph Bruneau displays an attractive high tenor as Mike. Broadway notables Mark Linn-Baker and Barbara Andres get their chances, too, though the latter is paired with the vocally uncertain Kate Burton in an unmoving mother-daughter reconciliation number. A bit small-scale for Broadway, which may have accounted for its short run, the show is nevertheless an evocative, cheeky time capsule. If there were some way to divorce Trudeau's lyrics from Swados' music, I might revisit it more often. —MARC MILLER

DO RE MI
Original Broadway Cast, 1960 (RCA) ★★

Right after *Gypsy,* you'd have expected Jule Styne to test his powers of composition in another meaty Broadway project. Instead, he regressed to formula musical comedy with this minor hit, reuniting with frequent collaborators Betty Comden and Adolph Green and his *High Button Shoes* star, Phil Silvers. As Ralph Kramden in everything but name (and even that was pretty close—he played one Hubie Cram), Silvers played opposite another great clown, Nancy Walker, in a jukebox-industry spoof that may have had some resonance in the wake of the payola scandals. But the score lets the stars down: "Waiting, Waiting," "Take a Job," "Ambition," and "Adventure" sound oddly unfinished, neither conforming to standard song structures nor having any special reason for avoiding them. Second couple John Reardon and Nancy Dussault fare somewhat better, and Reardon even gets to introduce "Make Someone Happy." But the blaring Styne overture is all fanfare and no substance, and the eleven-o'clock number "All of My Life," sung by a heavy-breathing Silvers, doesn't earn its right to breast-beat. Apparently, a lot of the show's virtues were visual: Silvers' shtick, Walker's reactions, and a nubile assortment of chorus girls. None of that comes through on disc.

Original London Cast, 1961 (Decca/TER) ★★★

The middling Styne score doesn't sound any more impressive as performed on the other side of the Atlantic, but it picks up some arresting oddities in this briskly conducted album. Most jarringly, in a very New York show filled with lyrical references to Far Rockaway, Brooklyn, and Dinty Moore's, this mostly Brit cast makes no attempt at New York accents. Billed above the title is Max Bygraves, a mugging music-hall comic who manages to be a restrained and affecting Hubie; there's real wistfulness in his "All of My Life." The comedienne Maggie Fitzgibbon's vocal part lies uncomfortably for her and she makes some very painful noises. Jan Waters, an attractive ingenue, is sturdily partnered by the big-voiced American Steve Arlen in a sweet duet. The cuts in the overture and the slightly thinned-out orchestra hurt this thin score not a bit.

Encores! Concert Cast, 1999 (DRG) ★★★

City Center's enterprising musicals-in-concert series had a go at *Do Re Mi,* and the cast album of that production improves markedly on the original. For starters, Nathan Lane has more voice than Phil Silvers, and he probably inhabits this type of burlesque-influenced conniver better than anyone alive today. This is also a more complete recording than RCA's; the lead-in dialogue and extra songs ("He's a VIP," "Who Is Mr. Big?") help us make more sense of the flimsy plot, and the score is followed by a ten-minute interview with the songwriters from the 1960 recording session. Brian Stokes Mitchell's creamy baritone sells the ballads, and Heather Headley is sweetly understated opposite him. She's also fine in the send-up of 1950s pop-awfulness "What's New at the Zoo?" As Kay Cram, Randy Graff works hard, but she's not the intuitive comedic genius that Nancy Walker was. Paul Gemignani conducts with his customary snap, and the slight tape hiss of the RCA original cast album is happily absent here. — MARC MILLER

DRAT! THE CAT!
Original Broadway Cast, 1965 (Blue Pear/no CD) ★★★

It's a cliché among cast-album collectors to hear a good score to a flop musical and ponder, "Why wasn't this a hit?" But the recording of this eight-performance 1965 tuner is truly mystifying in that respect; released in 1984, it's taken from a live tape and the audience is plainly having a marvelous time. Ira Levin's daffy book concerns a bumbling cop pursuing a seductive jewel thief in circa-1890s New York. The snatches of dialogue on the record are met with appreciative chuckles and outright guffaws. Milton Schafer's score is tuneful and spirited, and Levin's deft lyrics go heavy on the comedy. Elliott Gould's rendition of the one hit song, "She Touched Me," wins what sounds like a thunderous ovation. Even Joe Layton's comic ballet "The Upside-Down Thief" elicits gales of giggles. Best of all among the cast is a teenage Lesley Ann Warren as the diamond-pinching heiress: She's a giddy delight in "Wild and Reckless," a charmer in the tongue-twisting "Holmes and Watson" duet with Gould, and quite the pensive balladeer in "I Like Him." Jane Connell turns up as Warren's mother, making her inimitably odd noises in the waltz ensemble "Dancing With Alice" and raging engagingly at Jack Fletcher in "It's Your Fault." The score and the performances are super; I would have upgraded my rating if it weren't for the sound quality, which is pretty wretched overall.

Studio Cast, 1997 (Varèse Sarabande) ★★★

The good folks at Varèse Sarabande assembled a top-drawer cast and a full orchestra to give *Drat! The Cat!* the recording it deserved, and this CD improves on the above album—but not in all respects. Certainly, the sound is a dozen times better; there are superior liner notes by TheaterMania's own Peter Filichia and an appreciation by author Ira Levin. Jason Graae (in the role created by Elliott Gould) makes a fine lead and is even disarming in a hidden "bonus" track. There's luxury casting all around: Judy Kaye, with an intentional put-on of an Irish accent, is his widowed mother; Elaine Stritch is his lady love's harpy of a mama; and Tony Randall is the object of Stritch's considerable scorn. This CD retains the original orchestrations of Hershy Kay and Clare Grundman and includes even more lead-in dialogue. On the debit side: As Alice, the jewel-thief "cat" of the title, Susan Egan weighs every line carefully and sings excellently, but there's little of the giddy, naughty rich girl (a Paris Hilton of the 1890s) in her portrayal. For all of its assets, this *Cat* album lacks a certain theatrical spark. You can't really go wrong with either recording, although the original has a very slight edge. If you can find it—and if you still own a turntable—pounce. — MARC MILLER

DREAMGIRLS
Original Broadway Cast, 1982 (Geffen/Decca) ★★

What were they thinking? The most exciting Broadway score of the 1980s was carved up to fit on one disc, stripped of its narrative drive and emotional punch. But what a score! Under the whip hand of director-choreographer Michael Bennett, librettist-lyricist Tom Eyen and composer Henry Krieger created a musical loosely based on the story of Diana Ross and the Supremes. This is no trashy tell-all; rather, *Dreamgirls* is an American epic, tracking no fewer than eight characters as they climb to the top of the music industry. It's a musical melodrama about ambition, adultery, lies, corruption, and betrayal, set to an irresistible Motown beat. Moreover, the authors have much to say about show business as a pathway to assimilation and the high cost of success. The disc preserves Harold Wheeler's nonstop orchestrations and Cleavant Derricks' electrifying vocal arrangements. The cast, including Sheryl Lee Ralph, Loretta Devine, Ben Harney, and Derricks, is first-rate—but Jennifer Holliday's performance as Effie, the Dreamgirl who is cast out of the group and betrayed by her scheming lover/manager, seems more and more mannered upon repeated listening. Her rendition of the first-act finale, "And I Am Telling You I'm Not Going," caused standing ovations in the theater; hearing it today, you may be unnerved by her wild, unrestrained vocalizing. Still, the big disappointment of this disc is what's missing from it: Among the cuts are "Heavy," the number that signals trouble brewing in the group; "It's All Over," the dramatic scene that sets up "And I'm Telling You I'm Not Going"; and much of the dazzling opening sequence that introduces all of the major characters. While there are moments of excitement here, this groundbreaking musical didn't get the treatment it deserved in the recording studio.

Concert Cast, 2002 (Nonesuch, 2CDs) ★★★★★

This live recording of a benefit concert is an embarrassment of riches. The cast is led by divas Audra McDonald, Heather Headley, and Lillias White, and even the smaller roles are filled by the likes of Alice Ripley, Emily Skinner, Brian Stokes Mitchell, Malcolm Gets, Norm Lewis, and Patrick Wilson. Most important, this set redresses a historical injustice by recording the show in its entirety, giving listeners full access to the dramatic reach of the Krieger-Eyen score. It also preserves the Effie of Lillias White, a veteran of the original Bennett production. White's sassy, spiky, yet deeply vulnerable performance is tops; she sings "And I Am Telling You I'm Not Going" as a hair-raising aria of heartbreak and rage. Her rendition of Effie's Act II anthem "I Am Changing" is triumphant. McDonald and Lewis turn the duet "When I First Saw You" into a shattering confrontation, and Headley stirs up a whirlwind of comic fury when she tells off her married lover in "Ain't No Party." When all three ladies tear into the title number, you'll be in Diva Heaven. There's also fine work from Billy Porter as a James Brown-like figure whose career is skidding and Darius de Haas as the group's ambitious songwriter. This live recording shows the galvanizing effect that *Dreamgirls* inevitably has on audiences: It's pure gooseflesh from beginning to end and one of the few really essential cast albums of the decade. —DAVID BARBOUR

DUDE

Original Cast Members, 1972 (Kilmarnock/Original Cast) ★★★

Here's one of Broadway's legendary disasters, described by Otis Guernsey, Jr. in the *Burns Mantle Yearbook* as "an ardent questing for eternal verities of heaven and earth, life and death, youth and maturity, in the form of an unruly rock musical." Perhaps, but it plays well on this disc, which was made some months after the show's sixteen-performance run ended. You'll be surprised that it was such a terrible flop when you hear the overture, which starts out majestically. The score is more bluegrass than rock, but Galt MacDermot's music is always tuneful. Some show songs make you tap your toes, while more forceful ones make you briskly nod your head in tempo; Leata Galloway's rendition of "I Am What I Am" is in the latter category, and so is Nell Carter's "So Long, Dude." The melody of the title song is quite good, although Gerome Ragni's lyrics for it aren't so special. Ragni is also responsible for Musical Theater's Most Unlikely Song: "I'm Small," in which a guy confesses to being terribly unwell-hung. The CD also includes ten cuts from a separate album of songs from the show that was recorded by the androgynous-sounding Salome Bey. All of those songs display MacDermot's great gift for melody. We must mourn the fact that, throughout his career, he didn't work with better collaborators and pick his projects more carefully. Whatever was wrong with *Dude,* MacDermot's music wasn't the problem. —PETER FILICHIA

EATING RAOUL
Original Off-Broadway Cast, 1992 (Bay Cities/Original Cast Records) ★★★★

Paul Bartel wrote the book for this musicalization of his cult-classic film and found ideal collaborators in lyricist Boyd Graham and composer Jed Feuer; their score displays the same campy, goofy insanity as the flick. This tale of a couple repulsed by sex and the Mexican stud who joins in their scheme to murder swingers in order to raise cash to buy a restaurant (really, don't ask!) is told through a series of terrific, often hilarious numbers. Chief among them are the title song (the title phrase of which is rhymed with "kids in school," "don't be a fool," and "rabbis in shul"), two great trios ("Think About Tomorrow" and "Trio"), and a pair of late-show knockouts: a song-and-dance number called "Momma Said," sung by a large man in a flowing dress, and the eleven-o'clock stunner "One Last Bop." Everything is well sung by the cast of nine, led by Eddie Korbich, Courtenay Collins, and Adrian Zmed. M. W. Reid plays the guy in the dress, among other characters. Joseph Gianono's orchestrations are overly synthesized—the band consists of two keyboards, guitar, bass, and percussion—but they can't mask the undeniable fun of the score. —SETH CHRISTENFELD

EILEEN
Ohio Light Opera Cast, 1997
(Newport Classics, 2CDs) ★★★

Victor Herbert's 1917 "romantic comic opera" is a beauty, every bar of it suffused with the master's love of his native Ireland. Although *Eileen* ran but two months on Broadway, it left behind the classics "Thine Alone" and "The Irish Have a Great Day Tonight," plus a crowded program of heartfelt ballads, comic duets, and a half-dozen outpourings of Irish nationalism, all gorgeously orchestrated by Herbert. So this first-ever complete recording of the show, taken from a live performance, should be a cause for celebration. It is, but distractions keep spoiling the party. First, the recording includes *all* the dialogue, and while Henry Blossom's libretto isn't bad for its florid type, it's not the sort of thing you'll want to listen to again. The acting and singing are brogue-heavy and variable in quality, with some real screeching on the high notes. The sound level is generally too low, yet the clomp-clomping of the chorus across the stage is loud and clear. J. Lynn Thompson's conducting is melodramatic; Herbert himself probably wouldn't have inserted so many portentous *rallentandi* and *crescendi*. Still, this is a great operetta score, one likely to win friends for the underappreciated genre. The production even exhumed "Blarney Is Our Birthright," which probably hadn't been heard since 1917. The Ohio company's dedication is spectacular even when its execution doesn't quite measure up.   —MARC MILLER

ELEGIES: A SONG CYCLE
Original Off-Broadway Cast, 2003 (Fynsworth Alley) ★★★★★

In his songs for the theater, William Finn insists on being pointedly autobiographical; he seems happiest when dissecting his own thoughts with a sharp scalpel. Shying away from nothing, particularly not from death and grief, his *Elegies: A Song Cycle* is breathtaking in the depth of its commentary on the rewards and woes of being part of a family, a group of friends, and a society in good times and bad. "I wrote this song to not forget Mark's all-male Thanksgiving," he reports at the end of one number, and that statement is indicative of his tell-all compulsion as expressed in often free-form melodies and sometimes carefree rhyming. Though there are references here to people and places from Finn's upbringing, he's really chronicling the period of time bracketed by the advent of AIDS twenty years back and the Twin Towers' collapse ("Goodbye" includes remarks by someone phoning from the doomed buildings). There's no denying that much of the piece's brilliant content is painful, yet the songwriter invokes laughter amid tears. "Infinite Joy" may be the best song Finn has ever written—a marvel as delivered by Betty Buckley, for whom this sort of gloriously positive, soaring anthem is ideally suited. The other classy warblers on this cast album, for which Vadim Feichtner did the musical arrangements and Gihieh Lee the vocal arrangements, are the lustrous-voiced Carolee Carmello; the commanding yet easy-going Michael Rupert; the earnest Keith Byron Kirk; and the delightful Christian Borle. It all adds up to infinite joy.   —DAVID FINKLE

ELEGIES FOR ANGELS, PUNKS AND RAGING QUEENS
Original London Cast, 1993 (First Night) ★★★★★

An alternately moving, exciting, and hilarious program of songs and monologues about AIDS victims and their loved ones, this show premiered Off-Broadway in 1987, but no cast album of that production was released. Inspired by the enormous Names Project quilt that memorializes those lost to AIDS, and also by Edgar Lee Masters' *Spoon River Anthology,* the piece is a brilliant collaboration between Bill Russell (book and lyrics) and Janet Hood (music). The London cast recording includes none of the show's monologues but all of its songs—and what songs they are. In an uncommonly strong score, a highlight is "And the Rain Keeps Falling Down," the lament of a man who can't let himself cry over a friend's illness. Mindful of the fact that an evening made up entirely of sad songs would be unbearable, Russell and Hood came up with some numbers that are humorous ("I Don't Do That Anymore," "Spend It While You Can"), rousing ("Celebrate"), and/or inspirational ("Learning to Let Go"). This disc begins with the almost-title song "Angels, Punks and Raging Queens" in a touching rendition by Kim Criswell, who also excels in the score's most famous number, the heartbreaking "My Brother Lived in San Francisco." The other three singers—Miguel Brown, Simon Green, and Kwame Kwei-Armah—are equally fine.

New York Concert Cast, 2001 (Fynsworth Alley) ★★★★★

This is a live recording of a concert version of *Elegies . . .* that was performed as an AIDS benefit. Featuring a cast of fifty-two, the concert was conducted by Janet Hood and directed by Bill Russell. The CD begins disappointingly with Alice Ripley's forced rendition of "Angels, Punks and Raging Queens," a song that wants a much more simple, less showy performance, but the rest of the singers are wonderfully well matched to the material: Brian d'Arcy James lends his gorgeous voice to "And the Rain Keeps Falling Down"; Clent Bowers and Doug Eskew offer blessed comic relief in "I Don't Do That Anymore"; and Emily Skinner's reading of "My Brother Lived in San Francisco" is very special. (Skinner also duets with Ripley, her erstwhile *Side Show* sister, in "Celebrate.") On hand as well are such talents as Alton Fitzgerald White, Orfeh, Amy Spanger, Stephanie Pope, Kane Alexander, Kathy Brier, Sharon Wilkins, and Kelli Rabke. The disc ends grandly with the amazing Norm Lewis soaring through "Learning to Let Go" as the entire company sings backup and the audience claps along. Given that this is a live recording with no touch-ups, some of the performance sounds a bit raw—but that's entirely appropriate to the subject matter. A major selling point of the disc is that it includes six of the show's monologues, delivered to full effect by Steve Burns, Erin Torpey, Veanne Cox, Bryan Batt, Christopher Durang, and Mario Cantone.   —MICHAEL PORTANTIERE

ERNEST IN LOVE
Original Off-Broadway Cast, 1960 (DRG) ★★★
Following the success of *My Fair Lady,* it seemed that witty and teddibly literate entertainment was what the theatergoing public craved, so lots of songwriters began plowing through all things British for anything that would allow a similar tuner to be extracted. In light of that mad scramble, it's not surprising that Oscar Wilde's *The Importance of Being Earnest* attracted lyricist-librettist Anne Croswell and composer Lee Pockriss. This is the romp in which the incomparable Victorian playwright twitted a couple of twits who woo two young damsels, one of whom has an inordinately proper mother. Luckily, copycats Croswell and Pockriss brought sufficient élan to bear on a derivative score that nevertheless has charm and lilt. While it does not necessarily approach Wilde's genius with an epigram, it's not a travesty. Although the show produced no chart climbers, it does boast "A Wicked Man," which got some attention. Even "How Do You Find the Words?"—which sounds like something salvaged from the Lerner and Loewe discard bin—is a bit of all right. The speak-singing leading man that Rex Harrison validated in *My Fair Lady* is represented here by John Irving (not the novelist). Far superior chanting is done by the pursued soubrettes, Gwendolyn (Leila Martin) and Cecily (Gerrianne Raphael). Sarah Seegar as Lady Bracknell delivers Croswell's best rhyme—"satchel or" with "bachelor"—upon learning that, as a baby, her daughter's suitor was found in a handbag. Gershon Kingsley provided the lively arrangements.   —DAVID FINKLE

EUBIE!
Original Broadway Cast, 1978 (Warner Bros./no CD) ★★
The resurrection of Eubie Blake's music in the 1970s was a joyous affirmation of the fact that even if genuine talent fades for a while, it usually makes a comeback. Blake's career had peaked in 1921 with the all-black Broadway hit *Shuffle Along.* But he was still around more than a half-century later—a charming nonagenarian making appearances on talk shows, telling great stories, and playing a mean piano. Blake also had some fine songs to his credit. While "I'm Just Wild About Harry" (lyrics by Noble Sissle) and "Memories of You" (lyrics by Andy Razaf) are the only two that most people remember, many others are worth reprising. In 1978, a few months after the Fats Waller tribute *Ain't Misbehavin'* opened, it was Blake's turn. Forty years' worth of his songs were performed by an energetic, all-black group of singer-dancers in a revue

that just had to be titled with the composer's euphonious, unforgettable first name—plus an exclamation point! The company included Gregory and Maurice Hines, so it would be nice to report that the cast album is a winner—but, alas, its success is intermittent. Part of the problem is that the material is limited in range. Blake was not Fats Waller, and while his melodies go from rags to blues to Tin Pan Alley, they aren't always top-drawer. The arrangements are overblown and the recording sound is often unpleasant, as was the sound amplification in the theater. Many of the performers seem to have been directed to give subtlety a holiday and try to stop the show at every opportunity. "My Handy Man Ain't Handy No More," with its cheerfully dirty lyrics by Razaf, is a case in point. A song like this shouldn't be blasted out, as Alaina Reed does here; double entendres are usually funnier when they're not hammered home. Blake's songs require more care than they received in this revue.   —RICHARD BARRIOS

EVITA

Studio Cast, 1976 (MCA, 2CDs) ★★★★

This final collaboration (to date) of composer Andrew Lloyd Webber and lyricist Tim Rice is also the last really good musical theater piece to come from ALW's pen. *Evita* is based on the life of Argentinean dictator Juan Perón's wife, Eva Perón, who was idolized by the nation and perhaps was as powerful as her husband. The score is bursting with scintillating melodies and exciting rhythms written in a modified rock idiom. Although that idiom is historically inaccurate for a musical whose action takes place between 1936 and 1952, and literal-minded listeners may balk at the anachronism, the songs are wonderfully enjoyable in their own right. There is also a piquant Latin tinge to some of the tunes. Singing the tour-de-force role of Evita, Julie Covington is very much in the rock mode—but her performance is dynamic, committed, and highly theatrical. As Che, a character based on Che Guevara, C. T. (later Colm) Wilkinson is terrific. Paul Jones sounds too young, too attractive, and too straightforward for the role of Juan Perón, but Tony Christie as Magaldi and Barbara Dickson as Perón's mistress contribute vivid, well-sung cameos. Among the recording's best tracks are Covington's soulful delivery of the gorgeous "Don't Cry for Me Argentina" and her full-throttle belting of "Buenos Aires"; the coruscating "Waltz for Eva and Che"; Dickson's lovely, plaintive rendition of "Another Suitcase in Another Hall"; and the haunting "High Flying Adored," another great Eva-Che duet. Throughout the recording, the London Philharmonic sounds magnificent as conducted by Anthony Bowles. When the full orchestra really lets loose for the first time in "Requiem for Evita," the torrent of sound is worthy of what was, by most accounts, the funeral of the century.

Original London Cast, 1978 (EMI) ★★

Elaine Paige has one of the greatest musical theater voices ever, but much of her performance on this cast album of the world premiere stage production of *Evita* is disappointing; it almost sounds as if she's holding back at times so as not to blow out her voice. To give only one example: When she reaches the high-lying bridge of "Buenos Aires," she finesses the passage rather than delivering it in the gleaming belt for which she's famous. (It's understandable that Paige would make vocal adjustments in this killer role to get through eight performances a week onstage, but its hard to imagine why she didn't give her all for the recording.) The other featured soloists—Joss Ackland, David Essex, Siobhàn McCarthy, and Mark Ryan—are fine, but their roles have been more persuasively recorded by others. Another big strike against the album is that it presents only highlights, and this is a score you'll want to hear *in toto*.

Original Broadway Cast, 1979 (MCA, 2CDs) ★★★★

With her amazing, industrial-strength singing voice and serious acting chops, Patti LuPone might have been born for the part of Evita. She belts "Buenos Aires," "A New Argentina," and other songs to thrilling effect, yet she's vulnerable and moving in "Don't Cry for Me, Argentina," "Eva's Final Broadcast," and "Lament." Simply put, she's definitive in this role. Mandy Patinkin brings to Che a unique combination of sweet, Irish-tenorlike high notes and a cantorial *geshrei* when he belts. Bob Gunton gives a sly, skillful performance as Juan Perón; he leads "The Art of the Possible," a neat song that wasn't on the concept album of *Evita*, and he has great chemistry with LuPone in "I'd Be Surprisingly Good for You" and "Dice Are Rolling." Jane Ohringer offers a lovely lyric-soprano rendition of "Another Suitcase in Another Hall"; she really does sound like a teenager, which helps the song dramatically. Mark Syers, who died soon after this recording was made, is a fine Magaldi. The more rocklike sounds of the original arrangements and orchestrations were toned down for the stage version of the score; for example, the electric guitars in "Requiem for Evita" are replaced by trumpets. Also, the jarringly anachronistic rock 'n' roll number "The Lady's Got Potential" is gone entirely. The orchestra, augmented for this recording, sounds huge and exciting. Rene Wiegert is the music director. If you want only one recording of *Evita* in your collection, this is the one to choose. (Note: This is actually labeled the "Premiere American Recording" of the score; it was recorded in Los Angeles, where the show played prior to reaching Broadway.)

Film Soundtrack, 1996 (Warner Bros., 2CDs) ★★

A film version of *Evita* was in the planning stages for years. When the movie was finally ready to roll with Madonna as Eva Perón, there was widespread consternation at the casting; none of the pop star's recordings gave anyone any reason to believe that she would be able to handle the vocal demands of such a tough role. As it turned out, much of the score had to be transposed downward and otherwise rearranged for her to get through it. Not surprisingly, she sounds best in the more lyrical sections. Although "Don't Cry for Me Argentina" takes a lot of getting used to in a lower key, Madonna sings it pretty well if not with great feeling. She also does a lovely job with "Another Suitcase in Another Hall," but it's too bad that this song was taken away from the one-scene character of Perón's mistress in order to give Eva/Madonna yet another number. Madonna flattens some of the neat rhythms in "Eva and Magaldi" / "Eva, Beware of the City" (Jimmy Nail sings Magaldi), and she also seems to have some pitch problems in this sequence, although the music keeps modulating so wildly to accommodate her vocal range that it's hard to be sure. Also, Madonna gets the vowels and diphthongs of the words "Buenos Aires" all wrong, rendering the city name as if it were spelled "Buenes Arres." For a plausible Spanish accent, look to Antonio Banderas, who sings Che's songs with fire and charisma. Jonathan Pryce is an authoritative presence as Juan Perón—a brilliant bit of casting. The orchestrations are by the composer, with additional work by Andrew Cullen. As presented here, the score sounds a lot like it does on the concept album: There are some twanging electric guitars in the "Requiem" and "The Lady's Got Potential," the latter reinstated with new lyrics, and that works against the more authentic sounds engendered by some rescoring for acoustic guitar and accordion. The movie and its soundtrack album are notable for including a new Lloyd Webber-Rice ballad, "You Must Love Me"—yes, another song for Eva/Madonna! As conducted by John Mauceri, David Caddick, and Mike Dixon, the score sounds impressive despite the jarring transpositions.　　　—MICHAEL PORTANTIERE

FADE OUT—FADE IN
Original Broadway Cast, 1964 (ABC-Paramount/Decca) ★

This musical spoof of Hollywood in the 1930s is best known for its star's attempts to bail out of it. Betty Comden and Adolph Green tailored the book to the comic talents of Carol Burnett. She plays a Broadway chorine who is packed off to Hollywood and transformed into screen legend Lila Tremaine. (When Burnett tried to buy out her contract, the show closed, reopened, and quickly closed again.) Comden and Green's lyrics here seem a little tired; Jule Styne's music is always professional, but this is far from his best score. Burnett gets the most out of her numbers, including the witty "Call Me Savage," in which the chorine is reinvented as a sex symbol; the defiant "Go Home Train"; and "You Musn't Be Discouraged," in which the star riotously spoofs Shirley Temple while Tiger Haynes conjures Bill "Bojangles" Robinson. The rest of the cast—including Jack Cassidy as a narcissistic leading man, Lou Jacobi as the neurotic studio boss, Tina Louise as a dim starlet, and Dick Patterson as Burnett's love interest—are all fine, and the orchestrations by Ralph Burns and Ray Ellis are bouncy. Still, this is the sort of thing that Burnett did better a few years later on her TV variety series. —DAVID BARBOUR

FALSETTOS (MARCH OF THE FALSETTOS/FALSETTOLAND)
Original Off-Broadway Casts, 1981/1990 (DRG, 2CDs) ★★★★★

Although the second and third installments of William Finn's *Marvin* trilogy were originally produced nine years apart (the first was *In Trousers*), they're now better known as the united work *Falsettos,* which reached Broadway in 1992. The closest that we're ever likely to get to a cast album of that show is this two-disc set of material that eventually made up its two acts, but it doesn't preserve the rewrites made for Broadway. These are, nevertheless, definitive performances of Finn's brilliant scores; there will probably never be a better Marvin than Michael Rupert, a better Whizzer than Stephen Bogardus, or a better Mendel than Chip Zien. Alison Fraser's Trina in *March of the Falsettos* is only slightly superior to Faith Prince's Trina in *Falsettoland.* James Kushner and Danny Gerard, as the two iterations of Marvin and Trina's young son, are both terrific, and so are Heather MacRae and Janet Metz as the "lesbians next door." The scores are sublime; Finn was able

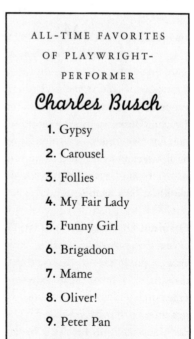

ALL-TIME FAVORITES
OF PLAYWRIGHT-
PERFORMER

Charles Busch

1. Gypsy

2. Carousel

3. Follies

4. My Fair Lady

5. Funny Girl

6. Brigadoon

7. Mame

8. Oliver!

9. Peter Pan

10. The Music Man

to write quirky patter songs and compose beautiful melodies. It's hard to believe that the man who wrote "Four Jews in a Room Bitching" (a great opening number), "Please Come to My House," and "Days Like This" was also responsible for "The Games I Play," "Father to Son," "What More Can I Say?" and the astounding "What Would I Do?" among myriad other songs on both ends of the spectrum.
— SETH CHRISTENFELD

FAME THE MUSICAL
Original London Cast, 1995 (Polydor) Not recommended.
Fame was successful as a movie and TV series but landed with a thud when it hit the stage. All about students at New York City's legendary High School for the Performing Arts, the source material seemed perfect for a musical. If only creators José Fernandez (book), Jacques Levy (lyrics), and Steve Margoshes (music) had had something more in mind than an After-School Special version of *A Chorus Line.* They use every cliché imaginable to tell of ambitious kids dealing with drugs, sex, and angst; no new dramatic or musical ideas are found here. Aside from the famous Dean Pitchford-Michael Gore title song, which somehow found its way into the score, the music mostly consists of flavorless beats and vamps. The lyrics say very little, very loudly. The song titles alone speak volumes: "Hard Work," "I Want to Make Magic," "Let's Play a Love Scene," and so on. Miquel Brown, as the teacher who wants to nurture the kids' minds rather than their talents, performs the gospellike "These Are My Children" with something akin to real emotion, though lyrics such as "These are my children / My saving grace / I see my calling in every face" don't make it easy for her. At least she's not in the position of Marcos D'Cruze, who's saddled with one of the most embarrassing "comedy" songs of the 1990s: "Can't Keep It Down." (As he sings, "You know what it's like / When you wake up in the mornin' and it's hard / Standin' up straight at attention / Like the changin' of the guard?")

Original American Cast, 1999 (DRG) ★
Despite the inadequacies of *Fame* as a musical, its first American touring production did boast some top-notch talent. Gavin Creel, Jennifer Gambatese, Kim Cea, Nadine Isenegger, Robert Creighton, Clyde Alves, and Natasha Rennalls are among the cast members who went on to bigger and better career things. They make the most of the material, and some credit goes to Jo Lynn Burks for her energetic musical direction. This recording has more energy than the London cast album—but since it features the same insufferable songs, that makes little difference. Creel and Gambatese's numbers come off well, and Rennalls is fine in the title track and in her falling-apart number, "In L.A." As with the London cast recording, "These Are My Children" is a relative standout, here sung with heartfelt passion by Regina Le Vert.

Original Off-Broadway Cast, 2003 (Q Records) Not recommended.
When *Fame* finally landed in New York, it was renamed *Fame on 42nd Street*—as if a title change would save it! But no time was spent fixing the show's ridiculous lyrics and trite sentimentality. Unlike the other recordings, this one boasts no exceptional cast members. Cheryl Freeman tries hard but can't make much of anything out of "These Are My Children," though her duet with Nancy Hess in "The Teacher's Argument" has an energy that previous renditions lack. Nicole Leach's Carmen is decently sung but somewhat lifeless, as are most of the other performances. Two items of note: This disc includes a second-act pas de deux and

a "Romantic Suite" of songs from the show performed by the Budapest Symphony Orchestra. These tracks suggest that *Fame* might be a much better show if it were only danced and not sung.

— MATTHEW MURRAY

A FAMILY AFFAIR
Original Broadway Cast, 1961 (United Artists/no CD) ★

This recording begins with the strains of "Here Comes the Bride," then the first words we hear are "Will you marry me?" The story goes on to trace what happens between those words and "I do." Noteworthy as composer John Kander's first Broadway show (collaborating with James and William Goldman) and Harold Prince's first Broadway directing credit, *A Family Affair* is about how the Siegels and Nathans of Chicago deal with their kids' impending nuptials. Top-billed Shelley Berman as the bride's uncle has a second-act number, "Revenge," that incorporates the sort of telephone sketch for which this comic was well known at the time. Berman manages not to obscure the prettiness of "Beautiful" and, backed by the male chorus, he does well with the cliché-ridden "Right Girls." With costars Eileen Heckart and Morris Carnovsky (as the groom's parents), he puts over "I'm Worse Than Anybody." Carnovsky, best known for his Shakespearean roles, is a game participant in "Kalua Bay" with Heckart, whose exuberance compensates for her vocal insufficiencies (she's very touching in "Summer Is Over"). The vocal honors go to Larry Kert and Rita Gardner as the marriage-bound kids; they excel in their duets ("Anything for You" and "There's a Room in My House," the latter as fine a ballad as Kander ever wrote) and in the now politically incorrect "Every Girl Wants to Get Married" (Gardner) and "What I Say Goes" (Kert). Bibi Osterwald runs riot as a wedding planner, leading her cohorts in the show-stopping "Harmony." According to the liner notes, *A Family Affair* was the "first Original Cast Album made on 35mm magnetic film . . . resulting in the most lifelike tone quality ever achieved." It would sure be nice to hear how that would translate to CD!

— JEFFREY DUNN

FANNY
Original Broadway Cast, 1954 (RCA) ★★★★

This nearly forgotten show has a beautiful score worthy of the golden era of Broadway from which it comes. Harold Rome's music and lyrics are full of gorgeous tunes and excellently crafted, character-specific lyrics. The performances by the great opera singer Ezio Pinza and the young Florence Henderson are also tops. This was the first Broadway venture of theater impresario David Merrick, and the cast album suggests how impeccably he produced *Fanny*. The musical is based on Marcel Pagnol's Marseilles trilogy about love and abandonment on the French Riviera. Joshua Logan directed, and the show was a solid success. Lush, large, and operatic, Pinza's voice is thrilling; William Tabbert's tenor has a legit timbre that may sound overwrought by today's standards but is nonetheless beautiful; Henderson (long before her TV stint as Mrs. Brady) displays a compelling soprano voice. The Hollywood character actor Walter Slezak portrays Panisse with charm and joie de vivre. The appealing songs include "Restless Heart," "Why Be Afraid to Dance?" and "Welcome Home"—one of the most touching ballads ever written for a musical. However, some of the atmospheric numbers, such as "Shika, Shika" and "Octopus Song," are less than pleasant. Also unfortunate is the flat, fuzzy mono sound that underlines the antique nature of the album. Still, there is much to enjoy here.

— GERARD ALESSANDRINI

THE FANTASTICKS
Original Off-Broadway Cast, 1960 (MGM/Decca) ★★★★★

There's a reason why this show ran for more than forty years; the prototype for every little Off-Broadway musical with big hopes, it has never been equaled. Tom Jones, adapting a little-known play by Edmond Rostand, spun a slender fable about a young couple whose fathers scheme to bring them together by pretending to separate them. What's important, however, are Jones' casually poetic words, Harvey Schmidt's elegantly understated melodies, and the simple, piercing insight that no one can appreciate happiness until they lose it. Schmidt's witty, melancholy tunes and jazz-piano harmonies mesh beautifully with Jones' lyrics, which are alternately tender, tart, ironic, and full of feeling. The leads are superb: Kenneth Nelson and Rita Gardner capture the young lovers' wide-eyed idiocy without a trace of condescension. As their fathers, William Larsen and Hugh Thomas are a pair of cheerful fools, doling out parental advice in "Never Say No" and "Plant a Radish." Best of all is Jerry Orbach as El Gallo, the narrator and catalyst; his rendition of "Try to Remember" sets the show's tone beautifully. In a score that includes the gorgeous "Soon It's Gonna Rain," the acidic "This Plum Is Too Ripe," and the driving "I Can See It," it's hard to choose favorites. Shot through with romance, irony, and sadness, *The Fantasticks* is unique among musicals.

Japan Tour Cast, 1993 (DRG) ★★

This is the cast album of a Japanese touring production of *The Fantasticks* that featured Jones as Henry and Schmidt at the piano. It's a competent performance but it never delves into the show's deep feelings of loss and regret. Alfred Lakeman (El Gallo), Sam Samuelson (Matt), and Chiara Peacock (Luisa) are all acceptable in their roles if somewhat lacking in personality. The disc contains many dialogue sequences that add little to one's enjoyment; in fact, some scenes are quite tedious. A bonus track offers "A Perfect Time to Be in Love," written for Robert Goulet as El Gallo to sing in a thirtieth-anniversary tour of the show. It's a sweet tune that fits in well with the rest of the score.

Kings College School Wimbledon Cast, 2000 (JAY) ★

This is a pleasant, competent, totally undistinguished production. The young cast is enthusiastic, but the El Gallo, Andrew Nicolaides, is vocally weak, while Ian Goodman and Mark Lowe sound far too young to be playing the fathers. As Matt and Luisa, Robin Chalk and Amber Sinclair are reasonably good; still, this is one of the least necessary cast albums ever. (Note: *The Fantasticks* was televised in 1964, starring Susan Watson, John Davidson, and Ricardo Montalban, and a movie version was released in 2000, starring Jean Louisa Kelly, Joseph McIntyre, Jonathan Morris, and Joey Grey—but neither version yielded a cast album. That's too bad, for we could use some more recordings of this oft-produced classic.) —DAVID BARBOUR

FERMAT'S LAST TANGO
Original Off-Broadway Cast, 2002 (Original Cast Records) ★★★

A musical about a math problem? It's a crazy notion, but composer-lyricist Joshua Rosenblum and librettist-lyricist Joanne Sydney Lessner make it work. Their show was inspired by the controversial last theorem of French mathematician Fermat, which has the mythic qualities needed to support a dramatic framework. *Fermat's Last Tango* is a bizarre, surprisingly effective, mostly true musical detective story. The creators changed few of the facts beyond renaming the central figure Daniel Keane. Fermat himself appears, taunting and yet assisting Keane throughout the show; if the device seems a bit silly at first, it works because of the epic scope of the musical. (Euclid, Newton, Pythagoras, and other mathematicians also appear.) The score is often operatic in weight, but the talented cast is more than up to the challenge. Chris Thompson displays a booming baritone as Keane, Jonathan Rabb's pompous Fermat is lots of fun, and members of the ensemble (Christianne Tisdale, Carrie Wilshusen, Gilles Chiasson, and Mitchell Kantor) are excellent. Perhaps the best performance is by Edwardyne Cowan, who plays Keane's wife. With her beautiful voice, Cowan puts over the show's one concession to traditional musical comedy, a terrific number titled "Math Widow." But there are several other enjoyable songs here. *Fermat's Last Tango* is not recommended as light background music but is definitely worth a listen or two. After all, how many musicals make math seem like fun? —MATTHEW MURRAY

FIDDLER ON THE ROOF
Original Broadway Cast, 1964 (RCA) ★★★★★
One of the greatest cast albums in the RCA catalogue, this is a treasured memento of the original production of the Jerry Bock-Sheldon Harnick-Joseph Stein masterpiece *Fiddler on the Roof,* based on stories by Sholom Aleichem. It's well documented that Zero Mostel, the show's hugely talented star, became impossible as *Fiddler* settled into its long run, ad-libbing outrageously. According to some reports, his antics were partly responsible for his being passed over for the film version of the musical. So we can be thankful that "Z" was on his best behavior for the cast recording, made just after the show opened. His Tevye is a force of nature, a portrayal of the role unlikely ever to be equaled. The rest of the company is marvelous: The late, great Maria Karnilova is simultaneously sharp, funny, and warm as Golde; Julia Migenes delivers a heart-tugging "Far From the Home I Love"; Austin Pendleton sings "Miracle of Miracles" like he really means it; and Bert Convy displays a lovely voice in "Now I Have Everything." The sound quality of the recording is superlative and the latest CD edition has bonus tracks, all but one of them featuring lyricist Harnick, who performs "If I Were a Rich Man" and two cut songs from the show, "How Much Richer Could One Man Be?" and "When Messiah Comes." He also shares stories of the original production. The remaining bonus item is an instrumental version of "If I Were a Rich Man" as played by the Moscow Virtuosi.

Original London Cast, 1967 (Columbia/Sony) ★★★
This is a fine recording if you don't mind the British accents of most of the singers and the strange, hard-to-pin-down accent of Topol in the role of Tevye. Topol fans may actually prefer his performance here to the one he gives on the film soundtrack album (see below) if only because it's less mannered and has more theatrical energy. The other soloists here are Miriam Karlin, Linda Gardner, Cynthia Grenville, Rosemary Nicol, Jonathan Lynn, Sandor Elès, and Paul Whitsun-Jones. They're all fine but not distinctive enough to warrant special note, except to say that Karlin is an extremely baritonal Golde. Although the Broadway orchestrations are used here, they intriguingly sound a bit different because of the way the score was conducted (by Gareth Davies), recorded, and mixed.

Studio Cast, 1968 (London) ★★
Here is an odd but intermittently enjoyable recording made in "Phase 4 Stereo." Aside from overload distortion in certain passages, the sound quality is terrific. Although the orchestrations seem to be the Don Walker originals with a few enhancements, the score sounds quite immense as recorded in full, weighty, reverberant acoustic. Conductor Stanley Black sets some

very slow tempi but his pacing does bring out the melodic beauty of "Sunrise, Sunset," "Sabbath Prayer," and "Far From the Home I Love." As Tevye, we have opera star Robert Merrill, who toured in the role and comes across on the recording as a fine actor as well as a great singer. Playing opposite him is Molly Picon, a treasured artist of the Yiddish theater—but she was too old for the role of Golde, further hampered by Black's tempi and by having to switch back and forth between octaves to accommodate her voice to the range of Golde's songs. Still, Picon has many engaging moments. Gary Cole sounds too operatic and too British in Motel's "Miracle of Miracles," but Mary Thomas sings Hodel's "Far From the Home I Love" well, even if she indulges in an ill-advised high note at the end. There is no Perchik to be found here; the character's "Now I Have Everything" has been eliminated. On the other hand, we do get to hear Merrill sing one of the "monologues" that Tevye delivers upon learning that his daughters are planning to marry against his wishes. The most controversial aspect of this recording is that it features an annoying "narrative" written by Jacob Kalich and spoken by Picon and Merrill. This was presumably intended to give dramatic thrust to the album—but, if that was the goal, why was the order of the first several songs shifted around?

Film Soundtrack, 1971 (United Artists/EMI) ★★★

Although the film version of *Fiddler on the Roof* is a fine adaptation of the show, the soundtrack recording doesn't stand up too well on its own. The music is adapted and conducted by John Williams, and the violin soloist is the great Isaac Stern, but many of the vocal numbers fall short as enjoyable listening experiences. Topol's Tevye has lots of personality yet, again, his odd accent is disconcerting. Also, he delivers his spoken lines in "Tradition," "Tevye's Dream," and elsewhere v-e-r-y slowly. Norma Crane is a fairly bland Golde, and Michele Marsh as Hodel goes overboard trying to make "Far From the Home I Love" sound "natural" rather than musically expansive. But when Rosalind Harris and Neva Small join Marsh in "Matchmaker," it's a delightful performance. Also, the "Chava Ballet Sequence" is gorgeous, thanks to Stern's achingly beautiful solo. The unquestionable highlight of the recording is Leonard Frey's rendition of "Miracle of Miracles"—two minutes and four seconds of utter joy. The latest CD edition includes cuts that are not on the original two-LP set or on the first CD edition. One of them is "Any Day Now," a song that was written for Perchik to sing in place of "Now I Have Everything" but didn't make it into the movie.

Broadway Cast, 2004 (PS Classics) Not recommended.

This revival of *Fiddler* was horribly misdirected by David Leveaux. We can be grateful that the cast album doesn't preserve such bits of staging as Tevye's daughters sponge-bathing themselves during "Matchmaker, Matchmaker," Tzeitel and Motel dangling from the flies during "Tevye's Dream," and the formerly minor character of Nahum the beggar taking over the spotlight in every big number. From a purely musical standpoint, the production wasn't terrible, so the cast album is not difficult to listen to—but that's certainly not to say that there's any reason to purchase it. As Tevye, Alfred Molina seems to have a bit more life here than onstage; still, he's pretty bland in a role that requires a good bit of personality and humor. Sally Murphy, Laura Michelle Kelly, and Tricia Paoluccio as (respectively) Tzeitel, Hodel, and Chava are colorless, and Kelly's singing is shaky. Randy Graff is good as Golde, but it's difficult to enjoy her work in the context of what's going on around her. And although John Cariani does a fine job with Motel's "Miracle of Miracles," Robert Petkoff doesn't have the voice for Perchik's "Now I Have Everything." Larry Hochman's rewrites of the Don Walker orchestrations are always unnecessary and often annoying; the fillips he adds to "Tradition" are especially egregious. Conductor Kevin Stites distorts such great songs as "Matchmaker" and "Far From the Home I Love" with silly internal shifts in tempo. For what it's worth, the recording includes a fair amount of Joseph Stein's wonderful dialogue. —MICHAEL PORTANTIERE

THE FIELDS OF AMBROSIA
Original London Cast, 1996 (First Night) ★★★

A curious musical with a curious history: It opened in New Jersey to respectable reviews, traveled to London for a sort of protracted New York tryout, was critically trounced there, and left behind this cast album. It's also unusual in that the lyricist-librettist, Joel Higgins, is the star—and did he write himself a juicy part! As Jonas Candide (perhaps too symbolically named?), a "traveling executioner" who carts a primitive electric chair to penitentiaries in the American South of 1918, Higgins possesses one of the finest voices in musical theater—though it has generally been confined to flops and replacement casts. Here, he makes an indelible impression early on in the title number as he offers con-man comfort to a death-row inmate just before throwing the switch. Jonas has the misfortune of falling in love with another doomed inmate, a German immigrant accused of murder. Since she's portrayed by Christine Andreas, who also possesses a great legit voice, you know you're in for an earful. With her vocal finesse and considerable acting chops, Andreas shines in the intense "Who Are You?" and in two fine duets with Higgins, "Too Bad" and "Continental Sunday." The uneven but often strong music is by Martin Silvestri; this is a score that glows when it focuses on the principals but goes somewhat slack in the ensembles. As Jonas' adoring disciple, Marc Joseph has another stunning solo, "Alone," and the orchestrations by Harold Wheeler are first-rate throughout. But both acts open with chorales for the prisoners that are as predictable as they are one-dimensional, and when Jonas tries to scare up some money to save his ladylove by appealing to American jingoism ("All in This Together"), the number has a perfunctory air to it. British critics objected mainly to the show's now-tragic, now-comic tone and its moral ambiguity, qualities (or deficiencies) that don't really help or hurt this CD. What does emerge is a flawed but intriguing, ambitious attempt at a serious, original, large-scale American musical. Given most of the product of the mid-1990s, that's nothing to scoff at. —MARC MILLER

FIFTY MILLION FRENCHMEN
New York Concert Cast, 1991 (New World Records) ★★★★★

Anything Goes may be rated the most fun Cole Porter score, but consider this 1929 hit: a whoop of joy from the late Jazz Age that makes relentless fun of Ugly Americans abroad. This sparkling concert version, performed by a fine cast at the Alliance Française in New York, was fortunately recorded on a CD that seems to capture every subtlety in the orchestrations. Since those orchestrations are by a variety of practiced hands, including Hans Spialek and Robert Russell Bennett, it was well worth the effort: Check out the happy flutes in "You Do Something to Me," the klaxons in "Do You Want to See Paris?" and the saxophones everywhere. Evans Haile's conducting is pure buoyancy; when he picks up the tempo for the orchestral interlude of "Let's Step Out," you'll want to get up and Charleston. Howard McGillin, an unusually soulful juvenile, gets one of Porter's best ballads ever: "You Don't Know Paree." Jason Graae catches all the innuendo in "You've Got That Thing." Kim Criswell is both a vocal powerhouse and an ideal Porter interpreter, making "The Boy Friend Back Home," "Find Me a Primitive Man," and "I'm Unlucky at Gambling" sound even dirtier than they are. Even Peggy Cass, hardly a singer, amusingly croaks something called "The Queen of Terre Haute." A couple of songs don't land: "Where Would You Get Your Coat?" is a one-joke affair that goes on and on; "Why Can't I Have You?" is a too-obvious riff on "Let's Do It." But the good stuff in this one is so good, and much of it so little-known, that you'll want to play the whole recording over again the moment it's done.   —MARC MILLER

FINE AND DANDY
Studio Cast, 2004 (PS Classics) ★

PS Classics' recording of this 1930 musical presents a fairly conventional score by Kay Swift and Paul James (a nom de plume for Swift's husband, James Warburg). The show was a vehicle for comedian Joe Cook. It features a catchy title tune that became a standard; a big ballad ("Can This Be Love?"); and a new-dance-craze number ("The Jig-Hop"). In those and other numbers, Swift's hot-jazz rhythms and bluesy chords are pretty good imitations of the work of her sometime boyfriend George Gershwin. James' lyrics, while illogical and a little casually rhymed, have an infectious, early-Depression optimism. If the material is decidedly second-tier, the execution is first-rate. Working from the one surviving fragment of Hans Spialek's orchestrations, Russell Warner and Larry Moore wrote sensational period charts that are played here by an excellent twenty-eight-piece orchestra, energetically conducted by Aaron Gandy. If you can get past Mario Cantone's screeching of the title song and Anne Kaufman's amateur-night line readings, many of the performances are enjoyable. Gavin Creel ingratiates instantly in "Starting at the Bottom"; Jennifer Laura Thompson is an appealing ingenue; and Andrea Burns exudes musical-comedy snap in "The Jig-Hop" and "I Hit a New High." Best of all is Carolee Carmello: If this were a live stage show, her "Nobody Breaks My Heart" would surely stop it. The score is shortish, but the disc generously includes an appendix of guest stars warbling other Kay Swift tunes. The Jessica Molaskey-John Pizzarelli duet "Can't We Be Friends?" is so contemporary cool, you'd never guess that the song dates from 1929.   —MARC MILLER

FINIAN'S RAINBOW
Original Broadway Cast, 1947 (Columbia/Sony) ★★★

The mélange of singing styles heard on the first recording of *Finian's Rainbow* is intriguing, but what hits the ears of those not familiar with the show may be confusing. Ella Logan is a Scottish singer playing an Irish lass; she caresses "How Are Things in Glocca Morra?" and "Look to the Rainbow" in a way not heard on Broadway before or since. As the leprechaun Og, David Wayne makes voice-cracking sounds in "When I'm Not Near the Girl I Love." Donald Richards displays a stalwart baritone in "Old Devil Moon" and other songs. Then there are the totally non-Broadway sounds of supporting cast members who deliver the soul-flavored "Necessity" and gospel-flavored "The Begat." After repeated listening, the score begins to shine through the mixture of singing styles, leavened as it is with more standard Broadway tunes such as "If This Isn't Love." Burton Lane's music is endlessly melodic and E. Y. "Yip" Harburg's lyrics are alternately satirical, whimsical, and romantic. The songs stand on their own and that's a good thing, because this recording doesn't give a clear picture of the musical as a whole; it's best to hear it after seeing a staging of the show and/or listening to other recordings of the score. The latest CD edition includes Harburg singing "How Are Things in Glocca Morra?" and "When I'm Not Near the Girl I Love"—his performances of both are revelatory. The final bonus track is the deleted song "Don't Pass Me By," sung by Harburg, with Lane on piano.

Broadway Cast, 1960 (RCA) ★★★★

The City Center revival of *Finian's Rainbow* moved to Broadway for a brief run; happily, the cast album exhibits a more theatrical approach to the score than was taken on the original recording. Jeannie Carson is a vibrant Sharon in "Look to the Rainbow" and "How Are Things in Glocca Morra?" while Biff McGuire is an effortlessly romantic Woody in "Old Devil Moon." They team with the excellent chorus for rousing performances of "That Great Come-and-Get-It-Day" and "If This Isn't Love." Howard Morris as Og is particularly funny in "When I'm Not Near the Girl I Love" and in the reprise of "Something Sort of Grandish." The monumental Carol Brice leads the ladies in "Necessity," and "The Begat" is given a gleeful rendition by Sorrell Booke, Jerry Law, Tiger Haynes, and Bill Glover that reveals all the humor and wit in this number. The CD features the cover art of the first LP edition and includes a previously unreleased track—a finale reprise of "How Are Things in Glocca Morra?" that brings the disc to a suitable conclusion. This is one of those cases where a revival cast recording is preferable to the original.

Film Soundtrack, 1968 (Warner Bros./Rhino) ★★★

It took more than twenty years for *Finian's Rainbow* to get from stage to screen. This was the first and only musical film directed by Francis Ford Coppola, and though it's surprisingly faithful to the Broadway script and score, it really doesn't work. Yet the soundtrack, disconnected from the film, has many delightful things to recommend it. The most important contributions come from Petula Clark, who brings her pop-singing style to Sharon McLonergan's songs in a way that seems altogether appropriate. The recording starts with her beguiling performance of "Look to the Rainbow"; equally charming is her rendition of "How Are Things in Glocca Morra?" and she's a pleasure to hear throughout the album. The character Finian, Sharon's father, doesn't sing in the stage version of the musical, but Fred Astaire was given a fair amount of singing to do as Finian in this, his final movie musical—and he sounds wonderful. Don Francks sings Woody's songs handsomely, and Tommy Steele plays Og with enough energy to burst through the speakers. Some of the movie's arrangements try too hard to be "up-to-date" (for 1968). Still, this soundtrack album is definitely worthy of attention.

Off-Broadway Cast, 2004 (Ghostlight) ★★★

The Irish Repertory Theatre's 2004 production of *Finian's Rainbow* reduced the script and the cast, and the score was presented in a two-piano arrangement. Very few overtures can truly survive that sort of reduction, so this recording gets off to a shaky start. But it recovers quickly with a spirited "This Time of the Year" and continues to grow in strength right through to finale. Melissa Errico is a wonderful Sharon; her "Look to the Rainbow" (with some lyrics not heard on previous cast albums) is ravishing. She and Max Von Essen (Woody) caress "Old Devil Moon," giving it a romantic, sexy, and tastefully swung performance. Malcolm Gets sings the role of Og very well and is a charmer throughout, especially in "When I'm Not Near the Girl I Love." Terri White's "Necessity" is hot and her vocal improvisations around the melody are thrilling; "The Begat" is notable for the complete clarity of the witty lyrics. For this production, the musically undernourished title role was enriched with a "Look to the Rainbow" reprise, and Jonathan Freeman performs it beautifully. The score, in its most complete recording to date, is not compromised by the two-piano arrangement, thanks to wonderfully clean musical direction by Mark Hartman. The CD has a healthy helping of dialogue (including

some narration) that aids in the storytelling, and there are several previously unrecorded bits of songs and reprises. There is also a delightful bonus track of lyricist E. Y. Harburg singing "Old Devil Moon."
—JEFFREY DUNN

FIORELLO!
Original Broadway Cast, 1959 (Capitol/Angel) ★★★★

In an earlier era of musical theater, it was not uncommon for an overture to start with a sound effect. Here, we have the sound of a fire-engine siren—appropriate for a musical about the New York City mayor who famously showed up at fires riding with the firemen. *Fiorello!* tied with *The Sound of Music* for the Tony Award for Best Musical, and won the Drama Critics' Circle Award and the Pulitzer Prize for Drama. Guided by veteran George Abbott, who directed and cowrote the book, the show featured the second Broadway score by composer Jerry Bock and lyricist Sheldon Harnick. (Their first, *The Body Beautiful,* wasn't recorded.) The score displays an excellent feel for both period and character. While none of the clever songs ever achieved popularity outside of the show, many are Broadway classics. The numbers are evenly distributed among the principals, and the story is fairly easy to discern by listening to this album. In the title role, Tom Bosley isn't required to sing much; there's his campaign song, "The Name's LaGuardia" (which he sings in three languages!) and he leads the energetic female ensemble in "Unfair!" Bosley also makes an impact with some brief but moving dialogue during the finale. As his long-suffering secretary Marie, Patricia Wilson is outstanding, especially in the bracing "The Very Next Man." Howard Da Silva as a political boss leads the strong-voiced men's ensemble (listen for the distinctive voice of Ron Husmann) in the classic showstopper "Little Tin Box"; the plot-driven "Politics and Poker"; and "The Bum Won," a contrapuntal, post-election lament. As Fiorello's first wife, Thea, Ellen Hanley uses her creamy soprano for nostalgia in "'Til Tomorrow" and for mature romanticism in "When Did I Fall in Love?" "I Love a Cop" is charmingly sung by Pat Stanley, and "Gentleman Jimmy" is belted out by Eileen Rodgers.
—JEFFREY DUNN

THE FIREBRAND OF FLORENCE
BBC Radio Concert Cast, 2003 (Capriccio, 2CDs) ★★

Capriccio and the BBC left no manuscript unturned in reconstructing Kurt Weill's biggest Broadway flop, a 1945 operetta about Benvenuto Cellini with lyrics by Ira Gershwin. The accompanying booklet describes in detail the quest for the right tempi, the full orchestrations (mostly by Weill, assisted by Ted Royal), and the missing songs. It's scrupulously assembled, excellently conducted by Sir Andrew Davis, and judiciously produced. In place of Edwin Justus Mayer's verbose book, we have Sam Brookes' witty rhyming couplets to connect the songs, and they are read with aplomb by Simon Russell Beale. The Weill-Gershwin score has its undeniable delights ("You're Far Too Near Me," "Sing Me Not a Ballad," "The Nosy Cook"), but the show is hampered by needless plot detours and extraneous ensembles. The tone is now lighthearted, now heavyhanded, as if the creators couldn't decide if we're to care about these characters or not. Rodney Gilfry, for all of his vocal resources, can't turn the bellicose braggart Cellini into a charmer; nor can Lori Ann Fuller overcome a mixed bag of songs, and George Dvorsky is at sea as the bumbling Duke.
—MARC MILLER

FIRST IMPRESSIONS
Original Broadway Cast, 1959 (Columbia/ DRG) ★

There may be a beguiling musical to be coaxed out of *Pride and Prejudice,* but Abe Burrows' attempt isn't it. Like several shows of the era, this one spends most of its time wishing it were *My Fair Lady*. Indeed, Elizabeth Bennett's exuberant "This Really Isn't Me" is so close to "I Could Have Danced All Night" that Lerner and Loewe probably could have sued. Other songs are ungainly stabs at hyperliteracy by the writers (music by Glenn Paxton, lyrics by Robert Goldman and George David Weiss): "I Suddenly Find It Agreeable," "A Gentleman Never Falls Wildly in Love," and "Wasn't It a Simply Lovely Wedding?" There are casting problems everywhere: Farley Granger's Darcy is off-key and listless, and what does Hermione Gingold's music-hall presence have to do with Jane Austen? As Elizabeth, Polly Bergen is game but miscast; at one bizarre point, in "Fragrant Flower," she actually has to trill in contralto. The album comes to life a bit when Phyllis Newman lilts through "I Feel Sorry for the Girl," and again when Ellen Hanley soars through that wedding number. But the overall effect is of spending a long afternoon at an English aunt's home and choking on the crumpets.   —MARC MILLER

FIRST LADY SUITE
Original Los Angeles Cast, 2002 (PS Classics) ★★★
Although Michael John LaChiusa's *First Lady Suite* premiered Off-Broadway in 1993, it did not receive a recording until it was staged in Los Angeles nine years later. While the resulting disc reveals a show packed with the kind of lyrical and musical invention that LaChiusa displays in all of his work, it can be a dense listen, difficult to fully absorb even on multiple hearings. Once assimilated, however, the show sticks with you. LaChiusa's musicalization of emblematic moments in the lives of Jacqueline Kennedy, Mamie Eisenhower, and Eleanor Roosevelt is full of trenchant emotional insights. Most creative is the Eisenhower sequence, distilled to musical comedy proportions, with Eydie Alyson hilarious as Mamie; Gregory Jbara is effective as her husband. Also impressive is Paula Newsome as the legendary opera singer Marian Anderson. The remaining material makes less of an impression, with the other performers more functional than exceptional; some moments that may have been brilliant in the theater were not successfully captured for the CD. Regardless, much of this show remains moving, not only in its portrayals of significant figures in American history, but also because LaChiusa was willing to take the sort of chances that are rarely taken by other contemporary musical theater composers.   —MATTHEW MURRAY

FIVE GUYS NAMED MOE
Original London Cast, 1991 (First Night) ★★★
Super producer Cameron Mackintosh found this little revue of Louis Jordan songs at the Theatre Royal Stratford in London's East End and liked it so much that he revamped the physical production, kept the cast intact, and transferred *Five Guys Named Moe* to the West End, where it ran for more than four years. This live recording of the London production is a festive disc and much preferable to its Broadway counterpart (below), although it has slightly less content and chatter. Dig Wayne is Nomax and the Five Moes who come to help him are Big Moe (Kenny Andrews), Four Eyed Moe (Clarke Peters), Little Moe (Paul J. Medford), No Moe (Peter Alex Newton), and Eat Moe (Omar Okai). They're a dynamic group of performers. In the theater, audience participation was practically mandated; at home, you can clap and sing along or let the audience heard on the disc do it for you. Highlights are the title song, "I Like 'Em Fat Like That," "What's the Use of Gettin Sober," and "Reet Petite and Gone." An augmented band (nine additional musicians were engaged for the recording) contributes significantly by adding new instrumental colors, giving each song a more distinctive, swingier groove and

lighter touch than is heard on the Broadway cast album. The vocal sound is also smoother and better blended (listen to "Saturday Night Fish Fry" and the title song), yet the voices are easy to tell apart, so you don't have to keep consulting the booklet to figure out who's singing.

Original Broadway Cast, 1992 (Columbia/Sony) ★★

It must have seemed that *Five Guys Named Moe* had "Broadway cash cow" written all over it: a transfer of a tried-and-true, small cast, West End hit in an era when the most popular shows on the Great White Way were British imports. But this celebration of a distinctly American musical legend, Louis Jordan, ran little more than a year in New York. Comparing the Broadway cast album with the London recording, it's apparent that something hard to define has been lost. The reduced instrumentation (only six onstage musicians) gives this performance more of a jazz-combo feel. Broadway professionalism is everywhere in evidence, but true spontaneity and joy are in shorter supply; the licks sound rehearsed, the group singing is muddy, the tempi are slower in places. Even the audience, faded in and out by the engineer, is less noisy. On the credit side, the Broadway CD booklet offers lyrics and more photos than the London insert, plus essays by David Hinckley, title-song author Larry Wynn, and Cameron Mackintosh himself.
— MORGAN SILLS

THE FIX
Original London Cast, 1997 (First Night/Relativity) ★★

An American political satire starring a Scotsman and an Australian, *The Fix* was a *succès d'estime* in the Sam Mendes-directed production staged at the Donmar Warehouse in London. That staging earned the show a small cult following and an Olivier Award or two, but there was no commercial transfer and, except for a regional production in the U.S. a few years later, *The Fix* has pretty much disappeared. The plot—an insane mélange of politicians, mobsters, drugs, and murder—is practically indescribable. The large cast is headed by John Barrowman (the Scotsman) as the nihilistic, pot-addled scion of a famous clan and Philip Quast (the Australian) as the young man's gay, crippled, stuttering uncle. They perform the score with aplomb, but there's not much there. Dana Rowe (music) and John Dempsey (book and lyrics) provided a few good songs, among them the bouncy "Two Guys at Harvard," the rock-and-roll anthem "One, Two, Three," and the rollicking "Simple Words." Inexplicably, the show's best song—the opening number, "Let the Games Begin"—was left off the album. At any rate, the plot of this musical ultimately becomes too convoluted to follow, and the score suffers for it.
— SETH CHRISTENFELD

FLAHOOLEY
Original Broadway Cast, 1951 (Capitol/DRG) ★★★★

With a title such as this, could you possibly expect something ordinary? The musical was the brainchild of E. Y. Harburg, who wanted to satirize big business, production, and workers' rights. Harburg cowrote and codirected with Fred Saidy; Sammy Fain provided the music. Because the show dealt with toy dolls (that's what Flahooleys were), Fain opted for fittingly childlike music. He also provided a spirited march in "The Spirit of Capsulanti" and a nifty square dance in "Jump, Little Chillin'." Harburg was still at the top of his wordplay game, pairing "Nicholas" with "ridic-u-lous" and "psychiatry" with "buy a tree." This was the first time that Broadway ever encountered Barbara Cook (she was twenty-three) and the first and last time that it heard Peruvian singing sensation Yma Sumac, with her eight-octave range. If her three selections seem not to be show tunes, that's because they weren't written by Fain but by Sumac's husband and muse, Moises Vivanco—and they are terrific.   —PETER FILICHIA

FLORA, THE RED MENACE
Original Broadway Cast, 1965 (RCA) ★★★

John Kander and Fred Ebb's first show together tells the story of Flora Meszaros (Liza Minnelli), who is thrilled to get a garment-district job during the Depression and even more thrilled to find a boyfriend in Harry Toukarian (Bob Dishy). She isn't thrilled to find that he's a Communist, but she doesn't seem to experience much more than embarrassment over this state of affairs. True, there are three wince-inducing songs here ("Knock, Knock," "Palomino Pal," and "Hello, Waves"). But "A Quiet Thing" and "Sing Happy" are stunners, especially as delivered by Minnelli when she was young and full of potential. Don Walker's orchestrations enhance the songs, and if the swingin' overture sounds more like a medley, it was actually the entr'acte in the theater.

Off-Broadway Cast, 1987 (JAY) ★★

More than two decades after the failure of *Flora,* Kander and Ebb—and new book-writer David Thompson—reworked the show for a revival at the Vineyard Theatre, where it was staged in the manner of a Federal Theatre Production of the 1930s. The recording of the revised version would be the reference for a staging of the show, but if you're only interested in hearing *Flora,* you need not buy this disc, which is quite inferior to the original album. Granted, three of the score's silliest songs have been excised, and it's nice to have an extra snippet of a song before "A Quiet Thing," a verse for "Dear Love," and some good dialogue leading into "Sing Happy." But Veanne Cox and Peter Frechette are limp substitutes for Minnelli and Dishy. While John Kander himself plays the piano, his solo accompaniment can't compare with the original disc's lush, full orchestra. "The Kid Herself" track makes it clear why the song was dropped from the original production. Worst of all, a most annoying thematic melody—which would have been a chore to hear even once—interrupts the action six times!   —PETER FILICHIA

FLORODORA
Original London Cast, 1900-15 (various labels/Opal) ★★

The blurb on the CD cover calls this "the world's first-ever original cast album!" Well, the cast of the 1899 success did enter the Gramophone Company recording studios in 1900 and commit several songs to wax, including the famous sextet "Tell Me, Pretty Maiden." But the tracks here range in sound quality from barely audible to unlistenable; indeed, several sound like messages from extraterrestrials. Nearly all are performed to tinny piano accompaniment. Few of the lyrics by Paul Rubens and Frank Clement can be deciphered, and those that can aren't any great shakes. Still, allowing for the otherworldly quality of the audio, this is a valuable document of the performance styles and stars of the day—stars such as Ada Reeve and Kate Cutler. Leslie Stuart's melodies have a nice lilt. There's a goofy track of Louis Bradfield duetting with himself in "Tell Me, Pretty Maiden," affecting a falsetto for the women's parts. The album is filled out with solo piano recordings from the show and a track from a 1915 revival that sounds more modern. As an archaeological dig, the CD is a noble attempt and occasionally pleasant listening.   —MARC MILLER

FLOWER DRUM SONG
Original Broadway Cast, 1958 (Columbia/Sony) ★★★★

Rodgers and Hammerstein explored East-West relations so often that they deserved their own subcommittee at the United Nations. Although this show doesn't have the substance of *South Pacific* or *The King and I,* it features one of their most enjoyable scores. The book (by Hammerstein and Joseph Fields, based on C. Y. Lee's much grittier novel) presents an affectionate portrait of an assimilating Chinese-American middle class and its attendant generation-gap problems. Miyoshi Umeki shines as Mei Li, the Chinese picture bride who finds a new life in America; her renditions of the poetic "A Hundred Million Miracles" and "I Am Going to Like It Here" are marvels of delicacy. Larry Blyden, in a 1950s version of nontraditional casting, is Sammy Fong, the thoroughly Americanized nightclub owner who doesn't want to marry her; he adds some Broadway zip to "Don't Marry Me." Pat Suzuki livens up the proceedings as nightclub star Linda Low, sashaying through "Grant Avenue" and the politically incorrect "I Enjoy Being a Girl" ("I talk on the telephone for hours / With a pound and a half of cream upon my face!"). As Wang Ta, the faithful Chinese son who chafes at parental strictures, Ed Kenney offers a fresh rendition of "Like a God." Juanita Hall as the fun-loving, Americanized matron Madame Liang delivers "Chop Suey," a witty inventory of American culture circa 1958 ("Hula hoops and nuclear war / Dr. Salk and Zsa Zsa Gabor / Harry Truman, Truman Capote, and Dewey / Chop Suey!"). Arabella Hong, as the lonely seamstress who bears unrequited love for Wang Ta, sings the operatic "Love, Look Away." The show is lively, dated, slightly silly, and a good introduction to Richard Rodgers and Oscar Hammerstein for those who might resist their more ambitious (and sententious) efforts.

Original London Cast, 1960 (HMV/Angel) ★★

With its multiethnic cast, this version is even less authentically Chinese than the Broadway original. Furthermore, as Mei Li and Sammy Fong, Yau Shaun Tung and Tim Herbert aren't as distinctive as their Broadway counterparts. Surprisingly, the recording really comes to life in the nightclub sequences: Such numbers as "Grant Avenue," "Fan Tan Fannie," and "Gliding Through My Memoree" are even bolder than before. This is partly due to the vivacious performance of Yama Saki as Linda Low. With her strong belt and aggressive manner, she makes the second half of the disc more fun than the first. (There's one particularly amusing textual interpolation: On the Broadway album, in "Gliding Through My Memoree," the nightclub singer tells a chorus girl to say something in Irish and she replies, "Elin Go Blah." On the London album, the same request is met with "Blendan Beehan.") While this recording is no substitute for the original, it makes a nice supplement to it.

Film Soundtrack, 1961 (Decca) ★

Ross Hunter's film adaptation of *Flower Drum Song* is a camp classic. You know you've departed from reality in the first scene, when Mei Li and her father emerge from a shipping crate (smuggled in from China) looking perfectly coiffed and made up. It gets sillier from there, with a grotesquely overblown dream ballet attached to "Love, Look Away" (the vocal dubbed by Marilyn Horne) and "Sunday" is equally blown up. The disc disappoints in eliminating "Like a God" and in padding the running time with instrumental tracks. Umeki and Hall, retained from Broadway, are still charming; Jack Soo is fine as Sammy Fong; and B. J. Baker, dubbing Linda Low's songs for Nancy Kwan, provides lively vocals. A CD bonus track features Rosemary Clooney singing "Love, Look Away."

Broadway Cast, 2003 (DRG) ★★★★

In David Henry Hwang's new, politically corrected libretto, Mei Li is an escapee from Communist China who takes refuge in a San Francisco-based Chinese opera theater run by Ta's father. Madame Liang is now an enterprising agent who turns the theater into a nightclub that panders to Western audiences with "exotic" shows. Thankfully, Linda Low is still belting "I Enjoy Being a Girl," and all in all, this disc presents a luxuriously sung version of a delightful score. Lea Salonga's sweetly seductive voice and powerful belt are tailor-made for Mei Li's numbers and José Llana is more than a match for her as Ta, especially in "Like a God." As Madame Liang, Jodi Long leads a zesty version of "Grant Avenue" and partners amusingly with Randall Duk Kim (as Ta's father) in "Don't Marry Me." As Linda, Sandra Allen has plenty of oomph. Don Sebesky's inventive new orchestrations make extensive use of Chinese harmonies; he really goes to town in the nightclub sequences, turning "Fan Tan Fannie" into a production number with an irresistible pop beat. Despite the fact that some of the numbers are over-extended here, this is probably the most accessible recording of the *Flower Drum Song* score for modern ears.   —DAVID BARBOUR

FLOWERS FOR ALGERNON
Original London Cast, 1980 (Original Cast Records) ★

Flowers for Algernon—or, as it was called onstage, *Charlie and Algernon*—is based on the Daniel Keyes novel about a retarded man, a mouse, and an experimental intelligence-increasing procedure that they undergo together. Charles Strouse's score contains one terrific song (the title number, a song-and-dance duet), another that could be described as pretty ("Whatever Time There Is"), and two that might be called interesting ("The Maze" and "Charlie"). But on the whole, it's rather boring and occasionally becomes unpleasant; the lyrics, by David Rogers (who also wrote the libretto), are no better. Michael Crawford plays Charlie and is utterly annoying for the first half of the disc; once the character achieves a level of intelligence, Crawford mercifully lightens up on the squeak factor in his voice. A few of the songs are almost saved by Cheryl Kennedy's singing (her character is both doctor and love interest to Charlie) and/or Philip J. Lang's orchestrations, but only almost, and the album's sound quality is weak. The London staging was no hit and a later Broadway version, with P. J. Benjamin and Sandy Faison replacing Crawford and Kennedy, was even less successful.   —SETH CHRISTENFELD

FLOYD COLLINS
Original Off-Broadway Cast, 1996 (Nonesuch) ★★★★★

In telling this bleak story of a Kentucky man trapped in a cave and the media circus that surrounds him and his family during the ordeal, composer Adam Guettel (the grandson of Richard Rodgers and a poster boy for the new wave of musical theater composers) married bluegrass and classical strains to create an utterly unique musical theater sound that echoes with Appalachian authenticity. Many "old school" enthusiasts will not appreciate the composer's musical audacity, whether it's the theatrical yodeling of "The Call" or the meandering gorgeousness of "Daybreak." But the title folk ballad, the rollicking "Riddle Song," and Floyd's intensely moving spiritual vision "How Glory Goes" may win over even the most hardened of purists. And Guettel's colloquial lyrics are character-perfect. (Additional lyrics were contributed by Tina Landau, the author of the show's book.) This excellent recording preserves the performances of an outstanding cast that includes Christopher Innvar in the title role, the clarion-voiced Jason Danieley as his brother Homer, and the incomparable Theresa

McCarthy as their touched-in-the-head sister. Bruce Coughlin's orchestrations—which make use of acoustic guitar, banjo, and harmonica in concert with more traditional musical theater instrumentation—are exquisite. —BROOKE PIERCE

FLY BLACKBIRD
Original Off-Broadway Cast, 1962 (Mercury/no CD) ★★

The cast album of this virtually forgotten musical by C. Jackson and James Hatch is notable for two of its leading performers: Avon Long, whose lengthy and distinguished career included stage performances and recordings of the role of Sportin' Life in *Porgy and Bess;* and Robert Guillaume, whose Broadway credits—*Kwamina, Purlie,* the 1976 production of *Guys and Dolls*—preceded his fame as the star of TV's *Benson. Fly Blackbird* concerns the struggle for civil rights as seen from the differing points of view of an older black man and members of a younger generation. The Long character counsels patience and forbearance in achieving racial equality while his daughter (Mary Louise), her boyfriend (Guillaume), and the other kids advocate a more aggressive stance; the song titles ("Everything Comes to Those Who Wait," "Now," "Who's the Fool?" and "Wake Up") pretty much tell the story. The show's lyrics by Jackson are often pedestrian but always earnest, and they are set to some attractive if unmemorable Hatch melodies. —MICHAEL PORTANTIERE

FLY WITH ME
Columbia University Cast, 1980 (Original Cast Records/no CD) ★★★

It's like dredging up riches from the Titanic: An unknown Rodgers and Hart score, their Columbia University varsity show from 1920, delivered intact. And the seventeen-year-old Richard Rodgers and twenty-five-year-old Lorenz Hart are already their inimitable selves. Here's Rodgers' famous "wrong note" trick snuck into "Dreaming True," thereby enhancing an already fine waltz. Here's Hart rhyming extravagantly ("ecclesiastics," "bombastics," "icon-oclastics," "plastics," and "gymnastics" in four bars of the opening number), moving the plot along, joking slyly ("Don't love me like Salome / I'd hate to lose my head"), and going senti-mental when the story calls for it. There's also one lyric by Rodgers and one by a young Columbia grad named Hammerstein. The score is so varied—waltzes, foxtrots, a Charleston, a rousing school song—and so frisky, it's a marvel that it took Rodgers and Hart five more years to be noticed. And Bruce Pomahac's orchestrations, while not authentically 1920, are authentically Broadway; that socko overture alone justifies the album. But here's the rub: This LP was taken down from a live performance at Columbia, and it's clearly a varsity show with varsity talent. The undergrads seem like nice kids, but they hardly display trained voices or make the most of the material, although Avi Simon and Marci Pliskin get a nice rapport going in "Don't Love Me Like Othello." The silly book, set in the distant future (1970), peddles eth-nic stereotypes, so you have to put up with Rod McLucas' bad French accent and Peter Cromarty and Annie Laurita pretending to be Chinese (in "Peek in Pekin'). This is all forgiv-able, but what hurts is that many of Hart's lyrics are unintelligible. The small-voiced actors are too far away from the mikes and an appreciative audience sometimes drowns them out. Still, the recording shouldn't be passed up; just settle down with a copy of *The Complete Lyrics of Lorenz Hart,* turn to 1920, and prepare to be dazzled. —MARC MILLER

FOLLIES

Original Broadway Cast, 1971 (Capitol) ★★★★

To many, this is one of the greatest of all shows, possibly the ultimate musical theater piece. Others find it cultishly "interesting," its magnificent Stephen Sondheim score compromised by a difficult book. And some, especially those seeking "pure entertainment," cannot grasp the show's then-and-now, fact-and-fantasy structure or the juxtaposition of clever pastiche songs with those emanating from four unhappy people. In short, *Follies* will always be controversial, but those who love it do so with the fiercest devotion. One aspect of the show's legend that is not open to dispute is that its original cast album is a pale (yet frequently wonderful) reflection of a legendary production. All the great performers are here—Alexis Smith, Dorothy Collins, Gene Nelson, Yvonne De Carlo, Mary McCarty, and the rest—but the decision to edit this lengthy score to fit it on one LP disc was penny-wise and posterity-foolish. On the startling list of total omissions are "Loveland," "Rain on the Roof," and nearly all of the show's dance music. ("One More Kiss," originally left off the LP, was reinstated for the CD.) What is present here is very fine and irreplaceable, including Collins' aching "Losing My Mind" and De Carlo's gutsy "I'm Still Here." But this condensed version of one of the most varied and intelligent scores in Broadway history allows precious little of the flavor of the original Harold Prince-Michael Bennett production to come through.

New York Concert Cast, 1985 (RCA, 2CDs) ★★★★

This concert performance (two, actually) at Lincoln Center featured an all-star cast, and the results were dazzling if not perfect. All of the show's strengths are clear in this nearly complete recording of the *Follies* score, but there are so many opportunities for big moments by stellar performers that it takes some doing to keep everything in balance. In fact, the balance is decidedly off when Elaine Stritch makes "Broadway Baby" a weird, disenchanted cousin to "The Ladies Who Lunch." More in line with the overall concept is a sweet memento from Betty Comden and Adolph Green, who chirp "Rain on the Roof." And a grand memento of operatic glories past is diva Licia Albanese in "One More Kiss" (she's beautifully matched up with the clear-voiced Erie Mills). Phyllis Newman as Stella is no match for Mary McCarty, nor does Carol Burnett, good as she is, offer a more definitive "I'm Still Here" than Yvonne De Carlo's original. But Barbara Cook is up to the Dorothy Collins standard; not surprisingly, "Losing My Mind" is one of the highlights of the disc. Lee Remick is engaging as Phyllis, and George Hearn does well as Ben. As Buddy, Mandy Patinkin offers his strange combination of fine singing and irritating self-indulgence. Everyone else delivers the goods acceptably and the orchestra is no less than the New York Philharmonic, conducted splendidly by Paul Gemignani.

Original London Cast, 1987 (First Night, 2CDs) ★★★★

Sondheim made considerable alterations to the score for this production: The Prelude and "Bolero d'Amour" were dropped; "The Story of Lucy and Jessie" was replaced by an "intellectual striptease" called "Ah, but Underneath"; "The Road You Didn't Take" was dropped in favor of the intricate Ben/Phyllis duet "Country House"; there was an entirely different "Loveland"; and Ben's "Live, Laugh, Love" became his exhortation to "Make the Most of Your Music." In the leading roles, Diana Rigg is a predictably strong Phyllis, Julia McKenzie is a moving Sally, David Healy does fine as Buddy, and Daniel Massey is very solid as Ben. The smaller roles are cast, at least in part, with the resonance necessary to any production of *Follies*. Dolores Gray sings "I'm Still Here" with much of her plush vocal tone intact, and operetta veteran Adele Leigh quavers her way poignantly through "One More Kiss." Some of the others struggle too hard to sound American, and the show as a whole seems a little reserved and earthbound. British reticence? Perhaps. But perhaps an ideal *Follies* resides only in the minds of those who adore the show.

Paper Mill Playhouse Cast, 1998 (TVT, 2CDs) ★★★★

As production costs skyrocketed in the 1990s, a full-scale revival of *Follies* seemed an ever-decreasing possibility. But the Paper Mill Playhouse—that adventurous, forty-five-minutes-from-Broadway company—mounted a well-received revival in 1998. Some of the show's scenic and sartorial values might have been stinted, but the casting was rich, imaginative, and crammed with Broadway/Hollywood talent: Kaye Ballard, Eddie Bracken, Laurence Guittard, Dee Hoty, Donna McKechnie, Ann Miller, Lilane Montevecchi, Phyllis Newman, Tony Roberts, and Donald Saddler. Some aspects of this revival were certainly arresting. Who, after all, was more qualified to sing "I'm Still Here" than Ann Miller, well into her seventies and still going strong? Who was a more apt "Broadway Baby" than Kaye Ballard? Who could be a more winsome Sally than *Chorus Line* sweetheart Donna McKechnie? If not all of this two-disc set lives up to those highlights, it is good enough to prove an ongoing truth: Every recording of *Follies* is fascinating and absolutely necessary in its own way. One caveat about this one: It's labeled "The Complete Recording" and an appendix section does offer a wonderful array of songs written for but not included in the original production, but since most of the numbers created for the London version are not here, it's not truly complete. Still, why carp? The cast ranges from competent to magnificent, the atmosphere is theatrically solid, and the resonant acoustic is gracious to some of the older singers. —RICHARD BARRIOS

FOOTLOOSE

Film Soundtrack, 1984 (Columbia/Legacy) ★★★

Directed by Herbert Ross from a screenplay by Dean Pitchford, *Footloose* is about some small-town teenagers who attack a municipal ordinance and do battle with a fundamentalist pastor in an effort to have dancing allowed at their high-school prom. (The plot was inspired by a controversy in Elmore City, Oklahoma, where the 1980 repeal of an anti-dancing law led to the town's first sock hop in over a hundred years.) It has a superb cast: Kevin Bacon as a big-city kid transplanted to a no-dancing hamlet; Lori Singer as his love interest; John Lithgow as the pinheaded preacher; and Dianne Wiest, Sarah Jessica Parker, and Chris Penn in supporting roles. Pitchford, an accomplished rock lyricist, enlisted Kenny Loggins and several others to collaborate on and perform songs for the movie's soundtrack. Those songs include Loggins' rendition of the title number and "I'm Free (Heaven Helps the Man)"; Mike Reno and Ann Wilson doing Eric Carmen's "Almost Paradise"; Deneice Williams singing Tom Snow's "Let's Hear It for the Boy"; Karla Bonoff's rendition of "Somebody's Eyes"; Shalamar's "Dancing in the Sheets"; Sammy Hagar's "The Girl Gets Around"; Moving Pictures' "Never"; and Bonnie Tyler's delicious "Holding Out for a Hero." The "remastered and enhanced" CD offers four bonus tracks: John Mellencamp's "Hurts So Good," Foreigner's "Waiting for a Girl Like You," Quiet Riot's "Bang Your Head," and a remix of Shalamar's "Dancing in the Sheets."

Original Broadway Cast, 1998 (Q Records) ★

When *Footloose* was adapted as a stage musical, it turned out that the movie's vintage rock songs, wonderful as they may be, were too closely identified with the performers on the soundtrack to seem anything but odd in the hands of show-music veterans like Dee Hoty and Broadway babies like Jeremy Kushnier and Jennifer Laura Thompson. Even if their idiom weren't foreign to this context, the songs from the film—as compared with the ones that Pitchford and Tom Snow wrote expressly for the stage version—are shoehorned, rather than integrated, into the action. On this original cast CD, the really good songs—that is, the ones from the movie—aren't given their due and the additional numbers don't live up to what's on the film soundtrack.

—CHARLES WRIGHT

FORBIDDEN BROADWAY
Original Off-Off-Broadway Cast, 1982 (DRG) ★★★

For more than two decades, Gerard Alessandrini's Off- and Off-Off-Broadway revues lampooning Broadway hits and personalities have been a reliable source of merriment. "Wicked" is the adjective most often applied to these knowing parodies of show tunes and celebrities, but there's usually affection at their base; more than that, Alessandrini's a considerable lyricist in his own right, particularly adept at turning a well-known lyric or show title on its head with a subtle tweak—e.g., "I Wonder What the King Is Drinking Tonight," "Into the Words," "Rant." And his revues spotlight some of New York's brightest young talents, theater pros with great gifts for mimicry. Of course, there's no way to duplicate the visual components that send audiences into uncontrollable laughter—among them, hilarious costumes (often by the legendary Alvin Colt) and tiny sets spoofing enormous ones. Since these are essentially comedy albums and too many listenings can diminish the jokes, the discs may linger on your CD shelf for long intervals, but they're fun to revisit as a reminder of the ridiculous foibles of a given season. This first *Forbidden Broadway* album is one of the best though by far the shortest at forty minutes. Alessandrini writes one entirely original title song for most editions of the show and there's a particularly apt one here: "There's a Great White Way / Where the white is gray / And the great is only okay . . ." He's also in the cast, doing a killer Topol in "Ambition." The invaluable Nora Mae Lyng is a brassy Ann Miller and a brassier Merman, future indie-film star Chloe Webb a pert Andrea McArdle, Bill Carmichael a funny emcee announcing, "Hats off, here they come, those . . . bankable stars." As always, the one-piano accompaniment (here by musical director Fred Barton) manages to sound like a whole orchestra. Subsequent *Forbidden Broadway* albums are more complete and more nastily funny, but this one has a hottest-new-show-in-town oomph. It also has that great *Merrily We Roll Along* parody poster art on its cover.

Compilation Album, 1991 (DRG) ★★★

For the best stuff in this compilation of *Forbidden Broadway* material from 1985 to 1991, check out Toni DiBuono capturing Patti LuPone to the last self-indulgent nuance ("I Get a Kick Out of Me"); an ingenious *My Fair Lady* parody ("I Strain in Vain to Train Madonna's Brain") inspired by Madonna's Broadway stint (in *Speed the Plow*); and Kevin Ligon as an amazing Mandy Patinkin ("Somewhat Overindulgent"). There are also winning performances by Michael McGrath and Karen Murphy. Not all of the tracks are for everybody; you have to have seen the original *M. Butterfly,* for instance, to appreciate the satiric puzzlement over its success. A backhanded salute to *The Phantom of the Opera* is a bit compromised because Lloyd Webber wouldn't allow his music to be used without alteration, but the righteous indignation expressed over a relatively fallow era in Broadway musical history makes for a winning hour-plus.

Off-Off-Broadway Cast, 1993 (DRG) ★★

This third edition's opening number is weak: a CD-only appearance by Carol Channing and a stageful of imitators. But some first-class stuff follows: devastating slaps at Petula Clark and David Cassidy in *Blood Brothers,* Suzanne Blakeslee's astonishing evocation of Julie Andrews, and Craig Wells' hilarious put-down of Michael Crawford. On the whole, however, that season's shows weren't as ripe for parody as those of other seasons: Dustin Hoffman as Shylock filtered through *Rain Man* doesn't hold up, and Topol's stodginess in *Fiddler* was old news even in '93; so was Robert Goulet's Vegas slickness. But the incidental pleasures keep coming: quick riffs on the scenery chewing of Nathan Lane and Faith Prince in *Guys and Dolls,* a knockdown punch at Liliane Montevecchi, an efficient torching of *Miss Saigon,* and so on.

Forbidden Broadway Strikes Back! Off-Broadway Cast, 1996 (DRG) ★★★★

A luxurious seventy-three minutes of what might be Alessandrini's most consistent bouquet of parodies, this edition benefits from top-flight talent. The opening number ("Parody Tonight") serves up Tom Plotkin's expert Nathan Lane, Christine Pedi's gurgling Liza, Donna English's sneering Zoe Caldwell, and Bryan Batt's vapid John Davidson in *State Fair,* beaming through "Oh, What a Beautiful Moron!" It's an auspicious start, and the CD seldom flags from there. There are digs at Harold Prince's enormous *Show Boat,* the failed promise of *Big,* and casting prospects for the upcoming *Kiss Me, Kate* revival (Pedi's Bernadette Peters and Batt's Mandy Patinkin duet in "So Miscast"). English does the best Julie Andrews you've ever heard in an extended pummeling of *Victor/Victoria* (with the Tony nominating committee warbling, "Victor/Victoria, we will ignore-ee-ya"), and a brilliant parody of *Rent* encapsulates all of its dissenters' frustrations. Even the arrangements are funny: Listen to the Sondheimisms in the *King and I* send-up. The album is a hoot and there's a terrific bonus track: English as Julie again, in a parody of *Star!* that's hilarious.

Forbidden Broadway 2001: A Spoof Odyssey. Off-Broadway Cast, 2000 (DRG) ★★★

This edition averages out slightly below the series' general level of inspiration. The first few tracks evaporate; the CD doesn't score a direct hit until the disembowelment of *The Music Man* (featuring a very funny Danny Gurwin). Other choice bits: a number that deals with Disney's downsizing of *Beauty and the Beast;* Christine Pedi's slaughtering of Liza Minnelli (plus her uncanny Patti LuPone and Gwen Verdon turns); and an extended riff on *Aida* that will tickle even those unfamiliar with the show. Alessandrini's take on Cheryl Ladd in *Annie Get Your Gun* ("I've No Business in Show Business") epitomizes his art, and Tony Nation's spoof of James Carpinello in *Saturday Night Fever* ("Stayin' Away") is a deft shot at an easy target, but the digs at Sondheim and Streisand don't land as smoothly as usual. Finally, the disc sends customers out on a high note with "76 Hit Shows"—but there wasn't much to celebrate on Broadway in 2000, so it seems disingenuous to pretend there was.

20th Anniversay Edition, 2000 (DRG) ★★★★

If you're not a *Forbidden Broadway* completist but want to know what all the fuss is about, this compilation, featuring eight previously unreleased tracks, is just the thing. Both the strengths and slight weaknesses of the format come through ringingly, and the prodigiously talented cast offers more variety than a single-edition album would. Not all the spoofs are top-drawer; that Carol Channing parody really should be retired. What a pleasure, though, to reencounter Christine Pedi's flawless invocations of Liza and Stritch, Toni DiBuono's uncanny Patti LuPone, and Alessandrini's particular distaste for Broadway Disneyfication. Among the bonus tracks are some of his very best vignettes, such as Terri White's glorious "Screamgirls" and the total demolition of *Aspects of Love* ("Love Changes Everything" becomes "I Sleep With Everyone"). Note how the various musical directors/accompanists throughout the history of *Forbidden Broadway* express entire orchestrations with one keyboard. Note also how they exaggerate cast-album affectations—languorous tempi for *Les Miz,* the heavy bass tread of a Rodgers 4/4 tempo—to great effect.

— MARC MILLER

FORBIDDEN HOLLYWOOD
Los Angeles Cast, 1995 (DRG) ★★★

Here, Gerard Alessandrini has as much fun with Hollywood excess as with Broadway idiocy. But this recording differs from the *Forbidden Broadway* albums in one crucial respect: It's live, and that's a mistake. The audience keeps howling at sight gags listeners can't fathom (like Dietrich's arm falling off in "Falling Apart Again"). The satirical targets are a little strange, too: some numbers aim at then-up-to-the-minute movies (*Braveheart, Pulp Fiction, Forrest Gump*), but nearly half the material clobbers decades-past Broadway musicals that were ruined on film (the color filters in *South Pacific,* Streisand's miscasting in *Hello, Dolly!*). That said, much of it is a riot, and Jason Graae's impression of Brando singing is as hilarious the twentieth time as the first. Gerry McIntyre is a flawless Louis Armstrong, a funny Whoopi Goldberg, a catatonic Keanu Reeves, and more. Christine Pedi, an unparalleled Liza in several *Forbidden Broadways,* gets unusually rich material here ("Mein Film Career"). And Suzanne Blakeslee, as Marni Nixon dubbing Audrey Hepburn, does justice to one of the funniest pieces of material Alessandrini has ever written.

— MARC MILLER

FOREVER PLAID
Original Off-Broadway Cast, 1990 (RCA) ★★★★

In its New York incarnation, Steve Ross' "Heavenly Musical Hit" *Forever Plaid* was—if you'll pardon the expression—a divine tribute to close harmony of the Brill Building-era. The book is about a "guy group," the Plaids, whose four members perished in a car crash on their way to pick up custom-tailored plaid tuxes for a gig that should have been their first big break. The date was February 9, 1964, and the Plaids were slammed broadside by a school bus filled with Catholic teens bound for Manhattan to join the studio audience for the Beatles' debut on the Ed Sullivan Show. Now, "through the Power of Harmony and the Expanding Holes in the Ozone Layer in conjunction with the positions of the Planets and all that Astro-Technical stuff," the deceased Plaids have returned to perform the big show they never got to do. *Forever Plaid* ran on the Upper West Side for years. Under the direction of writer Ross (who also choreographed), the show's original cast—Stan Chandler (tenor), David Engel (bass), Jason Graae (baritone), and Guy Stroman (tenor)—was wonderful. The recording was produced by the show's musical director, James Raitt, with Bill Rosenfeld supervising for the label; it captures the performers' unimpeachable intonation and their verve and comedic flair. The show is a rare combination of wit, hokiness, double entendre, and assured musical taste—and, in the hands of the original ensemble, it was even touching. The medleys combining "Gotta Be This or That" with "Undecided" (featuring Graae) and "Shangri-La" with "Rags to Riches" (featuring Engel) are standouts, but there's not a dud track on the disc, which also includes what is surely the most clever, delicious rendition of the Hoagy Carmichael-Frank Loesser chestnut "Heart and Soul" (here featuring Stroman) ever heard. During the 1990s, *Forever Plaid* became a fixture in several major cities and toured the hinterlands, providing employment to an army of young Equity actors. Too bad it's no longer playing on West 72nd Street, but at least we'll always have the CD.　　　　　　　　　　　　　　　　　　　　　　—CHARLES WRIGHT

42ND STREET
Original Broadway Cast, 1980 (RCA) ★

This wasn't the first Hollywood musical to be adapted to the stage, but its success established a trend that has reached well into the twenty-first century; whether or not this transfer process is a good thing will always be a cause for argument. The Broadway incarnation of *42nd Street* was the final work of Gower Champion, whose death was announced in a shocking and show-manlike gesture by producer David Merrick immediately after the opening-night bows. Champion had transformed the movie into an enjoyable theatrical pageant with nonstop glitter, an occasional nod to Busby Berkeley, and very little of the film's drive and desperation. Fueled by all that audience-grabbing spectacle and song, the production ran for years, but its manufactured nature is pretty obvious on the cast recording. The Harry Warren-Al Dubin score has been padded out with songs from other films and the wonderful period sound of the original Warner Bros. orchestrations has been replaced with the expert playing of a punched-up pit band. Fortunately, there are some seasoned pros in the cast—Jerry Orbach, Tammy Grimes, Lee Roy Reams, and Carole Cook—to provide true musical theater resonance. In the role of Peggy Sawyer, the chorine who's told "you've got to come back a star," Wanda Richert is sweet and sings better than Ruby Keeler. (Of course, it can also be said that coyotes sing better than Ruby Keeler.) There are things to enjoy in this recording, even though we might wish that the gifted Champion had expended his final energy upon something more substantial.

Broadway Cast, 2001 (Atlantic) ★

Two decades after the original show was a smash, the revival did it all over again. Done in "tribute" to the original Champion staging (i.e., they stole the best parts), this *42nd Street* was even more spiffed-up and brassy. There's an intense air of overkill here, those relentless tapping feet even more threatening than in Busby Berkeley's original "Lullaby of Broadway" number. "Shuffle Off to Buffalo," in particular, is a vulgar nightmare, but several other cuts are also objectionable. Fortunately, a genuine star performance emerges from the excess: Christine Ebersole, who won a Tony for her work as the fading diva Dorothy Brock. Amid a herd of screechers and belters, Ebersole is the classy, real thing. For her trouble, she is rewarded (and rewards the listener) with an added song, "I Only Have Eyes for You." Onstage, Michael Cumpsty seemed miscast in the Warner Baxter/Jerry Orbach role, and he sounds equally uncomfortable on the recording. As for Kate Levering, she serves up chilly efficiency in place of Ruby Keeler's clunky charm. If you want twenty-first-century Broadway brass, it's here in spades; if you're looking for something more, play the Ebersole tracks and then go out and rent the movie.　　　　　　　　　　　　　　　　　　　—RICHARD BARRIOS

FOSSE
Original Broadway Cast, 1999 (RCA) ★★★

Bob Fosse captured the revolutionary sexual politics of the 1960s and 1970s in a voluptuous mix of dance forms based on jazz, tap, and ballet. The show that bears his name traces (though not in chronological sequence) his choreographic career from *The Pajama Game* (1954) to *Big Deal* (1986). *Fosse* was conceived by codirectors Richard Maltby, Jr. and Ann Reinking, along with Chet Walker, who's credited as having "recreated" the master's choreography for the occasion. When it arrived on Broadway from Toronto after tryouts in Boston and Los Angeles, the show proved to be an eye-popping amalgam of ultra-fit Broadway dancers like Jane Lanier and Scott Wise, slick design elements by Santo Loquasto and Andrew Bridge, and amazing choreography overseen by Reinking, Walker, and "artistic advisor" Gwen Verdon. The show's score is a compilation of numbers from theatrical and nontheatrical projects to which Fosse was attached, including a 1968 Bob Hope television special and the unsuccessful 1974 movie musical of Antoine de Saint-Exupéry's *The Little Prince*, yet the cast recording is highly enjoyable. The numbers, written by various composers and lyricists, create a clear sense of what the opening ensemble terms "Fosse's World." And the show's melodies, rhythms, and lyrics, lovingly brought to compact disc by record producer Jay David Saks and legendary A&R man Bill Rosenfield, stand admirably on their own as an aural counterpart to Fosse's dance vocabulary. The vocal performances and a twenty-person pit band, under the baton of musical director Patrick S. Brady, display the level of professionalism that distinguishes Broadway at its best from musical theater anywhere else in the world. The disc is capped with a thrilling arrangement (over thirteen minutes' worth) of Louis Prima's "Sing! Sing! Sing!"—seemingly all brass and percussion—that would still leave the listener wanting more at four times its length.   —CHARLES WRIGHT

FOXY

Off-Broadway Cast, 2002 (Original Cast Records) ★★

Here was a wonderful idea for a musical: Bert Lahr in an adaptation of *Volpone,* with the action of that Ben Jonson classic moved to gold-rush Alaska. But the project was seemingly cursed from its inception. The creators of *Foxy* included the great lyricist Johnny Mercer; the wrong director, Robert Lewis; a constantly changing line-up of ineffective producers; and an inexperienced pair of bookwriters, Ring Lardner, Jr. and Ian McLellan Hunter, who refused to listen to Bert Lahr or pay attention to Jerome Robbins when he came in to help. The 1964 result was a ramshackle construction in which about half the score consisted of undramatic, shockingly trite numbers. But even when the ideas for the songs were poor, Mercer had great fun playing with words; and when the ideas were good—as in "Respectability," "Many Ways to Skin a Cat," "Money Isn't Everything," and "Bon Vivant"—he and composer Robert Emmett Dolan hit them out of the park. ("Bon Vivant" is a highlight as the chorus serenades a fake English Lord with "Yoicks and zounds / And Elizabethan sounds / What a bon vivant is he!") Unfortunately, this recording of the Musicals Tonight! staged concert presentation of the show falls short. John Flynn is much too sweet as the scheming Doc; Rudy Roberson, given the impossible task of following Bert Lahr, seems to have no comic chops at all; and the single-piano accompaniment is dull. (Note: Bruce Yeko's private label S.P.M. released a live LP of the Broadway cast, but it has sound problems. Box Office Records issued both *Bert Lahr on Stage, Screen and Radio,* which includes two very good, live *Foxy* tracks, and *Johnny Mercer Sings,* featuring a delightful ten-song demo of the score.)   —DAVID WOLF

THE FROGS/EVENING PRIMROSE

Studio Cast, 2001 (Nonesuch) ★★★★★

Based on a play by Aristophanes, *The Frogs* was written by Stephen Sondheim and Burt Shevelove to be performed by the Yale Repertory Theatre in the university's swimming pool. It had a one-week run with an ensemble that included three Yale School of Drama students who would be heard from again: Meryl Streep, Sigourney Weaver, and Christopher Durang. The show harkens back to the Sondheim-Shevelove-Larry Gelbart musical *A Funny Thing Happened on the Way to the Forum* in that both were freely based on ancient comic classics. This excellent recording of the brief score of *The Frogs* benefits from the luxury casting of Nathan Lane as the god Dionysos ("an aging juvenile of great charm") and Brian Stokes Mitchell as his slave, Xanthias. The comic chemistry between these two is terrific, never more so than in the droll "Prologos: Invocation and Instructions to the Audience": "Please don't cough / It tends to throw the actors off," Dionysos begs of the assembled theatergoers, going on to make further requests: "Please refrain / From candy wrapped in cellophane," and "Please, don't fart—there's very little air and this is art." In the equally funny title song, the chorus alternates between froggy noises and side-splitting self-assessment ("Frogs! / We're the frogs / The adorable frogs! / Not your hoity-toity intellectuals / Not your hippy-dippy homosexuals"). The only unconvincing moment of this world-premiere recording of the show comes when Shakespeare shows up in the person of Davis Gaines to sing the beautiful ballad "Fear No More" (with a text by the Bard himself, from *Cymbeline*). Gaines has displayed a powerful baritone in myriad musical theater roles over many years, but he sounds tired and affected here. (Note: As this book was being edited, *The Frogs* was playing at Lincoln Center in a production with new Sondheim songs and a revised book by its star, Nathan Lane.) The second part of this disc is devoted to songs from *Evening Primrose,* an hour-long musical that aired on ABC-TV in 1966. The teleplay by James Goldman is about a struggling poet who remains in a Manhattan department store after closing time and there discovers—in the words of Frank Rich, who wrote notes for the Nonesuch recording—"a mysterious nocturnal society of eccentric shutins as well as the muse he's been searching for, a sort of modern Rapunzel named Ella." (In the telecast, Charles was played by Anthony Perkins.) Since it was never a stage musical and is unlikely ever to be one, *Evening Primrose* doesn't warrant a lengthy review here, but it must be said that the four-song score contains two of the best ballads Sondheim ever wrote: Ella's touching reminiscence "I Remember" and the gorgeous duet "Take Me to the World." For this recording, Charles and Ella are sung persuasively by Neil Patrick Harris and Theresa McCarthy. Both the *Evening Primrose* and *Frogs* tracks feature the American Theatre Orchestra, brilliantly conducted by Sondheim specialist Paul Gemignani. The CD boasts Nonesuch's typically stunning recorded sound—powerful but not harsh, ambient but not overly reverberant, with enormous dynamic range. —MICHAEL PORTANTIERE

THE FULL MONTY
Original Broadway Cast, 2000 (BMG) ★★★★

A great pleasure of experiencing this show live was seeing how well Terrence McNally's script melded with show-tune novice David Yazbek's music and lyrics. Based on a hit English film, *The Full Monty* concerns a group of unemployed guys who resort to stripping to earn some dough. The property really needed a contemporary voice to make it believable as a musical— and, in Yazbek, that's what it got. The pop-tinged songs sound effortless, the lyrics as natural as dialogue coming from the mouths of these working-class men and their wives. Contemporary though the music sounds, Yazbek writes marvelously well along traditional musical theater lines, from the comically confessional "Scrap" (that's what these laid-off steel workers feel like) to "Jeanette's Showbiz Number," sung with world-weary pizzazz by the late Kathleen Freeman. Irreverence abounds in André DeShields's "Big Black Man" and in the show's shining gem, "Big Ass Rock," in which antihero Jerry (Patrick Wilson) and best-buddy Dave (John Ellison Conlee) use darkly humorous reverse psychology to talk a fellow worker and soon-to-be fellow stripper out of committing suicide. The show also has its poignant moments in "You Walk With Me" and "Breeze Off the River." While the songs don't pack the same punch here as they do onstage, this is still a great score to enjoy on disc.   —BROOKE PIERCE

FUNNY FACE
New York and London Casts, 1927 and 1928 (Columbia, etc.) ★★★

Purists who require the Gershwins' *Funny Face* untainted by songs written by others have no choice but to brave these primitive recordings made by cast members of the original New York and London productions of 1927-28. Not yet gathered on a single CD, individual tracks among these may be hunted down by rabid show-tune lovers on various compilations. The performances are pure gold from an archival standpoint: They offer the rare chance to hear Fred Astaire singing while he was still in his twenties, and there are also two priceless duets with his sister, Adele: "Funny Face" and "The Babbitt and the Bromide." Two Arden-Ohman piano medleys serve as a prologue and entr'acte, and we have George Gershwin himself playing "My One and Only," which Fred croons and taps on a separate track. Adele and Bernard Clifton get the love songs "He Loves and She Loves" and "'S Wonderful." Comedy is here too, as Leslie Henson performs "Tell the Doc." If one can get past the imperfect sound and travel back to another era of performance style, there's much pleasure to be found in this collection.

Film Soundtrack, 1956 (Verve) ★★★★★

One of the most fashionable films ever made is the classic *Funny Face* starring Fred Astaire, Audrey Hepburn, and Kay Thompson. Highlights from the score of the Gershwin brothers' Broadway musical of the 1920s, in which Astaire had starred three decades earlier, are inserted into a new plot and augmented with a trio of up-tempo numbers by composer-producer Roger Edens and lyricist-screenwriter Leonard Gershe. We know that this is a terrific recording as soon as Astaire's unmistakable voice launches into the title tune on the first track. Not much later, Thompson socks out the Edens-Gershe showstopper "Think Pink." Hepburn offers a deeply felt, subtle reading of "How Long Has This Been Going On?" Astaire's ballad "He Loves and She Loves" is given an equally uncluttered and sincere rendition. The disc also boasts some delightful duets: Thompson and Astaire's "Clap Yo' Hands" and Thompson and Hepburn's "On How to Be Lovely." Especially apparent without the film's visuals to distract the eye is the brilliance of the writing/arranging in the star trio's extended musical sequence "Bonjour Paris." The songs have been fitted with perfect orchestrations by Alexander Courage, Conrad Salinger, Van Cleave, and Skip Martin, and the entire performance is crisply conducted by Adolph Deutsch. In the words of Ira Gershwin as heard in the recording's final track, " 'S Wonderful! 'S Marvelous!"   —MORGAN SILLS

FUNNY GIRL
Original Broadway Cast, 1964 (Capitol/Angel) ★★★★★

"Essential" is a good word to describe the original recording of *Funny Girl,* with its wonderful suite of Jule Styne-Bob Merrill tunes and its terrific performances. Then-rising star Barbra Streisand, in the role of theatrical legend Fanny Brice, has never been fresher or more appealing than she is here in "I'm the Greatest Star," "Cornet Man," "Don't Rain on My Parade," "The Music That Makes Me Dance," "Who Are You Now?" and her definitive rendition of "People." The supporting cast is ideal: Sydney Chaplin, though no great shakes as a singer, is perfectly cast as Nick Arnstein, while Kay Medford as Fanny's mother and Danny Meehan as friend Eddie Ryan bring some nice vaudevillian touches to "Who Taught Her Everything?" and "Find Yourself a Man." (Jean Stapleton makes brief but enjoyable appearances in the latter song and the opener, "If a Girl Isn't Pretty.") Ralph Burns' orchestrations are superb, as usual, and it's difficult to imagine the orchestra sounding better than it does under Milton Rosenstock's direction.

Film Soundtrack, 1968 (Columbia/Sony) ★★

Barbra Streisand is almost unbearably *on* here, lacking the innocent exuberance that makes her performance on the Broadway recording of *Funny Girl* so special. Strictly in terms of vocal quality, she probably sounds better on the soundtrack, but who can penetrate the mile-thick shell of artifice to really find out? This show is no longer about the songs, it's about the singer. The film removed "Cornet Man" and "The Music That Makes Me Dance" by Styne and Merrill in favor of actual Fanny Brice songs such as "I'd Rather Be Blue Over You" and "My Man." There are other unfortunate changes to the score, with boredom-inducing rewrites of the Ziegfeldian "His Love Makes Me Beautiful" and a stupid number titled "The Swan" to replace the rousing show-stopper "Rat-Tat-Tat-Tat." A superfluous new title song is here, and even though it won an Oscar, there's no heart in it. If you'd like to hear cast members other than Streisand sing on this disc, you can pretty much forget it. There are brief flashes of Kay Medford, a few moments of Omar Sharif's Nicky, and the odd chorus member occasionally gets a word in edgewise but, otherwise, it's all Barbra all the time. Her fans probably won't mind—but I find the heartfelt emotions that she summons on the original Broadway album eminently preferable to the affected, manufactured performance she gives here. —MATTHEW MURRAY

A FUNNY THING HAPPENED ON THE WAY TO THE FORUM

Original Broadway Cast, 1962 (Capitol/Angel) ★★★★

Except for the "House of Marcus Lycus" sequence and the courtesans' dances, every important piece of music in this playful, skillful Stephen Sondheim score is included here, along with just enough dialogue to allow the listener to appreciate the songs in context. The album captures the indelible performances of the great clowns Zero Mostel, Jack Gilford, David Burns, and their co-low vaudevillians. Brian Davies and Preshy Marker imbue the romantic couple Hero and Philia with sweetness, although the recording misses the daffy humor that they brought to these roles onstage. As the stentorian Domina, Ruth Kobart finally explodes in "That Dirty Old Man" and makes it clear why she received a Tony Award nomination for her performance. The album is dominated by Mostel in "Comedy Tonight," "Free," and other gems, but almost all of the principals have their shining moments, especially Ron Holgate as a hilarious Miles Gloriosus in "Bring Me My Bride." The visual gags that convulsed audiences cannot be found here, of course, but this delightful recording will give your imagination a prod. Listening to "Everybody Ought to Have a Maid," you can almost picture Messrs. Mostel, Gilford, Burns, and David Carradine ambling across the stage of the Alvin Theater.

Original London Cast, 1963 (HMV/Angel) ★★

Typical of many London cast recordings, this one includes more dialogue than the Broadway album. Frankie Howerd stars as Pseudolus, leading a . . . *Forum* cast made up of Britain's comic hierarchy under the direction of the great George Abbott; the original orchestrations by Sid Ramin and Irwin Kostal are conducted by Alyn Ainsworth, and the sound quality here is excellent throughout. "Comedy Tonight" is almost complete (only the introduction of the Proteans is missing) and there are full dialogue lead-ins to "Free," "Lovely," "Pretty Little Picture," "Bring Me My Bride," "That'll Show Him," the "Lovely" reprise, and "The Funeral Sequence." But how do the London cast members stack up against their Broadway counterparts? Well, these actors seem reserved in their approach to the high art of low comedy. Also, Howerd often misses the mark as a singer. The others are reasonably musical, but they lack comic impact. As Philia, Isla Blair has a thin voice that is tremulous and colorless in "That'll Show Him." Hero is played by John Rye with a mature baritone voice that sounds much more suited to Miles Gloriosus; that part is sung by Leon Greene with comic credibility, but without the stentorian tones required. Linda Gray's adequate "That Dirty Old Man" is totally outclassed by Ruth Kobart's rendition on the Broadway album. While this disc wins points for completeness, it loses points for its several lackluster performances.

Film Soundtrack, 1966 (United Artists) Not recommended.

The film version of *A Funny Thing Happened on the Way to the Forum* was directed by Richard Lester in the style of a Marx Brothers movie, making the music virtually superfluous. This very funny film deleted any song that did not have overt comedic value. Those that remain are "Comedy Tonight," "Lovely" (both versions), "Everybody Ought to Have A Maid," "Bring Me My Bride," and "The Funeral Sequence" (listed here as "The Dirge"). The rest of the recording consists of music by Ken Thorne, who only utilizes Sondheim's themes in two selections. Zero Mostel (Pseudolus) and Jack Gilford (Hysterium) recreated their Broadway roles and Leon Greene (Miles) his London role; they make solid contributions. It's also of interest to hear a young Michael Crawford as Hero singing "Lovely." Still, this disc is only for collectors who feel they need to have every single Sondheim recording.

Broadway Cast, 1996 (Angel) ★★★

If you weren't happy with the original Broadway cast album of *Forum,* this zing-y revival CD may be for you. There are new orchestrations by Jonathan Tunick, plus quite a few new lyrics by Sondheim and other musical changes that were integral to the production. The entire "House of Marcus Lycus" sequence (not on the original cast album) is included and, while much of the dance music for the courtesans is new, the song itself has been preserved, performed by the always funny Ernie Sabella with musical assists from the ladies and connecting dialogue by Pseudolus (Nathan Lane) and Hero (Jim Stanek). Lane was the *raison d'être* for this production; it was inevitable that he and the role of Pseudolus would eventually meet. The actor does not disappoint, making good on the character's promise to "employ every device we know in our desire to divert you." He even recorded the tongue-twisting "Pretty Little Picture," which was cut from the stage production. Conductor Edward Strauss keeps everything surging forward, allowing us just enough time to savor the details of words and music before hurtling ahead. The supporting cast is variable: Stanek and Jessica Boevers as Philia are on the dull side (the humor of their characters is hard to capture on a recording), but their singing is lovely. Although the shoes of Jack Gilford and David Burns are hard to fill, Mark Linn-Baker (Hysterium) and Lewis J. Stadlen (Senex) do their best. Cris Groenendaal isn't as funny as Ron Holgate's original portrayal of Miles Gloriosus, but Mary Testa puts her own stamp on the role of Domina and delivers a smashing "That Dirty Old Man." This is a highly enjoyable, energetic recording of a classic musical farce. —JEFFREY DUNN

THE GAY LIFE
Original Broadway Cast, 1961 (Capitol/Angel) ★★★

After the film *Gigi,* nobody was interested in another tale of a virgin and a rake in belle-époque Europe, but Fay and Michael Kanin went ahead and adapted Arthur Schnitzler's *The Affairs of Anatol* anyway. Even with Barbara Cook singing a score by Howard Dietz and Arthur Schwartz, *The Gay Life* ran only 113 performances, yet this is one of those flops that shines on disc. Cook is Liesl, a respectable girl who was raised to make a good marriage but who prefers the rakish Anatol (Walter Chiari). As Liesl's brother, Max, Jules Munshin offers wry commentary on mating rituals in "Bring Your Darling Daughter" ("Who knows how many bows she will have upon her string? / She may annex a sexy sauerbraten king!"). Chiari, with his mush-mouthed diction, can be hard to take; but Cook is at her peak, delivering such thoughtful ballads as "Magic Moment" and "Something You Never Had Before." She's a spitfire in "I Wouldn't Marry You" and "The Label on the Bottle." Thanks to her superb work and the first-class songs, Liesl is no standard-issue ingenue; she's a fascinating young woman. The sumptuous, worldly score wittily analyzes the characters' hypocrisies even as it brims with emotion. Don Walker's orchestrations add an extra level of plush enjoyment. This is a rarity worth seeking out.

— DAVID BARBOUR

GENTLEMEN PREFER BLONDES
Original Broadway Cast, 1949
(Columbia/Sony) ★★★★★

This is a buoyant performance of a top-notch score by Jule Styne (music) and Leo Robin (lyrics), based on the popular 1920s novel and play of the same name by Anita Loos. Don Walker's orchestrations and Milton Rosenstock's musical direction are exciting, a great mixture of Roaring '20s jazz and Broadway pizzazz. Crowning it all is the legendary performance of Carol Channing as Lorelei Lee, the ultimate blonde gold digger. Her satiric portrayal is as funny and delightful today as it was when the show premiered in 1949; her hysterically funny renditions of "A Little Girl From Little Rock" and "Diamonds Are a Girl's Best Friend" beg for repeated listening to hear how she twists the phrases and inflects the words. The rest of the cast is also stellar, with Yvonne Adair and George S. Irving lending particularly strong support. As recorded here,

---

ALL-TIME FAVORITES
OF *New York Post*
REPORTER

Michael Riedel

1. My Fair Lady

2. She Loves Me

3. Movin' Out

4. A Little Night Music

5. Promises, Promises

6. The Lion King

7. Titanic

8. Nine

9. Sweeney Todd

10. West Side Story

---

the choral work and dance music do not seem dated at all; the mono sound is excellent even by today's standards. Even though the show itself is something of a trifle, the score and this cast album are first-rate.

Film Soundtrack, 1953 (MGM/various CD labels) ★★★

With the most voluptuous blonde of all cast as Lorelei Lee, *Gentlemen Prefer Blondes* became a fine piece of Hollywood fluff, made classic by Marilyn Monroe's presence. Six cuts from the soundtrack were originally released by MGM records (oddly, since this was a 20th Century-Fox film) and have been reissued on several albums by various labels over the years. They're great fun, but by no means representative of the Broadway score; only three of the Styne-Robin songs are included and the new material is middling Hollywood musical fare. Jane Russell shares star billing with Monroe and is vocally appealing. The highlight of the recording is "Diamonds Are a Girl's Best Friend" in an overtly sexual performance by Monroe that's extremely different from Channing's brilliantly funny rendition.

Broadway Cast, 1995 (DRG) ★★

Although this recording features a talented, enthusiastic cast, it's almost heartbreaking to hear Jule Styne's jazzy, brassy score played by what is basically a chamber orchestra. True, the orchestrations are skillfully reduced and expertly conducted, but this is not the type of score that lends itself to an intimate sound. The good-natured performers KT Sullivan (as Lorelei Lee), Karen Prunzik, George Dvorsky, and Allen Fitzpatrick simply don't have the proper musical setting in which to shine. Their singing is fine but never delivers the rush of excitement that comes from a big Broadway show or the feel of the Roaring '20s. Also, the small cast compromises the sound of the big choral numbers "High Time" and "Bye, Bye, Baby." This album does have some pluses, however. The classic "Diamonds Are a Girl's Best Friend" is performed uncut by Sullivan, so lovers of witty lyrics can enjoy every spicy verse of the song. Also note the interpolated Styne number "A Ride on a Rainbow," an ingenious little charm song, beautifully sung by Dvorsky and Prunzik. The performance is delightful overall but, as its earlier stage and film versions prove, this musical works better when it's played big. Since the original album with Carol Channing is still readily available, there's little reason to own this version other than curiosity.   —GERARD ALESSANDRINI

GEORGE M!
Original Broadway Cast, 1968 (Columbia/Sony) ★★★★

This is a brassy, heart-pounding (and ear-pounding!) show based on the life and songs of the great showman George M. Cohan. The title role is played by Joel Grey (fresh from his triumph in *Cabaret*) at the height of his talent, and he delivers a brash, charismatic performance. The recording was spectacularly well produced by the young Thomas Z. Shepard; the orchestra and chorus sound so huge and exciting that playing the album is like setting off a box of fireworks in your living room. As with fireworks, you should beware: Although the brassiness of the score is not inappropriate for the flag-waving aspects of the story, it is sometimes monotonously loud and it shortchanges the softer, more charming aspects of the era it's trying to evoke. But "Give My Regards to Broadway," "Over There," and other Cohan hits are as infectious as ever, and the dance music is thrillingly arranged. The overture and the instrumental "Popularity" are alone worth the price of the disc, which also offers the joy of hearing Bernadette Peters early in her career; it's easy to understand why her unique voice catapulted her to stardom. The recording contains many delightful Cohan songs that aren't featured in the famous bio-film *Yankee Doodle Dandy* and are hard to find elsewhere; the epilogue track is full of forgotten but wonderful numbers such as "The American Ragtime" and "It's All in the Wearing." Their presence makes the album even more appealing. —GERARD ALESSANDRINI

GIGI

Film Soundtrack, 1958 (MGM/Rhino) ★★★★★

This beloved Alan Jay Lerner-Frederick Loewe score is the most appealing ever written directly for a musical film, and the soundtrack album is one of the all-time great recordings of any screen or stage musical. Directed by Vincente Minnelli, *Gigi* won nine Academy Awards, including "Best Picture" of 1958. Time has been kind to this subtle adaptation of Colette's novella; it holds up well even today as a great feminist story. Leslie Caron's performance as Gigi adds believability and weight to the tale of a young girl who uses her intelligence and steadfastness of character to stand up against an entire society's misguided conceptions of sex and marriage—but it's the score that has made this film an enduring classic. Lerner's lyrics are among his most brilliantly crafted, while Loewe's dazzling music evokes Lehar, Ravel, and Brahms even as the composer retains his own distinctive melodic voice. Conductor André Previn, Conrad Salinger, Bob Franklyn, Alexander Courage, and others came up with arrangements/orchestrations that are widely regarded as among the best ever crafted for a movie musical; the gorgeous counter-melodies of the French horns and the Offenbachesque staccatos of the brass and percussion create spine-tingling effects. The vocal performances of Maurice Chevalier, Louis Jourdan, and Hermione Gingold are treasures. In his artful rendition of "Thank Heaven for Little Girls," Chevalier walks the fine line between great charm and eyebrow-raising naughtiness, and his performances of "I'm Glad I'm Not Young Anymore" and (with Gingold) "I Remember It Well" are supremely witty. Betty Wand dubbed the singing of the title character, and her voice adds just the right amount of sassiness to Caron's plucky Gigi. Rhino's CD offers Caron's unused vocal tracks (with solo piano accompaniment) as bonus cuts; you can judge for yourself whether producer Arthur Freed made the right decision in hiring Wand to post-dub Gigi's songs. Rhino also includes the film's magnificent background score plus several reprises and the "Gossip" number, none of which were on the original LP. Other outstanding selections are "The Waltz at Maxim's," "The Night They Invented Champagne," and the Oscar-winning title song, beautifully delivered by Louis Jourdan.

Original Broadway Cast, 1973 (RCA) ★★

This is the cast album of a stage production that came fifteen years after the film *Gigi*. The world had changed so in the interim that the stage musical seemed antiquated, aside from the flaws of the adaptation itself. The new orchestrations sound opaque and soporific; the show apparently had a kitschy, 1970ish operetta look, and this album reflects that ill-advised concept, although some of the performances sparkle. Maria Karnilova sounds charming as Grandmama, Agnes Moorehead must have been riveting as the tough-as-nails ex-courtesan Aunt Alicia, and Daniel Massey as Gaston is well cast, yet only Alfred Drake seems fully at ease and in his element. Amazingly, he is able to dispel the ghost of Chevalier's performance and offer a fresh characterization of Honoré. Although "Thank Heaven for Little Girls" will always conjure memories of Chevalier, Drake's other numbers—"I'm Glad I'm Not Young Anymore" and "Paris Is Paris Again," the latter written specifically for the stage version—

are high points of the disc. The major drawback is the tepid performance in the title role of Karin Wolfe, who displays none of the pluck and intelligence that are essential elements of Gigi's character.

—GERARD ALESSANDRINI

GIRL CRAZY

Film Soundtrack, 1943 (Rhino-Turner) ★★★

It's widely known that George and Ira Gershwin's *Girl Crazy* has a terrific score, and that Ethel Merman made her legendary Broadway debut in the show singing "I Got Rhythm." Many also know that Ginger Rogers, not Merman, was the heroine, and that the opening-night pit orchestra included Benny Goodman, Glenn Miller, and Gene Krupa. No one, however, knows or wants to know the script; even for 1930, this was a loose assemblage of ethnic humor, stock situations, and leftover shreds from cowboy movies. Small wonder that the musical's one major Broadway revival was so transformed that it needed a new title: *Crazy for You* (see the "C" list for a review of that cast album). Fortunately for home listeners, a timeless score matters far more than an unrevivable script. The property was filmed three times, never faithfully but twice with some interest. This 1943 version has Mickey Rooney and Judy Garland in their vocal prime. Their "Could You Use Me?" duet is an outstanding Gershwin cut, and so is Garland's sparkling "Embraceable You." Nor does June Allyson, in her feature film debut, hold anything back in "Treat Me Rough." The Tommy Dorsey Orchestra really swings out in "I Got Rhythm," and any recording that features Garland singing a definitive "But Not for Me" has its own built-in justification.

Studio Cast, 1951 (Columbia/Sony) ★

The first studio cast album of *Girl Crazy* is in no way a true reflection of the show. It might better be called "Mary Martin and Friends Do Songs From *Girl Crazy*." There is no theatricality here, simply an assured star blandly sailing through some favorite pieces. Martin is assisted by conductor Lehman Engel plus a chorus and supporting singers who evidently have no idea that the Gershwins intended these songs to have energy and fire; even "Treat Me Rough" sounds laid-back! This, then, is the Muzak version of *Girl Crazy,* and only Martin completists need give it their attention.

When the Boys Meet the Girls, Film Soundtrack, 1965 (MGM/no CD)
Not recommended.

When *Girl Crazy* made it to the big screen for the third time, it was a humdrum effort retitled *When the Boys Meet the Girls.* The flick starred two enjoyable singers, Connie Francis and Harve Presnell, but neither the orchestrations nor the new material were worthy of their talents, let alone those of the brothers Gershwin. All that need be added about this record is that it certainly is unique: Liberace and Sam the Sham and the Pharaohs perform material that is not from the show, and where else could you find a rendition of "Bidin' My Time" by Herman's Hermits?

Studio Cast, 1990 (Nonesuch) ★★★★

Six decades after its first hearing, the *Girl Crazy* score was finally given something like its due. This time there was a reconstruction of the orchestrations, and there is an almost time-capsule feel to the performances, ably conducted by John Mauceri. Although the singers work hard, the casting is not all it should be, so it's really the orchestra and the material that make this recording special. Judy Blazer is an attractive Molly, but the Danny of David-James Carroll (he later dropped the "-James") is too much in the sensitive juvenile vein; this show does not need a Candide! The toughest role to cast, of course, is the dramatically extraneous, musically necessary part of Kate—the Merman role. The character's songs have "self-assurance" written all over them from the very first note of "Sam and Delilah," and although Merman's brass isn't a requirement, some sort of magic is. Lorna Luft tries and has good moments, but something more is needed. (Maybe Bernadette Peters or Donna Murphy could make these songs work without imitating Merman.) At least Mauceri and his musicians hold up their end unfailingly, and there's a fun appendix included as well: "You've Got What Gets Me," written by the Gershwins for the 1932 *Girl Crazy* film. This is a worthy recording that will serve well until something even better comes along.   —RICHARD BARRIOS

THE GIRL FRIEND
Original U.K. Cast, 1987 (TER/no CD) ★
One of five Rodgers and Hart shows to open in 1926, *The Girl Friend* had a healthy run. In 1937, the show hit London, where two British writers—R. P. Weston and Bert Lee—replaced Herbert Fields' entire original book with a new plot from a comedy called *Kitty's Kisses*, which had been adapted as a London musical a year earlier. Most of the score was replaced with songs by Gus Kahn, Con Conrad, Will Donaldson, and Otto Harbach. Clear? A new version of *this* version was produced in Colchester, England, in 1987, with the old British script rewritten by director Michael Winter; it had a few Rodgers and Hart songs, plus tunes by others written for the 1927 production. In all, this record contains only three songs from *The Girl Friend* as originally staged on Broadway, plus a number that was cut during tryouts, two R&H songs from other shows, and four songs that—according to the credits on the album jacket—were collaborations of Rodgers, Hart, and Kahn. But the cast is lackluster and the orchestrations distractingly busy. The original New York score's biggest hits, "The Blue Room" and the title song, are here joined by another R&H delight, "Mountain Greenery," sung colorlessly by Barbara King and Mark Hutchinson. The rarely heard but appealing "Sleepyhead," "What's the Use of Talking?" and "Why Do I?" are also included.   —DAVID WOLF

THE GIRL IN PINK TIGHTS
Original Broadway Cast, 1954 (Columbia/DRG) ★★★★
Sigmund Romberg worked as a staff writer for the Shuberts, churning out twenty-two scores from 1914 through 1918 alone! Following his indentured servitude, he went on to compose such smash hits as *Blossom Time, The Student Prince,* and *The Desert Song.* In the 1940s, when his form of operetta had become passé, he changed gears and surprised everyone with a beautiful score (with lyrics by Dorothy Fields) for *Up in Central Park.* His next musical was a flop, but then a new Romberg score hit Broadway when *The Girl in Pink Tights* opened in 1954. The show ran only 115 performances—but what astounded theatergoers was that the composer had died in 1951. With jottings of an unfinished Romberg score found after his death, producer Anthony Brady Farrell had hired orchestrator Don Walker to complete the music. Walker admitted that there might have been more Walker than Romberg in the finished product, but the score is a delight. *The Girl in Pink Tights* is a fictionalized look at the creation of the nineteenth-century melodrama spectacle *The Black Crook.* The show's comic numbers are its standouts, thanks to lyricist Leo Robin (best known for *Gentlemen Prefer Blondes*). Robin skewered the acting profession in such hilarious songs as "We're All in the Same Boat" and "You've Got to Be a Little Crazy." The hit song was "Lost in Loveliness," but equally fine are the ballads "In Paris and in Love" and "My

Heart Won't Say Goodbye." Charles Goldner, Brenda Lewis, Jeanmaire, and David Atkinson shine in their numbers; deep down in the cast list you'll find Marni Nixon, Ted Thurston, Joshua Shelley, Dania Krupska, and Gregory and Maurice Hines. *The Girl in Pink Tights* is a favorite for its beautiful Romberg melodies and witty, sophisticated Robin lyrics. The cast album's riches are all the more exciting as the final work of a great composer. —KEN BLOOM

THE GIRL WHO CAME TO SUPPER
Original Broadway Cast, 1963 (Columbia/Sony) ★★★

This Cinderella story is set during the coronation of George V, adapted by Harry Kurnitz (book) and Noël Coward (music and lyrics) from Terence Rattigan's *The Sleeping Prince*. As the libidinous Prince Regent of Carpathia, José Ferrer is a gloomy presence on the cast album with his post-nasal-drip baritone and his singular lack of charm. As the American chorus girl in London who attracts his royal eye, Florence Henderson hits all the notes and has one wonderful showpiece, "The Coconut Girl," in which she performs an entire, ridiculous, period musical comedy in under eight minutes. But Henderson is a bit too on-the-nose, capable without idiosyncrasy, so this unlikely couple's doomed affair doesn't resonate as it should. However, the score itself is woefully underrated. Sir Noël contributed a cartful of appealing ballads, elegant waltzes, and satirical numbers, the latter exhibiting his customary lyrical sangfroid. He even whipped up an eleven-minute music-hall sequence for Tessie O'Shea, utterly irrelevant to the action but so fetching that O'Shea collected a Tony Award for it. Listen carefully to Sony's CD—which rearranges the tracks from the LP into their proper stage order—and you'll hear a big, old-fashioned show crashing as it docks in Manhattan. But if you step back just a bit, it emerges as a warm, witty musical with, unfortunately, two romantic leads who were not made for each other. (Note: Coward may be heard singing the show's songs himself, including several cut numbers, on the DRG disc *Noël Coward Sings His Score for The Girl Who Came to Supper*. If anything, he makes a better case for the property than does the cast album.) —MARC MILLER

GOBLIN MARKET
Original Off-Broadway Cast, 1996 (JAY) ★★

Goblin Market was a snob hit of the 1985-86 Off-Broadway season. Based on a fairy tale in verse by the pre-Raphaelite Christina G. Rossetti, this two-character "music theater piece" was the public's introduction to composer Polly Pen. With a libretto by Pen and Peggy Harmon, *Goblin Market* premiered at the Vineyard Theatre, which had commissioned it; that staging, directed by André Ernotte, subsequently transferred to Circle in the Square. Rossetti's lengthy poem concerns two young sisters, the bold Laura and the fainthearted Lizzie, who are tempted by specters proffering fruits that are luscious-looking but dangerous. Written in 1862, the poem is an angst-driven fantasy of early Victorian sexual wish fulfillment; Pen and Harmon transformed it into a story of grown-up siblings who visit the nursery of their childhood to ponder their developmental years from an adult perspective. The score, which reflects a variety of influences from baroque vocal literature to nineteenth-century parlor songs and twentieth-century theater music, often matches the morbidity of Rossetti's verse. Pen has a knack for creating tonal configurations and rhythmic patterns that seem anodyne until, repeated as themes, they reveal an eccentric complexity and burrow into the listener's consciousness. On the recording, Terri Klausner as Laura and Ann Morrison as Lizzie handle the arias with vivid expressiveness and musical accuracy. James McElwaine's orchestrations, though performed by a combo of only four, lend a cello-rich heft to the delicate melodies. In the years since *Goblin Market*, Pen has been showered with awards and grants; her well-deserved success illustrates how effectively the nonprofit resident theater system and charitable funding for the arts have combined, despite attacks from the political right, to nurture a branch of American musical theater that has no connection to mainstream tastes.　　　　　　　　　　　　　　　　—CHARLES WRIGHT

GODSPELL
Original Off-Broadway Cast, 1971 (Bell-Arista) ★★★★

Godspell, with music and new lyrics by Stephen Schwartz and a book by John-Michael Tebelak based on the Gospel according to St. Matthew, was for many years a perennial on the stock, amateur, college, and high-school theater circuit. The show's simple, wonderfully tuneful songs have an inevitability that makes them sound like old friends even upon first meeting. The cast of this original recording is strong, so it's surprising to realize that not one of these performers went on to a significant musical theater career. Stephen Nathan sings the role of Jesus in an oddly smoky but appealing voice and David Haskell is excellent as Judas/John the Baptist. Robin Lamont's lovely recording of the score's strongest song, "Day By Day," became a popular hit. On the debit side, Lamar Alford sings the glorious anthem "All Good Gifts" with a throaty tone that some listeners will find off-putting. Another beautiful song is "By My Side," written not by Schwartz but by cast member Peggy Gordon with Jay Hamburger; it's given a moving rendition by Gordon. The other cast members are Joanne Jonas, Gilmer McCormick, Jeffrey Mylett, Sonia Manzano, and Herb Braha. The band consists of Steve Reinhardt on keyboards, Jesse Cutler on acoustic and lead guitar, Richard LaBonte on bass, and Ricky Shutter on drums and percussion; those first three gentlemen sing the heartbreaking "On the Willows" as Jesus and his disciples say their final goodbyes to one another. *Godspell* is one of the very best of the seminal rock musicals of the late 1960s and early 1970s.

Original London Cast, 1972 (Bell-Arista/no CD) ★★

Because the tune stack and the arrangements are virtually the same, this *Godspell* sounds very much like the Off-Broadway cast album, except for the singers' British accents. The company includes Jeremy Irons, who later became a movie star and only rarely returned to musical theater (e.g., as Henry Higgins in a 1987 studio cast recording of *My Fair Lady*), and Julie Covington, who sings the title role on the concept recording of *Evita.* Jesus is the strong-voiced David Essex and Marti Webb is also in the cast. Several lines of dialogue help to give this long out-of-print LP a certain theatricality.

Film Soundtrack, 1973 (Bell-Arista) ★★★★

With several of the original singers and all of the original musicians on hand, augmented occasionally by strings and trombones, this recording also sounds a lot like the Off-Broadway cast album, with a few notable differences: As Jesus, Victor Garber has a sweeter voice than Stephen Nathan; Lynn Thigpen sings "Bless the Lord, My Soul" with a more authentic gospel style than Joanne Jonas; and Merrell Jackson's lyrical "All Good Gifts" is a significant improvement on Lamar Alford's rendition. One new song has been added: the joyous "Beautiful City." Set on deserted Manhattan streets, the *Godspell* movie is rather hard to watch on DVD because the film prominently features the World Trade Center in its opening shot and in the "All for the Best" number. But this CD definitely has its pleasures.

Off-Broadway Cast, 2000 (Fynsworth Alley) ★★★★

Here's a terrific recording of a fabulously well-sung, hilariously funny, deeply moving production of *Godspell* that started out Off-Off-Broadway under the aegis of a group called the Third Eye Repertory and later had an Off-Broadway run in the Theater at Saint Peter's Church. The show boasted a wonderful cast, intelligent direction by Shawn Rozsa, and sensitive musical direction by Dan Schachner. Barrett Foa's clear, youthful tenor brings a wonderful dimension to the role of Jesus. As Judas/John the Baptist, Will Erat adapts his full, rounded, legit voice to a pop/rock idiom impressively; he was wisely handed the haunting "On the Willows" to sing in this production. Other highlights of note: Eliseo Roman deserves a special nod for his magnificent rendition of "All Good Gifts"; Catherine Carpenter's "Day by Day" is warm and sincere; Capathia Jenkins' "Turn Back, O Man" is great fun; and Shoshana Bean's "Bless the Lord" is a roof-raiser. Foa leads the cast in a slow version of "Beautiful City" notable for lyrics that are eerily and movingly prescient of the 9/11 attacks on the Twin Towers: "Out of the ruins and rubble, out of the smoke, out of our night of struggle, can we see a ray of hope?"

National Touring Cast, 2001 (DRG) ★

Instead of the original guitar- and piano-based arrangements, there's a whole lotta synth going on in this cast album of a 2001 *Godspell* tour. Such an approach is not inappropriate, for example, in the opening "Tower of Babble" ensemble; but it soon becomes tiresome, causing the listener to yearn for the more natural, more melodious sound of previous recordings. Scott Schwartz—son of Stephen Schwartz and director of this production—wanted the flavor of alternative-rock and folk-rock artists to be evoked by Alex Lacamoire's new orchestrations and arrangements. Whether that goal was achieved and if the score is better for it is a matter of opinion. Joe Carney shows off a strong, sexy voice as Jesus, but he can't seem to find the beat at the top of "Save the People" and he's way off pitch in "Alas for You." (In his defense, the latter number's dissonant accompaniment would make it hard for any singer to hit the right notes.) Michael Yuen is a light-voiced Judas/John the Baptist and Sal Sabella's crooning approach to "All Good Gifts" is unpersuasive. One of the best cuts on the disc is a terrific up-tempo version of "Beautiful City" but, here once again, Carney falls prey to some pitch problems. Ditto Jessica Carter in "Turn Back, O Man." —MICHAEL PORTANTIERE

THE GOLDEN APPLE
Original Broadway Cast, 1954 (RCA) ★★★

One of the greatest of all cult musicals, this Jerome Moross-John Latouche collaboration has never really commanded the attention it deserves—and, unfortunately, the cast album may be one reason why. This reworking of Homer's *Odyssey* and *Iliad,* set in Washington State just after the Spanish-American War, bristles with smart ideas, thoughtful lyrics, tart commentary, distinctive melody, and a dream cast. But the show is sung-through, and anything less than a complete rendering would sell it short. In 1954, that would have taken at least two LPs. While RCA's single-disc album packs in as much music as the technology then allowed, it's still a sampler at best. To tie the plot threads together, RCA had cast member Jack Whiting recite a rhymed-couplet synopsis; he's personable, but the whimsical concept feels forced. The recording sounds hurried, with fast tempi and echoes being abruptly cut off to make room for the next track. Of the two finales Moross wrote, the label went with the reprise of the hoped-for hit ballad "It's the Going Home Together" rather than the more challenging, less conventional ending. With all of these caveats, there's still huge enjoyment to be had from the recording, especially from the ladies: Kaye Ballard's "Lazy Afternoon," Priscilla Gillette's "Windflowers," Bibi Osterwald's "Goona-Goona," Portia Nelson's "Doomed, Doomed, Doomed." (As Ulysses' introspection intensifies, the material does court pretentiousness.) But *The Golden Apple* is a greater work than the cast album conveys. What the show really needs is a definitive concert version à la Encores! and a two-CD digital recording. Then everyone would savvy what all the fuss was about in 1954.　　　　　　　　　　　　　　　　　　　　　　　—MARC MILLER

GOLDEN BOY

Original Broadway Cast, 1965 (Capitol/Bay Cities/Angel) ★★★★

This is a tale of two CDs and two LPs. *Golden Boy* was released initially by Capitol on LP shortly after the Broadway opening, which followed an extended preview period beset by changes to the show and missed performances by Sammy Davis in the title role of boxer Joe Wellington. With music by Charles Strouse and lyrics by Lee Adams, the show has a book based on the Clifford Odets drama of 1937, adapted for the musical by Odets and William Gibson. For the cast album recording sessions, Davis' voice was tired and strained at times, yet his singing is dynamic and exciting: "Night Song" becomes a cry of pain from the gut; "Stick Around" is devil-may-care yet thrilling; "Colorful" is pungent, funny, and decidedly angry beneath the surface; and "I Want to Be With You," sung with Paula Wayne as Lorna Moon, is heartfelt and moving. When Davis was in better voice a few months later, he rerecorded his solos and his duet with Wayne for a new LP that replaced the first one. The differences are many. For example, the finale of the first LP was a reprise of "Gimme Some" that was not in the opening-night stage version. In it, Joe's brother (Louis Gossett) gives the news of Joe's death to his father and Lorna, then Gossett sings a few lines from "Gimme Some," joined by Joe from the great beyond. (This may sound cheesy, but it was an effective ending to the album.) The final track on the second LP is the show's climactic fight, which may have been exciting in the theater but barely registers musically. Also, Davis' new recording of "Night Song" is smoothly sung with interpolated notes but dull in comparison with his brilliant first effort. Other songs that are more effective on the first LP include "Stick Around," "Can't You See It", and "I Want to Be With You." Unfortunately, both CD versions contain the re-recordings. *Golden Boy* is fascinating in that Strouse wrote it in a more mature, jazzy style than his earlier works (*Bye Bye Birdie*, *All American*) and the Adams lyrics are colloquial, pungent, and witty. In "Don't Forget 127th Street," Davis, Johnny Brown as his brother-in-law, and their friends boisterously rag on their Harlem neighborhood with smart-ass humor. Another powerful track is the gorgeously sung, gospel-style protest song "No More." "Everything's Great" is well sung by Lorna and her loser boyfriend (Kenneth Tobey), and Billy Daniels is deliciously evil as Eddie Satin (Joe's manager), using his famous jazz chops to excellent effect in "This Is the Life" and "While the City Sleeps." In sum: The two CDs and the second LP of the *Golden Boy* cast album score technical knock-outs, but the true champ is the first LP version.　　　　　　　　　　—JEFFREY DUNN

GOLDEN RAINBOW

Original Broadway Cast, 1968 (RCA/GL Music) ★★★

The ultimate in "guilty pleasure" musicals, *Golden Rainbow* took Arnold Schulman's charming little play *A Hole in the Head* and pumped it up into a glitzy, glamorous musical set in—where else?—Las Vegas. Walter Marks' score yielded a smash hit for Steve Lawrence, "I've Got to Be

Me." Lawrence costarred in the show with his wife, Eydie Gormé. Though her acting ability was decidedly limited, Gormé could really belt out a ballad, and Marks gave her a good one: "He Needs Me Now." Like Vegas itself, *Golden Rainbow* glitters but doesn't have a lot of depth; just read the song titles and you can pretty much tell what they're all about. Still, it's an upbeat score that's perfect for listening and singing along. The album is high in energy, moving along with rapid momentum. Some of that is due to the orchestrations of Jack Andrews and Pat Williams and the conducting of the esteemed Elliot Lawrence—but it's also because the finished master tape wouldn't fit the time limitations of a vinyl LP, so they just sped up the tape! And when Steve and Eydie themselves released the CD in the early 2000s, they kept the pace exactly as it was: breathless. Again, it's a guilty pleasure.　　　　　—KEN BLOOM

GOLDILOCKS

Original Broadway Cast, 1958 (Columbia/Sony) ★★★

Here, Elaine Stritch plays a pre-World War I stage star entangled with a fly-by-night silent movie director (Don Ameche) who yearns to make an epic about ancient Egypt. The hilarious book by Walter and Jean Kerr was dismissed by the critics, but the urbanely amusing score by composer Leroy Anderson, with lyrics by the Kerrs and Joan Ford, provides a droll showcase for Stritch. She's a ball of fire in "Give the Little Lady" and rollicking in the comic lament "Who's Been Sitting in My Chair?" ("Who's been sleeping in my bed? / Just me, just moi / I'd like a two-fisted biped / For my boudoir"). She's a riot when criticizing a too-reasonable lover ("The Beast in You") and ruefully touching in the confessional "I Never Know When to Say When." Ameche is suitably sardonic as her love/hate object, and Nathaniel Frey and Margaret Hamilton as Ameche's moviemaking cronies score in a pair of clever comedy numbers, "Bad Companions" and "Two Years in the Making." Anderson's music neatly blends period music styles into a standard 1950s Broadway sound, and the lyrics are dryly witty throughout. (Anderson himself wrote the orchestrations in collaboration with Philip J. Lang.) Romantics looking for soulful ballads needn't bother; for everyone else, this album is good, sophisticated fun, with Stritch at her peak.　　　　　—DAVID BARBOUR

THE GOODBYE GIRL

Original Broadway Cast, 1993 (Columbia/Sony) ★★★

The Goodbye Girl is a fine movie that was never a sound choice for adaptation as a stage musical, even if crafted by gifted, intelligent people: The Neil Simon plot is too uncomplicated and event-free, the characters too "small" and too few. The resulting show featured three major characters and an irrelevant landlady wandering through massive sets, twice running into some chorus dancers who might have come from a musical playing down the block. Composer Marvin Hamlisch and lyricist David Zippel certainly know how to write good songs, and their score is never less than professional; but instead of helping to progress the plot, the numbers just slow things down. Martin Short got the best of the songs: "Elliot Garfield Grant," "I Think I Can Play This Part," and "Paula: An Improvised Love Song," all of which gave him plenty of room to clown. Top-billed Bernadette Peters wasn't as lucky, having been handed some fairly generic ballads; but she does very well when the material is there for her, as in "A Beat Behind" and "Good News/Bad News." The orchestrations of Billy Byers and Torrie Zito are slick and sharp, and the album is quite pleasant to listen to even if the score is never inspired.

Original London Cast, 1997 (First Night) ★

Four years after the failure of *The Goodbye Girl* on Broadway, Neil Simon tried again, this time in London. He brought along composer Marvin Hamlisch but, for whatever reason, not lyricist David Zippel. So, except for the two best Zippel songs—"Elliot Garfield Grant" and "Good News/Bad News"—this is an entirely new score with lyrics by Don Black, and it's much worse. Zippel, an extremely clever wordsmith, wrote lyrics that were always believable extensions of the script. Black's are just pop songs. For the most part, they're vague, uninteresting, and difficult to understand. (One lyric goes: "I'll take the sky / I'll take the moon / I'll take the child with the yellow balloon.") The basic flatness of the characters doesn't help—nor does Ann Crumb as Paula, whose diction is simply terrible, and Gary Wilmot is unimpressive as Elliot. Marvin Hamlisch's new music is loud and, in an attempt to be more "contemporary," uncharacteristically ugly—at least, as heard in these trashy arrangements. On Broadway, *The Goodbye Girl* was a classy failure, but this version sounds like just another flop.   —DAVID WOLF

GOOD NEWS

Film Soundtrack, 1947 (MGM/Rhino) ★★

The first movie written by Betty Comden and Adolph Green for MGM, *Good News* has a smart and funny script. Only six songs were retained from the original 1927 hit stage musical by Ray Henderson, Lew Brown, and B. G. DeSylva; three of them—the title song, "The Varsity Drag," and "He's a Ladies' Man" (here changed to "Be a Ladies' Man")—were extensively reworked by vocal arranger Kay Thompson and coproducer Roger Edens. In addition, Edens wrote two new songs with Comden and Green: "The French Lesson," a real highlight, and "An Easier Way," which didn't make it to the final cut of the film. Also interpolated was the Edens-Hugh Martin-Ralph Blane number "Pass That Peace Pipe." Leads Peter Lawford and June Allyson sing passably well. The third major player, Broadway dancer and comedienne Joan McCracken, was more comfortable dancing than singing and is perhaps more effective in the film than on this recording. Though the show and the movie take place in the 1920s, no attempt was made to capture the feel of that era in the musical arrangements, which sound like '40s pop. The Rhino CD marks the first complete release of the soundtrack. It includes Mel Tormé's outtake reprise of "Lucky in Love" and the deleted "An Easier Way," an interesting piece that contrasts the characters played by Allyson and Patricia Marshall. The CD also has a dopey interview with Allyson and two numbers—"The Varsity Drag" and the title song—from the apparently lost 1930 film version of the stage musical.

Studio Recording With Cast Members of the Music Theatre of Wichita Production, 1996 (JAY) ★★

Some months after the closing of an unsuccessful 1975 Broadway revival of *Good News,* cast member Wayne Bryan produced a privately issued album of that production from a tape of a live performance, plus a second LP containing items that had been cut during the show's tryout. In an ideal world, this is the recording that would be widely available. Bryan never lost his fondness for this material and in 1992, as producing director for the Music Theatre of Wichita, he and writer-director Mark Madama got permission to write a new version of the show. That successful 1993 production was the basis for the disc at hand. Though it presents the basic, original stage score plus seven more Henderson-Brown-DeSylva songs, including "Button Up Your Overcoat," "You're the Cream in My Coffee," "Life Is Just a Bowl of Cherries," and "Keep Your Sunny Side Up," the recording is a little pale. Craig Barna's orchestrations are thin and his musical direction doesn't have much spirit. The performers—Ann Morrison, Michael Gruber, Kim Huber, Linda Michele, and Jessica Boevers—are fairly colorless. They are joined by Wayne Bryan himself, who was probably too old by then to play an undergraduate but who still sounds terrific, especially in "Never Swat a Fly." With its irresistible score and archetypal plot about a football player who must pass his astronomy final if he wants to play in the Big Game, *Good News* is good fun, and though this disc isn't bad by any means, the material deserves to be performed with a little more sass. —DAVID WOLF

GOODTIME CHARLEY
Original Broadway Cast, 1976 (RCA) ★★★

As he did with *Ben Franklin in Paris,* librettist Sidney Michaels—this time leaving the lyrics to other, more expert hands—tried to give old European history new Broadway pizzazz in this somewhat cumbersome retelling of Charles VII's relationship with Joan of Arc. If that sounds to you like a topic that doesn't naturally sing, you're right; there are abrupt shifts of tone between heavy, Old World seriousness and musical-comedy silliness. And, oddly for a big Broadway score, nearly all of Larry Grossman and Hal Hackady's songs are given to Charles (Joel Grey) or Joan (Ann Reinking), leaving little for the chorus or for the large, interesting supporting cast (Susan Browning, Richard B. Shull, Grace Keagy, Louis Zorich, Jay Garner, and others) to do. Still, Grossman and Hackady offer an enterprising attempt at an old-style score of wit and substance; there are no inappropriate rock posturings here, but there are some quite wonderful lyrics in such numbers as "Why Can't We All Be Nice?" and "Voices and Visions." Speaking of voices: Reinking's has an unpleasant, pseudo-Gwen Verdon rasp; and Grey—outfitted with all the accoutrements of a big-musical leading role, including a heavy-breathing eleven-o'clock number—tends to overemote. But this is a score of which connoisseurs of musical theater are understandably fond, and the CD is a lively, tuneful history lesson bolstered by Jonathan Tunick's excellent orchestrations. —MARC MILLER

GRAND HOTEL
Broadway Cast, 1992 (RCA) ★★★★

Based on the Vicki Baum novel that inspired the classic MGM film, *Grand Hotel* traveled a crooked road to Broadway. The first pass at the material, by librettist Luther Davis and song-writers Robert Wright and George Forrest, was titled *At the Grand;* it closed out of town in 1958. Decades later, the project was resurrected by director-choreographer Tommy Tune. When trouble set in on the road, Tune brought in Peter Stone to rewrite the book and Maury Yeston to write seven new numbers and revise existing ones—with no and little credit, respectively. Even with mixed reviews, *Grand Hotel* ran over a thousand performances. It was widely felt that Tune's brilliant staging had triumphed over weak material. But, as this disc shows, the score is no cut-and-paste job; every song meshes perfectly in this drama of life, death, and reversals of fortune in a Weimar Berlin hotel. In fact, it's hard to tell who composed which songs without referring to the notes, especially since it's not indicated which of the Wright/Forrest songs were revised by Yeston. Peter Matz's orchestrations merge sinister Kurt Weillesque downbeats with tinselly tea-dance rhythms and soaring melodies to create a brooding score that perfectly mirrors the fatalistic narrative. There are some routine items here, but the best of them are thrilling, including the romantic "Love Can't Happen," the sizzling jazz duet "Maybe My Baby Loves Me," and "I Want to Go to Hollywood," a bouncy number with dark undertones (of those, the first and third are by Yeston, the second by Wright/Forrest). Recorded late in the show's run, the disc features most of the original cast, including Liliane Montevecchi as an aging ballerina, Karen Akers as her devoted companion, Jane Krakowski as a sexy stenographer, and Michael Jeter as a dying bookkeeper. Sadly, David Carroll, who played Montevecchi's doomed lover, died of AIDS before he could record his performance; his songs are covered by his capable replacement, Brent Barrett. (A bonus track features a live recording of Carroll singing "Love Can't Happen" in a cabaret revue.) Overall, *Grand Hotel* is a potent musical soap opera.　　—DAVID BARBOUR

A GRAND NIGHT FOR SINGING
Members of the Broadway Cast, 1994 (Varèse Sarabande) ★★

A revue of songs from Rodgers and Hammerstein musicals, *A Grand Night for Singing* was directed by Walter Bobbie with musical direction by Fred Wells. It opened at the now-defunct, high-class cabaret venue Rainbow & Stars at Rockefeller Center in 1993, then later that year, the show had a brief run on Broadway at the Roundabout Theatre. It's an amiable compilation of beloved standards: "Hello, Young Lovers," "If I Loved You," "Some Enchanted Evening," "Oh, What a Beautiful Mornin'," and "It Might as Well Be Spring," along with several of the team's songs that are not as famous but just as terrific, such as "So Far" and "Don't Marry Me." Some of the songs are performed in full while others are excerpted in medleys. The show received Tony Award nominations for Best Musical and, believe it or not, Best Book of a Musical. This recording features the Broadway company—Victoria Clark, Jason Graae, Alyson Reed, Lynne Wintersteller—plus Gregg Edelman filling in for Martin Vidnovic. The songs of Rodgers and Hammerstein, like the songs of Stephen Sondheim, tend not to work very well in a revue format because they were so skillfully tailored to specific characters and situations. Two that suffer greatly when taken out of context are the comedic "I Cain't Say No" from *Oklahoma!* and "Honey Bun" from *South Pacific.* Others stand better on their own, such as the ballads "Do I Love You Because You're Beautiful?" and "This Nearly Was Mine." This CD can't hold a candle to any cast recording of a full Rodgers and Hammerstein musical, but it can be enjoyed as a sampler of the legendary team's work.　　—MICHAEL PORTANTIERE

THE GRAND TOUR
Original Broadway Cast, 1979 (Columbia/Broadway Redux) ★★

This is the cheeriest musical ever written about escaping from the Nazis. Jerry Herman has dismissed the show as a mistake ("It just didn't have the energy and excitement to be a real hit"), but no Herman score is without interest. Michael Stewart adapted S. N. Behrman's play *Jacobowsky and the Colonel,* itself an adaptation of a work by Franz Werfel. Set in 1940, the plot centers on a Jewish refugee (Joel Grey) trying to get out of German-occupied France in the company of a chilly, anti-Semitic Polish colonel (Ron Holgate) and his girlfriend Marianne (Florence Lacey). Some of Herman's work is extraordinary, including Jacobowsky's signature tune "I'll Be Here Tomorrow," rendered unforgettably by Grey; Marianne's hymn to her home, "I Belong Here"; and Holgate's lovely ballad "Marianne." But Herman's perennially bouncy attitude has an undermining effect on what is, after all, a very dramatic story. A number on a train, "We're Almost There," is disconcertingly upbeat. So is "You I Like," sung when the two men finally bond. "For Poland," in which Jacobowsky coaxes the colonel into letting him come along, sounds like the football fight song of a Midwestern university. (Philip J. Lang's orchestrations only accentuate the positive.) All three leads are superb, however, and the score is never less than easy to take.　　—DAVID BARBOUR

THE GRASS HARP
Original Broadway Cast, 1971 (Painted Smiles/Varèse Sarabande) ★★★★★

Even if it didn't star Barbara Cook, in resplendent voice in her last Broadway musical, this would be the most glorious cast album that you've never heard. A messy book (from Truman Capote's novella) and underfinancing shuttered the poorly received show after five performances in 1971. But this disc, made some months later with almost the entire original cast (a chorus of adults subbed for a chorus of children), preserves the lustrous music of Claibe Richardson and the sharp lyrics of Kenward Elmslie that combine to conjure up the rustic South in the early part of the twentieth century. Cook plays Dollyheart, who tends the home of her breadwinner sister Verena (Ruth Ford), who's fallen in love with Dr. Morris Ritz (Max Showalter). The doc wants to market the dropsy cure that Dollyheart's been making in the backyard with nephew Collin (Russ Thacker) and maid Catherine (Carol Brice). But Dollyheart won't give up her secret formula, and this causes Verena to lash out at her. So Dollyheart takes Collin, Catherine, and the cure with her on what becomes a modest adventure with a faith healer (Karen Morrow). It's all set to a fine score with orchestrations split among old master Robert Russell Bennett, new master Jonathan Tunick, and jazz specialist J. Billy Ver Planck. Cook has two beautiful ballads—"Chain of Love" and "Reach Out." Brice gets one that's a bolt of lightning, "If There's Love Enough," and another that's top-notch comedy, "Marry with Me." Thacker delivers the raucous "Floozies" and the more tender "This One Day," while Morrow gets the twelve-minute masterpiece "The Babylove Miracle Show," in which the faith healer encourages her listeners to "hang a little moolah on the washline." It might seduce you into opening your wallet; you'll be glad you did so in order to buy the cast album of *The Grass Harp.*   —PETER FILICHIA

GREASE
Original Broadway Cast, 1972 (MGM/Polydor) ★★★★

Those who know *Grease* only from its inexplicably popular, sophomoric film version or its pumped-up, wrongheaded 1994 Broadway production will be surprised the first time they hear this album. As first seen Off-Broadway and then on Broadway after a run in Chicago, the show was an affectionate little musical about the teenage lifestyle of the late 1950s—when rock-and-roll was aborning, the cool boys sported heavily gelled hair and motorcycle jackets, and their girls favored beehives and pedal pushers. The original staging was Broadway's long-run champ for a time, racking up 3,338 performances before it closed in 1980. With book, music, and lyrics by Jim Jacobs and Warren Casey, *Grease* skillfully walks the line between parody and *hommage*. The melodies, rhythms, harmonies, and arrangements of the songs are clever knockoffs of popular '50s hits, very catchy and buoyed by some clever lyrics. (Example, from "Freddy, My Love": "I treasure every giftie / The ring was really nifty / You said it cost you fifty / So you're thrifty / I don't mind.") Other highlights include "Summer Nights," which amusingly presents a boy's and a girl's disparate descriptions of their summer romance; the infectious "Magic Changes," sung by a kid who's thrown himself wholeheartedly into guitar lessons; "It's Raining on Prom Night," a cute lament over a lost high-school love (sample lyric: "I don't even have my corsage, oh gee / It fell down a sewer with my sister's I.D."); and "We Go Together," a bouncy anthem of teenage unity. The score does contain one serious number, and it's a good one: "There Are Worse Things I Could Do," sung by Rizzo, a girl whose outward toughness masks her vulnerability. Adrienne Barbeau gives a moving, well-sung performance of the number. Barry Bostwick is terrific as lead greaser Danny and Carole Demas sounds just right as Danny's sweet girlfriend, Sandy. Among the other standouts in the cast are Katie Hanley, Walter Bobbie, and Kathi Moss.

Film Soundtrack, 1978 (Polydor) ★

The first cut on this album, a new title song (there was none in the stage show), cues you into the silly, anachronistic style of the film version of *Grease.* It's a disco number, of all things, written by Barry Gibb of the Bee Gees and sung by Frankie Valli. Although *Grease* is set in the 1950s, director Randal Kleiser and colleagues apparently thought it necessary to add a disco song to the score just because that type of music was so popular when the film was made. Other major additions to the song stack aren't as objectionable. Louis St. Louis wrote "Sandy," a new lost-love song for Danny that's pretty but not as much fun as "Alone at a Drive-In Movie," the Jacobs-Casey song it replaced. John Farrar wrote "Hopelessly Devoted to You," a pretty ballad for Sandy, and "You're the One That I Want," a catchy tune, but still somewhat out of place as sung by John Travolta and Oliva Newton-John as Danny and Sandy. In Rizzo's songs, Stockard Channing relies on vocal mugging and overinflection rather than solid singing; she seems to have a perfectly fine voice but doesn't trust it. (One wag comments that the first time he heard Channing's rendition of "There Are Worse Things I Could Do," he was tempted to respond, "No, there aren't!") On the other hand, a plus for both the movie and the album is Frankie Avalon's performance of "Beauty School Dropout." Note that "Greased Lightnin'" is sung here by Danny rather than Kenickie, perhaps to give Travolta another song. Also note that some numbers in the show score, such as "Those Magic Changes" and "It's Raining on Prom Night," are performed on the soundtrack album by various artists, but aren't actually included in the film or are heard only as background music.

Original London Cast, 1993 (Epic) ★★

Producer Robert Stigwood included the songs that were written expressly for the *Grease* film in his London staging of the musical. The anachronistic title number, sung here by the full company, still rankles, but other, more innocuous songs from the movie are well performed. Deborah Gibson is perfect for the role of Sandy, and Craig McLachlan is right-on as Danny. As Rizzo, Sally Ann Triplett overplays "Look at Me, I'm Sandra Dee" (and mispronounces Troy Donahue's last name) but does a fine job with "There Are Worse Things I Could Do." Charlotte Avery offers a regrettable Marilyn Monroe impersonation in "Freddy, My Love." Of the others, Shane Richie's Kenickie and John Combe's Doody are especially commendable.

Broadway Cast, 1994 (RCA) ★★

The nonsensical addition of an exclamation point to the show's title is emblematic of how overblown this production of *Grease!* was. The vocals of Sam Harris and Billy Porter in (respectively) "Those Magic Changes" and "Beauty School Dropout" are the clearest examples of the show's exaggerations; both men have amazing voices, but they perform these songs as aggressive power ballads rather than the charming, little ditties they used to be. As Rizzo, Rosie O'Donnell sounds OK in "Look at Me, I'm Sandra Dee" but not OK in "There Are Worse Things I Could Do." Ricky Paull [sic] Goldin and Susan Wood are fairly nondescript as Danny and Sandy, but Megan Mullaly is a hoot in Marty's "Freddy, My Love." Producers Barry and Fran Weissler couldn't get the rights to the new numbers that were thrown into the movie, so the song stack of this recording is the same as that of the original Broadway album, except that the old favorite "Since I Don't Have You" by Joseph Rock, James Beaumont, and the Skyliners is added for Sandy and "All Choked Up" is cut. Let the record show that, in an incredibly strange and deplorably misleading move, this was billed as "the Tommy Tune production of *Grease!*" even though it was directed and choreographed by Tune protégé Jeff Calhoun.

Studio Cast, 1994 (JAY) ★

This recording would be superfluous if not for the participation of John Barrowman, a Scottish-born singing actor who became a star of the London musical stage as a young man but who, as of this writing, has had only two brief stints on Broadway (in *Putting It Together* and *Sunset Boulevard*). Barrowman brings his strong, clear, sexy tenor to Danny's songs and to the ridiculous "Grease" disco number added to the movie. The other three song additions to the flick are also included here. As Sandy, Shona Lindsay makes unpleasant sounds when belting at the top of her range. There's nothing distinctive about the rest of the cast members, some of whom are less successful than others at masking their Brit accents.   —MICHAEL PORTANTIERE

THE GREAT WALTZ
Original West Coast Cast, 1965 (Capitol/no CD) ★★★★

Edwin Lester of the Civic Light Opera Company of Los Angeles and San Francisco was known for bringing Broadway's first national tours to the West Coast and for mounting revivals with as many original Broadway cast members as possible. He was also famous for creating and producing such successful "modern" operettas as *Song of Norway* and *Kismet.* This show began in Vienna in 1930 as an operetta (*Walzer aus Wien*) based on the lives and music of Johann Strauss Sr. and Jr. As *The Great Waltz,* it traveled abroad successfully, then opened on Broadway in a new version in 1934. The credits on the album reveal the complicated history of the show: music by the two Strausses; musical adaptation by Erich Wolfgang Korngold, Robert Wright, and George Forrest; lyrics by Wright and Forrest; additional lyrics by Forman Brown; book by Jerome Chodorov, based on versions by Moss Hart (1934) and Milton Lazarus (1949). The book of the Lester version involves the father/son conflict that actually existed between Strausses *père* and *fils.* The melodies are, of course, ravishing, and the adaptations are scintillatingly orchestrated. Metropolitan Opera stars Giorgio Tozzi (as the elder Strauss) and Jean Fenn (as an opera singer who had a serious flirtation with Strauss in his youth) are wonderful in their respective introductory solos, "I'm in Love With Vienna" and "Philosophy of Life." And when they raise their voices together in their duets "Of Men and Violins" and "The Enchanted Wood," they are simply grand. The role of Strauss Jr. is sung with ringing tenor tone by Frank Porretta; the character has no solos in *The Great Waltz,* but his duets with Fenn and with Anita Gillette in the ingenue role of Resi are thrilling. Gillette delightfully joins with Wilbur Evans (as Herr Dommayer) in the infectious "A Waltz With Wings." There is also a fine quartet of conflict for the four principals, "No Two Ways"; a trio titled "Music," performed with verve by Evans, Leo Fuchs, and Eric Brotherson; and the effective "Blue Danube" finale.

London Cast, 1970 (Columbia/no CD) ★★

Edwin Lester's *Waltz* was the impetus for this production at London's famous Theatre Royal, Drury Lane. With a few textual changes (Julius Bittner is added to the songwriting credits), it ran 706 performances. The cast album features an overture that's not included on the earlier recording and there are other differences in the song stack. Sari Barabas, a genuine European operetta star, exudes Continental flair in a gorgeously sung, heavily accented "I'm in Love With Vienna" and could not possibly be more playful or charming in "Teeter-Totter Me" with the sturdy-voiced David Watson as Strauss, Jr. Watson also works well with the Resi of Diane Todd, whose soprano is fluttery yet attractive. As the elder Strauss, Walter Casell displays a huge, mature baritone of great authority. The quartet for the principals gets a little wild, but the finale has Todd and Barabas doing some lovely trilling of the famous "Blue Danube."

Film Soundtrack, 1972 (MGM/no CD) Not recommended.

The location filming in Austria was pretty much the only thing that was appealing about this movie. The soundtrack, featuring the voice of Mary Costa, offers the great Strauss melodies in new arrangements and orchestrations, but there's really not much of interest here, not even for the most devoted operetta fans. —JEFFREY DUNN

GREENWICH VILLAGE, U.S.A.

Original Off-Broadway Cast, 1960 (20th Century Fox/no CD) Not recommended.

Some of us have a blind affection for 1950s and 1960s revues, but being blind doesn't mean that you have to be deaf and dumb, too. There isn't anything in *Greenwich Village, U.S.A.* that's worth five seconds of your time. Although New York City's West Village was admittedly more distinctive in the '50s than it is now, it was never exactly Borneo, yet the authors consistently depict its residents as some rare breed of exotics. This basic lack of honesty is one major reason why nothing here is funny; another reason is the creators' sheer lack of talent. Those responsible for this fiasco are Jeanne Bargy, composer-lyricist; Frank Gehrecke, bookwriter-lyricist; and Herb Corey, lyricist. The only item of (minor) interest in this recording is that one of the performers, ballad singer Dawn Hampton, was an early influence on Bette Midler. —DAVID WOLF

GREENWILLOW

Original Broadway Cast, 1960 (RCA/DRG) ★★★★

Composer-lyricist Frank Loesser was determined never to repeat himself in his musicals. In between his operatic *The Most Happy Fella* and his satirical *How to Succeed in Business Without Really Trying,* he created a bucolic, whimsical score set in the village of Greenwillow—perhaps located a few miles due east of the equally mythical Brigadoon. The show seemed to perplex and confuse people, its charms eluding both critics and audiences. As a result, it lingered on Broadway for just under a hundred performances. We should be grateful that it opened at a time when most Broadway musicals were recorded on the first Sunday after opening, before it was known if the show would have a successful run. The album begins with church chimes and then, after a lovely prelude, moves into the syncopated opening number "A Day Borrowed From Heaven." This sequence introduces the villagers and, eventually, the central character Gideon Briggs, played by Anthony Perkins in his first and last Broadway musical. His is not a legit musical theater voice but, having made some pop albums for RCA prior to *Greenwillow,* Perkins was quite secure in his singing. He combines that talent with powerful acting to excellent effect in the ebullient "Summertime Love" and the dramatic "Never Will I Marry." Pert Kelton and Lee Cass practically steal the album with the uproarious "Could Have Been a Ring," in which they sing about the relationship they never had with each other. The ingenue, Ellen McCown, sounds fine in the haunting ballads "Walking Away Whistling" and "Faraway Boy," while Cecil Kellaway and William Chapman do fine work as two very different clergymen. There is also a Frank Loesser Christmas Carol ("Greenwillow Christmas") and a glorious song celebrating "The Music of Home." One can forgive the occasional clunkers (such as "Clang Dang the Bell," in which a cow gets baptized) because they are surrounded by so much good material from one of Broadway's greatest composer-lyricists. This is a recording you are likely to love. —JEFFREY DUNN

GRIND

Original Broadway Cast, 1985 (JAY) ★★★

Grind, which opened during director Harold Prince's 1980s slump, was one of the most hated shows of the period. It's easy to see why: Fay Kanin's overloaded book (based on her own unproduced screenplay *This Must Be the Place*) deals with racism, the Depression, feminism, riots, murder, suicide, and Irish Republicanism, while the score (music by Larry Grossman, lyrics by Ellen Fitzhugh) rides one's nerves with its harsh truths and dissonant chords. Nevertheless, this is the decade's most fascinating misfire. It's set in a Chicago burlesque house in 1933 where, thanks to payoffs, both black and white performers appear. Much of the action centers on the triangle between LeRoy, an Uncle Tom-like comedian (Ben Vereen); Satin, a tough-minded stripper (Leilani Jones in a Tony-winning performance); and Doyle (Timothy Nolen), a drunken bum with a brogue and a terrible secret. Stubby Kaye as Gus, a comedian who's losing his sight, acts as the plot's catalyst. For many, the score is too shrill and confrontational—Bill Byers' orchestrations are nerve-jangling—but the best stuff grabs you by the throat. Jones sizzles in the angry strip number "A Sweet Thing Like Me," commands in "All Things to One Man," and (with help from Vereen) wrings every bit of humor out of "Why, Mama, Why," in which she imagines confronting her bitter mother. Nolen's opera-level voice makes the most of "Katie, My Love" and "Down," in which Doyle recalls his sad family history. An ensemble number, "The Grind," acridly describes daily life in burlesque; and there's a knockout gospel tune, "These Eyes of Mine," led by Carol Woods. This is a CD that absolutely deserves your attention.   —DAVID BARBOUR

GUYS AND DOLLS

Original Broadway Cast, 1950 (Decca) ★★★★

While subsequent recordings of Frank Loesser's *Guys and Dolls* are superior to this one in certain respects, the performances here are definitive and remain the template for all future productions. Almost every Nathan Detroit is better than Sam Levene as far as singing is concerned, but just listen to Levene's barely on-pitch pleas to Adelaide in "Sue Me" and you may well feel that his Nathan is unbeatable. In "Adelaide's Lament," Vivian Blaine is completely natural, touching, and funny at the same time. In "A Bushel and a Peck" and "Take Back Your Mink," Blaine makes it clear exactly what kind of performer Miss Adelaide is and what kind of joint she works in. In "Sue Me," she and Levene give us a textbook example of how a comedy duet should be performed. Robert Alda and Isabel Bigley as Sky Masterson and Sarah Brown do very well in their duets "I'll Know" and "I've Never Been in Love Before" and are impressive in their respective solos, "Luck Be a Lady" and "If I Were a Bell." The supporting players, especially the irreplaceable Stubby Kaye in "Sit Down, You're Rockin' the Boat," are also distinctive. While we have Alda's "My Time of Day" on the album, it's regrettable that the dialogue and underscoring that connects the song to "I've Never Been in Love Before" were not recorded. Included as bonuses on the latest CD edition are four commercially released tracks from the film version, so we can savor the undubbed performances of Jean Simmons and Marlon Brando in "I'll Know" and in "A Woman in Love"; the latter is one of the songs that Loesser wrote for the movie. Simmons' "If I Were a Bell" is one of the best-acted versions of this song you are likely to find, and Brando's "Luck Be a Lady" is unexpectedly effective. No complete soundtrack album was ever released due to Frank Sinatra's contractual restrictions. However, an "unofficial" soundtrack came out on CD and then disappeared quickly. As the DVD of the film is readily available, only completists will feel the need to track down that disc.

Original London Cast, 1953 (Parlophone/Sepia) ★

Since most of the original Broadway cast of *Guys and Dolls* repeated their roles in London, a full-length recording of that production was considered unnecessary. Sky (American Jerry Wayne) and Sarah (Brit Lizbeth Webb) were new to the show, so studio recordings were made of most of their songs without the theater orchestrations, and without each other: We get two separate recordings of "I've Never Been in Love Before" but only Wayne's solo version of "I'll Know." The 1950s pop arrangements and Wayne's crooning sound in "Luck Be a Lady" and "My Time of Day" result in performances that lack a sense of theatricality. The one lovely surprise here is Webb's brassy belt, which makes her "If I Were a Bell" a true delight. Future London leading man Edmund Hockridge was a replacement for Sky, and his more legit voice is shown off in "Luck Be a Lady" and "I've Never Been in Love Before" on a three-CD set titled *The Greatest Musicals* (EMI Gold). Another West End star-to-be, Joyce Blair, was an Adelaide replacement; she can be heard singing "A Bushel and a Peck" on a British World Record Club LP that pairs *Guys and Dolls* with *West Side Story*.

Broadway Cast, 1976 (Motown) ★★★

For this *Guys and Dolls* revival with an all-black cast, the original orchestrations were rewritten to achieve a funkier sound. Some of the songs resist that kind of treatment, but one of the times when it really works is in the first duet for Sky and Sarah. Ernestine Jackson sings "I'll Know" with a solid soprano in a standard Broadway arrangement; then James Randolph swings into an R&B chorus of the song, and the two very different styles of singing tell us much about who these characters are. Later, Jackson's Sarah loosens up in "If I Were a Bell" and her voice meshes attractively with Randolph's in "I've Never Been in Love Before." The new orchestrations may not please traditionalists but their bounciness and the sense of joy that they create cannot be denied. Robert Guillaume portrays a very dry, leading-mannish Nathan Detroit and Norma Donaldson is an entertaining Adelaide; her shrieks at the end of "Adelaide's Lament" are unexpected and very funny. This is the only recording of the show that includes "Adelaide Meets Sarah"—a brief sequence in which "I've Never Been in Love Before" is sung in counterpoint with "Adelaide's Lament"—as it appears in the score. Ken Page's "Sit Down, You're Rockin' the Boat" is a foot-stomping showstopper with a gospel-style encore included. Though this is by no means a definitive *Guys and Dolls,* it's a highly enjoyable listening experience.

National Theatre Cast, 1982 (Chrysalis/Music For Pleasure) Not recommended.

Perhaps it's necessary to have seen this production of *Guys and Dolls* to understand why it was a resounding hit in London. The "band" was onstage, playing new orchestrations intended to evoke the Big Band sound of the 1940s. But this disc sounds like a cheaply produced studio recording rather than a first-class cast album, and much of what Loesser wrote seems to have been lost. The performances were reportedly wonderful onstage but did not translate well to CD. Ian Charleson as Sky never pretended to be a singer and his acting does not compensate for his lack of vocal power. Julie Covington's fluttery vibrato makes her renditions of Sarah Brown's songs virtually colorless. The Adelaide of the usually brilliant Julia McKenzie doesn't really register, nor does the Nathan Detroit of Bob Hoskins. David Healy's "Sit Down, You're Rockin' the Boat" is standard issue, and when he duets with Barrie Rutter in the title song, it's hard to tell that two people are singing until they break into harmony. Overall, this disc is a huge disappointment. At least Music For Pleasure is a budget label!

Studio Cast, 1986 (JAY, 2CDs) ★★★★★

If you must choose only one recording of *Guys and Dolls* to own, this gem should be it. It contains almost every note of the score as originally heard on Broadway and presents the original orchestrations and dance arrangements in stereo for the first and, so far, only time. It also has bonus tracks of songs written for the film ("Pet Me, Poppa," "Adelaide," and "A Woman in Love"), with excellent orchestrations by Larry Moore, and the deleted Sky/Nathan duet "Travelin' Light." Gregg Edelman's Sky and Emily Loesser's Sarah are nothing less than superb, both vocally and dramatically: To hear them navigate their way through the "I'll Know" sequence is almost as if to experience it for the first time. Another joy of this two-disc set is that it includes the entire musical scene of "My Time of Day" into "I've Never Been in Love Before" as Loesser conceived it. This is also the only recording of the show to include the entire original "Havana" sequence. Kim Criswell is a divine Adelaide, both brassy and touching. As Nicely-Nicely, Don Stephenson successfully accomplishes the unenviable task of following in Stubby Kaye's massive footprints. If Tim Flavin is not ideal as Nathan, he's suitable enough, and Ron Raines is a strong-voiced Sky Masterson. While some listeners may prefer a cast album of *Guys and Dolls* that represents an actual stage production, this recording offers so much in the way of theatrical atmosphere and excellent performances—not to mention completeness— that it should be a part of every musical theater CD collection.

Broadway Cast, 1992 (RCA) ★★★

Reaction to this recording will be largely based on one's feelings about the hugely successful *Guys and Dolls* revival that yielded it. Nathan Lane may not be everybody's idea of Nathan Detroit but he is wonderfully comic, sings better than the role's requirements, and is especially effective in "Sue Me" with Faith Prince as Adelaide. Prince's characterization is somewhat lacking in vulnerability, but her comedic instincts are dead-on; she does a bang-up job with "Adelaide's Lament" and is obviously having a ball in "A Bushel and a Peck" and "Take Back Your Mink." Josie de Guzman's lackluster Sarah lets Prince down in "Marry the Man Today" and is even more harmful in her duets with Peter Gallagher, who is suave, tough, and in fine voice as Sky Masterson. Gallagher does justice to the rousing "Luck Be a Lady" (heard here with new dance music) and "My Time of Day." The CD includes chunks of dialogue that give it a nice sense of theatricality. Walter Bobbie is an unconventional choice for the role of Nicely-Nicely Johnson but he makes the role his own; he leads a rousing "Sit Down, You're Rockin' the Boat," and he and J.K. Simmons give an excellent rendition of the title song. The cuts, however small, and reorchestrations of much of the score (Michael Starobin is billed after the original orchestrators) may limit some listeners' enjoyment of this performance, which is, in any case, strongly conducted by Edward Strauss.

Touring Cast, 2001 (DRG) ★

This fiftieth-anniversary recording of *Guys and Dolls* features the cast of a touring production that began at Washington, D.C.'s Arena Stage, with Maurice Hines top-billed as Nathan. Musical supervision and additional arrangements are by Danny Kosarin; the orchestrations sound like scaled-down versions of the originals with some alterations. Overall, it's a pretty lifeless affair with the exception of the Sky and Sarah, very well sung by real-life newlyweds Brian Sutherland and Diane Sutherland. Alexandra Foucard is bland in Adelaide's two performance numbers and makes dreadful attempts at humor. Even worse is Foucard's duet with Hines: To say that this rendition of "Sue Me" is of a community theater level would be insulting to community theaters everywhere. The recording goes further downhill with the worst "Sit Down, You're Rockin' the Boat" ever captured on disc and an awful "Marry the Man Today" with an inexplicable female back-up chorus at the end. The bonus tracks are a plus: Frank Loesser sings seven *Guys and Dolls* songs, including the deleted "Travelin' Light" and "Adelaide" from the film version. His revelatory performance of "Luck Be a Lady" should be required listening for any would-be Sky Masterson; his original verse-and-chorus ballad version of "Sue Me" is fascinating, and it's fun to hear his renditions of "I'll Know," "I've Never Been in Love Before," and "Sit Down, You're Rockin' the Boat." These selections are also available on DRG's *An Evening With Frank Loesser,* which includes Loesser's performances of many other songs from other shows of his. That CD would be a much better purchase than this touring cast album of *Guys and Dolls.*   —JEFFREY DUNN

GYPSY

Original Broadway Cast, 1959 (Columbia/Sony) ★★★★★

From the blaring trumpets that begin the overture to the final chords of "Rose's Turn," this is a recording that grabs you and never lets go. Representing Jule Styne, Stephen Sondheim, and several other great musical theater artists at the peak of their powers, the flawlessly integrated musical *Gypsy* is further elevated by this album's breathtaking performances. It's clear that Ethel Merman knew she had the role of her career and was going to make certain that the audio document of her performance would jump off of the vinyl on which it was originally released. In "Some People," she just about shakes you by the shoulders with Rose's ambition—and then she touches your heart with the character's yearning in "Small World." Later on, she both thrills and terrifies you in "Everything's Coming Up Roses." Finally, there's her "Rose's Turn," a performance that may someday be equaled but will almost certainly never be surpassed: It's a moment-to-moment exploration of an emotional breakdown and breakthrough, the equivalent of several years of therapy in five minutes. The supporting cast is worthy of the star. Sandra Church is a totally convincing Louise, from her heartfelt "Little Lamb" to "Let Me Entertain You." On Sony's most recent CD edition of the original cast album, Church can be heard squealing with delight at the end of Paul Wallace's flawless "All I Need Is the Girl," a magnificent theatrical moment previously thought to be lost in time. Jack Klugman's contributions to the recording are wonderful if not extensive. Maria Karnilova, Faith Dane, and Chotzi Foley make a feast of "You Gotta Have a Gimmick," and the CD happily gives us the previously deleted sections of the number: Tessie's "ballet" and the round before the final section. The disc is filled out with demo recordings of several of the show's songs, some with lyrics that were later changed, sung by Merman with Jule Styne at the piano. Oddly, there's no introductory dialogue on the recording, and it's too bad that Merman's orchestra-punctuated spoken lines into "Some People," her dialogue with Jack Klugman before "Small World," and her speech before "Rose's Turn" weren't recorded. You may also question the reorchestration of "Small World" for the album. Still, this CD deserves an honored place in every collection of musical theater recordings.

Film Soundtrack, 1962 (Warner Bros./Rhino-Turner) ★★★★

It took a long time for the *Gypsy* soundtrack to show up on CD, but this Rhino release proved to be well worth the wait. George Feltenstein did an excellent job of producing the disc and writing the informative notes. The recording was remastered and the complete version of "Dainty June and Her Newsboys" is included. The biggest bonus of all is the added tracks of Rosalind Russell singing Rose's songs, which were almost entirely dubbed for the film by Lisa

Kirk. In Russell's autobiography, she insists that she did all of her own singing in *Gypsy*, but that is simply not true: Only her vocals for "Mr. Goldstone, I Love You" and some sections of "Rose's Turn" made the final cut of the film, but Kirk's dubbing of the other songs is very skillful. In general, Russell acts the songs wonderfully well, yet her singing leaves much to be desired. However, in "Together," which was cut from the movie, she sings delightfully, as do Natalie Wood and Karl Malden. Wood's "Little Lamb" is touching if not pretty, and she sounds fine duetting with Ann Jillian in "If Momma Was Married." As Tulsa, Paul Wallace recreates his Broadway performance of "All I Need Is the Girl." The Broadway cast's Faith Dane leads the strippers in "You Gotta Have a Gimmick," and Malden handles Herbie's minimal vocals well enough. This CD offers "Rose's Turn" in two versions: the "album version," which is all Lisa Kirk, and the film version, which is part Kirk and part Russell. The thrilling overture is conducted by composer Jule Styne.

Studio Cast, 1969 (Music For Pleasure/no CD) ★

This is the oddest *Gypsy* recording of all. Kay Medford had played another showbiz mama (Mrs. Brice, in Jule Styne's *Funny Girl*), so it may have seemed a good idea to give her a shot at Rose in *Gypsy*. Produced by Norman Newell and featuring something close to the original orchestrations, this record's first quirk comes in "Some People," when Medford sings a rarely heard lyric ("Some people can sit and stare, living life in a rocking chair"). Her sliding into notes here is regrettable, but then she begins to capture you with a "Small World" that's nicely sung and well interpreted. Medford works hard in "Everything's Coming Up Roses," but her acting doesn't compensate for her singing, especially not at the climax of the number. In "If Momma Was Married," the Louise is boring while the June sounds very British and doesn't sing too well. Tulsa, in "All I Need Is the Girl," comes over like a London chorus boy rather than a would-be vaudevillian. The strippers are fine—but after all, "You Gotta Have a Gimmick" is almost indestructible. Finally, Medford's "Rose's Turn" is rather grim.

Original London Cast, 1973 (RCA) ★★★★

London didn't get to see *Gypsy* until 1973, when Angela Lansbury starred as Rose under the direction of the show's librettist, Arthur Laurents. When the eagerly awaited cast album arrived on these shores, listeners were immediately taken with the star's fresh approach to the character. Lansbury's Rose was electric in a totally different way from Merman's, and on this recording, we hear textual changes—some of which have remained in subsequent stagings. Herbie does some singing in "Small World," turning that song into a duet, and "The Strip" ("Let Me Entertain You") now has Louise/Gypsy speaking to the audience in addition to singing and changing outfits. Barrie Ingham, as Herbie, makes the most of his musical moments, and Zan Charisse is perfect as Louise. The vaudeville sequences have been telescoped into something called "Let Me Entertain You" (Montage) that gives us some of Bonnie Langford's hilarious Baby June and some of Debbie Bowen's Dainty June. On the LP, Lansbury's tracks were a bit raw but amazingly vital; she was also the first Rose on record to sing the final note of "Some People" as written in the score, to thrilling effect. However, when the album was issued in the United States, it was apparent that Lansbury had rerecorded some of her solo tracks. Those performances, retained on the CD, are somewhat lacking in immediacy and excitement as compared with the others. Still, in both versions, Lansbury's "Everything's Coming Up Roses" is powerful and her "Rose's Turn" is classic.

Broadway Cast, 1990 (Elektra-Nonesuch) ★★

Tyne Daly was reported to be having vocal problems when this recording was made, but if that's true, it doesn't seem to have daunted her in the role of Rose. The disc includes some dialogue which enhances the enjoyment of her performance. She and Jonathan Hadary turn "Small World" into a gem of a duet. While Daly's voice does show some signs of wear in "Everything's Coming Up Roses," the introductory spoken lines propel her into singing with a desperation that really makes the number land. Crista Moore is mostly good as Louise, but "The Strip," in a rewritten version, is weak. The strippers—Barbara Erwin, Jana Robbins, and Anna McNeely—display loads of showbiz savvy in "You Gotta Have a Gimmick," and Robert Lambert is a solid Tulsa. As for "Rose's Turn," it begins almost as a toss-off; then Daly gradually gains intensity and growls her way to an almost defeated ending.

Television Film Soundtrack, 1993 (Atlantic) ★★★

The TV movie of *Gypsy* starring Bette Midler is textually faithful to the stage version of the musical. The production was controversial; it took many fans of the show a second viewing to begin to accept Midler as Rose, but hers is an estimable performance and this soundtrack disc has much to offer. To start with, Michael Rafter does a fine job with the beloved overture—but now the quibbles begin. The recording includes almost no dialogue. (We do get to hear Ed Asner's recognizable voice as Pop in "Some People.") The lack of spoken lines limits the dramatic impact of "Small World," "You'll Never Get Away From Me," and "Together," though all three of these numbers benefit greatly from the very pleasant presence of Peter Riegert as Herbie. For some reason, much of what's good about the film doesn't translate to the CD. Cynthia Gibb doesn't make a strong vocal impression as Louise; her "Let Me Entertain You" is only saved by some voiceovers tracing her climb to Minsky's. Also, neither "All I Need Is the Girl" nor "You Gotta Have a Gimmick" register strongly without the visuals. But then there is Midler. According to producer Craig Zadan's notes, the star performed most of her vocals live. The spontaneity and verve that she brings to this classic score must be partly credited to that wise choice, one that's so rarely made when musicals are filmed. "Some People" bristles, "Small World" allows Rose to melt Herbie with a creamy vocal, and "Everything's Coming Up Roses" is suitably scary. The glory of the disc is Midler's superb "Rose's Turn": She acts her way through every moment of the number with enormous guts, bringing it to a searing climax.

Broadway Cast, 2003 (Angel) ★★★

Whatever one may have thought of this production, the cast album is the most complete preservation of the *Gypsy* score to be found on CD. Almost every track includes dialogue, and there is a great deal of incidental music and underscoring. Bernadette Peters' Rose is as unique to her personality as her predecessors' takes on the role were to theirs; she defines the character in her own special way. What comes through on the recording is her variance between charm ("Small World"), strength ("Some People"), vulnerability (the "Small World" reprise), ferocity ("Everything's Coming Up Roses"), and grit ("You'll Never Get Away From Me"). Peters skillfully juggles all these aspects of the role, finally allowing them to collide brilliantly in "Rose's Turn." Tammy Blanchard is not fully convincing as Louise in yet another version of the "Gypsy Strip," nor is she very effective in "Little Lamb," and she's only a little bit better when singing "If Momma Was Married" with Kate Reinders. John Dossett and David Burtka are far more persuasive as Herbie and Tulsa, respectively. The three strippers—Kate Buddeke, Julie Halston, and Heather Lee—are right-on in "You Gotta Have a Gimmick." —JEFFREY DUNN

H

HAIR

Original Off-Broadway and Broadway Casts, 1967/1968 (RCA, 2CDs) ★

Many traditionalists were nonplussed when the seminal rock musical *Hair* became a big hit Off-Broadway and then on Broadway in the late 1960s. Those productions were deplorable in that they featured lots of substandard singing, as is proved by RCA's rerelease of their cast albums in a two-CD Broadway Deluxe Collector's Edition. On both discs, the singing ranges from OK to execrable. The few listenable performances of songs from Galt MacDermot's wonderful score are to be found on the Broadway disc; among them are Lynn Kellogg's "Easy to Be Hard" and Shelley Plimpton's "Frank Mills." It's fun to hear a young Diane Keaton and Melba Moore in "Black Boys" and "White Boys," respectively. Leads Gerome Ragni and James Rado (who wrote the lyrics and book) sing well enough, but their interpretations lack theatrical charisma. On the Off-Broadway recording, "Aquarius" and "Good Morning Starshine" are sung so far off-pitch that you'll gasp; Jill O'Hara is the hapless soloist in "Starshine." In his notes for the CD release, series producer Daniel Guss writes that the Off-Broadway *Hair* LP "co-existed with the Broadway cast album for a few years, but soon was deleted and slipped into obscurity." One is tempted to add, ". . . where it belonged!"

Original London Cast 1968 (Decca) ★

Decca released two LPs worth of performances from the original London production of *Hair*, "the American tribal love-rock musical." As Peter Knight explains in his notes for the CD release, "the show contains some 34 titles but, when the initial recording [of the London *Hair*] was made in 1968, it was impossible to cram them all onto one 12-inch vinyl pressing . . . *Fresh Hair* [a follow-up album] was conceived to resolve the problem." Both albums are included in full on the CD, which is nothing if not complete. Unfortunately, the singing here is often as out of tune as on the original RCA albums—which means that it's very ragged and unpleasant. If you want to hear *Hair* at its best, go with the movie soundtrack album (see below).

Film Soundtrack, 1979 (RCA) ★★★★★

The film version of *Hair* is an indescribably vast improvement over the stage show, not only in terms of its script (a brilliant adaptation by Michael Weller) but also for the excellent representation of the score. To begin with, the

---

ALL-TIME FAVORITES OF
LYRICIST-LIBRETTIST

Betty Comden

1. Guys and Dolls

2. Sunday in the Park
   With George

3. Oklahoma!

4. Wonderful Town

5. The King and I

6. Show Boat

7. A Little Night Music

8. My Fair Lady

9. On the Town

10. On the Twentieth
    Century

songs are sung very well—and all of the voices you hear are actually those of the performers you see on screen. Treat Williams is an ideal Berger, positively bursting with subversive energy in "Donna" and "I Got Life." John Savage sings "Where Do I Go?" with great beauty of tone as well as great depth of feeling, and he engagingly duets with Williams in "Manchester." Don Dacus is funny and appealing as Woof in "Sodomy" and "Hair." Annie Golden is delightful as Jeannie on screen but does no solo singing in the film—and it's unclear if she does any on the soundtrack album, although it includes several songs not found in the flick. (It's annoying that none of the vocalists are specifically credited anywhere on the CD package.) Cheryl Barnes sings the hell out of "Easy to Be Hard." And, in her one brief solo spot, Beverly D'Angelo brings a sweet voice to "Good Morning, Starshine" even if she does have some minor pitch problems. Two alums of the Broadway staging of *Hair*, Melba Moore and Ronnie Dyson, sing powerfully in the terrifying "3-5-0-0," while Nell Carter and Ellen Foley turn up elsewhere. Best of all, the phenomenal score is thrillingly arranged and conducted by composer Galt MacDermot himself. (Tom Pierson is the vocal arranger/conductor.)   —MICHAEL PORTANTIERE

HAIRSPRAY
Original Broadway Cast, 2002 (Sony) ★★★★
The CD itself is gussied up to look like a Phil Spector 45, and that's typical of the attention to detail in this lively aural document of an irresistible musical comedy. Though based on John Waters' 1988 movie of the same title, *Hairspray* plays more like a faux-naif *Bye Bye Birdie*, propelled by '60s rock 'n' roll pastiche songs with just enough irony lurking at the edges. Marc Shaiman and Scott Wittman's score has a lot of heart, along with a sincere plea for tolerance, beneath all that jive. When Marissa Jaret Winokur kicks off with "Good Morning Baltimore," sung to perfection, we're all hers. From there, the album is pretty much a nonstop delight that employs every color of the era's pop palette, from girl-group bubblegum ("Mama, I'm a Big Girl Now") to gospel soulfulness ("I Know Where I've Been"). As Edna Turnblad, Harvey Fierstein sings with verve, bringing the house down in his "Timeless to Me" duet with the indispensable Dick Latessa. Mary Bond Davis, Corey Reynolds, Linda Hart, Matthew Morrison, and Kerry Butler all help out loads. A bonus track allows us to hear a cut song, the giggly-grisly "Blood on the Pavement," but it's unnecessary; we've long since been won over. Salutes also to Lon Hoyt's energetic musical direction and Harold Wheeler's fab orchestrations; the Ronettes never had it so good!   —MARC MILLER

HALF A SIXPENCE
Original Broadway Cast, 1965 (RCA) ★★★★
Whenever I feel depressed, I listen to *Half a Sixpence*, which always makes me smile. Composer-lyricist David Heneker is a wonderful craftsman and his work has real heart. The musical's book is by Beverly Cross, based on the novel *Kipps* by H. G. Wells, and the score reflects its British underpinnings; it's gently commanding and sweet through and through. Even the showstoppers—"Money to Burn," "Flash, Bang, Wallop," and "The Party's on the House"—are completely free of the knock-your-socks-off overkill that so many shows resort to. And the ballads—especially the touching "Long Ago," "He's Too Far Above Me," and "I Know What I Am"—are all the more emotional because of their innocence, understatement, and honesty. Star Tommy Steele, for whom the show was created, sings with great energy and comes across as a right amiable bloke. And there's no more heartfelt, sweeter performance

than that of Polly James as Ann, his love interest. (Note to trivialists: John Cleese had a featured, nonsinging role in this show!) So, when you're down and out, lift up your head and listen to *Half a Sixpence*. —KEN BLOOM

HALF-PAST WEDNESDAY
Original Off-Broadway Cast, 1962 (Columbia, reissued as *Rumplestiltskin*/no CD)
Not recommended.
The success of *Once Upon a Mattress* inspired several other fairy tale musicals, including this one—but the authors of *Mattress* knew how to adapt their source material for the stage so that it would appeal to adults. In contrast, the writers of *Half-Past Wednesday*—Robert Colby, Nita Jonas, and Anna Marie Barlow—took the story of Rumpelstiltskin and changed almost nothing. This is the original tale: straight, unadorned, and very involving if you're six years old. The songs aren't even run-of-the-mill. There's not a fresh idea to be found here and, despite the fact that the score contains a number of "comic" songs, there are no jokes. Columbia tried to repackage this LP and sell it as a children's album, but it's not even clever enough for kids—and they'll hate the soppy love songs. The only cast member you're likely to have heard of is Dom DeLuise, most of whose mannerisms were already in place by the time of this recording. —DAVID WOLF

HALLELUJAH, BABY!
Original Broadway Cast, 1967 (Columbia/Sony) ★★
Here's the gimmick: The show (book by Arthur Laurents) takes us from a Southern plantation in 1900 to New York in the '60s, yet the four main characters never age. Three of them are black and the entire story is an allegory of the changing roles of blacks in American society. Sounds clever but, in 1967, *Hallelujah, Baby!* pleased nobody. What was intended as progressive came off as patronizing. (Walter Kerr's tart assessment: "A course in Civics One when everyone in the world has already got to Civics Six.") Yet Leslie Uggams scored a personal triumph, and the score—music by Jule Styne, lyrics by Betty Comden and Adolph Green—is filled with distinctive songs. Uggams' first number, "My Own Morning," with its assertive lyrics and oddly loping melody, gets things off to a fine start. Later, she has the raucous, self-aware "I Wanted to Change Him" and the unsentimental, oddly minor-keyed "Being Good." Then there's the melancholy trio "Talking to Myself" and the kicky title tune. Not everything is at this level; the first act sometimes seems to be marking time with numbers pointing out the silliness of racism. And shockingly, one tune—"Witches Brew"—is a recycled version of "Call Me Savage" from *Fade Out—Fade In*. Still, Uggams is divine throughout, the rest of the cast is strong, and the good far outweighs the bad. —DAVID BARBOUR

HANK WILLIAMS: LOST HIGHWAY
Original Off-Broadway Cast, 2003 (Fynsworth Alley) ★★★
Fans of country-music icon Hank Williams may hesitate to buy the album of this Off-Broadway biomusical when there are so many recordings of the real deal available. But it's a fine CD nonetheless and a good introduction to the music of Williams, whose numerous hits— "Jambalaya (On the Bayou)," "I'm So Lonesome I Could Cry," and "Your Cheatin' Heart," to name only a few heard here—captured numerous hearts during his brief career. The recording preserves many of the show's dramatic moments, interspersing dialogue with its two dozen

tunes. ("Hey Good Lookin'," first heard in a purposefully bad rendition that's meant to illustrate Williams' descent into drunkenness, appears again unsullied in a bonus track.) The amazing Jason Petty, whose crooning and yodeling could almost be mistaken for Williams' own, delivers crisp renditions of these classic songs with the help of a tight instrumental ensemble featuring Myk Watford on guitar, Drew Perkins on violin, and Stephen G. Anthony on bass. Michael W. Howell, a blues singer who inspires Williams, lends his rich voice to the soulful "This Is the Way I Do" and "The Blood Done Sign My Name."   —BROOKE PIERCE

HANNAH . . . 1939
Original Off-Broadway Cast, 1992 (JAY) Not recommended.
Produced by the Vineyard Theatre, this show was much more serious—and much weaker—than composer-lyricist Bob Merrill's earlier work, notably, *New Girl in Town, Take Me Along, Carnival, Funny Girl* (for which he provided lyrics only to Jule Styne's music), and a few other quickly closed flops. In *Hannah,* Julie Wilson plays a famous Jewish clothing designer whose dress business is commandeered by the Nazis for the purpose of making uniforms. Perhaps because of the seriousness of the characters and the milieu, the energy that marked Merrill's previous shows is not in evidence here. Linked to the drably plotted book, which includes a number of unenlightening flashbacks, the score sounds like one long, dreary song.   —DAVID WOLF

THE HAPPIEST GIRL IN THE WORLD
Original Broadway Cast, 1961 (DRG) ★★★★★
"Ev'ry man, I must alert you / When seeking a lady fair / Always gravitates to virtue / Still hoping it won't be there." These four lines, echoing W. S. Gilbert, are only a meager sampling of the wit that E. Y. Harburg brought to this musical adaptation of Aristophanes' *Lysistrata,* in which the title character persuades the ladies of Greece to withhold sexual favors until their bellicose spouses stop pursuing war. When they do, all hell (and heaven) breaks loose. Perhaps all good lyricists are philosophers; if so, Harburg, forever contemplating man's inhumanity to man, was one of the most philosophical. Moreover, he never forgot to keep 'em laughing while sending the message. Known for trying his collaborators' patience, Harburg must have found this one of his smoothest assignments: working with the lilting music of the long-deceased Jacques Offenbach, who couldn't talk back. Harburg's words sit on Offenbach's melting tunes in the way a gondola glides on a cosmic sea in the masterful lyricist's "Adrift on a Star," a setting of the beloved barcarole from *The Tales of Hoffman.* Hearing this virtually flawless, operettalike score, you might wonder why *The Happiest Girl in the World* only played ninety-six performances. Explanation: The Fred Saidy-Henry Myers book made for a listless, substrata *Lysistrata.* The show's high points are on the CD, and that definitely includes Cyril Ritchard—the personisfication of "fey"—performing as both a highborn Greek and the troublemaking Pluto. Janice Rule, not known for musicals, sings well here as the goddess Diana, who's on the girls' side. Dran Seitz as the title character and Bruce Yarnell as General Kinesias warble beautifully. So does everyone in the large chorus, Lainie Kazan among them. The orchestrations are by the great Robert Russell Bennett with the equally great Hershy Kay; conductor Robert DeCormier did the vocal arrangements. In other words, top professional work all around.   —DAVID FINKLE

HAPPY HUNTING

Original Broadway Cast, 1956 (RCA) ★★★

Ethel Merman's only flop cast her as Liz Livingston, a wealthy, rough-at-the-edges widow from Philadelphia who decides to beat Grace Kelly at her own game and marry off her daughter to Spanish royalty (Fernando Lamas). The flimsy book by Howard Lindsay and Russell Crouse, who apparently hoped to repeat the topical success of *Call Me Madam,* wasn't loved by critics. However, the score—written by a pair of Broadway neophytes, composer Harold Karr and lyricist Matt Dubey, in a style that can only be called School of Irving Berlin—does contain a number of tasty items. Merman's voice turns everything to gold, especially her jubilant introduction number "Gee, But It's Good to Be Here," in which she holds one note for an impossible length of time and then goes up a step without taking a breath. Also fun are the risqué "Mr. Livingstone," in which Liz recalls her marriage, and the balled "This Is What I Call Love." Lamas scores with the lushly romantic "It's Like a Beautiful Woman." The numbers for the inevitable young lovers (Virginia Gibson and Gordon Polk) are disposable and the topical lyrics, as in "The Wedding of the Year Blues," are dated and silly. Still, even the weakest of songs benefit from Ted Royal's orchestrations with their swingy undertones.　　　　　　　　　—DAVID BARBOUR

THE HAPPY TIME

Original Broadway Cast, 1968 (RCA) ★★★★

This is a charming if inconsequential cast album of a show that missed the mark onstage. The score by John Kander and Fred Ebb (*Chicago, Cabaret*) lives up to their reputation as the kings of great opening numbers. In this case, it's the title song, so magnificently sung by Robert Goulet that you will think you're about to hear one of Broadway's all-time great musicals. Melodic, evocative, and dramatic, "The Happy Time" is a joyous ode to the wonders of childhood and memories of hometown life. The show that follows that number was not, however, embraced by the public, which had its mind on less innocent events in 1968. Whether or not the timing of this sweet, simple musical is what led to its obscurity remains a mystery. What's left behind is a lovely recording of a beautiful score that includes little-known but inspired ballads such as "I Don't Remember You" and "Walking Among My Yesterdays," plus showstoppers like "The Life of the Party" and "A Certain Girl." Goulet's Tony Award-winning performance shows why he was a great singing star of the 1960s; David Wayne is also excellent as the curmudgeonly Grandpapa. Although *The Happy Time* is not regarded as a precious gem from the golden era of musical theater, this album is a must for Kander and Ebb fans.　　　　　　　　　—GERARD ALESSANDRINI

HARLEM SONG

Original Cast, 2002 (Columbia/Sony) ★★★

George C. Wolfe's love letter to Harlem played the legendary Apollo Theater. It was less a full-fledged musical, or even a revue, than a museum installation. If many of the new tunes in *Harlem Song* by Wolfe and his *Bring in 'Da Noise, Bring in 'Da Funk* collaborators Zane Mark and Daryl Waters don't quite live up to their esteemed ancestry, what could possibly compare favorably to Billy Strayhorn's "Take the 'A' Train"—even when it's sung in Spanish, as here? The show never gets more daring than that, but with songs by a diverse range of artists, including Duke Ellington, Harold Arlen, and Count Basie, it comes across as a mostly exciting, mostly seamless retrospective of Harlem's rich cultural and musical heritage. The band (led by Mark) and the fine cast of sixteen performers, particularly the redolent Queen Esther and B. J. Crosby, are more than capable of smoothing over the rough edges and creating a listening experience that's alternately cool and hot. A few tracks—"Well Alright Then" by Jimmie Lunceford, performed by Queen Esther; "For Sale" by Clarence Williams and Henry Troy, knocked out of the park by Crosby; and "Linda Brown" by Alvin Cowens, sung by the whole company—ignite more quickly than others. But, even on this disc, Wolfe and company never let the heat die down for too long.

—MATTHEW MURRAY

HAZEL FLAGG
Original Broadway Cast, 1953 (RCA/Sepia) ★

A credible case could be made that, on any given project, Jule Styne was only as good as his lyricist. Give him Sondheim and you get *Gypsy;* give him Bob Hilliard and the result is *Hazel Flagg.* This musical adaptation of *Nothing Sacred,* Ben Hecht's classic 1937 film satire, was intended as Helen Gallagher's stepping-stone to stardom in the title role of a Vermont lass who's thought to be dying of radium poisoning and is transported to New York by *Everywhere* magazine for a supposed last fling. (Guess what happens to her prognosis.) Gallagher works very hard here, and her contralto belt is strong and secure. She's supported by such Broadway reliables as Benay Venuta, Jack Whiting (introducing "Every Street's a Boulevard in Old New York"), and Thomas Mitchell (who doesn't sing a note but took home a Best Musical Actor Tony anyway). Unfortunately, the star's luck ends there. Asked to carry most of the songs and dances, Gallagher opens with a dull ballad ("The World Is Beautiful Today") and closes with an equally dull eleven-o'clocker ("Laura de Maupassant"). Most of what's in between is dull as well, including romantic interest John Howard, Don Walker's by-the-book orchestrations, and several ho-hum ensemble numbers—though the show does sport amusingly elaborate vocal arrangements by Hugh Martin. The main problem seems to have been that Hilliard's lyrics failed to inspire Styne. Well, if you had to set "Autograph Chant" or "Salome (With Her Seven Veils)," you'd be uninspired, too.

—MARC MILLER

HEDWIG AND THE ANGRY INCH
Original Off-Broadway Cast, 1998 (Atlantic) ★★★

Here is a rock-music performance piece about an East German transsexual who submits to the knife out of love for an American serviceman and then escapes to Kansas, where s/he launches a pimply, self-hating teenager as an arena-rock sensation, only to be left bitter and abandoned. This, umm, unique storyline is shot through with crackpot philosophical ruminations about the nature of love, male and female identities, and the fall of the Berlin Wall. *Hedwig* is a terrific piece of work, by turns scathing, campy, and soulful. John Cameron Mitchell, who wrote the script, is indelible in the title role; it's astonishing how the listener can come to understand and sympathize with the character and his/her outlandish problems. At least three of Steven Trask's songs—"Wig in a Box," "Wicked Little Town," and the gritty, downbeat "The Long Grift"—are minor classics. This is possibly the only rock musical in which the music is authentic rock. It's a brilliant one-off and well worth your attention.

Film Soundtrack, 2001 (Hybrid) ★★★★

Here is one of those very rare instances in which the film improves on the stage original, as evidenced by this disc. The *Hedwig* song list is slightly altered and rearranged, but all the good stuff is here, and the lyrics are far more understandable than on the original cast recording. John Cameron Mitchell's vocals are, if anything, more confident, and the overall sound mix is more balanced. The disc preserves the score's scalding cynicism and dark romanticism, its Brecht-meets-power-rock sensibility. "Wig in a Box," in which Hedwig recalls his/her trailer-trash life in Kansas, is given an especially ebullient rendition. This is the most original musical theater score in years, a tribute to survivors everywhere. —DAVID BARBOUR

HELLO AGAIN

Original Off-Broadway Cast, 1994 (RCA) ★★★

The emergence of the "new wave" of American theater composers might be traced back to this 1994 musical—inspired by Arthur Schnitzler's *La Ronde*—about a series of sexual encounters that link ten characters in a circle "across time and place," to quote the CD booklet (which contains all of the show's lyrics and some nice production photos). Written by Michael John LaChiusa and staged by Graciela Daniele, *Hello Again* moves through the decades of the twentieth century, beginning with a prostitute's liaison with a soldier in the early 1900s and coming full circle when a U.S. senator meets a prostitute played by the same performer in the 1990s. LaChiusa creates some intriguing situations, as when the character Young Thing is propositioned by an older man on the *Titanic* and a lonely housewife has a rendezvous with a college boy in a movie theater. Like much of LaChiusa's work, *Hello Again* is more of an opera than a traditional musical—not in the style of singing but in how the music winds in and out of the dialogue, occasionally punctuated by a brief chorus number or solo. Although some of the sequences are more interesting as dramatic scenes than as songs, there is some marvelous stuff here: a World War II-era vignette of a soldier having a last fling before shipping out; the housewife's tale of meeting a stranger called "Tom"; the Young Thing's plaintive paean to "The One I Love" following a one-night stand; and the senator's dream of finding real love in "The Bed Was Not My Own." The cast is impressive: Donna Murphy, Carolee Carmello, John Dossett, Michele Pawk, Judy Blazer, John Cameron Mitchell, and Malcolm Gets each have at least one great song in which they demonstrate why they've become musical theater stalwarts. —BROOKE PIERCE

HELLO, DOLLY!

Original Broadway Cast, 1964 (RCA) ★★★★

If one composer's name leaps to mind when the phrase "show tune" is spoken, it's probably Jerry Herman; and if one show epitomizes Herman's work, it's *Hello, Dolly!* The prologue of this recording—a brief but thrilling orchestral arrangement of the monster-hit title song, created especially for the album—lets you know that you're in for quite a ride. From there to the finale, it's one terrific number after another, with "Put on Your Sunday Clothes" registering as one of the most exciting songs ever written for the American musical theater. This recording is a cornerstone of many people's collections but, upon hearing it for the first time, you may be struck by the fact that the whole is far greater than the sum of its parts. Charles Nelson Reilly, so fabulous as Bud Frump in *How to Succeed in Business Without Really Trying,* is less persuasive here as the more leading mannish Cornelius Hackl. Opposite him, Eileen Brennan sings "Ribbons Down My Back" and other songs in a stilted soprano that worked for her campy role in *Little Mary Sunshine* but is inappropriate for the straightforward Irene Molloy. On the plus side, David Burns is a delightful Horace Vandergelder. Of course, the album's *raison d'être* is Carol Channing's portrayal of Dolly Gallagher Levi—a one-of-a-kind, daffy, mercurial comic performance that's more well sung than this performer is often given credit for. The chorus members sing with energy, but in an oddly clipped fashion that sometimes makes them sound angry; however, the orchestra is terrific throughout as recorded in super-duper stereo. (Shepard Coleman is listed as musical director/vocal arranger.) Note that the songs "Motherhood" and "Elegance" were written at least in part by Bob Merrill, who pitched in when the show was in trouble out of town. The first of his numbers is a throwaway to cover some comic business, but "Elegance" has a catchy melody and such delightful lyrics as "All who are well bred agree / Minnie Fay has pedigree." Despite its flaws, this recording deserves a place in any cast album collection. (Note: Included as bonus tracks in the "Broadway Deluxe Collector's Edition" are two cuts each from the London cast album starring Mary Martin and the 1967 Broadway cast album starring Pearl Bailey, along with Ethel Merman's renditions of two songs that were reinstated when she starred as Dolly at the end of the show's marathon Broadway run. There's also an amusing interview with Carol Channing.)

Original London Cast, 1965 (RCA/no CD) ★★★★

This album has not yet been released on CD and was never readily available on LP in the United States—puzzling, since it's very well done and it stars Mary Martin, a true legend of the American musical theater. Martin apparently declined to have her songs transposed to lower keys to accommodate the changes in her voice as she aged, so there are a few less-than-lovely high notes to be heard here. But, overall, this beloved performer seems to be having such a great time in the role of Dolly that it's easy to overlook her vocal limitations. The supporting cast is strong, with Marilyn Lovell especially appealing as Irene.

Broadway Cast, 1967 (RCA) ★★★★★

In order to rekindle interest in *Hello, Dolly!* three years into the show's run, producer David Merrick brought in an all-black cast headed by two iconic performers, Pearl Bailey and Cab Calloway. The recording begins with a gorgeous, full-length overture that's almost too symphonic for this basically bouncy show. (Like the "Prologue" of the original cast album, this overture was created specifically for the recording.) Throughout the album, Philip J. Lang's revamped orchestrations are fabulous. This performance of the title song is the best ever recorded: Bailey and the boys have the time of their lives as saxophones wail, trumpets blare, a banjo strums, and the xylophone player goes nuts. A real pistol as Dolly, Bailey is very funny, but just as strong when delivering a serious song like "Before the Parade Passes By." Cab Calloway makes the role of Horace Vandergelder his own, even if he's heard only in a reprise duet of "Hello, Dolly!" with Bailey and in leading the male-ensemble number "It Takes a Woman." Jack Crowder's rich baritone voice isn't exactly right for the callow Cornelius, but Crowder sings so beautifully—especially in "It Only Takes a Moment," one of Herman's loveliest ballads—that it's foolish to carp. He is superbly partnered by Emily Yancy, who brings just enough jazz/pop style to Irene's songs to make them come alive without distortion. This is, without question, the finest recording of the *Hello, Dolly!* score.

Film Soundtrack, 1969 (20th Century-Fox/Philips) ★

The best that can be said for the *Hello, Dolly!* soundtrack album is that it's not as awful as the misbegotten film itself. Barbra Streisand's voice was at its zenith at the time of this recording, which may be enjoyed for the sheer pleasure of hearing her rather than as a representation of a musical theater property. Streisand's voice is beyond criticism, however stylistically inappropriate to the music as originally conceived. Her best number is "So Long, Dearie," heard here in a terrific up-tempo arrangement. She also sounds great in the title song, despite her ultra-slow delivery of the first chorus, and she belts the hell out of "Before the Parade Passes By." Walter Matthau is no great shakes as a singer, but he does well enough for Horace Vandergelder's one-and-a-half numbers and is truly funny in the part. On the other hand, Michael Crawford's thin, cartoonish voice is quite off-putting in "Put On Your Sunday Clothes," "It Only Takes a Moment," and Cornelius' other numbers. Whoever dubbed for Marianne McAndrew sounds lovely and sweet in Irene's songs, and it's a great gift to have the legendary Louis Armstrong on hand for one chorus of the title tune. The arrangements and conducting, by the well-respected Lennie Hayton and Lionel Newman, are fine for the most part. But given Streisand's miscasting and Crawford's uncommonly weird sound, this is one of the most problematic recordings of *Hello, Dolly!* on the market.

Touring/Broadway Cast, 1994 (Varèse Sarabande) Not recommended.

This album of a touring production that eventually got to Broadway is most unfortunate. Recorded when she was over seventy, Carol Channing sounds even older here; I heard her sing far better in live performance several years later, so she must have been tired and/or under the weather for the recording sessions. Jay Garner is lots of fun as Vandergelder, and Michael DeVries, with his ringing tenor, is probably the most felicitously cast Cornelius on record, but the poorly controlled belting of Florence Lacey is all wrong for Irene's songs. The orchestra sounds relatively small and is not very well recorded, with the percussion far too prominent. Skip it. —MICHAEL PORTANTIERE

HENRY, SWEET HENRY
Original Broadway Cast, 1967 (ABC-Paramount/Varèse Sarabande) ★★

Nora Johnson's novel *The World of Henry Orient* and the subsequent film that she wrote with her father, Nunnally, were marvelous stories of two girls enjoying and anguishing over their adolescence, but the stage-musical version was a big disappointment. That's mostly because of Bob Merrill's score, his first misfire after several good outings. Val (Robin Wilson) and Gil (Neva Small) have a schoolgirl crush on avant-garde pianist Henry Orient (Don Ameche), who is—to his credit!—more interested in women his own age. The ballad "In Some Little World" is melodious, and "Here I Am" is rather pretty. "I Wonder How It Is (to Dance With a Boy)" is a nice waltz that makes you hunger to see what choreographer Michael Bennett must have done with it. All this sweetness is interrupted by a genuine Nazi anthem sung by Alice Playten: "Nobody Steps on Kafritz," in which Val and Gil's nemesis makes her position known. Eddie Sauter's orchestrations try hard to lend some excitement to the songs, but by the time you reach "Weary Near to Dyin'"—a condescending comment on hippie life—you may be shaking your head in sympathy with the song's title. And there are still five cuts to go. —PETER FILICHIA

HERE'S LOVE
Original Broadway Cast, 1963 (Columbia/Sony) ★★

Here is an industrial-strength musical version of the Christmas movie classic *Miracle on 34th Street*. Directed by its producer Stuart Ostrow after Norman Jewison departed during the tryout, *Here's Love* was Meredith Willson's third Broadway effort, following *The Music Man* and *The Unsinkable Molly Brown*. It was helped along to a 334-performance run by a fine cast, a healthy advance sale, and a sumptuous production that featured choreographer Michael Kidd's re-creation of the Macy's Thanksgiving Day Parade. The album magnifies the show's major flaw: its middling score, which will likely remind the listener of better songs from previous musicals by Willson, who wrote this show's book, music, and lyrics. Things start off promisingly enough with "The Big Clown Balloons." There's also a perky title song that's determined to blast its way into every theatergoer's heart. But then Willson resorts to interpolating his old hit "It's Beginning to Look a Lot Like Christmas," a Yuletide chestnut and the most memorable tune on the album. Otherwise, the score consists of generic songs that could work just as well in Act I or Act II or even be dropped into any other so-so musical. But, uninspired as the score is, at least it's well presented here in bright orchestrations by Don Walker and dance-music arrangements by Peter Howard. Janis Paige brings considerable warmth and zest to such mediocre material as the "Look, Little Girl" reprise. Her pitch-approximate intonation and frequent switching of vocal registers in "My State" make for a highly individual sound, but her charisma is irresistible. Craig Stevens and the men gamely work to put over "She Hadda Go Back," salvaged from what must have been the bottom drawer of Willson's trunk. Laurence Naismith and Valerie Lee also give appealing performances. — MORGAN SILLS

HER FIRST ROMAN
Studio Cast, 1993 (Lockett-Palmer) ★

Ervin Drake's score for this show doesn't actually contain terrible songs; it's just that they're terrible for an adaptation of George Bernard Shaw's *Caesar and Cleopatra*. The title of the opening number—"What Are We Doing in Egypt?"—might well prompt us to ask: What are these *songs* doing in Egypt? That mismatch is why a quarter-century had to pass before someone made a full-fledged recording of this 1968 flop. As Caesar, Richard Kiley sings of being in "The Dangerous Age," where he's smitten with the sex-kitten Cleopatra, played by Leslie Uggams. Her songs include "I Cannot Make Him Jealous (I Have Tried)," with its frustrating stop-and-start melody; "Many Young Men From Now," which sounds like a running-up-and-down-the-scale vocal exercise; and, most atrociously, "The Wrong Man's the Right Man for Me," which calls to mind a snazzy nightclub song and has absolutely nothing to do with ancient Egypt. Similarly, the title song is far too Jerry Hermanish for the period—not to mention that a Shaw-inspired musical should have opted for a more elegant title. Just when the listener is convinced that things could not possibly get worse, out comes the most awful item of all: "I Fell in With Evil Companions," an anachronistic rouser that Caesar and his soldiers sing for no apparent reason. It was dropped during the Boston tryout, but it's included here for better or worse—with an emphasis on the latter. — PETER FILICHIA

HIGH BUTTON SHOES
Original Broadway Cast, 1947 (RCA) ★★★

This twenty-four-minute cast album of *High Button Shoes* contains only eight of the score's fourteen tunes; that's all that could fit on both sides of four 78-rpm records. Two of the show's numbers became very popular: the soft-shoe "I Still Get Jealous" and the polka "Papa, Won't You Dance With Me," both duets for Nanette Fabray and the now-forgotten Jack McCauley. But these songs have pretty much faded from memory; they and the score as a whole, with music by Jule Styne (his first Broadway hit) and lyrics by Sammy Cahn (his only Broadway hit), are as old-fashioned as the show's title. The secondary lovers get two very arch love ballads and McCauley sings lead in a nice, swirling waltz. The other three songs feature Phil Silvers: He plays (what else?) a lovable con man who's fixing a football game in "Nobody Died for Dear Old Rutgers," giving a family a new car (because he traded them out of their valuable land) in "There's Nothing Like a Model T," and extolling the charms of the beach (because he's managed to escape the law) in "On a Sunday by the Sea." That beach is the setting for the still-talked-about, much-praised "Mack Sennett Ballet" choreographed by Jerome Robbins; alas, the music for it is not on this disc, but that's what the cast album of *Jerome Robbins' Broadway* is for. (Note: RCA's CD transfer of *High Button Shoes* was only briefly available.)   — PETER FILICHIA

HIGH SPIRITS
Original Broadway Cast, 1964 (ABC-Paramount/MCA) ★★★

Noël Coward's martini-dry farce *Blithe Spirit* was turned into a brassy, uptempo musical by songwriters-librettists Hugh Martin and Timothy Gray; if the result is a bit disconcerting, it's still a droll entertainment, directed by Coward. Edward Woodward is Charles Condomine, whose experiments with spiritualism accidentally conjure the spirit of his first wife, Elvira (Tammy Grimes), much to the horror of his current spouse, Ruth (Louise Troy). Along for the ride is Beatrice Lillie as the bizarre medium Madame Arcati. The songs are generally very aggressive—Harry Zimmerman's orchestrations are hell-bent on turning this piece of fluff into a blockbuster—yet they're also witty and melodic. Grimes gets the choice material, including the lighthearted warning "You'd Better Love Me," the introspective "Something Tells Me," and the wacky jet-set spoof "Faster Than Sound." She absolutely sizzles when describing her social life on the astral plane in "Home Sweet Heaven" ("Delilah's dreary / But Samson's handsome / And with his good looks / Robin Hood looks fit for ransom"). Fans claim that you had to see Lillie perform to get her, but she's fun in her recordings of "Go Into Your Trance" and "Something Is Coming to Tea," and especially when singing sweet nothings to her Ouija board in "Talking to You." In less flamboyant roles, Woodward and Troy are models of urbanity.

Original London Cast, 1964 (Pye) ★★★

Coward tried again, this time without Lillie, and what was a nervous hit in New York was a flat-out flop in London. This cast album isn't bad but it lacks the exciting personalities of the New York original. Tammy Grimes, with her smoky voice and singular delivery, is much missed. Her replacement, Marti Stevens, does not for a moment suggest the eccentric, ectoplasmic Elvira. Cicely Courtneidge is fun as Madame Arcati and Dennis Quilley is a really first-rate Charles but, as Ruth, Jan Waters lacks Louise Troy's apt world-weary manner. Still, the recording is worthwhile for several reasons: "Home Sweet Heaven" has some new, even more riotous lyrics ("The King of Prussia / I call him Freddy / Is living by mistake / With Mary Baker Eddy"), and a set of bonus tracks features Coward himself singing "Something Tells Me," the ballads "If I Gave You" and "Forever and a Day," and what may be the definitive version of "Home Sweet Heaven."   —DAVID BARBOUR

HIT THE DECK!
Film Soundtrack, 1955 (MGM/TCM) ★★★

Hubert Osborne's *Shore Leave,* a dull sailors-in-port comedy from 1924, was incessantly reincarnated: as a silent movie, a Broadway musical that was filmed twice, and another movie musical with a different score. The 1936 film was the Astaire-Rogers gem *Follow the Fleet,* for which Irving Berlin wrote great songs; but Vincent Youmans' *Hit the Deck!* stage show came first (1927). With songs like "Hallelujah!" and "Sometimes I'm Happy" (lyrics by Clifford Grey and Leo Robin), this show doesn't deserve complete extinction, but in the realm of sailor musicals, it ain't *On the Town.* MGM's 1955 film version is plodding—yet the Youmans score, with others of his standards tossed in, sounds fine here as performed by a large cast full of musical pros. Perhaps it was because of CinemaScope that the script was padded with three musical couples, all of whom get a crack at the songs: Jane Powell and Vic Damone, Tony Martin and Ann Miller, Debbie Reynolds and Russ Tamblyn (dubbed by Rex Dennis). Also on hand is the enormous-voiced Kay Armen. Damone and Martin were singers, not actors, so there is more vocal tone than theater in their performances—though it's certainly gorgeous tone. But there's sure plenty of theatricality in Ann Miller's "Lady From the Bayou." Miller also has fun with "Keepin' Myself for You," written by Youmans for the first (1930) film version of *Hit the Deck!* Powell and Reynolds are no slouches either, and the ear-popping early stereo soundtrack is given a fine TCM presentation on CD.   —RICHARD BARRIOS

HOLD ONTO YOUR HATS
Studio Cast, 1980 (Painted Smiles) ★★★

This Ben Bagley recording, originally issued as *E.Y. Harburg Revisited,* is neither terrific nor terrible; it sounds rather like a mid-'60s Off-Broadway flop revival cast album of the 1940 Al Jolson vehicle *Hold Onto Your Hats* with a bunch of other Harburg songs thrown in. It has some marvelous tunes by Burton Lane. When you hear "The World Is In My Arms" in the overture, you'll wonder, "Where has this song been all my life?"—but when you hear the "Yip" Harburg lyric, which is not very good, you'll know why the number never became a standard. Some of the songs, such as "Life Was Pie for the Pioneer," may not amount to much but are filled with lyrical fun. And some of the other songs are simply swell: "Walking Along, Minding My Business," "There's a Great Day Comin' Mañana," the rhythmically irresistible "Don't Let It Get You Down," and "Would You Be So Kindly?" Helen Gallagher, Carlton Carpenter, and Arthur Siegel are the saucy principal performers. Siegel, Tammy Grimes, Patrice Munsel, and Harburg himself sing the remaining thirteen obscure songs that fill out the rest of the disc.   —DAVID WOLF

HONK!
Original Scarborough Cast, 1998 (Dress Circle) ★★★

Welcome to the duck yard, "Where life is nice and steady / Till we're plucked and oven-ready" and where Ida, a young mom, hatches an egg containing a distinctly odd duck—he is, in fact, the Ugly Duckling. Welcome also to the English songwriting team of George Stiles (music) and Anthony Drewe (lyrics), whose charming adaptation of the Hans Christian Andersen tale was one of the most interesting British musical theater pieces in years. (The show caused a stir in 2000, when it took the Olivier Award for Best Musical away from *The Lion King*.) *Honk!* follows the Ugly Duckling as he grows up scorned, wanders away, is menaced by a cat, meets a lovely swan, and undergoes various adventures before reuniting with his loved ones. The songs radiate optimism and humor; they're clever and sophisticated without being showy. There's also real feeling in such numbers as "Hold Your Head Up High" and "Every Tear a Mother Cries." Other highlights include "Look at Him," about the perils of being different, and "You Can Play With Your Food," sung by that evil cat. The main problem here is length: There are too many songs for this slender tale to bear. The cast, from the Stephen Joseph Theatre in Scarborough, England (run by playwright Alan Ayckbourn), is appealing, especially Richard Dempsey as the Ugly Duckling and Kristin Marks as Ida. But the names to remember are Stiles and Drewe. Let's hope we'll be hearing more from them.

Music Theatre of Wichita Cast, 2001 (MTW) ★★★

In this debut American production, some of the distinctively English humor of *Honk!* is lost, but John Cameron's expanded orchestrations are even more enjoyable. A solid cast of pros puts over the material with brio: Arthur W. Marks provides touching vocals as the Ugly Duckling; Susan Hofflander is a lovely Ida; Josh Prince has a campy sneer as the Cat; and La Quin Groves, as a bullfrog, has a field day with "Warts and All," an anthem to self-love that comes complete with children's chorus. Some of the more whimsical numbers play better on this disc—especially "The Wild Goose Chase," which spoofs airline-travel clichés as a flock of geese prepare for takeoff. Marks also offers a heartfelt rendition of "Now I've Seen You," the Ugly Duckling's declaration of love to a fetching female swan. It's still an overlong and perhaps oversophisticated children's musical, but *Honk!* should be embraced by family audiences everywhere, and this disc contains many moments of fun for all to enjoy.　　　　　—DAVID BARBOUR

HONKY-TONK HIGHWAY
Original Off-Broadway Cast, 1994 (Boebe) ★★

How much mediocre country music can you take if it's terrifically well performed? That's the barometer of how much you'll enjoy this recording. Robert Nassif-Lindsey (a.k.a. Robert Lindsey Nassif and other variations on his name) wrote a series of old-style country-western songs for this "mountain musical." Richard Berg is credited as librettist, with Nassif-Lindsey listed for "additional dialogue," but the CD gives no hint of a plot. As for the songs themselves: "Follow Where the Music Goes" is reasonably catchy, "Baby, I Love Your Biscuits" is sort of fun; and "Easier to Sing Than Say" is kind of pretty. The cast of actors-singers-musicians includes a few stage notables in Sean McCourt, Erin Hill, and Matthew Bennett—alongside Rick Leon, Kevin Fox, and musical director-arranger-performer Steve Steiner. Rich Blacker and Andy Taylor are heard in a few tracks as extra instrumentalists, with Nassif-Lindsey occasionally popping up on piano a few times. The disc is certainly a testament to the composer-lyricist's range, *Honky-Tonk Highway* being very different from his work on two other musicals: *3hree* and *Opal*.　　　　　—SETH CHRISTENFELD

HOUSE OF FLOWERS
Original Broadway Cast, 1954 (Columbia/Sony) ★★★★★

The five stars are for this fine 2003 CD reissue. Accept no imitations. The cast album of Harold Arlen and Truman Capote's flop musical set in a West Indian bordello had always been stunning and unique; the steel drums and whistles of the overture announce a 1950s musical with a sound like no other. The opening number, a slow lament for the girls of the house, promises an unusual frankness for the era, and Capote's lyrics ("Drowsin', dreamin,' moonbeamin' / 'bout the thing we're supreme in") are amazing for a beginner. Pearl Bailey, owning the stage as Madame Fleur, throws her weight around in "One Man Ain't Quite Enough" and caps the number with an outrageous ad lib that passed instantly into cast-album legend. A teenaged Diahann Carroll, nursing a cold for the recording session, nonetheless oozes charm and unselfconscious allure in "A Sleepin' Bee." And that's just the first fifteen minutes! (More oddball cast album history is made later, when Carroll's voice gives out near the end of "I Never Has Seen Snow," and Arlen has to dub her last high note.) It's a spellbinding score, quirkily orchestrated by Ted Royal and thrillingly conducted by Jerry Arlen. For this CD edition of a treasured recording, Columbia/Sony remastered everything: made the audio crisper; put the tracks in their stage order; found a longer, more sumptuous take of "Mardi Gras"; let the tape run a few seconds longer on "Waitin'"; and inserted a "Mardi Gras Waltz" from a Percy Faith album. There are bonus tracks—a single of "Two Ladies in de Shade of de Banana Tree" by cast member Enid Mosier, a tape of Arlen's first draft of "A Sleepin' Bee," and Capote reading an excerpt from his source-material short story—plus a booklet that contains some long-unseen photos from the gorgeous original production. The cumulative effect is compelling. For a half-century, people have heard this amazing score and wondered why such a show failed. We're lucky, at least, that *House of Flowers* yielded one of the great cast albums.

Broadway Cast, 1968 (United Artists/no CD) ★

Original producer Saint Subber unwisely ordered a major rewrite of *House of Flowers*, scaled the new production down, then coughed out this hard-to-find cast album in shrill stereo. These islanders appear more willfully ignorant than disarmingly unworldly. Some great songs ("One Man Ain't Quite Enough," "Gonna Leave Off Wearin' My Shoes") are missing, some lackluster new ones (not entirely by Harold Arlen and Truman Capote) are inserted, and the modest calypso-band arrangements sound like toy whistles next to Ted Royal's great originals. The musical director, Joe Raposo, plays it so safe that it sounds like he's warming up for *Sesame Street*. It's not the cast's fault: Yolande Bavan is a charming Ottilie, Thelma Oliver and Hope Clarke are lusty sidekicks, and Novella Nelson gamely grunts out something called "Madame Tango's Particular Tango." Replacing Pearl Bailey as Madame Fleur, Josephine Premice is deprived of some of the character's best material; "Don't Like Goodbyes," which was evidently written for Ottilie and swiped by Bailey, is here restored to its rightful owner. Premice's unidentifiable accent and inimitable, scratchy singing are ingratiating. Still, the squirm-inducing moments in this wilted *Flowers* far outweigh the soul-satisfying ones. If there's an object lesson in how to ruin a classic score, this is it. —MARC MILLER

HOWARD CRABTREE'S WHOOP-DEE-DOO!
Original Off-Broadway Cast, 1995 (RCA) ★★

This show was the brainchild of costume designer Howard Crabtree, whose outlandishly funny costumes were the real stars of the production—each outfit more elaborate than the last yet all looking as if they cost pennies to build. Throughout, Crabtree (playing himself) is heckled by Jay Rogers, who questions his taste and preaches that "less is more." This gives the revue a sort of structure and also a good finish: Howard uses "Less Is More" as a finale that belies its title, going on and on and on. The songs include one about the much-married Elizabeth Taylor; one featuring the Invisible Dance Company ("They're the biggest no-talents I've never seen," complains Rogers, "I can see right through them!"); and a piece about "Sgt. Sirloin and his corps of patriotic potatoes" being shaken by the arrival of Private Banana ("The new recruit is a fruit!"). There's also a mini-musical about Nancy Reagan's life and a number called "You Are My Idol," in which an airplane accidentally drops a crate of cast albums on a tribe of primitives who assume it's an offering from the gods and begin worshipping/imitating Ethel Merman, Carol Channing, and Rex Harrison. The sensibility throughout is matter-of-factly gay but not so much as to make straight folks uncomfortable. The material was mostly written by Mark Waldrop and Dick Gallagher but there are also contributions by David Rambo, Peter Morris, Brad Ellis, Eric Schorr, Bruce Sussman, and Jack Feldman. —DAVID WOLF

HOW NOW, DOW JONES
Original Broadway Cast, 1968 (RCA) ★★★

The story of a misfit who, rather than committing suicide, decides to try his hand at selling stock, this show made audiences laugh for one season and is hardly remembered today. But the cast album reveals what a creative collaboration the prolific film composer Elmer Bernstein had with the devilishly clever lyricist Carolyn Leigh. *How Now, Dow Jones* begins with a clever explanation of the workings of Wall Street ("ABC"), then deals with various characters' romantic problems. The talented belter Marlyn Mason and the wonderfully zany Brenda Vaccaro raise their voices in "They Don't Make 'Em Like That Anymore." After spending the night with the suicidal Charley (Tony Roberts), Mason's character sings the excellent ballad "Walk Away." Charley decides not to jump out of a window when some Wall Streeters tell him that all he must do to succeed is "Gawk, Tousle and Shucks." He goes off to sell stocks to widows, which leads to the show-stopping ensemble march "Step to the Rear." Also among the score's highlights are "Rich Is Better," "Shakespeare Lied," and "He's Here." —JEFFREY DUNN

HOW TO STEAL AN ELECTION
Original Off-Broadway Cast, 1968 (RCA/no CD) ★

A young black man (Clifton Davis) and a young white woman (Carole Demas), both veterans of the disastrous 1968 Democratic National Convention in Chicago, somehow meet Calvin Coolidge (D. R. Allen), who essentially gives them a lesson in the various forms of chicanery that resulted in the election of many American presidents. Combining authentic songs from past political campaigns with Oscar Brand's new book songs for the two young idealists, *How to Steal an Election* has Cal trying to convince the kids that at least some trickery is necessary for the system to work. (After the young woman sings "Mr. Might've Been," about President Kennedy, Coolidge reveals that her hero was not above some questionable political maneuvers.) The new songs are of varying quality, the old songs are interesting and sometimes funny, and the show's subject matter is surprisingly topical in the early years of the twenty-first century. But, of course, the lesson imparted here—that stealing elections is somehow a good thing— is highly debatable. —DAVID WOLF

HOW TO SUCCEED IN BUSINESS WITHOUT REALLY TRYING
Original Broadway Cast, 1961 (RCA) ★★★

George S. Kaufman said that "satire is what closes on Saturday night," but that certainly did not apply to *How to Succeed in Business Without Really Trying*. In its original Broadway run, the show saw three-and-a-half-years' worth of Saturday nights. With an incisive book by Abe Burrows, Jack Weinstock, and Willie Gilbert, this is a musical comedy that's truly funny—and it's got a great Frank Loesser score, from the mock-romantic "Happy to Keep His Dinner Warm" and the intentionally syrupy "Love From a Heart of Gold" to the caffeine-inspired "Coffee Break." Other highlights are the business-philosophy numbers "The Company Way" and "A Secretary Is Not a Toy." Judging by this recording, the original cast was energetic, but star Robert Morse is an acquired taste—and there's a lot of him here. Although he has the right kind of youthful ebullience for go-getter J. Pierrepont Finch, his singing is best described as "characterful" rather than good. Morse's leading lady, Bonnie Scott, tends to bray Rosemary's songs with an affected tone. But Charles Nelson Reilly as Finch's rival Bud Frump and Rudy Vallee as company president J. B. Biggley come across much better, as do Sammy Smith and Virginia Martin in their supporting roles. Overall, *How to Succeed . . .* succeeds nicely.

Film Soundtrack, 1967 (United Artists/MGM) ★★

Several of the original Broadway cast members appear in the film version of *How to Succeed,* but Michele Lee plays Rosemary and she does a much better job with the songs than Bonnie Scott, sounding warmer and far more natural. However, she doesn't have many songs: "Happy to Keep His Dinner Warm" and "Paris Original" were both cut from the movie score. Lee does perform a solo version of "I Believe in You" but is otherwise heard only in the trio "Been a Long Day." Robert Morse, Rudy Vallee, Sammy Smith, John Myhers, and Ruth Kobart (as J. B. Biggley's executive secretary) all sound good here, and although Anthony Teague doesn't have Charles Nelson Reilly's nervous energy, he's fine as Frump. The "Coffee Break" number is on this soundtrack album (but is not in the film). Although the incompleteness of this recording diminishes its appeal, avid Loesser fans may value it.

Broadway Cast, 1995 (RCA) ★★

Completeness is certainly not an issue here; this CD has the most material of any *How to Succeed* recording. In addition to the voiceover passages (read by Walter Cronkite!), there's some incidental music, a number of reprises, and even the Pirate Dance. The disc also boasts new orchestrations by Danny Troob that are even brassier than the originals, a reworked "Brotherhood of Man" with a lot of scatting and a new second-act opener: and a reprise of the title song in place of the cut "Cinderella, Darling" (with new lyrics written by the production's director, Des McAnuff). If these changes aren't really improvements, neither are they significant detriments. The cast is pretty good, with Megan Mullally an ideal Rosemary and Victoria Clark providing the best-sung Smitty to date. Jeff Blumenkrantz is Frump, Lillias White is Miss Jones, and other roles are well done by Ronn Carroll, Gerry Vichi, and Jonathan Freeman. Luba Mason's Hedy is a bit too vacant, though she makes quite a vocal effect when she slides up a full octave at the end of "Love From a Heart of Gold." But then there's Matthew Broderick, singing and acting in the same constipated style that he would later bring to *The Producers.* Although he hits all the right notes in Finch's songs and only sounds strained a couple of times, he never sounds real.   —MATTHEW MURRAY

THE HUMAN COMEDY

Original Cast, 1984 (Kilmarnock Records, 2CDs) ★★

This show flopped big-time when producer Joseph Papp transferred it to Broadway after a run at his Public Theater. Although billed as "a modern opera by Galt MacDermot and William Dumaresq," *The Human Comedy* is really more of an oratorio, complete with a Greek-style chorus. Based on a novel by William Saroyan, this musical tale of a small-town American family during World War II might be considered overly sentimental. Some of the lyrics are poetic, but many are awkward if not borderline illiterate—for example, "Your voice is in fine, fine fetter." (What?) However, MacDermot's music is so divine throughout that the show's flaws seem relatively unimportant. Among the many highlights: "Ulysses Reaches the Crossing," "Beautiful Music," "I've Known a Lot of Guys," and the boogie-woogie duet "I Let Him Kiss Me Once." The score contains at least two hymns, "When I Am Lost" and "Everlasting," that have absolutely nothing to do with the action, but they're so lovely that you probably won't mind. The cast is a mixed bag: Bonnie Koloc, Stephen Geoffreys, Mary Elizabeth Mastrantonio, and Don Kehr are all fine as various Macauley family members. Also good are Leata Galloway as Diana Steel, Caroline Peyton as Mary Arena, and David Johnson as the trainman. On the other hand, young Josh Blake is almost unlistenable as Ulysses Macauley and Rex Smith is vocally miscast as Spangler. The sound quality of the recording is odd (apparently, it was made onstage with no audience present). As for the CD transfer, be aware that these two discs are not tracked at all, so the only way to access particular songs is to use search buttons on your player. Contributing to the slapdash feel of the enterprise, the accompanying booklet leaves out the recording date and repeatedly misspells Saroyan's name (as "Saroyen"). *The Human Comedy* definitely deserves to be heard but, given all that's wrong with this expensive, privately produced recording, you might want to borrow it from a friend rather than buy it.

—MICHAEL PORTANTIERE

I CAN GET IT FOR YOU WHOLESALE
Original Broadway Cast, 1962 (Columbia/Sony) ★★★

This show has gone down in history for having launched the career of Barbra Streisand, but there's so much more here. Jerome Weidman adapted his own novel about a Seventh Avenue go-getter who sells his soul for *shmattehs*. Composer-lyricist Harold Rome's score percolates with soul. Elliot Gould stars as schemer Harry Bogen, displaying plenty of nasty vitality in numbers like "The Way Things Are" and "The Sound of Money." This is, however, an ensemble show filled with vividly etched character portraits. Marilyn Cooper, as the girl who loves Harry, delivers two wry ballads: "When Gemini Meets Capricorn" and "Who Knows?" Lillian Roth, as Harry's doting mother, offers chicken soup for the soul in the introspective "Too Soon" and the chilling "Eat a Little Something." And yes, Streisand hits the comedy number "Miss Marmelstein" out of the park. Rome's lyrics evoke a world of middle-class Jews who work in the garment trade, while his music merges jazz with Yiddish harmonies and a touch of Leonard Bernstein. Sid Ramin's percussive orchestrations are among the most unique of the period. It's an underrated, distinctive achievement. —DAVID BARBOUR

I CAN'T KEEP RUNNING IN PLACE
**Original Off-Broadway Cast, 1981
(Painted Smiles) ★**

This musical about a six-week women's assertiveness training workshop was little more than an audition piece for Barbara Schottenfeld, who wrote the book, music, and lyrics. The songs are decent enough, even if the music disappears from your mind the moment after you've heard it, but the book just isn't there, and the characters are minimally delineated: the rich and acerbic one, the fat one, the smug student, the doormat, and so on. They occasionally take part in telephone conversations with husbands and children, but none of them really does anything except sing. The songs are sincere and spirited. As performed by Helen Gallagher, Joy Franz, Evalyn Baron, Phyllis Newman, and especially Marcia Rodd in the role of the troubled therapist, they are momentarily effective. But the musical numbers are out there on their own, without plot or characters to back them up. —DAVID WOLF

ALL-TIME FAVORITES OF
PLAYWRIGHT-LIBRETTIST

Terrence McNally

1. The Pajama Game
2. A Funny Thing Happened on the Way to the Forum
3. Gypsy
4. My Fair Lady
5. Show Boat
6. Annie Get Your Gun
7. The King and I
8. Guys and Dolls
9. The Music Man
10. Porgy and Bess

I DO! I DO!
Original Broadway Cast, 1966 (RCA) ★★★★

A two-character musical based on the play *The Fourposter* by Jan de Hartog, *I Do! I Do!* contains numerous moments that may cause listeners to exclaim "Ah hah!" in recognition of similar moments in their own lives—as when Robert Preston sings, "My daughter is marrying . . . an idiot!" This is a score kindred to the best work of stand-up comics in that it holds a mirror up to the audience, allowing us to revel in the universality of our experiences and to feel the enjoyable shock of recognition. Of course, it doesn't hurt to have Mary Martin and Robert Preston as your leads. This energetic, highly theatrical recording is a knockout; you'd think that listeners would grow tired of a two-person musical, but Tom Jones and Harvey Schmidt have lots of surprises up their respective sleeves. Schmidt varies his rhythms and melodies wonderfully while Jones offers some rich, poetic lyrics and some remarkably funny ones as well, such as "A Well Known Fact" and "Nobody's Perfect." The requisite romantic songs include the hit "My Cup Runneth Over." Then there are the wry numbers, among them, "Where Are the Snows of Yesteryear?" and "Someone Needs Me."

Off-Broadway Cast, 1996 (Varèse Sarabande) ★★

This disc stars Broadway stalwarts Karen Ziemba and David Garrison as the long-married Agnes and Michael. Both sing well, but many listeners will feel that the piano reduction of the score renders this cast album noncompetitive with the original disc. —KEN BLOOM

IF LOVE WERE ALL
Original Off-Broadway Cast, 1999 (Varèse Sarabande) ★★★★

In a small-print introductory note, this diversion's creator Sheridan Morley recalls that Noël Coward and Gertrude Lawrence acted together only twice, in *Private Lives* and *Tonight at 8:30.* At that, their performances in those vehicles were in limited London and New York runs. Yet the two were in love with each other from their first meeting, when he was thirteen, she was fourteen, and they were leaving town for a tour. The word "platonic" hardly begins to explain their devotion. In Morley's soigné revue, Harry Groener is Noël and Twiggy is Gertie. Together and separately, they toss off the master's ditties as if strewing rose petals about the luxe set of a boulevard comedy. Groener doesn't imitate Coward's purr because he needn't do so; he's got his own casual stylings. Since Lawrence was herself rather twiggy, Twiggy is a wonderful choice to sub for the legendary star. Her voice—nasal but always on pitch—is actually an improvement on Lawrence's. Twiggy solos in "Parisian Pierrot" and duets with Groener in "You Were There" and "I'll See You Again." Groener slides through "Mad Dogs and Englishmen" and "Don't Put Your Daughter on the Stage, Mrs. Worthington." The talented pair also croon, banter, and tap-dance in "Has Anybody Seen Our Ship?" —DAVID FINKLE

I HAD A BALL
Original Broadway Cast, 1964 (Mercury/Decca) ★★★

With Buddy Hackett starring as a Coney Island psychic who screws up his friends' love lives, it's safe to say that *I Had a Ball* doesn't have a thought in its silly little head. Nobody really liked Jerome Chodorov's libretto, but the score by Jack Lawrence and Stan Freeman is enjoyable. The songs often seem shoehorned into the plot, yet the melodies are jazzy with an edge of dark sophistication—and with Richard Kiley and Karen Morrow on board, what could be bad?

The flop-plagued Morrow, one of Broadway's most distinctive voices, delivers thrilling renditions of the title tune and the mordantly cynical "I've Got Everything I Want." Kiley scores with the rueful eleven-o'clock number "Fickle Finger of Fate." Other fun items include the gospel rouser "Faith," the biting "Neighborhood" (delivered with gusto by Rosetta La Noire), and the moody quartet "Can It Be Possible?" Hackett is barely present on the disc but, after hearing his big comedy number "Dr. Freud," we can only be happy about that. Philip J. Lang's brassy, jazzy orchestrations add to the fun. This is the kind of score that makes show fans treasure flops. Bonus tracks include two studio versions by Morrow of the title tune and the ballad "Almost," plus instrumental renditions of two cut numbers—"Lament" and "Be a Phony"—by the Lester Lanin Orchestra.   —DAVID BARBOUR

ILLYA DARLING
Original Broadway Cast, 1967 (United Artists/no CD) Not recommended.
Having had an art-house film hit with *Never on Sunday,* writer-director Jules Dassin and the Mrs., otherwise known as Melina Mercouri, teamed up again for the stage musical version, which ran over three hundred performances before vanishing from Broadway's collective memory. The cast album—available only in the original LP format and hard to find—doesn't contain a plot synopsis, but if you've seen the glorious film, you'll get the idea. Once again, Mercouri is Illya, the happiest prostitute on the island of Piraeus. This time, Orson Bean is Homer, the dopey American intellectual who wants to introduce her to culture and the finer things in life. The score, with music by Manos Hadjidakis (who did the film) and lyrics by Joe Darion, is heavy with bouzoukis (Ralph Burns orchestrated) and lusty, life-affirming numbers. The only song that stands out is "Never on Sunday"—which, of course, comes from the movie. Mercouri's smoky voice and sexy intonations are fun to hear; but Bean's numbers, "Golden Land" and "I Think She Needs Me," are pretty dire. And "Medea Tango," which tries to replicate one of the funniest moments in the film (when Illya explains Greek tragedy to Homer), falls flat. The actress Despo, playing a character named Despo, sings "I'll Never Lay Down Anymore"—a title that tells all. There are also silly local-color items such as "Heaven Help the Sailors on a Night Like This."   —DAVID HARBOUR

I LOVE MY WIFE
Original Broadway Cast, 1977 (Atlantic/DRG) ★
Wife-swapping in Trenton, New Jersey, was already a dated topic in 1977, but this miniature sex farce was the surprise hit of the season. Audiences were taken with the zippy score by Cy Coleman and Michael Stewart (the latter also wrote the book) and by Gene Saks' clever staging, which featured four onstage musicians commenting on the action involving two inept pairs of married swingers. The show launched the career of comic actor Lenny Baker, who sadly died a few years later without attaining stardom. But, a quarter-century on, many of the songs—with their coy sex jokes and titles like "Love Revolution," "Sexually Free," "Ev'rybody Today Is Turning On," and "Married Couple Seeks Married Couple"—come across as so many outtakes from a PG-13 version of *Oh! Calcutta!* Coleman is, as always, a true pro, and Stewart's lyrics are generally nimble and literate; a few numbers are first-class, including the rueful country ballad "Someone Wonderful I Missed" and the touching title tune. The second-act opener, "Hey There, Good Times," is classic Coleman—an irresistible ragtime stomp with delicious Stewart lyrics—but has virtually nothing to do with the show. The cast, including the young Joanna Gleason, James Naughton, and Ilene Graff, is fine.   —DAVID BARBOUR

I LOVE YOU, YOU'RE PERFECT, NOW CHANGE
Off-Broadway Cast, 1996 (Varèse Sarabande) ★★★★

"Oh my God, that's *me* up there!" is an audience whisper heard often at this forever-running musical revue, the winning work of Joe DiPietro (lyrics) and Jimmy Roberts (music). Unapologetically middlebrow and critic-proof, it's not the wittiest or most profound examination of male-female relationships ever written, but it's a parade of good revue ideas smartly developed: nerds on a date, macho posturing, the straight-single-man shortage, baby-talking parents, geriatric romance, and more. Roberts relies on pastiche—some Lite-FM rock here, a sweet ballad there—and the music supports rather than overwhelms the lyrics. DiPietro rhymes a bit lazily and sometimes stumbles to weak endings, but the general tenor of the songs is likeable. No one in the cast of four stands out, but they all sing well and slip effortlessly in and out of varied characterizations: Danny Burstein as an alpha male blubbering through a chick flick; Jennifer Simard as a mousy date; Melissa Weil bemoaning a bridesmaid's plight ("For Tabitha, I wore taffeta / You never should, people laugh at ya"); and Robert Roznowski in the generic but affecting "Shouldn't I Be Less in Love With You?" Roberts did his own vocal and instrumental arrangements, which are as modest and to the point as the show itself.   —MARC MILLER

I'M GETTING MY ACT TOGETHER AND TAKING IT ON THE ROAD
Original Off-Broadway Cast, 1978 (Columbia/Fynsworth Alley) ★★

The book and lyrics are by Gretchen Cryer, who also plays the lead character, Heather; the music is by Nancy Ford. The two teamed previously on unsuccessful shows, but *I'm Getting My Act Together* finally put them on the map. Heather—well played and sung by Cryer—is a soap-opera star who's rehearsing for the opening of her cabaret act. All the songs are presented as part of the rehearsal, which is attended by Heather's manager and old friend, Joe (a nonsinging role). Heather and her two female backup singers do all the vocalizing with an occasional assist from a band member. The year was 1978, when many women were working toward self-actualization; so the songs, all ostensibly written by Heather, are autobiographical, and Joe has issues with them. The song titles suggest their content: "Miss America," "Strong Woman Number," "Smile (for Daddy)," "Lonely Lady," and "Old Friend," now a cabaret classic. Cryer's terrific backup ladies are Betty Aberlin and Margot Rose. The band includes Don Scardino as the young guitarist Jake, who sings "In a Simple Way, I Love You" sweetly. The eleven songs (plus one reprise) are all in a late-1970s pop vein and are given no theatrical context on the recording, which is an easy listen but not a theatrically engaging one.

Original London Cast, 1981 (JAY) ★★★★

This recording tries to impart a feeling of the entire show. Much dialogue is included, and the nonsinging character Joe is an essential part of the proceedings. The song list is augmented by a version of "In a Simple Way, I Love You" for Heather and a fun throwaway number for Jake, "If Only Things Was Different." Diane Langton is Heather and Ben Cross is Joe. Langton's singing is solid throughout; she belts "Happy Birthday" and "Natural High" with conviction and is remarkably touching in "Old Friend" and "Dear Tom" (about Heather's ex-husband). Throughout the recording, she receives strong vocal support from Nicky Croydon and Megg Nicol. Gregg Martyn sings attractively as Jake, who flirts with Heather but is rejected because she finds him too young. (To get this plot point from the Off-Broadway cast album, you must read the synopsis.) All the songs are very well set up by the dialogue and therefore seem to have more of an emotional center; having Cross as Joe fully participate in the recorded action gives

Heather an obstacle to play against, so the listener is aware of what is at stake within each number. The argument over whether cast albums should include dialogue is endless, but comparing this recording with the one reviewed above demonstrates how a show's songs come across with greater strength on disc when put in their dramatic context.　　—JEFFREY DUNN

INNER CITY
Original Broadway Cast, 1971 (RCA/no CD) ★★★★

Perhaps the source material was too obscure for audiences to really understand what this show was about. What poet Eve Merriam originally wrote was *Inner City Mother Goose,* a new take on nursery rhymes from an urban, sometimes violent perspective. So the familiar "Fee Fi Fo Fum" was followed by the less-expected "I smell the blood of violence to come"; and "Now I lay me down to sleep" was joined with "and I pray the double lock will keep." Helen Miller set the poems to theatrical rock music; most of them last a minute or less, but they're memorable minutes. In "Hushabye Baby," an unwed teenager sings about the child she'll soon have, and it sounds like something that Brecht and Weill might have written had they been around in the early 1970s. There are also "On This Rock," a statement of urban pride; the jaunty "City Life"; and the pulsating "Law and Order," which the TV series of the same title should have used as its theme song. "Deep in the Night" and "It's My Belief" are solid anthems that helped win Linda Hopkins a Tony Award as Best Featured Actress. Then there's "The Hooker," in which a prostitute sings, "If they want to hear a story, then I give out with a story . . . I need ten dollars for grandma, who is coughing and spitting up blood. But whaddaya say we cut the crap?" The same socko melody is used for both "The Pusher" and "The Pickpocket," but that last one didn't make the album. That's all right: We should be grateful that this short-run show yielded a cast recording at all.　　—PETER FILICHIA

INSIDE U.S.A.
Original Cast Members, 1948 (SHB-Show-Biz Productions/no CD) ★★★

Almost forgotten today but the second-longest-running revue of 1948, this Howard Dietz–Arthur Schwartz opus inspired by John Gunther's best-seller had a starry cast, two minor hit ballads ("Haunted Heart" and "Rhode Island Is Famous for You"), and some of the old ingenuity that peppered the team's 1930s revue output. The reconstituted cast album, assembled from scratchy 78s and topping out at twenty-eight minutes, boasts no rediscovered gems but shows off its cast ably; and the opening title number, with a lobotomized-sounding chorus exuding "The USA is gay, uproarious / In a glorious way," fully evokes mid-century nationalism. Pearl Bailey exudes her patented lazy hauteur in "Protect Me" and "Blue Grass," while Jack Haley puts over all of the playful "Rhode Island" puns ("Pencils come from Pennsylvania / Vests from Vest Virginia / And tents from Tentassee"). Beatrice Lillie plays a happy convict in "Atlanta," a deranged choral director in "Come, O Come," and a jolly reveler in "Mardi Gras." Billy Williams, not of the original company, somehow landed on the album; he delivers an undistinguished cowboy ballad. The cast of the show also included Jack Cassidy in the chorus and Carl Reiner delivering monologues but, alas, you won't hear them here.　　—MARC MILLER

INTO THE WOODS
Original Broadway Cast, 1987 (RCA) ★★★

One of Stephen Sondheim's most commercial shows, *Into the Woods* has one of the least distinctive scores he's ever written. Perhaps he wasn't really inspired by the fairy tale setting or characters, most of them lifted from famous stories, or perhaps he and librettist-director James Lapine thought that making the characters self-aware and having them face the realities of "happily ever after" was enough? Aside from an interesting song or two—"No One Is Alone" and "Children Will Listen"—there's not a lot of "here" here. Considering the setting, the tunes aren't particularly magical and some of the forced-clever lyrics ("There's no time to sit and dither / While her withers wither with her") come at the expense of character. The recording itself sounds somewhat hollow but is redeemed by a cast of top-notch performers: Bernadette Peters milks the role of the worldly wise witch for all it's worth; Joanna Gleason brings a thrilling vibe to the part of the Baker's Wife; and Chip Zien is a neurotic joy as the Baker himself. Tom Aldredge as the narrator, Kim Crosby as Cinderella, Ben Wright as Jack, Danielle Ferland as Little Red Ridinghood, and Kay McClelland and Lauren Mitchell as Cinderella's bitchy stepsisters are also great. The video recording of the original Broadway cast is a better representation of *Into the Woods,* but if you can't find it, this CD will do.

Original London Cast, 1991 (RCA) ★★★

This is a nice complement to, but not an adequate replacement for, the original Broadway album. With the exception of Julia McKenzie's fiercely acted and sung Witch, there's a stodginess exhibited by many of the leads: Ian Bartholomew and Imelda Staunton lack the distinctive personalities that Zien and Gleason brought to the roles of the Baker and Wife, and other cast members are similarly challenged by the material. A new song here for the Witch and Rapunzel—"Our Little World"—is musically attractive, but it spoils the original show's joke about Rapunzel never singing real lyrics, and it doesn't further the relationship between the two characters.

Broadway Cast, 2002 (Nonesuch) ★

Almost nothing that made the original production of *Into the Woods* charming survived in the misbegotten revival that yielded this disc. With the exception of Laura Benanti, who brings a purity to Cinderella, these performers are weak. Stephen DeRosa and Kerry O'Malley as the Baker and his Wife are personality-free, and Marylouise Burke massacres much of Jack's Mother's music. Vanessa Williams is the dullest Witch imaginable—her singing is adequate at best and grating at worst. Add to all that the thinned-down sound of Jonathan Tunick's orchestrations and the relentless tinkering with the script and score. Changes include the unnecessary (adding a second wolf and three pigs to "Hello, Little Girl"); the superfluous ("Our Little World"); the bizarre (letting Jack and Little Red chime in on what used to be Cinderella's big solo, "On the Steps of the Palace"); and the damaging (all of the venomous drama of the Witch's final number, "Last Midnight," has been removed). —MATTHEW MURRAY

IN TROUSERS
Original Off-Broadway Cast, 1979 (Original Cast Records) ★★★★★

Long before Marvin and Whizzer sang and were sung about in *March of the Falsettos, Falsettoland,* or the amalgam known and celebrated as *Falsettos,* the two guys met and experienced joy and pain in this 1979 work. The show never achieved the prominence of William Finn's other "Marvin Musicals," but it's by far the most tuneful. The Finn lyrics are tougher to understand; the opening song, "Marvin's Giddy Seizures," suggests that the show will be about an epileptic rather than a bisexual who's leaving his wife for a man (Whizzer). But, oh, what a glorious set of Finn melodies! "High School Ladies at Five O'Clock" is an infectious number that will have you rushing to your CD player to press the "Repeat" button. "Whizzer Going

Down" might be described as an Americanized version of Edith Piaf's irresistible "Milord" — and what could be a higher compliment than that? "How Marvin Eats His Breakfast" doesn't just have a memorable melody but also a fascinating lyric: We get a young child's point of view in wanting to eat *right now.* In this song and all others, Chip Zien—best known as the Baker in *Into the Woods*—is sensational. This was his first major role.   —PETER FILICHIA

I REMEMBER MAMA
Studio Cast, 1985 (Polygram) ★★★

Richard Rodgers' musical imagination persisted throughout his life, despite depression, a heart attack, and cancer of the vocal cords. His final show opened just seven months before he died. It was based on *I Remember Mama,* a play written by John Van Druten and adapted from *Mama's Bank Account,* a collection of stories by Kathryn Forbes; the play had also inspired a movie and a television series. In all its incarnations, the story is about a Norwegian family living in San Francisco around 1910. But, foremost, it's about Mama, a woman of little education who has a naturally liberal turn of mind. Rodgers wrote the musical version with librettist Thomas Meehan and lyricist-director Martin Charnin; film actress Liv Ullmann, who was not a gifted singer, played the title role. During the out-of-town tryout, producers Alexander Cohen and Hildy Parks brought in a new director, Cy Feuer, and a new lyricist, Raymond Jessel. Amid the chaos of the pre-Broadway tour, Rodgers created six new songs in two weeks. The show opened on Broadway in May 1979 to largely disparaging reviews and closed three months later. Still, *Mama* proves that even a lower-tier work by Rodgers is superior to almost anyone else's best effort, and in songs such as "You Could Not Please Me More" and "Time," the fresh music soars above the pedestrian lyrics. No cast album of the show was made; this studio recording was produced by Norman Newell, with John Yap as executive producer and Theodore S. Chapin as coordinating producer. Parts of it were recorded on either side of the Atlantic to accommodate a dream cast of American and British performers. George Hearn as Papa and George S. Irving as Uncle Chris recreate their Broadway roles; Sally Ann Howes replaces Ullmann as Mama; Ann Morrison plays Katrin, the writer who immortalizes Mama in magazine fiction; Gay Soper is Mama's benevolent sister; Patricia Routledge is Aunt Jenny; Elizabeth Seal is Aunt Sigrid; and Siân Phillips plays a British novelist. In the lively "Easy Come, Easy Go" and the acidic "It's Going to Be Good to Be Gone," Irving shows off the stuff that makes him one of the theater's great comedic assets. The recording's high point is the Routledge-Seal duet "A Most Disagreeable Man."   —CHARLES WRIGHT

IRENE
Broadway Cast, 1973 (Columbia/Sony) ★★★★

Encouraged by the success of the 1970 revisal of *No, No, Nannette,* producer Harry Rigby and colleagues reworked and mounted *Irene,* a musical that had been a hit in 1919 but had hardly ever been performed since the 1930s—even though it included such Harry Tierney-Joseph McCarthy songs as the monster hit "Alice Blue Gown." The buoyant headliner of the new *Irene* was Debbie Reynolds, who gave her pluckiest performance since *The Unsinkable Molly Brown* and helped turn the show into a hit. Happily, her gutsy portrayal is well preserved on the cast album. Reynolds' rendition of "The World Must Be Bigger Than an Avenue," a new song by Wally Harper, is dynamite. Other outstanding moments belong to George S. Irving (in a Tony Award-winning performance) and Patsy Kelly (direct from her Tony-winning triumph in *No,*

No, Nanette). More star presence is provided by Monte Markham as Donald S. Marshall III and Ruth Warrick as his mother. The recording was artfully produced by the great Thomas Z. Shepard at the peak of his expertise.

London Cast, 1976 (EMI/no CD) ★★★★

This bouncy, well-performed London *Irene* stars the excellent Australian performer Julie Anthony. The arrangements and orchestrations are almost identical to those of the Broadway revisal, and they sound bright and crisp as recorded here. Under conductor Ralph Burns' excellent baton, the chorus numbers are particularly spirited and exciting. As Irene, Anthony shows off a thrilling voice with much gusto, and she can belt out a show-stopper and then turn around and deliver a soft, tender ballad. The strong supporting cast includes Jon Pertwee, Jessie Evans, and Eric Flynn. As Donald, Flynn does an excellent job with a lovely song that wasn't in the Broadway production, "I Can Dream Can't I?" Another added treat is the ballad "If Only He Knew," persuasively rendered by Anthony. This is an unusual London cast album in that the singers sound like authentic American musical theater performers—and the sound quality of the recording is superb.

— GERARD ALESSANDRINI

IRMA LA DOUCE

Original London Cast, 1958 (Philips/no CD) ★★★★

This recording will come as something of a revelation to those who only know *Irma la Douce* from the original Broadway cast recording. While the three London stars—Elizabeth Seal, Keith Michell, and Clive Revill—and director Peter Brook were all imported to Broadway, the London recording offers a great deal of dialogue that reveals the story with more clarity than on the subsequent Broadway disc (see below). Many of the lyrics are different and there is a truly charming Act II reprise of "Our Language of Love," in which Irma expresses her feelings about Nestor while he is in prison. In the ballet, we can hear the prison break and learn of Irma's pregnancy and other plot details. The only disappointment is Seal's delivery of the title song; she does a much better job on the Broadway album. Other than that, the London LP captures the essence of a most unusual show, and the three leads are perhaps a little warmer and less slick here than they became by the time the show reached New York.

Original Broadway Cast, 1960 (Columbia/Sony) ★★★★★

One of very few French musicals to earn success in London and in New York, *Irma la Douce* went through some changes in each country, but this recording retains enough Gallic charm mixed with Broadway know-how to satisfy all but the most curmudgeonly Francophiles. That's particularly evident in the orchestrations of André Popp (additional orchestrations by Robert Ginzler, dance music by John Kander), with the obligatory accordion and a stylish xylophone often dominating. The overture is an old-fashioned attention-grabber. The opening number is "Valse Milieu," in which Clive Revill as Bob-le-Hotu—who narrates the story and plays numerous other roles—sets up the plot and defines the French words that are sprinkled throughout the piece: *poule* for prostitute, *mec* for pimp, *grisbi* for money, and so on. The fanciful tale tells how one of Irma's clients, Nestor, falls so in love with her that he wants to become her only client. The music is by Marguerite Monnot, composer of many songs popularized by Edith Piaf; the original French book and lyrics by Alexandre Breffort were cleverly adapted into English by Julian More, David Heneker, and Monty Norman. London leads Elizabeth Seal, Keith Michell, and Clive Revill also starred in the Broadway production. Seal, who won a Tony Award for her performance, is a singing actress whose personality jumps from a recording. Michell as Nestor has a beefy, full-bodied sound in the love duets, is comedic in "Wreck of a Mec," and is magnificent in the haunting "From a Prison Cell." Revill is especially funny in the climactic "But." The all-male ensemble is excellent in "Sons of France," "She's Got the Lot," and "Christmas Child." There is also an extended sequence that ends up in an Arctic Ballet complete with penguins! It doesn't make much sense, but the dance music is terrific. In his *New York Herald Tribune* review of *Irma la Douce*, Walter Kerr wrote: "If an original cast album is made available in your neighborhood, get it." Take Mr. Kerr's advice.　　　　　　　　　　　—JEFFREY DUNN

IS THERE LIFE AFTER HIGH SCHOOL?
Original Broadway Cast, 1982 (Original Cast Records) ★★★★
If this show had opened Off-Broadway instead of at the Ethel Barrymore Theatre in 1982, it might still be running. *Is There Life After High School?* represents the best work of Craig Carnelia, an extraordinarily talented composer-lyricist who has recently limited himself to writing lyrics to the music of Marvin Hamlisch. With a book by Jeffrey Kindley, the show is about the painful, wonderful experience of high school as viewed in retrospect by a bunch of young adults. A highlight is the opening (and closing) number "The Kid Inside," with its spot-on observations about adults who cling to their inner children; the soaring musical phrase that is sung to the words "There (s)he goes again" will not soon be forgotten once heard. One of the show's cleverest sequences is "Second Thoughts," in which five folks wonder what would have happened if they'd said or done things differently at pivotal moments in high school. Another standout is the beautiful song in which four women recall every detail of their earliest romantic encounters even though "Nothing Really Happened." Then there's the hilarious "I'm Glad You Didn't Know Me" (in high school), sung by a couple to each other. ("Picture a phony / Doin' the pony," she sings; "Speaking of fears / I had an erection the whole four years," he admits.) But the most glittering gem in the score is probably "Fran and Janie," a gorgeous tearjerker about two inseparable high school friends encountering each other years later. Given the acting and singing talent on display here, it's odd that only one of the cast members—Harry Groener—went on to have anything close to a major musical theater career. The other estimable performers are Maureen Silliman, Alma Cuervo, Sandy Faison, Raymond Baker, Cynthia Carle, David Patrick Kelly, Philip Hoffman, and James Widdoes.　　　　　　　　—MICHAEL PORTANTIERE

THE IT GIRL
Original Off-Broadway Cast, 2002 (JAY) ★★★
Based on *It,* the 1927 film that starred Clara Bow, *The IT Girl* is a small-scale 1920s-style musical comedy; it was presented Off-Broadway by the York Theatre Company almost a year before the Broadway opening of *Thoroughly Modern Millie,* but it covers much of the same ground. Jean Louisa Kelly stars as Betty Lou Spence, a spitfire flapper-type who sets New York aflame with her unique brand of style and sexual appeal. The cast also includes Jonathan Dokuchitz as the object of her affection, Jessica Boevers as the object of his semi-affection, and Stephen DeRosa as the dandy who sets the frantic plot in motion. All of the performers are talented if not exactly bursting with charisma, and the songs provided by composer Paul McKibbins and lyricist B.T. McNicholl are drenched in '20s rhythms and lively ragtime arrangements. The score's standout is Boevers' comic number "A Perfect Plan," in which she details the peaks and valleys of

her troubled love life. A tribute to "Coney Island" is about as bouncy and tuneful as the amusement park itself, "Why Not?" is a cheerfully upbeat entry, and the almost title song "It" is catchy enough to get stuck in your head.

—MATTHEW MURRAY

IT'S A BIRD . . . IT'S A PLANE . . . IT'S SUPERMAN
Original Broadway Cast, 1966 (Columbia/Sony) ★★★

This show seemed to have so much going for it, based as it was on the beloved comic books and popular television series known to millions. So composer Charles Strouse and lyricist Lee Adams asked David Newman and Robert Benton to write a book for a proposed musical with Superman as its central character; Harold Prince agreed to produce and direct the show. *It's a Bird . . . It's a Plane . . . It's Superman* opened to four good reviews, including a rave from *New York Times* critic Stanley Kauffman. But, for some reason, audiences did not flock to the show; it lasted only 129 performances. The show's lack of success was surely not the fault of the songs: This is a good-natured, humorous score, as colorful as the comic book characters it portrays. Reporter Jimmy Olsen is missing and Perry White is a small, nonsinging role, but many new characters were created for the musical. Gossip columnist Max Mencken was played by Jack Cassidy to a fare-thee-well, and the role of his secretary marked a major career step for Linda Lavin. These two get the best of the songs: Cassidy's suave, amusing seduction of Lois Lane, "The Woman for the Man," is a true showstopper as is Lavin's counter-attempt to seduce Clark Kent with "You've Got Possibilities." This number and her "love song" to Max, "Ooh, Do You Love You," allow Lavin to unleash her powerful belt voice, heard too infrequently on Broadway. Cassidy has two other terrific numbers, "So Long, Big Guy" and his vaudeville-style duet with the villainous Dr. Sedgwick (Michael O'Sullivan), "You've Got What I Need." The songs for Superman/Clark Kent are mostly tongue-in-cheek; Bob Holliday, a good physical match for the role, possesses a first-class baritone and delivers "Doing Good" and "The Strongest Man in the World" impressively. The character of Lois Lane, played by Patricia Marand, is treated pretty much like a traditional musical comedy heroine. She pines for you-know-who in "It's Superman," a lament that is both wistful and amusing. (In Act II, this song becomes a super ensemble number.) Marand also has a nifty duet with Don Chastain (as scientist Jim Morgan) titled "We Don't Matter At All" and, after he becomes her love interest, she sings the plaintive "What I've Always Wanted." As bonus tracks, the CD edition offers demos of three deleted songs plus a version of "You've Got Possibilities" with notably different lyrics, all performed stylishly by Strouse and Adams.

—JEFFREY DUNN

J

JACQUES BREL IS ALIVE AND WELL AND LIVING IN PARIS
Original Off-Broadway Cast, 1968 (Columbia) ★★★

This is the show to blame! The success of *Jacques Brel Is Alive and Well and Living in Paris* began the songwriter-revue revolution—but it would be a full decade before another good example of the genre showed up. (That show was *Ain't Misbehavin'* and it propelled a spate of glorified cabaret acts masquerading as musicals.) The Brel songs are performed with brio by a marvelous cast: Mort Shuman, who also adapted the French lyrics into English, costars with Shawn Elliot, Elly Stone, and Alice Whitfield. *Jacques Brel* introduced American audiences to a sophisticated romanticism blended with more than a soupçon of Gallic cynicism. After the initial run, a few regional productions, and a film version that featured Brel himself, the show slid into semi-obscurity—but Columbia thought enough of the revue to issue the cast album as a very fancy, boxed, two-record set.
— KEN BLOOM

JAMAICA
Original Broadway Cast, 1957 (RCA) ★★

During the 1950s, successful Broadway shows were mainly of two types: those that were and are revivable, some even timeless, and those that spoke only to their era and audience and then were silenced forever. *Jamaica* is decidedly in the latter category. It was a hit for Lena Horne and the matchless team of Harold Arlen and E.Y. "Yip" Harburg; then, after a year-plus run, it vanished without a trace. Calypso was a fifties phenomenon and this score is so full of it that it was originally written to star America's calypso singer of choice, Harry Belafonte. When he proved unavailable, a rewrite gave Horne a big-time Broadway debut. Her costars were notable as well: Interesting color-blind casting put Ricardo Montalban (a Mexican playing a West Indian) opposite Horne. Support was provided by Josephine Premice (husky-voiced and very entertaining), the personable Ossie Davis, and the veteran Adelaide Hall. The cast album is full of spirit and style, although the Jamaican patois sounds heavy-handed and phony coming out of Horne's mouth. Arlen's music is attractive but forgettable. Harburg failed to come up with a strong book (written with Fred Saidy and an uncredited Joseph Stein) and, in his lyrics, he mostly settles for a mix of faux-Caribbean attitude and obvious satire of Yankee consumerism and customs; not even the sultry "Coconut Sweet" is a truly

---

ALL-TIME FAVORITES

OF CHOREOGRAPHER

Jerry Mitchell

1. A Chorus Line

2. West Side Story

3. Gypsy

4. Follies

5. Hairspray

6. Dreamgirls

7. Fiddler on the Roof

8. Guys and Dolls

9. Sweet Charity

10. The Wiz

worthy entry in the Arlen-Harburg canon of standards. While the cast recording cannot reproduce the show's opulent designs and spicy Jack Cole choreography, it does give us a good idea of how *Jamaica* functioned: showing off the dynamic Horne to optimum advantage, moving swiftly, and providing very little for us to remember.

—RICHARD BARRIOS

JANE EYRE
Original Broadway Cast, 2000 (Sony) ★★★★

Based on Charlotte Brontë's classic novel of *sturm und drang* on the English moors, *Jane Eyre* represented the last gasp of the pop-opera cycle on Broadway. It managed to hang on for 209 performances, but tastes had shifted toward more lighthearted entertainments. The presence of director-librettist-colyricist John Caird (of *Les Misérables* fame) further emphasized how times had changed. Oddly—perhaps because of its intimate, introspective nature—a show that seemed stiff and uninvolving onstage fairly overflows with feeling on this superbly produced disc. Composer-lyricist Paul Gordon has a knack for melodic lines that are romantic and neurotic at the same time, and the lyrics are exceptionally literate. As Jane and Rochester, Marla Schaffel and James Barbour are the whole show, delivering abundant vocal thrills in such arias as "Sweet Liberty" and "The Pledge." The song "As Good As You," in which Rochester ruefully recalls his rakish past, is a gem of character revelation; so is the slashing, tormented "Painting Her Portrait," in which Jane struggles to accept living life as a spinster. Throughout, Larry Hochman's orchestrations have a plangent emotional transparency. This is a fine record of a show that will be heard from again.

—DAVID BARBOUR

JEKYLL & HYDE
Studio Cast, 1990 (RCA) ★★

As a musical theater composer, Frank Wildhorn writes great pop songs. That's amply demonstrated by this "concept" recording of *Jekyll & Hyde,* which lacks any theatrical context. The score, with lyrics by Leslie Bricusse, evokes *Les Misérables* and *The Phantom of the Opera* but is less interesting musically and dramatically. Colm Wilkinson and Linda Eder costar in this two-person recording; in grand pop-opera style, they let few vowels go unmodified and never exercise emotional shading where reckless overemoting will do. Eder seems clueless as to character nuance; still, her robust voice can overcome the sentiments of Bricusse's lyrics, sell a soft ballad such as "Once Upon a Dream," and deliver the power ballads "Someone Like You" and "A New Life." This show was always less about Jekyll or Hyde than about showcasing Eder's voice. Although Wilkinson sinks his teeth into his songs, particularly "This Is the Moment," his performance is so laughably over the top that we're forced to just grin and bear it until it's Eder's turn to sing again. We never have to wait very long.

Studio Cast, 1994 (Atlantic) ★★★

Linda Eder returned for the second *Jekyll & Hyde* recording (the complete score at that point), but here she sings only the songs of the prostitute Lucy; Carolee Carmello was brought in to belt her way through the songs for Jekyll's fiancée, Lisa. The title roles are superbly filled by Australian actor-singer Anthony Warlow. However, the fine actors Warlow and Carmello bring an unwanted subtlety to the score, which doesn't cast this material in a good light; trying to make these pop tunes theatrical is a lost cause. The disc boasts a huge orchestra and tons of songs, so if you simply must own one *Jekyll & Hyde,* this should probably be it. The plot is difficult to follow, mainly due to the paucity of dialogue on the CD, but certain tracks are fun: Chief among them are Eder's saucy "Bring on the Men" and her powerful "Someone Like You"; Warlow's dynamic "This Is the Moment"; and the Eder/Carmello duet "In His Eyes." Many other numbers are silly—"Facade" and "Murder, Murder!" in particular—but, overall, *Jekyll & Hyde* has never sounded better.

Original Broadway Cast, 1997 (Atlantic) ★

By the time *Jekyll & Hyde* got to Broadway, it was more a parody of itself than a serious show. This recording is decent enough, but the numbers that ended up in the production are unwieldy. Linda Eder is still Lucy and her pop affectations are hilariously out of place amid the theatrical acting/singing style of the Broadway cast members. This doesn't stop Robert Cuccioli from giving the title characters their most ridiculous performances yet; his "This Is the Moment" is a new high (or low) point in the number's already hefty catalog of self-indulgent renderings. Happily, he does a better job with Hyde's songs. Of the leads, only Christiane Noll as Emma (the renamed Lisa) makes her character believable; she performs with sweetness, sensitivity, and a legitimately beautiful voice. Unfortunately, her songs are among the show's dullest. "Murder, Murder" and the endlessly reprised "Facade" remain unintended comic highlights, and some newer numbers—"Pursue the Truth," "Emma's Reasons," "I Must Go On," and "Letting Go"—aren't much better. The score reaches a new nadir with "Good 'n' Evil," featuring such lyrics as "The key thing about good 'n' evil / Each man has to choose! / Heaven 'n' Hell / Is a helluva gamble to lose!" —MATTHEW MURRAY

JELLY'S LAST JAM
Original Broadway Cast, 1992 (Mercury) ★★★★

Inventively cobbled together from Jelly Roll Morton's musical catalogue, *Jelly's Last Jam* tells the composer's life story in a show that is as moving as it is entertaining. Luther Henderson (musical adaptation), Susan Birkenhead (new lyrics), and George C. Wolfe (director) used songs not originally written for the theater to propel the plot forward, and this recording proves the excellence of their efforts. The show benefited enormously from ideal casting. Gregory Hines, who received a well-deserved Tony, knocked 'em dead with his star turn as Morton. Hines' crisp tapping and smooth vocals quicken the pulse and gladden the soul in one highlight after another: "Doctor Jazz," "That's How You Jazz," the hauntingly sung and acted "Creole Boy," and others. Tonya Pinkins as Anita sings "Play the Music for Me" and "Last Chance Blues," a tough duet with Hines. There's also notable ensemble work by "The Hunnies": Mamie Duncan-Gibbs, Stephanie Pope, and Allison Williams. The accompanying booklet includes a concise synopsis and all the lyrics. —MORGAN SILLS

JENNIE
Original Broadway Cast, 1963 (RCA) ★★★

A star vehicle for Mary Martin, *Jennie* is a prime example of how a musical with wonderful ingredients can fail to jell. Arnold Schulman's book, a fictionalization of the life of Laurette Taylor with the character's name changed to Jennie Malone, is insufferably dull, but the Arthur Schwartz-Howard Dietz score boasts many captivating numbers; Martin is featured in ten of the fourteen vocal tracks on the recording. She rips into "Waitin' for the Evening Train" (a catchy vaudeville number with George Wallace) and caresses "I Still Look at You That Way." She is almost as corny as Kansas in August in the exuberant "Born Again" and in the inspirational "The Night May Be Dark" (sung with Ethel Shutta as her mother). Martin even shines in "Over Here," a duet with Robin Bailey. Finally, the star's "Before I Kiss the World Goodbye" is exceptionally well performed and then reprised as her solo finale. Jack DeLon's ringing tenor is heard in the catchy ensemble number "When You're Far Away From New York Town," and Shutta gives her all to the mediocre "For Better or Worse." Also noteworthy are the sparkling orchestrations of Philip J. Lang and Robert Russell Bennett and the dance arrangements of Trude Rittman: "Sauce Diable" is one of the most invigorating dance numbers ever captured on a Broadway cast album.

—JEFFREY DUNN

JEROME KERN GOES TO HOLLYWOOD
Original London Cast, 1985 (Safari/First Night) ★★

It's hard to understand the rationale or need for *Jerome Kern Goes to Hollywood,* a songwriter revue that was devised by one of its British costars, David Kernan. He, Liz Robertson, Elaine Delmar, and musical theater veteran Elisabeth Welch sing twenty-two Jerome Kern songs that may have appeared in films but weren't necessarily written for them—for example, the selections from *Show Boat.* Virtually all of these numbers are well known: "Smoke Gets In Your Eyes," "I Won't Dance," "The Last Time I Saw Paris," "Bill," "I'm Old Fashioned," and "All the Things You Are." They are certainly well sung, particularly by Delmar. But Welch is the drawing card for fans of legendary British performers, and although her four solos here are fine, it's hard to get worked up over them. (Note: A 1986 Broadway production of this revue with the same cast lasted only nine performances.)

—DAVID WOLF

JEROME ROBBINS' BROADWAY
Original Broadway Cast, 1989 (RCA, 2CDs) ★★★

Lovers of dance music should snap up this cast album of the 1989 Tony-winning Best Musical *Jerome Robbins' Broadway,* an assemblage of genius choreographer Robbins' greatest hits. Classic numbers from his shows were lovingly recreated by top-notch performers. Collectors will be especially interested in the material that has not otherwise been recorded with modern sound technology, or at all. Robbins won a Tony for Best Direction for this show and the cast swept the musical performance Tonys; they are well represented by this album. Jason Alexander (Best Actor) does "Comedy Tonight" and duets with Faith Prince on "I Still Get Jealous." Charlotte D'Amboise (Best Actress) knocks out "I'm Flying" and "America." Scott Wise (Best Featured Actor) does "Cool." A sultry pre-Gravitte Debbie Shapiro (Best Featured Actress) wails the seldom-heard Irving Berlin gem "Mr. Monotony" and leads the surefire "You Gotta Have a Gimmick." Also found here are longer pieces such as the "Small House of Uncle Thomas" ballet from *The King and I* and "On a Sunday by the Sea" from *High Button Shoes.* It all adds up to more than two hours of some of the brightest moments in musical theater history. The folks at RCA outdid themselves with a lavish, sixty-four-page booklet including more than forty color photographs, detailed notes, and mini-essays about each show.

—MORGAN SILLS

JERRY'S GIRLS
Original Broadway Cast, 1984 (Polygram/JAY) ★★★

When *Jerry's Girls* opened on Broadway in 1985, it starred Dorothy Loudon, Chita Rivera, and Leslie Uggams. No Broadway cast album was released. But in 1984, when Uggams, Carol Channing, and Andrea McArdle were on a lengthy pre-Broadway tour with the show, the stars made this two-LP set. Now it's a CD that includes—to no one's surprise—the familiar eight songs from *Mame,* six each from *Hello, Dolly!* and *Mack & Mabel,* four from *La Cage aux Folles,* two each from *Parade, Dear World,* and *A Day in Hollywood,* and one from *Milk and Honey* (none from *The Grand Tour*). The over-familiarity of the material and the fact that the orchestra is quite small almost make this recording expendable. Almost—for there is "Take It All Off," a humorous ditty that Herman wrote specifically for *Jerry's Girls*. This is also the only place where you'll find the parody lyrics written for the commercial "Hello, Deli" and the Democrats' 1964 campaign song, "Hello Lyndon." Plus it's fun to hear McArdle sing songs other than those from *Annie*, and she's marvelous in all of them. So is Uggams, even when she crosses the gender line to sing "I Won't Send Roses." As for Channing—this was the show where we first saw that the great lady had passed her prime. By the time she reaches "The Best of Times Is Now," her voice is somewhat unpleasant. Clearly, we all lose our charms in the end.   —PETER FILICHIA

JESUS CHRIST SUPERSTAR
Studio Cast, 1970 (Decca, 2CDs) ★★★★
Jesus Christ Superstar, the tour-de-force rock opera by Andrew Lloyd Webber and Tim Rice, presents Jesus Christ as a man at the center of a cult of celebrity while tracking the last week of his life in a respectful fashion. The composer-lyricist team succeeds in bringing the problems of both revered and reviled figures down to earth. Some of the songs examine the relationship of Jesus with his disciples ("Heaven on Their Minds") and his doubts about doing what's expected of him ("Gethsemane"), while others delve deeply into the character of the betrayer Judas, viewing his actions and their effects from multiple perspectives. The excellent cast conveys the richness of the story on the concept album that gave birth to the stage show. As Jesus and Judas, respectively, Ian Gillan and Murray Head are perfect for their roles; their rangy, powerful voices are capable of handling the demanding score and complex characterizations. Yvonne Elliman, barely eighteen at the time of the recording, is just right as the reformed sinner Mary Magdelene and scores a major success with her definitive version of "I Don't Know How to Love Him." Although Barry Dennen is hardly a spectacular singer, he finds plenty of nuances in Pontius Pilate; his repudiation of Jesus in the "Trial Before Pilate" sequence is particularly powerful. Conductor Alan Doggett keeps the orchestra and the singers working at top form from beginning to end.

Original Broadway Cast, 1971 (Decca) ★★★
Elliman and Dennen, the only two principal performers held over from the concept recording, remain ideal on the Broadway cast album; if anything, they improved on their performances. The other singers are good, if generally lacking the hard-rock voices that make the original recording so exciting. Jeff Fenholt's Jesus is dramatically astute but underpowered vocally; Ben Vereen is a magnetic Judas; Bob Bingham's bass makes his Caiaphas an often terrifying standout. The only major addition to the score is the lovely "Could We Start Again, Please?" for Mary Magdelene and Peter (Michael Jason). Unfortunately, this one-disc recording amounts to little more than a highlights album: Omitted are the overture, "What's the Buzz/Strange Thing Mystifying," "The Last Supper," and about six other songs and sequences.

Film Soundtrack, 1973 (Decca, 2CDs) ★★
The film version of *Jesus Christ Superstar* is faithful to the original property, with minor changes (mostly in lyrics) and no major cuts. One song, "Then We Are Decided," was added for Caiaphas and the priests, to limited effect. Director Norman Jewison plays up the story's intimacy but, as this soundtrack album reveals, the dramatic power of the tale is greatly lessened by that approach; everyone sounds restrained, and the energy that can drive the show is only intermittently present. Conducted by André Previn, the fine cast has Elliman and Dennen back

again, joined by Broadway's Bob Bingham, still imposing as Caiaphas, and Ted Neeley (from the original Broadway company) as Jesus. Of all the principals, Neeley suffers the most; robbed of the chance to let go during the biggest musical moments (particularly "Gethsemane"), he radiates little authority. Carl Anderson's Judas comes across more effectively, but this imbalance dampens the overall impact of the recording.

20th Anniversary London Cast, 1992 (RCA, 2CDs) ★★

Paul Nicholas, who played the title role in the first London stage production of *Jesus Christ Superstar,* should probably have avoided revisiting the part twenty years later. His acting is fine here, but his voice betrays his age, and he doesn't come across very well opposite the fresher-sounding Keith Burns as Judas and Claire Moore as Mary Magdelene. Gary Martin is an effectively creepy Caiaphas, and Jeff Shankley's contemplative Pilate is also good. While this cast recording is never outstanding, it's solid enough until its final track, "Could We Start Again Please?" The song is not presented in its proper slot in the show, and it's given an awful Muzak-like rendition, complete with new Tim Rice lyrics that sound like just another bland pop song.

Studio Cast, 1996 (JAY, 2CDs) ★

With its legit-sounding chorus and inappropriately leisurely tempos, this is one of the score's most ineffective presentations. There are a few good things here—the priests, led by Billy Hartman's Caiaphas, sound truly threatening rather than just silly, and Ethan Freeman's Pilate is good—but most of the recording comes across as a musical experiment gone terribly awry. Numerous questions arise: Why does Clive Rowe's Judas lack almost all the role's familiar pop inflections, however sumptuous his voice, and why is he nearly unintelligible? Why does Dave Willetts' Jesus sound ten times as vicious as any of the people who want him crucified? Why does Issy van Randwyck spoil her otherwise fine Mary Magdelene with laughable embellishments in "I Don't Know How to Love Him?" Why does the "Crucifixion" sequence sound like a lounge piano player having an epileptic seizure? And why has "Could We Start Again Please?" again been moved out of the actual song order to the end of the disc?

Studio Cast, 1996 (Decca, 2CDs) ★★★

Joanna Ampil is one of the weakest Mary Magdelenes on record, and her performance prevents this recording of *Jesus Christ Superstar* from being excellent. Never has it been more clear how much the contrast of Mary's emotions affects the balance of the show; Ampil has so little bite in her songs that the character essentially becomes insignificant. But there are no flaws in the rest of the casting. Steve Balsamo's Jesus and Zubin Varla's Judas are terrific, and David Burt's Pilate, while similar to Barry Dennen's, is painted with a variety of vocal and emotional colors; his performance in "Trial Before Pilate" is especially powerful. In a surprisingly enjoyable turn, Alice Cooper appears as Herod, lending authority and subtle humor to a role that is often over-played. The orchestra here sounds a bit thin—but despite that fact, a few lyric changes, and Ampil, this album is quite good.

Video Soundtrack, 2000 (Sony) ★★

This disc of highlights from a television production of *Jesus Christ Superstar* may be lacking in content—no "This Jesus Must Die" or "Damned for All Time/Blood Money"—but certainly not in energy. It also has a great Judas in Jérôme Pradon, who, if not one of the most vocally accomplished on record, gives a performance of significant dramatic power. Renee Castle as Mary

Magdelene, Tony Vincent as Simon Zealotes, and Frederick B. Owens as Caiaphas perform admirably, but the casting is otherwise less sure. Although Glenn Carter acts well enough in the title role, his singing is weak; his high notes do not bespeak a well-supported falsetto and his rendition of "Gethsemane" is particularly gutless. Fred Johanson is superb in "Pilate's Dream" but he overemotes destructively in "Trial Before Pilate." —MATTHEW MURRAY

JIMMY
Original Broadway Cast, 1969 (RCA/no CD) ★

This misbegotten musical biography of New York Mayor Jimmy Walker has three unsympathetic protagonists, a leading man who can barely hold a note, and a score that aspires to Jerry Herman-like friendliness but can't come up with a single memorable melody or impressive lyric. Producer Jack Warner probably selected Frank Gorshin to star because his compact Irishness reminded him of Jimmy Cagney. Unfortunately, Gorshin exhibits a wavery, raspy voice and has no sense of how to shape a song. This isn't to say that the songs, by Bill Jacob and Patti Jacob, are in any shape for shaping; the best they can do is wallow in New York platitudes, as in "Riverside Drive," or try to overlay some trendy, soft-rock sounds onto the Prohibition milieu, as in "What's Out There for Me?" Anita Gillette is hard-edged as Jimmy's mistress and, as his neglected wife, Julie Wilson hard-sells the torcher "I Only Wanna Laugh." They're pros, but they're wasting their time. The relentlessly bright sound of the RCA Dynagroove LP makes the whole thing seem even worse than it is. —MARC MILLER

JOHN & JEN
Original Off-Broadway Cast, 1996 (Varèse Sarabande/Fynsworth Alley) ★★

Talk about intimate: *John & Jen* is a three-character musical for two actors. Unfortunately, in its relentless focus on a single dramatic situation, the piece is perhaps too small. Carolee Carmello is Jen, who grows up protecting her younger brother, John, from their abusive father. Jen goes off to college, becomes a hippie, and falls in love with a draft-dodger. To please his father, John enlists in the Army and is killed in Vietnam. In Act II, Jen is now a single mother with a son named—you guessed it. Jen smothers the young John with unwanted attention, driving their relationship to the breaking point. Rated "S" for Sensitivity, *John & Jen* is a tearjerker that nevertheless leaves listeners surprisingly dry-eyed. The songs by Andrew Lippa (music) and Tom Greenwald (lyrics) are workmanlike, but the book (by both) is too schematic, so the characters and their airless existence soon become tiresome. Still, the final three numbers—"The Road Ends Here," "That Was My Way," and "Every Goodbye Is Hello"—do approach the emotional payoff that the authors hoped for. Carmello, one of our best singing actresses, works wonders with the material, and James Ludwig is also fine as the two Johns; in fact, they probably make the score sound better than it actually is. Still, it's an interesting calling card for two young writing talents and for orchestrator Jason Robert Brown—who, soon after this, wrote some really ripping songs for *Parade*. —DAVID BARBOUR

JOHNNY JOHNSON
Studio Cast, 1955 (MGM-Heliodor/Polygram) ★★★★★

Kurt Weill's first American musical, with lyrics by Paul Green, gets a thrillingly theatrical workout in this recording. Musical director Samuel Matlowsky is in firm control of a remarkable cast that includes Burgess Meredith, Thomas Stewart, Evelyn Lear, Hiram Sherman, Jane Connell, Scott Merrill, and Lotte Lenya. Weill's score features tangos, cowboy songs, Victorian-era love songs, group numbers, marches, torch songs, French cabaret numbers, German lullabies, and an abundance of orchestral and dance music. The score is much more sophisticated than Green's book, which is a victim of bad timing and overwriting about the wartime plight of innocent soldiers. Anti-war pieces were a staple of the post-World War I years, but by 1936, when *Johnny Johnson* opened on Broadway, the theme wasn't as valid. Johnny's sweet, anti-war gropings paled when compared with the genuine evils of Hitler. Still, this is a score filled with imaginative moments. Because attempts at revival have failed, this genuinely exciting album may remain the best way to fully appreciate Weill's considerable achievement.

Studio Cast, 1997 (Erato) ★★★

This *Johnny Johnson* is in stereo, versus the earlier version in monaural, and it has more music than its predecessor. Still, my vote still goes to the first release, which has an extraordinary cast of singing actors, a more theatrical feel, and sharper musical direction. Joel Cohen's musical direction here is soft, and though all of the performers sing well, they are noticeably uncomfortable when they have to speak dialogue. —DAVID WOLF

JOSEPH AND THE AMAZING TECHNICOLOR DREAMCOAT
Studio Cast, 1974 (MCA) ★★★

Inspired again by biblical lore, composer Andrew Lloyd Webber and lyricist Tim Rice—whose *Jesus Christ Superstar* drew on the New Testament—turned to the Old Testament for this soft-rock comedy based on the Genesis story of a young man who's betrayed by his brothers before becoming a powerful figure in Egypt. The score is clever, with plenty of variety. Joseph's brothers get most of the humorous songs: a western tune, "One More Angel in Heaven"; a French-style drinking song, "Those Canaan Days"; and the "Benjamin Calypso." An Elvis takeoff for the Pharaoh is thrown in for good measure. Peter Reeves is a competent Narrator; Gary Bond is fine as Joseph, and his "Close Every Door" is a highlight of the disc. Although this recording doesn't represent the score as later expanded, it's a nice piece of history and a good listen.

Original Broadway Cast, 1982 (Chrysalis) ★★★★

In its first Broadway staging, *Joseph . . .* had a female Narrator. And what a Narrator she was! Laurie Beechman, with her vivacity and wonderful high belt, steals the show from Bill Hutton as Joseph and sets the standard for this role. That's saying a lot, because Hutton is one of the best Josephs ever recorded; his earthy low notes and secure upper register bring more colors to the character's music than is often the case. Beechman, Hutton, the brothers, the female ensemble, and the fine orchestra—skillfully led by David Friedman—make this the most dazzling recording of the show, despite the few cuts in the score. Highlights are numerous, among them, Beechman's "You Are What You Feel," Hutton's "Close Every Door" and "Any Dream Will Do," and Tom Carder's rendition of the Pharaoh's number.

London Cast, 1991 (Polydor) ★★

This disc is most notable for its inclusion of the extensive "Joseph Megamix," a finale reprise of the score's best numbers. The recording represents the show's final version, but it's far from definitive. Jason Donovan, as Joseph, is bland throughout, and Linzi Hateley lacks authority as the Narrator. The supporting players are also lukewarm; even David Easter's Pharaoh doesn't score because his Elvis impersonation is so overdone. The CD is recommended only to diehard fans of the show.

Original Canadian Cast, 1992 (Polydor) ★★★

Donny Osmond began his lengthy stint as Joseph in the show's premiere Canadian staging. He's hardly the best vocalist to take the part, yet he brings to the role a likeability and tremendous sense of fun that keeps audiences invested in the character from start to finish. His "Any Dream Will Do" and "Close Every Door" are among the most moving renditions of those songs. Aside from anchoring the show, his performance reclaims star status for Joseph; as the Narrator, Janet Metz displays vocal finesse but lacks the charisma needed to make the character stand out from the ensemble. Even so, there's a lot to like on this disc, particularly the men playing Joseph's brothers. Among them are such future Broadway names as Jeff Blumenkrantz, Timothy J. Alex, Vance Avery, Michael Berresse, and Rufus Bonds, Jr.

Los Angeles Cast, 1993 (Polydor) ★★★

This recording's Joseph, soap-opera star Michael Damian, compensates for his vocal shortcomings with acting ability and charisma. Kelli Rabke's Narrator has vocal strength, but the singers to listen for are Broadway pros Clifford David (as Jacob and Potiphar), Bill Nolte (as the Baker and a brother of Joseph), and Marc Kudisch and Willy Falk (as two other brothers). Robert Torti's Pharaoh is excellent.

Video Soundtrack, 1999 (Really Useful Records) ★★★

Donny Osmond returned to the title role in this video production of *Joseph* . . . and gave another joyous performance. Joining him as the Narrator is the eminent West End star Maria Friedman, who sings brilliantly and exudes enough star presence to match Osmond's. Richard Attenborough and Joan Collins are a hoot as Jacob and Mrs. Potiphar, respectively. The strong ensemble helps make this a fine recording of the expanded score.   —MATTHEW MURRAY

THE JULIUS MONK REVUES

Julius Monk was the major domo and artistic director of a series of legendary revues that showcased young talents at the start of their careers. The then-unknown contributing composers/lyricists/writers/performers included such future greats as Schmidt and Jones, Coleman and Leigh, Portia Nelson, William Roy, Michael Brown, and Claibe Richardson. Monk's stock company of players boasted such urbane actors-singers as Jane Connell and Gordon Connell, Jack Fletcher, Ceil Cabot, Gerry Matthews, Mary Louise Wilson, Rex Robbins, and Susan Browning. Each show had dual pianists for accompaniment. All but three of the revues were recorded, often live, and the LPs capture the ambience of Upstairs at the Downstairs and other intimate Manhattan *boîtes* at a unique moment in entertainment history. The recordings, none of which are available on CD, are reviewed below in chronological order:

JULIUS MONK REVUE: TAKE FIVE
1957 (Offbeat/no CD) ★★★

Take Five was unusual in that it had a featured performer: Ronny Graham. Also along for the ride was future arranger extraordinaire Jonathan Tunick, who, with lyricist Steven Vinaver, composed three songs for the show. Graham's song "Doing the Psycho-Neurotique" is a Freudian hoedown, and WASPy Connecticut suburbs are given the once-over by Carolyn Leigh and Phil Springer in "Westport."

JULIUS MONK REVUE: DEMI DOZEN
1958 (Offbeat/no CD) ★★★★

Demi Dozen may be the best of the bunch—a delicious, stylish concoction. As in all Monk shows, topicality was at the forefront here, with Tom Jones-Harvey Schmidt offerings about the battle to make Hawaii a state and the rat race of the Lexington Avenue Express. Cy Coleman and Carolyn Leigh contributed "You Fascinate Me So," and Bill Dana wrote a sketch lampooning Madison Avenue ad-men.

JULIUS MONK REVUE: PIECES OF EIGHT
1959 (Offbeat/no CD) ★★★

Pieces of Eight boasts a couple of wonderful Bud McCreery songs, "Steel Guitars and Barking Seals" and "The Night the Hurricane Struck." Rod Warren's "Season's Greetings" would become one of Mabel Mercer's best-loved numbers, and for good reason. Monk's shows could impale the most pretentious people with impunity, but they also had a good deal of heart—the hallmark of any good show of any type.

JULIUS MONK REVUE: DRESSED TO THE NINES
1960 (MGM/no CD) ★★★

Dressed to the Nines offers as its best number "The Hate Song." Don't miss it! Michael Brown's "Bring Back the Roxy to Me" is an elegiac hymn to the beloved movie palace, while William Roy and Michael McWhinney's "The Theatre's in the Dining Room" explores the ever-tinier spaces of Off-Off-Broadway venues.

JULIUS MONK REVUE: FOUR BELOW STRIKES BACK
1960 (Offbeat/no CD) ★★★

Four Below Strikes Back is a typically excellent Monk revue with a soupçon of politics ("The Castro Tango"), a smidgen of social commentary ("Payola" and "Family Fallout Shelter"), a pinch of nostalgia ("Jefferson Davis Tyler's General Store"), and a touch of romance ("Love, Here I Am").

JULIUS MONK REVUE: SEVEN COME ELEVEN
1961 (Columbia/no CD) ★★★

Seven Come Eleven is the rarest of these albums because Columbia never distributed the LPs to record stores; they were sold only at Upstairs at the Downstairs. "John Birch Society" became a hit for songwriter Michael Brown, and Jacques Urbont and Bruce Geller's "I Found Him" later turned up in their Off-Broadway musical *All in Love.*

JULIUS MONK REVUE: DIME A DOZEN
1962 (Cadence 2LPs/no CD) ★★★

Dime a Dozen, the last Monk show to be recorded, was captured in its entirety in a two-LP set. It boasts a song that became quite popular: "Barry's Boys," a lampoon on the followers of Barry Goldwater, later recorded by The Kingston Trio. Along the way, Robert Moses, Newton Minnow, Plaid Stamps, Banlon (the wonder fiber), *The New York Times,* NASA, and other 1960s hot topics are examined, skewered, and dissected to humorous effect.   —KEN BLOOM

JUMBO
Film Soundtrack, 1962 (Columbia/Sony) ★★★

In these days of Broadway mega-musicals costing $12 million or more, it's interesting to note that a 1935 show nearly created a scandal because it was budgeted at $350,000. High-rolling producer Billy Rose was responsible for that near-obscene outlay of cash, which he lavished upon a musical spectacle—literally a circus—called *Jumbo*. It ran at the mammoth Hippodrome, refitted as a three-ring arena for a number of circus acts, a Romeo-and-Juliet-under-the-big-top plot, the antics of Jimmy Durante, and a wonderful score by Richard Rodgers and Lorenz Hart. The show was too expensive to recoup its investment and it soon passed into legend. Three of its songs—"My Romance," "The Most Beautiful Girl in the World," and "Little Girl Blue"—became standards. When *Jumbo* made it to the screen in 1962 (with *Billy Rose's Jumbo* name included in the title), not even the world's top box-office draw, Doris Day, could turn the film into a financial success. Nevertheless, the soundtrack recording is bouncy and enjoyable, with Day in strong voice. Durante repeated his stage role, and his reprise of "The Most Beautiful Girl in the World" is captivating. Martha Raye is a delight as his long-suffering fiancée. Most often remembered as a wide-mouthed clown, Raye was an accomplished vocalist; this becomes clear when she duets with Day in "Why Can't I?"—one of several R&H interpolations. Leading man Stephen Boyd's songs were dubbed by the strong-voiced James Joyce (how's that for an Irish name?) and the score was further padded with Roger Edens' "Sawdust, Spangles, and Dreams." Since there is no cast album of the stage production of *Jumbo,* it's nice to have selections from the entertaining film soundtrack on disc. —RICHARD BARRIOS

JUNO
Original Broadway Cast, 1959 (Columbia/Fynsworth Alley) ★★★★

For years, cast album collectors begged Columbia to issue this heartbreaker on CD. Finally, Fynsworth Alley got the rights and issued a CD in 2002. In adapting Sean O'Casey's Dublin tragicomedy *Juno and the Paycock* to the musical stage, composer-lyricist Marc Blitzstein and librettist Joseph Stein showed considerable theatrical savvy and the utmost integrity. Their thrilling score opens with "We're Alive," a jaunty march that ends in tragedy and turns into a dirge. Immediately after it comes "I Wish It So," one of three arresting ballads assigned to the lucky singer Monte Amundsen. Then Shirley Booth acts "Song of the Ma" to the core (its verse is by O'Casey himself), her approximate note-hitting just right for this overburdened character. The rest of the cast is also amazing: Melvyn Douglas (like Booth, no conventional singer but a wonderful actor), Tommy Rall, Jean Stapleton, Nancy Andrews, Sada Thompson, Jack MacGowran, and Loren Driscoll (who holds one of the longest notes ever attempted at the end of "One Kind Word"). First-class all the way, the album was produced by Goddard Lieberson; the orchestrations are by Robert Russell Bennett, Hershy Kay, and Blitzstein; and the conductor is Robert Emmett Dolan, an underappreciated Broadway composer himself. Blitzstein does overreach toward the end with a pompous "Hymn" and some noisy ballet music (Agnes De Mille choreographed), but even here, one admires his ambition and his refusal to cheapen the material with standard audience-pleasing tactics. —MARC MILLER

K

KAT AND THE KINGS

Original London Cast, 1998 (First Night/Relativity) ★★

The good thing about this disc, recorded live at London's Vaudeville Theatre, is that it allows you to forget about the show's well-meaning but hackneyed book and focus on what gave the Olivier Award-winning musical its spark: its peppy doo-wop music. The songs, by David Kramer and Taliep Petersen, may be only pale imitations of the classic '50s-'60s music that inspired them, but they do exhibit pleasant harmonies and toe-tapping beats. And they're delivered with enthusiasm by the musical's wonderful young cast members in this story of a group of friends in apartheid-era South Africa who aspire to rock stardom but encounter obstacles at every turn. Happily, the CD booklet contains all the lyrics; but even more welcome would have been a synopsis and background on the show, which was apparently a labor of love for its South African company and creators. Sadly, their good intentions are not enough to make *Kat and the Kings* essential for your cast album collection. —BROOKE PIERCE

KEAN

Broadway Cast, 1961 (Columbia/DRG) ★★★★★

Robert Wright and George Forrest may be thought of as mere "adapters" because they took the works of classical composers and massaged them into such musicals as *Song of Norway* and *Kismet,* but here's proof positive that they could craft their own wonderful music and lyrics. Based on a play by Dumas, the show tells the somewhat true story of Britain's greatest actor, Edmund Kean. In the title role, Alfred Drake is in top form as he delivers the romatic ballads "Sweet Danger" and "To Look Upon My Love" and the comedic "Civilized People," proving again that he could do it all. As for the song "Elena," had that name been as popular in 1961 as Maria was in 1957, the *Kean* tune might have become as popular as that little number from *West Side Story.* There's much more: the rollicking "The Fog and the Grog"; the swirling waltz "Swept Away"; and, in "Penny Plain, Twopence Colored," the most glorious melisma in all musical theater—six measures long and exquisitely sung by Alfred De Sio. Finally, Drake gets to put over a highbrow version of "Rose's Turn" in "Apology," conceived by the songwriters and librettist Peter Stone. *Kean* is an underrated musical that's worth a listen. —PETER FILICHIA

ALL-TIME FAVORITES

OF PERFORMER

Marni Nixon

1. My Fair Lady

2. West Side Story

3. A Funny Thing Happened on the Way to the Forum

4. Gypsy

5. Little Shop of Horrors

6. The King and I

7. Carousel

8. Oklahoma!

9. The Sound of Music

10. Sweeney Todd

KELLY

Studio Cast, 1998 (Original Cast Records) ★

Kelly closed on opening night, and this disc shows why it was one of the biggest flops of the 1960s. Eddie Lawrence's book focuses on the title character, who plans to jump off the Brooklyn Bridge for fame and profit, but the sketchy notes in the CD booklet provide few clues as to how the plot develops. The score, by Lawrence and Moose Charlap, is a raucous evocation of 1880s New York that reaches for a Brecht-Weill astringency without achieving it. There is a standout in "I'll Never Go There Anymore," an ambitious musical-dramatic scene with a haunting melody. As Kelly and his love interest, Angela, Brian d'Arcy James and Sally Mayes make their material seem better than it is. (Mayes shares Angela's numbers with pop singer Sandy Stewart.) Lawrence himself appears in several numbers, and there are contributions from solid pros Marcia Lewis, Jane Connell, Conrad John Schuck, and George S. Irving, although they're generally defeated by the monotonous melodies and subpar lyrics. A bonus track features Stewart in a lovely 1965 rendition of "I'll Never Go There Anymore." —DAVID BARBOUR

THE KING AND I

Original Broadway Cast, 1951 (Decca) ★★★

Although the quality of Gertrude Lawrence's singing as Anna in Richard Rodgers and Oscar Hammerstein's *The King and I* was widely criticized, the effectiveness of her performance onstage was never questioned. While listeners may find the star's vocal quality somewhat quivery here, the drama she brings to her songs gives substance to the superlatives that are still thrown around regarding her performance. Owing to space limitations on LPs of the 1950s, this recording has no dialogue lead-ins, little internal dialogue, and edits in many songs; the "Small House of Uncle Thomas" ballet and "Western People Funny" numbers are cut entirely. The exquisite Doretta Morrow as Tuptim wins the vocal prize with her solo "My Lord and Master" and her two duets with the stalwart but American-sounding Lun Tha of baritone Larry Douglas. Dorothy Sarnoff is wonderfully dignified in her rendition of "Something Wonderful," and Yul Brynner's first recording of "A Puzzlement" is essential although abridged. The sound has been improved for reissue on CD, and the preservation of the songs as originally performed, orchestrated by Robert Russell Bennett and conducted by Frederick Dvonch, shows this score to be a masterwork. Although subsequent recordings of *The King and I* are more complete and offer better sound, it would be a mistake to overlook this album.

Original London Cast, 1953 (Philips/Sepia) ★

Listening to Valerie Hobson as Anna, we can only wonder why, when so many people had issues with Gertrude Lawrence's singing in the Broadway production, a stronger vocalist was not engaged for the role in London. Hobson has charm but fails to soar in her songs, except when she duets with Herbert Lom in "Shall We Dance?" Lom's "A Puzzlement" is even further abridged than Yul Brynner's on the original Broadway album and not nearly as interesting. As Tuptim and Lun Tha, Doreen Duke and Jan Mazarus are generically legit singers. The only performance that rises above the level of "adequate" is Muriel Smith's "Something Wonderful." The Sepia CD is filled out with songs from two British musicals, *Golden City* and *Bet Your Life.*

Film Soundtrack, 1956 (Capitol/Angel) ★★★

One of the best stage-to-screen adaptations, the film version on *The King and I* is largely responsible for the musical's enduring popularity. To begin with, it captured Yul Brynner's performance for posterity. Marni Nixon's vocal dubbing for Deborah Kerr is so uncannily perfect that it's hard to believe, watching the film, that those gorgeous tones are not coming from Kerr's mouth. The soundtrack album contains three songs that are not in the film: "My Lord and Master," "I Have Dreamed," and "Shall I Tell What I Think of You?" On the other hand, the "Small House of Uncle Thomas" ballet is performed almost complete in the film but is not on the soundtrack recording—not even on the most recent, expanded CD edition. Orchestrations are credited to Robert Russell Bennett plus three others. Supervised by musical directors Alfred Newman and Ken Darby, these orchestrations provide a majestic sound. Terry Saunders (Lady Thiang) does her own singing, while Rita Moreno (Tuptim) and Carlos Rivas (Lun Tha) are dubbed by others.

Studio Cast, 1964 (Columbia/Sony) ★★

Unfortunately, this album features new orchestrations by Philip J. Lang, even though the originals for this Rodgers and Hammerstein score were among the best that Robert Russell Bennett ever created. Lang went out of his way to go his own way but, ironically, his orchestrations work best when they are most reminiscent of the originals; when he seeks to improve, he fails. Nevertheless, this is a noteworthy recording in that it documents a superb performance by Barbara Cook in a critically acclaimed 1960 staging of *The King and I* by the City Center Light Opera Company, run by Jean Dalrymple and devoted to faithful revivals of great musicals. While all of Cook's performances on this studio recording are wonderful, her "Hello, Young Lovers" and "Shall I Tell You What I Think of You" are among the best on record, and her "Shall We Dance?" with Theodore Bikel as the King has great verve. Bikel sings "A Puzzlement" in a stalwart manner; Jeanette Scovotti and Daniel Ferro are appropriate if unexciting as the young lovers; and Anita Darian is fine as Lady Thiang.

Music Theater of Lincoln Center Cast, 1965 (RCA/no CD) ★★★

The King and I was the inaugural production of the regrettably short-lived Music Theater of Lincoln Center—Richard Rodgers, producer. The major news about this album was that it contained the first recording of the "Small House of Uncle Thomas" ballet, supervised by Rodgers and featuring Lee Venora as a superb Tuptim. Risë Stevens is a gushingly operatic Anna, Darren McGavin as the King makes a strong showing in "A Puzzlement," Frank Poretta lends his glorious tenor to the Lun Tha/Tuptim duets, and Patricia Neway is a supremely stately Lady Thiang. This pleasant recording is certainly worth tracking down on LP and would be welcome, if not essential, as a CD reissue.

Broadway Cast, 1977 (RCA) ★★★

A lot of previously unrecorded music from *The King and I* (but not the "Small House of Uncle Thomas" ballet) can be heard here. Included are the offstage chorus that leads into "I Whistle a Happy Tune"; the crossover scene of monks chanting in counterpoint to the King's children singing "Home Sweet Home"; the charming "Royal Bangkok Academy" song; the reprise of "A Puzzlement" for Anna's son, Louis, and Prince Chulalongkorn; the droll "Western People Funny"; the lovely instrumental "Dance of Edward and Anna"; and the entire finale of Act II. The completeness of this recording gives Yul Brynner a much stronger presence than displayed on the original Broadway album or the film soundtrack. Constance Towers is in excellent voice as Anna, even if she's defeated occasionally by some of conductor Milton Rosenstock's slow tempi. June Angela and Martin Vidnovic are fine as the "young lovers," but this is the first recording to make adjustments in "I Have Dreamed," giving Lun Tha more and Tuptim less of the second chorus. A wiser "new tradition" was the casting of an Asian actress as Lady Thiang, and Hye-Young Choi's beautiful singing helped make this concept *de rigueur* for subsequent stagings. The original orchestrations sound excellent here, and the inclusion of so much music and dialogue earns this recording a worthy place next to the original Broadway cast recording.

Studio Cast, 1992 (Phillips) ★★★

Despite its dream cast, this recording of *The King and I* is strangely underpowered. It uses the arrangements and orchestrations from the film version, which had internal cuts in many of the songs; but several sections of dialogue are included, lending dramatic context to some numbers. The casting of Julie Andrews as Anna benefits this recording greatly, but the original orchestrations and the complete "Shall I Tell You What I Think of You?" are sorely missed. Ben Kingsley offers a well-sung, dramatic King, Marilyn Horne sings a majestic "Something Wonderful," and if we must have a pop-vocalist approach to Tuptim and Lun Tha, Lea Salonga and Peabo Bryson at least sound tasteful and pleasant. If you are a fan of Andrews and *The King and I* and have always longed to hear Julie as Anna, this recording is a must. The fact that her voice is not in pristine shape here matters little; her mere presence in the role, which fits her like a glove, makes up for any deficiencies.

Broadway Cast, 1996 (Varèse Sarabande) ★★

The 1996 revival of *The King and I* starred Donna Murphy and Lou Diamond Phillips. While their singing was fine, what made their performances noteworthy was the revelatory acting that they brought to many scenes. Happily, a good amount of their dialogue is included on this recording. It gets down to business immediately with an overture that is really no more than a brief prelude and goes right into the Anna/Louis scene that contains "I Whistle a Happy Tune." Some listeners may have problems with Murphy's use of chest-oriented tones rather than the expected soprano for Anna, but her "Hello, Young Lovers" comes from a place of great depth and her "Shall I Tell You What I Think of You?" is compelling. However, "Getting to Know You" seems painfully slow, even if Murphy's performance almost justifies the tempo. Phillips explores "A Puzzlement" with such spontaneity that you may feel you are hearing it for the first time. Together, the stars score quite well in the scene leading into the finale of Act I and in the "Shall We Dance?" sequence—but, somehow, that song does not soar musically. This disc also boasts many rarely recorded inclusions: "Confrontation" (between Anna and the Kralahome); "Procession of the White Elephant," with dialogue from the Kralahome, Captain Orton, and Prince Chulalongkorn; "The Letter," read by Anna to Lady Thiang; and the final scene, wherein Jimmy Higa as the Prince makes a game attempt at becoming kingly. As Tuptim and Lun Tha, Joohee Choi and José Llana were heartbreaking lovers onstage but come across as bland on disc. On the plus side, Taewon Yi Kim makes an impact as Lady Thiang; her "Something Wonderful" is enhanced by the related scene with the Kralahome, in which Randall Duk Kim's presence is strong. Still, what was a thrilling stage experience is not fully captured on this CD.

Studio Cast, 1997 (JAY, 2CDs) ★★★★

In this two-disc set, *The King and I* is note-complete, with a very suitable cast superbly conducted by John Owen Edwards. British opera star Valerie Masterson and film star Christopher Lee fill the roles of Anna and the King well. Here is the first absolutely complete recording of the "Small House of Uncle Thomas" ballet and only the second recording of the charming "A Puzzlement" reprise for Louis and Prince Chululongkorn. Overall, the score is very well sung and a very valid attempt was made to create a dramatic listening experience. Masterson sings earnestly throughout, Lee is suitably grave (if a bit humorless), and Sally Burgess' "Something Wonderful" is splendid. As the lovers Lun Tha and Tuptim, Jason Howard and Tinuke Olafimihan might have been oddly matched in a stage production but sound terrific here. This is a necessary recording for anyone who truly loves *The King and I*.

Animated Film Soundtrack, 1999 (Sony) Not recommended.

If you think of this as a studio cast recording, rather than a soundtrack recording, you might get through it without grimacing. The singing, by Christiane Noll and Martin Vidnovic, is excellent. But anyone who has seen the animated film that yielded this CD will find it impossible to shake off that awful memory. Here's a scary thought: One day, a kid will be sitting in a theater at a revival of *The King and I,* and when "I Whistle a Happy Tune" begins, the child will ask: "Mommy, where's the dragon?"

London Cast, 2000 (WEA-Warner Music) ★★★★

With the casting of Elaine Paige as Anna, it was evident that this London revival and cast recording would be defined by the sterling vocal powers of the leading lady. Not only is Paige's singing expectedly excellent, her acting is top-notch, and all other elements of this disc are so strong that it probably ranks as the best available recording of *The King and I*. Instead of slavishly imitating the 1996 Broadway CD, producer Mike Moran took a fresh approach with this disc, giving it a dramatic tension that is sustained throughout its seventy minutes. The brief prelude is rich, taking us into the Captain Orton scene with Louis, then to Anna's entrance as Paige sings a beguiling "I Whistle a Happy Tune." Her magic continues in "Hello, Young Lovers" and "Getting to Know You." Paige's "Shall I Tell You What I Think of You?" reveals a mixture of humor, anger, warmth, and bottled-up fury. As the King, Jason Scott Lee delivers "A Puzzlement" and "Song of the King" with brio, and he and Paige wring everything possible out of "Shall We Dance?" As Lady Thiang, Taewon Yi Kim, who was also in the 1996 cast, evinces a deeper understanding of the character now; this influences her singing of "Something Wonderful" to stunning effect. Tuptim's "My Lord and Master" is sung with intensity and some welcome anger by Aura Deva, who also adds urgency to "We Kiss in a Shadow." Sean Ghazi is equally impressive as Lun Tha; the well-played scene following the song gives the reprise enormous weight. Then this Tuptim and Lun Tha bring a totally different quality to "I Have Dreamed": No longer fearful, their voices glide to a sweeter place as they caress this glorious Rodgers and Hammerstein song ardently. Other delights: Alexander Deng is an excellent Prince who will be King, and the entire "Small House of Uncle Thomas" ballet is included under the direction of John Owen Edwards' skillful baton. So, what's missing that was on the Broadway CD? "Royal Dance Before the King," "Procession of the White Elephant," the reprise of "Something Wonderful," and some dialogue. But with the excitement that this recording whips up, let's not quibble. —JEFFREY DUNN

KING OF HEARTS
Original Broadway Cast, 1978 (Original Cast Records) ★

When the charming film *King of Hearts,* a cult hit of the 1970s, was adapted as a Broadway musical extravaganza, it curled up and died. Don Scardino starred as Johnny, a young American soldier in World War I. Sent to a French village in search of a time bomb, Johnny doesn't know that all the townspeople have evacuated and the folks he encounters are actually the escaped inmates of the local lunatic asylum. The story is afflicted with the ridiculous notion that crazy people are beautiful visionaries, while the score lacks dramatic punch and variety. For the recording, composer Peter Link replaced the original Broadway orchestrations with more intimate arrangements that make the whole thing sound like a collection of cutouts from French cabaret albums. Jacob Brackman's lyrics are OK, but the score is simply too weak, although Scardino's sweet rendition of "Close Upon This Hour" does have a nice folk-pop quality. Also on hand are Millicent Martin as one of those soulful European madams, Pamela Blair as a virginal prostitute, and Bob Gunton as a circus master. It all begins pleasantly enough, but everything sounds alike—and the recording sounds like a demo.　　　—DAVID BARBOUR

KISMET

Original Broadway Cast, 1953 (Columbia/Sony) ★★★★★

Based on the themes of composer Alexander Borodin, this is the classic Arabian Nights musical. Starring the magnificent Alfred Drake as Hajj the poet, *Kismet* is one of the greatest cast albums ever recorded—unsurpassed and indispensable. The show is a poetic fantasy about fate, an almost operatic treatment of the belief that a man can control his own destiny through industry and wit. Drake is at the height of his powers here, his every moment of brio, wisdom, and romantic musicality bursting from this excellent-sounding monophonic recording. Seldom has a score been as well conducted as this one is by Louis Adrian. Drake's exceptional performance is ably supported by Richard Kiley as the Caliph, with his rich, sexy baritone voice. Soprano Doretta Morrow is lovely in "Baubles, Bangles, and Beads," "And This Is My Beloved," and Marsinah's other musical moments. The amazing Joan Diener is on hand to hit Lalume's numbers out of the park; her vocal gymnastics in "Not Since Nineveh" still can make jaws drop. And Henry Calvin is powerful in "Was I Wazir." Through the genius of Robert Wright and George Forrest, Borodin's classic melodies have been transformed into great theater music. The team's lyrics still crackle with the intelligence, wit, and craft of a Cole Porter or Stephen Sondheim. The few melodies that Wright and Forrest created from scratch—such as "Rahadlakum" and the bridge to "Stranger in Paradise"—are so excellent and so authentic-sounding that they combine seamlessly with the Borodin music.

Film Soundtrack, 1955 (MGM/Rhino-Turner) ★★★★★

When the movie version of *Kismet* hit the Cinemascope screen, the results were pallid compared with the spectacular stage production, but the film soundtrack is a triumph. It is led by the young André Previn, a classical musician who had also established himself as an accomplished jazz pianist; Previn fully comprehended the score's serious roots, and having musically supervised many MGM films, he was also able to enhance the glitzy elements of the score. Rhino's expanded soundtrack CD is a fabulous treat. It even includes "Rhymes Have I," recorded by Howard Keel and Ann Blyth but deleted from the film, and the reprise of "Fate" and the "Dance of the Three Princess of Ababu" are spectacular. Keel and Blyth are nearly as good as Alfred Drake and Doretta Morrow on the Broadway cast album. Dolores Gray surpasses all other Lalumes; she brings tremendous color and vivacity to "Not Since Nineveh," while her delivery of the reinstated song "Bored" is smooth and sensual. Her chemistry with Keel is titillating and their "Rahadlakum" duet is wonderfully erotic. Unfortunately, the only disappointing selection on this *Kismet* edition is the score's most famous song, "Stranger in Paradise." It's conducted at a very slow tempo, and Vic Damone as the Caliph croons and slides through this operatic ballad as though he's singing in a wee-hours piano bar. When Blyth joins Damone for the second chorus, she sounds precious and stilted. Even the arrangement of the number is lethargic. But, other than that misguided performance, the soundtrack is glorious and highly recommended as a companion to the original Broadway recording.

Studio Cast, 1963 (London) ★★★★

The popular conductor Mantovani received top billing when this album was released, but he isn't the only star here: Opera great Robert Merrill sings Hajj to great effect and diva Regina Resnik is Lalume. This *Kismet* has a very "classical" sound, yet the nuances of musical comedy are intact; the performance captures both the lyrical and showbiz glitz elements of the show. Merrill handles the big baritone passages and witty patter songs of his role equally well; next to Alfred Drake, he's the best Hajj on records. Resnik's "Not Since Nineveh" may be a bit high-toned, but she is nonetheless sexy and fun. Adele Leigh and Kenneth McKellar show off their lovely, operetta-style voices in "Stranger in Paradise" and "This Is My Beloved." This was the first stereo recording of *Kismet* and, as heard on CD, it definitely measures up to more recent digital recordings of the score.

Music Theater of Lincoln Center Cast, 1965 (RCA) ★★★★

Recorded in beautiful stereo, this *Kismet* features the show's original star, Alfred Drake. It's a joy to hear him recreate his most colorful role, and the elapsed years only add weight to his intelligent performance. One difference between this recording and the 1953 Broadway album is that the thrilling overture has been replaced by a watered-down section of Borodin's "Polyvetsian Dances." Still, Franz Allers' conducting certainly has musical expertise. Most of the supporting cast is excellent, particularly Lee Verona as Marsinah. Anne Jeffreys, a major musical theater talent who rarely had the good fortune to be recorded, is Lalume; although not as witty as Joan Diener in the role, she has a versatile voice and gets to sing the sensual "Bored." As for the Caliph, Richard Banke displays a wonderful tenor in his renditions of "Stranger in Paradise" and "Night of My Nights." On the whole, this is a more intimate statement of the score than the original cast album and is fine as a second choice for your collection.

Studio Cast, 1989 (JAY, 2CDs) ★★

This is a nearly complete British studio recording of *Kismet*. Although parts of the score may benefit from a semi-operatic interpretation of the Borodin melodies, the performance is stodgy and lacks presence. The brassy Broadway elements of the score are sabotaged and, as a result, those sections simply seem old-fashioned. The usually wonderful Judy Kaye displays a certain amount of showbiz flamboyance as Lalume, but even she sounds too cautious. Donald Maxwell, Valerie Masterson, and especially David Rendall are first-rate singers, yet they all sound too stuffy for the score's witty numbers and sensually romantic ballads. The fabulously talented Rosemary Ashe is fine in the small role of Ayah, momentarily bringing the proceedings to life. John Owen Edwards' conducting is rather sloppy and never bouncy. The only real recommendation of this recording is the inclusion (on the two-disc version) of five Wright-Forrest songs from *Timbuktu*, a 1979 rewrite of *Kismet*. Also included is "Bored" from the film version, here sung by Judy Kaye.

Studio Cast, 1991 (Sony) ★★★★

The colorful, vocally demanding role of Hajj the poet is taken here by Samuel Ramey. This opera star's expansive bass voice sounds thrilling in "Fate," "The Olive Tree," and the rest of

Kismet's more legit-type numbers, but his stalwart style leaves something to be desired in such lighter songs as "Rhymes Have I" and "Gesticulate." On the other hand, Julia Migenes is equally at home in opera and musical theater; her performance as Lalume is vocally spectacular and loaded with sex appeal. Jerry Hadley, as the Caliph, has a magnificent voice, but his interpretations of "Stranger in Paradise" and "Night of My Nights" are more stilted than romantic. Ruth Ann Swenson is far more successful as Marsinah; her gorgeous rendition of "Baubles, Bangles, and Beads" is a highlight of the disc. Dom DeLuise is an amusing Wazir and Mandy Patinkin does a weird cameo as the "Marriage Arranger," singing his number in falsetto. Broadway veteran Paul Gemignani conducts expertly.   —GERARD ALESSANDRINI

KISS ME, KATE
Original Broadway Cast, 1948 (Columbia/Sony) ★★★★★
Here is Cole Porter's greatest score—fresh, groundbreaking, and oh, so naughty. The show's book, by Bella and Sam Spewack, has a rousing backstage plot matched by a spirited play-within-the-play—Shakespeare's *Taming of the Shrew*—which turns up in excerpts here and there, giving the principals dual roles. As Fred/Petruchio and Lilli/Kate, the great stars Alfred Drake and Patricia Morison are at their professional peak; they deliver every word distinctly and caress every note magnificently. As Lois/Bianca, Lisa Kirk acts and sings her numbers impeccably; her performance of "Why Can't You Behave?" is unsurpassed as her sultry voice pours over great lines like "There I'll care for you forever / Well, at least till you dig my grave." Porter's raunchy lyrics for "Always True to You in My Fashion" are also meticulously rendered by Kirk. Harold Lang is on hand as Bill/Lucentio to sing the silly but charming "Bianca." Pembroke Davenport conducts skillfully. *Kiss Me, Kate* arguably contains more famous songs than any other Broadway score: "So in Love," "Wunderbar" "Another Op'nin', Another Show," "Too Darn Hot," and one of the cleverest comedy numbers ever written for the stage, "Brush Up Your Shakespeare." And let's not forget the delightfully nasty "I Hate Men," performed here by Patricia Morison as if she really means it! (Note: *Kiss Me, Kate* opened on December 30, 1948, but the cast recording was actually made in January 1949.)

Film Soundtrack, 1953 (MGM/Rhino-Turner) ★★★★★
MGM gave *Kiss Me, Kate* the royal treatment. The soundtrack is thrilling, even if this is more a flashy movie musical than a faithful transfer of the stage show. As Fred/Petruchio, Howard Keel sings with bravura. Katherine Grayson as Lilli/Kate is less adequate; her vocal trills are flashy but she doesn't have the acting or belting chops for "I Hate Men." The cast member who shines the brightest is Ann Miller as Lois/Bianca. Besides being a great dancer, Miller was also a fine singer, and her brassy renditions of "Always True to You in My Fashion" and "Too Darn Hot" are terrific. Another delight is the musical scoring by Saul Chaplin and André Previn; although the treatment is as Hollywoodish as can be, Porter's splendid melodies and urbane lyrics shine through. The score was transferred to the screen almost in its entirety. Sadly, "Another Op'nin', Another Show" was dropped, but another great Porter song was added: "From This Moment On," here in a spectacular jazz arrangement for full orchestra. That track alone is worth the price of the disc, but Rhino's expanded CD includes the entire film score in glorious early stereo.

Studio Cast, 1959 (Capitol/Angel) ★★★★★
This recording is nearly identical to the original cast album made ten years earlier, the only major difference being that this version is in stereo. The stars reunited to rerecord the score in

state-of-the-art "Full Dimensional Stereo" soon after the airing of a CBS-TV version of *Kiss Me, Kate* that starred Alfred Drake and Patricia Morison; the telecast featured Bill Hayes as Bill/Lucentio and Julie Wilson as Lois/Bianca, but this studio cast recording brought back Lisa Kirk and Harold Lang along with the Broadway conductor, Pembroke Davenport. All of the performances are as fresh and vibrant as on the original album; except for the improved sound quality, it's sometimes hard to tell one version from the other. But the orchestra seems augmented a bit here, and original cast member Lorenzo Fuller as Paul the valet gets to lead "Another Op'nin', Another Show" in addition to "Too Darn Hot." Note that the show's gangster roles are sung by Aloysius Donovan and Alexis Dubroff—both a.k.a. Alfred Drake!

Studio Cast, 1990 (Angel) ★★★

Conductor John McGlinn spearheaded this recording of *Kiss Me, Kate,* starring Josephine Barstow and Thomas Hampson in a fine edition but one that is less effective and less theatrical than other recorded performances of this great show. Still, it's historically important because of its completeness; aside from the original overture, it offers every song verse and fully orchestrated versions of songs dropped from the show before it opened, plus an excellent booklet filled with background information. Hampson and Barstow are magnificent opera singers, but a Cole Porter score needs performers with a more theatrical edge. Kim Criswell is also a wonderful talent but miscast as Lois/Bianca. George Dvorsky, David Garrison, and Davis Gaines are effective in their roles, but, on the whole, this recording sounds somewhat cold. Ultimately, it short changes the jazzier, wittier aspects of the score.

Studio Cast, 1996 (JAY, 2CDs) ★★★

Thomas Allen and Diana Montague are well cast as Fred/Petruchio and Lilli/Kate, with beautiful voices that never overpower the songs and acting that suits the material nicely. Diane Langton as Lois/Bianca is somewhat less effective vocally and comically, but Graham Bickley as Bill/Lucentio is quite appealing. The score is excitingly conducted by John Owen Edwards: His tempi are bright and bouncy, and the orchestra sounds full and lush. The complete, original Robert Russell Bennett orchestrations are heard in all of the jazzy dance numbers, the overture, and the entr'acte plus the scene-change music and underscoring. This two-disc set also contains bonus tracks of the overtures to Porter's *Can-Can, Jubilee,* and *Out of This World.*

Broadway Cast, 2000 (DRG) ★★★★

This recording of *Kiss Me, Kate* stars Brian Stokes Mitchell and Marin Mazzie, and their stellar performances help to make it one of the most delightful cast albums of recent years. Although reorchestrated for today's much smaller pit bands, Cole Porter's music still sounds great, and the story and songs haven't aged a bit. Mazzie's rendition of Lilli's "So in Love" is a particular standout as she captures all of the angst and passion inherent in one of Porter's greatest love songs. Mitchell does an especially fine job with Fred's/Petruchio's love songs; his rendition of "Were Thine That Special Face" is at once poignant and thrilling. On the comedy side, Mazzie takes the honors with the most wonderfully overwrought version of Kate's "I Hate Men" imaginable. Amy Spanger and Michael Berresse are less effective as Lois/Bianca and Bill/Lucentio on this recording than they were onstage, but their performances remain solid. In fact, the entire cast—including Michael Mulheren and Lee Wilkof as the gangsters—performs with great vigor. If you're looking for an excellent contemporary interpretation of this timeless show, look no further.

—GERARD ALESSANDRINI

KISS OF THE SPIDER WOMAN
Original Toronto/London/Broadway Cast, 1992 (First Night) ★★★★★

Surely one of the most original and haunting musicals of the decade, *Kiss of the Spider Woman* is also one of the strangest and most surreal shows ever to enjoy a long Broadway run. Terrence McNally's adaptation of Manuel Puig's novel and film unfolds with the terrible logic of a dream. The action is set in a prison in an unnamed Latin American country: Brent Carver is Molina, a gay window dresser under arrest for having had sex with a minor; his cellmate is Valentin (Anthony Crivello), a fierce, homophobic revolutionary. Their relationship is complex, sexually charged, and fraught with ambiguity. Hovering over them both is Aurora, the film goddess of Molina's fantasies who is also the Spider Woman—the spirit of death—played by Chita Rivera. The drama moves in and out of the prison cell into a series of movie narratives, dreams, and memories that enmesh both men in a web of seduction, treachery, and death. The astonishingly rich score by composer John Kander and lyricist Fred Ebb captures every shifting mood and level of reality. "Dressing Them Up" and "I Draw the Line" establish the troubled Molina-Valentin relationship clearly. "Dear One" is a gorgeous quartet for the two men plus Molina's mother (nice work by Merle Louise) and Valentin's girlfriend Marta (Kirsti Carnahan). Equally fine is the heartbreaking "You Could Never Shame Me," also featuring Molina's mother. There is room for wild movie parodies ("Gimme Love," "Russian Movie/Good Times"), and such dark, surreal numbers as the "Morphine Tango." Once again, however, a Kander-Ebb score is afflicted with an overblown anthem—in this case "The Day After That." Carver and Crivello are first-rate, but the miracle here is Rivera. At an age when most of her contemporaries have retired, she is a stunning presence—alternately campy, sinister, maternal, and mysterious. She's particularly electrifying in the show's best song, "Where You Are," a creepy yet hilarious portrait of the movies' power to obliterate reality (brilliantly orchestrated by Michael Gibson). Rivera is also alluring and frightening in "I Do Miracles" and commanding in the sinister title tune. She, and the disc, are simply not to be missed.

Broadway Cast, 1995 (Mercury) ★★★

Few replacement casts get their own album, but Vanessa Williams was a popular recording artist when she went into *Kiss of the Spider Woman* as Aurora—hence, this disc. Something is lost and something gained here. Williams' singing is formidable but her performance falls short. Aurora isn't really a character; she's an idea, a projection of Molina's fantasies about the movies, his feelings about his mother, his fascination with death. Chita Rivera brought every watt of her star power to bear on the role, with memorable results. Williams simply doesn't have the same overwhelming personality. On the other hand, Brian Stokes Mitchell is now Valentin and the power of his voice is, as always, stupendous; he even makes something stirring out of "The Day After That." As Molina, Howard McGillin is a little too leading mannish—Brent Carver was far closer to the desperately sad character envisioned by Terrence McNally and Manuel Puig—but his singing is beyond reproach. The disc is out of print as of this writing; don't go out of your to way find it, but if you're a Williams fan, you'll certainly enjoy it.   —DAVID BARBOUR

KNICKERBOCKER HOLIDAY
Original Broadway Cast, 1938 (Joey/AEI) ★★★

Boiled-down radio broadcasts of Broadway musicals were not unheard of in the 1930s and the few that have been released commercially in subsequent decades generally provide interesting, if scratchy, listening. This one is especially valuable, since there are no other recordings of Kurt

Weill and Maxwell Anderson's 1938 political satire; as a bonus, AEI's CD also incorporates material from a 1945 radio version with a studio cast. In a little under an hour, the recording spins a diverting yarn of old New Amsterdam and its autocratic mayor, Peter Stuyvesant, as filtered through the imagination of narrator Washington Irving (played by a young Ray Middleton). In the process, Anderson has fun with jokes about old New York and scores still-trenchant political points about media censorship and totalitarianism in democracy's clothing. Best of all, Walter Huston preserves for posterity his debut role in musical theater, whispering "September Song" unforgettably and making every syllable count. His comic timing is also impeccable, even though he's playing against the tepid Tina Tienhoven of Jeanne Madden. The bad news, aside from the decidedly predigital sound, is the heavy editing of the musical program: Included here are just four complete songs and slivers of others, along with the briefest of overtures. At least the other principal ballad, the tender "It Never Was You," gets a complete rendering by Madden and Richard Kollmar. This score, Weill's second for the Broadway stage, demands a more complete recording. (You can get an additional taste of it on Thomas Hampson's Weill album.) Till that happens, the AEI disc is a useful stopgap.   —MARC MILLER

KUNI-LEML
Off-Broadway Cast, 1998 (Slider Music) ★★

Avrom Goldfadn's Yiddish farce *The Two Kuni-Lemls* is all but forgotten today. Even so, New York's Jewish Repertory Theatre (JRT) commissioned a musical version of it in 1984 and it turned out to be a success. But it wasn't until the JRT revived *Kuni-Leml* fourteen years later that the musical was recorded. The album reveals this to be a charming show; Raphael Crystal's music is bouncy and Richard Engquist's lyrics are solid, but that's pretty much the best that can be said for the score. The strength of the recording lies in the casting: Danny Gurwin as the title character, a pious student who's roped into marrying a rich man's daughter; and Farah Alvin as a matchmaker's daughter who's unlucky in love. These two are hilarious in their solos ("What's My Name?" and "Don't Worry, Darling") and delightful in their duet ("Do Horses Talk to Horses?"), so much so that they rise above the middling material. Paul Harman is suitably over-the-top as the boisterous matchmaker. David Wolfson leads a four-piece band through the nicely orchestrated score.   —SETH CHRISTENFELD

KWAMINA
Original Broadway Cast, 1961 (Capitol/Angel) ★★★★

So, which Broadway composer stretched himself the most in writing a score that no one would have guessed he had in him? Jerry Herman with *Dear World*? Good answer. Stephen Schwartz with *The Baker's Wife*? Better answer. Richard Adler with *Kwamina*? Best answer! Adler, who had previously cowritten two hits—*The Pajama Game* and *Damn Yankees*—here took on African tribal music and scored astonishingly well. The album starts off arrestingly with "The Cocoa Bean Song," in which African laborers tell what they have in common with their crop ("One does the drinkin'; the other gets drunk"). "Nothing More to Look Forward To" has a glorious, Bantu-inspired melody, and it's a shame that the Kingston Trio's cover version wasn't included as a bonus track. Both music and lyrics sparkle in "One Wife," which gives us the tribe's atypical views on monogamy, and "Something Big," the African colony's cry for independence from England. But—and a big but it is!—much of the show deals with two doctors: Kwamina (Terry Carter), an African educated in England, and Eve (Sally Ann Howes), a British woman. And, alas, most of their songs are routine.   —PETER FILICHIA

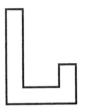

LA CAGE AUX FOLLES
Original Broadway Cast, 1983 (RCA) ★★★★★

Harvey Fierstein's book closely follows Jean Poiret's stage farce (which became a huge film hit) about the chaos unleashed when the son of a St. Tropez gay couple, one of whom is a drag-nightclub star, becomes engaged to the daughter of a conservative politician. But this *La Cage aux Folles* is the only version—including the American film remake *The Birdcage*—that portrays the two men, Georges and Albin, as deeply in love. Indeed, Jerry Herman's touching "Song on the Sand" is still one of the few gay love ballads to come out of Broadway. Among the other choice songs are Albin's delightful paean to drag, "I Put a Little Mascara On," and the title tune about the nightclub ("You go alone to have the evening of your life / You meet your mistress and your boyfriend and your wife!"). Additional highlights of the score: "Look Over There," an angry defense of gay parenting, and "The Best of Times," with its live-for-today philosophy. The first-act closer, "I Am What I Am," is in a class by itself, and George Hearn's savage rendition of it is one of the great Broadway performances of the decade. Gene Barry does sensitive work as Albin's seen-it-all spouse. Jim Tyler's brassy orchestrations add a touch of Jacques Brel to Herman's melodies. This show sends Sondheim fans into a tizzy for having snatched away the Best Musical Tony Award from *Sunday in the Park With George,* but in my book, the Tony voters were right. —DAVID BARBOUR

LADY, BE GOOD!
Original Broadway Cast Reconstruction, 1977 (Smithsonian/no CD) ★★★★★

Here is one of the great artifacts of the American musical theater—and it's also a great listen. One of a series of Smithsonian reconstructions released during the 1970s, this album of the 1924 George and Ira Gershwin musical *Lady, Be Good!* is probably the best of all. After Fred and Adele Astaire finished the show's Broadway run, they repeated their roles in London, where they recorded six of their songs (and English cast member William Kent recorded one more). George Gershwin himself played piano for four of the sides and all of them are simply delightful. To be able to hear Fred and his legendary sister perform "Hang On to Me," "Fascinating Rhythm," "So Am I," "Swiss Miss," "I'd Rather Charleston" (added for the London run), and "The Half-of-It-Dearie Blues" (in which Fred dances and clowns

---

ALL-TIME FAVORITES OF
THE NEW YORK TIMES
THEATER CRITIC

Ben Brantley

1. Carousel
2. Chicago
3. Follies
4. Gypsy
5. My Fair Lady
6. Oklahoma!
7. Pal Joey
8. Show Boat
9. Sweeney Todd
10. West Side Story

with Gershwin) is simply remarkable. In addition, Cliff Edwards—mostly remembered as Jiminy Cricket's voice in Disney's *Pinocchio*—sings a couple of numbers, and the duo-piano team of Phil Ohman and Victor Arden is also heard. A few Gershwin piano solos, drawn from old radio broadcasts and a 1924 piano roll, add more delights.

Studio Cast, 1992 (Roxbury/Elektra-Nonesuch) ★★★

This recording, like others of the well-intentioned Gershwin releases from Roxbury, fails to recreate the musical comedy spirit that made *Lady, Be Good!* a touchstone of the Roaring Twenties. Too often, it feels like an academic exercise, busily reconstituting original orchestrations and performing styles. It may be authentic, but it isn't very enjoyable. Except for female lead Ann Morrison, most of the cast, especially the male principals, sing everything very squarely and right on the beat. However, John Pizzarelli is charming in emulating the vaudeville looseness of Cliff Edwards, the show's original lead. And when Jason Alexander arrives near the end of the first act with the title song and some terrible jokes, he offers a welcome burst of energy. As always with this label's releases, the booklet accompanying the CD is extensive and terrific. —DAVID WOLF

LADY IN THE DARK

Original Cast Recordings Without Original Orchestrations, 1941; collected on *Kurt Weill From Berlin to Broadway,* Volume 1 (Pearl /Pavilion, 2CDs) ★★★

Why do we always read that Gertrude Lawrence was a poor singer? (Kurt Weill was quoted as saying that she had "the greatest range between C and C-sharp.") Perhaps she was inconsistent in live performances, but as heard in her studio recordings of songs from *Lady in the Dark,* Lawrence is in command and on pitch most of the time. (OK, there are a few questionable notes in "My Ship.") On these recordings of Lawrence and Danny Kaye performing selections from the show, the arrangements and orchestrations are watered-down versions of what composer Weill wrote. With lyrics by Ira Gershwin, all of the songs in the score, save one, appear in dreams that Liza Elliott recounts to her analyst; each dream becomes a mini-opera, but these first recordings from the show feature only its major numbers. The exception is a medley from the "Glamour Dream" that includes "Oh, Fabulous One," "Huxley," and "Girl of the Moment." (It's fun to hear Lawrence handle the patter of "Huxley" with a vocal quartet culled from the show's chorus; it gives us some sense of the original production.) The "Glamour Dream" continues with Lawrence blithely swinging through "One Life to Live." The "Wedding Dream" presents the star in a romantic ballad, "This Is New," and a fairytale, "The Princess of Pure Delight." Kaye delivers "It's Never Too Late to Mendelssohn" and a big showstopper: "Tschaikowsky (and Other Russians)," in which he races through the names of fifty Russian composers in a tongue-twisting tour de force. Then Lawrence scores with another showstopper, "The Saga of Jenny"; unfortunately, for this recording, Ira Gershwin had to sanitize many of his lyrics for the ribald song. The show's final number, "My Ship," is the only one sung outside of the dream sequences, and it marks the conclusion of Liza's therapy: She recalls the words to the song from her childhood and is instantly cured! While these vintage recordings do not really convey the theatricality of *Lady in the Dark,* they are a valuable record of a show that earned a major place in the development of the modern musical. (In addition to the eight tracks from *Lady in the Dark,* this two-disc compilation includes four more Danny Kaye recordings of songs from the show, the incomparable Hildegarde singing "The Saga of Jenny," and selections from other Weill scores.)

Television Production Soundtrack, 1954 (AEI) ★

Taken directly from the kinescope soundtrack of a Max Liebman television production, this *Lady in the Dark* stars Ann Sothern as Liza. The orchestrations are by Irwin Kostal and they bear little resemblance to Weill's originals; the musical style is more 1950s Hollywood than 1940s Broadway. Sothern handles her dialogue well and has the right glamour and archness for the role. Her "One Life to Live" is jaunty and cool, her "My Ship" is smooth if not overly complex, but her "Saga of Jenny" is incomplete and cleaned up for TV. The disc includes three long, extraneous dances to variations on Weill's music; they were performed in the ninety-minute TV special by Bambi Linn and Rod Alexander. These annoying entries aside, the bonus tracks on this CD make it worth purchasing; among them are Lawrence's studio recordings of several songs from the score, plus her live broadcast performances of "Jenny" and "My Ship" with MacDonald Carey of the original Broadway cast.

Studio Recording with TV Cast, 1954 (RCA/no CD) ★★

The cast of the *Lady in the Dark* TV production went into a studio before performing the show live to make this album. Irwin Kostal's orchestrations sound much better here without all the background noise and hubbub of the AEI release reviewed above. Ann Sothern comes across well, while Carleton Carpenter does a fine job as Beekman in the "Glamour Dream" and does not disappoint with the Ringmaster's "Tschaikowsky." Robert Fortier gets to sing a little as Randy Culver, the character's name having been inexplicably changed from Randy Curtis.

Studio Cast, 1963 (Columbia/Sony) ★★★

When originally released, this was the first full-length representation of the classic Kurt Weill-Ira Gershwin score for *Lady in the Dark.* While the notes claimed the recording to be "musically intact . . . complete with Kurt Weill's original orchestrations," there are many internal cuts that were probably made to fit the songs onto a single, forty-five-minute LP, and some of the orchestrations were fiddled with. Still, the recording gives listeners a sense of how the dream-sequence songs hung together to form mini-operettas—one of the things that made the show such a groundbreaker. While this recording has its flaws, Sony's beautifully remastered CD has many virtues. The orchestra and chorus are jauntily conducted by Lehman Engel. As Liza, Risë Stevens brings requisite glamour to "One Life to Live," some beautiful tones to "My Ship," and does her darnedest to shed her operatic mannerisms in "The Saga of Jenny" (but ends the song with a glorious high note). If she is not fully convincing in the more dramatic moments of dialogue and recitative, this is still a hearty and well-sung performance. Adolph Green works too hard at times, but he's still enjoyable and makes the most of "Tschaikowsky." John Reardon is heard as film star Randy Curtis, the role originated by a barely musical Victor Mature; he sings the big ballad that Mature never sang, "This Is New," with ringing baritenor tones. The smaller roles are also well handled.

Original London Cast, 1997 (JAY) ★★★★

Of all *Lady in the Dark* recordings, this one must be perceived as the genuine article. The original Weill orchestrations were used with some augmentation and there are no cuts in the score. As a result, this recording is nothing less than revelatory. In the pivotal role of Liza Elliot, we have Maria Friedman, a brilliant, established musical theater star in London. Friedman is a much stronger singer than Gertrude Lawrence, possessing a very strong belt voice with a soprano extension. Her "One Life to Live" is belt-y—but that sound of confidence, shaken at the end of the "Glamour Dream," creates its own mystique. When she offers lighter soprano tones in "My Ship," Friedman's Liza sounds as if she is truly rediscovering the words and realizing for the first time what they mean to her. She does an equally great job with the "Saga of Jenny." Another lovely discovery is that we can finally hear "This Is New" as originally conceived; singing it with Friedman, the American baritenor Steven Edward Moore sounds wonderful. James Dreyfuss won an Olivier Award for his performance as Russell Paxton and The Ringmaster (the Danny Kaye roles) and he comes across fairly well on the recording, which also boasts excellent choral work.

—JEFFREY DUNN

THE LAST 5 YEARS
Original Off-Broadway Cast, 2002 (Sh-K-Boom) ★★★★★

Although the Off-Broadway production that yielded this recording received mixed to negative reviews and closed quickly, *The Last 5 Years* has proven to be extraordinarily popular on the regional theater circuit—in part because this two-character musical requires minimal sets and costumes, but also because it offers the excellence of Jason Robert Brown's score. Somewhat autobiographical, Brown's story charts the five-year relationship between a writer (Jamie) and an actress (Catherine). The show is really more of a song cycle than a traditional musical, which doesn't mean that it's lacking in emotion or theatricality. Through Jamie's songs, we see the couple's relationship moving from beginning to end, while Cathy's songs progressively take the story backward in time from the couple's breakup to the first flush of romance. Both characters are fully rounded human beings with their own virtues and flaws: Jamie is smart, witty, and a real charmer but also rather full of himself while Cathy is warm, loving, and funny but tends to see herself as a victim. The forward/reverse concept adds immeasurably to the emotional content of the score: The exact moment when the couple's stories overlap chronologically, while they're in a boat on the lake in Central Park, is breathtaking, and the final sequence is indescribably moving. The show also has comic relief: Cathy's "A Summer in Ohio" is a hilarious vision of summer-stock hell, while "Shiksa Goddess" is Jamie's very funny spiel about his mother's anticipated reaction to his dating a non-Jew. Another highlight is "The Schmuel Song," in which Jamie tells Cathy a sweetly humorous story that makes a point about their relationship. On this recording, Norbert Leo Butz and Sherie René Scott bring Jamie and Catherine to life in all their joy and pain, and the band—basically a string quartet plus Brown as pianist-conductor—sounds beautiful. *The Last 5 Years* is a modern masterpiece of the American musical theater, and the cast album is essential to the collection of anyone who loves the art form.

—MICHAEL PORTANTIERE

THE LAST SESSION
Original Off-Broadway Cast, 1997 (EMG) ★★★★

By the mid 1980s, plays about AIDS began to surface and continued to emerge through the '90s, but with only a few musicals among them. Nevertheless, this one would likely stand out in a large field. At the request of his partner, librettist Jim Brochu, composer-lyricist Steve Schalchlin wrote ten songs about his experiences battling the plague. Brochu slotted them into a script about Gideon, a dying rock musician who intends to commit suicide after recording a final album. Not surprisingly, the recording session—for which three other singers and an engineer are present—and its aftermath do not go entirely as planned. Granted, the situation that triggered the show's creation and the storyline is rife with potential pitfalls, but Schalchlin avoids them all with his unflinching lyrics: Examples are "Somebody's Friend" (about cure rumors) and "The Group" (about support circles). Schalchlin's melodies are unflaggingly propulsive. Since AIDS may not be as topical now as it was during its urgent-headline days, the musical is now something of a period piece—but there's nothing dated about these performances. Bob Stillman has all of the passion needed for Gideon. The others, singing at the top of their lungs about their feelings, are Stephen Bienskie, Dean Bradshaw, Amy Coleman, and Grace Garland. Schalchlin did the arrangements, which were enhanced by Stillman (an expert rock pianist).   —DAVID FINKLE

THE LAST SWEET DAYS OF ISAAC
Original Off-Broadway Cast, 1970 (RCA/no CD) ★★
Three years after their debut show (*Now Is the Time for All Good Men*), which was studded with well-crafted lyrics and lovely ballads, composer Nancy Ford and librettist-lyricist Gretchen Cryer appeared to have struck gold with *The Last Sweet Days of Isaac*. Very well reviewed and the winner of Obie, Drama Desk, and Outer Critics Circle awards, the show seemed a shoo-in headed for a long run, but there was just one problem: It didn't have a second act, and audiences balked. Act I—the first side of this LP—is literate, odd, and very funny. It introduces us to the self-dramatizing Isaac, convinced that every moment on earth is his last, and Ingrid, an inhibited secretary who has always longed to be a poet. These two are stuck together in an elevator. Onstage, Austin Pendleton was genuinely hilarious and wildly endearing as Isaac. His recorded performance and one of Isaac's songs, the terrific "My Most Important Moments Go By," earn this entry its two stars. As Ingrid, Fredricka Weber was quirky and appealing, sang well, and even played the trumpet! Still, this was Pendleton's show, if "show" is the correct word. I don't think there's a coherent moment in the second act, which again focuses on Isaac and Ingrid. Here, they're locked in individual prison cells fourteen years earlier, able to communicate only through video cameras.   —DAVID WOLF

LATE NITE COMIC
Studio Cast, 1988 (Original Cast Records) Not recommended.
This vaguely autobiographical musical by composer-lyricist Brian Gari, with a book by Allan Knee, lasted for only fifteen previews and four performances on Broadway—and it's not hard to understand why. The plot, such as it is, concerns the off-and-on relationship between a pianist who wants to be a standup comedian and an "off-the-wall" (so the synopsis says) ballet dancer who keeps changing her name. Most of the songs are performed by Gari, whose thin, squeaky voice is even worse than his songs, and Julie Budd, whose singing almost manages to transcend the poor material. Michael McAssey (from the Broadway production) and Robin Kaiser put in special appearances: He and Gari function as the male chorus; she sings a terrible song in the guise of a hooker. The capper is the "bonus track," an unintentionally hilarious number titled "Late Night Saga" in which Gari melodramatically recounts the sob story of his musical's fate. It offers the disc's sole moment of genuine enjoyment in the form of a quote from an unidentified theater critic: "*Late Nite Comic*, my friends, is so bad that when I went outside for intermission, I stood under the marquee of another theater."   —SETH CHRISTENFELD

LEAVE IT TO JANE
Off-Broadway Cast, 1959 (Strand/AEI) ★★
The "Princess Theater" musicals of Jerome Kern, Guy Bolton, and P. G. Wodehouse form an

important chapter in musical theater history that is badly underrepresented on CD. Although *Leave It to Jane,* a 1917 college musical, didn't actually play the Princess, its tight construction, modest production values, and good humor make it a close relative. So let's be grateful for the cast album of this revival, a big hit in a tiny theater. (The actors actually had to go out to the street, down a transom, and through the audience to make their entrances.) That said, the album is largely a botch. Kern's graceful, lilting melodies are indestructible and Wodehouse's lyrics have their signature good humor and self-effacement. But Joseph Stecko, conducting an underpopulated orchestra, wreaks havoc with the tempi: "The Crickets Are Calling" is supposed to be slow and reflective, not a slapstick chase. Conversely, "There It Is Again" plods here. Kathleen Murray as Jane must have been very charming onstage, because she certainly can't sing. Dorothy Greener puts "Cleopatterer" across but doesn't convey the funny-sad pathos of "Poor Prune." A young George Segal is in the chorus, but you won't hear him. The show itself remains entirely stageworthy, with a laugh-out-loud book and a score that's eminently lovable. — MARC MILLER

LEAVE IT TO ME!
San Francisco Cast, 2001 (42nd Street Moon) ★★★★
With political satire a mainstay of 1930s musicals (the Gershwins' *Of Thee I Sing,* Rodgers and Hart's *I'd Rather Be Right,* Irving Berlin's *Louisiana Purchase*), Cole Porter's turn came in 1938 with *Leave It to Me!*—an amusing if none-too-penetrating look at U.S.-Soviet relations. The show was both a critical and financial success, but history remembers it only as the musical that made Mary Martin a star as she sang and stripteased her way through "My Heart Belongs to Daddy." Martin's role was subsidiary to those of Sophie Tucker, Victor Moore, William Gaxton, and Tamara; in hindsight, her success overshadowed the contributions of the stars and the rest of Porter's score, which included "Get Out of Town" and the cheeky "Most Gentlemen Don't Like Love" (with its references to Sappho and rolls in the hay). As with many other Porter shows, *Leave It to Me!* was neither recorded (except for a couple of Martin cuts) nor filmed, and it is almost never revived. Fortunately, sixty years after the fact, San Francisco's 42nd Street Moon company tackled it. While most of the original arrangements did not survive, musical director Dave Dobrianksy did a fine job of piecing together the enjoyable score—dance breaks and all. Of course, the lyrics are incredibly witty; in "I'm Taking the Steps to Russia," Porter rhymes "Harlem rhythm" with "Communithm." The cast is accomplished, the scaled-down orchestra is dandy, and Marc Miller's notes are clever and informative. — RICHARD BARRIOS

LEGS DIAMOND
Original Broadway Cast, 1989 (RCA) ★★★
This show did not work onstage, but some of the songs and performances on the CD are fun. Peter Allen, woefully miscast as a tough-guy gangster, rips joyfully into "When I Get My Name in Lights" and is very effective in the big ballad "Sure Thing, Baby." He swings through "Steal From Thieves" with Randall Edwards, seems to be having a ball with Julie Wilson in "Only an Older Woman," and makes the most of "Now You See Me, Now You Don't." Wilson takes the mediocre number "The Music Went Out of My Life" and wrings lots of emotion from of it, but the female trio "The Man Nobody Could Love" doesn't quite land. This out-of-print recording preserves a mediocre Peter Allen score with a few bright spots; you'll probably want to use your remote to get to the good stuff. The disc has some added interest in that quite a few of the *Legs Diamond* songs wound up in the Allen biomusical *The Boy From Oz.* — JEFFREY DUNN

LES MISÉRABLES
Original London Cast, 1985 (First Night/Relativity, 2CDs) ★★

In 1980, Claude-Michel Schönberg ("musique") and Alain Boublil and Jean-Marc Natel ("textes") wrote what amounts to a song cycle that was inspired by Victor Hugo's massive novel *Les Misérables.* The French-language "concept album" of that work contains less than ninety minutes of material. Evidently realizing that every self-respecting Frenchman knows *Les Misérables* well, the creators did not try to cover the entire plot in the songs they wrote. But when British producer Cameron Mackintosh saw a stage version of the work in Paris, he had the artistically (if not financially!) foolish idea that *Les Miz*—as it would come to be known the world over—should be translated into English and turned into an epic musical that would attempt to tell the full story of the novel. Herbert Kretzmer was hired to do the English adaptation, and he performed the impossible task as well as anyone could have done. The problem is that, although the Mackintosh *Les Misérables* is fully twice as long as the original French version, Schönberg wrote only a comparatively small amount of new music for it; the extra hour-and-a-half contains endless reprises and fillers of banal sung dialogue. To offer only two examples: The tune of the prostitutes' Act I song "Lovely Ladies" recurs in Act II in a completely unrelated context, sung by a group of women mourning the dead revolutionaries; and the gorgeous melody that's first heard in Fantine's deathbed lament "Come to Me" is later repeated note-for-note as Eponine's "On My Own," with only the key and lyrics changed. *Les Miz* is a sung-through show, but probably it would have been much better as a book musical with some spoken-dialogue scenes. That would have served the double purpose of allowing more of the plot to be covered in less time while avoiding the repetition of so many melodies with alternate lyrics. Among the score's best moments are "At the End of the Day," the moving song of the wretched masses; the students' stirring anthem "Do You Hear the People Sing?"; and Marius' "Empty Chairs at Empty Tables," affectingly performed by the young Michael Ball. Colm Wilkinson displays a magnificent, versatile voice in the role of Jean Valjean, but some listeners will find it hard to adjust to his odd accent and mannerisms. As Eponine, Frances Ruffelle sounds mush-mouthed and whiny. On the plus side, Patti LuPone is magnificent in the brief role of Fantine, singing the beautiful "I Dreamed a Dream" for all its worth; and Roger Allam is dramatically committed as Inspector Javert if a little insecure from a vocal standpoint. Finally, Sue Jane Tanner and Alun Armstrong are amusing enough as the Thenardiers—but the fact that these evil characters are used for comic relief in this ill-advised musical version of *Les Misérables* is indicative of the show's problems.

Original Broadway Cast, 1987 (Decca, 2CDs) ★★

There are a few reasons to consider this recording as an alternative/addendum to the one reviewed above. Randy Graff is a wonderful Fantine, quite the equal of Patti LuPone; Terrence Mann, as Javert, has better vocal technique than Roger Allam; and Michael Maguire is a stalwart Enjolras. There is also some new music on this recording, notably, Jean Valjean's gorgeous "Bring Him Home"—even if the song's main melody sounds like that of the "Humming Chorus" from Puccini's *Madama Butterfly,* a debt that Claude-Michel Schönberg has allegedly acknowledged. Otherwise, this two-disc set isn't a whole lot different from its predecessor: Colm Wilkinson returns as Valjean and, unfortunately, Frances Ruffelle is back as Eponine.

The Complete Symphonic Recording, 1988 (First Night, 3CDs) ★

The star here is Gary Morris, an American country-western singer who had played Valjean early in the run of the Broadway production. Unfortunately, Morris' accent and mannerisms are just as weird as Colm Wilkinson's in the role, and his voice isn't nearly as good. Morris has a vibrato so wide that it's really a wobble; every sustained note that he sings is really two notes, and it ain't pretty. Given that his singing of the show's central role is unlistenable, the strengths of this recording seem beside the point. Still, for what it's worth: Philip Quast as Javert and Anthony Warlow as Enjolras are excellent. Michael Ball is back as Marius and Tracy Shayne sings prettily as Cossette. Also, Debbie Byrne as Fantine delivers the high notes of "I Dreamed a Dream" without belting, and some listeners may therefore prefer her performance to Patti LuPone's and Randy Graff's. As Eponine, Kaho Shimada has a better voice than Frances Ruffelle—but, annoyingly, she seems to imitate Ruffelle's inflections and enunciations. The London Philharmonia orchestra sounds huge and impressive. This is a complete recording of the score, but none of the extra music you'll find here is worth writing home about.

London Concert Cast, 1995 (First Night, 2CDs) ★★

This is a live recording of a concert given at the Royal Albert Hall to mark the tenth anniversary of the opening of *Les Miz* in London, and there's quite a sense of occasion about it. In total, some two-hundred-and-fifty performers took part, and the orchestra is no less than the Royal Philharmonic, conducted by David Charles Abell. At the end of the second disc, Jean Valjeans from many worldwide companies may be heard delivering various lines of "Do You Hear the People Sing?" in various languages. So, if you want to choose only one recording of *Les Misérables* for your library, this may be your best option. To begin with, it's the only one that gives you Colm Wilkinson as Valjean while not giving you Frances Ruffelle as Eponine. Here, Eponine is Lea Salonga, whose lovely, unaffected singing goes a long way toward wiping out memories of Ruffelle in the part. Other major roles are filled by some of the most talented performers to have played them: Philip Quast as Javert, Ruthie Henshall as Fantine, Michael Ball as Marius, Michael Maguire as Enjolras, and Judy Kuhn as Cossette. Note that a video recording of this concert is also available.

—MICHAEL PORTANTIERE

LET 'EM EAT CAKE

New York Concert Cast, 1987 (Sony, 2CDs, paired with *Of Thee I Sing*) ★★★★

This performance doesn't vary much in character from the dully dutiful reading of the Gershwins' *Of Thee I Sing* that accompanies it. But *Let 'Em Eat Cake,* a 1933 George and Ira Gershwin-George S. Kaufman-Morrie Ryskind sequel to that Pulitzer Prize winner, is so darkly different and the music so fascinating that it's easily the more rewarding listening experience. (Most of the score was previously unrecorded.) The show pokes fun at unions, socialists, capitalists, influence brokers, the League of Nations, and baseball. You can understand why critics and audiences rejected it—it's too acerbic and almost hysterically bitter, with none of its predecessor's sly good humor—but it's stupendous from a musical standpoint. The riches start immediately as a dissonant, percussive overture segues into "Tweedledee for President," and the score throughout is highly adventurous. (It's as if we can hear George warming up for *Porgy and Bess.*) Maureen McGovern leads "Mothers of the Nation," a real find with a mock-sanctimonious lyric wedded to a soaring, anthemlike melody. Incidental numbers and ensembles like "Union Square," "They're Hanging Throttlebottom in the Morning," and the ferocious title song show two geniuses pushing against the walls of musical theater convention with all their might. As they are in *Of Thee I Sing*, Paige O'Hara and David Garrison are enormous assets here, and Michael Tilson Thomas' conducting sounds energized by the prospect of reintroducing so much marvelous material to the world. —MARC MILLER

LET IT RIDE
Original Broadway Cast, 1961 (RCA/no CD) ★

Apologies to songwriters Jay Livingston and Ray Evans, but here's the show with arguably the worst title song in the history of Broadway—and that includes *Happy Hunting*. While the doleful tune isn't heard until track six of the first side of the LP, by then, this pallid adaptation of *Three Men on a Horse* has already proven its lack of worth. The show starts with a chorus singing about how they must "Run, Run, Run" the rat race, but the melody erroneously suggests joy. Then comes the saccharine "The Nicest Thing," in which a wife tells her husband why she loves him, followed by "Hey, Jimmy, Joe, John, Jim, Jack," sung by George Gobel in his horribly nasal voice. That voice also spoils the score's ace trump, "His Own Little Island," a song that should be better known—which is more than can be said for "Broads Ain't People." You'd expect that a song titled "Love, Let Me Know" would be plaintive, but the melody for it is brisk. There is an item that would spark the dullest party: The kitschy stripper's song "I Wouldn't've Had to Shake It." Still, by the time you reach "There's Something About a Horse," you'll have realized that little about *Let It Ride* is worth the trip. —PETER FILICHIA

THE LIFE
Original Broadway Cast, 1997 (Sony) ★★★★

The Life opened just as Times Square was being cleaned up and turned into a tourist-friendly theme park. It captured the Best Musical prize from the Drama Desk, Drama League, and the Outer Critics Circle and ran for 465 performances. This tasty cast album preserves the two best elements of the show: its largely terrific, tuneful score by composer Cy Coleman and lyricist Ira Gasman, and vivacious, charismatic performances that practically leap from the disc. The score's pulsating, rhythmic, lowdown groove is very different from other shows of the period. One peak follows another: Sam Harris and company hit a home run early on with "Use What You Got"; Pamela Isaacs, the hooker with a head voice, gives out with a funky "A Lovely Day to Be Out of Jail" and the gorgeous ballad "He's No Good"; and the show-stopping, comedic "The Oldest Profession" is sung for all its worth by Lillias White. Chuck Cooper won a Tony for his performance as a "cold-blooded, sweet talkin', jive ass, motherfuckin' son of a bitch" pimp called Memphis; his "My Way or the Highway" and "Don't Take Much" are here to be savored. Other delights of *The Life* include the show's ensemble numbers, especially the toe-tapping "Hooker's Ball," led by Vernel Bagneris, and the ladies' rocking, high-belt anthem "My Body." The album concludes beautifully with Isaacs and White performing the touching duet "My Friend." A few passages of recitative may strike some listeners as an uneasy fit with the overall style of the piece. But, all things considered, *The Life* strikes me as a welcome breath of grimy New York City air in an era when Times Square has been sanitized. —MORGAN SILLS

LI'L ABNER
Original Broadway Cast, 1956 (Columbia/Sony) ★★★★

The cast album of this hit, faithfully adapted from Al Capp's deep-fried comic strip, has a complicated history that's worth telling because this disc warrants attention. One of the last monaural cast recordings, it made a brief appearance on CD around 1990 in a no-frills transfer that quickly became a collectors' item. Rumor had it that the entire album had been recorded in stereo, but it turned out that the binaural tracks were unusable because the orchestra was recorded on the left channel, the singers on the right. Sony cleaned up the monaural tracks and added several things for this CD reissue: a full-stereo overture; a stereo version of the "Sadie Hawkins Ballet"; missing finale material; and some never-heard-before original-cast moments. To top it off, folded in are a Rosemary Clooney single of a fine song that was cut from the show ("It's a Nuisance Having You Around") and a Percy Faith instrumental of another out-of-town casualty ("The Way to a Man's Heart"), all of which stretches the CD's length to a generous seventy-two minutes. The result is a first-class Goddard Lieberson recording of a quintessential Golden Age smash. The score boasts strong Gene DePaul melodies and incomparable Johnny Mercer lyrics. The rhymes are ingenious, the satire still pertinent (there's even a funny song about genetic engineering), the Dogpatch idiom even more resonant than it was in Capp's strip. Peter Palmer, though slightly stiff, is so ideal as Li'l Abner that he had a hard time thereafter getting casting agents to picture him as anything else. Edith (Edie) Adams sings sweetly and sexily as Daisy Mae, and Stubby Kaye's Marryin' Sam shines in show-stopping material. One only wishes that Charlotte Rae, as Mammy Yokum, had a whole song to herself instead of just a few bars of the opening number. Lehman Engel's musical direction displays enormous verve from the overture's first rockabilly note. By the way, note the gaffe in "Put 'Em Back," when a chorus girl comes in early and then stops herself short.

Film Soundtrack, 1959 (Columbia/no CD) ★★

Paramount's film version of *Li'l Abner* was among the most faithful of its era, retaining a lot of the Broadway score and several of the leading players as well as a stage-bound production design. So there are few surprises on this soundtrack album. Among the pluses: Peter Palmer has loosened up a lot, Nelson Riddle's new arrangements are fresh and snazzy, and this recording is in end-to-end stereo. But there are minuses: Several stage songs are missing; the one new ballad ("Otherwise") doesn't equal the one it replaces ("Love in a Home"); some of Mercer's lyrics have been dumbed down for the movies; and Imogene Lynn, the voice double for Leslie Parrish's Daisy Mae, hasn't as much style as her stage counterpart, Edith (Edie) Adams. Not yet released on CD, the album is a pleasant souvenir of one of the better '50s stage-to-screen transcriptions, but it's hardly worth traipsing to Dogpatch and back to track it down.

—MARC MILLER

THE LION KING
Film Soundtrack, 1994 (Walt Disney Records) ★★★

The mega-hit animated Disney movie *The Lion King* spawned this mega-selling soundtrack recording, which includes the Oscar-winning best song "Can You Feel the Love Tonight?" A large orchestra with that distinctive, latter-day Disney-pop sound plays the five Elton John-Tim Rice songs, including "Circle of Life" and "I Just Can't Wait to Be King." Some of the celeb voices featured in the film can be heard on the soundtrack disc: Jeremy Irons does "Be Prepared" with Whoopi Goldberg and Cheech Marin, and that's Nathan Lane singing with Ernie Sabella in "Hakuna Matata." The accompanying booklet helpfully includes lyrics to all of the songs for those who choose to sing along. The disc includes tracks of instrumentals by the gifted Hans Zimmer and ends with three of the songs in distinctive, electric renditions by Elton John. More often than not, you can indeed "feel the love" on this recording.

Original Broadway Cast, 1997 (Walt Disney Records) ★★★★

The Lion King is more than a musical; it's a juggernaut. This time, Disney didn't follow the route it had taken with *Beauty and the Beast,* for which the Broadway staging was mostly a replication of the film with a few extra songs. Instead, Julie Taymor directed a show packed with visual splendor that creatively reimagined and expanded upon the movie (and won the 1998 Tony Award for Best Musical). Composer Elton John and lyricist Tim Rice's pop-hit songs are thrillingly performed, and they sit very well next to the chanted pieces and new songs that the team wrote for the stage show. (There is some additional material by other writers.) That stylistic unity is aided by lush orchestrations by Robert Elhai, David Metzger, and Bruce Fowler that utilize authentic African rhythms and instruments. "Circle of Life" and "Can You Feel the Love Tonight?" retain their effectiveness, though their presentation here differs somewhat from that of the film's soundtrack. "Hakuna Matata" is charmingly performed, and Geoff Hoyle as Zasu does a clever new number, "The Morning Report." The best of the additions are "They Live in You" (sung by Samuel E. Wright, reprised by Tsidii Le Loka) and "Shadowland" (warbled by Heather Headley). One quibble, which applies to many cast albums these days: The rough edges of a live performance have been so thoroughly fixed and mixed in the studio that the whole thing is an inch short of freshness. But that's a tiny complaint about this glorious audio souvenir of an enchanting Broadway perennial. —MORGAN SILLS

LISTEN TO MY HEART: THE SONGS OF DAVID FRIEDMAN
Original Cast, 2003 (Midder Music, 2CDs) ★★★★

Skillfully programmed and directed by Mark Waldrop, this revue had an all-too-brief run Upstairs at Studio 54. Happily, it yielded a terrific "live" cast album that will bring pleasure to those who saw the show and introduce some wonderful music to those who missed it. As presented onstage and in this two-disc set, *Listen to My Heart* demonstrates that David Friedman's range as a composer-lyricist is much greater than he's often given credit for. His best-known songs were popularized by two late, irreplaceable singers, Laurie Beechman and Nancy LaMott. Most of his material falls into two general categories: life-affirming anthems and heart-on-the-sleeve love ballads. Some of the lyrics can be difficult for the more cynical among us to take, but Friedman's sincerity is genuine, and his talent and versatility are much in evidence here. "Live It Up," for example, is a funny up-tune that's very different from two standout, country-inflected numbers: the witty "If You Love Me, Please Don't Feed Me" (written with Robin Boudreau and Scott Barnes) and the heartfelt "My White Knight" (not to be confused with the *Music Man* song of the same title). Given that so many of Friedman's songs mark him as a paragon of positive thinking, one of his most surprising creations is "Catch Me," a poignant plea for help from a person on the brink of suicide. Then there are Friedman's hysterically funny "Jewish humor" songs, performed to the hilt by Alix Korey. Happily, her rendition of "My Simple Wish," aka "My Simple Christmas Wish"—long the stuff of cabaret legend—is preserved here. Thanks to this disc-set's excellent sound quality, every performance can be fully appreciated: Allison Briner's soulful delivery of "My White Knight"; Joe Cassidy's powerful "Catch Me"; Michael Hunsaker's sympathetic response, "I Can Hold You"; and Anne Runolfsson's "What I Was Dreamin' Of" and "We Can Be Kind," which show her to be one of the finest singing actresses of her generation. First-rate ensemble work and three songs played and sung beautifully by Friedman himself complete the listening experience. —MICHAEL PORTANTIERE

LITTLE MARY SUNSHINE

Original Off-Broadway Cast, 1959 (Capitol/Angel) ★★★★★

Not too long after Sandy Wilson proved with *The Boy Friend* that audiences enjoyed spoofs of old musicals, Rick Besoyan wrote the book, music, and lyrics to this hilarious send-up. It ranks with the Wilson opus as head-and-shoulders above every subsequent satire of the genre. Besoyan's target is operetta of the type that Sigmund Romberg and Victor Herbert were turning out circa 1910-'20s. Throughout the narrative about forest rangers, finishing-school maidens, and a few Native Americans, the clever author lines up every cliché of the art form as if setting ducks in a row, then shoots every one down with great delight. There's the love chant ("Colorado Love Call"), the cheer-up ditty ("Look for a Sky of Blue"), the marching song ("The Forest Rangers"), the fun-time contrapuntal choral pieces ("Playing Croquet," "Swinging," "How Do You Do?"), the salute-to-the-old-country tune ("In Izzenschnooken on the Essenzook Zee"), the novelty number ("Mata Hari"), and a darling title song. All are tuneful and amusing. Leading the large cast, Eileen Brennan became the toast of downtown as the sunny title character, instigating lots of laughs with her silvery voice and cunning delivery. John McMartin and Elmarie Wendel played the secondary love interests. Onstage, the score was played on twin pianos, but for this recording, Capitol provided a full orchestra. — DAVID FINKLE

LITTLE ME

Original Broadway Cast, 1962 (RCA) ★★★★★

The album starts with one of the most exciting overtures ever and takes off from there, thanks to orchestrator Ralph Burns. With Cy Coleman's tough, sophisticated melodies perfectly matched to Carolyn Leigh's mind-bending word games, the entire score of *Little Me* is a treat. Neil Simon's libretto, based on Patrick Dennis' spoof of tell-all celebrity bios, is a raucous series of burlesque blackouts tracing the rise, fall, and rise of Belle Poitrine (née Schlumpfert). Our heroine's search for "wealth, culture, and social position" leads to numerous misadventures, including the annihilation of most of her lovers—all of whom are embodied by Sid Caesar. In terms of energy and wit, the score is simply unforgettable. The opening number, in which "Miss Poitrine, Today" (Nancy Andrews) announces her plan to pen her memoirs, sets the perfect tone of genial satire. Other gems include the poor-girl's manifesto "The Other Side of the Tracks," in which Virginia Martin as Young Belle unleashes her astonishing belt, and "Deep Down Inside," with Young Belle innocently vamping a superannuated miser played by Caesar. In the hands of Swen Swenson, the sizzling "I've Got Your Number" is one of the sexiest tracks on any cast album. Three ballads also stand out: the Tinseltown lament "Poor Little Hollywood Star," the delightful "Real Live Girl," and the notably fatalistic "Here's to Us." And when the two Belles merge to sing the title song, watch out! One irony is that Caesar, in his only Broadway musical, is somewhat overshadowed on disc by Martin and Andrews; but every number is guaranteed to chase the blues away.

Original London Cast, 1964 (Pye/DRG) ★★★

A fair copy of the Broadway original, the London cast album of *Little Me* features Brit comedy star Bruce Forsyth in Sid Caesar's roles, with Eileen Gourlay as Young Belle. They're enthusiastic, to say the least—and the disc contains the dance number "Rich Kids Rag," which the Broadway edition does not. Forsyth is a better singer than Caesar but he can't approach his predecessor's hilarious performance as French cabaret star Val du Val in "Boom-Boom." Swen Swenson is still on hand but, for some reason, this recording of "I've Got Your Number" lacks excitement. Still, the cast is strong, and this is one London recording of an American musical that doesn't suffer from slow tempi. It's a good complement to the Broadway version but harder to find; if you do come upon it, note the many changes in the lyrics for Brit audiences.

Broadway Cast, 1999 (Varèse Sarabande) ★★

Never really a hit, *Little Me* is one of those musicals that its creators can't let alone. (An early-'80s Broadway revisal that divided Sid Caesar's roles between Victor Garber and James Coco was a quick flop.) For the 1999 Roundabout Theatre production, Simon again rewrote his book, combining Belle and Young Belle into one role for Faith Prince. Martin Short appeared as all the men in her life. The overall performance is brassy and far too knowing: Short's hamming is shameless (his mangled French accent in "Boom-Boom" is very unfunny) while Prince's breathy, overemphatic singing underlines each joke with the vocal equivalent of a magic marker. On top of all that, Harold Wheeler's orchestrations lack the metallic exuberance of Burns' originals. However, the disc does contain the "Rich Kids Rag" and a zesty rendition of "Deep Down Inside." Also, thanks to the inclusion of some amusing dialogue sequences, we get a better sense of the show's plot line than what may be gleaned from the original Broadway album.　　　　—DAVID BARBOUR

A LITTLE NIGHT MUSIC

Original Broadway Cast, 1973 (Columbia/Sony) ★★★★★

This show is emblematic of composer-lyricist Stephen Sondheim's work in that it sounds like none of his other scores and yet is clearly the creation of musical theater's reigning genius. Based on Ingmar Bergman's film *Smiles of a Summer Night,* with a book by Hugh Wheeler, *A Little Night Music* features songs that are romantic, witty, and heartbreaking by turns—and Jonathan Tunick's orchestrations are lush. The cast album is disappointing in that the vocal limitations of Glynis Johns as Desirée Armfeldt and Patricia Elliott as Countess Charlotte Malcolm prevent them from full-out acting of their songs. Elliott sings "Every Day a Little Death" with little nuance; Johns gives flat readings of her semi-spoken lines in "You Must Meet My Wife," and although her rendition of "Send in the Clowns" is heartfelt, it's difficult to listen to because the bulk of the music lies right around her register break. The rest of the cast is superb, however. Len Cariou and Laurence Guittard sing beautifully as Fredrik Egerman and Carl-Magnus Malcolm, respectively. Victoria Mallory is vocally resplendent as Anne Egerman, yet she manages to sound convincingly young, as the character must be for the plot to make sense; ditto tenor Mark Lambert as Henrik, whose singing in "Later" and "A Weekend in the Country" is really quite something. Hermione Gingold's performance of Madame Armfeldt's "Liaisons" is full of personality, and be sure not to miss D. Jamin-Bartlett's definitive rendition of one of the best, most profound songs in the score: "The Miller's Son."

Original London Cast, 1975 (RCA) ★★★

This recording boasts fewer legit voices than the Broadway album; even some of the Liebeslieder singers fall short. More damagingly, Joss Ackland just doesn't have the vocal goods for the role of Fredrik. The key of "You Must Meet My Wife" has been lowered for him, but he's still unable to sustain high notes for more than one beat, and he's perfectly awful in "It Would Have Been Wonderful." As Anne, Veronica Page sings prettily enough except above the staff, where her voice thins out. David Kernan sounds fine as Carl-Magnus, as does Terry Mitchell as the tormented Henrik. Although Maria Aitken has even less voice than Patricia Elliott, her contribution to "Every Day a Little Death" has much more emotion to it. Jean Simmons is lovely as Desirée, even if her voice seems much lower than it is on the film sound-track of *Guys and Dolls;* her "Send in the Clowns" is very persuasive. Finally, Diane Langton rather thrillingly belts "The Miller's Son" in a higher key than her Broadway predecessor, D. Jamin-Bartlett. Gingold is back as Mme. Armfeldt. The orchestrations are the originals for the most part, but this version of Fredrik's "Now" includes some clever little brass and woodwind interjections that are not on the Broadway album.

Film Soundtrack, 1977 (Columbia/no CD) ★

A film that might have been wonderful was hampered by the casting of Elizabeth Taylor as Desirée. *A Little Night Music* was also sabotaged by moving the action from Sweden to Austria, with some of the characters renamed to conform to the new locale. The switch to Vienna may not seem a bad idea, given the score's many waltzes, but it just doesn't work. The movie score does include a brilliant new version of "The Glamorous Life" for Fredrika, winsomely sung by Elaine Tomkinson (dubbing for Chloë Franks)—but since a bonus track of that song is now to be found on the more accessible original Broadway album, why search for a long out-of-print LP? Tomkinson also dubs Anne Egerman's songs for Lesley-Anne Down; she does a beautiful job in both cases, but the fact that one singer ghosts two separate roles indicates how misguided this film is. Better than expected is Taylor's "Send in the Clowns"; while her voice is quite tremulous, it adds to the character's emotional vulnerability. (Taylor's singing is also dubbed by Tomkinson in the rewritten opening number, "Love Takes Time" and also, it seems, for Desirée's final line in "You Must Meet My Wife.") Another plus is Diana Rigg—a fabulous Charlotte; not only does she act the character's songs better than others who preceded her in the role, she sings them better, too. Len Cariou and Laurence Guittard recreate their original roles but rein in their big voices for the film medium, so you'll probably enjoy them more on the Broadway album. Among the great songs not included in the film or on the soundtrack LP are "In Praise of Women," "Liaisons," and "The Miller's Son." Gingold is back once again as Mme. Armfeldt but, with "Liaisons" gone, she doesn't have much to do here.

Royal National Theatre Cast, 1995 (Tring) ★★★

This recording features two major, controversial additions to the score: Fredrika's solo version of "The Glamorous Life," which Sondheim wrote for the film version of *A Little Night Music,* and Charlotte's "My Husband the Pig," which was cut from the show before it opened on Broadway. Trying to shove those songs into a stage production is questionable to begin with, and it's done here with a consummate lack of skill: Fredrika's "Glamorous Life" is broken up into sections that are interrupted by bits of the original version sung by Desirée, Madame Armfeldt, and the Liebeslieder singers, while "My Husband the Pig" is stuck into the middle of Carl-Magnus' "In Praise of Women." It's shocking that Sondheim allowed any of this; the new "Glamorous Life" conglomeration, in particular, is hard to listen to because it contains several bizarre modulations of key. Not surprisingly, the best thing about this recording is the versatile, stellar Judi Dench in the role of Desirée. Her performance of "Send in the Clowns" is truly special, most noteworthy for the bitterness and anger that she adds to the song's mix of emotions. Laurence Guittard (the original Carl-Magnus) has graduated to the role of Fredrik, which he sings very well; here, Carl-Magnus is capably sung by Lambert Wilson. Other accomplished principals are Joanna Riding as Anne, Patrica Hodge as Charlotte, Issy van Randwyck as Petra, and the great Siân Phillips as Mme. Armfeldt. The glaring exception is Brendan O'Hea as Henrik, screaming the high notes that are sung so beautifully by Mark Lambert on the original Broadway album. —MICHAEL PORTANTIERE

LITTLE SHOP OF HORRORS

Original Off-Broadway Cast, 1982 (Geffen) ★★★★

Who would have thought that Roger Corman and Charles B. Griffith's campy 1960 horror flick about a bloodthirsty plant out for world conquest would make such a delightful musical? The original cast recording of *Little Shop of Horrors* beautifully demonstrates why this show has become a modern classic. The score, with lyrics by Howard Ashman and music by Alan Menken, is a treasure; it charmingly combines evocative early-'60s song styles with theatricality so solid that the "girl group" sound of the catchy title song and the driving Motown beat of "Git It" don't sound out of place next to the sweetly heartfelt "Somewhere That's Green" or the soaring duet "Suddenly Seymour." Then there's the cast: Lee Wilkof has just the right combination of hardness and softness for the nebbishy Seymour, who works at the behest of the carnivorous Audrey II (soulfully voiced by Ron Taylor); Hy Anzell is fine as flower-shop owner Mushnik; Franc Luz plays a variety of bit parts successfully, including the sadistic biker dentist; and Sheila Kay Davis, Jennifer Leigh Warren, and Leilani Jones are great as the close-harmony singing, Greek-choruslike urchins. Finally, there's Ellen Greene, her unique talents perfectly matched to the role of ever-hopeful yet abused Audrey; Greene melds trashiness with vulnerability while singing beautifully. Unfortunately, one full song, an important reprise, and small sections of other numbers are omitted from this disc, and included is a version of "Mushnik and Son" that was later replaced. These changes make it an incomplete record of the material that most people will see performed today, but what's here is presented well enough to forgive what's not.

Film Soundtrack, 1986 (Geffen) ★★★

All things considered, the film adaptation of *Little Shop of Horrors* is excellent: bright, funny, thoughtfully directed (by Frank Oz), and well performed by a cast that features Rick Moranis as Seymour, the irreplaceable Ellen Greene as Audrey, and Steve Martin in a riotous performance as the dentist. Changed for the film: All of Mushnik's songs are cut and "Some Fun Now" replaces "Ya Never Know"; the new song "Mean Green Mother from Outer Space" is fine but not as exciting as "Don't Feed the Plants." Note also that the soundtrack album's spoken prologue and "Skid Row" have minor but noticeable differences from what's heard in the film, and "The Meek Shall Inherit" doesn't reflect the movie's cuts. Happily, while the score retains most of its original intimacy, it sounds better than ever with the full orchestrations by Bob Gaudio, Thomas Pasatieri, and original orchestrator Robby Merkin. ("Suddenly Seymour" is particularly thrilling.) Though this recording doesn't capture all the magic of the movie itself, it does a pretty commendable job.

Broadway Cast, 2003 (DRG) ★★★★

This is the cast recording that *Little Shop of Horrors* always needed. Everything is here: "Mushnik & Son" (with the now-standard lyrics); "Call Back in the Morning"; Audrey's "Somewhere That's Green" reprise; and even the "Shing-a-ling" first act finale! While some of the show's sweet simplicity was sacrificed in favor of bigger takes on everything in the Broadway revival, *Little Shop* fans will want this disc to be part of their collection despite its minor flaws. There are a few musical changes—most significantly, the use of the movie version's extended title song. Danny Troob's orchestrations lack the appeal of Robby Merkin's, and some of the casting—particularly Hunter Foster as Seymour and Kerry Butler as Audrey—is more functional than ideal. Still, the recording is a winner, and it includes five bonus tracks of demo/cut songs sung by Menken, Ashman, and original Audrey II-voice Ron Taylor.　　—MATTHEW MURRAY

THE LITTLEST REVUE
Original Off-Broadway Cast, 1956 (Painted Smiles) ★★★★

The vibrant overture on this disc tells us that we're about to hear one of the tangiest revues of the 1950s. Ben Bagley produced the show. Most of the songs are by Vernon Duke and Ogden Nash, and those that aren't are by unknowns who wouldn't stay unknown for long: Charles Strouse, Lee Adams, and Sheldon Harnick, to name just three. The hilarious "Backer's Audition" opener is the work of orchestrator John Strauss, Kenward Elmslie, and John Latouche. The cast is uneven but pretty terrific overall. A young Tammy Grimes is already mannered and throaty, but who cares when she's introducing "I'm Glad I'm Not a Man," with Nash rhymes like "battle-axe" / "Cadillacs." Joel Grey has fun with the mock-Belafonte number "I Lost the Rhythm" (music and lyrics by Strouse). And everything Charlotte Rae touches turns to gold: She's warm and distinctive in the Duke-Nash song "Summer Is a-Comin' In," zany in Harnick's "The Shape of Things," devastating in Bud McCreery's "The Power of Negative Thinking," and triumphant in "Spring Doth Let Her Colours Fly." That last-named item, an impudent Strouse-Adams spoof of Helen Traubel's Las Vegas act, may be the single funniest song from any '50s revue. The other performers aren't quite of the Grimes-Grey-Rae caliber: Beverly Bozeman over-belts "Good Little Girls," and Tommy Morton, more a dancer than a singer, bobbles the fine, odd Duke-Nash ballad "Born Too Late." But the material (including a couple of CD bonus tracks) is so strong that one columnist was moved to call the show "the *My Fair Lady* of the intimate revue." That's not much of an exaggeration.　　—MARC MILLER

LOOK, MA, I'M DANCIN'!
Original Broadway Cast, 1948 (Decca) ★★★

Based on an idea by Jerome Robbins, *Look, Ma, I'm Dancin'!* was a broad musical comedy about a touring ballet company. It starred the incredibly gifted Broadway clown Nancy Walker, best remembered as Rhoda's mother on *The Mary Tyler Moore Show;* at 4'10", she made her entrance leading a Russian wolfhound that was nearly as tall as she was. Walker played an heiress whose money pays for the tour, thereby securing her place as the latest addition to the corps de ballet. The other main character, played by Harold Lang, is a brilliant but disliked young choreographer, loathed even by the girl who loves him. The show comprised three love stories, but the eight Hugh Martin songs on this album, all lightly swinging, do not reveal any sense of plot. Walker gets two solid comic pieces, "I'm the First Girl in the Second Row in the Third Scene in the Fourth Number, in Fifth Position" and "I'm Tired of Texas," plus the more romantic, upbeat "If You'll Be Mine." Lang sings the irrepressible "Gotta Dance" and the self-reflective "I'm Not So Bright." Composer Martin performs the odd "Little Boy Blues" with Sandra Deel, who also sings "Shauny O'Shea," though Deel did neither in the New York production. Bill Shirley didn't make it to opening night, but he has two numbers on the album, which was recorded during rehearsals to avoid a pending musicians' strike. If you're looking for more of this show, Robbins' "Mlle. Scandale Ballet" is on the Ben Bagley CD *Ballet on Broadway.*

Off-Broadway Concert Cast, 2000 (Original Cast Records) ★★

Musicals Tonight! is a very well-meaning New York company that mounts concert performances of old musicals. It consistently chooses the most interesting titles of all the NYC concert-musical series, and its tickets are far less expensive than any of the others. This recording documents the group's presentation of *Look, Ma, I'm Dancin'!*— apparently, the first since the original Broadway run. I'm fond of this material and Hugh Martin's writing in general, but I can't say that this disc is very impressive, even if it does include five songs that are not to be found on the original Broadway album. Except for Rob Lorey, none of the performers here sings with any distinctive sense of character. —DAVID WOLF

LORELEI

Original Broadway and Touring Cast, 1973-74 (MGM/Decca) ★★★

Sort of a "revisal" of *Gentlemen Prefer Blondes,* though that term had not yet been coined when this show was staged, *Lorelei* had a new book and many new songs by *Blondes* composer Jule Styne, with lyrics by Betty Comden and Adolph Green. The star of both shows was the same and so was the plot; a prologue and epilogue were added wherein central character Lorelei Lee reminisced about her life, to help justify the fact that Carol Channing was now too mature to play the role she had created twenty-four years earlier. The cast recorded the show before launching a year-long tour that was to precede the Broadway opening, but changes on the road led to a second recording. The first album, labeled "The Original Cast Recording" in big red letters and featuring a large drawing of Channing's face, had three new Styne-Comden-Green songs: "Looking Back," "Lorelei," and "I Won't Get Away." There were also new lyrics for the original score's "Sunshine," retitled "Paris, Paris." (Leo Robin wrote the lyrics for *Gentlemen Prefer Blondes.*) The second album was labeled "The Original Broadway Cast Album" in big *blue* lettering, with the same drawing of Channing. It added four tracks that were recorded a year after the first sessions: "It's Delightful Down in Chile"; "Men"; a reprise of "Looking Back" leading into a reprise of "Diamonds Are a Girl's Best Friend"; and a new overture. Inexplicably, some songs that were in the show when it reached New York were not on the album; but a new title song not performed on Broadway was included, probably to give leading man Peter Palmer more of a presence. The CD edition of *Lorelei* has everything that was recorded for both albums. Although the remastering is excellent, some of the tracks still sound hollow. Channing is in great voice and top form throughout. There is not much opportunity for the other cast members to score on disc, but Lee Roy Reams does a bang-up job with the jazzy "I Won't Let You Get Away," Tamara Long is a fine Dorothy, and Dody Goodman makes the most of her occasional comedic interjections. —JEFFREY DUNN

LOST IN THE STARS

Original Broadway Cast, 1949 (Decca) ★★★

Lost in the Stars, by playwright Maxwell Anderson and composer Kurt Weill, deals with racial discrimination and segregation—unlikely territory for a Broadway musical in 1940s America. With its operatic dimensions and somber tone, the show elicited mixed but largely approving notices. Weill and Anderson based their musical play on Alan Paton's *Cry, the Beloved Country,* a 1948 novel that contrasts the natural beauty of South Africa with the brutality of that country's apartheid policy. As in the novel, the protagonist of *Lost in the Stars* is a Zulu (played by Todd Duncan) ordained to the Anglican priesthood, whose son kills a white man in the course of committing a robbery and is tried for murder, convicted, and hanged. The story concludes with the reconciliation of two bereaved fathers—the black priest and the white man whose son was killed. Anderson's libretto and Weill's magnificent score take liberties with Paton's material; in fact, after seeing *Lost in the Stars,* the novelist wrote that he regretted giving its adapters the rights to his book. The musical featured a Greek chorus narrating and commenting on the action. The resultant show is what Virgil Thomson, in his review for the *New York Herald-Tribune,* called a *singspiel;* the chorus performs an inordinate amount of the score, leaving little for the principals to do. The recording contains about forty-five minutes of music, with Maurice Levine conducting a twelve-piece chamber ensemble, orchestrations by Weill. The spoken dialogue is somewhat wooden and some of the singing is weak.

Studio Cast, 1993 (MusicMasters Classics) ★★★★

As general director and principal conductor of the New York City Opera in the late 1950s, Julius Rudel rescued *Lost in the Stars* from obscurity by introducing it into his company's repertoire. Thirty-five years later, Rudel conducted this definitive recording of the beautiful Weill-Anderson score. Leading the Orchestra of St. Luke's, he utilized more musicians than Weill ever envisioned, and he searched the worlds of opera and musical theater to find a dream cast. Notable among the vocalists are Arthur Woodley, who not only sings exquisitely but also brings poignancy to Stephen Kumalo's Act II soliloquy; Cynthia Clarey, who executes "Stay Well" and "Trouble Man" with tenderness; and Carol Woods, who belts "Who'll Buy?" with flair. But the true stars of this recording are the members of the Concert Chorale of New York and tenor Gregory Hopkins as chorus leader. While the original Broadway album retains considerable historical interest, the superior vocalism and the ample orchestral sound of Rudel's studio version eclipses the earlier release.   —CHARLES WRIGHT

LOUISIANA PURCHASE
New York Concert Cast, 1996 (DRG) ★★★

This is a biting and funny satire of Louisiana's byzantine politics in general and of Huey Long in particular. Although *Louisiana Purchase* opened on Broadway in 1940 with a delightful sung disclaimer that all of its incidents were fictitious, composer-lyricist Irving Berlin and book-writers Morris Ryskind and B. G. DeSylva—and, no doubt, delighted theatergoers—reveled in the show's doses of reality-based topical material. This spirited musical had to wait more than a half-century for a recording. Fortunately, the wait was worth it. Based on a concert presentation at Weill Recital Hall in New York City, this is a zingy and infectious performance that is more than complete: A number of cut songs, some of them quite good, were reinstated. (Who besides hard-core scholars knew of "I'd Love to Be Shot From a Cannon With You?") Michael McGrath is aces as the wisecracking hero, Judy Blazer (with a hilarious German accent) makes a good partner for him, and veteran George S. Irving is predictably good in the role originally played by Victor Moore. Another veteran, Taina Elg, is charming if perhaps less assured than her part's creator, Irene Bordoni. In a role that's more Greek chorus than integral character, Debbie Gravitte offers some fine Broadway can-belto. Score-wise, this is not *Annie Get Your Gun* or *As Thousands Cheer,* but it's a lot of fun.   —RICHARD BARRIOS

LUCKY IN THE RAIN
Studio Cast, 2000 (DRG) ★

For this musical, seen at the Goodspeed Opera House in 1997, librettist Sherman Yellen wrapped a yarn about the romances of expat American journalists in 1927 Paris around a batch of songs by Jimmy McHugh (with lyrics by Harold Adamson and Dorothy Fields). Don't expect much; Yellen's idea of historical realism includes Gertrude Stein singing "On the Sunny Side of the Street" and a newsroom full of reporters performing a musical tribute to Charles Lindbergh with "Comin' In on a Wing and a Prayer." Others passing through include Josephine Baker and Isadora Duncan. With its easily ignorable plot and most of the lead roles sung by more than one performer, the album works best as a nod to McHugh by Broadway A-listers. Barbara Cook has several lovely tracks, but they appear to have been taken directly from her tribute album to Dorothy Fields, *Close as Pages in a Book.* Other notable participants are Malcolm Gets, Patrick Wilson, Debbie Gravitte, and Lillias White, but Peter Matz's orchestrations are more evocative of a pop album than a Broadway show. —DAVID BARBOUR

LUCKY STIFF
Original Off-Broadway Cast Members, 1994 (Varèse Sarabande) ★★★
"Promising" is the obvious word for *Lucky Stiff,* the first produced musical by composer Stephen Flaherty and lyricist Lynn Ahrens, but that would sell it short. It's also professional, assured, and entertaining, if not entirely successful. The show tells the trivial story of a meek British shoe salesman who will inherit six-million dollars if he agrees to take his uncle's corpse, in a wheelchair, for one last holiday in Monte Carlo. The two are pursued (and occasionally kidnapped) by all kinds of people who, essentially, want the salesman's money, although the pursuers each have their own particular farcical motivation. Perhaps because there's so much convoluted plotting and exposition in *Lucky Stiff,* it's hard not to wish that the score was a little less "integrated." The songs are occasionally so busy doing plot work that they aren't as much fun as they might have been; still, they exhibit genuine skill and craft. Flaherty's great gifts for melody and humor are already clearly in evidence, and some of Ahrens' neatest and most effortless lyrics are to be found here. Partly because the characters are broad but not terribly rich, the accomplished farceurs who make up the cast don't get the kind of musical moments that would elevate this show to another level—but the redoubtable Mary Testa, Evan Pappas, Judy Blazer, and Debbie Shapiro Gravitte come close.

Off-Broadway Cast, 2003 (JAY) ★★★
This recording, which followed a five-performance "Musicals in Mufti" run of *Lucky Stiff* at the York Theatre, is better than the original. The Varèse Sarabande album was made years after the show had closed at Playwrights Horizons, without the participation of the director and with only a few of the original performers. The JAY disc has much more of a real cast album feel to it, with a company that sounds like they've been through rehearsals and performances together; in fact, six of the ten performers here were also in the first production, though only two of them are heard on the original recording. All of their performances are looser, less frantic, and funnier here, with Mary Testa unleashed most triumphantly. Among the newcomers, Janet Metz and Malcolm Gets make an appealingly believable leading couple, even if his British accent is a sometime thing. Musical director David Loud's single-piano accompaniment is more attractive than the elaborate orchestrations of the first recording, which too often strain for comic effect. The material—silly but, unfortunately, never wonderfully silly—is mostly the same on both discs, though this one has a little more spoken dialogue as well as the previously unrecorded Act I finale and "A Woman in My Bathroom." In a bonus track, we get the charming "Shoes," which was cut from the show. Both CD booklets feature uncommonly ugly cover art. —DAVID WOLF

M

MACK & MABEL

Original Broadway Cast, 1974 (ABC/MCA) ★★★★

Everybody's favorite flop starred Robert Preston as silent-movie pioneer Mack Sennett and Bernadette Peters as his leading lady/lover Mabel Normand. In spite of numerous revisions and revivals, the show never works. Michael Stewart's downbeat book tells the story of a failed romance ending with Normand's early death, while Jerry Herman's witty, hooray-for-Hollywood songs belong to another musical altogether. The promised cocktail of tough humor and glossy tears is, in fact, a mélange of unpalatable opposites. Nevertheless, it's a hell of a score that provides a deluxe showcase for two of Broadway's greatest stars. Preston's gritty singing is ideally suited to the clever lyrics of "Movies Were Movies," "Hundreds of Girls," and "My Heart Leaps Up," all of which lay out Sennett's philosophy of filmmaking. Peters' Betty Boop-style belt is perfect in the galvanizing "Look What Happened to Mabel," the furious "Wherever He Ain't," and the wounded torch song "Time Heals Everything." Both stars score in different versions of the ballad "I Won't Send Roses." Other plusses include Lisa Kirk belting her way through the vivacious "Big Time," "Tap Your Troubles Away," and the inevitable Herman salute to the female star, "When Mabel Comes in the Room." All of the melodies sparkle in Philip J. Lang's orchestrations. This is a classic case of a show album that outclasses the show itself.

London Concert Cast, 1988 (First Night) ★★

This live recording of a concert version of *Mack & Mabel* has George Hearn and Denis Quilley lending their big voices to Mack's songs, Debbie Shapiro Gravitte walloping the daylights out of "Big Time" and "Wherever He Ain't," Georgia Brown's eccentric but touching version of "Time Heals Everything," and Tommy Tune's ebullient "Tap Your Troubles Away." Debits include the replacement of "My Heart Leaps Up," Mack's tribute to the Keystone Kops, with the inferior "Hit 'Em on the Head." Jerry Herman narrates.

Original London Cast, 1995 (Angel) ★★★

Although the leads are not ideal, this disc contains plenty of material not found on the Broadway album, including both act finales, an entr'acte, some reprises, and a title song that uses the melody of "Look What Happened to Mabel." Howard McGillin is vocally

---

ALL-TIME FAVORITES OF PERFORMER

John Raitt

1. Carousel
2. Oklahoma!
3. My Fair Lady
4. Porgy and Bess
5. The Pajama Game
6. Annie Get Your Gun
7. West Side Story
8. Fiddler on the Roof
9. Man of La Mancha
10. The Phantom of the Opera

overqualified as Mack; in "I Won't Send Roses," he laments the lack of romance in his soul in a voice that throbs with feeling. Caroline O'Connor as Mabel sounds eerily like Bernadette Peters (or an impersonator of her). Still, McGillin makes a very good case for "Hit 'Em on the Head," and O'Connor is appealing throughout. Kathryn Evans provides lusty renditions of "Big Time" and "Tap Your Troubles Away." And, if anything, Larry Blank's revisions of Philip J. Lang's orchestrations improve upon the originals.   —DAVID BARBOUR

THE MAD SHOW
Original Broadway Cast, 1966 (Columbia/no CD) ★★★★
Marshall Barer is the unsung genius lyricist of the musical theater; his output was slight in terms of quantity, but he could write a ballad or comic song with a felicity equal to anyone in the field. *The Mad Show,* a reunion with his *Once Upon a Mattress* collaborator Mary Rodgers, is one of the funniest recordings in cast album history. Of course, it helps if you're tuned in to the anarchic (and New York Jewish) humor of *Mad Magazine.* The excellence of the revue, the unity of its components, and its terrific cast all shine through on this recording. Here are Linda Lavin, JoAnne Worley, MacIntyre Dixon, Richard Libertini, and Paul Sand in the show that propelled their long, distinguished careers. A highlight of the album is "The Boy From," which all good musical comedy queens (err, fans) know was credited to Rodgers and "Esteban Ria Nido"—a pseudonym for Stephen Sondheim. *The Mad Show* ran for almost nine hundred performances. Unfortunately, when the show was released for production by regional groups, it was in a bowdlerized version. To add insult to injury, the recording has never been transferred to CD. But it's definitely worth the trouble to find a copy of the original LP.   —KEN BLOOM

THE MADWOMAN OF CENTRAL PARK WEST
Original Broadway Cast, 1990 (DRG) ★★★
I remember having a very good time at *Madwoman,* but the maddening thing is: I can't remember it in any detail. And this disc, only thirty-seven minutes long, is of little help in bringing back the experience. The show is about Phyllis Newman trying to get her life together. It begins as she drags herself out of bed, singing "Up! Up! Up!" (written for an unfinished *Skin of Our Teeth* adaptation by Leonard Bernstein, Betty Comden, and Adolph Green). Other numbers are "What Makes Me Love Him?" (from the Jerry Bock-Sheldon Harnick-Jerome Coopersmith musical *The Apple Tree*); Ed Kleban's irresistible "Better"; and a very funny version of the Bruce Sussman-Jack Feldman-Barry Manilow hit "Copacabana." But the one item that makes the album essential is "Don't Laugh," written by Mary Rodgers and Martin Charnin for the musical *Hot Spot* starring Judy Holliday, then doctored on the road by Rodgers' friend Stephen Sondheim, who added the wonderful "show me" sections: "Show me a glass of water, I'll show you a soggy dress / Show me a tube of toothpaste, I'll show you a mess / Show me a fresh-laid sidewalk and guess where my footprints are / Show me a fire hydrant, I'll show you my car," and so on. (Note: There was a TV adaptation of *The Madwoman of Central Park West,* so you may be able to find a copy and see it for yourself.)   —DAVID WOLF

MAGDALENA
New York Concert Cast, 1988 (CBS) ★★★★
This is a musically adventurous, complex, and unruly Columbian stew by Heitor Villa-Lobos—a flop in 1948, though an admired one—brought back decades later in this concert version. The melodies, harmonies, and intricate rhythms of *Magdalena* sound like no other Broadway score,

and the composer's use of contrapuntal rhythms and strains—a player piano in the middle of a priest's reverie, a pagan uprising amid a state ceremony—is as sophisticated as in any opera. His orchestrations are dazzling, too, combining South American folk motifs with the sounds of late-'40s Broadway. Unfortunately, the story that librettist Homer Curran and lyricists Robert Wright and George Forrest concocted is incomprehensible and annoyingly pious; the dull, religious heroine triumphs, but the fun-loving heathens have the best material. The witty "Food for Thought" lyrics, trilled to perfection by villainess Judy Kaye, and her later "Pièce de Résistance" stand out. But the ballads and recitatives are faux-naif and bogus. If you can endure those failings, you'll be rewarded with a lavish, well-sung musical presentation based on a Lincoln Center concert. There's especially fine work from Kaye and from George Rose in one of his last roles, hamming it up lustily as a corrupt general. The romantic leads, Faith Esham and Kevin Gray, seem a little pallid by comparison, but they're unfairly weighted down by all that shallow dialogue. Evans Haile conducts an enormous orchestra and chorus masterfully, and the flow of imaginative Villa-Lobos music is unending. A special nod to percussionist Patrick Smith, who is probably recuperating still.   —MARC MILLER

MAGGIE FLYNN
Original Broadway Cast, 1968 (RCA/no CD) ★★★

Hardly remembered today, this show has had only one small-scale revival and is rarely performed. It marked the return of Shirley Jones to Broadway, where she began her career in choruses before going on to star in the film versions of great musicals. Playing opposite Jones was her husband, Broadway veteran Jack Cassidy. *Maggie Flynn* was directed by Morton DaCosta, who had helmed such hits as *The Music Man, Plain and Fancy,* and *Auntie Mame.* The book, music, and lyrics were a collaboration of Hugo Peretti, Luigi Creatore, and George David Weiss. With encouraging out-of-town reviews, the musical seemed to have everything going for it, but it opened in New York to decidedly mixed notices. "The Thank-You Song" may seem to be a poor man's "Do-Re-Mi," but there's more to *Maggie Flynn* than that number. Cleverly using the New York City draft riots of 1863 as background for a romance as well as a story of racial tolerance, the show has a tuneful score that made for a really fine cast album. "Why Can't I Walk Away?" is powerfully sung by Cassidy as Maggie's ex-husband Phineas. Whether delivering the lullaby "Pitter Patter" or the rousing "Mr. Clown," Cassidy uses his voice to great advantage. As Maggie, who runs an orphanage for black children, Jones sings beautifully in the clear-as-a-bell soprano that helped make her a star, and she's just as engaging when belting out the cheery "Nice Cold Morning" and the sly "I Wouldn't Have You Any Other Way." Among the orphans are future stars Stephanie Mills, Irene Cara, and Giancarlo Esposito; the group as a whole sounds glorious, especially in the chilling "The Game of War." Robert R. Kaye is in fine voice as Colonel Farrady (Maggie's beau). The title tune is introduced as a ballad for Cassidy and later turns into an up-tempo production number. The recording concludes with Jones singing "Mr. Clown" while Cassidy sings "Maggie Flynn," the two songs fitting together perfectly. A beautiful gatefold album, *Maggie Flynn* is worth seeking out on LP.   —JEFFREY DUNN

THE MAGIC SHOW
Original Broadway Cast, 1973 (Bell/January Records) ★★★

This musical got the worst reviews imaginable but ran five years, thanks to its star, who could not act, sing, or dance but was a magician unlike any we'd ever seen. A skinny little hippie in jeans with a fresh, artless, chipmunk-cheeked persona, Doug Henning created illusions so startling and imaginative that the show's hideous physical production and the basic crumminess of its book didn't matter. The Stephen Schwartz songs jump lightly from one pop genre to another in a casual, genial style of writing. This is a brief score and a minor one, but it's not without its pleasures. The only interestingly conceived character is a beautiful young woman named Charmin, who materializes before our eyes in a plexiglass box. Whenever any magician needs to conjure up a beautiful woman, it's her—and she's sick of it. "Charmin's Lament," a mock country-western number, was performed by the funny, genuinely sexy Anita Morris. Although "Lion Tamer" may be a bit too on-the-nose as ingenue Dale Soules' first song, it's still appealing. David Ogden Stiers' villainous set piece "Style" is helped by the cheerful oddness of its music, as is "Two's Company." The most remembered number of the score is "West End Avenue," which pops up frequently on recordings and in cabaret. Belted intently by Soules, the number is skillful and effective if a tad overwrought. Henning doesn't sing at all; his entire performance on the cast album consists of one line, spoken unsurely.   —DAVID WOLF

MAKE A WISH
Original Broadway Cast, 1951 (RCA/Sepia) ★★★★
A spiffy overture, a swell opening chorus ("The Tour Must Go On"), then out comes our heroine (Nanette Fabray) with an even better character-establishing number, "I Wanna Be Good 'n' Bad." In Hugh Martin's musical update of Ferenc Molnar's *The Good Fairy,* Fabray is a Parisian orphan who breaks away from the orphanage and runs smack into an aspiring barrister, played by Stephen Douglass. Fabray and Douglass are strictly A-list. As the second couple, Helen Gallagher and Harold Lang play a bickering nightclub duo. The cast album is generous with song-setting dialogue, and Martin's score is up-tempo and unpretentious, offering lots of chances for this gifted quartet to shine. The ballads are also choice, particularly Fabray's "What I Was Warned About" and Douglass' "When Does This Feeling Go Away?" Yet even with a Preston Sturges book and show-stopping Gower Champion dances (one ballet is included here), this musical wasn't a hit—and you can hear why. Halfway through the recording there's a silly march ("Paris, France"), and most of what follows sounds like filler. By the time Fabray, Lang, and Gallagher are slamming across "Take Me Back to Texas With You" ("My poor eyes will get all watery / When I see Monsieur Gene Aut-e-ry"), you know what a hodgepodge the score is, its ambience careening uneasily between Paris and Passaic. Martin's vocal arrangements, so much fun when he's serving other composers, just sound garish when he's working his own stuff into the ground (as in "That Face!"). Still, the four leads are tops and the gold in this mixed bag outweighs the dross.   —MARC MILLER

MAME
Original Broadway Cast, 1966 (Columbia/Sony) ★★★★★
Seldom has a cast recording captured the thrill and excitement of a smash Broadway musical as well as this one does. From the spectacular opening bars of the overture to the huge finale, you can hear and feel the joy of the entire company. The album is so well produced that listening to it is almost like having the entire show performed in your living room. And what a cast! Angela Lansbury, in perhaps the greatest role of her long career, is an unsurpassed Mame. Her voice is rich and melodic, and her wit comes through clearly; it's a treat to hear such a wonderful blend of acting and singing talent. Beatrice Arthur delivers a droll Vera Charles that will have you laughing out loud; "Bosom Buddies," her duet with Lansbury, is magnificently exe-

cuted. Frankie Michaels as Young Patrick has an amazing singing voice, while Jane Connell's rendition of "Gooch's Song" is one of the great comedic performances in musical theater history. Jerry Herman's music is among his very best and his lyrics are sharp, funny, and impeccably crafted. The orchestra is thrillingly conducted by Donald Pippin. This *Mame* actually improves upon the wonderful novel on which it was based, Patrick Dennis' *Auntie Mame,* and its subsequent straight play and film adaptations. As wonderful as those versions may be, you can't help missing great songs like "It's Today," "We Need a Little Christmas," "If He Walked Into My Life"—and, of course, the show-stopping title tune of the musical. All of these are rendered definitively here, and there are interesting bonus tracks of Jerry Herman singing demo versions of several numbers.

Film Soundtrack, 1974 (Warner Bros./Rhino) Not recommended.
All elements of the Broadway smash hit pointed toward *Mame* being turned into a wonderful movie musical, but it misfired. The soundtrack album reveals how Lucille Ball's lack of musicality sabotaged the film more than any of its other flaws. As much as we all love Lucy, her singing here is unlistenable; she sounds ill at ease performing numbers written for someone with the vocal chops of a Judy Garland. When Lucy isn't singing, some of the choral work is very nice, but the orchestral arrangements sound wanting. And while Bea Arthur and Jane Connell reprise their original roles, even they sound uncomfortable on this disc. Only Robert Preston as Beau Burnside has a stellar moment when he sings "Loving You," an excellent song that Jerry Herman composed expressly for the movie.　　　—GERARD ALESSANDRINI

MAMMA MIA!
Original London Cast, 1999 (Decca) ★★
Diehard musical theater fans love to hate this international megahit, which showcases two dozen pop hits by the 1970s Swedish pop group ABBA. In truth, it's arguably the only musical that succeeds in working preexisting tunes into a new libretto. Well, sort of new: Catherine Johnson's book is remarkably similar to the screenplay plot of *Buona Sera, Mrs. Campbell,* which also inspired the flop Broadway musical *Carmelina.* The heroine of *Mamma Mia!* is Donna, who keeps a taverna on a tiny Greek island and makes plans for the wedding of her daughter, Sophie. Wanting to find out who her father is, Sophie invites the three most likely candidates to the wedding, setting the stage for farcical complications. The songs by Benny Andersson and Björn Ulvaeus (the male half of ABBA; Stig Anderson also contributed) often have only the barest acquaintance with the libretto, but this Europop is irresistible and the no-star London cast performs with verve. Annoyingly, the album contains no plot synopsis. Even though the songs are arranged by Martin Koch, the recording isn't really necessary, given the existence of the greatest hits collection *ABBA Gold.* Still, who can resist the lure of "Dancing Queen"?　　　—DAVID BARBOUR

MAN IN THE MOON
Original Broadway Cast, 1963 (Golden Records/no CD) ★★
Many readers will remember Bil and Cora Baird, whose puppets were all over early television (and were featured in the musical *Flahooley*). In the 1960s, Bil Baird attempted a series of theatrical musicals for kids; some of them were performed in his Greenwich Village jewel-box theater, but *Man in the Moon* actually played on Broadway. The director was Gerald Freedman, the book was by Arthur Burns (based on Baird's story), and the songs were by

composer Jerry Bock and lyricist Sheldon Harnick. They wrote five numbers for this one-act musical, all of them modest but delightful. (The second acts of Baird's shows were puppet revues.) In one of the numbers, "I Got an Itch," the gangster-villain sings about having "an itch for a rich, ripe rube I can rob" and tells us that "When night-time comes a-stealing, so do I." The plot centers on a young boy who goes to the moon by riding a moonbeam but doesn't realize that gangsters on the lam are right behind him. The gangsters are defeated, and everyone leaves happy—except for Bock and Harnick's numerous fans, who can't help thinking about all the wonderful shows that they might have written if only the team had kept working together after *The Rothschilds.* —DAVID WOLF

MAN OF LA MANCHA

Original Broadway Cast, 1965 (Kapp/Decca) ★★★★★

This first recording of the Mitch Leigh-Joe Darion score for their musical inspired by Miguel de Cervantes' *Don Quixote* is definitive. Richard Kiley is so vocally and dramatically brilliant as Cervantes/Quixote that he set the bar impossibly high for all future interpreters of the role. Playing opposite him as Aldonza, Joan Diener gives an amazing vocal performance; she was one of those rare singing actresses who boasted a strong chest voice with a full soprano extension. When Diener ends her powerfully belted performance of "It's All the Same" with a flight into the soprano stratosphere or when she switches back and forth between registers in "Aldonza," the effect is breathtaking. Completing the musical's central triumvirate, Irving Jacobson's Sancho Panza is warm and funny. In the excellent supporting cast, Robert Rounseville is the Padre and Ray Middleton is the Innkeeper. Harry Theyard as a muleteer offers two starkly contrasting performances of "Little Bird"—one gorgeously lyrical, the other frighteningly violent. Even though the flamenco style employed by Leigh is inappropriate to the period and some of Darion's lyrics are ungrammatical, there is much to love about this score. If there's anything to regret in the CD transfer of the recording, it's that the "I, Don Quixote" number eliminates the terrifying Inquisition theme that begins this track on the LP. On the plus side, the technical quality of the CD is superb.

Original London Cast, 1968 (Decca, 2LPs/no CD) ★★★

While this is not really a "complete" *Man of La Mancha,* the two-LP set does give us a vivid sense of the show through its inclusion of much dialogue and some nice sound effects. Keith Michell is almost as magnificent a Cervantes/Quixote as the role's creator, Richard Kiley. Joan Diener is back as Aldonza, but her performance here is quite mannered and lacking in spontaneity; it sounds as if she had given up on playing the character, having decided instead to deliver a star turn. Despite this major caveat, the London *Man of La Mancha* deserves a CD release: The supporting cast is fine, especially Alan Crofoot as the Padre, and the sound quality of the recording is excellent. Oh, and another plus is that we get to hear that wonderfully scary Inquisition theme more than once.

Film Soundtrack, 1972 (United Artists/no CD) Not recommended.

What a disaster this is. On paper, Peter O'Toole and Sophia Loren would seem like excellent casting for a film version of *Man of La Mancha,* providing that their singing voices were skillfully dubbed by others. Alas! Simon Gilbert, who ghosts for O'Toole, has a nice enough voice but strange mannerisms of enunciation; just listen to him sing the lyric "thou art base and debauched as can be," hitting every "b" with a sledgehammer. As for Loren, she was unwisely allowed to do her own singing and the results are borderline embarrassing. Her voice has about one-third the range required for Aldonza's music and her weirdly modified Italian accent is a further liability. Up against these two, James Coco manages to retain his dignity as Sancho, although he sings his part in "I, Don Quixote" down the octave from where it's written. Ian Richardson has far too thin a voice for the Padre, but this is a moot point: The beautiful "To Each His Dulcinea" has been cut. The one good thing about this recording is that the orchestrations for symphony-sized forces were done skillfully; it's nice to hear strings playing this score even if the original orchestrations for a much smaller band remain superior.

Studio Cast, 1972 (Columbia/no CD) ★

This recording was only briefly in print and it's hard to find. Jim Nabors, famous for his TV sitcom *Gomer Pyle, USMC,* possessed a legit baritone voice that gave him some additional career mileage. But his sound is affected and ponderous to the point of camp—certainly not the effect that a good Cervantes/Don Quixote is supposed to make. The Aldonza here is superstar diva Marilyn Horne in a frustrating performance; her magnificent mezzo is right for the role, but she sings "It's All the Same" and other songs so squarely that they make little impression. By far the best of the three principals is Jack Gilford, a wonderfully endearing Sancho. The supporting cast—Madeline Kahn as Antonia, Ron Hussman as the Innkeeper, and the great opera tenor Richard Tucker as the Padre—is uniformly excellent and the original orchestrations are wisely used, but the performances of Horne and especially Nabors make this album little more than a curiosity.

Studio Cast, 1990 (Sony) ★

There's nothing terribly wrong about this recording aside from the presence of the outrageously mannered Mandy Patinkin as Sancho Panza. But, somehow, the whole thing doesn't jell, even though the original orchestrations are expertly conducted here by Paul Gemignani. Opera icon Plaçido Domingo sings Quixote's songs with all of the glorious tone you'd expect, but his Spanish accent is distracting—even though he is playing a Spanish character. Julia Migenes is well cast and has many fine moments, but her performance isn't as mercurial as Joan Diener's on the original Broadway recording; she just doesn't use her chest register in the same full-out way as Diener. Jerry Hadley does a good job as the Padre, but though Samuel Ramey has one of the most voluminous bass voices in operatic history, it's not a voice that's appropriate to the Innkeeper. This isn't the worst recording of *Man of La Mancha* but it's far from the best.

Broadway Cast, 2002 (RCA) Not recommended.

To say that Brian Stokes Mitchell does not have the range for Cervantes/Don Quixote in *Man of La Mancha* is to put it mildly. Mitchell possesses an impressive baritone, but his singing style is ill-suited to this dual role. He annoyingly slides off of notes like a pop/jazz singer throughout this CD and his grandstanding rendition of a foolishly extended version of "The Impossible Dream" is off-putting. Even less successful is Mitchell's attempt to handle the show's dialogue. When playing Cervantes, he sounds like a genial TV-sitcom actor; when he morphs into the Quixote characterization, he assumes a laughably ponderous tone. Also unequal to their roles are most of this production's costars and supporting players. As Aldonza, Mary Elizabeth Mastrantonio displays a beautiful soprano voice when she doesn't have to push (as in the moving "What Does He Want of Me?") but there are some harrowing moments when she switches vocal registers to negotiate the more challenging sections of the score (as in the final measures of "It's All the Same"). Also, her delivery of dialogue is just as giggle-inducing as Mitchell's; this Aldonza sounds as if she comes from Brooklyn. Ernie Sabella as Sancho Panza has so much trouble with breath support that he chops up phrases willy-nilly. On the other hand, Mark Jacoby has the vocal goods for the role of the Padre, and Don Mayo sounds fine as the Innkeeper. It's ironic that one of the best singers in the show—Stephen Bogardus—has very little to sing as Sanson Carrasco. One final reason not to bother with this recording: It doesn't include the show's exciting overture!   —MICHAEL PORTANTIERE

A MAN OF NO IMPORTANCE
Original Off-Broadway Cast, 2002 (JAY) ★★
Roger Rees did first-rate work as Alfie, a Dublin bus driver who revels in amateur theatricals and yearns for a male coworker, but this show was a disappointment. The 1994 film (of the same title), a melancholy comedy about Irish eccentrics, was notable for its light touch. In contrast, Terrence McNally's libretto for the musical consists of much hand-wringing over the fate of closeted, middle-aged, 1960s gay Irish bachelors. Still, Stephen Flaherty's seductive tunes and Lynn Ahrens' sharp, economical lyrics are hard to dismiss. High points include the opening title-tune sequence, the rousing yet acrid "Streets of Dublin" (sung by Steven Pasquale as Alfie's unwitting love object), and the forlorn "Love Who You Love." Faith Prince, as Alfie's spinster sister, has to cope with substandard material, and a pair of songs about community theater—"Going Up" and "Art"—belong in a different show. Still, the score does cast a certain spell and, when it works, it can bring tears to your eyes. A bonus track offers "Love's Never Lost," an expanded version of a song fragment heard in the show.   —DAVID BARBOUR

MAN WITH A LOAD OF MISCHIEF
Original Off-Broadway Cast, 1966 (Kapp/no CD) ★★★★
For a tantalizing glimpse of the talent and creativity spawned Off-Broadway in happier times, seek out this 1966 hit, a Restoration-style comedy (based, though, on a minor twentieth-century play) that is by turns bawdy, witty, satirical, and as romantic as fine Madeira shared by the fire. It led observers to expect great things of composer-lyricist John Clifton (librettist Ben Tarver helped on the lyrics), whose melodies and harmonies are distinctive and alluring without straying too far from tradition. Sadly, one later Off-Broadway fiasco aside, Clifton hasn't worked much in the theater since. That's a pity, since such vocal showpieces as "Lover Lost," "Goodbye, My Sweet," and "Once You've Had a Little Taste" mark their composer as a natural musical storyteller with unfailing instincts as to which dramatic moments should be turned into song. Reid Shelton's reedy tenor sails easily above the staff in "Hulla-Baloo-Balay" and "Come to the Masquerade." Virginia Vestoff acts as well as she sings in the title track and "A Wonder." Raymond Thorne exudes patrician hauteur in "You'd Be Amazed" and "Forget!" The other three—Alice Cannon, Tom Noel, and Lesslie Nicol—are less skilled vocally but well cast. This recording demands a CD release.   —MARC MILLER

MARIE CHRISTINE
Original Broadway Cast, 2000 (RCA) ★★★
Michael John LaChiusa turns out songs quickly—so quickly, he boasts, that he can sometimes knock off several in a day. There's nothing necessarily wrong with that, but it is a problem when

the songs don't sound so much effortless as hurried, and there's a strong whiff of that here. LaChiusa has a gift for ravishing melody but cuts corners by not bothering to develop the themes and motifs into rounded songs. Seemingly allergic to the thirty-two-bar ditty, he prefers to construct his scores as if they're ever-evolving fragments of music. Sometimes it works, and sometimes it can strike the listener as continual *songus interruptus*. Parts click and other parts don't in *Marie Christine,* the creator's transplant of Euripides' *Medea* to New Orleans and Chicago at the turn of the nineteenth century. The murderous mom here is a Creole with magical powers who gets involved with a politically ambitious man. When the cad realizes that the liaison could stymie his career, he dumps Marie Christine for a politico's daughter and suffers the dumpee's wrath. LaChiusa's great fortune is in having Audra McDonald apply her gorgeous mezzo-soprano to his concoctions. She sings beautifully in "Beautiful" and tops herself in a flowing chanson titled "C'est l'amour." Also shining like diamonds in a flawed setting are Darius de Haas in "Complainte de Lord Pierrot" (from a Jules LaForgue poem) and the always lusty Mary Testa as a toddlin' town madam. The orchestrations, subtle and authoritative throughout, are by Jonathan Tunick. —DAVID FINKLE

MARRY ME A LITTLE
Original Off-Broadway Cast, 1981 (RCA) ★
Stephen Sondheim compilation shows have always seemed silly to me; doesn't the appeal of his work lie largely in its specificity? This is one of the most plodding, monotonous, and annoying recordings of Sondheim's songs ever released. *Marry Me a Little* doesn't have much of a story but it does have a concept: On a Saturday evening, a man and a woman who don't know each other (and who never meet) sit home in their respective apartments and sing Sondheim songs. Among them: "Can That Boy Foxtrot!" and "Uptown, Downtown" (both cut from *Follies*), the title song and "Happily Ever After" (both cut from *Company*), and "There Won't Be Trumpets" (cut from *Anyone Can Whistle*). These items are interesting and worth knowing, yet they are of primarily historical value; in many cases, it's easy to understand why they were cut from their respective scores in the first place. The only truly unbearable section of the disc is an insufferable combination of "All Things Bright and Beautiful" (*Follies*) and "Bang!" (*A Little Night Music*), sung by Suzanne Henry and Craig Lucas. Although their voices are generally lacking in distinction, these two are slightly better in other numbers—but they're never aided by the cool, impersonal, distant-sounding accompaniment of a lone piano. —MATTHEW MURRAY

MARTIN GUERRE
Original London Cast, 1996 (Dreamworks) ★★★★
By the time this latest epic from composer Claude-Michel Schönberg and lyricist Alain Boublil arrived on the scene, the serious pop-opera genre was fading away. That's too bad, as this is one of the best scores of its type. The Boublil-Schönberg book was inspired by a historical incident best known for its dramatic treatment in the film *The Return of Martin Guerre.* The title character, a sixteenth-century French farmer, is forced into marriage with a young woman, Bertrande, in order to consolidate their Catholic families' hold on their farmland near the village of Artigat. The marriage is a disaster and produces no children, so Martin runs off to war. Seven years later, he apparently dies on the battlefield; his companion-in-war, a man named Arnaud, subsequently visits Artigat and is mistaken for Martin. Then he falls in love with Bertrande. This tale of deception is set against a background of smoldering conflict between Catholics and Protestants. It's a grim piece, carried along by the sweep of Schönberg's frequently ravishing melodies.

Boublil's lyrics—translated by Herbert Kretzmer, Edward Hardy, and Stephen Clark—are often cruelly pointed and serve the story well. The best numbers include the title song; "Here Comes the Morning," a duet for Martin and Arnaud; "Tell Me to Go," Arnaud's plea to Bertrande; and the stunning choral number "The Imposters." These and some grandly scaled orchestral interludes give *Martin Guerre* the scale of a true opera. (Skip the one egregious attempt at humor, "Sleeping on Our Own," delivered by a trio of comic crones.) As Arnaud and Bertrande, Iain Glen and Juliette Caton sing beautifully; they receive strong support from Matt Rawle in the title role and Jerome Pradon as Guillame, who loves Bertrande from afar.

Touring Cast, 1999 (Dreamworks) ★★★

After *Martin Guerre* failed in the West End, producer Cameron Mackintosh tried again. He had Boublil and Schönberg create a new touring version that represents one of the major overhauls of a musical. Even though it follows the same general plot line, it's an almost total rewrite, with many new songs and with melodies from the 1996 version reassigned and given new lyrics. The overall result is harsher, focusing even more on the religious strife that is tearing Artigat apart; if at times the score is shrill, even hysterical, there's plenty of dramatic power here. Alas, Stephen Clark alone translated the lyrics and they're much weaker. For example, the new ballad "Live With Someone You Love" is a thesaurus of clichés. On the other hand, "Without You as a Friend" is a canny addition to the score. The title song and "The Imposters" are both still here (albeit with new lyrics), along with many other effective numbers, but William David Brohn's orchestrations lack majesty. The new cast (Stephen Weller as Martin, Matthew Cammelle as Arnaud, Joanna Riding as Bertrande, Maurice Clark as Guillaume) is vocally skilled and dramatically apt. —DAVID BARBOUR

MATA HARI
Off-Broadway Cast, 2001 (Original Cast Records) ★★★★

The legendary 1967 out-of-town closing performance of this show is notorious for its Mata Hari, one Marissa Mell, being shot by a firing squad, falling, dying—and then rubbing her itchy nose when she was supposed to be stone-cold dead. In a strange way, Mell's move has proven to be a good metaphor for this musical, which has refused to die. In 2001, the cast of the York Theatre Company revival recorded the stirring score—unfortunately, with synthesizers. (No show should use synthesizers if it's set in an era before synthesizers were invented!) But even those machines can't destroy Edward Thomas' strong melodies and the deft, incisive lyrics of Martin Charnin. Mata Hari (Robin Skye) has a terrific opening song, "Everyone Has Something to Hide," and the equally effective "Not Now, Not Here." Captain LaFarge (Michael Zaslow), Mata Hari's would-be capturer/romantic interest, has the pungent "Is This Fact?" and the wistful "How Young You Were Tonight." The jewel of the score is "Maman." If only it didn't sound like the singers were accompanied by automobile horns! —PETER FILICHIA

MAYOR
Original Off-Broadway Cast, 1985 (Harbinger) ★★

When *Bye Bye Birdie* exploded on Broadway in 1960, it was an announcement that a brand-new generation had arrived in just about every department; even the cast album was physically different from any that had come before. Since then, composer Charles Strouse has had an interesting time of it. He's written more shows than any of his contemporaries, most of them failures—although his three big hits, *Bye Bye Birdie, Applause,* and *Annie,* have more than made up for the missteps. Even his flops have been filled with terrific songs. That said, *Mayor* has what may be the least interesting tunes of Strouse's career. Based on Ed Koch's book and produced while he was still in office, the musical doesn't take advantage of the spikiness of Mayor Koch's personality; it's a bland, fairly generic revue that covers familiar New York subjects, attitudes, and stereotypes. Unusually, Strouse wrote his own lyrics and they're OK, but there's not much in the way of a fresh point of view here. The book is by Warren Leight, who won a Tony Award for his play *Side Man* fourteen years later. —DAVID WOLF

ME AND JULIET
Original Broadway Cast, 1953 (RCA) ★★★

It's hard to believe, but Rodgers and Hammerstein did have a few flops in addition to their many hits. *Me and Juliet* was one such failure and the team's only foray into the backstage musical genre. Still, these great men of the theater hardly ever wrote a bad song, and even this show contains flashes of brilliance. "Marriage Type Love" is a tuneful charm song with a wonderfully romantic lyric, while "That's the Way It Happens" has just the right pithiness and showbiz nonchalance called for. Probably the best and most famous item in the score is "No Other Love," based on a theme that Rodgers originally wrote for the background score of *Victory at Sea,* a television documentary on World War II. It's a lovely song with a beguiling melody but indicative of the non-character-specific writing in *Me and Juliet.* Many of the songs are misfires, particularly "We Deserve Each Other" and "Keep It Gay," both of which are leaden. There is one showbiz song that succeeds: "Intermission Talk." Isabel Bigley heads the cast, fresh from her starring role in *Guys and Dolls;* Bill Hayes displays a very appealing voice; and Joan McCracken steals the show with her brand of sassiness. —GERARD ALESSANDRINI

ME AND MY GIRL
London Cast, 1985 (EMI) ★★★★

This production took a very charming, very old musical, gussied up the book, the score, and the arrangements, and presented it to the public as a nostalgia fest. *Me and My Girl* had originally opened in London in 1937 and enjoyed a very long run. With music by Noel Gay and book and lyrics by L. Arthur Rose, the show tells the sweet tale of Bill Snibson, a cockney ne'er-do-well who turns out to be an earl and is pressured to forsake his Lambeth girlfriend, Sally Smith, when he assumes his title. Director Mike Ockrent, producer Richard Armitage, and executive producer David Aukin supervised the tuner's rebirth, incorporating revisions by playwright Stephen Fry and Ockrent and interpolating several Gay songs from other sources. The new production proved to be a big success in London and, a year later, on Broadway. Among the best numbers are the title song, Bill's "Leaning on a Lamp Post," and the catchy "Lambeth Walk," which was a huge international hit in 1937 and then delighted a new generation of audiences when resurrected in the 1980s. The recording is skillfully produced by Norman Newell. As Bill, Robert Lindsay is a real charmer, and so is his Sally: Emma Thompson, who went on to a brilliant career as a highly respected actress in nonmusical films.

Broadway Cast, 1986 (MCA) ★★★★

The Broadway transfer of the hit London revival of *Me and My Girl* inaugurated the Marquis Theatre, located within a new hotel whose building entailed the destruction of the venerable

Helen Hayes and Morosco theaters, which predisposed many Broadway old-timers to hate the show. But *Me and My Girl* was so much fun that it was impossible to harbor any ill will toward it. Robert Lindsay repeated his West End role of Bill Snibson and received a Tony Award for his efforts; Maryann Plunkett, an utterly winning Sally Smith, also won a Tony. Among the old pros on hand in supporting roles are Jane Connell as Maria, Duchess of Deane; George S. Irving as Sir John Tremayne; Timothy Jerome as Herbert Parchester; and Justine Johnson as Lady Battersby. That superb cast, plus the fact that the CD booklet notes by musical theater expert Stanley Green are far more extensive than those for the London album, will make this the preferable recording of the show for many listeners.   —MICHAEL PORTANTIERE

MEET ME IN ST. LOUIS
Film Soundtrack, 1944 (MGM/Rhino-Turner) ★
Based on a series of stories by Sally Benson that originally appeared in *The New Yorker,* Vincente Minnelli's *Meet Me in St. Louis* is one of the glories of MGM's Arthur Freed unit. Unfortunately, the film doesn't have enough noteworthy music or interesting vocal performances to fill a compact disc. Judy Garland renders Hugh Martin and Ralph Blane's "The Boy Next Door," "The Trolley Song," and "Have Yourself a Merry Little Christmas," plus Richard Rodgers and Oscar Hammerstein's "Boys and Girls Like You and Me" with an exquisitely light touch. (The R&H song wound up on the cutting-room floor.) About half of this CD consists of musical underscoring from the movie, which means that a few vocal gems alternate with long stretches of orchestral tedium—even though the instrumental tracks do feature luxurious orchestrations by Conrad Salinger.

Original Broadway Cast, 1989 (DRG) ★★
Back when this stage version of *Meet Me in St. Louis* opened, who could have ever foreseen that, fifteen years later, Broadway would be reduced to a theme park full of musical revivals and adaptations of Hollywood movies? This recording combines the small handful of standards contained in MGM's 1944 film with additional numbers by Hugh Martin and Ralph Blane. Ironically, the paucity of invention on Broadway over the past decade makes this technically splendid recording of a so-called "New Broadway Hit Musical" worth a second listen. A revision of a stage adaptation that Martin, Blane, and Sally Benson had concocted in 1960 as summer fare for the Municipal Opera of St. Louis, the Broadway *Meet Me in St. Louis* was quite overproduced; its lavish set design by Keith Anderson included a frozen pond on which dancers executed intricate skating choreography by Michael Tokar. In addition to its visual excesses, the show offered a sprightly mix of Martin-Blane songs and old chestnuts like "Skip to My Lou" and "Under the Bamboo Tree" (both in the film version as well), sumptuously orchestrated by Michael Gibson and well performed by a plucky, talented cast. It's hard not to feel an uplift of spirit when the large pit band, under Bruce Pomahac's baton, soars through the lush overture with its antiphony of brassiness and schmaltz; or when Donna Kane, the show's ingenue, lets rip her energetic rendition of "The Trolley Song." The show didn't last long in New York, but its thoroughly listenable score is a reminder that Martin and Blane deserve a page in the Great American Songbook.   —CHARLES WRIGHT

THE ME NOBODY KNOWS
Original Broadway Cast, 1970 (Atlantic/150 Music) ★★★
Based on Stephen M. Joseph's book of the same title, *The Me Nobody Knows* is a collection of

writings by inner-city students turned into a musical by composer Gary William Friedman, lyricist Will Holt, and playwright Herb Schapiro. Holt did his best to create lyrics without making big alterations to the material; the result is a collection of poetic songs that describe the dreams of kids growing up in the ghetto. With their defiantly hopeful voices, the show's energetic company of twelve brings truth to songs like "If I Had a Million Dollars," "How I Feel," and "Black." The cast album was belatedly released on CD; its sound quality isn't very clean and some of the kids' voices are pretty rough. Still, these elements give *The Me Nobody Knows* an authentic feeling of time and place, while the material itself—concerning drugs, poverty, and other challenges faced by city youth—is still sadly relevant. Even those who don't appreciate the funky rock score will likely be moved by the infectious melody and imagery of "Light Sings" or the musical's beautiful finale, "Let Me Come In." —BROOKE PIERCE

MERRILY WE ROLL ALONG

Original Broadway Cast, 1982 (RCA) ★★★★★

Stephen Sondheim's biggest flop boasts one of his best scores. George Furth's book, drawn from a George S. Kaufman-Moss Hart disappointment, follows two writers and a composer backward in time from adulthood to their idealistic salad days in New York, reviewing the missteps, betrayals, and compromises made along the way. With its lurid "inside" view of showbiz, the musical was dramatically unworkable; the production design was disastrous; and the performers, playing gin-swilling, backstabbing sophisticates, were too young. But none of this matters when you're listening to the disc. Savor the heartbreaking melodies and trenchant lyrics or analyze the score's jigsaw-puzzle construction in which themes and ideas are quoted and reworked, creating a solid emotional substructure. (The melody that's first heard as "The Hills of Tomorrow" is reused several times and serves as a strong musical through-line.) Jonathan Tunick orchestrations are brassy and driving, and the three leads are marvelous. As composer Franklin Shepard, Jim Walton displays a piercing tenor that shines especially in "Not a Day Goes By," one of Sondheim's most wounding ballads. Lonny Price is appealing as Charley, Frank's collaborator; he easily navigates the tortuous lyrics of "Franklin Shepard, Inc." and gives a heartfelt reading of the rueful "Good Thing Going." Another plus is a young Jason Alexander as Joe. But the big revelation is Ann Morrison, devastating as Mary, the novelist who descends into alcoholism while pining for Frank. She brings an overwhelming warmth and sadness to "Like It Was" and "Not a Day Goes By," and is just as strong in the invigorating "Now You Know."

Leicester Haymarket Theatre Cast, 1993 (JAY, 2CDs) ★★★★

This is presumably the final version of *Merrily We Roll Along* and the most complete recording of the score to date, with substantial dialogue sequences included. The story line is still plagued by a breathless view of showbiz mores and the idea that writing Broadway musicals is a career for noble souls while working on a Hollywood film is iniquitous. New material includes "That Frank"; a reworking of "Rich and Happy"; "Growing Up," sung by Frank and his second wife, Gussie; and the entr'acte, bows, and exit music. Also included is "The Blob" (cut from the original Broadway staging), Gussie's disenchanted description of guests at her New York party. This lively, up-tempo performance has strong work from its mostly British cast, especially Michael Cantwell as Frank and Jacqueline Dankworth as Beth, Frank's first wife. Maria Friedman strains for brittle sophistication as Mary but partners nicely with Dankworth and Cantwell in "Not a Day Goes By." American performer Evan Pappas is a very capable Charley, especially in "Good Thing Going." Louise Gold is an aptly cynical Gussie. Minor flaws include some shaky American accents and occasionally overemphatic performances, but it's interesting to hear the score performed by an adult cast.

Off-Broadway Cast, 1994 (Varèse Sarabande) ★★★★

The York Theatre production of *Merrily We Roll Along* is preserved on this disc, which presents a slightly condensed version of the material heard on the Leicester Haymarket album and has a slight edge over that version because it boasts superb singing and warmer performances overall. Malcolm Gets and Adam Heller are in fine form as Frank and Charley; Amy Ryder is quite wonderful as tough-talking, heartbroken Mary; Michele Pawk is a gutsy Gussie (her brassy rendition of "Good Thing Going" is a riot), and Anne Bobby is the most touching Beth on record, especially in "Not a Day Goes By." Jonathan Tunick's more intimate orchestrations work well, giving the entire performance energy and bite. A particular standout is "Opening Doors," one of Sondheim's most dazzling numbers in an extended sequence that shows us Frank, Charley, and Mary at the beginning of their careers. — DAVID BARBOUR

MEXICAN HAYRIDE
Original Broadway Cast, 1944 (Decca) ★★★

Cole Porter, Herbert Fields, and Dorothy Fields enjoyed a long run with this silly piece of wartime escapism, but the major force behind the show was producer Mike Todd. First, he saturated the stage with showgirls. Then he got Porter to write a song about them for the stolid baritone Wilbur Evans to sing—"Girls (to the Right of Me, Girls to the Left of Me)"—while the chorines wiggled and shrieked around him. Disappointingly, the show's star, the great comic Bobby Clark, is absent from this twenty-one-minute cast album. The lead female comic, June Havoc, plays a lady bullfighter, wailing Porter's "Count Your Blessings" (about the advantages of death), "There Must Be Someone for Me" (a Porter list song), and "Abracadabra." Like so many 1940s comediennes, Havoc sounds hoydenish and too pleased with herself, but such was the style. While none of the material is classic, Decca's recording of highlights conveys the incidental charms of a loud, throw-it-in-if-it-works, wartime success: Evans drones the hit ballad "I Love You" without inflection, but the chorus scampers through "What a Crazy Way to Spend Sunday," and Corinna Mura hits stratospheric notes with ease in "Sing to Me, Guitar" and "Carlotta." As musical theater, it's forgettable; as a crash course in tired-businessman entertainment of the period, it's peachy. — MARC MILLER

MILK AND HONEY
Original Broadway Cast, 1961 (RCA) ★★★

Jerry Herman's first Broadway score is surely one of his best, an atmosphere-soaked tour through contemporary Israel in service of a tired soap opera plot. At thirty, Herman was already a melody master. Note his gift for well-judged production numbers (the minor/major-key intricacies of "Independence Day Hora"), stirring title songs (dancer-singer Tommy Rall delivers this one with vigor), eleven-o'clock showstoppers ("Hymn to Hymie," with Molly Picon socking across a funny lyric), and warmly appealing ballads (the ardent, chromatic "There's No Reason in the World"). The orchestrations, by Eddie Sauter and Hershy Kay, are more interesting than Herman's scores generally commanded—even his bigger hits. Robert Weede, fresh from *The Most Happy Fella,* can still play an aging romantic lead with the best of them. Unfortunately, this time he has less to play off of; leading lady Mimi Benzell is vocally precise but terminally dull and doesn't let her hair down even when the lyrics demand it. The whole album feels a little hurried, incomplete, and short on dance interludes. But Herman comes out swinging: The opening number, "Shalom," announces an unusually promising Broadway songwriter. That was this score's hit song, but there's plenty more to appreciate here. —MARC MILLER

MINNIE'S BOYS
Original Broadway Cast, 1970 (Project 3) ★★

"Good MORN-ing, ladies!!" Shelley Winters' entrance line in this musical biography of the Marx Brothers and their indomitable mother is brayed rather than spoken, and most of her subsequent readings on this shrill cast album are snorted rather than sung. Winters had sung before (she was a replacement Ado Annie in the original *Oklahoma!*), but she's hoarse here and more pushy than the role requires. The part, a Mama Rose Lite without subtext or character growth, ultimately defeats the star. Other components of this Larry Grossman-Hal Hackady work, their first for Broadway aside from a couple of revue songs, are tuneful though frequently mired in showbiz cliché: Harpo's (Daniel Fortus') love ballad to his mother, "Mama, a Rainbow"; a wry brothers' lament, "Where Was I When They Passed Out Luck?"; and father Frenchy's (Arny Freeman's) torch song "Empty," cut before opening night but included here. A duet between Lewis J. Stadlen as Groucho and Julie Kurnitz as a Margaret Dumont type is glorious, and an ambitious finale depicting the progression of the brothers' characters gets an "A" for effort. But the score lacks a certain something and is not well supported by garish orchestrations that are, shockingly, the work of the great Ralph Burns. —MARC MILLER

MISS LIBERTY
Original Broadway Cast, 1949 (Columbia/Sony) ★★

Irving Berlin's highly anticipated follow-up to *Annie Get Your Gun* was one of those can't-miss packages that missed. It had thick postwar nostalgia, Jerome Robbins choreography, direction by Moss Hart, sets by Oliver Smith, and a book by the distinguished playwright Robert E. Sherwood. The plot is slight: Reporter travels to 1885 Paris to interview Bartholdi's model for the Statue of Liberty, bags the wrong girl, and hilarious complications ensue. Apparently, one of the show's problems was that audiences rooted for the reporter to end up with his American girlfriend, not the *jeune fille* who ultimately lands him. But the real trouble may have been the unexciting principals and Berlin's lackluster score. Eddie Albert, a Broadway pro by 1949, was capable but hardly one to set a stage ablaze. The girls fighting for his affections, Allyn Ann McLerie and Mary McCarty, were promising young talents, the former more a dancer than a singer (Exhibit A: her high notes on "Just One Way to Say I Love You") and the latter an ideal best-pal sort overselling middling material. Berlin packs some good foreign-relations jabs into "Only for Americans," and the show's finale, "Give Me Your Tired, Your Poor," has the required dignity, though McLerie's thin soprano undercuts it somewhat. Otherwise, the album is interesting as a document of how deeply ingrained sexism was in 1949. In "Homework," career gal McCarty admits that her real dream is "Staying / At home and crocheting / And meekly obeying / The guy who comes home." In "You Can Have Him," she says that her greatest desire is to "give him babies, one for every year." Sheesh! —MARC MILLER

MISS SAIGON
Original London Cast, 1989 (Geffen, 2CDs) Not recommended.

Like its equally Eurotrashy predecessors *The Phantom of the Opera* and *Les Misérables, Miss Saigon* followed a crooked path to enormous popular and financial (but not artistic) success: Create a stage musical based on a story that has been beloved for generations and, with the help of shrewd marketing, it will run for years even if the adaptation is third-rate. The plot of *Miss Saigon* is based on that of the Puccini opera *Madama Butterfly,* with the action reset at the time of the Vietnam War. But the Claude-Michel Schönberg-Alain Boublil show built around that brilliant idea has one of the worst scores ever contrived for the musical theater. "Why, God, Why?" begins with a beautiful tune; however, that tune was originally written by Richard Rodgers for "There's a Small Hotel." The melody that Kim sings later to the lyrics "You will not touch him, don't touch my boy" is the tune of the song "Hang Down Your Head, Tom Dooley." The French-speaking librettist Boublil's collaboration with Richard Maltby, Jr. yielded lyrics that are awkwardly phrased to the point of semi-literacy. (A few examples among scads: "God, the tension is high, not to mention the smell," "My parents got themselves killed in the week you changed sides," and "You must decide upon which side you're really on.") The song "Movie in My Mind" illustrates the chasm between the creators' goals and their abilities: The idea of the Vietnamese prostitutes imagining an alternate reality in order to bear the selling of their bodies is interesting, but Schönberg's music and the Boulbil/Maltby lyrics are pedestrian. Although it's difficult to pick the nadir of the score, a good candidate is "Bui Doi," a shamelessly manipulative plea on behalf of children sired by American servicemen and left behind in Vietnam. At least experiencing *Miss Saigon* on CD spares you having to view the tasteless film that was projected onstage during this number. Listeners are also spared the spectacle of the utterly Caucasian-looking Jonathan Pryce in the role of the Engineer, an oily Eurasian pimp; even from an aural standpoint, though, Pryce is badly miscast. On the other hand, Lea Salonga sounds lovely and winsome as Kim. As her lover Chris, Simon Bowman sings well but doesn't sound American, which is a problem in terms of the plot.

Studio Cast, 1995 (Angel, 2CDs) Not recommended.

The CD booklet notes assure us that there was much more to the success of *Miss Saigon* than the stunning onstage simulation of the landing and takeoff of a helicopter—yet this recording begins with the whirring of chopper blades as if to admit, "Yes, that special effect is what most people will remember about the show." Billed as a "complete recording," it includes revisions of the score that were made following the London production. The material is performed by a cast drawn from several of the show's worldwide productions, backed by a huge orchestra. Joanna Ampil's Kim is very much in the Lea Salonga mold, which is a good thing. The partly-Asian Kevin Gray brings credibility to the role of the Engineer, but even he can't triumph over such dreck as "The American Dream," a hit-them-over-the-head number in which the title phrase is repeated eighteen times. Peter Cousens—from the Sydney cast—has a fine voice but is unable to sound convincingly American as Chris. Hinton Battle sings John's "Bui Doi" for all it's worth, which is very little, and the thankless role of Ellen is well handled by Ruthie Henshall. The large orchestra, conducted by David Charles Abell, plays beautifully and the sound quality of the recording is superb, but it's all in the service of a score that deserves to be consigned to the musical theater trash heap.   —MICHAEL PORTANTIERE

MISS SPECTACULAR
Studio Cast, 2002 (DRG) ★★★★

Talk of a stage presentation of Jerry Herman's *Miss Spectacular* continues to be heard on the Rialto grapevine, but a Las Vegas production that was planned for May 2001 never materialized. This concept recording is a doozy, featuring the kind of cast that a Broadway producer would have to empty his and many others' wallets to sign: Chirping at their best are Debbie Gravitte, Michael Feinstein, Faith Prince, Christine Baranski, Karen Morrow, Davis Gaines, and Steve Lawrence; the latter robustly sings a paean to Las Vegas that cutely includes the names "Steve and Eydie." The plot of the musical concerns Kansas expatriate Sarah Jane Hotchkiss, who's come to Vegas to enter a competition to become spokeswoman for the Spectacular Hotel, all the while remaining emotionally tied to the boy back home. Herman's songs are on a par with the composer-lyricist's best work. Not only is there a banjo-heavy anthem called "Sarah Jane" to rank with the title songs "Hello, Dolly!" and "Mame," there's also a love song, "No Other Music," that's one of Herman's finest ballads; happily, it gets a perfect reading by the great Karen Morrow. Michael Feinstein beautifully delivers the lush "Ziegfeld Girl," a tribute to showgirl pulchritude. An eighteen-member chorus and a large orchestra are conducted by the redoubtable veteran Donald Pippin, who also did the vocal arrangements; Larry Blank provided the string- and brass-prominent orchestrations. The plot of *Miss Spectacular* isn't a world-beater, so this may be the best realization for which the irrepressible Herman and his admirers can hope.　　　　　—DAVID FINKLE

MRS. PATTERSON
Original Broadway Cast, 1954 (RCA) ★

Is it a musical or a straight play with incidental songs? *Mrs. Patterson* was a hybrid oddity of the 1954-55 Broadway season. Having seen Eartha Kitt create a sensation in his revue *New Faces of 1952,* producer Leonard Sillman resolved to showcase the new star's versatility in a role far from her kitten-fatale persona. The result—a play by Charles Sebree and Greer Johnson, with songs by James Shelton—was disappointing. The story of a young daydreamer, *Mrs. Patterson* ran for several months and was quickly forgotten except for Kitt's Tony nomination and this cast album. There are long dialogue patches that alternate with Shelton's six songs, and while Kitt works hard to capture the voice and manner of a teenaged innocent, the material is weak; the fey lyrics and wispy vocal lines of the songs seldom allow the star to have any fun. Ironically, the only number that is at all striking ("I Wish I Was a Bumble Bee") is sung not by Kitt but by Helen Dowdy in the role of an over-the-hill blues singer. It's unlikely that *Mrs. Patterson* will ever turn up again onstage, so this recording is a bona fide hothouse curiosity. It's available on CD only as part of the Bear Family boxed set *Eartha Quake.*　　　—RICHARD BARRIOS

MR. PRESIDENT
Original Broadway Cast, 1962 (Columbia/Sony) ★

Irving Berlin's final show should have been a natural—it's a look at a JFK-like First Family with mild social satire and plenty of flag-waving—but, from the listless opening fanfare to the desperate finale, it's a bust. There's scarcely a fresh idea in *Mr. President,* just a lot of recycling of old ones that were better executed the first time: the latest dance craze ("The Washington Twist"); the contrapuntal duet ("Empty Pockets Filled With Love"); and the novelty number to wake up a drowsy Act II ("The Only Dance I Know"). One character even announces, "The girl that I marry will have to be / Meat and potatoes, potatoes and meat like me." (Huh?) Robert Ryan's light tenor hardly conveys Chief Executive authority. As his First Lady, Nanette Fabray—always a pro—puts over "Let's Go Back to the Waltz" and "They Love Me." First Daughter Anita Gillette is fine in "The Secret Service." The rest of the score is a disappointment, and the Broadway talent delivering it has no chance against such feeble material. Even orchestrator Philip J. Lang can't spark the dispiriting arrangements; these songs just end. Berlin went on to prove that he could still write by supplying the show-stopping "An Old-Fashioned Wedding" for the 1966 revival of *Annie Get Your Gun.* But here, he sounds terribly, terribly tired.   —MARC MILLER

MR. WONDERFUL
Original Broadway Cast, 1956 (Decca/MCA) ★★★★

From the moment the overture fires up, strings sawing away and trumpets blaring, you know that this is a mid-'50s schlock musical comedy. Produced by Jule Styne and written by lesser lights to showcase the talents of Sammy Davis Jr., *Mr. Wonderful* leaves no convention unturned: There's the frantic opening chorus ("1617 Broadway"); the second couple's silly duet ("Without You I'm Nothing"); Davis' swinging nightclub specialty ("Jacques D'Iraq"); the leading lady's adoring title song; the comedienne's pointless choral ensemble ("Miami"); and the other comedienne's irrelevant song and dance number ("I'm Available"). So feeble is the score that when Davis needs a socko eleven-o'clock number, he simply pulls an old standard out of the trunk ("Sing, You Sinners"). Act II is basically his nightclub act, so how much story has to be told? What makes all of this special is the cast. That "I'm Available" comedienne just happens to be Chita Rivera. The other comic gal is Pat Marshall, so funny and leather-lunged that you wonder why she didn't have more of a career. (Answer: She married Larry Gelbart and lived happily ever after.) Davis' love interest, Olga James, displays a sweet soprano, but she can also wow us when given good comedy material ("Talk to Him," "I've Been Too Busy"). And there are some good songs here: The score is by a young Jerry Bock and George David Weiss, who keep things unfailingly tuneful. As for Davis, he's so eager to show off his versatility—tapping, doing impersonations, hard-selling the hit song "Too Close for Comfort"—that he's almost frantic. But it's pleasing how little fuss is made about having a black leading couple (Davis and James), a white second couple (Marshall and Jack Carter), and making them all best friends. If you love the sound of boilerplate musical comedy from the Golden Age, here's a Grade-A specimen. If not, downgrade the rating to three stars.   —MARC MILLER

THE MOST HAPPY FELLA
Original Broadway Cast, 1956 (Columbia/Sony, 2CDs) ★★★★★

When Frank Loesser's adaptation of Sidney Howard's *They Knew What They Wanted* opened on Broadway, the composer-lyricist quickly corrected those who suggested that he had written an opera: "Actually," he said, "it's just a musical with a lot of music." Happily, *The Most Happy Fella* was recorded complete and released in a three-LP album (and as a single LP of highlights). The two-CD edition gives us a rare chance to sample a mid-'50s hit in its entirety. The recording is noteworthy for Don Walker's lush orchestrations and underscoring, the cast's emphatic line readings and rich voices, and Loesser's stretching of the art form's borders in terms of both musical style and morality. (The plot of *Happy Fella* concerns a bride who is unfaithful on her wedding night yet doesn't get struck by lightning.) Yes, the score careens between musical comedy silliness and operatic intensity, some of the acting is artless, the lyrics repeat and repeat, but none of that matters because Loesser's musical storytelling is so passionate, his sympathy for his characters is so limitless, and the show is so sincere a portrayal of adult romance. As Tony, ex-Met baritone Robert Weede is superb; no one has ever surpassed him in the role. Jo Sullivan as his pretty Rosabella uses her thin top notes effectively to communicate vulnerability. (In a real-life romance, Sullivan and Loesser courted and married during the show's run.) Susan Johnson is the definitive Cleo, while Art Lund captures Joe's restlessness in "Joey, Joey, Joey" and his ambivalence in "Cold and Dead." Herbert Greene conducts with all of the sweep that this unique score requires. Although the album was recorded before Columbia switched to stereo, the mono sound is crisp and resonant. For those who value a good love story, this is a tremendously moving performance—so much so that when Tony asks, "Young lady, what's-a you name?" in the final scene and Rosabella offers her surprising reply, you may weep with happiness for both of them.

Original London Cast, 1960 (His Master's Voice/no CD) ★★★

The first stereo recording of Frank Loesser's great romantic musical is a fine one, though it's limited to one LP. The West End production wisely imported several of its principals from New York, ensuring authentic American accents. Helena Scott is an authentic-sounding, lovely Rosabella. Libi Staiger is a superb, rafter-raising Cleo and is well partnered by Jack DeLon's Herman. The Maori basso Inia Te Wiata has voice to spare and the requisite sincerity for Tony, but he overdoes the hearty peasant thing: Hear him burble "Omma so happy-happy omma t'ink omma gonna bust!" Reprising his New York role of Joe, Art Lund seems a little tired and makes some horsey noises in "Joey, Joey, Joey." But the editing of the score is judicious and the luscious stereo sound brings out vocal and instrumental subtleties that the mono original couldn't capture. "How Beautiful the Days," for instance, sounds more beautiful than ever.

Broadway Cast, 1992 (RCA) ★★

Goodspeed Opera House's vest-pocket-size revival of *Happy Fella* was successful enough to transfer to Broadway's cozy Booth Theater, where it ran out the season. The justification for turning the musical into a smaller show was that the material would feel "more intimate" and the substitution of two pianos for a full orchestra would bring audiences "closer" to the material. Excuse me, but Don Walker's original orchestrations have never been emotionally distancing, nor do the two pianos (plus an accordion in "Sposalizio" and a guitar in "Song of a Summer Night") bring out any qualities previously lacking in Loesser's music. The production was well acted and sung for the most part, although Spiro Malas as Tony is sometimes below pitch and often resorts to head voice, and Claudia Catania's Marie is downright unpleasant. On the plus side, Sophie Hayden's Rosabella is a fresh take on the role; she's more tired, more resigned at first and, eventually, more transformed by love. The score has been edited for this single-CD recording yet, somehow, nothing crucial seems to be missing. But pretending that "smaller is better" for this grandly ambitious piece is disingenuous.

Studio Cast, 1999 (JAY, 3CDs) ★★★★★

This is a well-cast, well-conducted *Happy Fella*. The bonus tracks of cut songs tell us more about the character Marie, Tony's possessive sister, beautifully sung here by Nancy Shade. "House and Garden," which was included in the unrecorded (but videotaped) 1979 Broadway revival, offers a peek into Rosabella's wistful side. And "Wanting to Be Wanted," an earlier draft of "Somebody Somewhere," is given a sensitive reading by Jo Sullivan. Mrs. Loesser should be proud of her daughter Emily, whose Rosabella is vocally secure and acted with great range. The one casting letdown is the lead: Louis Quilico interprets Tony solidly, if unimaginatively, but there's vocal strain in his performance. And Richard Muenz, who was a sexy Tony in the '79 revival, sounds like he's walking through the role here. But Karen Ziemba's Cleo is wonderful and Don Stephenson's Herman is enormously ingratiating. Overall, this is a detailed, loving recording, with expert performers such as George Dvorsky, Walter Charles, and even Kristin Chenoweth taking tiny roles. Conductor John Owen Edwards doesn't over-sentimentalize the score—and we can be grateful, too, for the stirring exit music. Generous packaging offers the complete libretto and numerous photos from both the original production and the recording sessions for this release. If I could have only one version, I'd still take Columbia's Broadway cast album, but there's value added in this luxurious tour.   — MARC MILLER

MOVIN' OUT
Original Broadway Cast, 2002 (Sony) ★★★★
In the old days, composers hoped that theatergoers would go out humming what they'd just heard. With *Movin' Out,* however, the idea is that the audience will be humming the show's melodies on the way in. Sure, this is an original cast recording, but the singer featured on it did not introduce the songs that make up the score; every rock 'n' roll number that Michael Cavanaugh warbles and plays on piano with exuberance was popularized by singer-songwriter Billy Joel on albums that have sold in the millions. Cavanaugh hews to Joel's phrasing and inflections while bringing his own distinctive talents to the likes of "Just the Way You Are," "Uptown Girl," "We Didn't Start the Fire," "Captain Jack," and "I've Loved These Days," and there's some thrilling instrumental work by the sidemen, particularly by saxophonist John Scarpulla. While this is an expertly produced aural document of a spectacular and important show, it's obviously incomplete in one major respect: Director-choreographer Twyla Tharp created a visual masterwork around Joel's triumphs as a troubadour-chronicler of his troubled pre- and post-Vietnam times but, of course, there was no way for CD producers Tommy Byrnes and Mike Berniker to make an audio recording of Tharp's extraordinary choreography. So this cast album is a must-have with that qualification, and another: If you want the definitive recordings of these songs, pick up Joel's versions.   — DAVID FINKLE

MUSICAL CHAIRS
Original Broadway Cast, 1980 (Original Cast Records) Not recommended.
After only fourteen performances, *Musical Chairs* vanished from sight. But, inexplicably, it yielded a cast album. The episodic "plot" concerns the folks in the audience on opening night of a play. Everyone, it seems, gets a song: the playwright (Tom Urich); two bitter playgoers (Brandon Maggart and Joy Franz) who have been dragged to the show by their spouses; another playgoer (Scott Ellis) whose date (Susan Stroman!) shows up very late; some amateur divas; and a trio of tap-dancing critics. There's even a song about hitting the ladies' room—which, naturally, closes the first act. Composer-lyricist Tom Savage, who's also one of the three bookwriters credited, provided a few better-than-mediocre pop-ballad melodies, but the up-tempo numbers are silly and most of the lyrics are pretty terrible. (Example: "Give me some time for analysis / I'll find their strengths and their fallacies.") Unless you're a Brandon Maggart completist, this one isn't worth your time.   — SETH CHRISTENFELD

THE MUSICAL OF MUSICALS: THE MUSICAL!
Original Off-Broadway Cast, 2004 (JAY) ★

This is Eric Rockwell and Joanne Bogart's attempt to parody hit musicals by taking one melo-dramatic story (a landlord trying to secure his tenant's rent) and presenting it in the "styles" of famous composers and lyricists. What might have been fun in the right hands proves a cata-strophe, for these send-ups of Rodgers and Hammerstein, Stephen Sondheim, Jerry Herman, Andrew Lloyd Webber, and Kander and Ebb lack real wit. A few decent laughs are derived from the similarities between Webber tunes and Puccini melodies, but that's about it; the bulk of the score is dreary, taking shots so obvious as to defy humor. For example, the R&H spoof—entitled "Corn!"—includes "I Couldn't Keer Less About You," "Sowillyquey," and "Clam Dip." Other segments capitalize on tired stereotypes, with little creative ribbing achieved. All of the performers—Rockwell, Bogart, Craig Fols, and Lovette George—are fine, but they can only do so much with the material. This recording receives one star only because it's superior to the show that spawned it; the faster pace is a plus and the narration is less distracting than it was in the theater.
—MATTHEW MURRAY

MUSIC IN THE AIR
Radio Broadcast, 1952 (AEI) ★

If *Music in the Air* sounds like the title of a hokey operetta, that's intentional: The 1932 show—music by Jerome Kern, book and lyrics by Oscar Hammerstein—took an amused look at that genre and the egos toiling in it. Two small-town lovers journey to Munich with the score of her father's show and promptly tangle with an egotistical composer-star and his muse, an over-the-top diva. The couples trade partners, but when the village girl fails to make the grade as an operetta star, the natural order of things is restored. Meanwhile, the audience is treated to such gems as "The Song Is You" and "I've Told Ev'ry Little Star." This CD is based on the transcript of a cut-down radio version of the show, complete with a narrator and overwrought actors who speak the lines while other performers take care of the songs. Musically, it's not a bad performance; there's decent singing by people you've never heard of plus an adequate orchestra and chorus, all in listenable sound. But the dialogue and plot have been mangled beyond recognition, and there's no option for skipping over the "drama" tracks to hear just the songs. It's fortunate that this doc-ument of the show exists, but *Music in the Air* deserves better. (An LP of a 1954 Broadway revival is long out of print and was unobtainable for review.)
—RICHARD BARRIOS

THE MUSIC MAN
Original Broadway Cast, 1957 (Capitol) ★★★★★

This is among the greatest of all cast albums. Meredith Willson, in his first Broadway effort, wrote the colorful, varied music and lyrics. *The Music Man* score is full of innovation, begin-ning with the unconventional opening "Rock Island," in which a group of traveling salesmen rhythmically discuss how Harold Hill is ruining their business—instant exposition in a musi-cal number with no actual singing! There follows an excellent chorale that introduces the "Iowa Stubborn" townspeople before any of the principals do any singing. After having been turned down by song-and-dance men Danny Kaye and Gene Kelly, Willson gave the role of Professor Harold Hill to Robert Preston, an established stage/screen actor who had no prior musical cred-its. And what a blessing that turned out to be! Preston is mesmerizing in what might be considered one of the world's first "rap" numbers, "Trouble," and he sings "Seventy-Six

Trombones" with enormous skill and gusto. His rendition of the "Sadder-but-Wiser Girl" reveals a vaudevillian's pizzazz, yet he also sounds fully at home in the soft-shoe-tempo love song "Marian the Librarian" and holds his own in the ballad "Till There Was You." Most of that ballad is sung by Barbara Cook, arguably the greatest soprano leading lady/ingenue in Broadway history. After a delightful "Piano Lesson" (Marian telling her mom, played by Pert Kelton, about Harold Hill), Cook takes the beautiful "Goodnight My Someone" and makes it shimmer. When she sings about the man of her dreams in "My White Knight," it's a perfect expression of romantic yearning. And when Marian's emotions explode in the discovery of "Till There Was You," it's one of those rare moments when a cast album gives you the thrill of a live performance. The Buffalo Bills do excellent barbershop-quartet singing; Eddie Hodges as little brother Winthrop lisps charmingly through "Gary, Indiana" and adds to the excitement of "The Wells Fargo Wagon"; and Iggie Wolfington as Marcellus has great fun with "Shipoopi." The one thing missing is the complete original overture. While it may be hard to comprehend how *The Music Man* won the Tony Award for Best Musical over *West Side Story,* this album does make it clear why the show was such a hit.

Original London Cast, 1961 (HMV/Laserlight) ★★
In the London production of *The Music Man,* Van Johnson played Harold Hill. The film star was a selling point at the box office and also brought a real American presence to the British cast. This recording is a fun listen, if not distinctive. Johnson is more than pleasant and Patricia Lambert sings beautifully as Marian. A particular standout is the Winthrop, Denis Waterman. A regrettably abridged version of this recording was released on CD by Laserlight in 1995; missing from it are "Iowa Stubborn," "Piano Lesson," "Sincere," "The Sadder-but-Wiser Girl," "My White Knight," and "Shipoopi." But since it's unlikely that a more complete version will appear on compact disc, this budget item is worth buying.

Film Soundtrack, 1962 (Warner Bros.) ★★★
Your enjoyment of this disc will depend on several things: Do you prefer Hollywood's Shirley Jones to Broadway's Barbara Cook? Do you favor the souped-up movie arrangements/orchestrations or the stage originals? Do you think the conventional ballad "Being in Love" is an improvement over the more complex "My White Knight?" Would you rather hear Robert Preston's Harold Hill as he sounded when the show first opened or after he had been playing the role for a few years? Since responses to all of those questions are highly subjective, I won't try to convince you one way or the other. Anyway, of primary importance is Preston—and on this disc, his Harold Hill is as spontaneous and irreplaceable as ever. Buddy Hackett is an engaging Marcellus, Hermione Gingold makes a major impact in her few vocal moments, and Ronnie Howard is delightful as Winthrop. Pert Kelton wonderfully reprises her Broadway role as Mrs. Paroo, and The Buffalo Bills are also on hand—so answer the above questions, then make your decision based on your budget and how much shelf space you have available.

Studio Cast, 1991 (Telarc) ★
This recording features Erich Kunzel conducting the Cincinnati Pops Orchestra; it uses a mixture of Broadway and film orchestrations of *The Music Man* score. Included are "My White Knight," "Being in Love," and Harold Hill's version of "Gary, Indiana." The orchestrations are credited to Don Walker (Broadway), Ray Heindorf (film), and four other gentlemen—so if the

album doesn't sound consistently theatrical, small wonder. The movie's overture is also here, along with dance music that seems an amalgam of the stage and film versions, none of it played with much excitement. There is a huge chorus, the Indiana University Singing Hoosiers. Timothy Noble plays the title role; the notes refer to him as a leading operatic baritone, but his portrayal of Harold Hill is way off the mark. Marian is played by Kathleen Brett, a Canadian soprano who has a pure, pretty voice but does not ignite any sparks. Doc Severinsen plays Marcellus and leads "Shipoopi" with some energy, but the rest of the supporting cast is uninteresting. So, why does this recording deserve even one star? The "It's You" Ballet, previously unrecorded, is included here. Also of interest is a counterpoint version of "My White Knight" and "The Sadder-but-Wiser Girl."

Broadway Cast, 2000 (Q Records) ★

Onstage, Craig Bierko sounded so astonishingly like Robert Preston in the title role of *The Music Man* that the actor's own personality never emerged. On this CD, the similarity is unnerving enough to be spooky; you may wonder, "Which disc did I put on?" Since any successful production or recording of this show must have a dynamic Harold Hill, Bierko is a handicap. But Rebecca Luker's performances of "Goodnight, My Someone" and "My White Knight" are beautifully sung. The barbershop quartet is also fine, but adding Harold and Mrs. Paroo (Katherine McGrath) to "Gary, Indiana" barely allows Michael Phelan to register as Winthrop. Finally, while the CD contains almost every bit of music in this revival, along with dialogue to add dramatic punch, the new orchestrations (by Doug Besterman) and dance arrangements (by David Crane) aren't improvements on the originals; in fact, adding accompaniment to "Rock Island" is harmful, for the lyrics don't fall as pungently on the ear.

Television Film Soundtrack, 2003 (Disney) ★

The casting of Matthew Broderick as Harold Hill in *The Music Man* was controversial. Some viewers of this TV film may have gradually fallen under Broderick's spell and, by the final scenes, may have bought into his subtle characterization. On the CD, however, his performances of "Trouble" and "Seventy-Six Trombones" are simply too low-key. He does a little better with "The Sadder-but-Wiser Girl" and "Marian the Librarian," but Hill's first two songs must establish the character strongly for the show to work. On the plus side, Kristin Chenoweth's Marian is enchanting. The supporting players are all good actors who sing well, but their vocals don't have much éclat and often seem muted. Some of the musical changes for the big-screen version are included here, but how nice that Chenoweth sings "My White Knight" instead of the inferior "Being in Love."   —JEFFREY DUNN

MY FAIR LADY
Original Broadway Cast, 1956 (Columbia/Sony) ★★★★★

My Fair Lady is regarded by many as the supreme achievement of the American musical theater. Lyricist-librettist Alan Jay Lerner and composer Frederick Loewe did such a superb job in adapting George Bernard Shaw's *Pygmalion* to the musical stage that critics have been inclined to forgive the grammatical errors in Lerner's lyrics. (One example of many: "I'd be equally as willing for a dentist to be drilling than to ever let a woman in my life.") The original performances of Rex Harrison as Henry Higgins, Julie Andrews as Eliza Doolittle, Stanley Holloway as Alfred P. Doolittle, and Robert Coote as Colonel Pickering are considered definitive. The show was the biggest hit of its era and you can practically hear the excitement of everyone involved on this recording, made in the flush of a huge success. Harrison has the time of his life as Higgins; his obvious enjoyment of the role makes an overbearing character likeable. The young Andrews is a dream Eliza, equally effective as the squawking guttersnipe and the grand lady with pear-shaped tones; her shining moments are "I Could Have Danced All Night," "Show Me," and "Wouldn't It Be Loverly?" Holloway, as Eliza's dad, masterfully leads the ensemble in "With a Little Bit of Luck" and "Get Me to the Church on Time." Coote is a charmer as Pickering, and John Michael King does a fine job with Freddy Eynsford-Hill's "On the Street Where You Live." Franz Allers conducts the score with skill and energy (orchestrations by Robert Russell Bennett and Philip J. Lang); "The Rain in Spain" as recorded here is electrifying, and if the first few measures of the overture don't start your pulse racing, you've probably already shuffled off this mortal coil.

Original London Cast, 1959 (Columbia/Sony) ★

The peerless original album of *My Fair Lady* was recorded just months before stereo was established as the industry norm. Since the four leads of the Broadway production were set to repeat their roles in London, Columbia Records decided that a new cast album in true stereo would be highly marketable. Alas, the London recording turned out to be a dud. Harrison overinflects much of the role, as if he were bored with it. Andrews sounds tired and droopy but, on the plus side, her Cockney accent seems more organic than on the prior album. Holloway often indulges in talk-singing. Coote rushes "You Did It," which is surprising, since Cyril Ornadel's tempi are rather brisk to begin with. On the plus side, Leonard Weir sings Freddy's "On the Street Where You Live" beautifully. The irony is that the sound quality of this recording is actually inferior to that of its predecessor. Yes, the London album is stereophonic, but there are distortions in certain tracks (most lamentably, the overture) and the general timbre of the sound is less warm than the monophonic original.

Film Soundtrack, 1964 (Columbia/Sony) ★★★

This *My Fair Lady* boasts fabulous orchestrations by Alexander Courage, Robert Franklyn, and Al Woodbury, created under the supervision of conductor André Previn. The film soundtrack is lush without ever seeming gimmicky or overblown. Oddly but happily, Rex Harrison's Henry Higgins sounds fresher here than on the London cast recording. As for Eliza Doolittle, apparently an attempt was made to use Audrey Hepburn's singing voice for much of the role, so she recorded "Wouldn't It Be Loverly?" and "Show Me," transposed to keys in which she was most comfortable. Even after it was decided that Marni Nixon would dub almost all of Eliza's songs (except for the first and last sections of "Just You Wait" and two lines at the beginning of "I Could Have Danced All Night"), the Hepburn keys were retained. As a result, Nixon's singing is compromised, and Eliza's songs don't come across well on this recording. But Stanley Holloway, back again as Alfie Doolittle, is delightful as ever; Wilfrid Hyde-White is an ingratiating Pickering; and vocal ghost Bill Shirley ardently sings "On the Street Where You Live" on behalf of actor Jeremy Brett's Freddy. The CD is a much-expanded version of the original LP: Extras include background music for the flower market scene, the servants' chorus lead-in to "The Rain in Spain," intermission and exit music, and—best of all—the gorgeous "Embassy Waltz."

Broadway Cast, 1976 (Columbia/no CD) ★★★★

What a shame that this cast album of the twentieth-anniversary Broadway revival of *My Fair Lady* has never been released on CD; it's second only to the original recording of the score in overall excellence. Ian Richardson is a mercurial Higgins; Christine Andreas is superb as Eliza; and as Alfie P. Doolittle, George Rose has a rousing time. It's great to have Robert Coote back as Colonel Pickering, and Jerry Lanning is the most vocally resplendent Freddy on record; when he sings "On the Street Where You Live," you'd expect Eliza to throw herself into his arms. The sound quality is somewhat dry but sharp and clear.

Studio Cast, 1987 (London) ★★

As Eliza Doolittle, the Maori operatic soprano Kiri Te Kanawa affects a convincing Cockney accent and her voice sounds beautiful in the higher reaches of the score; still, there's a studied quality to her performance. The salient point about Jeremy Irons' portrayal of Higgins is that this role should not be played by someone with a notably sibilant "s"; Irons is assuredly a great actor, but not in the role of a professor who's a stickler for the perfect pronunciation of English. Sir John Gielgud sounds ancient as Pickering, but the opera tenor Jerry Hadley has just the right voice for "On the Street Where You Live," Warren Mitchell is a colorful Alfie Doolittle, and the London Symphony Orchestra is ably led by John Mauceri.

Studio Cast, 1993-94 (JAY, 2CDs) ★★★

This note-complete recording is essential if only for archival purposes. In the case of *My Fair Lady,* completeness is particularly important for the dance music, largely omitted on other recordings of the score but included here. Other plusses: Alec McCowan is a delightful Higgins and Tinuke Olafimihan is an excellent Eliza, fully credible in the Cockney numbers and singing "I Could Have Danced All Night" gloriously. As Freddy, Henry Wickham sings "On the Street Where You Live" with sincerity even if his voice is rather shaky; and as Pickering, Michael Denison is OK even if he makes little attempt to match pitches in "You Did It." But Bob Hoskins, a fine actor, doesn't have enough voice for Alfred P. Doolittle's songs; he's raspy and almost inaudible when he tries to sing low notes. The National Symphony Orchestra plays beautifully under John Owens Edwards and is recorded in state-of-the-art sound.

London Cast, 2001 (First Night) Not recommended.

This CD begins without the pulse-quickening music that began every previous production and recording of *My Fair Lady,* so you know from the start that you're in for an awful experience. Aside from the fussy rearrangements/reorchestrations by the normally reliable William David Brohn, the recording suffers from some weak casting. As Eliza, Martine McCutcheon displays an exceedingly thin voice, and Mark Umber's rendition of Freddy's "On the Street Where You Live" is full of superficial, heavy-handed effects but lacks real emotion. Jonathan Pryce gives a fine performance as Henry Higgins, deftly walking the line between singing and speaking, and his imitation of Zoltan Karpathy's Hungarian accent in "You Did It" is genuinely funny. As Pickering, Nicholas Le Prevost is also fine and his byplay with Pryce is charming, but these two worthy performers are done in by their surroundings.

—MICHAEL PORTANTIERE

MY FAVORITE YEAR
Original Broadway Cast, 1992 (RCA) ★★★

No two Stephen Flaherty-Lynn Ahrens scores sound remotely alike. Here, the flavor is bright, clever, and wonderfully varied. In adapting the popular film *My Favorite Year,* the team did first-rate work, from the dynamite opening number "Twenty Million People" to the hilarious and touching "Funny" to the warm "Shut Up and Dance." Michael Starobin's orchestrations reflect the show's setting with just the right 1960s New York brassiness. Ted Sperling conducts with great verve; would that the cast were as up to par. True, Andrea Martin lands every joke, and Tim Curry's self-loathing Alan Swann (read: Errol Flynn) comes through vividly on disc. But Lainie Kazan's Jewish mama is over the top. Tom Mardirosian's King Kaiser (read: Sid Caesar) should be side-splitting but is merely unpleasant. And leading man Evan Pappas tries too hard to be liked; his relentless niceness nearly kills the affecting "Larger Than Life." Still, this recording shows off the work of two supremely gifted songwriters.   —MARC MILLER

MY LIFE WITH ALBERTINE
Original Off-Broadway Cast, 2003 (PS Classics) ★★★

Directed by Richard Nelson, also the show's librettist-lyricist, *My Life With Albertine* has a powerful and distinctive score. Composer Ricky Ian Gordon's work here, ranging from near-operatic arias to comic songs, bursts with musical invention and is given a French flavor by Bruce Coughlin's tasty orchestrations. The top-notch cast is led by Kelli O'Hara and Brent Carver. O'Hara is particularly impressive, displaying great dramatic and musical range—and she gets most of the score's best songs. Carver's numbers are more varied in quality, but his layered performance makes even his odder songs sound natural for his character. Although Chad Kimball doesn't quite reach his costars' level of achievement, the overqualified members of the ensemble—including Emily Skinner, Donna Lynne Champlin, and Brooke Sunny Moriber—sound almost perfect throughout.   —MATTHEW MURRAY

MY ONE AND ONLY
Original Broadway Cast, 1983 (Atlantic) ★★★

This "new" musical was written around old George and Ira Gershwin songs. During its troubled pre-Broadway tryout, bookwriter Peter Stone and the uncredited Mike Nichols oversaw an extensive reworking of the show, with star Tommy Tune taking over as director. They surprised everybody by pulling it off: By the time *My One and Only* reached New York, it was delightful. The cast album is not a fully accurate representation of the show; it was much more fluid than this recording suggests, with witty dance numbers popping up from the ensemble as well as the stars. (This is the show in which Twiggy and Tommy Tune tap-danced in water during "'S Wonderful.") Several songs have been left off the disc, including the chorus number "Just Another Rhumba." A more serious omission is dancer Honi Coles' big first-act showcase, "High Hat"—a skillful weave of dialogue, singing, and dance that has inexplicably been replaced on the album by a straightforward version of "Sweet and Lowdown." On the other hand, Twiggy and Tune duet in "Little Jazz Bird," even though it was cut from the show. Throughout, the stars are charming and the songs incomparable. A partial list of highlights: "I Can't Be Bothered Now," "Boy Wanted," "Soon," "He Loves and She Loves," "How Long Has This Been Going On?" and, of course, the fabulous title song.   —DAVID WOLF

THE MYSTERY OF EDWIN DROOD
Original Cast, 1986 (Polydor/Varèse Sarabande) ★★★

Composer-lyricist-librettist Rupert Holmes folded a tribute to the English music hall into a musicalization of Charles Dickens' unfinished novel and came up with *The Mystery of Edwin Drood,* an intriguing whodunit. The original cast, as preserved here, is exemplary; it includes the great George Rose and the one-of-a-kind Cleo Laine, along with heavy-hitting Broadway pros Howard McGillin, Patti Cohenour, Judy Kuhn, Donna Murphy, and belter extraordinaire Betty Buckley in the title role! "The Wages of Sin" is a specialty number delivered stylishly by Laine, and the haunting "Moonfall" is beautifully rendered by Cohenour. Other standouts are the boisterous opening number, "There You Are"; the breathless "Both Sides of the Coin"; the exciting "Don't Quit While You're Ahead"; and the finale, "The Writing on the Wall." The show's peculiar distinction is that it allowed audiences to vote on three different plot conclusions; the two editions of the cast recording offer varying material in regard to those choices. Another difference between the two is that Varèse reinstates "Ceylon" and the "Moonfall" quartet, which are not on the Polydor disc.
— MATTHEW MURRAY

MYTHS AND HYMNS (SATURN RETURNS)
Studio Cast, 1999 (Nonesuch) ★★★★

Adam Guettel's song cycle *Saturn Returns* had a brief run at the Public Theater but never got an original cast recording. *Myths and Hymns* comes pretty close, as this disc contains most of the show's songs and features the original cast joined by other wonderful performers: Billy Porter, Audra McDonald, and the dulcet-toned composer himself. Guettel delivers what the title promises, offering his—and, occasionally, lyricist Ellen Fitzhugh's—unique perspectives on Greek myths, musical settings of obscure hymnal lyrics, and original hymns. Most of the mythic songs are humorous, modern psychological deconstructions of such legends as the one about Icarus, while the hymns capture both the optimism and anguish of spiritual belief. (Listen to Porter's fiery "Awaiting You" for the best example of the latter.) One of the most striking pieces concerns an abortion. The style of composition varies greatly, from the funky electronics of "Icarus" to the joyful gospel sound of "There's a Shout," the angular "Children of the Heavenly King," and the soaring "Migratory V." "Hero and Leander" is a ravishing romantic ballad, but even more compelling is "Saturn Returns," a musical monologue in which the composer laments, "I don't know what I hunger for, I only know I feel the hunger more and more with every passing day."
— BROOKE PIERCE

N

NAKED BOYS SINGING!
Original Los Angeles Cast, 1998 (Café Pacific) ★★★

Obviously, the CD can't capture the *raison d'être* of this popular revue. Yet it does make conceiver-director Robert Schrock's case, as described in his notes, that *Naked Boys Singing!* is not a salacious show but, rather, a simple celebration of nudity. When you hear these charming tunes (by various songwriters) about nakedness in settings ranging from a bris to a locker room, you'll understand why many people who have seen the show claim it's more cute than crude. Still, with sometimes explicit mentions of male privates—most hilariously in "Members Only" and "Perky Little Porn Star"—even the CD version of the show is for mature audiences only. Other comic highlights include "The Naked Maid," "Nothin' but the Radio On," and a tribute to one-time movie sex symbol Robert Mitchum. The musical also has its more serious moments, notably the lovely ballad "Window to Window," about two men looking at each other from afar and contemplating meeting. —BROOKE PIERCE

THE NERVOUS SET
Original Broadway Cast, 1959 (Columbia/DRG) ★★

This investigation of beatnik culture ran twenty-three performances, and you'll know why when you hear the cast album. With a jazz quartet instead of an orchestra and song titles like "Man, We're Beat," *The Nervous Set* comes across more like a faded topical revue than a book musical about love among Greenwich Villagers. The libretto is by Jay Landesman and Theodore J. Flicker. The score, by Tommy Wolf and Fran Landesman, did yield a couple of attractive numbers in "The Ballad of the Sad Young Men" and "Fun Life" ("Shakespeare was a hack / So we read Kerouac!"). There's also a charming counterpoint duet, "What's to Lose/Stars Have Blown My Way," and the introspective "Laugh, I Thought I'd Die." But the comedy numbers are painful, especially the kinky "How Do You Like Your Love?" and the repetitive "Party Song." The cast isn't loaded with distinctive voices, although ingenue Tani Seitz's singing has a sweet, sad quality. A very young Larry Hagman gets a country-western hoedown, "Travel the Road of Love," but the song is only one curio in an album filled with them. —DAVID BARBOUR

ALL-TIME FAVORITES
OF PERFORMER

Barbara Cook

1. Carousel
2. The Unsinkable Molly Brown
3. Gypsy
4. The Most Happy Fella
5. Funny Girl
6. Fiorello
7. Sweeney Todd
8. The King and I
9. She Loves Me
10. Oklahoma!

A NEW BRAIN
Original Off-Broadway Cast, 1998 (RCA) ★★★★

Those who find William Finn's work too abrasive should check out this moving and original work about serious illness. With librettist James Lapine, composer-lyricist Finn brings comedy and feeling to this most unlikely subject. Malcolm Gets stars as Gordon, a frustrated songwriter; when he's diagnosed with a brain tumor, his family and friends rally around. The score mixes Finn's neurotic, hilarious brand of kvetching with some ballads that reflect a newfound serenity in his work. Among the comic highlights are "And They're Off," a recounting of Gordon's troubled family history; "Poor, Unsuccessful, and Fat," the lament of a nurse (Michael Mandell); and "The Homeless Lady's Revenge," sung by a resourceful derelict (Mary Testa). The album's real gems are "The Music Still Plays On," a torch song delivered by Gordon's mother (Penny Fuller), and the final ballad, "I Feel So Much Spring," in which many aspects of Gordon's life come into harmony. There's also good work from Chip Zien as a malevolent TV host and amusing contributions by the prestar Kristin Chenoweth. In the role of Gordon's lover, Norm Lewis fills in for original cast member Christopher Innvar and offers a dreamy performance of the love song "Sailing." —DAVID BARBOUR

NEW FACES OF 1952
Original Broadway Cast, 1952 (RCA/Jasmine) ★

Broadway once thrived on clever little revues in which clever young people satirized whatever was topical along the Great White Way. Once considered the height of sophistication, they might as well be written in Sumerian for all that they have to offer modern audiences. This one, with a score by legions of writers, including Sheldon Harnick, is considered a classic of the genre, perhaps because it launched so many careers. Alice Ghostley sings "The Boston Beguine," a moody Latin ballad about the city of beans and Brahmins, and a pre-*Hogan's Heroes* Robert Clary romps as a romantic Frenchman in "Lucky Pierre." A minor presence on the cast album is Paul Lynde, who had very little musical material. It's all very cute and negligible. Among the most enjoyable items, Virginia de Luce performs "He Takes Me Off His Income Tax," while Eartha Kitt sizzles her way through the faux-French "Bal Petit Bal" and vamps as a world-weary playgirl in "Monotonous." —DAVID BARBOUR

NEW FACES OF 1956
Original Broadway Cast, 1956 (RCA/no CD) ★★★★

While it didn't create as big a sensation as *New Faces of 1952*, this revue still had a roster of impressive performers. Front and center is T.C. Jones, a gifted mimic, comedian, and female impersonator, who opens the album as a boozy, befuddled Tallulah Bankhead. A grab bag of material written by various songwriters is performed by such talents as Amru Sani, a big-voiced belter; the slyly hep Tiger Haynes; baritone John Reardon; ingenue Inga Swenson; and the comediennes Billie Hayes and Jane Connell (the latter's "April in Fairbanks" recalls the beloved "Boston Beguine" of the 1952 edition). A young Maggie Smith is uproariously funny in "One Perfect Moment," a love ditty in which her voice becomes more piercing as her rapture escalates. "Isn't She Lovely?" is best of all, a devastating parody of a Bankhead-headlined edition of the *Ziegfeld Follies* that had been a recent flop. The wordplay here is hilarious, and so is Reardon's turn as a dreadful, off-key revue tenor. —RICHARD BARRIOS

NEW FACES OF 1968
Original Broadway Cast, 1968 (Warner Bros./no CD) ★★

If you want to know what killed the traditional Broadway revue, this cast album provides two answers: economics and a bankruptcy of imagination. *New Faces* impresario Leonard Sillman himself is on hand here to introduce the talent. And there *is* talent: Madeline Kahn, Robert Klein, the forgotten Marilyn Child. But even though much of the material is by *New Faces* veterans Ronny Graham, June Carroll, Arthur Siegel, and Murray Grand, it sounds like stuff you'd hear on the Straw Hat Circuit. A mistress of ceremonies, Gloria Bleezarde, reads her intros weakly, and what she's introducing seldom soars. The running gag of Brandon Maggart (he of the big, silly voice) singing terrible special material by composer-lyricist Clark Gesner collapses right out of the gate but plods on and on. Sociological historians might enjoy the pseudo-hipness of it all: The glimmerings of Women's Lib can be detected in Child's rendition of "Where Is Me?" and M. K. Allen's bad-black-dude turn in "Evil" sounds like a warm-up for *Super Fly.* Most of the rest sinks, but there is one moment of glory: Kahn's peerless Lotte Lenya sendup, "Das Chicago Song." Now, here was a New Face worth discovering!   —MARC MILLER

NEW GIRL IN TOWN
Original Broadway Cast, 1957 (RCA) ★★★★

Although rarely performed today, *New Girl in Town* is an adaptation of Eugene O'Neill's *Anna Christie* that sounds like a hit on this recording. The score, by composer-lyricist Bob Merrill, is bouncy and colorful. Highlights include the naughty "On the Farm," the catchy "The Sunshine Girl," and the beautiful "Look at 'Er" and "Did You Close Your Eyes?" The terrific performances of Gwen Verdon and Thelma Ritter in this show earned them a rare tie for Tony Awards as Best Actress in a Musical. George Wallace is fine in the big baritone role of Mat; Cameron Prud'homme is effective as Chris; and Lulu Bates and Mara Landi stand out in "Flings."   —GERARD ALESSANDRINI

THE NEW MOON
Original London Cast, 1929 (Columbia/Pearl) ★★★★

With wonderful lyrics by Oscar Hammerstien, Sigmund Romberg's frippery about New Orleans, the French Revolution, and love leveling all classes is one of his most melodious works—and the first London cast recording, which has never been long out of print in one form or another, is one of its best readings ever. It's not that the singing here is so impressive (much of it's quite awful), but the style is so confident and the choral work and conducting so excellent that it's a triumph of operetta spirit over technical considerations. Leading man Howett Worster sings some of "Wanting You" and "Stouthearted Men" an octave down, but he still comes across like an authentic operetta hero. Opposite him, Evelyn Laye is vocally and histrionically his superior, though she does have that late-'20s habit of overemphasizing her vowels. Comic leads Gene Gerrard and Dolores Farris have great fun with "Gorgeous Alexander" and "Try Her Out at Dances"; he's so callow and charmingly understated, with practically no vocal equipment, that you'd swear he's Peter Lawford.

Studio Cast, 1953 (Decca) ★

This *New Moon* is a greatest-hits version of the score, missing several incidental numbers and lacking in theatrical orientation. There's an overture that's at least marginally modeled on the original, but those muted trumpets and that augmented string section practically scream "1950s."

The best vocal work comes from Lee Sweetland, who sings "Stouthearted Men" and "Wanting You" like he means it. Leading lady Jane Wilson sounds like she's out to lunch, and Thomas Hayward is only somewhat more involved in "Softly, as in a Morning Sunrise." And what are those soft-shoe temple blocks doing in "Marianne"? They and the lobotomized chorus are decades away from authenticity; this *New Moon* is a little too new. Good CD remastering, though.

Studio Cast, 1962 (RCA/Reader's Digest) ★★★

Poor Peter Palmer: born too late for operetta's golden age, too early to play Jean Valjean. His supple, slightly syrupy tenor is ideal for classic Romberg and he gets to strut his stuff in this boiled-down version of *The New Moon*. With Lehman Engel conducting, the tempi are accurate enough and the cast fairly well acquainted with the form's bravado style. Palmer is personable and secure in "Marianne" and "Wanting You"; Arthur Rubin delivers thrilling high notes in "Softly, as in a Morning Sunrise"; but Jeanette Scovotti sounds a bit pinched in the upper register of her songs. The comic numbers of *The New Moon* are not to be found here. In fact, the editing is pretty schizo: Some seldom-recorded snatches of the show are included, such as the intro to "Marianne," while second choruses and familiar strains are omitted. Henri René's upholstered arrangements recall the 1960s rather than the heyday of operetta.

Studio Cast, 1963 (Capitol/EMI) ★★

Sigmund Romberg surely did not intend "Softly, as in a Morning Sunrise" for a marimba-band arrangement, but that's what it gets in this arthritic reading of his classic *New Moon* score. (Only a few songs from the original recording are included on the EMI CD, along with numbers from other Romberg shows.) The indignities don't end there: Van Alexander stiffly conducts some of his own godawful orchestrations and others by Warren Barker. But Gordon MacRae is in fine voice and Dorothy Kirsten's familiar timbre is well suited to the likes of "The Girl on the Prow" and "Lover, Come Back to Me." The Roger Wagner Chorale backs them up, sounding bored. The polka "Try Her Out at Dances," usually expurgated, is included; but with Alexander practically dozing off as he conducts an uninvolved band of choristers in Muzak-like arrangements, this is the Geritol version of the score. —MARC MILLER

NICK AND NORA
Original Broadway Cast, 1991 (JAY) ★★

As conceived by librettist Arthur Laurents, the ambitious *Nick and Nora* wanted to be a gripping murder mystery, an X-ray of Hollywood hypocrisies, a feminist investigation of marriage, and also a witty Broadway musical. That this overloaded ship capsized shortly after opening night is no surprise; but what remains is the work of gifted people, and the score by composer Charles Strouse and lyricist Richard Maltby, Jr. improves with repeated playings. As the title characters, taken from Dashiell Hammett's novel and movie series *The Thin Man*, Barry Bostwick and Joanna Gleason probe the murder of a blackmailing bookkeeper, played by Faith Prince in a performance of creepy comic intensity. The list of suspects includes a director of the Erich von Stroheim variety (Remak Ramsay), a Katharine Hepburn-ish actress (Christine Baranski), and a Boston matron based on Rose Kennedy (Debra Monk). There's also a corrupt union president played by Chris Sarandon. The score was woven in and out of the dialogue in a way that wasn't reproduceable on disc, so the songs aren't really heard as they were in the show. They're an odd blend of imitation movie music ("Is There Anything Better than Dancing" and "Let's Go Home") with sophisticated-but-sour items like "Men" (the victim's bitter tirade against the stronger sex), "People Get Hurt" (sung by Monk as the tough matron), and "Busy Night at Lorraine's" (in which Nick and Nora run through competing versions of the murder). The blue-chip cast cannot be faulted, and Maltby's lyrics are filled with cleverness and clues. Jonathan Tunick's orchestrations give Strouse's music a citrus bite, but the show's clashing agendas result in serious tonal problems. Frustratingly, the notes in the CD booklet don't reveal the solution to the mystery, so you'll have to wait for a (most unlikely) revival to find out who did it and why.   —DAVID BARBOUR

THE NIGHT OF THE HUNTER
Studio Cast, 1998 (Varèse Sarabande) ★★

Composer Claibe Richardson, best known for his remarkable score for *The Grass Harp*, worked unsuccessfully on a musical version of *Sweeney Todd* for several years before Stephen Sondheim produced his masterwork. Richardson then found similarly dark source material in *The Night of the Hunter*, a cult film of 1955 that starred Robert Mitchum as an ex-con "Preacher" with "L-O-V-E" tattooed on the knuckles of one hand and "H-A-T-E" tattooed on the other. This genuinely evil protagonist is a casual murderer who spends most of the story trying to kill two young children for their money. So the question is, "Can you draw sweet water from a foul well?" The score is filled with gorgeous, emotional numbers such as "Lookin' Ahead," "The River Jesus," "One More Harvest," and especially "Trading Secrets." Yet sometimes the material seems shapeless, and Stephen Cole's lyrics take too long to get the plot points made. But the real problem here is the Preacher. None of the songs written for this frightening sociopath really land—except for "Trading Secrets," which has a built-in dramatic situation. The music keeps building in volume and intensity but never really gets inside of the character. On the plus side, the cast of this recording is extraordinary, from George Lee Andrews' quietly desperate performance as the children's doomed father to Ron Raines as the Preacher and Sally Mayes as one of his victims. Marcia Lewis provides something akin to comic relief, and Dorothy Loudon makes something very special of "One More Harvest."   —DAVID WOLF

NINE
Original Broadway Cast, 1982 (Columbia) ★★★★★

The most original musical of its decade is both a dazzling exercise in style and a heartfelt tale of a middle-aged man's fear of maturity. Arthur Kopit's book for *Nine* is based on the Fellini film masterpiece $8^1/2$, about a famous director who holes up in a chic spa to retreat from his chaotic private life while he struggles to come up with an idea for his next project. The result is a wild, dreamlike, Felliniesque carnival in which Guido Contini—creatively stalled, his marriage collapsing—is besieged by all of the women from his past and present. Presiding over this fantasia is Raul Julia, a suave and saturnine presence throughout. He's witty in "Guido's Song," seductive in "Only You," full of self-loathing in "I Can't Make This Movie." And what women! As Guido's sorrowful wife, Luisa, Karen Akers is superb, especially in the resigned "My Husband Makes Movies" and the furious "Be on Your Own." Anita Morris as his lover, Carla, sizzles in "A Call From the Vatican." Liliane Montevecchi as his skeptical producer, Liliane La Fleur, vivaciously recalls a world of old-fashioned entertainment in "Folies Bergères." Taina Elg, as his mother, delivers the lovely title tune. And Shelly Burch, as his muse Claudia, movingly delivers the soulful "Unusual Way." Maury Yeston's kaleidoscopic music and lyrics are by turns satirical, biting, sentimental, and romantic; each song shines in the hands of orchestrator Jonathan Tunick. The CD is considerably expanded from the original recording, with longer versions of several numbers and bonus tracks of Yeston performing three numbers from the show.

London Concert Cast, 1992 (BMG/TER) ★★★★★

This recording of *Nine* benefits from the intelligent, probing, well-sung Guido of Jonathan Pryce. With Elaine Paige as Claudia and Ann Crumb as Luisa, you can expect a certain amount of belting, but that's in keeping with the expansive, rather grand work of conductor Timothy Higgs. The performance lacks some of the lightness and wit of the Broadway original but, thanks to the singers' crystalline diction, this is the disc to go with if you really want to savor Yeston's lyrics. Even the tongue-twisting "Germans at the Spa" is perfectly clear in this rendition, as is the notoriously difficult "Grand Canal" sequence that depicts Guido's disastrous attempts to shoot a film about Casanova. It's a robust and dramatic account of the score, easily the equal of the original recording.

Broadway Cast, 2003 (PS Classics) ★★★★

Armed with considerable sex appeal and acting skills, Antonio Banderas had a triumph as Guido in the Broadway revival of *Nine*. Banderas' accent is occasionally intrusive, but his boyish, tormented Guido is certainly effective. Overall, the recording is a little less strong than its predecessors. Mary Stuart Masterson's Luisa is a tad prosaic, although she delivers a powerful "Be on Your Own." As Carla, Jane Krakowski sounds sexy but not truly madcap. Chita Rivera is amusing but more than a little spurious as Liliane LaFleur. Laura Benanti is a lovely Claudia, and if her performance lacks the original's humor, it does have intelligence and skill. Jonathan Tunick's orchestrations were thinned out for this revival, and the disc omits "The Germans at the Spa" and "Waltz from Nine," a haunting instrumental that usually follows Guido's breakdown in "I Can't Make This Movie."

—DAVID BARBOUR

NITE CLUB CONFIDENTIAL
Original Off-Broadway Cast, 1983 (Confidential Recording Company/no CD) ★

This is a camp-fest, to say the least: a book musical with the feel of a revue, set in the demimonde of sophisticated 1950s cabarets and with a score made up of standards, semi-standards, and some new material. The plot concerns a young singer/stud who uses an aging chanteuse to advance his career, but the show revels so fully in its luridness that it doesn't bother to offer any real wit or insight. The few new songs by Albert Evans and Dennis Deal are fruity '50s pastiche, though there's a swell item called "The Canarsie Diner," belted by Denise Nolin. The Evans-Deal arrangements of some good old songs ("That Old Black Magic," "I Thought About You," "Something's Gotta Give") are in authentic Hi-Los style and the album does boast a glorious performance by Fay DeWitt, sounding much as she did in *Flahooley* more than thirty years earlier. Playing a Kay Thompson-like chanteuse, DeWitt avidly and sassily spoofs cabaret grande-dame conventions. When she sings a "Man That Got Away" knockoff called "The Long Goodbye," her vowels practically fly off the LP and into the wall. Her dead-on inflections are hilarious.

—MARC MILLER

NO FOR AN ANSWER
Original Cast, 1941 (Pearl/Koch/AEI) ★★★

Marc Blitzstein's follow-up to *The Cradle Will Rock* failed to coalesce and ran for only three performances—yet it earned a cast recording, with Blitzstein at the piano. Billed as a "new American opera" but closer to a pro-union revue with a few plot threads, the show is innovative in form and passionate about the plight of the disenfranchised. Some of the songs sound decades ahead of their time in their unusual construction: Consider "Francie," a hummed melody with spoken interjections but virtually no lyrics. The score is not easy listening and Blitzstein's agitprop concert production employed few real singers, but the social anger and commitment to reform come through. The writer's satirical gifts are fully apparent as well: "Penny Candy," "Dimples," and "Fraught" are sneaky parodies of the pop pablum of the day. It's a mostly no-name cast (future movie director Martin Ritt is in the chorus), but one soon-to-be famous performer stands out: Carol Channing, then an undergraduate at Bennington. In her two numbers, she sounds like nothing you've ever heard—she doesn't even sound like Carol Channing—but her comic style is already assured and assuredly bizarre. —MARC MILLER

NO, NO, NANETTE
Broadway Cast, 1971 (Columbia/Sony) ★★★★★

Pure heaven. This revisal of a nearly forgotten 1925 hit helped kick off the nostalgia craze on Broadway. Burt Shevelove adapted Otto Harbach and Frank Mandel's book, a typical farcical tangle involving three couples hiding out in Atlantic City, but the Vincent Youmans-Irving Caesar songs are everything here. And Ralph Burns' gloriously expansive orchestrations, complete with two pianos, are among the finest ever for a Broadway musical. The entire cast embraces both the silliness and sophistication of the material, and the leads are sublime. Helen Gallagher delivers the eccentric "Too Many Rings Around Rosie" and the scorching "'Where-Has-My-Hubby-Gone' Blues." Jack Gilford and Susan Watson are charming in "I Want to Be Happy," the reprise of which features the tapping of Ruby Keeler and chorus. Bobby Van partners with Gallagher in the amusingly hyperactive "You Can Dance With Any Girl at All," and Watson and Roger Rathburn offer a fresh rendition of "Tea for Two." This cast album, more than most, preserves the electric excitement of a Broadway performance. It's essential to any collection. —DAVID BARBOUR

NO STRINGS
Original Broadway Cast, 1962 (Capitol/DRG) ★★★

Does this sound like a Richard Rodgers musical? A black American fashion model, living in Paris with a rich older lover in attendance, falls in love with a washed-up American novelist who spends his time mooching off of rich patrons. Their romance is played out against an international background of poseurs, partygoers, and professional guests. Not only do they not stay together, librettist Samuel Taylor does not make it clear what will happen to them at the end of the show. But that's *No Strings*. Composer Rodgers, flying solo after the death of Oscar Hammerstein, furnished his own lyrics and found a style all his own. Richard Kiley and Diahann Carroll are the romantic pair, and though both are fine, she's the real star here—sassy in "Loads of Love," furious in "You Don't Tell Me," and eloquently angry at herself in "An Orthodox Fool." Her voice blends beautifully with Kiley's in ballads like "Nobody Told Me," the title tune, and "The Sweetest Sounds," which features one of Rodgers' oddest, most angular melodies. These are interspersed with such astringent items as "Be My Host," "Love Makes the World Go," and "Eager Beaver," most of them featuring Bernice Massi as an American heiress who gets taken for a ride by Kiley's fast-living friends. Ralph Burns' orchestrations are true to the title; in Joe Layton's staging, the wind and brass musicians freely roamed the stage with the actors, giving the score an improvisational, jazzy quality. *No Strings* is not considered a major Rodgers work, but this is one of the master composer's most distinctive scores and a significant historic document of his work as a lyricist. —DAVID BARBOUR

NO WAY TO TREAT A LADY
Off-Broadway Cast, 1997 (Varèse Sarabande) ★★★★

Douglas J. Cohen's chamber musical *No Way to Treat a Lady* received the American Academy of Arts and Letters' Richard Rodgers Award and two productions (in 1987 and 1996) by Off-Broadway nonprofits, but it never snagged a commercial New York staging. Fortunately, the musical component of the first-rate 1996 York Theatre production was lovingly preserved on this disc produced by Bruce Kimmel. The show is an adaptation of a novel by William Goldman about two mamas' boys: a warm-hearted detective and an erudite serial killer. Despite being adversaries, the two share a yen for the big-time public recognition that their ambitious mothers always wished for them. This cast is well-nigh perfect: Adam Grupper as the tough detective; Marguerite MacIntyre as the ingenue; Paul Schoeffler as the sinister thrill killer; and the astonishingly good Alix Korey, who plays the cop's overbearing mother, three murder victims, and the ghost of the murderer's mom. The musicality of the singers and the six-person combo, conducted by Wendy Bobbitt, is unimpeachable. But the recording's star is composer-lyricist Cohen, who has an impressive vocabulary that includes all the idioms of Broadway: jazz, pop, and even funk. The songs and the libretto (also by Cohen) are thoroughly integrated, with stretches of virtuosic material: Korey's snoopy "I Hear Humming," for instance, and Grupper's horny "The First Move." There are also numbers of wonderful melodic invention, such as "I Need a Life," "Safer in My Arms," and "So Far, So Good." —CHARLES WRIGHT

NOW IS THE TIME FOR ALL GOOD MEN
Original Off-Broadway Cast, 1968 (DRG) ★★★★

With a book and lyrics by Gretchen Cryer and music by Nancy Ford, *Now Is the Time for All Good Men* is set in a small town in the Midwest. Its central character is Mike Butler, a new teacher whose liberal views have a strong effect on the townspeople. In its attempt to be hard-hitting, contemporary, and relevant, the show was helped by a solid score written in a theatricalized late-'60s pop style. Heading the first-rate cast, David Cryer—then married to Gretchen—is splendid as Mike in two haunting solos: "What's in the Air?" and "All Alone." His leading lady is Gretchen Cryer, performing under the name Sally Niven. No vanity casting here; she's perfect as Sarah, a shy schoolteacher who's swept up in the events that Mike's liberalism sets in motion. Her growing affection for Mike is showcased in "He Could Show Me," a fine ballad, and her light soprano mixes with David Cryer's solid baritenor in the charming duets "Tea in the Rain" and "Rain Your Love on Me." Better still is "My Holiday," a poignant twin-soliloquies song about Christmas season loneliness; it's a gem that deserves to be a holiday standard. Other standouts: David Sabin offers a sweet rendition of "A Simple Life"; Judy Frank sings a raucous, country-rock-flavored "Stuck Up"; and Steven Skiles and Anne Kaye are impressive in "Down Through History." —JEFFREY DUNN

NUNSENSE
Original Off-Broadway Cast, 1986 (DRG) ★★★

This album preserves much of the straightforward charm of the show on which author Dan Goggin would eventually build a worldwide franchise. The story of *Nunsense* is eminently silly: Five nuns put on a revue to raise money to bury four sisters of their order who died from eating bad soup. With a score full of bounce and fun (under the musical direction of Michael Rice), the show capitalizes on religious themes and on the sisters' showbiz proclivities in songs that range from the reflective "Growing Up Catholic" to the toe-tapping "Tackle That Temptation With a Time Step." Plot numbers tell the story: "We've Got to Clean Out the Freezer," a reference to the place where the dead nuns' bodies are being stored preburial; and character numbers such as "The Biggest Ain't the Best," all about humility, are tossed in for good measure. The cast is fine: Marilyn Farina as the reserved Reverend Mother Mary Cardelia; the brassy Christine Johnson as Sister Robert Anne; the sweet-voiced Suzi Winson as Sister Mary Leo; and the energetic Edwina Lewis, who, as Sister Mary Hubert, delivers the terrific gospel rave-up "Holier Than Thou." Finally, there's the multitalented Semina De Laurentis singing legit soprano, a country-western ditty, and a duet with a puppet in her role of Sister Mary Amnesia, the forgetful nun whose search for her identity comprises the show's subplot. There's not much depth in *Nunsense,* but there's plenty of good-natured ribbing of the Catholic Church and the women who devote their lives to it.

Original London Cast, 1987 (JAY) ★★★

A bit more complete than the Off-Broadway recording, this one includes the full dance music and vocal in "Benedicite," the second-act "Dying Nun" ballet, and the brief "Gloria in Excelsis Deo." In most other respects, the London edition of *Nunsense* is on a par with the New York original; some of the singing is a bit more adventurous, but the performers' British accents lend the score a slightly stodgier feel. The cast includes Honor Blackman, Anna Sharkey, Pip Hinton, Bronwen Stanway, and Louise Gold. All are competent.   —MATTHEW MURRAY

NUNSENSE II: THE SECOND COMING
Original Off-Broadway Cast, 1993 (DRG) ★★

Can anyone blame librettist-composer-lyricist Dan Goggin for not wanting to mess with the formula that made *Nunsense* such a success? Of course not. Still, *Nunsense II* might have been more original. The score of the sequel does more than pay homage to its predecessor; again, there's an upbeat opening chorus, a nun ballerina song, an understudy's lament, a puppet-aided comedy number, a lengthy first-act finale dance, a gospel showstopper, and so on. Goggin even unapologetically quotes the prior show's music in "The Biggest Still Ain't the Best" and "Look Ma, I Made It." The numbers that incorporate new ideas—"We're the Nuns to Come To" (in which the sisters consider starting a burial service), the envious "Padre Polka," and the effervescent can-can "Yes We Can"—are more fun than the retreads. Kathy Robinson, Mary Gillis, and Lyn Vaux are acceptable replacements for the roles' originators, but returning cast members Christine Johnson and Semina De Laurentis shine most brightly, particularly in (respectively) the joyous "I Am Here to Stay" and the emotional "No One Cared Like You." Michael Rice's musical direction is, once again, just right. All in all, *Nunsense II* works best if you don't know the original.   —MATTHEW MURRAY

NYMPH ERRANT

London Concert Cast, 1990 (EMI) ★★★★★

Here is a rare find: a lost gem of a musical by Cole Porter that was produced in England but never on Broadway. This star-studded 1990 concert performance of the score was recorded live in London. The music is Porter at his melodic best, and the lyrics are so sublimely witty that they warrant repeated listening for one to fully grasp the sharpness and comedic effect of his remarkable word play. So much of the album is laugh-out-loud funny that you'll have to play many of the tracks repeatedly to hear and savor all the jokes. Among the luminaries in the cast are Alexis Smith, Larry Kert, Lisa Kirk, Kaye Ballard, Patrice Munsel, and Patricia Hodge, who pristinely sings that wonderful Porter paean to life and lust, "Experiment." Other standout cuts are "The Cocotte," "Solomon," the hilarious throwaway number "Sweet Nudity," and "How Could We Be Wrong?" The ballad "You're Too Far Away" is lovely, but the most famous song in the score is the comic marathon "The Physician," sharply performed by Lisa Kirk, who sails through the various choruses of this terrific number with glee and relish. For this performance, the entire score was reorchestrated by Jim Tyler and Michael Gibson; with Donald Pippin and David Firman at the twin pianos, the effect is gloriously authentic. Steven Hill's vocal direction is impeccable, and the recording culminates in a bouncy choral reprise of "Experiment." Those searching for a classic show score that's fresh, naughty, and not over-familiar should seek out this album.
— GERARD ALESSANDRINI

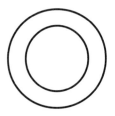

OF THEE I SING
Broadway Cast, 1952 (Capitol/DRG) ★★★

Of Thee I Sing (1931), the first musical to win a Pulitzer Prize, is glorious. With a book by George S. Kaufman and Morrie Ryskind, its George and Ira Gershwin Jazz Age score is exuberant and ingenious, and its skewering of American politics—particularly presidential campaigns—has, if anything, grown more relevant with the passing years. There is no cast album of the original production, but a 1952 revival, directed by George S. Kaufman himself, yielded this recording. All the principal music is here, with revised orchestrations by Don Walker and a few rewritten lyrics by Ira Gershwin. Jack Carson may have seemed an unlikely choice for presidential candidate John P. Wintergreen, but he sings smoothly, exhibiting real warmth in "Who Cares?" His Mary, Betty Oakes, is bland, and his running mate Throttlebottom, Paul Hartman, shares star billing but claims only one number. Jack Whiting's Chief Justice has this song-and-dance man's customary panache and, as Diana Devereaux, Lenore Lonergan offers a truly bizarre performance; throaty and off-key, she turns her vocal liabilities into character points and is quite funny and original. Maurice Levine conducts with energy and briskness.

Television Cast, 1972 (Columbia/no CD) ★

With "Archie Bunker for President" bumper stickers on every Ford Pinto and a theater-of-the-absurd presidential race in full swing, CBS decided to trot out *Of Thee I Sing* as a vehicle for some of its top sitcom stars. Carroll O'Connor played Wintergreen and the network advertised, "Tonight, Archie Bunker becomes President!" O'Connor displays a serviceable Irish tenor and a nice way with a lyric. His Mary, Cloris Leachman, is similarly passable, and Michele Lee is a high-voltage Diana Devereaux. Otherwise, this hard-to-find LP is not worth the search. It's garishly orchestrated and conducted. Worse still, the generous helping of laugh-track-supported dialogue confirms one's suspicions: This *Of Thee I Sing* is fatally dumbed-down, replacing the smart Kaufman-Ryskind dialogue with exchanges better suited to *Green Acres*.

New York Concert Cast, 1987 (Sony, 2CDs, paired with *Let 'Em Eat Cake*) ★★

Conducted by Gershwin scholar Michael Tilson Thomas and presented with great fanfare at the Brooklyn

ALL-TIME FAVORITES
OF COMPOSER-LYRICIST

David Friedman

1. Carousel

2. A Chorus Line

3. The King and I

4. West Side Story

5. The Sound of Music

6. My Fair Lady

7. Dreamgirls

8. Little Shop of Horrors

9. South Pacific

10. Boy Meets Boy

Academy of Music, a 1987 concert version yielded a studio recording that is the most complete, most faithful *Of Thee I Sing* album available. Unfortunately, gleeful as the material is, the presentation is a little stiff. Larry Kert as Wintergreen is a fine singer, but here has all the personality of tofu. Maureen McGovern as Mary Wintergreen has more presence but less to do. Jack Gilford, who had played Throttlebottom on TV, is endearing but, by this time, his voice had aged and weakened almost to a whisper. The best performance comes from Paige O'Hara, whose Diana Devereaux is vocally secure and dizzily funny, but even she overpunches her line readings; I smell a director who insisted on socking everything across the footlights, even in the recording studio. The digital stereo helps bring out the brassy orchestrations, and the notes in the accompanying booklet are authoritative.

—MARC MILLER

OH, BROTHER!
Original Broadway Cast, 1981 (Original Cast) ★★★

It may have been pure folly for Donald Driver and Michael Valenti to invite comparison to *The Boys from Syracuse* with this modern, Mideastern retelling of Shakespeare's *The Comedy of Errors.* In fact, they were rewarded with a three-performance run. Still, there's much to enjoy on this forty-nine-minute cast album, starting with Valenti's tuneful, singable melodies. Songs like "Everybody Calls Me by My Name," "OPEC Maiden," and "How Do You Want Me?" radiate goodwill. Driver's lyrics are good-natured throughout, sung by an exceptionally rich-voiced young cast, with David Carroll, Judy Kaye, Mary Elizabeth Mastrantonio, and Larry Marshall giving their all. (Listen to Mastrantonio's insane high note at the end of "That's Him." What planet is it from?) Not all of the material is golden, and the recording's inclusion of several cut songs ("Revolution," "It's a Man's World," "My World's Comin' Unwrapped") only advocates their excision. But this show was honest and unpretentious, and its best qualities are nicely captured on this brief, friendly disc.

—MARC MILLER

OH! CALCUTTA!
Original Broadway Cast, 1969 (Aidart/DRG) Not recommended.

Given that numerous scores by Cole Porter, Rodgers and Hart, and Jerome Kern remain unrecorded, the existence of this album—and its reissue on CD—is outrageous. *Oh! Calcutta!* was a good idea: an erotic revue written by such interesting and gifted people as Samuel Beckett, Jules Feiffer, John Lennon, and Sam Shepard. (Exactly who wrote what is revealed for the first time in Sherman Yellen's excellent CD booklet notes.) But the show was developed by people with no musical theater experience or skill. In fact, it's almost perversely unmusical in design and direction. *Oh! Calcutta!* famously played much of its marathon run to non-English-speaking tourists, who bought tickets not for the Beckett but because the cast members took off their clothes. The music recorded here isn't theatrical at all; rather, it's soft rock of no particular quality, like the background score of a movie. Professional actor-singers are featured in only three of the twelve cuts. The others are performed by composers Robert Dennis, Peter Schickele, and Stanley Walden, who—collectively known as The Open Window—make up the show's band. Only one of the selections, "I Like the Look," sounds like a theater song; I mention this because it's the last track on the disc, so you'll probably never hear it.

—DAVID WOLF

OH CAPTAIN!
Original Broadway Cast, 1958 (Columbia/DRG) ★★★★

For their Broadway songwriting debut, the Hollywood team of Jay Livingston and Ray Evans freely adapted the British film *The Captain's Paradise* and did outstanding work: It's a full, integrated score that nimbly tells the story of a sea captain (Tony Randall) with a prim English wife (Jacquelyn McKeever) just outside London and a sizzling French mistress (Eileen Rodgers) in Paris. True, some of the lyrics snicker sophomorically about sex or contort themselves wildly to rhyme ("This report is special on / How I achieve my echelon"). But consider the compensations: a tuneful, clever score with one hit ("All the Time") and some other fine writing ("You Don't Know Him," "Surprise"), plus a supercharged atmosphere and game principal performances. The supporting cast is strong, too: Edward Platt reveals a sturdy bass-baritone in the lovely "It's Never Quite the Same," and the great Susan Johnson gives all she's got to "Give It All You've Got." (Her inflection on "Save your strength for the honeymoon and give it all you've got" is so innuendo-packed!) *Oh Captain!* didn't run very long and the score isn't absolutely top-drawer, but the album is a lesson in how a recording produced by Goddard Lieberson makes second-rate material sound first-rate.   —MARC MILLER

OH COWARD!
Original Off-Broadway Cast, 1972 (Bell/no CD) ★★★★

After appearing in Noël Coward's last musical, *The Girl Who Came to Supper,* Roderick Cook compiled a revue of Coward's songs that was first produced as *Noël Coward's Sweet Potato,* a quick Broadway flop in 1968. Cook tried subsequent assemblages of Coward material in different cities with different titles and finally returned to New York with *Oh, Coward!* The revue enjoyed a successful Off-Broadway run. Coward's songs—and his verse, plays, and memoirs, excerpts of which serve as linking narration—are delightfully entertaining as presented here. No one ever wrote comic songs like Coward; he chose his words with specificity, using them with precision and a demented logic. When he turned serious, his work was almost as impressive if not nearly so unique. He is well served in *Oh, Coward!* by the layout of the material (roughly according to subject) and also by the three-member cast: Cook and comic actress Barbara Cason are very effective, and Jamie Ross is an only slightly weaker link.   —DAVID WOLF

OH, KAY!
Studio Cast, 1955 (Columbia/Sony) ★★

With a score by George and Ira Gershwin and a book by Guy Bolton amd P. G. Wodehouse, this 1926 lark is a tuneful jaunt through the then-familiar territory of Long Island rum-running, society marriages, and mistaken identities. The first attempt to set the score down intact was this recording, produced by Goddard Lieberson and conducted by Lehman Engel. Unlike some other titles in Columbia's 1950s series of studio recordings of significant shows, *Oh, Kay!* at least preserves the period sound of the score, with twin pianos and a Grapelli-like jazz violin. But the sluggish tempi and the casting don't do these nimble songs justice. Barbara Ruick is a sweet Kay and her "Someone to Watch Over Me" is heartfelt, if glacially slow, but her cooing soprano lacks variation. Jack Cassidy, always perfect as a shallow cad, doesn't sound like he's kidding his own oiliness here; he just sounds oily. The comic numbers assigned to Allen Case call not for voice but for personality, and Case seems to have left his outside the studio. The remastered CD has a few bonus tracks (Mary Martin singing "Maybe," two dizzy-fingers piano displays by Gershwin), not to mention one of those greatest-hits finales that rob the show's story of whatever cohesion it had. The disc is easy listening, but those padded tempi dominate, so much so that the whole thing seems to have been wrapped up in slipcovers.

Off-Broadway Cast, 1960 (20th Century-Fox/Stet) ★

When Stet picked up the rights to this long-forgotten revival cast album, it plastered the names of cast members Linda Lavin and Penny Fuller in big block letters on the cover—despite the fact that both were merely members of the chorus. On the other hand, Eddie Phillips, who has two big numbers, isn't billed at all. There are missing songs, interpolations from other scores, and new, slapdash lyrics by Wodehouse. ("You'll Still Be There," originally "Dear Little Girl," doesn't even scan neatly.) The snatches of dialogue included here show a certain patronizing attitude toward the material, as if to say: "Look, it's 1960 and we're much smarter now!" The arrangements for an anorexic combo are cutesy and the cast is uneven. David Daniels, his baritone as solid as ever, is a fine Jimmy; but his Kay, Marti Stevens, drifts in and out of her Mayfair accent, and she has the odd habit of speaking whole verses of her lyrics, though not for any lack of singing ability. The recording is over in thirty-six minutes and Gershwin's melodic magic does survive the mishandling. As background listening, it's OK—but it's not *Oh, Kay!* (The CD includes selections from *Leave It to Jane*.)

Studio Cast, 1995 (Nonesuch) ★★★★★

A sheer delight, this reconstruction of *Oh, Kay!* takes certain liberties: It has new orchestrations by Russell Warner; some of the songs are resequenced; and some cut material has been restored. Still, the recording is utterly faithful to its Jazz Age heritage. Dawn Upshaw's Kay is fervent, girlish, whimsical, and miles away from the opera-house haughtiness that sometimes is displayed when crossover artists attempt the Great American Songbook. Her "Someone to Watch Over Me" is melting and persuasive, her "Maybe" is pensive and touching, and her command of musical theater vernacular is total. Similarly, Kurt Ollmann's Jimmy is no opera snob slumming on Broadway; rather, he's a chipper juvenile with a lot of voice. Other cast members—Patrick Cassidy (ripping through "Fidgety Feet"), Robert Westenberg, and Liz Larsen—are thoroughly Times Square. There are some fun surprises, too: Susan Lucci pouts amusingly as Jimmy's bitchy fiancée and Fritz Weaver bloviates as her pompous pater. Eric Stern's twenty-three-piece orchestra is just the right size for this score and has a clean, unaffected sound; Kevin Cole and Joseph Thalken tear irresistibly through some twin-piano arrangements. The notes contained in the handsome CD booklet—by Lee Davis, producer Tommy Krasker, and Evan Ross—are informative and engaging. —MARC MILLER

OH! WHAT A LOVELY WAR
Original London Cast, 1963 (Decca/Must Close Saturday) ★★★★

A hit in London, a flop *d'estime* on Broadway, and the basis of a very odd film, *Oh! What a Lovely War* was a show that slotted vintage World War I tunes amid sketches/vignettes while the names of battles and numbers of war dead rolled by on an upstage flashing-lights billboard. Directed by Joan Littlewood, the show was billed as a "musical entertainment," but the material can be quite upsetting. This recording captures its essence to strong effect with lengthy sequences of the score and dialogue. Many of the tunes are familiar, but some of them are outfitted with special wartime lyrics. The numbers are alternately sardonic (a postwar parody of the famous Kern song "They Wouldn't Believe Me"), amusing (the saucy "Hitchy-Koo," the recruiting song "I'll Make a Man of You"), and moving (Ivor Novello's "Keep the Home Fires Burning," beautifully sung by Myvanwy Jenn). A particularly poignant sequence takes place on Christmas Eve in a trench, as English soldiers make temporary peace with German soldiers; it concludes with Victor Spinetti as an emcee leading a lighthearted "Goodbye-ee" that fades into sounds of distant gunfire.

Film Soundtrack, 1969 (Paramount/no CD) ★★

Directed by Richard Attenborough, the film version of *Oh! What a Lovely War* found its own way to interpret the kaleidoscope of scenes and songs from the dazzling stage show. Unlike the London cast album, which includes a lot of dialogue, the soundtrack LP has only the songs; some of them are given big, Hollywood-style orchestrations, others are arranged and performed more atmospherically, and there are also some medleys and instrumental tracks. "Belgium Put the Kibosh on the Kaiser" is charmingly sung by Jean-Pierre Cassel. In a recruiting sequence, Peggy Allen lends her bland soprano to "We Don't Want to Lose You," but then Maggie Smith takes over and grabs our attention with "I'll Make a Man of You." Smith has a commanding belt that will surprise listeners; this track alone makes the soundtrack album noteworthy. Most of the other singing on the LP is lacking in personality and, because the songs are heard out of context, they aren't as heartbreaking as they are on the stage cast album.   —JEFFREY DUNN

OIL CITY SYMPHONY
Original Off-Broadway Cast, 1988 (DRG) ★★

This is one of the most disappointing cast albums ever made. It utterly fails to capture any of the brilliance of this hilarious musical revue. *Oil City Symphony* was a straight-faced send-up of small-town musical programs. The cast/creative team consisted of Mike Craver, Debra Monk, Mark Hardwick, and Mary Murfitt. The show's great appeal lay in the ingenuous earnestness of a group of people trying their best to present a concert in their decorated high-school gymnasium but goofing up, rather than measuring up, all along the way. *Oil City* was performed with no winking and no irony, and after each show, lemonade and cookies were served in the lobby by the smiling cast. The score features new songs by the creative team as well as such ringers as "Baby, It's Cold Outside," "Dizzy Fingers," and "Stars and Stripes Forever." One interpolation was Ernest Gold's "The Exodus Song." For this number, Monk—a vision of ex-debutante propriety—played the drums with a vengeance. She really whacked the bejesus out of that trap set, unleashing what seemed to be millennium's worth of pent-up frustration. It was uproarious. Other songs were touching and charming, always presented in character. *Oil City Symphony* was the funniest musical revue of its time, but this lifeless recording captures none of its atmosphere. I give it two stars only because the material is top-notch; the disc itself should almost get a negative rating for reducing gold to dross.   —KEN BLOOM

OKLAHOMA!
Original Broadway Cast, 1943 (Decca) ★★★★

This thrilling, nearly complete album of Rodgers and Hammerstein's *Oklahoma!* score is the one, the only, the original that started it all. The show was a groundbreaking triumph in its day, and Decca pulled out all the stops to preserve its musical component; this was the first time a full score was recorded commercially by the entire original cast with the original orchestrations as heard in the theater. The album includes the show's overture and finale as well as some dance music, all delivered with enormous spirit and enthusiasm. In particular, the joyous performances of Alfred Drake as Curly and Celeste Holm as Ado Annie show us why these two stars launched major careers with this show. That said, there is an antique quality to aspects of the recording that may be jarring: The performers' enunciation is exaggerated as if for stage delivery, rather than being modified for the studio sessions, and the limitations of the era's technology also make the orchestrations sound a bit squeaky. Still, this is not only the first recording of a great American musical but also, for all intents and purposes, the *original* original cast album. As such, it's a must for any serious collector.

Original London Cast, 1947 (HMV/various CD labels) ★

The original London production of *Oklahoma!* was recorded with the songs laid down as medleys on 78-rpm platters—four medleys of twelve songs. Curly is sung by Howard Keel (or, as he was billed at the time, Harold Keel), whose strong voice is immediately identifiable. Betty Jane Watson as Laurey sings very nicely until the last note of "People Will Say We're in Love," when she hits a high Q-sharp above P. The result is the screechiest soprano sound since Janet Leigh screamed bloody murder in *Psycho*.

Studio Cast, 1952 (Columbia/Sony) ★★★

Produced by Goddard Lieberson, this fine recording is conducted by Broadway maestro Lehman Engel. Hollywood singing star Nelson Eddy is Curly; his strong, beautiful voice is a natural for this romantic baritone role, but he may sound a bit too operatic and stodgy for some listeners. Kaye Ballard's Ado Annie is a classic turn, her belt voice and comic genius making for one of the best recordings of "I Cain't Say No." Virginia Haskins is a lovely Laurey; the great Portia Nelson is on hand as Aunt Eller; and Wilton Clary rounds out the cast as Will Parker. With its high-fidelity sound, this album gives us a better sense of Robert Russell Bennett's orchestrations than does the 1943 recording. While it's not the best aural document of *Oklahoma!* overall, there is much to recommend it.

Film Soundtrack, 1955 (Capitol/Angel) ★★★★★

Although the original Broadway cast album of *Oklahoma!* is a treasure, the film soundtrack of the musical is more satisfying overall. Beautifully recorded in stereo, the score is even more complete, and the performances remain unsurpassed. The singing of Gordon MacRae and Shirley Jones is magnificent; with their melodic voices and naturalistic diction, they offer perfect examples of how to deliver musical theater material. MacRae's renditions of "Oh, What a Beautiful Mornin'" and "The Surrey With the Fringe on Top" are superb; Jones' singing in "People Will Say We're in Love" and "Out of My Dreams" is breathtaking. Neither of their performances nor those of Gloria Grahame as Ado Annie, Gene Nelson as Will Parker, and the rest of the cast sound the least bit dated. The grand orchestrations are expanded from the Broadway originals and a bit Hollywoodized, but never overblown. Angel's expanded CD contains two overtures and all of the film's (and show's) wonderful dance music, including the dream ballet.

Broadway Cast, 1979 (RCA) ★★★

This is a spirited performance led by Jay Blackton, conductor of the original Broadway production of *Oklahoma!* Christine Andreas is full of warmth and pluck as Laurey; Mary Wickes is perfect as Aunt Eller; Christine Ebersole is terrific as Ado Annie; but Laurence Guittard, though a fine singer, seems miscast as Curly. In fact, Martin Vidnovic as Jud sounds so much sexier that you almost wish Laurey would leave Curly and run off with him!

London Cast, 1998 (First Night) ★★★★

This is the cast album of Trevor Nunn's acclaimed National Theatre production of *Oklahoma!* As seen onstage, Nunn's reinterpretation of a great American musical brought forth elements of the Lynn Riggs play *Green Grow the Lilacs,* upon which *Oklahoma!* is based. As heard on the recording, Hugh Jackman may not sing with the beauty of Gordon MacRae, but he brings plenty of gusto and sex appeal to the role of Curly. Josefina Gabrielle was billed as the first woman ever to act, sing, and dance the part of Laurey, rather than yielding to a counterpart in the dream ballet. Of those three talents, her singing is the least impressive, but her delivery of Laurey's songs doesn't really compromise the cast album. Maureen Lipman as Aunt Eller and Shuler Hensley as Jud Fry are outstanding, the latter giving an emotionally complex, spine-tingling performance of "Lonely Room" that surpasses all other versions. The original orchestrations were revamped by William David Brohn to great effect, and new dance music was created by David Krane for the show's stunning new choreography by Susan Stroman.　　—GERARD ALESSANDRINI

OLIVER!

Original London Cast, 1960 (Decca) ★★★★

This musical adaptation of Charles Dickens' *Oliver Twist* was revolutionary in its day, beginning as a modest, fringe-type production in London and becoming an international smash hit. The show boasted a melodic score by composer-lyricist-librettist Lionel Bart; innovative sets by Sean Kenny; fluid direction by Peter Coe; and orchestrations and arrangements that were simple, clear, and direct. On this cast recording, the now-legendary performance of Ron Moody as Fagin is vibrant and unforgettable. Georgia Brown makes the part of Nancy her own; her husky voice throbs with emotion and she is entirely believable as a woman of the Victorian underworld. Her rendition of "As Long as He Needs Me" is definitive. Keith Hamshere as Oliver and Martin Horsey as the Artful Dodger are also excellent. Although the recording lacks the abandon of a real theatrical performance, this is still the best available *Oliver!* album.

London Studio Cast, 1962 (Capitol/Angel) ★★

On this recording, Stanley Holloway—famous for his portrayal of Alfred Dolittle in the original stage and film versions of *My Fair Lady*—is well cast as Fagin. As Nancy, Alma Cogan, a popular cabaret singer of the 1960s, does a fine job belting out "Oom-Pah-Pah," "It's a Fine Life," and a pop-style rendition of "As Long as He Needs Me"—and Tony Tanner makes a fine Artful Dodger. Still, this is less a cast album than a "Songs from *Oliver!*" disc.

Original Broadway Cast, 1963 (RCA) ★★★

Although Clive Revill gives a fine performance as Fagin, his characterization isn't as broad and eccentric as that of Ron Moody of the original London cast. But this Broadway album does have Georgia Brown recreating her landmark role as powerfully as ever. Bruce Prochnik sings well as Oliver, Michael Goodman is a fine Artful Dodger, and Willoughby Goddard is well cast as Mr. Bumble. With musical director Donald Pippin breathing new life into the score, the tempi are brighter than on the London album, although the earlier effort is fresher on the whole and more authentic in atmosphere. However, RCA's "Living Stereo" sound is superior. An interesting note is that this recording was made in Los Angeles, where the show's pre-Broadway tour began; by the time the production reached New York, Michael Goodman had been replaced as the Artful Dodger by David Jones, who went on to become famous as one of The Monkees.

Film Soundtrack, 1968 (Colgems/RCA) ★★★★

Earning six Academy Awards, including Best Picture, the film version of *Oliver!* was masterfully directed by Sir Carol Reed, with the grand score given a bigger-than-big, movie-musical treatment. Under the direction of maestro Johnny Green, the orchestrations and choral arrangements heard on the soundtrack recording are layered with counterpoint, but the overall effect is appropriate to the opulence and squalor of the story's various settings. Lionel Bart's songs stand up beautifully to the elaborate scoring, and the performances are as vivid as the orchestrations. At the forefront is Ron Moody, who outdoes his own fine performance as Fagin on the original London cast album. Equally excellent is Jack Wild as the Artful Dodger; with his charming Cockney accent, he offers the best account of the role on record. As Nancy, Shani Wallis sings magnificently; as Mr. Bumble, Harry Secombe displays a superb tenor that elevates the title song and "Boy for Sale" to classic level. The one off-note is Kathe Greene, who sounds a bit phony and overly sweet in her dubbing for Mark Lester as Oliver Twist.

London Cast, 1994 (Angel) ★★★★

An expanded production of *Oliver!* that combined the original version with elements of the film yielded this most complete aural document of the score. Many of the songs have additional verses not found on other recordings, and a lot of dialogue is included. But the new orchestrations by William David Brohn are heavy on the synthesizer, conjuring the 1990s rather than London of a century earlier. On the plus side, there is excellent musical direction by Martin Koch, and the cast is strong. Jonathan Pryce is a marvelous Fagin, Sally Dexter does a fine job as Nancy, and the Artful Dodger is well portrayed by Adam Searles. As Oliver, Gregory Bradley displays a lovely voice; indeed, his is the best vocal performance of the role on CD. Sam Mendes directed this production and Mathew Bourne did the musical staging. Although you can't enjoy their imaginative work on the CD, the packaging is loaded with pictures and extensive notes. Even better, the booklet contains all of the show's lyrics.   — GERARD ALESSANDRINI

OLYMPUS ON MY MIND
Original Off-Broadway Cast, 1987 (That's Entertainment/JAY) ★★

During the opening number of this musical based on *Amphitryon,* as the three-man chorus sings "We are the chorus / Please don't ignore us," a woman suddenly joins them and adds, "My name's Delores." Played by Joyce DeWitt, she is the wife of the show's principal backer, Murray the Furrier, and he has promised her a role. Sweet but untalented, this ex-showgirl pops up throughout the show to help with numbers or exposition, always while modeling Murray's furs. The joke is funny for a while, less so as *Olympus on My Mind* wears on. It distracts us from the main plot: the story of Jupiter, who comes to earth to win a beautiful woman by disguising himself as her husband, Amphitryon. In this version, Jupiter isn't satisfied with bedding her; he wants her to love him. His son, Mercury, warns him that, on Earth, he will start feeling human emotions—and, sure enough, Jupiter begins to experience real pain. But as soon as we start caring about him, Delores is back with her shtick. The main plot, involving disguises and double identities, is reminiscent of *The Boys From Syracuse,* and much of it is well written and quite funny. The songs, by composer Grant Sturiale and lyricist Barry Harman, are prankish and playful; among the best of them are "The Gods on Tap," "Back So Soon," "Wonderful," "A Little Something of Yourself," and "It Was Me!" The cast is strong: Martin Vidnovic sings well as Jupiter and Amphitryon; Frank Copyk is a funny Sosia; and Jason Graae is a very spruce Mercury.   —DAVID WOLF

ON A CLEAR DAY YOU CAN SEE FOREVER
Original Broadway Cast, 1965 (RCA) ★★★★★

This is a fabulous score. Alan Jay Lerner's lyrics are not only among his wittiest but also his most poetic, while Burton Lane's music is as melodic and moving as anything ever written for the stage. Although Lerner's libretto for *On a Clear Day You Can See Forever* has been deemed problematic, the show's songs have endured. Indeed, the title song became a standard. Robert Russell Bennett's beautiful orchestrations were augmented impeccably for this recording, masterfully conducted by Theodore Saidenburg. Barbara Harris is blissfully captured here in the dual-identity leading role, Daisy in the present and Melinda in a past life that emerges under hypnosis administered by Dr. Mark Bruckner. In the latter part, John Cullum with his strong, stalwart voice never sounded better than he does on this recording; particularly enjoyable are his renditions of "Come Back to Me," "Melinda," and the title song. William Daniels and Clifford David are also outstanding in supporting roles; Daniels' deadpan delivery of "Wait Till We're Sixty Five" makes this witty number a comic gem, while David does a beautiful job with the lovely ballad "She Wasn't You." The entire recording is a thrilling theatrical experience, from the magnificent fanfare that begins the overture to the spine-tingling finale in which the chorus joyfully sings "forever and ever and *e-ver-more!*"

Film Soundtrack, 1970 (Columbia) ★★★

On a Clear Day was reconfigured as a film vehicle for Barbra Streisand, with mixed results. A good bit of the score remained intact but some appealing songs are missing, such as the funny "Wait Till We're Sixty Five" and the catchy "On the S.S. Bernard Cohn." Also, Alan Jay Lerner's original lyrics for "She Wasn't You" have been replaced; Burton Lane's melody remains, but Lerner revamped the lyrics so that Streisand could sing the song as "He Isn't You," and the new version pales by comparison. While Streisand's great voice and solid acting talent are well suited to the leading role(s), the film soundtrack is marred by the limited acting ability of costar Yves Montand as the doctor, here named Marc Chabot. His singing on the album is not unpleasant, but his difficulties with the English language prevent him from communicating the nuances of Lerner's ingenious lyrics; "Come Back to Me" suffers greatly in this respect. More bad news: Nelson Riddle's musical arrangements are not up to snuff. So, even though Streisand's renditions of "Hurry, It's Lovely Up Here," "What Did I Have That I Don't Have?" and the title song are among the best things she's ever recorded, the soundtrack is less than terrific overall.   —GERARD ALESSANDRINI

ONCE ON THIS ISLAND
Original Broadway Cast, 1990 (RCA) ★★★★

The strongest work to date by lyricist Lynn Ahrens and composer Stephen Flaherty, *Once on This Island* is a juicy adaptation of the Rosa Guy novel *My Love, My Love.* The story, set in the

Antilles, is a simple one: A young, dark-skinned peasant girl named Ti Moune rescues a wealthy Beauxhomme (a lighter-skinned French descendant) named Daniel from a car wreck and offers her life to the gods in exchange for his. The tale is told with honesty, simplicity, and a wonderful musicality. From the opening number, in which the peasant storytellers explain their way of prayer ("We Dance"), to the jubilant finale ("Why We Tell the Story"), the songs are dramatically and emotionally acute. There's only one exception: "The Human Heart" is bland and completely extraneous to the score. The rest of the songs are transporting and gorgeous, and Michael Starobin's orchestrations are generally brilliant. Heading the strong cast are the shimmering LaChanze as Ti Moune; the romantic Jerry Dixon as Daniel; the enveloping Kecia Lewis-Evans as Asaka, Mother of the Earth; the menacing Eric Riley as Papa Ge, Demon of Death; and the charming Afi McClendon as Little Ti Moune.

Original London Cast, 1994 (JAY) ★★★

This CD contains much the same material as the original Broadway album but lacks some of the freshness and magic that makes its predecessor so special. Lorna Brown's Ti Moune is more serious and comes across as older and less energetic than LaChanze's portrayal. Except for Monique Mason, who doesn't sound up to the challenge of Little Ti Moune, the other performers are about on a par with their Broadway counterparts. One misfire on the recording is a "special mix" of "The Human Heart," sung by P. P. Arnold in a "pop" arrangement. Everything else here is perfectly enjoyable if never quite as exceptional as the Broadway recording.   —MATTHEW MURRAY

ONCE UPON A MATTRESS
Original Broadway Cast, 1959 (Kapp/MCA) ★★★★★

The fairy tale in question is "The Princess and the Pea," given a satirical fleshing-out. But *Once Upon a Mattress* was really a Cinderella show. Its composer was theatrical royalty: Mary Rodgers, daughter of Richard. Its lyricist, Marshall Barer, was unknown, and so was most of the cast. A big-league production team, led by director George Abbott, launched the show downtown and it soon moved up to Broadway. The score is charming and funny by turns, but the show's success hinged largely on its star. As Winnifred the Woebegone, Carol Burnett established herself as a strong singer and a peerless comic, and the proof is here on the recording. Burnett is fabulous as she caterwauls over "The Swamps of Home" or torches about the lucky princesses who end up living "Happily Ever After." The supporting cast is ideal: Joe Bova is an appealing Prince Dauntless; Jane White is the imperious Queen Aggravain; and Matt Mattox as the Jester does a fine job with one of the score's best numbers, "Very Soft Shoes." Apart from the necessary loss of Jack Gilford's priceless mime performance as the mute king, there's nothing at all amiss in this recording. Brava Burnett!

Original London Cast, 1960 (HMV/no CD) ★★★

Although Carol Burnett did not star in the West End production of *Once Upon a Mattress,* another funny American lady did. Jane Connell, who would later achieve musical theater immortality as Agnes Gooch in *Mame,* made a valiant stab at swimming Winnifred's moat. Her performance on this cast album differs from Burnett's: Connell shrieks where Burnett would bellow, and instead of inhabiting the role as her predecessor did, Connell comes through in her own way as a fine musical comedienne. Otherwise, the London cast is quite equally matched with the American, and Patricia Lambert's veddy-British diction adds an extra layer of mock-operetta charm to the role of Lady Larkin. The recording as a whole is slightly more decorous than the rather boisterously vaudevillian American original, but what matters most is that *Once Upon a Mattress* is a good enough show to work well either way.

Broadway Cast, 1997 (RCA) ★

After nearly four decades and two televised productions, *Mattress* made it back to Broadway, albeit with drab results. The charm was still evident, but more conspicuous was the by-the-numbers aura that permeates the cast recording. Alas, Sarah Jessica Parker was not an apt choice for the heroine. Although her musical theater experience goes back to *Annie* and her Winnifred was Tony-nominated, Parker just doesn't cut it. Setting aside the untouchable Burnett template, Parker can only manage to serve up makeshift vocalism and indifferent comic timing. The remainder of the cast, the chorus, and the orchestra perform in acceptable "Broadway generic" fashion, although Lawrence Clayton's vocal tone is very thin in "Many Moons Ago." The main virtue of this recording is that it's complete, even unto the Nightingale of Samarkand. Otherwise, stick with Burnett and company. (One final gripe: Whose crummy idea was it to shoehorn a disco break into "The Spanish Panic"?) —RICHARD BARRIOS

110 IN THE SHADE
Original Broadway Cast, 1963 (RCA) ★★★

A cultist's musical, *110 in the Shade* is the Harvey Schmidt-Tom Jones adaptation of N. Richard Nash's *The Rainmaker*. As heard on this recording, the songs are replete with simple, folksy melodies and lyrics that evoke the story's wide-open, Southwest setting. The score is enhanced by superb Hershy Kay orchestrations, but the conventionality of songs like "Love, Don't Turn Away" and "Is It Really Me?" prevents this score from being truly great. The album also reveals the cast to be underpowered: A certain coldness comes through in Inga Swenson's portrayal of Lizzie Curry; and her vis-à-vis, Robert Horton, isn't up to the considerable vocal demands of the rainmaking Starbuck. But Stephen Douglass, completing the triangle as File, is engaging; and teenager Lesley Ann Warren is delightful in her one song, squealing with high-school-girl naughtiness. The CD restores the previously unreleased overture, but it's blaring and sloppily played. The LP opened more appropriately with the scene-setting "Gonna Be Another Hot Day"—so here's one case where a bonus track is a liability.

Studio Cast, 1997 (JAY, 2CDs) ★★★

Sumptuously produced, this double-CD set may be *too* inclusive. With John Owen Edwards conducting England's National Symphony Orchestra, every note of the score that was missing from the original Broadway album of *110 in the Shade* is restored here, including a pointless soft-shoe interval in the already dull "Everything Beautiful Happens at Night." An appendix offers a couple of songs that were cut from the show and some other slightly rethought ones. But what this recording can rightfully boast over the original is a suitable Starbuck: Ron Raines is vocally velvety and a hell of an actor, capturing both this con man's bluster and the self-doubting poet underneath. In the role of Lizzie, Karen Ziemba is persuasive as a plain woman terrified of becoming a spinster, but Ziemba is insecure in her upper register—most noticeably when she sings the Act I finale "Old Maid," which should be a tour de force. Richard Muenz is fine as File, and the supporting cast is first-rate, particularly Kristin Chenoweth in the Lesley Ann Warren role. —MARC MILLER

ONE MO' TIME

Original Off-Broadway Cast, 1980 (Warner Bros./no CD) ★★★

A couple of decades ago, musical comedy turned a nostalgic and admiring eye on the black the-ater of earlier years—the imperishable music, the raucous humor, the artists who triumphed in spite of dire conditions and Jim Crow laws. A number of revue-type shows celebrated black vaudevillians and their music; *One Mo' Time* was set backstage at the fabled Lyric Theatre in New Orleans, circa 1926. The brainchild of writer-choreographer-costar Vernel Bagneris, the show had a tiny cast, a rudimentary plot, and a lot of exuberant music. It enjoyed a long run at New York's Village Gate, where this live recording was made. The singers exude scrappy energy and an obvious love of the material, which includes "Miss Jenny's Ball," "Kiss Me Sweet," and "Muddy Water." Much of the music derives from Bessie Smith's repertoire, including songs she wrote, so it makes sense to have a Smith-like character in the show. Unfortunately, Sylvia "Kuumba" Williams can't touch the genuine article, and both she and Bagneris are out-sung by fellow cast members Topsy Chapman and Thais Clark. Veteran trumpeter-singer Jabbo Smith makes a guest appearance, performing more in the style of '50s rhythm-and-blues than '20s vaudeville. What matters most, however, is the vitality and sincerity of all the performers as they pay homage to their predecessors.   —RICHARD BARRIOS

ONE NITE STAND

Original Broadway Cast, 1980 (Original Cast Records) ★★★

From overture to finale, *One Night Stand* is as dynamic a score as Jule Styne ever wrote. But Herb Gardner proved to be inept as a librettist-lyricist in this, his one run-in with musical theater. The plot has possibilities—a famous performer decides to give one last concert, then kill him-self onstage—but the lighthearted music is mismatched to it, and Gardner's lyrics would be wrong in any situation. Styne crafted top-notch melodies for "Don't Kick My Dreams Around," "A Little Travelin' Music, Please," "There Was a Time," and "Too Old to Be so Young." There's also a quartet of ingratiating leads—Charles Kimbrough, Catherine Cox, Jack Weston, and William Morrison—and a great set of orchestrations by Philip J. Lang. This was the last of Styne's Broadway scores to yield a cast album (*Treasure Island* and *The Red Shoes* followed, but both went unrecorded), so that's reason enough to buy the CD.   —SETH CHRISTENFELD

ONE TOUCH OF VENUS

Original Broadway Cast, 1943 (Decca) ★★★

Be aware that this incomplete recording of composer Kurt Weill's *One Touch of Venus* paints a very deceptive picture of the score. Of the show's seventeen songs, only ten are here, sung by only two members of the original cast: Mary Martin and Kenny Baker. While all of Martin's material is included, the songs of Paula Laurence and John Boles are not. (Actually, Baker inher-its one of Boles' songs, "Westwind.") Since the show is, for the most part, a low comedy, the fact that seven of the comic songs are missing from the album means that this *Venus* misses by more than a touch. But Martin is charming, particularly in the score's two best songs, "I'm a Stranger Here Myself" and "That's Him," and Baker's tenor will appeal to many listeners. The show's lyrics, by the talented light-versifier Ogden Nash, are witty and filled with amusing wordplay even if not well integrated with the book by Nash and S. J. Perelman. The music for the two Agnes De Mille ballets, "Forty Minutes for Lunch" and the climactic "Venus in Ozone Heights," is impressive; even edited as they are here, these pieces are quite stunning. Six songs from Martin's next show, *Lute Song,* are heard as bonus tracks.   —DAVID WOLF

ON THE TOWN
Original Broadway Cast Members, 1944 (Decca/MCA) ★★

Record companies treated Broadway musicals pretty poorly until the concept of the original cast album was firmly entrenched, so this CD is mainly of interest for its historical value. Rather than issuing an integral recording of the Leonard Bernstein-Betty Comden-Adolph Green musical *On the Town,* which was certainly a big hit, Decca produced 78rpms of Nancy Walker doing her solo "I Can Cook, Too" and performing the quartet "Ya Got Me" as another solo; Comden and Green in their duet "Carried Away"; the Lyn Murray Chorus in the show's opening sequence (including "I Feel Like I'm Not Out of Bed Yet" and "New York, New York" but with no dialogue); and Mary Martin crooning the two ballads that were sung in the show by John Battles as Gabey, "Lucky to Be Me" and "Lonely Town." All of these recordings plus an extended version of the opening sequence are included on the 1991 MCA CD, along with selections from *Fancy Free* (the Jerome Robbins ballet that inspired *On the Town*) as performed by the Ballet Theatre Orchestra under the direction of composer Bernstein.

Studio Recording With Original Cast Members, 1960 (Columbia/Sony) ★★★★★

In 1960, legendary cast-album producer Goddard Lieberson reassembled most of the original *On the Town* principals and brought them into a studio to record virtually the entire score with Leonard Bernstein conducting. Nancy Walker, Cris Alexander, Betty Comden, and Adolph Green were all present, and the excellent John Reardon joined them as Gabey, the third sailor. Two songs missing from the first LP release of this album, the female chorus number "Do Do Re Do" and Pitkin's "I Understand," sung by George Gaynes, were restored and are heard on the Sony CD. The performances are so fresh that the recording sounds as if it were made right after the show opened on Broadway; Bernstein's conducting is sensational in all of the ballet music and the wonderful songs, too. Walker and Alexander are perfect in "Come Up to My Place," as are Comden and Green in "Carried Away," and Reardon lends his warm, clear baritone to "Lonely Town" and "Lucky to Be Me." The choral work is fine, and we are even treated to Bernstein himself doing some singing as Rajah Bimmy in "The Real Coney Island" Ballet. An indispensable recording.

Original London Cast, 1963 (CBS/no CD) ★★

The first London production of *On the Town* was based on a critically acclaimed but unsuccessful Off-Broadway production; the principals of that staging were imported for the occasion, but the London edition also failed to become a hit. An LP was released and quickly became a collectors' item. The three male leads are much better than the rest of the cast: Don McKay is an excellent Gabey, Elliott Gould is a funny, underplayed Chip, and Terry Kiser is quite good as Ozzie. Less successful are Carol Arthur as Hildy and Gillian Lewis as Claire. The LP includes the show's rarely recorded overture, but almost all of the ballet music is abridged. Though well conducted by Lawrence Leonard, the album is a curiosity, not a necessity.

London Concert Cast, 1992 (DG) ★★★★

On the Town in concert, with an all-star cast from the worlds of Broadway and opera plus Michael Tilson Thomas conducting the London Symphony Orchestra, sounds like a great idea—and, indeed, it was. The orchestra is magnificent and the live-performance energy of the cast is palpable. Tyne Daly is tops as the tough Hildy, especially in "I Can Cook, Too." As Claire and Chip, Frederica von Stade and Kurt Ollman prove themselves to be opera singers who can successfully "cross over" to Broadway. When respectively paired with them in the comic duets "Carried Away" and "Come Up to My Place," musical theater veterans David Garrison (who plays Ozzie) and Daly blend with ease; and when these four team up for the rueful "Some Other Time," any barriers between Broadway and classical music are broken. Thomas Hampson uses his creamy baritone well in Gabey's songs; Evelyn Lear is very fine as Mme. Dilly; and basso Samuel Ramey's "I Understand" is impressive. Included are two previously cut songs: "Gabey's Comin'" ("Pickup Song") introduces tunes subsequently used as leitmotifs in the score, and its importance as a missing link is explained in the first-rate CD booklet notes written by Ethan Mordden. Cleo Laine sings the second restored song, "Ain't Got No Tears Left," and Adolph Green makes a cameo appearance as Rajah Bimmy in "The Real Coney Island" ballet. As an appendix, we get yet another cut song, "The Intermission's Great."

Studio Cast, 1996 (JAY, 2CDs) ★★★

This "First Complete Recording" of *On the Town* boasts a commitment to character truth that deeply engages the listener; the five singing principals are exactly right from a vocal standpoint and they illuminate the material. As Gabey, Ethan Freeman is vulnerable in "Lonely Town" (the previously unrecorded chorale section of the song after the "Pas de Deux" is haunting), and his "Lucky to Be Me" is exuberant. Gregg Edelman and Kim Criswell deliver the goods in "Come Up to My Place," and Criswell raises the roof with "I Can Cook, Too," complete with encore. Tim Flavin and Judy Kaye, in the roles that Betty Comden and Adolph Green wrote for themselves to play in 1944, are solid in "Carried Away." The two couples raise their voices joyously when cheering up Gabey in "Ya Got Me" and heartbreakingly when they prepare to part in the melancholic "Some Other Time." The ballet music is complete and excitingly conducted by John Owen Edwards—as are the overture, the entr'acte, the exit music, an amusing nightclub sequence, and even the deleted "Gabey's Comin'."
—JEFFREY DUNN

ON THE TWENTIETH CENTURY
Original Broadway Cast, 1978 (Columbia/Sony) ★★★★

Based on the stage farce *Twentieth Century*, best known as a Hollywood film starring John Barrymore and Carole Lombard, this 1930s spoof might have been written as a pastiche of the era's musicals. Instead, composer Cy Coleman and librettists-lyricists Betty Comden and Adolph Green had the inspired idea of treating it as an operetta. That extravagant musical style works brilliantly for this story of dueling egos and theatrical temperaments. John Cullum sings heroically and hilariously as Oscar Jaffe, a bankrupt Broadway producer who is desperate to sign his ex-lover, Hollywood star Lily Garland (née Mildred Plotka), to appear in a bloated stage epic about Mary Magdelene. The action takes place on a sixteen-hour train ride between Chicago and New York. Along for the ride are Kevin Kline, making an uproarious Broadway debut as Hollywood lounge lizard Bruce Granit, and Imogene Coca as the wealthy religious nut Letitia Primose, who offers to finance Oscar's show with a rubber check. The show is fast, furious, and over the top, its hilarity arising from the tension between Coleman's rich music and Comden and Green's skeptical lyrics. Madeline Kahn—who left the show soon after opening, thus giving understudy Judy Kaye the break of a lifetime—shines in two riotous numbers: "Veronique" recalls Lily's stage debut as a virtuous mademoiselle who says no to Bismarck and thereby launches the Franco-Prussian War, while in "Babbette" Lily alternately imagines herself in the role of the Magdalene and as the star of a play about a Mayfair love triangle. Cullum hams it up gloriously in "I Rise Again" and "The Legacy." Coca's big solo, "Repent," is riotous. Musical comedy is rarely this witty; the album is a civilized pleasure. —DAVID BARBOUR

ONWARD VICTORIA

Original Broadway Cast, 1981 (Original Cast Records) ★

Although the subject was ripe and the characters were fascinating, *Onward Victoria* was a one-performance disaster that nonetheless yielded a cast album. The story, by librettists-lyricists Charlotte Anker and Irene Rosenberg, centers on the nineteenth-century feminist Victoria Woodhull and her adventures in New York with Elizabeth Cady Stanton, Henry Ward Beecher, and other notables. Its stirring themes include religious hypocrisy and women's rights, but the characters tend to sing about these issues in shallow polemics ("Revolution's in the air like an impending storm"), and Keith Herrmann's music, while generally constructed as a traditional musical theater score, is styled mostly as soft rock. Jill Eikenberry is a thin-voiced Victoria, Michael Zaslow is treble-y as Beecher, but Lenny Wolpe has one good moment in "Unescorted Women." By the time Victoria is defending the good reverend on the witness stand with the striptease-like "A Valentine for Beecher," in which she sings about how "well-endowed" he is, credibility and good taste are out the window. —MARC MILLER

ON YOUR TOES

Studio Cast, 1952 (Columbia/Sony) ★★★

One of Lehman Engel's sturdier studio-cast efforts, this rendering of the 1936 hit by Richard Rodgers and Lorenz Hart tries harder than most in the series to sound like a cast album of a stage production. The orchestrations hew closely to Hans Spialek's originals; Engel even throws in a convincing entr'acte, and his conducting brings out all the urban excitement of the "Slaughter on Tenth Avenue" ballet. Jack Cassidy's tenor brings sensuousness to "There's a Small Hotel" and "It's Got to Be Love." Portia Nelson is equally effective with "Glad to Be Unhappy." Laurel Shelby, a wonderfully dry comedienne, chews her consonants stylishly in "The Heart Is Quicker Than the Eye" and "Too Good for the Average Man." The song order is quite inaccurate, some numbers are assigned to the wrong characters, and the album is capped by one of Engel's annoying greatest-hits finales. Still, it has plenty of theatrical personality—and, of course, the score is evergreen.

Broadway Cast, 1954 (Capitol/Angel) ★★

This revival of *On Your Toes* starred the 1936 production's original *premiere danseuse,* Vera Zorina. But she's not on the cast album, nor is this version at all faithful to the original. Don Walker's arrangements, adept enough in their brassy way, don't feel right for this comparatively gentle and witty score. Light-on-his-feet leading man Bobby Van is also light of voice, and his love interest, Kay Coulter, is a nonentity even in such can't-miss material as "There's a Small Hotel" and "Glad to Be Unhappy." Joshua Shelley, a reliable Broadway pro, is almost unintelligible in "Too Good for the Average Man." But this Capitol recording, long out of print and briefly reissued on CD (with too much treble), does have its ace in the hole: Elaine Stritch, serving up an unforgettable "You Took Advantage of Me." It's a rare instance of a Rodgers and Hart interpolation actually helping one of their scores.

Broadway Cast, 1983 (Polydor/JAY) ★★★★

George Abbott, at age ninety-six, returned to Broadway with this impeccably produced revival and was rewarded with a long run and critical adoration. Hans Spialek, almost as old as Abbott, was on hand to restore his orchestrations; they're as imaginative and distinctive in 1983 as in 1936, and John Mauceri conducts them like the authority he is. Ballerina Natalia Makarova danced gracefully in this show and also proved herself to be a knockout comedian, but you won't find her on the cast album. However, you will find Christine Andreas, offering a definitive "Glad to Be Unhappy." She overpowers her leading man, Lara Teeter, a brilliant dancer but an uncertain singer. Nor does Dina Merrill, thin of voice and not naturally very funny, quite measure up in "The Heart Is Quicker Than the Eye" or "Too Good for the Average Man," but, luckily for her, she's wonderfully partnered in "Average Man" by George S. Irving. Overall, this digital stereo recording is a fine preservation of a joyful production. The CD includes an extended "Slaughter on Tenth Avenue," the "Princess Zenobia" ballet, and a sensitive "Quiet Night" reprise by Irving.

— MARC MILLER

OPAL

Studio Cast, 1996 (Original Cast Records) ★★★

A Richard Rodgers Award-winner and a minor Off-Broadway hit, Robert Lindsey Nassif's chamber musical was adapted from the diaries of a French orphan who lived in an Oregon lumber camp circa 1904. It's a grim tale with a shipwreck, a forest fire, a nasty stepmother with a sad secret, a tragic blind girl, and a Bible-spouting old mystic lady, among other bizarre characters. Nassif's lyrics seldom rise above the functional and his appealing melodies are undercut by an annoying, synth-heavy orchestration. But what makes the score distinctive is its exploration of the macabre, as little Opal puzzles out the mysteries of death in song. Eliza Clark is refreshingly unaffected as Opal, and she has some formidable musical theater talent behind her: Marni Nixon as the mystic, Rachel York as the blind girl, and Emily Skinner in a small part. Nassif himself does very well as a lovesick lumberjack in the ballad "Sears and Roebuck Wedding Band." There are a few dreary numbers, especially those in which the Sunday sermonizing gets heavy. Still, this score has personality—and the 1990s brought forth few ensemble numbers as spirited and life affirming as "Everybody's Looking for Love."

— MARC MILLER

OUT OF THIS WORLD

Original Broadway Cast, 1950 (Columbia) ★★★★

For *Out of This World,* a modern-day retelling of the Amphitryon legend, Cole Porter produced a gorgeous score; unfortunately, it was tied to an unwieldy book that worked too hard to substitute dirty jokes for real wit. Despite a lush production, direction by Agnes De Mille, and the Broadway return of the beloved musical comedienne Charlotte Greenwood, the show managed only a four-month run. The songs are so great and the premise so enticing that there have been a few subsequent attempts to shore up that messy script. Still, the strength of this show lies solely in its songs. As Juno, Greenwood is wonderful; while the album can't deliver her high kicks, it does preserve her ringingly funny way with a lyric. William Redfield is competent as Mercury, zipping with ease through the risqué "list" song "They Couldn't Compare to You," but the rest of the casting is uneven. George Jongeyans (later Gaynes) is a wobbly Jupiter; Priscilla Gillette's voice has sufficient firmness for "Use Your Imagination," but the vocal inadequacies of her vis-à-vis in the show, William Eythe, led to the deletion of the score's best song: "From This Moment On." In short, this was one unlucky show, but Porter at his near-best is more than ample compensation for the cast album's disappointments.

Encores! Concert Cast, 1995 (DRG) ★★★★

Out of This World was obvious fodder for a big-league concert performance that could spotlight the songs and stars and elide the worst parts of the script. So it was that the New York City Center Encores! series tackled Cole Porter's problematic Greco-Roman extravaganza in 1995. The resulting recording doesn't always compare favorably with the original Broadway album, but some aspects of it are clearly better and, overall, it's sheer bliss. Happily, the star at its center is up to her assignment: Andrea Martin is just terrific, especially in her rendition of "I Sleep Easier Now." For the most part, Ken Page is strong if a dash overbearing as Jupiter; the character should be loud but there's always room for shading, isn't there? Marin Mazzie and La Chanze are outstanding, both singing with beauty and spirit. "From This Moment On" is back, and Mazzie and Gregg Edelman do a very good job with it. Peter Scolari is fine as Mercury, Ernie Sabella is a scrappily funny gangster, and Rob Fisher's Coffee Club Orchestra plays with its customary class.   —RICHARD BARRIOS

OVER HERE!

Original Broadway Cast, 1974 (Columbia /Sony) ★★★

Designed to do for the 1940s what *Grease* did for the 1950s, *Over Here!* is a supremely silly tale of romance and espionage on a cross-country train loaded with volunteers, war workers, and Nazi sympathizers. It was a vehicle for the two remaining Andrews Sisters, Patty and Maxene. The score, by Richard M. and Robert B. Sherman, is a pastiche of the period's hit parade; you'll hear echoes if not actual excerpts of "Take the A Train," "The Beer Barrel Polka," and "Boogie Woogie Bugle Boy," among other songs. It's all good fun thanks to the Andrewses, a very strong supporting cast, and electrifying orchestrations by Michael Gibson and Jim Tyler that create an irresistible, big-band frenzy. The opening ballad, "Since You're Not Around," strikes the right note of agreeable nostalgia; then April Shawhan and John Driver score with "My Dream for Tomorrow." The surprisingly tough-minded "Don't Shoot the Hooey to Me, Louie," delivered by Samuel E. Wright, touches on the period's racism. Janie Sell amusingly spoofs Marlene Dietrich in "Wait for Me, Marlena," and the young John Travolta is smooth as silk in "Dream Drummin'." The Andrews gals are ebullient in such numbers as "The Big Beat," "We Got It!" and the title tune. Most of their solos are also effective, but you'll weep for Patty when she is forced to deliver the sex-hygiene number "The Good-Time Girl," in which she urges soldiers to avoid "The VD Polka" ("The enemy can sock us / By spreading gonococcus"). Note that the incredible supporting cast of *Over Here!* included Ann Reinking, Treat Williams, and Marilu Henner, none of whom turn up on this recording in any recognizable way.   —DAVID BARBOUR

P

PACIFIC 1860
Original London Cast, 1946 (Decca/Encore Box Office) ★★★

Noël Coward's overstuffed postwar operetta plunked a visiting diva among some missionaries on the island of Samolo. It failed to ignite the box office, even with Mary Martin in her London debut. But the attractive score contains Sir Noël's singular lyrics and some original touches. It opens with two trenchantly satirical songs, "His Excellency Regrets" and "Uncle Harry." But then there's the unwittingly hilarious ensemble song "Fumfumbolo," when Brit missionaries get down with the natives. The cast album covers nearly the entire score. Martin is at her vocal peak, hitting fine coloratura notes, donning a credible British accent, and outclassing her leading man, Graham Payn. Bonus cuts present Martin and costar Wilbur Evans in their London run of *South Pacific.* The only drawback to the CD is the sound quality. The notes claim that the original recordings were "digitally edited and remastered," but large swatches of the lyrics remain unintelligible.
— MARC MILLER

PACIFIC OVERTURES
Original Broadway Cast, 1976 (RCA) ★★★★★

Only Harold Prince and Stephen Sondheim could find musical possibilities in the opening up of Japan to the West in 1853. Only Sondheim could make such a brilliant score out of such material, and only Prince would have the nerve to produce the show on Broadway. *Pacific Overtures* is based on a play by John Weidman about East-West diplomacy (Hugh Wheeler provided additional book material). Add a production utilizing Japanese theater techniques and (until the finale) an all-male, all-Asian cast and you have a perfect recipe for box office poison. Despite its failure to last beyond a few months, the show has a score that is unique even in Sondheim's oeuvre, bending clever and pointed lyrics to austerely beautiful melodies informed by Japanese harmonies. Some numbers, such as "There Is No Other Way" (a tense exchange between a fearful wife and her husband) and "Poems" (in which two men trade haikus) are tersely eloquent, aided by Jonathan Tunick's fine orchestrations. But the score also contains two of Sondheim's most elaborate set pieces: "Someone in a Tree," which recounts a treaty signing from multiple points of view, demonstrates that history is in the eye of the beholder; "Please Hello," in which Japan is

---

ALL-TIME FAVORITES OF
COMPOSER-LYRICIST

Michael John LaChiusa

1. South Pacific
2. The King and I
3. A Little Night Music
4. The Threepenny Opera
5. Candide
6. 110 in the Shade
7. Merrily We Roll Along
8. Follies
9. Nine
10. Pal Joey

invaded by diplomats from abroad, blends pastiches of various musical genres into a scalding satire. The final number, "Next," brings the story up to the present day and is devastating in its irony. The original cast, led by Mako and Sab Shimono, performs with notable skill. Sondheim may have written more moving scores, but none surpass the glittering intelligence and excitement of his work here.

Original London Cast, 1989 (BMG/JAY) ★★

Complete to the last word, this recording of the English National Opera production of *Pacific Overtures* offers the entire show, with its lengthy dialogue included. It may be archivally important, but it's an uphill battle for the average listener; the nonmusical sequences are tedious and lacking in authenticity. The score, with its intensively rhymed lyrics, doesn't really call for the skills of opera singers. Still, the cast sings well and the disc includes material not heard on the Broadway recording, such as the Kabuki lion dance that ends Act I. This version of "Next" updates the song to the late 1980s with new spoken lines that make ironic reference to Pearl Harbor. There is also some startlingly effective percussion work from the orchestra.
— DAVID BARBOUR

PAINT YOUR WAGON
Original Broadway Cast, 1951 (RCA) ★★★★

A show with a magnificent score but an inferior book, Alan Jay Lerner and Frederick Loewe's *Paint Your Wagon* tells of an 1853 California gold rush, the lonely men of the mining camp, the peripatetic Ben Rumson, and his daughter's love affair with a Mexican baritone. It's a combination that calls for a heap of singing from a lusty male chorus, and they sound great right from the opening number, "I'm on My Way." (That's Kay Medford as "Cherry," with an amusing faux-French accent.) A couple of songs are missing from the album, and where's Loewe's terrific music for those Agnes De Mille ballets? Still, what's here is of a very high order. James Barton, capping a career that extended back to vaudeville, doesn't offer much voice but whispers his way arrestingly through "I Still See Elisa," "In Between," and "Wand'rin' Star." Olga San Juan is a fun, fiery soubrette with a throaty belt in "What's Goin' on Here?" and "How Can I Wait?" And if Tony Bavaar's "I Talk to the Trees" is a little boring, his singing of "Another Autumn" makes up for it. Conductor Franz Allers does Ted Royal's orchestrations proud, and there's enough dialogue included to convey the contours of the plot.

Original London Cast, 1953 (Columbia/Sepia) ★

It sounds like ideal casting: the lovable British comic Bobby Howes as Ben Rumson and his up-and-coming daughter Sally Ann Howes as Ben's daughter, Jennifer. But this cast album, taken from some old 78-rpms, shows neither performer at best advantage. The recording is in medley form—one chorus each of such songs as "All for Him" and "There's a Coach Comin' In"—and adds up to barely thirteen minutes. Sally Ann Howes is a little raw, with stilted line readings and uncertain top notes. As her love interest, Ken Cantril is off-pitch and doesn't sound remotely Mexican. The one selling point is some tasty dialogue not heard on the Broadway album. The Sepia CD also includes selections from *Love From Judy, Pal Joey,* and *Wonderful Town.*

Film Soundtrack, 1969 (MCA) Not recommended.

There are not quite three minutes of fine singing here, when Harve Presnell, as the movie-invented character "Rotten Luck Willie," sings "They Call the Wind Maria" in the pouring rain. The rest is torture. Alan Jay Lerner and André Previn wrote five new songs for the movie, each more dismal than the next. All right: "A Million Miles Away Behind the Door" is an almost-good ballad, but Anita Gordon, dubbing for Jean Seberg, phones it in. When Clint Eastwood sings (!) "I Still See Elisa" in a toneless, hoarse tenor, he sounds even less engaged than Gordon. Lee Marvin's "Wand'rin' Star" is sleep-inducing, and so is Nelson Riddle's conducting. This album is for masochists only.   —MARC MILLER

THE PAJAMA GAME

Original Broadway Cast, 1954 (Columbia/Sony) ★★★

For a primer on the state of musical comedy in the mid-1950s, look no further than here. *The Pajama Game* was based on notably "unmusical" source material: a novel called *7 1/2 Cents* that took a light look at labor-management strife in a Midwestern pajama factory. Songwriters Richard Adler and Jerry Ross created a score full of songs that were tied to the action yet stood on their own as pop tunes: "Hey, There," "Steam Heat," and "Hernando's Hideaway." The show ran for well over two years, followed by Adler and Ross' next hit, *Damn Yankees*. (Alas, further triumphs would not be possible; Jerry Ross died in 1955.) The original cast album, while acceptable, is not the best souvenir of this show. Fortunately, John Raitt is in charge as the character Sid Sorokin, and that tenorial baritone of his can attack a mediocre number like "A New Town Is a Blue Town" and glorify it. When he gets a truly good song, such as "Hey There," the bliss factor rises accordingly. Opposite him as Babe, Janis Paige belts with gusto even if she's occasionally off-pitch. Dancer Carol Haney, who made a major impression in the show with "Steam Heat" and "Hernando's Hideaway," is not terribly comfortable as a singer. Showbiz veteran Eddie Foy, Jr. has no such problems, and he and Reta Shaw sail happily through "I'll Never Be Jealous Again."

Film Soundtrack, 1957 (Columbia/Collectables) ★★★★

Hollywood treated *The Pajama Game* grandly. Most of the songs, dances, and Broadway cast were retained. As Gladys, Carol Haney comes across much better here than on the prior recording; her smoky tone in "Hernando's Hideaway" now insinuates through the number's tango rhythms with ease. As Sid, Raitt is again exemplary; "New Town" is gone but not much missed, and his singing of "Hey There" and everything else he does is wonderful. Where the movie really trumps Broadway is in its Babe: Doris Day is so ideally cast that such songs as "I'm Not at All in Love" seem to have been written for her. Another Hollywood addition is the memorably squeaky-voiced Barbara Nichols as Poopsie. Eddie Foy, Jr. and Reta Shaw are again in fine form, and the album contains a fair amount of dance music.

Studio Cast, 1996 (JAY, 2CDs) ★★

The Pajama Game has remained a favorite of stock companies and community theaters; the show even enjoyed a staging by the New York City Opera in 1989, and the leading lady of that production heads this London studio cast recording. Every scrap of music was taped and, as a result, posterity now has a complete, two-CD set of the score. The most important addition is the "Jealousy" ballet, in which Carol Haney had shone in the original production. The mixed American-British cast sings enthusiastically. The finest of the leads is the solid pro Ron Raines; Kim Criswell sounds a bit uncomfortable as Gladys; Judy Kaye works hard as Babe, sometimes ratcheting up to overblown, but on balance, she comes through. All of the other singers are OK.   —RICHARD BARRIOS

PAL JOEY
Studio Cast, 1950 (Columbia/Sony) ★★★★★

Joey, a small-time entertainer bent on opening his own nightclub, drops his girlfriend, Linda, to bed Vera, a rich dowager who's bonkers for him and backs his venture. When this sophisticated saga premiered on Broadway in 1940 as *Pal Joey,* the production did not generate a cast album. But over the next decade, the Richard Rodgers-Lorenz Hart songs grew so in popularity that by 1950, the score was ripe for a complete recording. Conductor Lehman Engel and producer Goddard Lieberson recreated a cast album featuring the original leading lady, Vivienne Segal, as Vera. In place of Gene Kelly, who had been scooped up by Hollywood following his acclaimed stage portrayal of Joey, dancer Harold Lang—fresh from his triumph in the original *Kiss Me, Kate*—was brought in. The results are spectacular. The performances on this disc are definitive and, for the most part, the original orchestrations are intact. Rodgers' beloved melodies and Hart's witty lyrics are a joy. Segal delivers Vera's solos "What Is A Man" and "Bewitched, Bothered and Bewildered" to perfection, and her two duets—"In Our Little Den of Iniquity" with Lang and "Take Him" with Beverly Fite as Linda—are just as great. Lang's rendition of "You Mustn't Kick It Around" will set you to dancing in your living room.

Broadway Cast, 1952 (Capitol/DRG) ★★★

This is partly a stage-cast album (Elaine Stritch and Helen Gallagher) and partly a studio album (Jane Froman and Dick Beavers) of the first Broadway revival of *Pal Joey,* prompted by the solid success of Lehman Engel's 1950 recording (see above). Since that album was on the Columbia label, Capitol Records had to replace Vivienne Segal and Harold Lang with two singers from its stables—so, strangely, the cast album of the 1952 revival was recorded without its stars! Froman and Beavers sing the songs well from a musical standpoint but don't quite connect with the caustic aspects of Hart's lyrics. The score has been reorchestrated and the results are pleasant enough but inferior to the originals. The recording's ace in the hole is Stritch's unsurpassed performance of "Zip," which catapulted her to stardom. Gallagher's tracks are also brilliant and brassy. (Note that the CD concludes with tracks of Jane Froman performing selections from *With a Song in My Heart;* it's a nice match.)

Film Soundtrack, 1957 (Capitol) ★★★

Here's a terrific Frank Sinatra album that has little to do with *Pal Joey* as seen and heard on Broadway; the show's score and story are all but lost in the film version. The arrangements (by Nelson Riddle and George Dunning) are swinging and cool, making for some fine pop recordings of Richard Rodgers' music, but Lorenz Hart's brilliant work is not served as well; most of his caustic and/or risqué lyrics were changed, dropped, or "cleaned up" clumsily for the movies by an uncredited hand. Some of the background scoring is pleasant, owing more to the flexibility of Rodgers' music than to Morris Stolloff's musical direction. There is also a pleasant "Joey" theme running through the film and recording, but it doesn't seem to have been written by Rodgers (another uncredited mystery). The album's best selections are "The Lady Is a Tramp" and "I Didn't Know What Time It Was" as sung by Sinatra. Both are classics, but neither song is from the original *Pal Joey* score.

Encores! Concert Cast, 1995 (DRG) ★★

A worthy attempt at a complete stereo recording of *Pal Joey*—but even though it's well cast in theory and performed by solid pros, this disc is dull. The highlights are Patti LuPone's solo tracks. Perfectly cast as Vera, LuPone delivers Hart's wry lyrics with savvy, and her versatile, pitch-perfect voice serves Rodgers' music very well. Her standout number is "Bewitched, Bothered and Bewildered," complete and uncensored. On the other hand, Peter Gallagher is not in good vocal form here, however well cast he is as Joey in other respects. Many of his sustained notes in the ballads are slightly flat and, in the up-tempo numbers, he sounds lethargic. In the supporting role of Melba, Bebe Neuwirth doesn't come across with enough sass or brass. And while the original orchestrations are here, the orchestra sounds sloppy and sometimes lags behind the singers. In sum, this CD is worthwhile for LuPone's performance and for its inclusion of "I'm Talkin' to My Pal," a great Rodgers and Hart song that was originally slated to end the show, but was dropped during the pre-Broadway run in Boston. —GERARD ALESSANDRINI

PANAMA HATTIE
Original Broadway Cast, 1940 (Decca) ★★★
Piggybacked onto the Decca CD issue of the *Call Me Madam* studio album starring Ethel Merman are four selections from *Panama Hattie* in their first appearance since their original 78-rpm release in 1940. They certainly don't represent Cole Porter at his best in songs such as "My Mother Would Love You" and "Let's Be Buddies." Still, it's nice to have these recordings along with "I've Still Got My Health" (in a cut-down version) and "Make It Another Old Fashioned, Please." Merman performs them exactly as you'd expect, joined by eight-year-old Joan Carroll, who speaks her lines rather than singing them because of the child-labor laws of the era! Forgive me for admitting a preference for Kaye Ballard's more complete "I've Still Got My Health" on Ben Bagley's *Cole Porter Revisited* and Carmen Alvarez's more nuanced "Make It Another Old Fashioned, Please" on Bagley's *Decline and Fall* album, but I wouldn't want to be without these delightful Merman souvenirs. —DAVID WOLF

PARADE (Herman)
Original Off-Broadway Cast, 1960 (Kapp/Decca) ★★
This topical revue served as a calling card for a young composer-lyricist named Jerry Herman. It remains a pleasant diversion if you're in the right mood. By 1960, Herman's remarkable facility for songwriting was fully in place—although it's a little disorienting to hear the melody of "Show Tune," later used for "It's Today" in *Mame,* and an overture passage that was recycled for "I Want to Make the World Laugh" in *Mack & Mabel.* Dody Goodman and Charles Nelson Reilly deliver the comedy material, including the notably dirty "Save the Village," in which Goodman protests shutting down the Women's House of Detention on Sixth Avenue ("There's love in the laundry / There's love in the showers / There's love in the clinic"); "Confession to a Park Avenue Mother," in which Reilly shamefacedly admits loving a girl from the West Side; "Maria in Spats," about Maria Callas' banishment from the Metropolitan Opera ("Why can't I play the Palace / If Judy can play the Met?"); and "Jolly Theatrical Season," which spoofs flop shows. The uneven but generally enjoyable ballads are handled by a trio of big-voiced unknowns: Lester James, Fia Karin, and the astonishing Richard Tone, who has one number only: "Two a Day," a salute to vaudeville that brings down the house even on disc. —DAVID BARBOUR

PARADE (Brown)
Original Broadway Cast, 1999 (RCA) ★★★★
Jason Robert Brown earned a Tony Award for his work on *Parade,* his first Broadway score.

Although this dark musical about accused murderer Leo Frank had only a limited run at the Vivian Beaumont Theater, it yielded an excellent cast recording. Alfred Uhry's book for the musical is distancing, and so was Harold Prince's direction of the show; but Brown's score, his warmest to date, is what's preserved on the album. Note the evocative Southern flavor that's so vital to the story's Georgia setting in the beautiful opening anthem "The Old Red Hills of Home" and the heavy blues strains in the chain-gang song "Feel the Rain Fall." Also exciting: the eight-song trial sequence, which runs the gamut from sentimental to comic to soulful, and the show's dynamic second-act duets, "This Is Not Over Yet" and "All the Wasted Time." These are put across with gusto by Brent Carver and Carolee Carmello, who each have strong solo moments (his "How Can I Call This Home?" and her "Do It Alone") but truly soar when singing together. The rest of the cast is equally top-notch: Rufus Bonds, Jr., Don Chastain, John Hickok, Herndon Lackey, Jessica Molaskey, Evan Pappas, Christy Carlson Romano, John Leslie Wolfe, and the ensemble all come across beautifully. If not every song on the album is a gleaming gem, it's an impressive score overall. —MATTHEW MURRAY

PARDON MY ENGLISH
Studio Cast, 1994 (Elektra-Nonesuch) ★★★★

Surprisingly, *Pardon My English*—the 1933 musical that had the shortest run of any Gershwin show—makes for a most entertaining recording. The wonderful songs are mostly unfamiliar, but Eric Stern's conducting is lively, making the original orchestrations sound strong rather than distractingly antique. After a hellish gestation, during which the original cast members quickly departed, *Pardon My English* was totally rewritten by Herbert Fields and Morrie Ryskind; then Ryskind decamped as well. Jack MacGowan, who had scripted *Girl Crazy,* came in and did last-minute doctoring just before the New York opening. Of course, George and Ira Gershwin had to do considerable jiggering of the score to suit the revised plot and characters. Although the story makes little sense, the songs are delightful. The best of them is certainly "Isn't It a Pity?" But obscure numbers such as "Where You Go, I Go" and "I've Got to Be There" will be as enjoyable as Gershwin gems that you've been listening to and loving all your life. There are also a few "lyric fun" songs: "Freud and Jung and Adler," "He's Oversexed," and "My Cousin in Milwaukee." The first-rate cast of this recording is headed by John Cullum, William Katt, Arnetia Walker, and Michelle Nicastro. —DAVID WOLF

PASSION
Original Broadway Cast, 1994 (Angel) ★★★

One of Stephen Sondheim's most daring achievements, *Passion* is also one of his most divisive: Some people respond to the work's uncompromising nature while others find its story unbelievable from beginning to end. Nevertheless, the score is committed and, yes, passionate. The show is based on Ettore Scola's 1981 film *Passione d'Amore* (which was adapted from Igino Ugo Tarchetti's 1869 novel *Fosca*). It concerns an Italian officer named Giorgio who is obsessively pursued by and eventually falls in love with an unattractive, infirm woman named Fosca—much to the chagrin of his lover, the already-married Clara. While many of the show's situations border on the melodramatic, there's a brutal honesty about the characters' actions and feelings that gives *Passion* just the bite and heat that it needs. The recording runs under an hour and omits much dialogue and music, but what's included is lush and heavily emotional; these songs embrace or suffocate you as they define every facet of the intertwining relationships at the musical's core. Jere Shea (Giorgio), Donna Murphy (Fosca), and Marin Mazzie (Clara) give rich musical and dramatic performances, pulsing with blood and full of heart; Murphy, in particular, brings a startling intensity to her every spoken and beautifully sung word. The supporting cast members have little to do, but both Gregg Edelman as Fosca's cousin and Tom Aldredge as a military doctor are fine.

Original London Cast, 1997 (First Night) ★★★

This disc is almost twenty minutes longer than the Broadway album, containing more music as well as dialogue, but is roughly on a par with it in quality. Maria Friedman's Fosca is more strident than Donna Murphy's; her portrayal is not as well layered and, therefore, is less sympathetic overall. Michael Ball brings a raw sexual energy to the role of Giorgio. Helen Hobson, as Clara, presents a casting problem: She seems harsh, cold, and false in her declarations of love for Giorgio, which somewhat reduces the overall effect of the disc. But in supporting roles, Hugh Ross and Paul Bentley sound more dynamic than their New York counterparts. Overall, the performance sounds a bit too concertlike (it was recorded live); still, fans of *Passion* will want to have both the Broadway cast album and this one. —MATTHEW MURRAY

PERSONALS
Original London Cast, 1998 (JAY) ★★★

Before their huge success with TV's *Friends,* David Crane and Marta Kauffman wrote this amusing theater piece in collaboration with lyricist Seth Friedman and various composers. No cast album of the original 1985 Off-Broadway production was made; this is a recording of the 1998 London staging that featured David Bardsley, Martin Callaghan, Marcus Allen Cooper, Christina Fry, Ria Jones, and Summer Rognlie. As the title suggests, *Personals* is about people who run "personals" ads. The characters include a shy teenager who, believing that he's the last remaining virgin, advertises for a teacher of "extra-curricular activities" and gets nearly a hundred responses; a young woman who's open to dating for the first time since her marriage broke up; and a lonely man who's trying to concentrate on a book while hoping for the doorbell to ring. The typesetter who works on the ad page sings about the pleasures that he and his wife have found with their new partner, a bisexual dwarf: "So my wife and I have fallen for a guy who's three foot two—well, so would you!" Despite its seemingly absurd premise, the song becomes moving at the end. In the best piece, "Moving In With Linda," a man's old girlfriends pop out of his suitcases and trunks; the music and lyrics for this item are by Stephen Schwartz, who also wrote the impressive opening and closing numbers. The rest of the songs are by Michael Skloff, Alan Menken, Seth Friedman, Phillip Friedman, and William Dreskin. —DAVID WOLF

PETE 'N' KEELY
Original Off-Broadway Cast, 2001 (Fynsworth Alley) ★★★★

James Hindman's goofy, marvelous spoof/homage *Pete 'n' Keely* stars George Dvorsky and Sally Mayes as Pete Bartel and Keely Stevens, a pair of bitterly divorced songbirds who have been coerced into performing on a TV reunion special. Material that might have been overly campy in other hands is just right when delivered by the divine Mayes and Dvorsky. The song list combines standards ("This Could Be the Start of Something Big," "But Beautiful"), a patriotic classic ("The Battle Hymn of the Republic"), and new songs by director-lyricist Mark Waldrop and musical director-composer Patrick Scott Brady. "Wasn't It Fine?" is the one serious song among the new ones, and it's lovely. The comic highlights are the hilarious "Cross Country Tour" (a six-minute medley that mentions every state in the union, and

then some); "Tony 'n' Cleo" (highlights from the couple's one Broadway show, a stereotypical 1960s musical ostensibly based on Shakespeare's *Antony and Cleopatra*); and "Love" (not a funny song in itself, but interspersed with hilarious, rapid-fire rounds of jabs). Brady leads the crack eight-piece band, and production photos in the CD booklet offer a glimpse of Bob Mackie's lavish costumes.
— SETH CHRISTENFELD

PETER PAN (Bernstein)
Original Broadway Cast, 1950 (Columbia/Sony) ★

This is a little-known, unusually lackluster score by Leonard Bernstein, not the beloved *Peter Pan* musical of four years later (reviewed below). Except for students of its composer, it's hard to imagine anyone actually wanting this recording; here's a straightforward version of James Barrie's play, edited for records in the manner of a radio drama, with some songs interspersed. Only five musical selections are included here; the ballet music and "Never Land," written for two mermaids, were not recorded. A song for Captain Hook ("Walk the Plank") and one for the Pirates ("Pirate Song") are both exactly what you'd expect. The other numbers, sung by Wendy, are "Peter, Peter" (the only song with any dramatic function), "Build My House" (a soprano snooze), and "Who Am I?" Bernstein wrote both music and lyrics for the songs, which he wanted to reuse when he was asked to write the subsequent production of *Peter Pan* that would star Mary Martin. Here, Jean Arthur is rather charming as Peter; Boris Karloff is a surprisingly effective Captain Hook; and Marcia Henderson sings Wendy's songs in a soprano that you may appreciate more than I do.
— DAVID WOLF

PETER PAN (Styne, et al)
Original Broadway Cast, 1954 (RCA) ★★★★★

James M. Barrie's ever-young story of the boy who wouldn't grow up has been a favorite in print and on the stage and screen for more than a century. While Maude Adams was long the most celebrated of the stage Peter Pans, at least two generations of American kids had as their touchstone the all-singing, all-flying Mary Martin. The musical became legendary because of television, not Broadway, where it had a less than spectacular run; a West Coast tryout had been problematic, and before the show opened in New York, its Moose Charlap-Carolyn Leigh score was bolstered with some major new contributions from Jule Styne, Betty Comden, and Adolph Green. The result may not always be faithful to Barrie, but with Martin starring and director Jerome Robbins in charge, it was irresistible. The cast recording preserves most of the production's sparkle; the wonderful score includes "I Gotta Crow," "I'm Flying," and all the sing-along others. Martin is in peak form and far fresher vocally than she would be for the 1960 television taping (two earlier telecasts had been live), and a peerless Cyril Ritchard is Captain Hook. Happily, the recording has received a clear CD transfer. The album is pure magic, and not just because of Tinker Bell or fairy dust.

Studio Cast, 1997 (JAY) ★★★

Despite its difficult aeronautical demands, the Moose Charlap-Carolyn Leigh-Jule Styne-Betty Comden-Adolph Green *Peter Pan* became a stage and stock company perennial. Two Peters fared especially well: Sandy Duncan, who starred in a smash Broadway revival in 1979, and former Olympic gymnast Cathy Rigby, who toured extensively with the show in the 1990s and headlined four Broadway engagements. While the Duncan production did not yield a cast album, Rigby left both video and audio souvenirs of her performance. And guess what, kids:

She's good! Her voice has much of the sheen of Mary Martin's without some of the coyness, and her characterization is completely valid. "Mysterious Lady," which always seemed more a Martin showpiece than a fitting part of the show, is gone, but the rest of the score gets first-class treatment. Alas, Paul Schoeffler as Captain Hook is little match for his energetic adversary—let alone for his predecessor, Cyril Ritchard, whose humor and verve are nowhere to be found here. The rest of the cast is acceptable. Overall, the theatrical thrill of the 1954 recording is replaced by a more generic 1990s performance style; but, as even staunch Martin devotees might admit, Rigby soars.

—RICHARD BARRIOS

PHANTOM
Studio Cast, 1993 (RCA) ★★★★

Unfotunately, Maury Yeston (music and lyrics) and Arthur Kopit (book) began their own adaptation of the Gaston Leroux potboiler concurrently with the Andrew Lloyd Webber version, but Lord Andrew got his to the stage first; so this *Phantom,* with just as lush music and vastly superior lyrics, has never gotten any closer to Broadway than New Jersey. The whole sordid mess is recounted by Kopit in his notes for this recording, which was excellently produced by Yeston, Steve Vining, and Bill Rosenfield. Yeston's wide-ranging score roams from the Gothic breast-beating of "Paris Is a Tomb" to the lilt of "Melodie de Paris" to the foxtrot "Who Could Ever Have Dreamed Up You?" The sturdy Richard White, in the title role, doesn't really get to show his stuff till the revelatory eleven-o'clock number, "My Mother Bore Me"; but he gives that song the full treatment, going vocally and histrionically to the top, yet not over it. Glory Crampton, as Christine, sounds sweet but thin in her upper range. On the other hand, it's a pleasure to have the underemployed Meg Bussert as Carlotta, deliberately screeching her way through "As You Would Love Paree" and having some great, hammy fun with "This Place Is Mine." Jack Dabdoub and Paul Schoeffler are helpful in supporting roles, and Jonathan Tunick's orchestrations and conducting are, as usual, superb. Best of all, it's refreshing to hear a *Phantom* that is musically satisfying and not lyrically pinheaded.

—MARC MILLER

THE PHANTOM OF THE OPERA
Original London Cast, 1986 (Polydor, 2CDs) ★

Andrew Lloyd Webber's score for this through-sung musical contains many wonderful melodies; unfortunately, as has been pointed out by many sharp-eared critics, some of them are not quite original. Various tunes in *The Phantom of the Opera* owe much to the work of such composers as Claude Debussy, Giacomo Puccini, and Frederick Loewe. Of the *Phantom* songs that seem to be original, several are very pretty but stylistically inappropriate to the time period in which the show is set; for example, the lovely "Think of Me," with its dotted rhythms. For that matter, the arrangement of the title song makes it sounds like a disco number. Charles Hart's lyrics (additional lyrics by Richard Stilgoe) range from very good to very poor. The most successful sections of the score are its lighter moments, particularly the "Notes" / "Prima Donna" sequence. Given the general quality level of the material, the performance is not bad overall. Michael Crawford is quite compelling as the Phantom; his mannerisms and odd vocal timbre are well suited to a character who's supposed to be a freakish madman and, with the help of skillful audio engineering, Crawford delivers some spine-tingling high notes. His Christine, Sarah Brightman, sounds fine when singing in the middle of her range at a dynamic level no higher than mezzo forte, but her soprano thins out and become shrill when it rises in pitch and volume, and her vibrato is too heavy for the weight of her voice. Steve Barton sings well as

Raoul, especially in the beautiful "All I Ask of You." The recording gets one grudging star for its few nice moments, but don't take that as a recommendation to buy it. A final insult: In its initial release, this two-disc set wasn't tracked, so the only way you could skip to various sections of the score was to press and hold the forward or backward search buttons on your CD player. Reportedly, Lloyd Webber insisted on this, because he had conceived *Phantom* as a unified work and hoped listeners would experience it as such. (No comment!)

Original Canadian Cast, 1990 (Decca) ★

As the Phantom, Colm Wilkinson displays a strong vocal instrument, yet his mannerisms and Scottish accent are very intrusive on this recording, and the broad pseudo-British accents of several other members of the cast are laughably stilted. Rebecca Caine's voice is mediocre as heard in Christine's songs, and her pronunciation is very poor. Byron Nease's Raoul sounds fine when he's not overacting and artificially darkening his voice. For some reason, many of the lyrics as set down on this recording are revisions of the originals—but the new versions aren't superior, just different. This one-disc album of the score's "highlights" is a better option for purchase than the two-disc London album because it's shorter, it's cheaper, and the selections are tracked, which allows you to quickly access and enjoy the few songs that are well written and aren't based on the melodies of other composers. —MICHAEL PORTANTIERE

PHILEMON
Original Off-Broadway Cast, 1975 (Gallery/no CD) ★★★

Composer Harvey Schmidt has consistently written lovely, dramatic, and distinctive music. For *Philemon,* which concerns a street clown in ancient Rome who becomes ennobled enough to experience Christian martyrdom, Schmidt's songs are again striking and effective—as are the lyrics of his collaborator, Tom Jones. The opening number, "Within This Empty Space," establishes the raw theatricality and elements of ritual common to so many Schmidt-Jones shows while also introducing us to Cockian, the main character, and to the specific, vaguely primitive sound of this score. Jones' script and lyrics are more complex than usual, and all of the characters are distinctly limned musically. The cast is solid without ever being flashy. It's headed by Dick Latessa as Cockian; Howard Ross as the Roman Commander; Michael Glenn-Smith as a young prisoner whom Cockian betrays; Kathrin King Segal as Kiki, Cockian's performing partner; Virginia Gregory as the wife he has abandoned; and Leila Martin as the real Philemon's wife. If you're curious, you may be able to track down a tape of the TV version that featured the original cast. —DAVID WOLF

PIANO BAR
Original Off-Broadway Cast, 1978 (Original Cast Records/no CD)
Not recommended.

Time was when you could buy an original cast recording with a reasonable amount of confidence. If a score got recorded, it usually meant that it was a work of some quality. Not so here. This is a musical that takes place in—well, a piano bar. It throws together four strangers who sing about their pasts, their hopes, and their despair. The paper-thin characters and their petty problems are of extremely limited interest; Doris Willens' weak lyrics are predictable and undramatic, while Rob Fremont's music is simply monotonous. The high-powered cast features Kelly Bishop, Karen DeVito, Steve Elmore, Richard Ryder, and Joel Silberman (as the piano player), all for naught. —DAVID WOLF

PINS AND NEEDLES
Studio Cast, 1962 (Columbia/Sony) ★★★

This 1930s topical revue is legendary for its original cast of talented shop workers from the International Ladies' Garment Workers Union. Featuring songs by Harold Rome and sketches by Marc Blitzstein (among others), *Pins and Needles* wore its pro-labor, pro-union bias on its sleeve. But, in a bid for popularity, the writers pulled their punches. What began as mild political satire became anodyne as, over the course of a three-year run, new material—some of it by John Latouche—was interpolated. The show began performances in 1936 at the Labor Stage but didn't open officially until 1937. It later moved uptown, spawned a national tour, and ultimately was seen by more than a million theatergoers in New York and on the road. With a run of 1,108 performances, it held the longevity record for Broadway musicals prior to *Oklahoma!* This recording, made to commemorate the revue's silver anniversary, saved Rome's perky ditties from being lost (as were many of the show's sketches) and has ensured that *Pins and Needles* is one of the few early Broadway revues known for its entire score rather than just for the odd "standard." The music, originally arranged for two pianos, is played here on piano, guitar, bass, and drums under the direction of Stan Freeman. The vocalists—including Rome himself, Jack Carroll, Rose Marie Jun, Alan Sokoloff, and the twenty-year-old Barbra Streisand—are very engaging. The charm of numbers such as "Sing Me a Song of Social Significance," "Not Cricket to Picket," and "Doing the Reactionary" compensates for the recording's audio flaws. — CHARLES WRIGHT

PIPE DREAM
Original Broadway Cast, 1955 (RCA) ★★★

Rodgers and Hammerstein may not have been the ideal team to put the chippies and layabouts of John Steinbeck's Cannery Row onstage; it's tantalizing to consider what Frank Loesser, who was first approached to adapt Steinbeck's *Sweet Thursday,* would have wrought. Still, the score of the shortest-running R&H Broadway musical is lovely, full of Oscar Hammerstein's humanity and Richard Rodgers' surprising melodic turns; listen to the composer's wondrous harmonics in "Suzy Is a Good Thing," for example. Evidently, Helen Traubel's whorehouse madam failed to convince in the theater, but she's fine on disc. Even better are the young lovers, the soulful Judy Tyler and the always reliable William Johnson, genuinely sexy together and apart. As for the choral ensembles, they're lively and lusty. The overture is incomplete; second verses of each song, even the excellent "The Man I Used to Be," are missing; and the album is capped by an illogical finale that crams as many hopeful hits as possible into a few minutes. But as this is the only *Pipe Dream* disc we're ever likely to see, we'll take it. — MARC MILLER

PIPPIN
Original Broadway Cast, 1972 (Motown/Decca) ★★★

Stephen Schwartz wrote the score for this hippy-dippy medieval musical. John Rubinstein starred as the son of Charlemagne, roaming the Holy Roman Empire looking for the meaning of life and instead finding war, sex, patricide, and—finally!—the love of a good woman. The oddball story was all-that-jazzed up by Bob Fosse, whose sexy, inventive staging made it one of the biggest hits of the decade. Even with a fundamentally weak concept, there's much to like here, starting with the unique, folk-jazz sound of the score. "Magic to Do," led by narrator/emcee Ben Vereen, is the definitive band-of-strolling-players opening number; and Pippin's first solo, "Corner of the Sky" is a stirring piece of writing. Also hard to resist is that paean to pagan joys "No Time At All," which provided veteran trouper Irene Ryan with her career sign-off. A very young Jill Clayburgh offers a lovely reading of the clear-eyed ballad "I Guess I'll Miss the Man," and Vereen and Rubinsten demonstrate split-second timing in the duet "On the Right Track." The pure 1970s soft-pop orchestrations are, surprisingly, by Ralph Burns, who apparently could work in just about any style; as a result, this is the most intimate-sounding of Broadway albums.   —DAVID BARBOUR

PLAIN AND FANCY
Original Broadway Cast, 1955 (Capitol/DRG) ★★★★

Listening to a second-rank score, a longtime musical-lover will marvel at how often just-above-par tuners were a dependable source for Hit Parade clicks. "Young and Foolish," sung here by David Daniels and Gloria Marlowe, was a major chartbuster thanks to teens of the 1950s, who were becoming the largest segment of the 45-rpm record-buying public. But "It Wonders Me," "Plain We Live," and "It's a Helluva Way to Run a Love Affair" also turned up on the airwaves and in nightclubs—to the gratification, surely, of composer Albert Hague and lyricist Arnold B. Horwitt. Another big number, "This Is All Very New to Me," is interpreted by the wonderful Barbara Cook, who supplied notes for the most recent CD release of the *Plain and Fancy* cast album. The plot, hardly the stuff of great dramatic literature, concerns a couple of Manhattan so-so sophisticates who wander to Bird-in-Hand, Pennsylvania, and get mixed up in the restrained romantic entanglements of some stage-quaint Amish folks. The cast boasts a number of accomplished vocalists. Shirl Conway, who has an astringent approach to a comedy ditty, nails "It's a Helluva Way . . ." to the back wall. Cook, whose soaring tones are never flowery (as opposed to Marlowe's), shows up enthusiastically in the forefront of three tracks. Lively Nancy Andrews takes the lead in "Plenty of Pennsylvania" as well as in the extremely cute "City Mouse, Country Mouse." The impeccable Franz Allers conducts.   —DAVID FINKLE

PLAY ON!
Original Broadway Cast, 1997 (Varèse Sarabande) ★★★★★

Play On! is at least the fourth musical adapted from Shakespeare's *Twelfth Night* to play, albeit briefly, in New York. This version moved the action to Harlem, circa the 1940s. The noble Count Orsino of the original became the greatest jazzman of the time, a composer and band-leader named "the Duke"—and if there's any doubt as to who inspired the character, the musical's songs were all taken from the catalogue of Duke Ellington. The trouble with the show is that, even though the songs make dramatic sense as slotted, the book writing is deadly. But what you'll find on the disc is one terrific Ellington song after another, gorgeously arranged by Luther Henderson. There are famous titles—"Take the 'A' Train" and "Don't Get Around Much Anymore"—and others not-so-famous, such as "Hit Me With a Hot Note and Watch Me Bounce." All of them are wonderfully performed by Tonya Pinkins, Cheryl Freeman, Carl Anderson, Lawrence Hamilton, André De Shields, and Larry Marshall.   —DAVID WOLF

PORGY AND BESS
Original Broadway Cast Members, 1940/1942 (Decca) ★★★★★

Porgy and Bess may be the most fabulous failure in musical theater history, though this full-fledged opera can only be judged a failure in that its original 1935 run of 124 performances was brief by Broadway standards. Of course, a new work entering the repertoire of an opera house would probably have a dozen performances per season at most—so if you use that yardstick, 124 performances of *Porgy and Bess* are equivalent to a ten-year run. George Gershwin's iconic work is based on the play *Porgy* by Dorothy and DuBose Hayward; the latter was librettist-lyricist for *Porgy and Bess,* with Ira Gershwin collaborating on the lyrics. It might be argued that recordings of their opera should not be reviewed in this book devoted to musical theater, but *Porgy and Bess* has become part of the fabric of American culture in a way that *Regina, The Consul,* and other operas that played on Broadway never did. If critics and audiences didn't fully appreciate the work in 1935, they certainly came to do so in the years following Gershwin's tragic death in 1937. The first recordings reviewed here were made by members of the original Broadway cast years after the fact, under the leadership of the opera's original conductor, Alexander Smallens. Todd Duncan and Anne Brown sing gloriously in the title roles; indeed, their rendition of the beautiful duet "Bess, You Is My Woman Now" has served as a benchmark for every subsequent recording. Duncan and Brown also perform several songs that were written to be sung by other characters: She does Clara's "Summertime" and Serena's "My Man's Gone Now," he does Sportin' Life's "It Ain't Necessarily So" and Crown's part in "What You Want Wid Bess?" John Bubbles, the original Sportin' Life, is not among the singers; Avon Long, who played the part in the 1942 revival, does "There's a Boat That's Leavin' Soon for New York" and is also heard in a bonus track of Porgy's "I Got Plenty o' Nuttin" that features a jazzy arrangement for the Leo Reisman Orchestra. The only other original cast member represented here is the rich-voiced Edward Matthews as Jake, who sings "A Woman Is a Sometime Thing." This album represents only a small fraction of the three-hour score, with unfortunate cuts in some of those sections; for example, "Porgy's Lament" is bereft of the wonderful counterpoint parts for Maria and Serena. Still, the wonder of these recordings lies not in their completeness but in their authenticity. (Note: Three months before the opera's Broadway premiere, Gershwin conducted excerpts from the score in a CBS studio with several of the original cast members and a forty-three-piece orchestra. Some extraordinary sides of those sessions have been issued on the MusicMasters CD *Gershwin Performs Gershwin;* they are precious in allowing us to hear "Summertime" and "My Man's Gone Now" as conducted by Gershwin and sung by their original interpreters, Abbie Mitchell as Clara and Ruby Elzy as Serena.)

Studio Cast, 1951 (Columbia, 2CDs) ★★★★★
While this recording of the the Gershwins-Heyward masterwork is not "complete" as advertised, it contains so much more of the *Porgy and Bess* score than had previously been recorded that the exaggeration can be forgiven. Of the many fine musical theater albums conducted by Lehman Engel and produced by Goddard Lieberson, this one is the cream of the crop. Among the original cast members heard here are Edward Matthews (Jake), J. Rosamond Johnson (Frazier), and Helen Dowdy (who sings Maria in addition to her original role of Lily). Warren Coleman is marvelously frightening as Crown, but he lunges at a lot of the notes rather than hitting them. Avon Long is back as Sportin' Life, and though his voice isn't ideal for the part, his performance oozes with personality. Camilla Williams is an adequate Bess, if a bit droopy of tone, but Lawrence Winters is magnificent as Porgy. His ringing high-baritone voice sounds ideal throughout the recording and then, just when you think that he couldn't possibly top himself, his delivery of the climactic line "I gotta be wid Bess" in the final scene is thrilling beyond description.

Film Soundtrack, 1959 (Columbia/no CD) ★★★
This is an aural document of a troubled film. The album has been out of print for years; I somehow acquired a hiss-laden Japanese CD-pressing that sounds like it was transferred directly

from the LP master tape with no digital processing whatever. The movie stars Sidney Poitier as Porgy, Dorothy Dandridge as Bess, Sammy Davis, Jr. as Sportin' Life, Pearl Bailey as Maria, Brock Peters as Crown, Ruth Attaway as Serena, and Diahann Carroll as Clara, but only Davis, Bailey, and Peters do their own singing—and, for contractual reasons, Davis is not heard at all on the soundtrack album! Instead, the role is sung by Cab Calloway, whose engaging performances of "It Ain't Necessarily So" and "There's a Boat That's Leavin' Soon for New York" lack the sense of menace that the character needs. Despite its flaws, this recording is worth tracking down if only for baritone Robert McFerrin's extraordinary performance of Porgy's music, dubbed for Poitier, and Adele Addison's lovely singing for Dandridge; both rein in their operatic voices for the film medium but they still sing beautifully under the tasteful, respectful musical direction of André Previn and Ken Darby.

Studio Cast, 1963 (RCA) ★★★★

There are many recordings of excerpts from *Porgy and Bess,* but this one is exceptional for its superb singing, conducting, and sound quality. Diva Leontyne Price had one of the most beautiful voices of the twentieth century; she toured in the role of Bess for two years (1952-54) and posterity should be grateful that she recorded large portions of this score before political correctness prompted her to remove it from her repertoire. Her Porgy on tour and on the recording is William Warfield, to whom Price was briefly wed; the marriage may not have worked out, but they sure make beautiful music together, she with her glorious soprano and he with his warm baritone. Less successful is McHenry Boatwright, who brings a stuffy operatic sound to the role of the brutal Crown, but it's great to have original Sportin' Life John Bubbles on hand; although by the time of this recording his voice had weakened with age, Bubbles still had style for miles. The two leads sing sections of the score that were written for other characters, but this compromise of theatrical verisimilitude is justified when we hear Price's thrilling renditions of "Summertime" and "My Man's Gone Now." Skitch Henderson conducts with tremendous verve, and the technical quality of the recording is awesome; be sure to attenuate the volume control of your sound system during the orchestral postlude to "There's a Boat That's Leavin' Soon for New York" if you don't want to wake your neighbors.

Studio Cast, 1976 (London, 3CDs) ★★★

For forty years after the premiere of *Porgy and Bess,* no truly complete recording of the score was available; then two such recordings were released in 1976. This one features the first-rank conductor Lorin Maazel leading the Cleveland Orchestra. Willard White is an estimable Porgy, if perhaps a bit too bass-sounding for some tastes; Leona Mitchell is in fresh and lovely voice as Bess. McHenry Boatwright, who was Crown on the 1963 recording, is back and he sounds even stodgier here; but Barbara Hendricks as Clara, Florence Quivar as Serena, and François Clemmons as Sportin' Life are very well suited to their roles. In terms of technical quality, this is a full, rich, and exciting recording.

Houston Grand Opera Cast, 1976 (RCA, 3CDs) ★★★★★

A superb production of a great American work marked the country's bicentennial when the Houston Grand Opera's *Porgy and Bess* came to Broadway in 1976. Because this complete recording was based on an actual stage production, it has a palpable theatricality, and John DeMain's conducting of the score is magnificent. The solo singers are generally fine if only definitive in one case: Larry Marshall is the best Sportin' Life on records. Donnie Ray Albert displays a strong baritone as Porgy, but his voice may strike some listeners as too "operatic" for the part and his sibilant esses are distracting. As Bess, Clamma Dale sounds marvelous and more vibrant than her Porgy. But it's the singers in supporting roles who make this recording really special: Betty Lane offers what may be the most ethereally beautiful performance of "Summertime" ever; Wilma Shakesnider is immensely moving in Serena's "My Man's Gone Now"; Carol Brice's Maria is a force to be reckoned with; and Andrew Smith is an excellent Crown. The large chorus and pick-up orchestra sound fabulous throughout. Although Albert's Porgy is not all that we might wish it to be, this set still rates five stars because it's by far the most satisfying of the three note-complete recordings of a true American masterwork.

Studio Cast, 1989 (EMI, 3CDs) ★

What might have been an estimable recording of *Porgy and Bess* is sabotaged by Simon Rattle, a maddeningly willful conductor who seems more interested in self-aggrandizement than in interpreting this work according to the composer's intentions. Several of the tempi that Rattle sets for the London Symphony Orchestra are ridiculously fast and others are absurdly slow. That's too bad, because the singers are excellent: Willard White is back as Porgy, sounding even better than before, and he's superbly partnered by the Bess of Cynthia Haymon. Also happily on hand are Gregg Baker as the sexiest Crown imaginable; Damon Evans as a slick, very well-sung Sportin' Life; and Harolyn Blackwell as a pure-toned Clara. After the fact, this recording served as the soundtrack for a 1993 video version of *Porgy and Bess* that's deplorable not only because it's so badly lip-synched but also because it was apparently sanctioned by the Gershwin estate in lieu of a TV telecast of the excellent Metropolitan Opera production. —MICHAEL PORTANTIERE

PRETTYBELLE
Original Cast, 1971 (Original Cast Records/Varèse Sarabande) ★★★★

A woman who lives in the Deep South wants to repent for her husband's deplorable hostilities toward minorities—so she beds Hispanic and black men. With such a contrived plot, it's no surprise that *Prettybelle* folded quickly in Boston, but a tuneful, Southern-tinged score by the great composer Jule Styne survives. From the lazy waltz of the title tune to a rollicking Dixieland march, Styne's music, joined to wonderfully evocative lyrics by Bob Merrill, is performed on this recording by one of Broadway's greatest leading ladies, Angela Lansbury. She's absolutely brilliant in the plaintive "To a Small Degree," wherein Prettybelle describes her marriage; her angry delivery of "How Could I Know?" reveals the character's devastating discovery of her husband's vileness; and Lansbury really socks it to us with "When I'm Drunk, I'm Beautiful," the eleven-o'clock blockbuster. —PETER FILICHIA

THE PRINCE AND THE PAUPER
Original Off-Broadway Cast, 2002 (JAY) ★★

Based on Mark Twain's novel about a pair of sixteenth-century London look-alikes who swap identities, this adaptation of *The Prince and the Pauper* played a respectable 194 performances Off-Broadway. With music by Neil Berg, lyrics by Berg and Bernie Garzia, and libretto by Garzia and Ray Roderick, the show is an adventure-soaked musical with pop-opera inflections. The score is sprightly, performed by a strong cast of thirteen singing actors, many of whom play multiple roles and give their all on this album. Most notable for their talent and energy are Dennis Michael Hall as the Tudor prince who pretends to be a commoner and

Gerard Canonico as the slum lad masquerading as royalty. John Glaudini's orchestrations and arrangements, played by a three-person combo—Glaudini on piano, Anne-Marie Tranchida on cello, and Frank Basile on reeds—lend a full, swashbuckling sound to the proceedings. True to Twain's source material, this is a children's piece with enough satiric edge to be enjoyed by adults as well.

—CHARLES WRIGHT

PRODIGAL (SON)

Original Australian Cast, 2000 (Prodigal Son Productions) ★★★

Australian librettist-lyricist Dean Bryant and composer Matthew Frank took inspiration from the Bible for their musical *Prodigal Son.* They updated the story to present-day Australia and made the central figure of the straying son returning to the fold a young man named Luke, who's coping with his homosexuality. As the recording reveals, this is an intimate show, with only piano accompaniment played by the composer. The score deals with the larger implications of small issues, capturing the oppressive aspects of an everyday rural existence ("Happy Families") and the allure of a life with more choices ("Run With the Tide"). Several moving songs express the growing pains experienced by children ("Out of Myself," "Epiphany") as well as their parents ("My Boy," "Love Them and Leave Them Alone"). Bryant himself gives an engaging performance as Luke; Jules Hutchinson is persuasive as his mother; Barry Mitchell is a bit bland as Luke's father; Graham Pages is adequate in dual roles as Luke's brother and boyfriend; and Amanda Levy as Maddy, a performance artist, gives fine if undistinguished support. The disc includes a bonus track of a song from a subsequent Bryant-Frank musical, *Emoh Ruo,* sung by Levy.

Original Off-Broadway Cast, 2002 (JAY) ★★★

The title of Bryant and Frank's musical was shortened to *Prodigal* for its 2002 York Theatre production, but the show lost none of its emotional power on the journey from Australia to New York. In fact, this recording has more energy and humor than the original. Joshua Park embodies Luke's youth and naiveté very well, and Kerry Butler makes Maddy a force to be reckoned with. David Hess and Alison Fraser depict Luke's parents with plenty of outer strength to mask the fragility of their frightened inner selves; this is a true battle of wills, beautifully presented. The only weak link is Christian Borle in the boyfriend/brother roles, which seemed vital onstage but aren't well established through song. Australian musicals with original scores don't often show up in America, but this recording makes an excellent case for *Prodigal.*

—MATTHEW MURRAY

THE PRODUCERS

Original Broadway Cast, 2001 (Sony) ★★★★★

Mel Brooks' full-blown musical version of his semi-musical 1968 movie about a has-been Broadway producer's backfired scheme to bilk his show's investors by staging a colossal flop has all the excitement of a Broadway smash hit, and the star power of Nathan Lane and Matthew Broderick comes through on this recording—one of the brashest cast albums ever made. *The Producers* epitomizes Borscht Belt humor. Brooks' clever songs are charming and hilariously offensive at the same time; while many of the tunes are frank pastiches of Tin Pan Alley standards, they're sturdy enough to progress the uproarious plot rapidly and effectively. The musical opened to extravagant critical and audience acclaim, and it garnered twelve Tony Awards, the most ever won by a Broadway show. The performances of Lane as the frantic producer Max

Bialystock and Broderick as Leo Bloom, the panicky accountant who becomes Max's coproducer, display a comic brilliance unheard on cast albums since the days of Zero Mostel and Carol Channing. Also brilliant are Gary Beach as Roger De Bris—the effete, delusional director who ultimately portrays a Judy Garland-like Hitler in the show's outrageous centerpiece production number, "Springtime for Hitler"—and De Bris' common-law assistant, Carmen Ghia, played by the fabulous Roger Bart. Other outstanding tracks include Cady Huffman belting out "When You've Got It, Flaunt It," Brad Oscar singing "Haben sie Gehört das Deutsche Band?" and Nathan Lane's marathon "Betrayed." The finale, "Prisoners of Love (Leo & Max)," is spine-tingling in classic Broadway style. —GERARD ALESSANDRINI

PROMENADE
Original Off-Broadway Cast, 1969 (RCA) ★

Two prisoners identified as "105" and "106" escape from jail and wander through various settings, including a park, a banquet, and a battlefield. Among the people they encounter are Mr. R., Mr. S., Miss O, and a bereaved woman who thinks she's their mother. At the end of the day, they return to prison. Only in the 1960s could something like this get a commercial production, let alone achieve a half-decent run and earn a measure of critical respect. Obvious in its details (the usual comparisons are drawn between rich and poor, there's a scene spoofing the foolishness of war, and so on) and utterly impenetrable in its overall intentions, *Promenade* enjoyed a following in its seven-months' run at the theater of the same name. Nowadays, it's just another baffling artifact of an era when plot and character were regularly thrown to the wind. Maria Irene Fornes is the gnomic librettist-lyricist; composer Al Carmines' melodies owe a debt to Kurt Weill, but there are several catchy tunes. Among them are "Unrequited Love," "The Clothes Make the Man," and "Capricious and Fickle," the latter belted by Alice Playten. As recorded, the score is not unpleasant but neither is it compelling. —DAVID BARBOUR

PROMISES, PROMISES
Original Broadway Cast, 1968 (United Artists/MGM) ★★

Based on the film *The Apartment,* this show was the only Broadway effort of pop songwriters Burt Bacharach (music) and Hal David (lyrics), who had written such hits as "Alfie," "One Less Bell to Answer," and "Close to You." Unfortunately, this album of *Promises, Promises* is one of the worst ever from a performance standpoint. The usually wonderful Jerry Orbach sounds tired and pitch-shy as Chuck Baxter, especially in "She Likes Basketball" and in two duets, "Our Little Secret" (with Edward Winter as J. D. Sheldrake) and "A Young Pretty Girl Like You" (with A. Larry Haines as Dr. Dreyfuss); it's hard to tell who's singing farther below pitch in those last two cuts but, at any rate, they're almost unlistenable. As Fran Kubelik, the young woman caught between Baxter and Sheldrake, Jill O'Hara has a most unpleasant voice—raspy, coarse, and unequalized throughout its range. The score itself is marred by David's often ham-fisted lyrics; but the good songs ("Knowing When to Leave," "I'll Never Fall in Love Again," and others) finally outweigh the stinkers. One of the few completely successful tracks is the touching "Christmas Day," well sung by the ensemble. And Orbach does sound fine in the terrific title song. You can supposedly hear Donna McKechnie singing along with Baayork Lee and Margo Sappington in "Turkey Lurkey Time," but it sounds to me like the number was actually recorded by the show's "orchestra voices."

Original London Cast, 1969 (United Artists/no CD) ★★★

As of the fall of 2004, this recording had not been issued on CD, and it's hard to figure out why. The two leads, Tony Roberts and Betty Buckley, are now established Broadway stars. And, though it has its flaws, the album is far superior to the Broadway release. There are far fewer pitch problems overall, though there is some out-of-tune singing in the ensemble ballad "Christmas Day." Happily, Roberts is charismatic in Baxter's songs, and if Buckley's steely belt/soprano won't appeal to everyone, she's solid from a technical standpoint. Another plus of the recording is that its sound quality is superb; Jonathan Tunick's orchestrations sound magnificent here, whereas on the Broadway album the percussion is too heavy and the strings are barely audible. (Note: Donna McKechnie traveled to London with the show, but I can't make out her voice in "Turkey Lurkey Time" on this album, either!)   —MICHAEL PORTANTIERE

PUMP BOYS AND DINETTES
Original Cast, 1982 (Columbia/Sony) ★★★★

An unexpected delight when it opened, this revue of countryish songs doesn't have much in the way of a story line. The setup of a roadside stop populated by a quartet of service-station fellas and a pair of flirtatious waitresses was just an excuse to keep on singing. The cast members— Jim Wann, Mark Hardwick, John Foley, John Schimmel, Debra Monk, Cass Morgan—wrote material for the show and/or played instruments convincingly, performing with nice dollops of personality. The CD contains nineteen selections that would still perk up any country-music play list. Three of the tracks—"Be Good or Be Gone," "The Night Dolly Parton Was Almost Mine," and "Sisters"—were produced by Billy Sherrill, the rest by Mike Berniker. Don't try looking for conflict or character development in these songs; just kick back in your boots and listen up.   —DAVID FINKLE

PURLIE
Original Broadway Cast, 1970 (Ampex/RCA) ★★★

With music by Gary Geld and lyrics by Peter Udell, *Purlie* is based on the play *Purlie Victorious* by Ossie Davis, who adapted the musical in collaboration with Udell and the show's producer, Philip Rose. Both versions are seldom revived, probably because their portrayals of African-Americans living in the Deep South "in the recent past" are dicey according to current standards of political correctness. But the score of the musical is quite wonderful, from the rousing Gospel anthem "Walk Him Up the Stairs" to Purlie's character-establishing number "New Fangled Preacher Man" to the soulful duet "He Can Do It." In the title role, Cleavon Little is dynamic and charismatic; and as Lutiebelle, the sweet girl who's in love with him, Melba Moore displays a thrilling voice, especially in the roof-raising "I Got Love." Novella Nelson is a worthy partner to Moore in "He Can Do It," and it's fun to hear Sherman Hemsley, who later gained fame on TV's *The Jeffersons,* delivering the comedic "Skinnin' a Cat." The sound quality of the CD is marred by distortion in several sections, possibly caused by a defect on the original recording or by deterioration of the master tape prior to digital transfer.   —MICHAEL PORTANTIERE

PUTTING IT TOGETHER
Off-Broadway Cast, 1993 (RCA) ★★

There have been tons of Stephen Sondheim revues, but the big attraction of *Putting It Together* was unique: Julie Andrews singing Sondheim, live, in a tiny theater. It seemed like such a good fit: the sophisticated, elegant, warm-hearted superstar tackling Sondheim's sophisticated, elegant, ice-cold songs. Indeed, her work on this album is an unalloyed pleasure and a master class in theatrical clarity. Andrews is dryly funny in "Sweet Polly Plunkett," the goofy Victorian parlor song from *Sweeney Todd,* and her vitriolic "Could I Leave You?" from *Follies* makes you dream of the Phyllis that never was. In "Getting Married Today" from *Company,* Andrews gives a tour-de-force performance, singing the parts of both the frenzied, motormouth bride and the soprano who rains down churchly blessings. However, the rest of the cast is a mixed bag. Director Julia McKenzie had contrived a "let's party!" *mise-en-scène* for the show, but the characters' interactions feel less urbane than brittle. Playwright and sometime-performer Christopher Durang is no great singer, though he lends an impish, Oscar Levant quality to his songs. Stephen Collins is no great singer, either, but he brings grown-up gravitas to his numbers. Rachel York, as an oddly glamorous maid, is lush and sexy; she has a stratospheric vocal range and comic timing to spare. Michael Rupert's throbbing vibrato and tenor ping are characteristically intense. Adding to the problem that two of the five performers are not trained vocalists, the instrumentation for keyboards, bass, and percussion sounds thin. —ROBERT SANDLA

R

RADIO GALS
Original Cast, 1995 (Varèse Sarabande) ★★

In this comedy-concept musical by Mike Craver and Mark Hardwick, we're hearing a radio broadcast emanating illegally from the home of an Arkansas matron in 1927. (This album documents the premiere staging in Pasadena; the show subsequently had a brief Off-Broadway run.) Although no plot synopsis is included, the song titles almost speak for themselves: "Aviatrix Love Song," "Fairies in My Mother's Flower Garden," and the immortal "That Wicky Wacky Hula Hula Honka Wonka Honolulu Hawaiian Honey of Mine." These are interspersed with jokes about "Doc May and His Musical Goats" and a running series of commercials for "Horehound Compound." All in all, it's a heapin' helpin' of folksy humor. While *Radio Gals* was amusing onstage, the disc has a somewhat cloying effect, but there are some priceless bits, such as "The Tranquil Boxwood," a series of crashing piano chords reminiscent of the work of Béla Bartók. And considerable musical cleverness is heard in the songs "Edna, the Elephant Girl," "Dear Mr. Gershwin," and "Buster, He's a Hot Dog Now." For some reason, Craver and cabaret luminary Mark Nadler are cast as women; but the oddly named Helen Geller is effective as Hazel Hunt, mistress of the airwaves, and she and the rest of the cast sing well. The show consists entirely of novelty material, totally unconnected to plot; fans of the down-home whimsy heard on NPR's *Prairie Home Companion* will probably appreciate *Radio Gals* more than the average musical theater aficionado.   —DAVID BARBOUR

RAGS
Original Broadway Cast Members, 1986 (Sony) ★★★★

High on the list of flops that deserved better is this four-performance heartbreaker by composer Charles Strouse and lyricist Stephen Schwartz. The reviews ranged from respectful-bad to whiny-bad, with most of the bile reserved for Joseph Stein's fragmented book. Maybe the show, set on the Lower East Side of 1910-11, had too much happening in terms of plot: three love stories, multiple immigrant experiences, ward-heeler intrigue, and so on. To many, the leftist agitprop spirit got in the way of the story. But what a score! Like master illusionists, Strouse and Schwartz put a mirror up to early-twentieth-century song styles and produced a reflection brighter than the actuality. Irish ballads, Yiddish folk music, vaudeville specialty numbers, patri-

---

ALL-TIME FAVORITES OF
COMPOSER-LYRICIST

Andrew Lippa

1. The King and I
2. Dreamgirls
3. Gypsy
4. West Side Story
5. A Chorus Line
6. Ragtime
7. Falsettos
8. Fiddler on the Roof
9. Les Misérables
10. Sweeney Todd

otic marches, ragtime—they're all here, only smarter and more sophisticated than their original models and packed with meaty ideas. The show's top-billed star, Teresa Stratas, elected not to record the album, so Julia Migenes was brought in. With a stunning voice and plenty of fire, she makes an excellent Rebecca Hershkowitz. She's surrounded by an A-list company: Judy Kuhn is remarkable in the title song, pouring anger, regret, and contempt into a rollicking Strouse rag; Marcia Lewis and Dick Latessa wring laughs and poignancy out of "Three Sunny Rooms"; Terrence Mann and Lonny Price are fine in their roles; and Josh Blake is as nonirritating as child singers get. Only Larry Kert, as Rebecca's husband, doesn't quite convince; he's OK from a technical standpoint but doesn't seem to inhabit the character. The disc includes "Cherry Street Café" and "Nothing Will Hurt Us Again," two songs dropped from the show's brief run. They're welcome bonuses to a score that's a rich panorama of the American dream in old New York. If you alphabetize your cast albums (and who doesn't?) this one goes right before *Ragtime.* As sweeping musical storytelling, it's not far behind. —MARC MILLER

RAGTIME
"Songs from Ragtime," 1996 (RCA) ★★★★

One of the great gems of the American musical theater, *Ragtime* is replete with beautiful performances on this first recording of the magnificent score by Stephen Flaherty and Lynn Ahrens, released to coincide with the show's world premiere in Toronto. Most of the principals heard here—Brian Stokes Mitchell, Marin Mazzie, Peter Friedman, Audra McDonald, and others—were also in the New York production two years later (Camille Saviola, this album's Emma Goldman, was not), but there are many differences between this disc and the subsequent Broadway recording. As its title suggests, "Songs from Ragtime" gives us highlights from the score, including all of the show's major musical moments, movingly performed by the stellar cast. It also contains some material that didn't make it to New York: "The Show Biz," a song for Evelyn Nesbit and Houdini, and the stirring original bridge for "The Night That Goldman Spoke at Union Square." Since this disc was made and released while the show was still being developed, it lacks a certain theatricality heard on the very best cast albums, yet there's a decided freshness about it.

Original Broadway Cast, 1998 (RCA, 2CDs) ★★★★★

This spectacular recording documents what few other musicals have achieved: The show actually improves upon its source material, in this case, a best-selling novel by E. L. Doctorow. As adapted by librettist Terrence McNally, lyricist Lynn Ahrens, and composer Stephen Flaherty, *Ragtime* includes almost every vivid character and gripping plot point of the epic novel while expanding the emotions of the story with a superb score that underlines the sociological thrust of the story with great style and entertainment value. Unfortunately, the show did not receive the critical kudos and mass popular acceptance that it deserved during its Broadway run, but this recording adds to its legacy. Brian Stokes Mitchell has the role of a lifetime as Coalhouse Walker; his finely balanced mix of haughtiness and optimism turned to disillusionment is so compelling that the potentially unsympathetic character is transformed into a heartbreaking, tragic figure. Marin Mazzie's performance as Mother, who reacts nobly to a changing world, is just as expertly acted and sung and is the emotional heart of the musical. Audra MacDonald is phenomenal as Sarah, one of the four roles for which she has won Tony Awards (as of this writing). Judy Kaye is stellar as Emma Goldman, as are Peter Friedman, Mark Jacoby, Lynette Perry, and Steven Sutcliffe as Tateh, Father, Evelyn Nesbit, and Mother's Younger Brother, respectively. Recorded right after the Broadway opening, this two-disc set includes two numbers that were added to the show on its way to New York: "Atlantic City" brings pageantry and fluff to the proceedings while "Sarah Brown Eyes" is a tender musical moment for Mitchell and McDonald. Offered as an appendix is a "symphonic portrait" of *Ragtime,* arranged and performed by a symphony-size orchestra.　　　　　　　　—GERARD ALESSANDRINI

RAISIN
Original Broadway Cast, 1973 (Columbia/Sony) ★★★

Despite its healthy Broadway run and its Tony Award for Best Musical, *Raisin* is almost completely forgotten. Fortunately, the Robert Nemiroff-Charlotte Zaltzberg adaptation of Lorraine Hansberry's *A Raisin in the Sun,* with a score by composer Judd Woldin and lyricist Robert Brittan, yielded a wonderful cast album. Stunning vocals tell the story: The matriarch (Virginia Capers) of the ghetto-bound, black Younger family wants to use her late husband's insurance money to buy a nice house that is up for sale in a white neighborhood, but her son Walter (Joe Morton) and daughter-in-law Ruth (Ernestine Jackson) have different ideas about how to use the money. There's also fine work from Debbie Allen as Walter's striving sister and Ralph Carter as Walter and Ruth's son. The score is alternately soulful, driving, and tender. The pulsating prologue sets the tone, followed by "Man Say," Morton's explanation of the differences between men and women. Jackson shines in "Whose Little Angry Ma" and "Sweet Time." Other highlights are the lovely "Sidewalk Tree," the biting "Not Anymore," and the rousing gospel tune "He Come Down This Morning." Capers' eleven-o'clock number, "Measure the Valleys," is one of the most powerful theater songs of the period.　　—DAVID BARBOUR

REDHEAD
Original Broadway Cast, 1959 (RCA/Fynsworth Alley) ★★★

With a book by Herbert and Dorothy Fields, Sidney Sheldon, and David Shaw, music by Albert Hague, and lyrics by Dorothy Fields, *Redhead* is certainly among the least-well-known shows to have won the Tony Award for Best Musical, in addition to several other Tonys. RCA's initial "Living Stereo" release was missing "Essie's Vision," an exhilarating dream dance arranged by Roger Adams, but the cut was reinstated for a later stereo LP. The CD release includes three new recordings of songs that were cut from the show: "You Love I" (sung by Jennifer Piech and Mark Price), "It Only Takes a Minute" (sung by Liz Callaway), and "What Has She Got?" (sung by Faith Prince). The eighteen tracks from the original album may not enable you to follow the show's intricate murder-mystery plot but, once heard, many of the tunes will likely run through your head for weeks. Gwen Verdon as Essie scores strongly in the effusive waltz "Merely Marvelous" and the tongue-twisting "'Erbie Fitch's Twitch." Richard Kiley vacillates amusingly between "She's Not Enough Woman for Me" (a comic duet with Leonard Stone) and "My Girl Is Just Enough Woman for Me" (a solo ballad); he also does a great job with "I'm Back in Circulation," his character's paean to freedom. Together, Verdon and Kiley shine in the romantic "Look Who's in Love" and the climactic "I'll Try." Further delights include "The Simpson Sisters' Door," a sprightly opening chorale; "Behave Yourself," a funny duet for Essie's maiden aunts; and "The Pick-Pocket Tango," whose music conjures images of the choreography that a young Bob Fosse devised for Verdon and Buzz Miller in the role of a jailer. As the song says, "merely marvelous" is how you're likely to find this recording.　　　　　　　　—JEFFREY DUNN

RED, HOT AND BLUE

Ethel Merman With Studio Artists, 1936 (Liberty/AEI) ★★★★

Hoping for another *Anything Goes,* producer Vinton Freedley put Cole Porter and Ethel Merman together again, this time adding Jimmy Durante and Bob Hope to the mix; but *Red, Hot and Blue,* about a missing heiress who can only be identified by a waffle-iron brand on her buttock, ran only about half as long as its predecessor. Merman recorded her four major songs from the show with pianists Fairchild and Carroll and their orchestra, and she's in top form here—belting "Ridin' High" to high heaven, breaking your heart in "Down in the Depths (on the 90th Floor)," and insouciantly swinging her way through the title song and "It's De-Lovely." Also included are a Fairchild-Carroll instrumental medley and the amusing "The Ozarks Are Calling Me Home," performed by Ramona and her Grand Piano. AEI's CD also contains selections from *Stars in Your Eyes.* (Note: Other songs from *Red, Hot and Blue* can be found on Ben Bagley's *Cole Porter Revisited* album.)   —JEFFREY DUNN

REEFER MADNESS

Original Los Angeles Cast, 1999 (Madness Records) ★★

Musicals don't come any sillier than the Kevin Murphy (lyrics-book) and Dan Studney (music-book) adaptation of *Reefer Madness.* This wacky show based on the legendary 1938 "masterpiece" of film propaganda was a big hit in Los Angeles; an Off-Broadway production two years later only ran for two weeks. It would seem that the tale of teenagers whose lives are corrupted and ultimately destroyed by "the green menace" of marijuana would be a natural for musicalization, but the songs are devoid of sincerity and the whole thing gets tiresome quickly. A few moments stand out: the catchy title number, a terrific first-act finale, and one great song, "Listen to Jesus, Jimmy." The cast is uniformly terrific: Christian Campbell and Jolie Jenkins as the doomed young'uns; Robert Torti as both the villainous dealer Jack and Jesus Christ; the hilarious Harry S. Murphy in a variety of roles; the big-voiced Lori Alan as Jack's pot-addled mistress; Erin Matthews as a self-described "reefer slut"; and John Kassir as a couple of colorful characters. The company is rounded out by a lively ensemble that includes Gregg Edelman, Michele Pawk, and Kristen Bell. David Manning and Nathan Wang lead the strong six-man band, and the CD ends with a pair of bonus tracks, one of which is a nice ballad from a work-in-progress; the other is a song dumped from *Reefer Madness* early in its run.   —SETH CHRISTENFELD

RENT

Original Broadway Cast, 1996 (Dreamworks, 2CDs) ★★★★★

Rent is a heartbreaking work in more than one sense: First, it's a moving reimagination of *La Bohème* as a portrait of struggling artists on New York's Lower East Side, coping with poverty, drugs, and AIDS; second, composer-lyricist-librettist Jonathan Larson died before the first preview, depriving us of a major voice in the musical theater. Larson's rich, melodic gift is on full display here as he cunningly creates a Broadway opera in a modern musical idiom. Among the best items are "One Song Glory," sung by the creatively blocked, HIV-positive musician Roger; "Light My Candle," the seductive entrance for the sad, ailing Mimi; the clever catalogue song "La Vie Bohème" (surely the only lyric to reference Maya Angelou, Stephen Sondheim, Susan Sontag, and the Sex Pistols); and the time-spanning "Seasons of Love." But the score is filled with alluring, propulsive melodies and a fresh lyrical wit that undercuts any sentimentality. Larson's libretto, with its references to gentrification, performance art, and AZT, is already a period piece, but he captures the wounded idealism of his characters and makes you care deeply about them. The original production launched the careers of Adam Pascal (Roger), Daphne Rubin-Vega (Mimi), Anthony Rapp (Mark Cohen), Idina Menzel (Maureen), Taye Diggs (Benny), Jesse L. Martin (Tom Collins), and Wilson Jermaine Heredia (Angel). There's not a weak performance in the bunch. The two-disc recording preserves the entire score and therefore reveals the breadth of librettist-composer-lyricist Larson's ambition. This is a key work that has reached a generation of young new theatergoers.   —DAVID BARBOUR

REX

Original Broadway Cast, 1976 (RCA) Not recommended.

This late-career Richard Rodgers flop, about the marital problems of Henry VIII, revealed the composer to be out of touch with contemporary Broadway. He wasn't the only one: Librettist Sherman Yellen and lyricist Sheldon Harnick couldn't decide if Henry, played by Nicol Williamson, was a monster of ambition and ego or a misunderstood paterfamilias like Captain von Trapp. Yellen's big gimmick was to have Penny Fuller appear in Act I as Anne Boleyn and in Act II as her daughter, Elizabeth I; this created a neat psychological triangle with Henry, but the show's melodies are often slow and stentorian, while the lyrics explain themselves to death. The best items are the opening madrigal "No Song More Pleasing" and the Henry-Anne ballad "Away From You." The rest of the cast album is taken up by such awful numbers as "The Chase," in which the men of the court keep score of Henry's conquests, and "In Time," a solo for Elizabeth that sounds like a first draft of "Do-Re-Mi." (Irwin Kostal's orchestrations frequently have a pleasant Renaissance patina.) Williamson croons mournfully through seemingly dozens of songs wherein he complains about the lack of an appropriate heir. (Stargazer alert: Glenn Close can be heard in one or two numbers as Mary Tudor.)   —DAVID BARBOUR

THE RINK

Original Broadway Cast, 1984 (Polygram/JAY) ★★★★

For Broadway diva lovers, it's the Fight of the Century. In this corner: Chita Rivera as Anna, a feisty, middle-aged widow who's about to walk out on the decrepit seaside roller rink she inherited from her husband, Dino. In the opposite corner: Liza Minnelli as Angel, her estranged, ex-hippie daughter, who's racked up plenty of mileage on the road and in the bedroom. The stage is set for wisecracks, catfights, tears, and many flashbacks as Anna and Angel relive their tormented past, battle over the rink, and finally come to terms. Critics complained that Terrence McNally's book, with its profane leading ladies and its preponderance of ugly incidents including fraud, rape, and domestic abuse, was unpleasant and manipulative. It is a shock to hear Liza sing to Chita, "Your ass is in a sling!" Still, the show is a true original. The only possible complaint about the score by composer John Kander and lyricist Fred Ebb is that their songs are too knowingly tailored to the stars' talents; the same is true of Michael Gibson's orchestrations. But anyone who loves Rivera and Minnelli will find this cast album irresistible. Rivera has never been better, sardonically recalling her homemaking career in "Chief Cook and Bottle Washer" and belting her heart out in "We Can Make It." Cast as a wilted flower child, Minnelli movingly reflects on her aimless life in "Colored Lights" and wackily imagines the rink as "Angel's Rink and Social Center." The stars pair up beautifully, trading barbs in "Don't Ah Ma Me," ogling men through a pot-induced haze in "The Apple Doesn't Fall," and kicking up their heels in "Wallflower." The exclusively male supporting players, representing the wreckers who have come to tear down the rink, portray everyone in Anna and Angel's pasts; they include Scott Ellis and Jason Alexander. The score reaches its peak in "Mrs. A," featuring Anna, Angel, Lenny, and a clutch of leering neighborhood suitors; the number has the complexity of a one-act opera as it explores Anna's loneliness and frustration, her anger at God, and Angel's troubled awareness of her mother's sex life. The show climaxes on a sour note with "All the Children in a Row," a eulogy for the 1960s that sounds phony coming from Minnelli. Still, there are plenty of glitzy pleasures to be found here.

Original London Cast, 1988 (JAY) ★★

As Anna and Angel, Josephine Blake and Diane Langton are surprisingly good and, at times, they sound like their Broadway predecessors; clearly, *The Rink* works with other performers. Still, this is a star vehicle without stars, and the performances of the London leading ladies don't display Chita and Liza's tough, malicious wit and all-enveloping warmth. Blake and Langton don't get many laughs out of "The Apple Doesn't Fall," but Langton doesn't sound as silly as Minnelli when delivering "All the Children in a Row." Typical of many London recordings of Broadway musicals, the entire performance is a bit too slow and lacks a certain edge—a real debit in a show that's nothing if not edgy.   —DAVID BARBOUR

RIO RITA

Original London Cast, 1930 (Columbia/Pearl) ★★★

One of the quintessential musicals of the 1920s, *Rio Rita* was also a bit of an oddity, poised as it was on the brink between musical comedy and operetta. It has a typically lush and improbable plot (romance and intrigue on the Texas/Mexico border), a lot of comic relief, and an excellent score by Harry Tierney with lyrics by Joseph McCarthy. Florenz Ziegfeld thought enough of the show to use it to inaugurate his colossal Ziegfeld Theater, where it opened in 1927 and ran for a year, then inspired two movies—a musical and an Abbott and Costello comedy. The show has been in little evidence for over half a century; with its haciendas and banditos, it probably isn't a candidate for a politically corrected revival. This album of six selections from the score features members of the original London cast. ("You're Always in My Arms," a song that Tierney wrote for the first movie version, is interpolated here.) Edith Day is fine as Rita; Geoffrey Gwyther, as her romantic Texas Ranger, is virile of voice but so implacably British in manner that's it's a hoot to hear him singing of his patrols along the Rio Grande. The nationality of the chorus members is just as obvious, but this doesn't detract from their enthusiasm or from the enjoyment that these recordings still give a listener more than seven decades after they were made.   —RICHARD BARRIOS

RIVERWIND

Original Off-Broadway Cast, 1962 (London/no CD) ★★★

After a brief instrumental prelude of the title song, the sound of crickets is heard, a soft female voice sings hauntingly in the distance, and the juvenile begins a sweet lament about the girl he loves ("I Cannot Tell Her So"). This is how *Riverwind* gets going, and it gradually becomes an almost-Chekhovian piece as it explores the relationships of two couples visiting Riverwind, a bucolic getaway along the Wabash River. The older couple (played by Elizabeth Parrish and Lawrence Brooks) is returning to the site of their honeymoon; the younger couple (Brooks Morton and Lovelady Powell) are not married. Also on hand are the woman (Helon Blount) who runs Riverwind, her daughter (Dawn Nickerson), and a boy (Martin Cassidy) who works there. The songs by composer-lyricist John Jennings are highly entertaining, performed by seven wonderful singing actors. Blount practically steals the recording with two contrasting duets: "Sew the Buttons On," wherein she gives some homespun advice to her daughter, and "A Woman Must Never Grow Old," a drunken, barrel-house-style number with Parrish. Nickerson is all youthful exuberance in "I Want a Surprise" and Parrish is all delicate wistfulness as she lends her sure soprano to the title song. Morton and Powell get two excellent comedy duets, "American Family Plan" and "Almost, but Not Quite." There is also a sophisticated quartet called "Wishing Song." The recording is well produced, with just enough dialogue to give the songs a dramatic context.

—JEFFREY DUNN

ROADSIDE
Original Off-Broadway Cast, 2001 (JAY) ★★

Tom Jones and Harvey Schmidt first began work on a musical adaptation of Lynn Riggs' 1930 play *Roadside* in the mid-1950s but didn't complete it until almost a half-century later. In many ways, the musical still felt unfinished in its 2001 York Theatre production (the cast album was made in early 2002); it tells the meandering, bland story of a woman caught between a tough bad guy and a meek good guy, and the score is full of harmless but only intermittently memorable numbers. The recording nicely preserves the show's simple, country-tinged songs, but the score isn't on a par with that of the established Jones-Schmidt hits. The title song is attractive, as is the rustic ballad "The Way It Should Be." The bawdy "Personality Plus," energetically delivered by James Hindman, is a real highlight. Drab performances from just about everyone else, including leads Julie Johnson and Jonathan Beck Reed, keep the album mired in the dust—but songs like "Here Am I," "Smellamagoody Perfume," and "Another Drunken Cowboy" probably wouldn't sound great even if performed by Broadway's best.

—MATTHEW MURRAY

THE ROAR OF THE GREASEPAINT—
THE SMELL OF THE CROWD
Original Broadway Cast, 1965 (RCA) ★★★

Is that a car with a bad muffler or a lame rhinoceros rousing itself out of the mud? No, it's Anthony Newley, wallowing in self-pity and vibrato as he belt-bleats, "*WHOOO can I tuuhhn to if YOUUU tuuhhn AH-WHYYYY!!!*"— one of several fine songs in this unprofitable but tuneful follow-up to *Stop the World, I Want to Get Off*. Like that 1961 hit, *Roar* was a self-consciously "new-style" musical that starred Newley and featured a Newley-Leslie Bricusse score. There's little spine to the book except for Cyril Ritchard as Sir, constantly getting the better of Newley's Cocky, with a children's chorus spelling them from time to time. But the score is strong; it includes not only "Who Can I Turn To?" but also "On a Wonderful Day Like Today," "Look at That Face," "My First Love Song," and other goodies. Ritchard's dry prissiness works well here, and Philip J. Lang's orchestrations are super-bright; love those dissonant trumpets, a half-tone apart, in "Joker." Gilbert Price as "The Negro" (this was a well-meaning show but a naively symbolic one) offers a spine-tingling, nearly *a cappella* rendition of "Feeling Good," and the kids are cute in "The Beautiful Land" and "That's What It Is to Be Young." They help compensate for the moments where Newley's vibrato careens off the highway.

—MARC MILLER

THE ROBBER BRIDEGROOM
Original Broadway Cast, 1976 (Columbia/Original Cast Records) ★★★★

Let's face it: Country music is not where Broadway shines, but this show is a happy exception to the rule. Librettist-lyricist Alfred Uhry and composer Robert Waldman came up with a fiddle-filled score that beautifully enhances Eudora Welty's story of an innocent young lass who falls in love with the handsome, brooding anti-hero. The enjoyable score includes country waltzes, square dances, toe-tappers, and the most memorable "Two Heads (Are Better Than One)." Many musical theater fans will view this recording as a disappointment because it features the 1976-77 Broadway cast—Barry Bostwick, Rhonda Coullet, Barbara Lang, Lawrence John Moss, Ernie Sabella, Stephen Vinovich, Dennis Warning—rather than the original 1975 cast with Patti LuPone as the heroine. But it's still a swell album.
— PETER FILICHIA

ROBERTA
Studio Cast, 1944 (Decca) ★★★

Roberta is one of the best-remembered musicals of the 1930s, and it owes its fame solely to the efforts of Jerome Kern, whose rapturous music managed to triumph over Otto Harbach's regressive lyrics and an archaic plot in which the leading conflict is a dispute over an evening gown. When was the last time you heard music so gorgeous that it makes you forgive the howlers to which it's married? "So I chaff'd them" and "Happiness forsooth was mine" are only the tip of Harbach's purple-hued iceberg. When you hear the witty "I'll Be Hard to Handle," you may begin to forgive Harbach for his missteps; then you discover that he did not write the lyrics for that song. (They're the work of Bernard Dougall.) Still, a show that includes "Smoke Gets In Your Eyes" and "Yesterdays" can survive many things. The score has fared well in the recording studio, beginning with this album starring Kitty Carlisle, Alfred Drake, and Paula Lawrence. Carlisle's voice is well suited to the imperishable "Smoke Gets in Your Eyes," even though she sounds a bit tentative when she teams with Drake in "The Touch of Your Hand." Lawrence makes expert comic-soubrette sounds; and Drake, who takes the songs written for both the male leads, is in glorious voice. The CD includes Drake's *Vagabond King* set, so it's as much a tribute to this great Broadway star as it is to the dazzling artistry of Jerome Kern.

Film Soundtrack, *Lovely to Look At,* 1952 (MGM/Rhino-Turner) ★★

In venerable musical comedy tradition, the central couple in *Roberta* carries the plot and love songs while the secondary pair gets the zingy numbers and incidental shtick. For the MGM film version of the property, retitled *Lovely to Look At,* three couples are on hand: Howard Keel and Kathryn Grayson for the romance; Marge and Gower Champion for song and dance; and Red Skelton for shtick and Ann Miller for zing. The whole thing is dauntingly glossy, but there are some nice moments. Keel and Grayson perform in synch with their reputations: He's strong-voiced, she's shrill. The Champions could never replace Astaire and Rogers, but they're fun on their own terms, and Miller belts out "I'll Be Hard to Handle" in her best earthy style. The CD offers some interesting numbers that were cut from the film, and boasts crisply remastered sound.

Studio Cast, 1953 (Columbia/Sony) ★★★

This well-cast *Roberta* features Stephen Douglass making wonderfully virile sounds that come close to overpowering the sweetly tentative singing of Joan Roberts. Jack Cassidy and Kaye Ballard, a pair of pros recorded early in their careers, are perfectly attuned to the lighter Kern style; Cassidy's work in particular is effortlessly suave. Portia Nelson is a full-voiced Mme. Roberta (a.k.a. Aunt Minnie), and Lehman Engel's idiomatic conducting ensures that, unlike the MGM film soundtrack, Kern's work isn't smothered by too much schmaltz here. —RICHARD BARRIOS

THE ROCKY HORROR SHOW
Original London Cast, 1973 (First Night) ★

The first recording of Richard O'Brien's kinky cult classic is weak. The cast members include O'Brien himself, Patricia Quinn, Little Nell, Jonathan Adams, Rayner Bourton, and, of course, Tim Curry. Quinn sounds unpleasant singing "Science Fiction Double Feature"; Bourton is even squeakier in "Sword of Damocles." Richard Hartley's orchestrations for a five-piece band are guitar-heavy and unexciting. At under forty minutes, this *Rocky Horror* cast album is shorter than any of the others that follow; missing are "Charles Atlas Song," "Eddie's Teddy," and "Planet, Schmanet, Janet."

Original Roxy Cast, Los Angeles, 1974 (ODE) ★★★

Tim Curry is the only holdover from the London production, and the Stateside cast members do a better job with a show that's rooted in American monster-movie culture, even if it was written by a Brit. Jamie Donnelly gets things off to a great start with a giggly "Science Fiction Double Feature." If B. Miller is a weakish Brad and Bruce Scott a subpar Riff-Raff, the rest of the company shows high energy: Abigale Haness is enjoyable as a deliriously belty Janet; Meat Loaf offers his first blazing Eddie and also has a ball as Dr. Scott. Richard Hartley (billed as Richard Hartly) reorchestrated the score for a larger band that's led by D'Vaughn E. Pershing.

Film Soundtrack, 1975 (ODE/Rhino) ★★

The thing about *The Rocky Horror Picture Show*, as the property became known on celluloid, is that it's iconic and indelible but not very good. Apparent on this disc is the problem that plagues every recording of the score: Without an audience full of rowdy geeks screaming out callbacks, *Rocky Horror* feels incomplete. It's disconcerting to hear the actual lyrics rather than those revised by the audience: "He told us where we stand" should be followed by "on our feet," damn it! Still, some performances on this disc are definitive. Tim Curry is superlative as Frank, and several of the others are very good, but the best to be said about Susan Sarandon's singing is that she isn't totally awful. The first CD edition (ODE) is missing "Sword of Damocles" and "Once in a While" but has two versions of "The Time Warp"; one is a boring remix, the other a karaoke version. The other CD (Rhino) includes both songs dropped from the first CD, plus lots of dialogue—too much, in fact).

Studio Cast, 1995 (JAY) Not recommended.

Christopher Lee as the Narrator and Queen's Brian May as Eddie are, in theory, amusing stunt casting—but only in theory. Everyone else on this recording seems to be doing third-rate imitations of the film cast. The band plays the less-than-good arrangements from the original London production, and the cover art is terrible.

Broadway Cast, 2001 (RCA) ★★★★

At last, a really great recording of *Rocky Horror.* The Broadway revival was dazzling and the cast album is just as good: Tom Hewitt, Alice Ripley, Jarrod Emick, Raúl Esparza, Daphne Rubin-Vega, Dick Cavett, Sebastian LaCause, and Kristin Lee Kelly perform the hell out of the score. Hewitt is hilarious as Frank, especially in his "Sweet Transvestite" number. The one weak link in the cast is Lea DeLaria, a bad choice for Eddie/Dr. Scott. Doug Katsaros' new orchestrations for a six-piece band are terrific. All that's missing is the audience participation; Cavett was a deliciously funny Narrator who bantered regularly with the crowd. But what's here is fantastic.   —SETH CHRISTENFELD

ROMANCE ROMANCE
Original Broadway Cast, 1988 (MCA Classics) ★★

Romance Romance is intelligent and well crafted, yet I can't say that I'm eager to hear it again. The show consists of two one-act musicals. In the first, a pair of rich, bored, nineteenth-century Viennese masquerading as members of the bourgeoisie meet, become romantically involved, and finally reveal the truth. In the second piece, two contemporary couples sharing a house in the Hamptons ponder whether one of the couples is on the verge of adultery. The problem is an absence of defined characters: Alfred and Pepi in the first act are just a man and a woman, while the second-act foursome have no traits to distinguish them from one another or from anyone else. The score has careful writing by lyricist Barry Harman and composer Keith Herrmann. Their songs perform the narrative functions obediently, but we always hear a lyricist at work rather than a character portrayal being built. Cast members Scott Bakula, Alison Fraser, Robert Hoshour, and Deborah Graham all sing well, which does help.   —DAVID WOLF

THE ROTHSCHILDS
Original Broadway Cast, 1970 (Columbia/Sony) ★★★★★

Composer Jerry Bock and lyricist Sheldon Harnick were still at the peak of their productivity, following their great *Fiddler on the Roof* success, when they came up with this sort of rich-man's *Fiddler,* based on the true story of the wealthy and powerful Rothschild family. Listening to the impeccable cast album today, it's hard to believe that *The Rothschilds* was not a blockbuster hit. Happily, this aural document preserves a musical theater masterpiece. The score is exciting, richly melodic, full of intelligence, character, and passion. There are outstanding, Tony Award-winning performances by Hal Linden as Mayer Rothschild and Keene Curtis in multiple roles; also excellent are Paul Hecht as Nathan Rothschild and Jill Clayburgh as Hannah Cohen. "Pleasure and Privilege" and "Everything" are triumphs of ingenuity. The ballad "In My Own Lifetime," a strong comment on the futility of war, is movingly delivered by Linden, as is the wonderful character song "He Tossed a Coin." Bock's music is orchestrated masterfully by Don Walker. This album is a great addition to any collection.   —GERARD ALESSANDRINI

RUGANTINO
Original Broadway Cast, 1965 (Warner Bros./no CD) ★★★

One of the oddest musicals ever to hit Broadway, *Rugantino* first opened in Rome and became an enormous hit. On a visit to Italy, American producer Alexander H. Cohen became so enchanted with the show that he brought it to New York with its Italian libretto and lyrics intact. That was long before sub- or super-titles were in common use in opera houses or elsewhere, so the failure of this "Roman Musical Spectacle" on Broadway had more to do with the language barrier than with the quality of the show. The cast album was recorded in Italy, with the second leading lady replacing the original, and a different singer as the Troubadour. The souvenir program included with the LP provided an extensive synopsis but translations of only a few songs. The librettists-lyricists are Pietro Garinei and Sandro Giovannini; the music is by Armando Trovaioli, composer of numerous Italian film scores and song hits. The score is unique; it has an unclassifiable style that will either entrance you immediately or leave you cold. Added to the language barrier, the songs are not presented on the album in proper sequence; so, even if you follow the synopsis, you may have trouble following the plot. Many musical sections of varying length and importance were not recorded, but the material that's included is performed well. As Rugantino, Nino Manfredi clearly communicates emotion through the Italian lyrics, and so do the other featured singers: Ornella Vanoni, Aldo Fabrizi, and Bice Valori. One of the traditions of a Garinei-Giovannini musical was to take a single song and have it endlessly repeated, reflecting the different characters' points of view in the lyrics. In *Rugantino,* the song given such treatment is "Roma, non fa la stupida stasera," which was recorded by a few American singers as "The Lights of Roma" and became a standard in Italy.

Italian Television Cast, 1978 (CAM) ★★★

When *Rugantino* was revived in Italy, it was videotaped for TV; this soundtrack is the recording of the score that you're most likely to find, and its lavish booklet has a few of the lyrics translated into English. This is a more complete recording than the Broadway album, with extra dance music and so on. The new Rugantino is a crooning Enrico Montesano. Bice Valori and Aldo Fabrizi repeat the roles they originated; Alida Chelli is a fetching Rosetta; and Aldo Donati is a raspy-voiced Troubadour.

Italian Cast, 1998 (CAM) ★★★★

This is the most complete recording of *Rugantino.* The orchestrations are new, and the inclusion of some beautiful incidental music makes the score seem more cohesive. Valerio Mastandrea is strong as the leading man Rugantino; the top-billed Sabrina Ferilli is a fiery Rosetta; Maurizio Mattioli sings the Headsman's songs powerfully; and Fabrizio Rusotto's Troubadour is very effective. —JEFFREY DUNN

RUNAWAYS
Original Broadway Cast, 1978 (Columbia/DRG) ★★★

Elizabeth Swados' revue about street kids, developed by the Public Theater before opening on Broadway, was considered fresh and edgy when it debuted. *Runaways* is a collage of monologues and expressionistic songs featuring a young cast and "popular" music. Even if the occasional disco beats now sound dated, there's lots of great stuff here; the Latin rhythms of "No Lullabies for Luis" and the tribal rap of "Enterprise" are among the best of what composer-lyricist Swados offers up. She also offers some memorable melodies, as in the mesmerizing dirge "Every Now and Then" and the jaunty "Find Me a Hero." Serious subjects like street violence and child prostitution dominate the show, but humor also abounds. Especially funny are "Revenge Song," which has the runaways daydreaming about gruesome fates for their parents; "The Undiscovered Son," in which they imagine their family members as celebrities; and the mocking "Where Are Those People Who Did Hair?" The entire twenty-person ensemble radiates personality, passion, and intelligence; among what was then a largely unknown group are the now-familiar Trini Alvarado and Diane Lane. Karen Evans deserves a special mention for her unforgettable reading of the fiery song "To the Dead of Family Wars."

—BROOKE PIERCE

RUTHLESS!

Original Los Angeles Cast, 1993 (Varèse Sarabande) ★★

Ruthless! is a very campy show about a talented little girl named Tina Denmark who loves to sing and dance. She is surrounded by an all-woman cast, though you can't help wondering if some of them are being played by men (in fact, on this recording, one is). They include an aggressive talent agent named Sylvia St. Croix; Tina's mother, who identifies herself only as "Tina's mother"; Tina's third-grade teacher, who came to New York to be an actress but was mugged and raped before she left Penn Station; and several others, all of whom seem to exist only to exploit Tina. Near the end of the first act, the girl kills someone, which we know because her mother sings: "Oh, what's to become of my only daughter, who I have protected from croup and split ends? So many lessons that I should have taught her—like for example, to not kill her friends." Has Tina murdered another little girl who got a part she wanted? That's possible but, from the album alone, unknowable. Tina is sent away to school and, after that, it's hard to understand the additional characters we meet or anything that happens. The lyrics, by Joel Paley, are often clever and written with real craft; the music, by veteran dance arranger Marvin Laird, is brisk.

—DAVID WOLF

SAIL AWAY
Original Broadway Cast, 1961 (Capitol/Angel) ★★★★
Which show has the best opening and closing numbers for its star? A good bet is the Noël Coward musical *Sail Away.* The show-stopping songs—written expressly for Elaine Stritch—are "Come to Me" and "Why Do the Wrong People Travel?" Stritch is a stitch as a "professional pepper-upper" cruise director on an ocean liner, and her material is a hoot. Listen and guffaw at "Useful Phrases," Coward's clever parody of foreign guidebooks that give translations of sentences no one ever needs ("Please bring me some rhubarb"). Savor "The Little Ones' A-B-C," in which Stritch grapples with her passengers' children. And when romance comes her way, the star is utterly convincing and tender singing "Something Very Strange." Yes, the "Beatnik Love Affair" number, performed by Grover Dale, is an embarrassing attempt by Coward to be au courant. James Hurst is a disappointment as Stritch's young lover—he's supposed to be a breath of fresh air but comes across as uptight—and Patricia Harty is simpering as the show's soubrette. Still, Stritch keeps things happily afloat, so jump aboard for a good listen.

Original London Cast, 1962 (HMV/Fynsworth Alley) ★★★
A year after the show's disappointing few-months' run on Broadway, *Sail Away* crossed over to London, where it was slightly more appreciated. Stritch was still strong at the helm, with David Holliday showing panache as her lover. One of the better songs on the original album, "The Little Ones' A-B-C," is missing here—but this disc does have one word more, "ass," which was replaced in "Why Do the Wrong People Travel" by a trumpet bleat on the more demure Broadway album. Another addition is "Bronxville Darby and Joan," a witty ditty for two minor characters that was cut from the New York staging, restored in London, and included here. Sadly, Irwin Kostal's superb orchestrations have yielded to new, inferior charts by a person who is uncredited. We can understand why the culprit chose to remain anonymous. —PETER FILICHIA

ST. LOUIS WOMAN
Original Broadway Cast, 1946
(Capitol/Angel) ★★★★
Careening between musical comedy and musical tragedy, *St. Louis Woman* is a turn-of-the-century tale with an all-black cast and a score by Harold Arlen and

ALL-TIME FAVORITES
OF LYRICIST
Fred Ebb

1. Guys and Dolls
2. Carousel
3. The King and I
4. She Loves Me
5. The Threepenny Opera
6. Pal Joey
7. Gypsy
8. Kiss Me, Kate
9. Paint Your Wagon
10. The Wild Party (Lippa)

Johnny Mercer that reflects the tonal uncertainty at both ends of the comedy/tragedy spectrum. One minute, the score strives for *Porgy and Bess*-like grandeur ("Leavin' Time"), then it returns to standard-issue, albeit high-grade, Broadway ("Ridin' on the Moon"), and a young Pearl Bailey is always in the wings with another insinuating comic specialty number. But Arlen's music is amazing throughout, Mercer's lyrics are adult and idiomatic, Leon Leonardi's conducting is sensational, and the singers are terrific. June Hawkins infuses "I Had Myself a True Love" and "Sleep Peaceful, Mr. Used-to-Be" with operatic intensity. Ruby Hill is warm and appealing in "Lullaby" and sassy in "Anyplace I Hang My Hat Is Home." Harold Nicholas was a great dancer without much of a voice, but he comes through in "Come Rain or Come Shine." At just under thirty minutes, this is an uncommonly short cast album but also an uncommonly sweet one. And the sound quality, for its age, is excellent.

Encores! Concert Cast, 1998 (Mercury) ★★

This recording captures every note of a City Center Encores! concert staging of *St. Louis Woman* on a CD that's more than twice as long as the Broadway cast album. But from the first few bars—a portentous drum roll, a brassy fanfare, a showy parade of unrelated themes—it disappoints. The original orchestrations have been tarted up with Vegas obviousness, and the big songs are punctuated with even bigger "buttons" at the end; you'd think "Come Rain or Come Shine" was the *Eroica*. Rob Fisher's conducting is strangely cautious, as though applying some heat to the score might scorch it. (Listen to the middle section of "Leavin' Time," so deliberate that it sounds like a school band is playing it.) To be sure, it's terrific to have all the missing material restored; "I Feel My Luck Comin' Down" and "Li'l Augie Is a Natural Man" are joyous rediscoveries. But this cast doesn't make much of the score's riches. Vanessa Williams is a pleasant vocalist, but her much-vaunted va-va-voom doesn't carry over to disc and she's short on individuality in the role of Della. Helen Goldsby's Lila is a disaster as she mumbles her lyrics and sings stiffly. Leading men Stanley Wayne Mathis and Victor Trent Cook are competent but vapid. Only Yvette Cason measures up, offering a very different but equally valid take on Butterfly from that of Pearl Bailey.

—MARC MILLER

SALVATION
Original Off-Broadway Cast, 1969 (Capitol/Angel) ★★★

Unlike some other rock musicals of the period, *Salvation* had no dance or spectacle elements; the physical production was tacky and the show played in an ungainly Off-Broadway space. Yet the songs, by Peter Link and C. C. Courtney, are uncommonly sweet and melodic. The style of the music is so time-specific that, to some modern ears, it may be meaningless. Still, there's a touching simplicity in "Let the Moment Slip By," all about a young woman who didn't sleep with her boyfriend and regrets it after he's killed in Vietnam. "Daedalus" is at once an odd and ravishing tune, especially as performed by jazz singer Yolande Bavan. "In Between," "Gina," "Let's Get Lost in Now," and "If You Let Me Make Love to You, Then Why Can't I Touch You" are arresting '60s rock. The cast, which includes songwriters Link and Courtney along with Joe Morton, Chapman Roberts, Marta Heflin, and Annie Rachel, is vocally strong—and the CD edition of the cast album includes three songs that previously had been issued only on the eight-track tape version of the recording.

—DAVID WOLF

SARAFINA! THE MUSIC OF LIBERATION
Original Cast, 1988 (RCA) ★★★★

Conceived and directed by Mbongeni Ngema, *Sarafina!* is the "little musical that could." Despite considerable financial hardship in moving the show to production, it premiered in Johannesburg, South Africa, and within three months, was transported intact to New York for a limited engagement at Lincoln Center; it proved so popular there that it moved to Broadway, where it received five Tony Award nominations and ran for 597 performances. *Sarafina!* concerns apartheid and its repressive conditions as reflected in the lives of a group of high school students in Soweto during the 1980s. The title character is an endearing rebel who retains her zeal for civil rights despite harassment and incarceration. The score, by Ngema and Hugh Masekela, features the stomping dance rhythms, electronic keyboard, blasts of brass, and idiosyncratic vocal harmonies that are trademarks of Mbaqanga, the pop sound of South Africa's black townships. The album features exhilarating, letter-perfect performances that pulse and spin inexorably toward the climactic number "Bring Back Nelson Mandela," during which Sarafina (Leleti Khumalo) impersonates the imprisoned leader and imagines what he might say upon release.
— CHARLES WRIGHT

SARATOGA
Original Broadway Cast, 1959 (RCA) ★

Edna Ferber's *Saratoga Trunk* had already been adapted as a hit film, so the stage musical version, developed for Broadway as *Saratoga* and rumored to be the most costly production of its day, was eagerly awaited, but it turned out to be a crushing failure. Morton da Costa was in charge of both the book and the direction; Harold Arlen and Johnny Mercer supplied the songs. Tryouts were nightmarish and Arlen departed in disgust, leaving Mercer to compose some of the music. The recording doesn't reflect what was reportedly an exceedingly talky script, but it does reveal the score to have many incomplete musical statements: A nice melodic line suddenly stops without resolution; a jazzy rhythm has little to play against; and nothing is at all memorable. The cast was headed by Carol Lawrence, whose soubrettish manner falls flat, and Howard Keel, who sings well but without much individuality. The humorous "Finding a Man," given its full due by Carol Brice and Odette Myrtil, is the closest thing to a bigtime musical moment.
— RICHARD BARRIOS

SATURDAY NIGHT
Original London Cast, 1998 (First Night) ★

With music and lyrics by a twenty-four-year-old Stephen Sondheim and a book by Julius J. Epstein, *Saturday Night* was supposed to be produced on Broadway in the mid-'50s but didn't have its first fully staged performance until some decades later in London; so this is the world-premiere recording, documenting the show as presented at a fringe theater. The twelve British actors struggle with American accents, and although they aren't much as vocalists, they do exhibit great energy. Sam Newman is passable as Gene, but Anna Francolini is inept as a phony Southern belle. Six musicians play orchestrations that are competent but do not fully reveal the beauty of Sondheim's music.

Original New York Cast, 2000 (Nonesuch) ★★★★★

Stephen Sondheim has described *Saturday Night* as his "baby pictures." Although an anticipated move to Broadway for the 2000 Second Stage production did not happen, this lavish recording was made with thirty-six musicians! Jonathan Tunick's excellent orchestrations, conducted by Steven Freeman, have the thrust of a 1950s Broadway musical, yet they sound entirely appropriate for the 1929 setting of the show. In the evocative, beautifully delivered title song that opens the show, four young men—played by Kirk MacDonald, Greg Zola, Joey Sorge, and Michael Benjamin Washington—lament that they are dateless on the biggest night of the week. Gene, the show's "hero," is introduced in "Class," a complex melody perfectly sung by David Campbell. The young Australian leading man also uses his solid baritenor to excellent dramatic effect in the beautiful duet "Too Many People" with Lauren Ward and in the clever trio "A Moment With You," which Campbell and Ward sing in counterpoint with a record. Ward is delightful in "Isn't It?" and in the fine ballad "All for You." Other standouts are Christopher Fitzgerald in "Exhibit A," slyly explaining to his buddies his *modus operandi* with women, and Andrea Burns and Clarke Thorell as a married couple cutely reminiscing about their first date in "I Remember That." Wonderful group numbers—"Delighted, I'm Sure," "In the Movies," "One Wonderful Day," and "What More Do I Need?"—fully reveal who the characters are and give all of the cast members chances to shine.   —JEFFREY DUNN

SATURDAY NIGHT FEVER
Film Soundtrack, 1977 (Polydor) ★★

Iconic though this movie may be, the blockbuster soundtrack album of *Saturday Night Fever* is distressingly dated. Even if individual songs are terrific, how much disco can you stand in one sitting? That's the defining factor here: the Bee Gees' falsetto deliveries of "Stayin' Alive," "Night Fever," "How Deep Is Your Love?" and so on. In addition to two versions of "More Than a Woman," there's Walter Murphy's "A Fifth of Beethoven"—a disco version of Beethoven's Ninth Symphony—and "If I Can't Have You," performed by Yvonne Elliman. Also included are a few instrumental tracks written by David Shire.

Original London Cast, 1998 (Polydor) Not recommended.

This recording begins with an overture that quotes "Stayin' Alive," and then it just gets worse. The film soundtrack has better versions of all the songs even if it lacks the two new items that the Bee Gees wrote for the stage show: the unpleasant battle-of-the-sexes dance number "It's My Neighborhood" and the bad ballad "Immortality." Adam Garcia may have been charismatic as Tony Manero onstage, but on disc, he's just another mediocre singer. Tara Wilkinson's "If I Can't Have You" is an unmemorable performance by an unmemorable singer, and the other cast members aren't any better. The disc is mercifully brief, containing only about half of the score and none of Nan Knighton's "book" for the musical. In this case, less is definitely more.   —SETH CHRISTENFELD

SAY, DARLING
Original Broadway Cast, 1958 (RCA/no CD) ★★

First, novelist Richard Bissell wrote 7 1/2 *Cents*, which he turned into *The Pajama Game*. Then he wrote a novella about his experiences on that show, which in turn served as the basis for *Say, Darling*, a moderately successful "comedy about a musical." That designation clues us in: This is not really a musical at all, just a play with some incidental songs by Jule Styne, Betty Comden, and Adolph Green. Most of the numbers are performance pieces that don't advance the plot; some of them—such as "The Husking Bee" and "Chief of Love"—are intentionally cheesy. The two leads, Johnny Desmond and Vivian Blaine, are respectively oily and bland, although it's interesting to hear Blaine use her contralto belt instead of her Adelaide adenoids. David Wayne, playing a small-town innocent who mixes with Broadway sharpies, has more personality than either of the stars; he puts over the unimpressive "Something's Always Happening on the River" through sheer force of will. The title song and the "Dance Only With Me" waltz are sweet ballads, and the arrangements by Sid Ramin—created specifically for the recording—are supercharged. But, after a rousing Styne overture, there's just not much going on here.

—MARC MILLER

THE SCARLET PIMPERNEL
Original Broadway Cast, 1997 (Atlantic) ★★★

Despite the antipathy leveled at this effort by composer Frank Wildhorn and lyricist Nan Knighton to adapt the Baroness Orczy's classic novel into a lavish neo-operetta for Broadway, *The Scarlet Pimpernel* has its merits as heard on this disc. The score nods at current conventions but also loads up on fanciful eighteenth-century atmosphere. Wildhorn does occasionally stoop to cheap effects (he never met a key change he didn't like), and Knighton's lyrics wouldn't rob Sondheim of sleep, but they're at least competent and occasionally better; check out her genuinely witty "The Creation of Man," which has the nerve to rhyme "haberdashery" with "make a splash, cherie." Christine Andreas gets the best material, or maybe it's just that her lustrous soprano makes it sound that way: a luminous "When I Look at You," a lively "Vivez!" and a Piaf-like "Storybook." Douglas Sills, in a high-profile debut, brings a rangy tenor and an engaging brio to the title role. As Chauvelin, Terrence Mann growls his way through some lesser, *Les Miz*-knockoff material. The hard-sell big finishes, needless reprises, and all those key changes can be grating, but such is the stuff of operetta.

"Encore" Recording, 1999 (Atlantic) ★

Although it dropped millions, *The Scarlet Pimpernel* ran for two years, during which time its songs were rearranged, reassigned, and substituted; this lavishly packaged CD reflects all the revisions. The new version of the show featured not only new material but two new performers in the roles of Marguerite and Chauvelin: Rachel York and Rex Smith, the latter's rock-star snarls and posturings amusingly out of place amid all the Louis XVI trappings. The changes to the score are unabashedly populist: a new, heavy-breathing ballad called "I'll Forget You," the repositioning of "Storybook" at the top of the show, and so on. Although York is a pro, she hasn't quite the vocal finesse of Andreas, but Douglas Sills remains in fine, swashbuckling form as the hero. You may also enjoy Smith's sneering performance, which accomplishes a high-wire feat previously considered impossible: He's hammier than Terrence Mann!

—MARC MILLER

THE SECRET GARDEN
Original Broadway Cast, 1991 (Columbia) ★★★★★

The Lucy Simon-Marsha Norman musicalization of the beloved Frances Hodgson Burnett novel *The Secret Garden* worked its charm on Broadway for more than seven hundred performances. The writing, cast, and production were all first-rate, as is this cast recording. A generous helping of dialogue on the CD helps establish the show's atmosphere. Norman's intelligent, well-crafted lyrics (printed in the CD booklet) and Simon's masterful score are even more rewarding with repeated listening. Mandy Patinkin, Rebecca Luker, Daisy Eagan, Robert Westenberg, John Cameron Mitchell, and Alison Fraser give well-sung performances rich with musical nuance and detailed characterization. Among the disc's highlights: Fraser has the chipper "If I Had a Fine White Horse" and the closest thing in the show to an anthem, "Hold On." Patinkin and Westenberg sing the powerful "Lily's Eyes" to perfection. Mitchell is winning in a pair of quirky numbers, while Luker and Patinkin share the superb love duet "How Could I Ever Know?" Eagan is at the center of it all with her Tony Award-winning performance, well represented in dialogue and song on this splendid CD.

Highlights With Australian Cast, 1995 (Polydor) ★★

Anthony Warlow, Marina Prior, and Philip Quast lead the cast of this recording, which consists of only eight selections from the *Secret Garden* score. The performances run the gamut from excellent to troubling. Tom Blair starts things off with a sluggish "Winter's on the Wing." Warlow's "Race You to the Top of the Morning" and "Where in the World" are strong, and his "How Could I Ever Know?" with Prior is also effective. But Mary Lennox (Samantha Fiddes) is barely present, showing up only to do her half of "Wick," and Susan-Ann Walker doesn't have the necessary power for "Hold On." The orchestra, though full-sized, sounds strangely thin at times.

Original London Cast, 2001 (First Night) ★★★★

A radically different *Secret Garden* is heard here, the show having undergone major rewrites for tightening and focusing purposes. The restructuring does a great job of helping to tell the story. Other bonuses include a large and lush orchestra and a goodly amount of underscored dialogue with enhancing and evocative sound effects. On the whole, the singers are less successful than those on the Broadway album in terms of musicality and characterization, but there's one exception: the ultra-sharp performance of Linzi Hateley as Martha. Keeping her company on this disc are Freddie Davies as Ben and some impressive chorus boys in the "Garden Suite." But Craig Purnell struggles with the notes and lyrics of "Winter's on the Wing"; a thin-voiced Philip Quast lacks bravura; and Meredith Braun doesn't sound quite right in "How Could I Ever Know?"
—MORGAN SILLS

THE SECRET LIFE OF WALTER MITTY
Original Off-Broadway Cast, 1964 (Columbia/no CD) ★★★

Based on a popular short story by James Thurber that had already inspired a film starring Danny Kaye, *The Secret Life of Walter Mitty*—adapted by librettist Joe Manchester—features a score by composer Leon Carr and lyricist Earl Shuman, who have not had a musical produced since. Despite reasonably positive reviews, the production had a short run. Yet this is a score of high quality, filled with inventive melodies and clever lyrics, and the cast is wonderfully talented. In the title role, Marc London conveys an apt nebbishy quality but springs into exuberant life when needed. He excels in "Now That I Am Forty"; "Don't Forget," a funny harangue duet with the big-voiced Lorraine Serabian, who plays Walter's wife; and "Walking With Penninah," a charm song for Walter and his daughter (Christopher Norris). As Willa de Wisp, Cathryn Damon exudes star quality in "Marriage Is for Old Folks" and in the French-chanteuse fantasy "Fan the Flame." It's fun to hear Rue McClanahan share the duet "Two Little Pussycats" with Lette Rehnolds, and there are entertaining numbers for the denizens of the bar where Walter hangs out—especially Eugene Roche's "Hello, I Love You, Goodbye," a smug lesson for Walter on how to deal with women. Then there is the first-act-ending "Confidence," a march in which Walter makes the decision to change his life; if the tune sounds familiar, that's probably because it's been used as theme music for many sports telecasts. There are also some recurring themes, a few pleasant ballads, and a happy-ending finale.
—JEFFREY DUNN

SECRETS EVERY SMART TRAVELER SHOULD KNOW
Off-Broadway Cast, 1999 (RCA) ★★

Many composers and lyricists turned out a mixed bag of songs and sketches for this occasionally clever revue. In *Secrets Every Smart Traveler Should Know,* nearly all of the numbers fall into the category of special material that's more about the lyrics than the music. Given the show's title, the obvious choices for song content are here—from the cute "Naked in Pittsburgh" (about lost luggage) to the round-trip finale titled (you guessed it!) "Home." Musical supervisor-arranger Stan Freeman contributes the smart "See It Now" and the amusing running gag "This Is Your Captain Speaking." An enjoyable detour is a clever *Private Lives* spoof performed by Nick Santa Maria and Maribeth Graham. Several bits in Glen Kelly's "The French Song," sung by Graham and Denise Nolan, are also fun. Cabaret performers will find this CD chock full of potential comic material for their acts, but *Secrets* just doesn't know when to quit, getting to the end of the road with songs about Montezuma's revenge and traveling on "Aging Planes." Also, the cast's heavy-handed approach to comedy makes the ride bumpier; apparently, none of these secrets were meant to be whispered. As a result, the often-strident singing on this album becomes grating, so this is a trip that many listeners will want to take only once.   — MORGAN SILLS

SEESAW
Original Broadway Cast, 1973 (Buddah/DRG) ★★★

"Up, down; up, down" goes a lyric in the title tune, and that's a good barometer for this Cy Coleman-Dorothy Fields musical based on the William Gibson play *Two for the Seesaw.* First the good news: As the uptight Omaha lawyer Jerry Ryan, Ken Howard sings the nicely teasing ballad "You're a Loveable Lunatic" to his new-found girlfriend, the eccentric Gittel Mosca, played by Michele Lee. When he fully lets loose, Howard has an up-tempo gem in "We've Got It." (Note the joyous Larry Fallon orchestration when Howard says, "Fred Astaire came from Omaha, y'know" and the marvelous rideout that follows.) Gittel's numbers aren't as good, although "Nobody Does It Like Me" is a decent example of those self-deprecating songs that musical theater heroines sometimes sing. As for the bad material: "My City" is not inviting and "Chapter 54, Number 1909" is even less so. When musical theater buffs discuss the worst songs ever written for Broadway, this show's "Ride Out the Storm" comes up often. Still, "It's Not Where You Start, It's Where You Finish" (performed by Tommy Tune) is not only a good song but also an excellent metaphor for *Seesaw,* which started out shakily and righted itself only after director/show-doctor Michael Bennett came in.   — PETER FILICHIA

SEUSSICAL
Original Broadway Cast, 2000 (Decca) ★★★

Whatever was wrong with producers Barry and Fran Weissler's attempts to cobble a musical out of bits and pieces of Dr. Seuss' cherished children's books, it certainly wasn't the Stephen Flaherty-Lynn Ahrens score. Flaherty's unfailingly tuneful melodies run the gamut of always-appropriate pastiche, including soft rock, jazz, blues, salsa, folk, and, yes, a little ragtime. This composer is always good for a great ballad or two as well; here, there's the yearning, soaring "Alone in the Universe" and "Solla Sollew," a bewitching lullaby in the "Toyland" tradition. Ahrens' lyrics are Seussier than Seuss: for example, "If you're hungry, there's schlopp in the frig-e-merator!" Happily, the "life lessons" demanded of a children's musical aren't pounded into the ground—although "A person's a person, no matter how small" gets more airing than may be necessary. The sound effects-heavy cast album conveys all the ingeniousness of the score but also betrays some of the misjudgment that marred the short-lived Broadway production of *Seussical.* Making the Cat in the Hat the evening's emcee is sensible, but the gifted mime David Shiner isn't the man for the job; he's simply not a singer and his overemphatic line readings are out of Saturday-morning cartoons. Sharon Wilkins' Sour Kangaroo overshoots the runway, too, with her astringent blues inflections and contrived melismas. But most of the principals are just right: Kevin Chamberlin's sweet-souled Horton, Janine LaManna's hapless Gertrude McFuzz, Michele Pawk's brassy Mayzie LaBird, and Anthony Blair Hall's uncloying JoJo. And how nice to find Broadway veteran Alice Playten in the supporting cast as the Whoville mayor's droll wife. —MARC MILLER

SEVENTEEN

Original Broadway Cast, 1951 (RCA/no CD) ★★

"Willie, get a wiggle on!" That characteristic, gee-whiz, chorus-boy exhortation, in a song called "Weatherbee's Drug Store," opens the cast album of this aggressively homespun show chronicling the 1907 Hoosier romance of Willie Baxter (Kenneth Nelson) and flirty Lola Pratt (Ann Crowley). Based on a Booth Tarkington novel and positively wallowing in the same postwar nostalgia that sired so many movie musicals of the day, *Seventeen* aims for charm in its score by Walter Kent and Kim Gannon. The treacle gets thick in songs like "Summertime Is Summertime" and "A Headache and a Heartache," while the performances are often arch; get a load of the vocal preening in "This Was Just Another Day" and "Ode to Lola." Still, there are a couple of fine show tunes here—"I Could Get Married Today" and "Reciprocity"—supported by plush Ted Royal orchestrations. And though the cast isn't starry, the album does offer early audio peeks at *The Fantasticks'* Nelson and that distinctive *Greenwillow* ingenue, Ellen McCown. The recording is barely forty minutes in length, but what's there is a like a rich ice cream soda: too foamy and sweet, yet it still goes down easily. —MARC MILLER

1776

Original Broadway Cast, 1969 (Columbia/Sony) ★★★★

History teacher-turned-songwriter Sherman Edwards turned his idea for a musical about the writing and adoption of the Declaration of Independence into *1776,* one of Broadway's most distinctive hits. Although Peter Stone's libretto has garnered kudos, Edwards' score is seldom given its due, but it's replete with flavor, character, and stirring emotionalism. This recording documents that score—with Eddie Sauter's grand orchestrations and Peter Howard's top-notch musical direction—at its freshest and most exciting. William Daniels is the definitive John Adams, displaying a combination of fire, ice, desperation, and dry humor in songs like "Piddle, Twiddle, and Resolve" and "Is Anybody There?" Rex Everhart does quite well as the ribald Benjamin Franklin, spelling original cast member Howard da Silva, who had suffered a heart attack and was absent for the recording sessions but eventually returned to the show. Ken Howard brings an earnest likability to Thomas Jefferson; Ron Holgate's joyful bombast as Richard Henry Lee is infectious; and Paul Hecht and Clifford David make formidable opponents in Adams' quest for independence. "Molasses to Rum," in which David's Edward Rutledge takes on the infamous Triangle Trade, is the recording's most brilliant and frightening moment. Virginia Vestoff gives a vibrantly romantic performance as Abigail Adams, while future Broadway powerhouse Betty Buckley belts out Martha Jefferson's coyly suggestive "He Plays the Violin."

Original London Cast, 1970 (Columbia/no CD) ★★★

The London production of *1776* had a brief run and this recording is now a difficult-to-find curiosity, but a few of the performances are truly remarkable. Lewis Fiander's John Adams is sweeping and energetic, the best-sung Adams recorded, and Ronald Radd's booming baritone provides Franklin with that role's lustiest interpretation. Vocally challenging items like "Cool, Cool, Considerate Men" and "Momma Look Sharp" receive rich renditions by Bernard Lloyd and David Firth, respectively, while David Kernan's "Molasses to Rum" is first-rate. Under Ray Cook's musical direction, the ensemble is full of dynamic singers and the orchestra is clear and precise. Still, the recording is not without its problems: John Quentin has trouble with what little music Jefferson is asked to sing; Vivienne Ross's voice is distractingly thin for Abigail; and Cheryl Kennedy's Martha is somewhat cloying.

Film Soundtrack, 1972 (Columbia/no CD) ★★★

With so many of the original Broadway leads retained, the film version of *1776* is one of the most faithful film versions of a stage musical, and the soundtrack recording documents that very little was lost in transition. Daniels, Vestoff, Howard, and Holgate recreate their roles and they all sound better here than on the Broadway cast album. Howard da Silva finally got to record his Franklin and is so delightful in the role that it was well worth the wait. Blythe Danner is a softer, more tentatively sung, yet ultimately more effective Martha Jefferson than Buckley was. John Cullum assumes the role of Rutledge and provides a solid "Molasses to Rum."

Broadway Cast, 1997 (TVT) ★★

This is the most frustrating recording of the *1776* score. It's the most complete—with all of the usual songs, a fair amount of dialogue, "Compliments," all of "The Lees of Old Virginia," and the rarely heard lead-in to "Is Anybody There?"—but most of the performances lack drive. Brent Spiner sings well enough but his Adams always sounds annoyed; Pat Hingle's Franklin is frail and uncertain; Lauren Ward's Martha is somewhat flavorless; and a number of the other smaller supporting roles lack bite. On the plus side, Linda Emond sings Abigail quite attractively; Gregg Edelman's Rutledge and Michael Cumpsty's Dickinson are dependable; and Paul Michael Valley is the best-sung Jefferson on record. But Brian Besterman's orchestrations and a reduced number of musicians conducted too sedately by Paul Gemignani prevent the recording from ever really getting off the ground. — MATTHEW MURRAY

SEVENTH HEAVEN
Original Broadway Cast, 1955 (Decca) ★★

Seventh Heaven received mixed-to-negative reviews and closed fairly quickly, but the show's impressive music earned it this recording. Composer Victor Young's rich melodies are paired with Stella Unger's often catchy, but sometimes silly, lyrics. ("I'm richer than Midas, I'm high as a kite is" and "To all headwaiters named François, I wish you all a very cordial au revoir" are two examples.) Yet the stronger numbers outweigh the weaker ones and the performers put the material over skillfully. Robert Clary, as a pickpocket, performs the humorous "Happy Little Crook" and the delightful "Love Sneaks Up on You" with the baby-voiced Patricia Hammerlee as a prostitute. Clary also leads the ensemble in the rousing "C'est La Vie," which opens and closes the musical. Chita Rivera and Gerrianne Raphael as happy hookers join Hammerlee in a powerful rendition of "Camille, Colette, Fifi"—but they don't do as well with "Love, Love, Love." Leading lady Gloria DeHaven has a solid ballad in "Where Is That

Someone for Me?" but her "If It's a Dream" is not up to snuff; nor is Ricardo Montalban's "A 'Miss-You' Kiss" or "A Man With a Dream," although he does good work in the waltz "Remarkable Fellow." The one duet for Montalban and DeHaven, "Sun at My Window, Love at My Door," has lyrics that may give you the giggles but the melody and performances will satisfy. There's also some lovely dance music: "The White and Gold Ballet" as listed on the LP, "Chico's Reverie" as listed on the CD. One of the two bonus tracks is Marian Caruso singing "Blessings"; the other is DeHaven doing a pop version of "Where Is That Someone for Me?" with Victor Young and his orchestra. — JEFFREY DUNN

70, GIRLS, 70

Original Broadway Cast, 1971 (Columbia/Sony) ★★★

Despite its failure on Broadway, *70, Girls, 70* is too much fun on recording to pass up. Scored by composer John Kander and lyricist Fred Ebb, the musical has a book by Ebb and Norman L. Martin (with an adaptation credit for Joe Masteroff), based on the English play *Breath of Spring*. The show's characters are residents of a Manhattan hotel for the aged who turn to grand larceny to spice up their lives. Perhaps what doomed the musical was the overly complicated show-within-a-show concept, in which a gang of veteran performers frequently step out of the action to perform numbers about the vicissitudes of old age. These songs—such as "Old Folks," "Broadway, My Street," and "Coffee in a Cardboard Cup"—are the most enjoyable in the score, especially as delivered by this ball-of-fire cast. The title tune, with its rousing banjo passages, is a gem; less interesting are "The Caper," which lays out the plan for the first robbery, and "The Elephant Song," an overlong eleven-o'clock number in which leading lady Ida (Mildred Natwick) announces her own imminent death. Natwick, however, is delightful throughout, especially in "Home," an inviting rhumba, and "Yes," a lively tune that sums up the song-writers' live-for-today philosophy. Equally peppy are Hans Conreid, Lillian Roth, and Lillian Hayman. A standout number is "Go Visit (Your Grandmother)," featuring Yiddish-theater veteran Henrietta Jacobson with Tommy Breslin; the song includes some eyebrow-raising lyrics ("Go ahead and give the old lady a laugh / You went to Fire Island last summer? / For God's sake, show her the photographs!"). Don Walker's orchestrations make extensive use of onstage pianist Dorothea Freitag and provide a propulsive undertow for every number.

Original London Cast, 1991 (JAY) ★★★

This recording is an appealing alternative to the Broadway album. The London production of *70, Girls, 70* starred Dora Bryan and featured a new book by David Thompson and Norman L. Martin that eliminated some of the lesser numbers while adding pleasant new ones: "Well Laid Plans" and "I Can't Do That Anymore." Julian Kelly's new, more intimate orchestrations work nicely. The CD offers lively renditions of the score's highlights, sparked by Bryan's warbly but witty singing. — DAVID BARBOUR

SHE LOVES ME

Original Broadway Cast, 1963 (MGM/Polydor) ★★★★★

"Charming, romantic, perfect"—those words from the song "Dear Friend" define *She Loves Me,* a true masterpiece of the American musical theater. A two-LP recording transferred to one fabulous CD preserves almost the entire score. Based on a play that inspired the films *The Shop Around the Corner, In the Good Old Summertime,* and *You've Got Mail,* the show tells of warring Budapest shop clerks who don't realize they've been sending anonymous love letters to each other. The songs, by composer Jerry Bock and lyricist Sheldon Harnick, blend seamlessly with the work of librettist Joe Masteroff, and the recorded performances are flawless. Barbara Cook is so much more than a typical ingenue, finding nuance and complexity in the role of the needy, neurotic, vulnerable Amalia; her renditions of "Dear Friend," "Ice Cream," and "Will He Like Me?" exemplify what great musical theater singing is all about. When Cook does "I Don't Know His Name" with Barbara Baxley as "bad girl" Ilona, the vocal contrast is divine, and it's a moment to treasure when Cook raises her voice to a hysterical soprano-belt with Daniel Massey in the frenzied "Where's My Shoe?" As "Dear Friend" Georg, Massey is convincingly shy and nervous in "Tonight at Eight" and winning in the exultant title song. Baxley rips into "I Resolve" and then simply oozes out "A Trip to the Library." Jack Cassidy, as the suave roué Kodaly, caresses "Ilona" seductively and makes the grandest of exits in "Grand Knowing You." The roles of Maraczek ("Days Gone By"), Sipos ("Perspective"), and Arpad ("Try Me") are done to a turn by Ludwig Donath, Nathaniel Frey, and Ralph Williams, and Wood Romoff is very funny as the Headwaiter in "A Romantic Atmosphere." I defy you to listen to the finale of Act II as sung and acted by Cook and Massey without getting a tear in your eye.

Original London Cast, 1964 (HMV/Angel) ★★★★

An abridged recording of a great score, this *She Loves Me* lacks "Days Gone By," "Goodbye, Georg," "Tango Tragique," "Where's My Shoe," "Will He Like Me?" and the dialogue leading into the finale. "I Resolve" is replaced by a new song for Ilona titled "Heads I Win," sung here with blistering strength by Rita Moreno, who also does an amazing job with "A Trip to the Library." The "Three Letters" sequence for Amalia and Georg was also reconceived for London and features members of the ensemble as other lovelorn correspondents. Anne Rogers is a sweet if somewhat bland Amalia, Gary Raymond is a believable Georg, and Gary Miller is a dashing Kodaly. Gregory Phillips sings adorably as Arpad, but Carl Jaffe as the Headwaiter is shockingly off-key throughout "A Romantic Atmosphere." For this first London production, many of the show's lyrics were Anglicized and some were rewritten to rhyme with the British pronunciations.

Broadway Cast, 1993 (Varèse Sarabande) ★★★★

This energetic recording of the Roundabout Theatre's revival of *She Loves Me* has the skillfully reduced orchestrations by Frank Matosich, Jr. and David Krane that were heard in the theater, and there are a few changes to the original score: Georg's "Tango Tragique" is heard only as an instrumental; a brief reprise of "Days Gone By" is eliminated; and some adjustments are made in "Twelve Days to Christmas." A nice amount of dialogue, underscoring, and incidental music gives the album a real sense of theatrical flow. Diane Fratantoni (now known as Diane Sutherland) sings well as Amalia. Boyd Gaines may sound too emotionally secure as Georg but he's still charming, adding some nice touches to "Tonight at Eight" and "She Loves Me." As Kodaly, Howard McGillin makes deceit almost likable in "Ilona" and "Grand Knowing You." Louis Zorich, Lee Wilkof, and Brad Kane as Maraczek, Sipos, and Arpad are all fine in their solos. Sally Mayes is distinctive in Ilona's numbers, Jonathan Freeman is a terrific Headwaiter, and the ensemble is high-spirited.

London Cast, 1994 (First Night) ★★★★

The astonishingly versatile Ruthie Henshall is a delight as Amalia, and her chemistry with John Gordon Sinclair as Georg is palpable on this CD. The supporting cast is good, particularly Barry James as Sipos, Simon Connolly as Arpad, and Tracie Bennett as Ilona. Only Gerard Casey as

Kodaly is outclassed by his predecessors in the role. This is another highly theatrical recording of the *She Loves Me* score; intriguingly, the lyrics that were Anglicized for the original London production have reverted back to the American originals. —JEFFREY DUNN

SHELTER

Off-Broadway Cast, 1997 (Original Cast Records) ★★★

Seven years after the 1973 Broadway failure of *Shelter*, librettist-lyricist Gretchen Cryer and composer Nancy Ford rewrote the show, combining it with the first act of their earlier musical *The Last Sweet Days of Isaac*. In 1997, a newly titled revision, *The Last Sweet Days*, was presented by the York Theatre Company; that production was recorded here under the title *Shelter*. (Got that?) But rather than solving the problems of their two unsuccessful musicals, all the team did was create a third show that substitutes a certain verbosity for dramatic action. In the first act of *Shelter*, Isaac is more than a little crazy; in the second act, the character (who has changed his name to Michael) monstrously mistreats his wife, his girlfriend, and a woman named Ingrid, whom he had known earlier and has just met again and bedded, but this plot twist adds no resonance or meaning to the piece. In sum, *Shelter* is a tedious, sedentary soap opera about "relationships," albeit one filled with imaginative touches and a bunch of good songs, nicely sung here by Willy Falk, Ellen Foley, Ellen Sowney, and Romain Frugé as the voice of Arthur, a singing computer. —DAVID WOLF

SHENANDOAH

Original Broadway Cast, 1975 (RCA) ★★★

Based on a film of the same name, *Shenandoah* tells the story of Charlie Anderson, a widowed Virginian who tries in vain to keep his family uninvolved in the Civil War. Librettist James Lee Barrett adapted his screenplay in collaboration with Philip Rose and Peter Udell; the songs are by lyricist Udell and composer Gary Geld. The musical enjoyed a healthy run, due in part to the magisterial, Tony Award-winning performance of John Cullum as Anderson. The homey, country-tinged score is unfailingly tuneful, with the joyous "Freedom"—sung by Donna Theodore and Chip Ford—a standout. "Next to Lovin' I Like Fightin'"—a testosterone-infused number for the six Anderson sons—is rousing. (Sample lyric: "Next to poetry and prose, I like punchin' me a nose!") "Violets and Silverbells," "The Only Home I Know," and a few other songs are rather treacly, but Cullum's numbers carry the show: He's bracingly angry in "I've Heard It All Before," tender in "The Pickers Are Comin'" and "Papa's Gonna Make It Alright," and commanding in his two "Meditations." —MICHAEL PORTANTIERE

SHERRY!

Studio Cast, 2004 (Angel, 2CDs) ★★★

Every flop musical should be so lucky: A deluxe presentation with an all-star cast and a fifty-two-piece orchestra (sixty-seven for the overture!), this two-disc recording features every note and every cut song, plus some interviews. *Sherry!* is composer Laurence Rosenthal and librettist-lyricist James Lipton's 1967 tuner based on George S. Kaufman and Moss Hart's classic comedy *The Man Who Came to Dinner*. The diverting score—conducted by Marvin Laird and sumptuously played—is smartly orchestrated to sound like a 1930s movie musical, but the bitchiness of the material becomes monotonous and many of the numbers are extraneous. As for the cast, Nathan Lane hasn't the innate elegance for Sheridan Whiteside, and Carol Burnett is comically expert but vocally worn in Lorraine's songs. Bernadette Peters sounds lovely as Maggie in the ballads "Maybe It's Time for Me" and "Imagine That"; Tom Wopat partners her with relaxed assurance. Tommy Tune is excellent as Beverly Carlton, and smaller roles are taken by Phyllis Newman, Lillias White, and Mike Myers. Even Rosenthal and Lipton participate, performing like seasoned troupers.   —MARK MILLER

SHOW BOAT

Original London Cast, 1928 (Columbia/HMV/Pearl) ★★★

Composer Jerome Kern and librettist-lyricist Oscar Hammerstein's *Show Boat* premiered in New York in 1927, but the original Broadway cast was not recorded. Performed here by what is billed as "The Mississippi Chorus" are tab versions of "Cotton Blossom," "Queenie's Ballyhoo," "In Dahomey," and "Can't Help Lovin' Dat Man," all in their original choral arrangements. In "Make Believe," Edith Day is a charming Magnolia and Howett Worster a very fine Ravenal in all three of their duets. In London, Paul Robeson finally got to play the role of Joe that was written for him (though not played by him during the original Broadway staging), but unfortunately, the "Ol' Man River" chosen for inclusion here is Robeson's surprisingly casual, 1928 studio recording with the Paul Whiteman Orchestra. (Also represented on this disc is the Joe of the original Broadway production, Jules Bledsoe, who offers a suitably tough and angry "Ol' Man River.") Marie Burke's "Can't Help Lovin' Dat Man" and "Bill" are good, if unexceptional. Day's "Dance Away the Night," written for this production, is bright and bouncy. The Pearl CD includes selections from the London casts of Kern's *Sunny* and Rodgers and Hart's *Lido Lady.*

Original Broadway and Studio Casts, 1932 (Columbia-CBS/ASV-Living Era) ★★

Helen Morgan, who played Julie in the original Broadway staging and 1932 revival of *Show Boat,* sings "Can't Help Lovin' Dat Man" and "Bill." Paul Robeson (Joe in the 1932 revival) delivers a stirring "Ol' Man River." James Melton is overly florid in solo versions of "Make Believe" and "You Are Love," but Countess Olga Albani displays a nice soprano in "Why Do I Love You?" (with Frank Munn). An overture and finale are also included, with eight selections conducted by Victor Young.

Broadway Cast, 1946 (Columbia/Sony) ★★

For this revival, Oscar Hammerstein stripped away many of the comedy aspects of *Show Boat* and focused on the drama. Robert Russell Bennett gave his 1927 orchestrations a more 1940s Broadway sound. The new overture is well conducted by Edwin McArthur, but "Cotton Blossom" is rushed and sounds strangely old-fashioned on this recording. Jan Clayton is an earnest Magnolia, but Charles Fredericks lacks character as Ravenal. The orchestral lead-in to "Ol' Man River" is almost laughable; Kenneth Spencer restores some dignity to the song with his earthy approach but, unfortunately, the second verse is omitted. Carol Bruce began the tradition of Julies who are less soprano and more husky-voiced; she uses throaty sounds impressively in both "Can't Help Lovin' Dat Man" and "Bill." Colette Lyons is a conventional soubrette as Ellie, squeakingly cute in a very brisk version of "Life Upon the Wicked Stage" that includes some of "I Might Fall Back on You" as dance music. Jan Clayton's "Nobody Else but Me," reputedly the last song Kern ever wrote, brings this ten-track recording to a lively finish.

Film Soundtrack, 1951 (MGM/Rhino-Turner) ★★

This CD almost sounds like a *Show Boat* suite for voices and orchestra, played with very slow tempi. Howard Keel and Kathryn Grayson are in top form and the MGM Orchestra makes magnificent sounds as conducted by Adolph Deutsch. There is a powerful if turgid "Ol' Man River" by William Warfield and a lovely "Make Believe" (reprise) by Keel. Annette Warren sings Julie's songs for Ava Gardner, as in the film, but the final tracks of the Rhino CD give us Gardner herself singing "Can't Help Lovin' Dat Man" and "Bill" very well.

Studio Cast, 1956 (RCA/no CD) Not recommended.

Show Boat goes down in defeat here. One of the earliest "crossover" recordings of a musical, this entry features Metropolitan Opera stars Robert Merrill, Patrice Munsel, and Risë Stevens. Their singing is disappointingly colorless, as are Janet Pavek and Kevin Scott's turns as Ellie and Frank. The orchestrations aren't the originals and aren't very good. The LP includes the often-omitted "Till Good Luck Comes My Way," but Merrill makes this dull, too. "Dance Away the Night," written for the 1928 London staging, is given a lifeless performance here; but Merrill can't be blamed for his "Ol' Man River," a bad idea in the first place.

Studio Cast, 1958 (RCA/no CD) Not recommended.

From the overture on, this recording makes you feel like you're trapped in an elevator, so Muzak-like is Henri René's orchestra (no arranger credited). Howard Keel is in good voice but sounds detached, and Anne Jeffreys' usually lustrous soprano seems under wraps. Gogi Grant is a torchy Julie in too-slow renditions of "Can't Help Lovin' Dat Man" and "Bill." Although there are a few interesting inclusions—"Nobody Else but Me," "Till Good Luck Comes My Way," and "Where's the Mate for Me?"—this *Show Boat* sinks.

Studio Cast, 1959 (EMI/no CD) ★

A wild combination of disparate elements, this *Show Boat* recording has soupy arrangements, often woefully slow tempi, and awful orchestrations. Shirley Bassey is a restrained Julie; New Zealander Inia Te Wiata's "Ol' Man River" is well sung; Don McKay and Marlys Watters display lovely voices in their three big duets as Ravenal and Magnolia; Dora Bryan's Ellie exudes showbiz know-how in "Life Upon the Wicked Stage" and, with Geoffrey Webb, in "I Might Fall Back on You."

Studio Cast, 1961 (Columbia/Sony) ★

Theatricality is missing from this *Show Boat*. While John Raitt's Ravenal and Barbara Cook's Magnolia are nicely sung, their "Make Believe" seems incomplete. Their "You Are Love" is only adequate, and the singers are swamped by the orchestrations in "Why Do I Love You?" William Warfield is solid but unexciting in Joe's "Ol' Man River." Anita Darian's Julie is almost coquettish in "Bill," yet warm and honest when caressing "Can't Help Lovin' Dat Man." Fay DeWitt has a bubbly belt and is reasonably droll in Ellie's "Life Upon the Wicked Stage," but the female chorus drags down the number. In fact, every time the Merrill Staton Choir takes over, singing with little feeling, there is a deadening effect. The uncredited orchestrations are led by Franz Allers, and four bonus tracks on the CD reissue offer Tess Gardella in a bang-up version of "Can't Help Lovin' Dat Man" (recorded in 1928); Helen Morgan singing "Bill" with the Victor Young Orchestra (1932); Paul Robeson in a solo version of the duet "I Still Suits Me" (1947); and Jan Clayton singing "Nobody Else but Me."

Music Theater of Lincoln Center Cast, 1966 (RCA) ★★★★★

This fine, succinct recording of the *Show Boat* score deletes the opening chorus of "Cotton Blossom"—but from then on, most of the major songs are heard in fairly complete versions, very well sung and convincingly acted. Barbara Cook (Magnolia) and Stephen Douglass (Ravenal) do superlative work in their three duets: Broadway's greatest soprano and one of its greatest baritenors truly soar when they raise their voices in "You Are Love," "Make Believe," and "Why Do I Love You?" The latter song also has a comedic chorus sung by David Wayne (Captain Andy) to Margaret Hamilton (who played Parthy, but doesn't appear on the album). "Can't Help Lovin' Dat Man" is well handled by Constance Towers as Julie, with Rosetta LeNoire and the spirited chorus lending strong support; Towers' "Bill" is also lovely. Allyn Ann McLerie is definitive in Ellie's "Life Upon the Wicked Stage" and the Act II opening is well done, if brief. Finally, this recording is blessed with a sensational "Ol' Man River" sung by William Warfield, whose voice has incredible power and beauty throughout its range in a performance bursting with spontaneity. The Robert Russell Bennett reorchestrations are largely intact and lovingly conducted by the great Franz Allers.

London Cast, 1971 (Stanyan) ★★★

Although musically inauthentic in many ways, this *Show Boat* staging ran for more than nine hundred performances. What makes this recording most special is the presence of Cleo Laine as Julie: Her "Bill" is achingly beautiful and deeply felt; her "Can't Help Lovin' Dat Man" is rich in sultry tone and thrilling riffs, and her "Nobody Else but Me" is delivered as a soulful ballad. André Jobin as Ravenal and Lorna Dallas as Magnolia handle their songs beautifully. Kenneth Nelson and Jan Hunt are very lively as Frank and Ellie, performing in fine vaudeville style to enjoyable effect in the interpolated "How'd You Like to Spoon With Me?" Thomas Carey is good as Joe in "Ol' Man River" and Ena Cabayo makes a distinctive Queenie. Included in this recording (but not in the production itself) are "Life Upon the Wicked Stage," "Till Good Luck Comes My Way," "I Have the Room Above Her," and "I Still Suits Me."

Studio Cast, 1988 (EMI, 3CDs) ★★★★★

This complete set is the one indispensable recording of *Show Boat*. Five classic songs—"Make Believe," "Ol' Man River," "Can't Help Lovin' Dat Man," "You Are Love," and "Bill" (lyrics partly by P. G. Wodehouse)—have survived every permutation of the show, and "Why Do I Love You?" has survived most. Other songs of the score have varied in many productions. This album includes every extant piece of music ever written for *Show Boat*: the complete score as heard on Broadway in 1927; portions that had been deleted during road tryouts; songs added for various revivals and film versions; and a lot of dialogue, most of it underscored. Only some music for scene changes and a few incidentals are omitted. John McGlinn reconstructed the score and conducts this truly monumental recording; from the first chord of the original overture, which intermingles the musical's ever-changing moods, it's clear that the result is unique. Frederica Von Stade and Jerry Hadley, as Magnolia and Ravenal, act almost as well as they sing. Playing Julie is the magnificent Teresa Stratas, who combines the inner strength of the character with a touching vulnerability. Representing the (unrecorded) 1983 Broadway revival are Paige O'Hara as Ellie, Bruce Hubbard as Joe, and Karla Burns as Queenie—all of them terrific. Hubbard's "Ol' Man River" is warm, wise, and sung with the right amount of power mixed with resignation. Two other Broadway veterans, Robert Nichols and David Garrison, bring their talents and good humor to Captain Andy and Frank (respectively). The supporting roles are also luxuriously cast, which helps boost this recording to such a high level. It's a revelatory experience, whether one is hearing the astonishing "Mis'ry's Comin' Aroun'" for the first time or simply marveling at how the individual pieces of the score fit together.

Studio Cast, 1993 (TER) ★★★

This nearly complete recording of a revival based on the 1946 Broadway edition of *Show Boat* includes the rarely performed or recorded "In Dahomey" and a good deal of dialogue. John Owen Edwards does an excellent job of conducting. Janis Kelly sings Magnolia superbly, and Jason Howard is a heavy-voiced but romantic Ravenal; their "Make Believe" is particularly impressive. Sally Burgess has the right vocal heft for Julie and displays a legit voice with a lot of soul in her songs. Shezwae Powell is cutely sassy as Queenie, Caroline O'Connor is nice and brassy as Ellie, but Willard White's "Ol' Man River" seems a bit too ponderous.

Original Toronto/Broadway Cast, 1994 (Quality Music) ★★★★

Harold Prince and Susan Stroman created a new version of *Show Boat* that ran 946 performances on Broadway, beating the London record set in 1971. Recorded during the pre-Broadway Toronto run, this album features Robert Morse as Captain Andy. The fine orchestrations by Robert Russell Bennett and William David Brohn show respect for the originals while forging a *Show Boat* for the 1990s with restorations/inclusions such as "Mis'ry's Comin' Aroun'," "Till Good Luck Comes My Way," and "I Have the Room Above Her." Here, "Why Do I Love You?" is done as a solo by Elaine Stritch in the previously nonsinging role of Parthy. "Kim's Charleston" is a dance confection thrillingly whipped up by arranger David Krane. Also included is the music for both of Stroman's great Act II montages. Rebecca Luker and Mark Jacoby are excellent as Magnolia and Ravenal—no sugary nonsense in either interpretation but lots of beautiful vocalism—and "stunning" is the best word to describe Michel Bell's unadorned, heartfelt "Ol' Man River." Lonette McKee as Julie is believable and expressive in "Can't Help Lovin' Dat Man" and "Bill," neatly treading the fine line between legit authenticity and soul. The rich-voiced Gretha Boston won a Tony Award for her performance as Queenie. Under Jeffrey Huard's intelligent musical direction, the entire cast and the orchestra sound excellent throughout.

The Ultimate *Show Boat,* 1999 (Various labels/Pearl, 2CDs) ★★

This attempt to be the "ultimate" recording includes the cast album of the 1946 Broadway revival, the eight-song album of 1932, and a *Show Boat* orchestral "Scenario." It also offers nine (!) versions of "Ol' Man River": four by Paul Robeson and one each by Jules Bledsoe, Kenneth Spencer, Todd Duncan, Al Jolson (bizarre), and Bing Crosby (baffling). Helen Morgan's two recordings from 1928 are here and so is Tess Gardella's "Can't Help Lovin' Dat Man." Further inclusions: vintage recordings of two non-Kern songs usually heard in the Act II Trocadero scene, "After the Ball" and "Goodbye My Lady Love," the latter sung by its songwriter, Joseph E. Howard; and "I Still Suits Me" in a solo version by Robeson, plus another version that pairs him with Elisabeth Welch. Finally, there's some material featuring Allan Jones, Irene Dunn, and Charles Winninger, three of the stars of the 1936 *Show Boat* film.

—JEFFREY DUNN

SHOW GIRL
Original Broadway Cast, 1961 (Roulette/no CD) ★★★

Carol Channing spent many years between *Gentlemen Prefer Blondes* and *Hello, Dolly!* touring in a successful nightclub act that was gussied up for Broadway as *Show Girl*. Critics and audiences were cool to having a legit stage used for what they saw as an illegit show (little did they know what was to come!) so it didn't stay long, but the album is charming. The music, lyrics, and sketches by Charles Gaynor draw some material from the star's breakthrough 1948 Broadway show *Lend an Ear,* created by Gaynor. Channing was joined onstage in *Show Girl* by comedian Jules Munshin, but their sketches didn't make it to the recording; Munshin is only heard sharing two sly songs, "My Kind of Love" with Channing and "The Girl Who Lived in Montparnasse" with Les Quat' Jeudis, a French quartet. The rest is all Channing and she's wonderful, whether singing the faux Rodgers and Hammerstein number "This Is a Darn Fine Funeral" or enacting the tragic tale of silent film star Cecilia Sisson, whose career was doomed by a hilarious speech defect when talkies arrived. Channing fans should be aware that *Show Girl* also exists on video, having been taped way back when for TV.   —DAVID WOLF

SIDE BY SIDE BY SONDHEIM
Original London/Broadway Cast, 1976 (RCA) ★★

When *Side by Side by Sondheim* opened in London, it was heartily received, as half of Sondheim's shows had still not been seen in the West End. In New York, where the music was much more familiar, the show still had a healthy Broadway run with the transplanted London company. The cast album reminds us how incredibly fine these songs are; each included number from Sondheim's pre-1977 shows, *West Side Story* (music by Leonard Bernstein) to *Pacific Overtures,* is an extraordinary piece of work. Yet with all of the Sondheim cast albums available these days, there's little reason to revisit this one. Why, for instance, opt to hear Julia McKenzie and two pianists performing "Losing My Mind" when we can hear Dorothy Collins and a gorgeous Jonathan Tunick orchestration on the Capitol *Follies?* Millicent Martin has her moments, particularly in "I Never Do Anything Twice" from the film *The 7 Percent Solution,* but her renditions of other songs simply can't compare with recordings of the original performances. David Kernan, who conceived the show, is the third and least interesting member of the cast.   —DAVID WOLF

SIDE SHOW
Original Broadway Cast, 1997 (Sony) ★★

Based on the lives of Daisy and Violet Hilton, twins who were born joined at the hip and had minor show business careers that exploited their oddity, *Side Show* is one of the most overwrought musicals in recent memory. On Broadway, the exciting staging by Robert Longbottom distracted from all the heavy emoting; here, you have to deal head-on with Bill Russell and Henry Krieger's exhausting score. Russell's book follows the sisters as they fall in love with a pair of promoters, achieve mainstream celebrity, then realize that they will never find marriage and happiness. It's a touching story undermined by hysterical dramatics and weepy ballads harping on the loneliness of carnival freaks. Krieger's score is melodic, but every number is pitched at finale level, and Russell's lyrics constantly skirt the ridiculous. The acid test is the number "Tunnel of Love," in which Daisy and Violet take a spin on the eponymous amusement park ride along with their boyfriends, hopeful of having sex in the dark. Alice

Ripley and Emily Skinner are excellent as Violet and Daisy, screaming their heads off as the score demands. Jeff McCarthy and Hugh Panaro are OK as their men, Norm Lewis offers powerful vocals as a factotum who secretly loves Violet, and Ken Jennings strikes sinister notes as the creepy sideshow boss.

—DAVID BARBOUR

SILK STOCKINGS
Original Broadway Cast, 1955 (RCA) ★★★★

Cole Porter's last Broadway show is a charming and sophisticated musical version of the Greta Garbo film *Ninotchka*; only Porter could have given that heady cinematic masterpiece the urbane and romantic musical touch that it deserved. Set against an enticing Parisian background that inspired one of the great composer-lyricist's most sensual love songs, "All of You," the *Silk Stockings* score also includes the melodic and witty "Paris Loves Lovers"; the smoldering title song; the comedic "Stereophonic Sound" and "It's a Chemical Reaction, That's All"; the swinging "Satin and Silk"; and the jazzy "Red Blues." Hildegarde Neff as Ninotchka, a dour Russian official visiting Paris, and Don Ameche as a slick American talent agent head the strong cast. Gretchen Wyler in a supporting role is a particular delight, displaying plenty of spunk when belting out hilarious Porter lyrics in "Stereophonic Sound." (Sample: "If Zanuck's latest picture were the good, old-fashioned kind / There'd be no one in front to look at Marilyn's behind!") This recording has lots of sensational lyrics that were considered too risqué for the film version of *Silk Stockings,* yet it's not perfect; the production numbers sound a bit frantic and even the overture is rushed.

Film Soundtrack, 1957 (MGM/Rhino-Turner) ★★★★★

The treatment of Porter's score by André Previn and the MGM orchestra is flawless; in fact, the musical arrangements/orchestrations for the *Silk Stockings* film are far more dazzling than the Broadway originals. Fred Astaire was perfectly cast in the male lead, but Cyd Charisse was less well suited to the role of Ninotchka—a moot point on the disc, since Charisse's singing is dubbed by Carol Richards. Janis Paige, Jules Munshin, and Peter Lorre (!) in his only musical are all great fun. Although the movie itself isn't considered a top MGM musical, the soundtrack is definitely a winner. The tempi for "The Red Blues" and "Stereophonic Sound" are bright, the lush orchestrations for Astaire's vocal and dance in "All of You" are gorgeous, and added to the score are two songs that were written by Porter especially for Astaire; one of them, "Fated to Be Mated," is a special treat. The only disappointment of this recording is the ridiculous censoring of some lyrics that were considered too risqué for movie audiences of the day. How amazing that an American film released in 1957 couldn't contain the lines, "If Ava Gardner played Godiva riding on a mare / The people wouldn't pay a cent to see her in the bare."

—GERARD ALESSANDRINI

SIMPLY HEAVENLY
Original Broadway Cast, 1958 (Columbia/no CD) ★★★

Strong reviews kept *Simply Heavenly* on the boards for about four months in all. It opened Off-Broadway, later moved to Broadway for a while, then went back to Off-Broadway in a different venue and finished its run there. Sometime in the midst of all that, this album was cut. (The show was also telecast by WNET-Channel 13 for five consecutive evenings in 1959 as part of the "Play of the Week" series.) Langston Hughes fashioned the book and lyrics from "Simple Takes a Wife" and other stories he wrote about the life of Jess Simple in Harlem of the 1950s.

The evocative music is by David Martin, and the jazzy arrangements make good use of electric guitars and throbbing trumpets. As Simple, Melvin Stewart is not the greatest singer but he's effective in his three monologues, all included on the recording. Vocal honors go to Claudia McNeil, who sashays through her eleven-o'clock number, "I'm a Good Old Girl," with humor and style. Partnered by John Bouie, McNeil also rips into "Did You Ever Hear the Blues?" and "When I'm in a Quiet Mood." Other pleasures: the sweet title song sung by Marilyn Berry; "Let Me Take You for a Ride," an amusing duet for Simple and Anna English; and Brownie McGhee's artful interpretation of "Broken Strings." —JEFFREY DUNN

SINGIN' IN THE RAIN
Film Soundtrack, 1952 (MGM/Rhino-Turner) ★★★★

For many, *Singin' in the Rain* remains the greatest movie musical of all time. The mere image of Gene Kelly splashing around in those Hollywood puddles would be enough for some; for many others, the greatness of the film is that it's one of the rare musicals, on stage or screen, that has a script (by Betty Comden and Adolph Green) equal in quality to its musical moments. If it isn't possible to sock across the script on a soundtrack album, two CD releases do a great job with the music. As part of its ongoing releases of MGM musicals, Rhino and Turner scored big with *Singin' in the Rain*. A one-disc version gives us all of the songs plus a few extras; a two-disc set adds still more, including the original recordings of many of the wonderful old songs in the Arthur Freed-Nacio Herb Brown score. All of the movie tracks sound great, and it's quite interesting to hear the underscoring without dialogue and sound effects. Another treat is listening in on material that didn't make it to the final cut of the film: Debbie Reynolds' "You Are My Lucky Star," a "Dear Mr. Gable"-style apostrophe to a poster of Gene Kelly; Reynolds' original attempt at "Would You?"—a song that was dubbed in the final film; and the original fashion-show narration for "Beautiful Girl."

Original London Cast, 1984 (First Night) ★

The greatness of *Singin' in the Rain*—the movie, that is—was never more apparent than when it was adapted to the stage. First in London, then in the United States, people worked hard to do so: Both stage versions recreated most of the movie's best-remembered moments in a script retooled by Comden and Green themselves, with some songs and a lot of synthetic sparkle added. But it all simply fizzled out, because putting a movie musical about how movie musicals were invented onstage robs the story of its intimacy and what theorists call self-reflexivity. Plus, with those indelible movie performances firmly in all of our heads, who would be fool enough to try to copy Gene Kelly or Donald O'Connor? Tommy Steele sure would, at least in London, and his energetic performance had a big smile pasted on everything, but little going on below the surface. Although Steele is a better singer than Gene Kelly, his charm is synthetic. The rest of the cast works valiantly, but this recording stands as a splashy testimonial to the artistic bankruptcy of musical comedy in the 1980s.

Studio Cast, 1996 (JAY) ★

Following the London staging of *Singin' in the Rain* and the flop Broadway incarnation, there was an American tour, and then silence—except for this disc based on regional productions in Houston (Theatre Under the Stars) and New Jersey (Paper Mill Playhouse). The recording has a bit more heart and soul than that Tommy Steele thing, in part because it attempts to capture the spirit of the original. Once again, however, the sound of the wonderful movie soundtrack simply could not be duplicated—not even under the baton of this disc's hardworking conductor, Craig Barna. The cast is nearly faceless: Just listen to Michael Gruber delivering the "Dignity, always dignity" speech in the first scene, totally devoid of the charm, irony, and ego that Kelly gave it. Finally, as in the Steele version, this effort washes out in trying to duplicate a 1950s version of a 1920s score.

—RICHARD BARRIOS

SING OUT, SWEET LAND!

Original Broadway Cast, 1944 (Decca/no CD) Not recommended.

What's more surprising: That this "salute to American folk and pop music" was produced by The Theatre Guild or that it managed a thirteen-week run? With no dramatic content at all, *Sing Out, Sweet Land!* was a sort of pageant celebrating country and folk music, an Elie Siegmeister compilation of songs that he had collected while traveling the country. Their authorship mostly unknown, the songs include well-known pieces like "Frankie and Johnnie," "Big Rock Candy Mountain," "Casey Jones," and "The Blue-Tail Fly" ("Jimmy crack corn and I don't care") as well as others previously heard only in the Kentucky hills or sung by chain gangs—work songs, spirituals, and blues numbers. The show was directed by Walter Kerr, who went on to a career as one of Broadway's most respected drama critics. Alfred Drake stars along with Burl Ives; Bibi Osterwald, Juanita Hall, and Jack McCauley fill out the cast. This recording is of little interest to Broadway musical enthusiasts, whose main response upon hearing "Jimmy crack corn" will be "I don't care!"

—DAVID WOLF

SITTING PRETTY

Studio Cast, 1990 (New World Records, 2CDs) ★★★

Thanks to conductor John McGlinn, who chose to preserve this 1924 flop, we have a memento of *Sitting Pretty,* a show created by that legendary trio responsible for so many intimate, gentle comedies with music: composer Jerome Kern, librettist Guy Bolton, and lyricist P. G. Wodehouse. The plot, about orphaned twins mixing with the Long Island set, is a trifle; and the score, though easy to take, is overstuffed with what Lehman Engel would call "I want" songs in which the characters wish that they were on a desert island, in a Congo paradise (several numbers in the show would give the P.C. police pause), or back in Sing-Sing. Wodehouse's lyrics largely lack his usual curveballs: "A year from today, when I come back to you / The sun will be shining, the sky will be blue" must have sounded lame even in 1924. But there are some choice musical moments, courtesy of Kern: when "The Enchanted Train" (a tribute to the Long Island Railroad) launches into a full-throttle orchestration; when "Shufflin' Sam" quotes audaciously from the New World Symphony; and when "There Isn't One Girl" takes some wild melodic leaps. The cast, led by Paige O'Hara and Judy Blazer, knows its stuff—O'Hara even contributes slightly stilted lyric readings, as a 1920s vocalist might have done—and Roberta Peters drops in for a touching solo. The generous dialogue samplings reveal an uninteresting story, and the delivery is too cutesy by half. Still, this is a definitive *Sitting Pretty* with bonus tracks. (An instrumental titled "All the World Is Dancing Mad" is irresistible).

—MARC MILLER

SKYSCRAPER

Original Broadway Cast, 1965 (Capitol/DRG) Not recommended.

Peter Stone's book for this musical was adapted from Elmer Rice's *Dream Girl.* The show's leading role was bestowed on a nonsinging Broadway star, Julie Harris; she plays Georgina

Allerton, the kooky owner of "The Litterbug" antiques shop located in a Manhattan brownstone that stands in the way of a new skyscraper. Peter Marshall is the architect who romances her, and Charles Nelson Reilly is Harris' assistant, who tries to sell her out. The songs by composer James Van Heusen and lyricist Sammy Cahn are worse than routine: The lyrics strain for cleverness, and Fred Werner's metallic orchestrations overemphasize the clunky melodies. Among the oddities are "More Than One Way," Marshall's tribute to building ever-bigger skyscrapers; "Just the Crust," the first of Reilly's labored comedy numbers; "The Gaiety," about rude delicatessen waiters; and "Haute Couture," one of two weird songs sung by Rex Everhart as a construction foreman and his crew, commenting on unisex fashion trends: "You never know just who you may seduce / You think it's Helen but it might be Bruce!" Harris, croaking her way through her numbers, is no musical theater dream girl.   — DAVID BARBOUR

SMOKEY JOE'S CAFÉ
Original Broadway Cast, 1995 (Atlantic) ★★

Did Jerry Leiber and Mike Stoller write every great 1950s-'60s tune? That's the feeling you get when listening to *Smokey Joe's Café*, a greatest-hits revue of their songs that opened on Broadway in 1995 and ran for five years. "Spanish Harlem," "Kansas City," "I Who Have Nothing," "Love Potion # 9," "I'm a Woman," even novelty numbers like "Yakety Yak" and "Charlie Brown" are here, delivered by top-notch Broadway singer-dancers and backed by a Louis St. Louis-led band. Directed by Jerry Zaks, the production had a neon-hued party atmosphere that matched the pulsing, vintage-rock energy of the songs. On the recording, Ken Ard, Adrian Bailey, Victor Trent Cook (a tenor with a huge range), and Frederick B. Owens make a doo-wop group par excellence. Among the soloists, Pattie Darcy Jones has an appealing, slightly hoarse sound; B. J. Crosby's gospel growl is dynamite; and Brenda Braxton sizzles in everything she does. So why isn't this album more fun? Probably because these are theatrical performers putting over the songs, not singers who live and die by their sound the way real rock 'n' roll shouters and thumpers do when they deliver a "Hound Dog" that will send you crawling to the pound.   — ROBERT SANDLA

SNOOPY!!!
Original San Francisco Cast, 1976 (DRG) ★★

If you admire *You're a Good Man, Charlie Brown* as much as I do, you too may have trouble warming to its sequel, *Snoopy!!!* While the former captures Charles Schulz's comic-strip characters well in all of their endearing idiosyncracies and obsessions, the problem with *Snoopy!!!* (aside from those exclamation points) is that its songs are generic. The most appealing number, "Poor Sweet Baby," inspired by an actual Peanuts punch line, sounds like a pop song; "Don't Be Anything Less Than Everything You Can Be" and "Just One Person" could have come from any children's musical; and Snoopy's eleven-o'clock number, "The Big Bow Wow," is empty showbiz. It doesn't help that the bland Peppermint Patty is emphasized here as a substitute for the more dynamic character of Lucy. Lyricist Hal Hackady does connect with the comic strip successfully in "Clouds," where the kids talk about the shapes they see in the sky—one sees the ceiling of the Sistine Chapel, one sees the Fall of Rome, but Charlie Brown is forced to admit that what he sees is "a horsey and a ducky." Larry Grossman's music is melodic and filled with humor, and the fine cast includes Don Potter, James Gleason, Pamela Myers, Jimmy Dodge, Carla Manning, Roxann Pyle, and Alfred Mazza.

Original London Cast, 1983 (Polydor/JAY) ★★★

Five songs not heard on the San Francisco recording are welcome additions here, and this version of *Snoopy* (those silly exclamation points removed in London) relates more specifically to the characters. "Snoopy's Song" and "Mother's Day" especially lift the Larry Grossman-Hal Hackady score, and although "Hurry Up, Face," "Dime a Dozen," and "When Do the Good Things Start?" aren't as well targeted, they are so tuneful that we can forget about dramaturgy and simply enjoy the listening experience. Other improvements: Stuart Pedlar's musical direction; a small combo (versus only two pianos on the first album); a fine overture; and, singing with far more spirit than their American counterparts, a terrific British cast consisting of Terry Kempner (Snoopy), Robert Locke (Charlie Brown), Nicky Croydon (Peppermint Patty), Susie Blake (Sally Brown), Mark Hadfield (Linus), Zoe Bright (Lucy), and Anthony Best (Woodstock).
— DAVID WOLF

SO LONG, 174TH STREET
Studio Cast, 1980 (Original Cast Records) ★★★

Joseph Stein adapted his backstage comedy *Enter Laughing* (based on a novel by Carl Reiner) into a musical that had a dismal two-week run in 1976 but was recorded four years later with many of the original company members. Middle-aged Robert Morse is miscast in the central role of David Kolowitz, an eighteen-year-old Bronx boy who dreams of Broadway stardom. The show focuses heavily on the kid's fantasy life, especially his dreams of fame and sex: "I'm Undressing Girls With My Eyes," he confesses at one point. The best numbers include "You," a duet made up entirely of lines from 1930s pop songs ("There's a small hotel / Where you can do-do that voodoo you do so well"); "Bolero on Rye," an imagined romantic encounter at a deli; and "Men," a showstopper in which Loni Ackerman, as David's girlfriend, torchily recalls her former flames. George S. Irving, playing the seedy actor who mentors David, delivers the score's most notorious number, "The Butler's Song." A fantasy sequence of David as a Hollywood stud, it begins with the line, "He's screwing Dolores Del Rio / That's why he cannot speak to you" and continues with "At 5:30 he humps Alice Faye / Then Jean Harlow at seven / Mae West at eleven / And, somewhere between them, Fay Wray." As David's mother, Kaye Ballard belts out "If You Want to Break Your Mother's Heart." Stan Daniels' tunes are catchy, if a bit derivative, and his lyrics are full of good humor about Jewish families and adolescent angst.
— DAVID BARBOUR

SOME LIKE IT HOT
Original London Cast, 1992 (First Night) Not recommended.

Twenty years after the musical *Sugar* played on Broadway, this revised, retitled version showed up in London. Judging from the cast album of *Some Like It Hot,* Tommy Steele, who directed and starred, made some peculiar decisions—not the least of which was playing the wrong part. Instead of taking the role of Daphne (Robert Morse on Broadway, Jack Lemmon in the classic 1959 film *Some Like It Hot*), he opted for the romantic Tony Roberts/Tony Curtis part. Unfortunately, this character has the dullest material in the musical. Steele is all over the CD while Daphne and Sugar, the Marilyn Monroe character, have very few songs. The Jule Styne-Bob Merrill score has been treated cavalierly; for instance, the opening number is now Scott Joplin's (uncredited) "Maple Leaf Rag." Several songs have been cut, some have been combined with others, lyrics have been rewritten throughout, and there are odd interpolations: "I'm Naive," a fine song from a Styne-Merrill TV musical, has been inappropriately handed to Sugar; worse, the amusing "November Song" has been replaced by "Dirty Old Men" (music and lyrics by Merrill for *Breakfast at Tiffany's*). There's also an uncredited title song.

—DAVID WOLF

SOMETHING FOR THE BOYS

Ethel Merman and Original Cast Members, c. 1944 (AEI) ★★★

Perhaps the definitive wartime musical, *Something for the Boys* was a hit for Cole Porter and Ethel Merman; it offers an enjoyable score but not a major one. (Forget the book, which climaxes when the Merman character discovers that her dental work can intercept Axis radio messages.) You keep hearing echoes of earlier, better Porter in a number of the songs: "He's a Right Guy," for instance, bears more than a passing resemblance to "I Get a Kick Out of You." "By the Mississinewah" isn't clever enough to overcome its jarring political incorrectness; it might have been funny to watch Merman and Paula Laurence schlep through a faux-squaw routine, but the song itself doesn't cut it. Although the notes don't say so, these tracks were drawn from two radio broadcasts: Merman sings "I'm in Love With a Soldier Boy" (sung by Betty Garrett onstage), and Laurence has been replaced by Betty Bruce. But the CD does give us Merman in her star-spangled prime, plus the excellent Bill Johnson as her romantic interest.

San Francisco Cast, 1997 (Music Box) ★★

Even a second-rate work by a master such as Cole Porter is worth knowing, and *Something for the Boys* wasn't entirely neglected in later years. Several small-scale revivals have been staged; San Francisco's intrepid 42nd St. Moon company's production prompted this complete recording (with piano accompaniment). This show was never intended to be a piece for the ages; it's theatrical junk food that's pretty tasty and not wholly without nutrition. But it does require a pair of star voices, and here the San Franciscans come up somewhat short: Meg Mackay and Joseph Lustig are engaging, but the score needs more. At least the "Mississinewah" number, as performed by Mackay and Lesley Hamilton, has some of the bawdy sheen that must have caused folks to cheer back in 1943.

—RICHARD BARRIOS

SONG & DANCE

Original London Cast, 1982 (Really Useful Records, 2CDs) ★★

This two-disc album was recorded live during the show's opening-night performance, and it has a definite theatrical snap to it. *Song & Dance* is a unique show comprised of two very different parts—a one-woman song cycle and a ballet—that are only tangentially related. The first act, subtitled "Tell Me on a Sunday" after the best song in the score, concerns Emma, an English girl who goes to New York seeking a career as a hat designer. During her one-hour musical monologue, Marti Webb as Emma makes wry observations about life and men in Manhattan—sometimes expressed through letters written home to her mum, sometimes directly addressed to her unseen boyfriends. With music by Andrew Lloyd Webber and lyrics by Don Black, the show has two fine ballads in "Tell Me on a Sunday" and "The Last Man in My Life." Also affecting is the angry, sarcastic "Take That Look Off Your Face." Some of the other music sounds like filler, but the lyrics are generally fine, delivered by Webb with conviction. The second half of *Song & Dance* is subtitled "Variations." However entertaining the dance may have been onstage, hearing this music on CD is not quite the same experience as listening to ballet music by Tchaikovsky or Prokofiev. "Unexpected Song" is the most memorable melody in the ballet score, and "Variation 8" is also nice.

Original Broadway Cast, 1985 (RCA) ★★★

This disc preserves only "The Songs" of *Song & Dance.* The musical monologue was revised for Broadway by Richard Maltby, Jr., who directed the show and adapted and added lyrics. In this version, we hear about Emma's involvement with four different men, the most significant being a guy named Joe. In a major addition to the score, Emma sings the beautiful "Unexpected Song" upon falling in love with Joe; the number is so lovely that it alone justifies the purchase of this recording. "Nothing Like You I've Ever Known" from the London version is also included, even though it wasn't in the Broadway show. Bernadette Peters' British accent as Emma sometimes sounds natural, sometimes studied, but she's in fine voice and her performance is sympathetic throughout. The orchestrations sound cheesy, perhaps because they are so poorly recorded and mixed; there's even some audio distortion on Peters' vocals in "English Girls."　　　　　　　　　　　　　　　　　—MICHAEL PORTANTIERE

SONGBOOK
Original London Cast, 1979 (Pye/DRG) ★★★

The centerpiece of *Songbook,* a revue of songs written by a fictional Irish-Jewish composer named Moony Shapiro, is a seven-minute medley of "vocal gems" supposedly drawn from Shapiro's one, long-ago Broadway hit. It's silly but it works, and much the same can be said for the rest of the score. With music by Monty Norman and lyrics by Julian More, these songs are affectionate, clever pastiche; the result is genial fun, expertly performed. Particularly good are the Gershwin spoof "East River Rhapsody," the Spike Jones-ish "Nazi Party Pooper," the terrific ballad "Messages," and everything sung by Diane Langton. (Note: Under the title *The Moony Shapiro Songbook,* this show had a one-performance Broadway run in 1981, in a production that featured Judy Kaye, Jeff Goldblum, Tim Jerome, and Gary Beach.)　　　—SETH CHRISTENFELD

SONG OF NORWAY
Original Broadway Cast, 1944 (Decca) ★★★★

"Hurry, Countess! The boys' names are in the cakes! They're starting the drawing!" So runs a typical line of dialogue in this peerlessly fruity operetta that's supposedly based on the life of composer Edvard Grieg. *Song of Norway* was a smash hit and an auspicious Broadway debut for musical adaptors and lyricists Robert Wright and George Forrest. The fanciful plot—Grieg loves Nina but is intercepted by a temperamental diva, escapes her clutches and writes the A Minor Concerto—hasn't an original moment in it. The original production featured super singers, and this cast album, with its generous song-scenes and purple dialogue, certainly is an earful. Lawrence Brooks and Helena Bliss are appealing in the leads even if, after yodeling the hit ballad "Strange Music," Brooks has to rhapsodize: "Oh, Darling, to think we've just found each other!" And tenor Robert Shafer, as their poet comrade Nordraak, is spectacular. The role of the vexing diva Louisa Giovanni (played on Broadway by Irra Petina) is sung by Decca's house soprano, Kitty Carlisle. Although she doesn't possess a magnificent voice, Carlisle dives head-first into the ridiculous text and her classic vocal performance is something to treasure.

Jones Beach Marine Theatre Cast, 1959 (Columbia/no CD) ★★★

Brenda Lewis is a trouper of a Louisa here, savoring her character's temperament and attacking her high notes with mastery. Unfortunately, this cast album of a successful *Song of Norway* summer production—"One of the largest and costliest musicals ever presented on the living stage," the liner notes crow—stints on the ripe operetta dialogue, so we're left with a fairly straightforward presentation of material whose silliness shouldn't be masked. The recording also omits some of the show's most charming musical moments ("Midsummer Eve," "At Christmastime") to make room for the entire A Minor Concerto of Grieg. Still, as conducted by Lehman Engel and backed by a chorus of two hundred, it's a pretty grand performance. John Reardon is a rich-voiced Grieg; Helena Scott a pretty but brain-dead Nina; Sig Arno, a veteran of the original Broadway cast, still purrs ably through "Bon Vivant"; and, as Nordraak, William Olvis has a vibrato that could drill through cement.

Film Soundtrack, 1970 (ABC/no CD) ★★

The cinematic success of *The Sound of Music* inspired a parade of family-friendly movie musi-cals, but none followed the climb-ev'ry-mountain template as closely as this one: It features hillsides, streams, a very busy musical supervisor (Roland Shaw), and Florence Henderson standing in for Julie Andrews. While the film itself is an atrocity, the soundtrack, surprisingly, is not. Grieg is Grieg, after all, and his music is played here by the London Symphony. The film retains just a few songs from the stage version; Wright and Forrest raided the Grieg catalog fur-ther and set others of his melodies to florid but not unintelligent lyrics. Toralv Maurstad as Grieg has no voice, so most of the male vocals are assigned to Frank Porretta, a fine singer who nevertheless strains as the notes sail high above the staff. Fortunately, Harry Secombe steps in for three tracks, his ringing tenor as thrilling as ever. Henderson is her usual competent, unex-citing self, though unexpectedly affecting in "The Little House" and "Wrong to Dream."

Studio Cast, 1990 (JAY, 2CDs) ★★★

Spreading *Song of Norway* over two CDs has its advantages: more Grieg (with a smattering of Verdi in a *Traviata* excerpt), more imperishable dialogue, and more complete song-scenes. The Act I finale, for instance, builds and builds before fading into a satisfying pianissimo. But John Owen Edwards' conducting is slightly stolid, and the overall perfor-mance style is more dutiful than inspired. As compared with the cast of the 1944 record-ing, the singers heard here don't have the sort of natural artificiality that's required. Diana Montague comes close as Louisa, her killer soprano hitting the right notes of haughtiness. But Donald Maxwell's chirpy Grieg sounds like a first reading; David Rendall's Nordraak is resonant but flat-out boring; and the usually reliable Valerie Masterson is a so-so Nina, shrill in her upper register. The concert pianist Yit Kin Seow plunges avidly into the con-certo, and Wright and Forrest contribute an informative if self-serving essay to the accom-panying booklet.   —MARC MILLER

SONG OF SINGAPORE
Original Off-Broadway Cast Members, 1992 (DRG) ★

A tongue-in-cheek pastiche of 1940s pop culture, *Song of Singapore* had a substantial Off-Broadway run at a nightclub venue. It was whipped up by a quartet of composer-performers: Erik Frandsen, Michael Garin, Robert Hipkens, and Paula Lockheart, who wrote the songs and collaborated on the book with Allan Katz. Set in a Singapore gin mill, the plot deals with a jewel heist, a murder, an amnesiac female flier who's also a lounge singer, and a band called the Malayan Melody Makers; it includes elements of works by W. Somerset Maugham, Raymond Chandler, and numerous black-and-white movies. The songs work nicely within the context of the daffy libretto and benefit from first-rate execution by a five-person combo, with further instrumentation provided by the versatile cast. With tropical drinks flowing and table-seated spectators surrounded by dramatic action, *Song of Singapore* was a great night out but no one's idea of a landmark in musical theater. Nonetheless, the swinging score received Drama Desk and Outer Critics Circle citations and was preserved via this recording, which features the torchy Jacquey Maltby and three of the four composers. (The fourth composer, Lockheart, served as the production's "jazzaturg.") Donna Murphy, who was in the original cast, is not heard here. Director A. J. Antoon died during the production's run, so *Song of Singapore* is fondly remembered by theater folk as his swan song. — CHARLES WRIGHT

SONGS FOR A NEW WORLD
Original Cast, 1997 (RCA) ★★★

Perhaps the most perfect representation of Jason Robert Brown's work ever committed to disc, *Songs for a New World* documents the composer-lyricist's superb musicianship and knack for connecting with younger audiences who appreciate contemporary musical theater. Even though Brown's tendency toward self-indulgence in his work is apparent here, this recording of his inaugural revue makes it clear why Brown burst onto the New York theater scene in such a fiery way. As a writer of story songs, he's unequaled by any recent composer, and some of his most brilliant work is heard on this disc, for example: "Stars and the Moon" and the searingly funny Brecht/Weill parody "Surabaya Santa," both expertly sung by Jessica Molaskey; "I'm Not Afraid of Anything," movingly delivered by Andrea Burns; and the modern love duet "I'd Give It All for You," impressively performed by Burns and Brooks Ashmanskas. Ty Taylor, the fourth performer on the disc, is somewhat lacking in spark. The singers, the band (led by Brown), and the orchestrations (by Brown and Doug Besterman) keep all of the songs sharp, but many have a similar, inflated sound that grows wearisome in big doses—notably, "The New World," "American Flag, 1775," and "Hear My Song" (in which Brown sings). So, worthy as this recording is, it's most enjoyable when absorbed a little at a time. — MATTHEW MURRAY

SOPHISTICATED LADIES
Original Broadway Cast, 1981 (RCA) ★★★

Duke Ellington classics were well served by the incisive performances in *Sophisticated Ladies,* which received ten Tony Award nominations and ran for nearly two years. Without the show's visual elements, the recording sounds more like a greatest-hits anthology featuring the Duke Ellington Orchestra and fine Broadway performers than a traditional cast album, but composer Ellington's genius is amply evident in this disc's staggering array of hit songs: "It Don't Mean a Thing," "Don't Get Around Much Anymore," "Take the A Train," "I Let a Song Go Out of My Heart," "Satin Doll," "Mood Indigo," "I Got It Bad and That Ain't Good," "I'm Beginning to See the Light," and, of course, "Sophisticated Lady." Gregory Hines, Judith Jamison, Phyllis Hyman, P. J. Benjamin, Gregg Burge, and Hinton Battle are all top-notch, as is the musical direction by Mercer Ellington. — MORGAN SILLS

THE SOUND OF MUSIC
Original Broadway Cast, 1959 (Columbia/Sony) ★★★★★

Though excellent, this recording of the Rodgers and Hammerstein classic has been so over-shadowed by the popular film soundtrack album that it's difficult to judge it on its own merits. Mary Martin is in magnificent voice as Maria and seems perfectly matched to the material, yet her interpretation of the character differs a lot from that offered by Julie Andrews; Martin is more wistful, delivering the title song with a deeper, more plaintive quality. As conducted by Frederick Dvonch, the entire score has a more legit operatic tone here than in other recordings; fortunately, Martin, Theodore Bikel, and especially Patricia Neway as the Mother Abbess have the voices to support Dvonch's interpretation. Kurt Kasznar and Marion Marlowe as Max and the Baroness are also standouts; they perform "How Can Love Survive?" and "No Way to Stop It" delightfully. The children, headed by Lauri Peters as Liesl, exude warmth. From a technical and musical standpoint, this *Sound of Music* album is highly commendable, and as a record of Rodgers and Hammerstein's last score written together, it's a must for serious collectors of transcendent musical theater work.

Film Soundtrack, 1965 (RCA) ★★★★★

One of the principal reasons for the enduring appeal of the hugely successful *Sound of Music* film and soundtrack album is the fresh approach given to the material. Julie Andrews brings wit and spirit to the role of Maria and more buoyancy to the songs than Mary Martin musters on the Broadway album. Perfectly sung and brilliantly acted, Andrews' great performance is also notable for its clear but unaffected diction; the star knows exactly which lines to sing, which ones to exclaim. The songs of the Captain and the Mother Abbess are sung by Bill Lee and Margery McKay, respectively, dubbing for Christopher Plummer and Peggy Wood. McKay's rendition of "Climb Every Mountain" is notably stirring. Charmian Carr does her own singing as Liesl; she's charming in "Sixteen Going on Seventeen" with Dan Truhitte as Rolf and in all of her tracks with the children. The scoring of the film's music is light, bouncy, uplifting, and enjoyable—a delight from beginning to end.

London Cast, 1981 (Epic/no CD) ★★★★

Here's a fresh and vibrant reading of *The Sound of Music*. In fact, this is the only stage cast album of the show that seems to catch the joyous excitement of the forever popular movie, due in part to the rich new orchestrations and exceptionally clear sound quality of the recording. Petula Clark comes off very well as Maria and is firmly supported by her fellow cast members, who all excel in their roles: Michael Jayston as Captain Von Trapp, Honor Blackman as the Baroness, and June Bronhill as the Mother Abbess. "My Favorite Things," "Sixteen Going on Seventeen," and many of the show's other songs were moved around for this production, but it's all done tastefully and effectively.

Studio Cast, 1987 (Telstar) ★★

This *Sound of Music* recording features a large orchestra and many classically trained singers, so it has an operatic feel about it, sounding too meticulous and lacking the abandon often heard on stage cast albums. Frederica von Stade sings with rich, round tone; she may not be convincing as Maria from a dramatic standpoint, yet her lovely voice mostly lends itself well to the beautiful Rodgers and Hammerstein score. But the nuns, some of the children, and Rolf (Neil Jones) sound a little stiff, and the charm of the character roles Max and Elsa is obliterated by the hugely operatic performances of Lewis Dahle von Schlanbusch and Barbara Daniels; their rendition of the comic gem "How Can Love Survive?" is way off. As Captain Von Trapp, Håkan Hagegård sounds more appropriate but not very exciting. The vocal highlight of the recording is Eileen Farrell's exquisite rendition of "Climb Every Mountain." The Cincinatti Pops Orchestra is conducted by Erich Kunzel without particular zest. In sum, this disc is of interest primarily to those who are curious to hear what this musical might sound like if it entered the repertoire of the Metropolian Opera.

Broadway Cast, 1998 (RCA) ★★

Although this recording is pleasant and features competent work by Rebecca Luker as Maria and Michael Siberry as the Captain, there's nothing outstanding about it. Luker has a lovely soprano but she lacks a distinctive personality in the role. Patti Cohenour seems miscast as the Mother Abbess; her beautiful, ingenue-type voice is disconcerting in "Climb Every Mountain." The performances of the other cast members are tepid and the orchestrations sound weak.   —GERARD ALESSANDRINI

SOUTH PACIFIC

Original Broadway Cast, 1949 (Columbia/Sony) ★★★★★

Romantic and durable, this great Rodgers and Hammerstein score ranges from operatic to 1940s swing to exotic quasi-Polynesian to Americana, yet each song is perfectly appropriate in terms of character and situation. Hearing the unsurpassed portrayals of Emile de Becque and Nellie Forbush created by Ezio Pinza and Mary Martin is a sheer joy. Wonderful songs like "Some Enchanted Evening" and "I'm Gonna Wash That Man Right Outta My Hair" were written specifically for their talents, and their interpretations of these classics remain untouched; no subsequent recording presents a more glowing performance of *South Pacific.* Pinza's "This Nearly Was Mine" will give you goose bumps; in a bonus track, he also offers his own thrilling rendition of "Bali Ha'i." The charm and heartfelt optimism of Martin's Nellie leaps from the recording in every one of her songs, including two numbers dropped from the show and included as additional bonus tracks on the most recent CD edition of this album. Juanita Hall as Bloody Mary is also a terrific standout and, as Lt. Cable, William Tabbert sings "Younger Than Sprintime" and "You've Got to Be Carefully Taught" sweetly. Note that the *South Pacific* cast was recorded in two formats: on acetate discs, as heard on the latest CD, and on magnetic tape, as heard on a prior release. The disc drawn from the tapes is technically superior, but the other disc offers the bonus tracks, so collectors may want to own both.

Film Soundtrack, 1958 (RCA) ★★★★★

It's too bad that the film version of *South Pacific* isn't as fulfilling as the soundtrack album it yielded; this is a beautiful reading of the score. The vocal performances of Mitzi Gaynor and Giorgio Tozzi (dubbing for Rossano Brazzi) are excellent. Gaynor's "A Wonderful Guy" is especially good, but she has many other lovely moments. Tozzi's renditions of "Some Enchanted Evening" and "This Nearly Was Mine" differ from Pinza's but are very beautiful in their own right; often sung pianissimo, his performances are perfect for the intimacy of film and come across very well on the album. The vocal doubles for John Kerr and Juanita Hall—Bill Lee and Muriel Smith—deliver Lt. Cable's and Bloody Mary's numbers perfectly. (Hall did her own memorable singing as Bloody Mary on Broadway, so it's odd that her songs were dubbed for the movie.) Also heard on the soundtrack is "My Girl Back Home," a song dropped from the stage score but reinstated for the film, and other music that was cut before the movie's release. But the real triumphs of this album are the spectacular orchestrations, played by as many as 125 musicians, and Ken Darby's splendid choral arrangements, all under the supervision of Alfred Newman.

Music Theater of Lincoln Center Cast, 1967 (Columbia/no CD) ★★★

Produced by Richard Rodgers himself, this *South Pacific* revival starred Florence Henderson, a Broadway singer in her pre-TV-sitcom days, and Giorgio Tozzi, the acclaimed operatic bass-baritone who dubbed the singing voice of Emile for the film version. Both are very impressive in their roles, and except for some flaws in the sound quality of the LP, this is a fine recording. Irene Byatt is perfect as Bloody Mary and Justin McDonough does a good job with Cable's songs.

Studio Cast, 1986 (CBS/Sony) Not recommended.

Although it stars opera greats Kiri Te Kanawa as Nellie and José Carreras as Emile, this recording is an out-and-out failure. Te Kanawa's voice is too sophisticated and grand for the young, naive Nellie, while Carreras' romantic tenor is inappropriate for the older, wiser Emile. In supporting roles, Sarah Vaughn as Bloody Mary and Mandy Patinkin as Cable are also miscast. Although the disc features the London Symphony Orchestra conducted by Jonathan Tunick, the *South Pacific* score sounds lethargic here.

Studio Cast, 1997 (JAY, 2CDs) ★★

To date, this is the only complete recording of *South Pacific,* but surely not the best. It boasts operatic bass-baritone Justino Diaz as Emile and Paige O'Hara, the vocal star of Disney's animated *Beauty and the Beast,* as Nellie, but their renditions of the songs lack charisma. Pat Suzuki brings spunk and mystery to Bloody Mary's numbers, and Sean McDermott as Cable also comes across well, his beautiful tenor adding to the album's credibility. However, John Owen Edwards' conducting isn't up to his usual high standards; some of his tempi are sluggish and the performance lacks vibrancy. It's a big plus that this is a note-complete document of the score, including the full overture, the entr'acte, and the scene-change music. Still, it's more worthwhile for research than for its entertainment value.

Royal National Theater Cast, 2002 (First Night) ★★

Although the score is conducted with passion by Stephen Brooker, this cast album of Trevor Nunn's production of *South Pacific* features some less-than-stellar vocal performances. As Emile, Philip Quest is the most effective of the four leads; his rich baritone is melodic, despite the bleat in his vibrato at times, and he conveys the right romantic fervor in the role. But Lauren Kennedy's Nellie has a twang and nasality that can be cloying. Sheila Francisco is well cast as Bloody Mary but the throatiness of her voice is distracting after a while. Edward Baker Duly as Cable displays a tenor that's fine, yet not distinctive. On the plus side, this disc includes "Now Is the Time," a brisk marching-tempo song for Emile and Cable that was dropped from the score before the show's New York premiere. There is also a good amount of dialogue and underscoring, plus some reprises not usually included on earlier recordings. —GERARD ALESSANDRINI

THE SPITFIRE GRILL
Original Off-Broadway Cast, 2001 (Triangle Road) ★

About a third of the way through *The Spitfire Grill,* wherein a troubled young woman wanders into a sad Wisconsin hamlet and instills new hope, the sojourner and her local suitor sing the exquisite love song "This Wide Woods." That number and one other, "Forest for the Trees," are among the few magnets in this musical. Adapted from Lee David Zlotoff's 1996 movie of the same title, the show is overly warm and fuzzy; composer James Valcq and lyricist Fred Alley, who also collaborated on the book, needed to produce a more engaging score than this. For the most part, the ersatz folk tunes are quite tuneless and too often freighted with rhymed couplets. Worse, the rhymes are not only predictable but also scant: Anytime "town" is sung, "down" nips at its footsteps, and vice versa. One driving ditty, "The Colors of Paradise," has the characters chanting about how colorful the world has become, but this chamber piece is almost entirely monochromatic. The cast—including Garrett Long, Phyllis Somerville, Steven Pasquale, and the always-reliable Liz Callaway—is solid, but everyone seems to be performing in shades of brown.   —DAVID FINKLE

STARLIGHT EXPRESS
Original London Cast, 1984 (Really Useful Records, 2CDs) ★★

Starlight Express is one of the least objectionable shows that Andrew Lloyd Webber wrote after his partnership with Tim Rice broke up. With suitable lyrics by Richard Stilgoe, this fantasy about anthropomorphized trains is rather juvenile, but at least it's not pretentious. The pastichelike music is delightful; highlights include the opening "Rolling Stock" and "Pumping Iron," two homoerotic numbers in which the diesel engine "Greaseball" sings lead. The songs written for the female trains Belle, Dinah, and Pearl aren't as interesting, though Dinah's "Uncoupled" is a cute spoof of a country-western lament. The show's title song has a soaring melody that ranks among the very best that Lloyd Webber ever wrote. Oddly, while the entire company is listed on the back cover of the CD booklet, nowhere are we informed which roles they play or which songs they sing; and though all of the lyrics sung on the album are printed in the booklet, you'll need a magnifying glass to read them. In fact, the packaging is so awful that it makes what might have been a three-star recording a two-starrer at best.

Studio Cast, 1987 (MCA) ★★

In an introductory note for this recording, Andrew Lloyd Webber describes it as a "concept album" made after *Starlight Express* had already been staged in London and New York. Even though this is not really a cast album, it's worth a nod because it was produced by the great Phil Ramone, and some of the singers are terrific: for example, El DeBarge in a revised version of the title song, Richie Havens in "Light at the End of the Tunnel" and "I Am the Starlight" (a duet with Peter Hewlett). The other singers are Josie Aiello, Marc Cohn, Earl Jordan, and Harold Faltermeyer.

Studio Cast, 1993 (Hip-O) ★★★

The two-dozen tracks on this single CD encompass all of the music from *Starlight Express* that anyone needs to hear; the songs are well performed and there's also some fun dialogue by "Control" (the kid who's playing with the trains) and his mother, entertainingly delivered by Tara Wilkinson and Debbie Blankett. Happily, the booklet that comes with this recording matches the names of the singers with their roles. Greg Ellis does a fine job with the phenomenal title song (arranged/orchestrated by Andrew Lloyd Webber, Nigel Wright, and David Collen); Lon Satton is Poppa; Maynard Williams is Greaseball; and Caron Cardelle is Dinah.   —MICHAEL PORTANTIERE

STARMITES
Studio Cast, 1998 (Original Cast Records) ★

Starmites earned six Tony Award nominations in 1989, at the end of one of the leanest Broadway musical seasons in history. All about a shy teenager named Eleanor who builds a fantasy world around the sci-fi characters in comic books that she collects, the show has adequate music and lyrics by Barry Keating, who collaborated on the book with Stuart Ross. Some of the melodies are catchy, such as the title song (which calls to mind "Little Shop of Horrors"), and others are pretty enough—for example, the "Love Duet" between Eleanor and Spacepunk (the Starmites' "heartthrob captain"). As for the lyrics, some ("Call me macho, a hot-to-trot joe") are more skillful than others ("Her etiquette's so delicate"). This disc was made nine years after the fact, and missing are two of the original cast members—Brian Lane Green and Sharon McNight—who were the best things about the show. But Broadway cast member Liz Larsen is back as Eleanor, and, for better or worse, so is Gabriel Barre in the dual role of Trinkulus/Shak Graa. —MICHAEL PORTANTIERE

STARS IN YOUR EYES
Ethel Merman With Studio Artists, 1939 (Liberty, etc./AEI) ★★★

The first musical with a score by composer Arthur Schwartz and lyricist Dorothy Fields, *Stars in Your Eyes* reunited Ethel Merman and Jimmy Durante, who had worked together in *Red, Hot and Blue*. While *Stars* ran for only a few months, Merman recorded four of her songs with the show's musical director Al Goodman and his orchestra. "A Lady Needs a Change" is typically sassy, brassy Merman, but the other three numbers—"This Is It," "I'll Pay the Check," and "Just a Little Bit More"—require her to dig a little deeper than usual, and she's more than up to the challenge. Clear-voiced and impassioned, she makes these songs her own. Richard Smart, who was not in the show, sings "All the Time" and "Terribly Attractive," and Al and Lee Reiser offer an instrumental medley. It's nice to have seven selections from this mostly forgotten musical preserved on this CD, paired with songs from Cole Porter's *Red, Hot and Blue*. (Not included here is a radio broadcast recording of Merman and Durante doing their show-stopping "It's All Yours," but you can find it on Ben Bagley's *Arthur Schwartz Revisited* album.) —JEFFREY DUNN

STARTING HERE, STARTING NOW
Original Off-Broadway Cast, 1977 (RCA) ★★★★★

Few original cast recordings are as good as this one, made up of songs written by Richard Maltby, Jr. and David Shire for about ten-years' worth of unsuccessful shows. These actable showpieces are the best ever written by the team, and this assemblage is just about the best songwriter anthology ever created. The songs are mostly sharp vignettes about New Yorkers, performed by George Lee Andrews, Loni Ackerman, and Margery Cohen, who sing wonderfully well and are utterly charming. Both women share the irresistible "I Think I May Want to Remember Today," and Ackerman freaks out hilariously doing the "Sunday Times Crossword Puzzle." Cohen shines most brightly in "Song of Me," "A Little Bit Off," and "Autumn." Andrews provides a strong, masculine ballast in the explosive "I Don't Remember Christmas," the funny "We Can Talk to Each Other," and the touching "I Hear Bells." Of all twenty-one songs on this disc, only two are less than interesting: the title song and "What About Today?" With so much imitative musical theater writing out there, the best thing about these songs is that each of them is a fresh and original piece of work.

Original London Cast, 1997 (JAY) ★★★

If you like Maltby-Shire's *Starting Here, Starting Now* as much as I do, you may want to own this London cast recording as well as the original Off-Broadway album because it contains five additional songs (plus a little encore/reprise). But note that the British cast members not as fine as their American counterparts: Michael Cantwell is a little soft, Clare Burt is a little hard, and in general, the performers lack the effortless charm of the New York company. —DAVID WOLF

STATE FAIR
Selections From 1945 and 1962 Film Soundtracks (Varèse Sarabande) ★★

The Rodgers and Hammerstein score for the 1945 film version of *State Fair* is unlike any of the team's other efforts in that many of the songs are spotted as numbers performed at parties or nightclubs, rather than helping to develop the characters. Still, it's a fine score that includes "It Might as Well Be Spring," "It's a Grand Night for Singing," the less famous but wonderful "Isn't It Kinda Fun?" and the catchy title tune. This CD contains all of the songs from both the 1945 film and the 1962 remake. The six songs and various reprises from the earlier movie are performed in slower tempi and feature orchestrations by Alfred Newman. Louanne Hogan sings "It Might as Well Be Spring" (for Jeanne Crain) well, if impersonally, and Vivian Blaine and Dick Haymes sing almost everything else. The later movie cut one of the original songs and, with Hammerstein deceased, Rodgers wrote music and lyrics for five new ones—all very weak. Farmer Tom Ewell has a creepy love song to a pig that includes the line "Warm and soft affection lies / In your teeny-weeny eyes." Playing the mother, Alice Faye sings "Never Say No to a Man" as though apologizing for it. Pat Boone and Ann-Margret play one romantic couple, Bobby Darin and Pamela Tiffin (dubbed by Anita Gordon) are the other; they're all OK. Musical outtakes from the first film and some instrumental music from the second one, arranged by Newman with Ken Darby, are also included on the CD.

Original Broadway Cast, 1996 (DRG) ★★★★

The Broadway version of *State Fair* yielded an entertaining cast album. It includes all of the standards from the 1945 film, plus nine other Rodgers and Hammerstein songs: "So Far" (from *Allegro*); "The Man I Used to Be" and "The Next Time It Happens" (from *Pipe Dream*); "That's the Way It Happens" and the deleted "You Never Had It So Good" (from *Me and Juliet*); and "Boys and Girls Like You and Me" and "When I Go Out Walking With My Baby" (both cut from *Oklahoma!*). Rodgers' lamentable ode to a pig, "More Than Just a Friend," is less repellent as a barbershop quartet here than as the solo it was in the 1962 film. The recording features strong vocal performances by Donna McKechnie, Andrea McArdle, Scott Wise, John Davidson, Kathryn Crosby, and Ben Wright. Bruce Pomahac's orchestrations are terrific and so is Scot Wooley's dance music.
—DAVID WOLF

STEEL PIER
Original Broadway Cast, 1997 (RCA) ★

The idea of a John Kander and Fred Ebb musical set during a 1930s dance marathon sounds like a natural; this milieu would seem to be an ideal backdrop for the team's trademark blend of cynicism and tough romance. But David Thompson's book is a drippy, New-Age tale about a stunt pilot (played by Daniel McDonald) who comes back from the dead to save a naive dance contestant (Karen Ziemba) from the clutches of her boyfriend, a promoter (Gregory Harrison) who always makes sure that the fix is in. Ziemba's opening number, "Willing to Ride," and the scene-setting "Everybody Dance" are typical Kander and Ebb—simultaneously cynical and ebullient. McDonald's first big number, "Second Chance," benefits from a bouncy Kander melody and a clever Ebb lyric. But McDonald and Ziemba are saddled with a series of ballads that lack any real emotional punch. The authors' uncertain handling of Harrison's character is seen in "A Powerful Thing," which tries unsuccessfully to play the fellow's nastier qualities for laughs. Debra Monk, as a love-'em-and-leave-'em type, wrestles with two substandard numbers: the crude "Everybody's Girl" ("I could never be a cowhand's girl; I just can't keep my calves together!") and the maudlin "Somebody Older." Ziemba's big second-act solo, "Running in Place," falls flat. (Orchestrator Michael Gibson is on more solid ground during the lengthy dance sequences.) Ziemba herself is a treat and diva-watchers will enjoy Kristin Chenoweth, in an early Broadway appearance, demonstrating her coloratura in the wedding number "Two Little Words." Still, this is possibly Kander and Ebb's weakest show.   —DAVID BARBOUR

STOP THE WORLD—I WANT TO GET OFF
Original London Cast, 1961 (Decca/no CD) ★★★★

This may not be a great musical, but it has a great score by Leslie Bricusse and Anthony Newley. These are inventive, compelling songs. The lyrics are impeccable, full of fresh ideas and good jokes, sitting perfectly on the music and rhyming skillfully; the melodic music is whimsical on occasion but emotionally rich when it needs to be. A rather pretentious, abstract piece set in a circus ring, *Stop the World* tells the story of Littlechap (played by Newley) from birth to death, using musical theater, British music hall, and mime techniques. The songs chart this Everyman's rise from poverty to success in business and a run for public office. Littlechap marries the boss's daughter (Anna Quayle) after getting her pregnant. Though he is often unfaithful to her, all of the women with whom he dallies are essentially his wife: Quayle plays all of them with great comedic skill. In addition to funny material for Littlechap's romantic conquests, there are some nice musical scenes ("Nag! Nag! Nag!" and "Mumbo Jumbo") and three instant hit songs: "Gonna Build a Mountain," "Once in a Lifetime," and "What Kind of Fool Am I?"

Original Broadway Cast, 1962 (London/Decca) ★★★★★

I rate this the best recording of the wonderful *Stop the World* score if only for the drummer in the overture. It's a hotter record than the British cast album, with a tighter, seemingly larger orchestra that can really swing. Star Anthony Newley is sharper here than on the London recording, singing and acting Littlechap's songs with greater precision, insight, and flair. Anna Quayle is again wonderfully funny, and the unique score continues to be a marvel.

Film Soundtrack, 1966 (Warner Bros./no CD) ★

The original *Stop the World* orchestrations have been softened here, some of the tempi are slower, and the performers can't begin to compete with Anthony Newley and Anna Quayle. Tony Tanner, who replaced Newley onstage, comes through creditably but without his predecessor's dramatic singing style. As all of the women in his life, Millicent Martin, a talented performer, simply doesn't register in this role. The score is presented more or less as heard onstage in London and New York, except that the Typically German woman with whom Littlechap gets involved is a Typically Japanese one here, and a terrible song titled "I Believed It All" has been inserted for the chorus at the end.

Broadway Cast, 1978 (Warner Bros./no CD) ★

Since Sammy Davis, Jr. had made hit recordings of "Gonna Build a Mountain," "What Kind of Fool Am I?" and "Once in a Lifetime," it seemed reasonable to cast him as Littlechap in this *Stop the World* revival, but he was not really suitable for the role. The character was

Americanized and renamed "Littlecat," and the material was cheapened in many ways, from the new tempi and orchestrations to the staging to the crudely rewritten lyrics; the new "Jewish" section of "Mumbo Jumbo" is embarrassing and an entirely new song called "Life Is a Woman" adds nothing to the proceedings. "Family Fugue"/ "Nag! Nag! Nag!" has been cut entirely. Davis, a great pop singer who had previously proven himself in musical theater, comes across here as if he's giving a personal appearance rather than performing in a book show. The gifted comedienne Marian Mercer is a little understated as Littlecat's wife and the other women in his life, although she does find a new, amusing take on the Russian woman. This production was eventually filmed as *Sammy Stops the World* but the movie was never released.

Studio Cast, 1996 (JAY) ★★★

There's very little on this disc than can't be found on the wonderful original London and Broadway cast albums of *Stop the World*. "Welcome to Sludgepool" (introducing the Russian sequence), a reprise of "Once in a Lifetime" (leading into "Mumbo Jumbo"), the entr'acte, and playout music are the only real extras here. Still, it must be said that the extraordinary Newley-Bricusse score comes through with its ingenuity and wit intact. Mike Holloway is a perfectly adequate Littlechap but lacks the star presence required for the role. As Mrs. Littlechap and all the women with whom her husband has affairs, Louise Gold is fine but not innately comedic. The orchestra is well conducted by Michael Yates.

—DAVID WOLF

STREET SCENE

Original Broadway Cast, 1947 (Columbia/Sony) ★★★★

Composer Kurt Weill and lyricist Langston Hughes set Elmer Rice's 1929 Pulitzer Prize-winning play *Street Scene* to music as an opera, although there's plenty of dialogue in it. The music underscores the talk very much as if Weill had scored a film instead of a play. A paean to the aspirations and frustrations of the common man, the piece is set mostly in the communal area in front of a row of squalid tenements. For a work about the American melting pot, into which Weill himself had melted, he wrote great songs that sound unlike anything he'd written before; Hughes' lyrics are a complementary aspect of the drama. The central figures are Anna; her jealous husband, Frank; their daughter, Rose; and Rose's ardent suitor, Sam. The action takes place on a day when Frank's volatile behavior dims the future for the other three. This recording is well worth repeated listening; it was produced by Goddard Lieberson, who virtually invented the original cast album. But note that Anne Jeffreys as Rose, Brian Sullivan as Sam, and Polyna Stoska as Anna are only heard in excerpts from the score; some of the individual sections were edited and others eliminated entirely from the recording. Jeffrey's "What Good Would the Moon Be?" is vocally stunning, although her acting is routine. Sullivan sounds too mature for the young man he plays, but his "Lonely House" is lovely. Stoska's strong voice impresses, and the children in the second-act opener "One, Two, Three, Four, Superman" are terrific.

Original London Cast, 1989 (JAY, 2CDs) ★★★★

It took the English National Opera more than forty years to introduce *Street Scene* to British audiences. When conductor Carl Davis did so, he put together a cast that's stronger on the singing than the emoting, as most opera-house casts are. It doesn't help that the show calls for all sorts of accents because it's set in a New York City tenement that houses people of various ethnicities. But if some of the singers in supporting roles struggle with Langston Hughes' lyrics, the leads are intelligible and sing like angels. Kurt Weill worked in a number of musical modes when composing *Street Scene:* For example, "Moon-faced, Starry-Eyed" is his quite good notion of a jitterbug, performed here by Philip Day and Catherine Zeta-Jones. The other principals here include Kristine Ciesinski, Janis Kelly, Bonaventura Bottone, and Richard van Allen as the four characters caught up in the plot's climactic turn of events. They variously get to sing some truly exquisite arias, such as the poignant "Lonely House" and the equally stunning "What Good Would the Moon Be?" Because sections of *Street Scene* are melodramatic and/or sentimental, the piece as a whole may now seem dated—but the music isn't. And when two nursemaids sing a lullaby to their charges about the horrible newspaper headlines, Weill and Hughes are at their most scathing.

Studio Cast, 1990 (London) ★★★★

Street Scene is a nearly through-sung piece, and conductor John Mauceri's tangy, respectful treatment is its first complete recording. The score is sung beautifully and with appropriate passion by a cast led by Josephine Barstow, Samuel Ramey, Angelina Réaux, and Jerry Hadley; but the acting, which includes a turn by maestro Mauceri as a police officer, isn't quite so beautiful or passionate. Ramey does some particularly leaden emoting as the bullying husband in a melodrama that telescopes birth, death, and thwarted romance into a couple of hot June days. Perhaps because he's such a purist, Mauceri takes no liberties with tempi or meter; as a result, the awkward manner in which the words are sometimes set to the melodies is more noticeable here, and this must have presented a true challenge for the singers. On the other hand, in declaiming their lines with such fervor, the cast members see to it that the authors' political and social criticism comes across loud and clear. This is helped by the fact that the recording is very well engineered.   —DAVID FINKLE

THE STREETS OF NEW YORK
Original Off-Broadway Cast, 1964 (AEI) ★★★★★

For a long time, this was an extremely rare recording, so AEI's CD release is especially welcome. With music by Richard Chodosh and lyrics by Barry Alan Grael, *The Streets of New York* is based on the famous old play of the same title by Dion Boucicault. Its melodramatic story should keep us at arm's length from the characters, yet the songs are so compelling that the listener even comes to care about the so-called villains of the piece. The show begins with a through-sung prologue and then moves forward twenty years to 1890; each act concludes with an extended musical sequence utilizing reprises, leitmotifs, and some new melodies. The other eleven numbers represent some of the best musical theater writing of its day. Barbara Williams is deliciously evil if a tad shrill as Alida Bloodgood, giving outstanding performances of "He'll Come to Me Crawling" and "Laugh After Laugh." Hero and heroine David Cryer and Gail Johnston sing very well throughout and particularly in the duet "Love Wins Again." Ralston Hill is almost Shakespearean as principal villain Gideon Bloodgood, while coauthor Barry Alan Grael is funny as the undependable yet finally heroic Badger, leading three Mexicans in the comedic "California." A wonderful "Tourist Madrigal" reminds us that, in some respects, New York has changed very little in a hundred years. There's also the inventive "Where Can the Rich and Poor Be Friends?" sung by a dispossessed family while Bloodgood contrapuntally sings about how much money she will gain from their belongings. It's all quite delectable.   —JEFFREY DUNN

STRIKE UP THE BAND
Studio Cast, 1991 (Elektra, 2CDs) ★★★★★

The "Roxbury Recordings" series of restored Gershwin scores is a mixed bag, but this double CD of *Strike Up the Band,* recorded here in its unsuccessful 1927 version, is a joy. This was George and Ira Gershwin's first attempt to actually say something in a musical. They created a plot-heavy but delightful score in perfect synch with the cynical book by George S. Kaufman and Morrie Ryskind. This painstaking reconstruction, with John Mauceri conducting the work of eight orchestrators (!), conveys the excitement of using musical comedy to score political points—a novelty in 1927. The recording is beautifully cast, with Brent Barrett and Rebecca Luker simultaneously sardonic and sincere in "The Man I Love" and "Hoping That Someday You'd Care." Jason Graae and Juliet Lambert are youthful ardor personified in "17 and 21" and "Military Dancing Drill," while Beth Fowler is delicious in a Margaret Dumont-like role. Don Chastain plays a warmongering industrialist. There are two special bonuses here: a great, rediscovered Gershwin number, "Homeward Bound," and Burton Lane's gorgeous music for the verse for "Meadow Serenade" (the Gershwin melody couldn't be tracked down). An appendix to the disc adds six numbers from the rewritten (by Ryskind alone) 1930 version of the show, including the Gershwin perennials "Soon" and "I've Got a Crush on You." The 1927 version may have shuttered in Philadelphia, but it's a fascinating, acid satire on phony patriotism, unnecessary wars, and the corrupt military-industrial complex. Thank heaven we've outgrown such things!

—MARC MILLER

THE STUDENT PRINCE
Studio Cast, 1950 (Decca) ★★★

Operetta albums from decades ago often sound even more dated than the material itself, with white-bread orchestrations and stilted singers. You'd expect the 1924 warhorse *The Student Prince,* with music by Sigmund Romberg and lyrics by Dorothy Donnelly, to come across badly here; standards like "Serenade," "Deep in My Heart, Dear," and the "Drinking Song" can sound like parodies if mistreated. But this recording is quite good, thanks to Victor Young's conducting and Lauritz Melchior's singing. Although the heldentenor is thrice the age of an ideal Karl Franz, he sounds like he could step right into a pair of *lederhosen* and play the hell out of the role. His top notes are thrilling, his enthusiasm infectious, and his thick accent great fun. ("The sweet May moon" comes out as "this wheat May moon"; "perfumed of roses and dew" is "parv-youmed of roses and you.") Jane Wilson's American Kathie seems a little incongruous, but she's warm and bright, despite some shrill trills. The original orchestrations are mostly intact, and Lee Sweetland and Gloria Lane offer able support. (Note: This CD also includes songs from *The Merry Widow.*)

Studio Cast, 1952 (Columbia/DRG) ★★★

Lehman Engel crams everything important from Sigmund Romberg's landmark operetta into fifty-two minutes—quite a lengthy album for the time. The performance has a theatrical flair to it, right from the character-actor footmen in the opening number singing "By our bearing so sedate / We uphold the royal state." The recording is well cast, with Robert Rounseville an enthusiastic Karl Franz (if a bit desperate on the top notes of "Serenade") and Dorothy Kirsten a spirited Kathie. The choral singing is mushy at times and some of the lyrics are unintelligible—but, judging from the intelligible ones, we're not missing much. An unbilled George Gaynes is easily recognizable in a prominent supporting role.

Studio Cast, 1960 (RCA/no CD) ★★★

Oddly, when MGM made its 1954 film version of *The Student Prince* with Edmund Purdom lip-synching Mario Lanza's vocals to Ann Blyth, no actual soundtrack album was released; instead, RCA offered a recording that paired Lanza with Elizabeth Doubleday and featured three new songs by Nicholas Brodsky and Paul Francis Webster that were written for the movie. That album is rare today; somewhat easier to find is this 1960 retread with Lanza, the coquettish Norma Giusti, and uncredited but lush orchestrations conducted with spirit by Paul Baron. Lanza easily hits Karl Franz's high notes, even with the keys pushed way up to show off his tenor. His singing is nicely understated in the Brodsky-Webster "Summertime in Heidelberg" and fervent in "I'll Walk With God." Most of the original score's songs are here, too, though wildly out of order and exclusively the property of Lanza and Giusti. Considering the absence of a supporting cast, this barely qualifies as a cast album; but the superb sound quality of the recording brings Lanza beautifully into your living room, and that's worth something.

Studio Cast, 1962, *Music of Sigmund Romberg* (Capitol/Angel) ★★

Gordon MacRae's unforced high baritone is always pleasant to hear, but he sounds bored and not very princely here. This recording also suffers from impersonal arrangements and bloodless conducting by Van Alexander. Dorothy Kirsten returns as Kathie, sounding much as she did ten years earlier. Fully cast with no-name supporting players and capably backed by the Roger Wagner Chorale, the album zips through the score in thirty-five minutes and omits nothing major, reminding us how well Romberg spun standard-size scores into full-length operettas. With its safe tempi and American accents, this is sort of a summer-tent-theater rendering with a larger orchestra—agreeable enough, but more Harrisburg than Heidelberg. (Note: The *Student Prince* tracks are accompanied on the CD by excerpts from *The Desert Song* and *The New Moon*.)

Studio Cast, 1962 (Columbia/no CD) ★

Roberta Peters is a great lady of opera whose warmth and unpretentiousness should make her an ideal candidate for crossover recordings. Her entrance here, trilling in the "Drinking Song," is lovely, and her voice is in wonderful shape; but afterward, there's an excess of coyness that's accentuated by the snatches of dialogue included on the LP. Jan Peerce as Karl Franz is a mature prince, but he has conviction, and Giorgi Tozzi is excellent as Dr. Engel. There's just enough linking dialogue to propel the simple story. With a new set of orchestrations by the great Hershy Kay and musical direction by Franz Allers, this recording certainly has the personnel to revitalize operetta, but Allers' conducting is a trifle stiff and Kay's string-heavy charts don't entirely escape that Muzak-operetta sound of the '60s.

Studio Cast, 1990 (JAY, 2CDs) ★★★★

Emil Gerstenberger was one of the outstanding Broadway orchestrators of the 1920s, equally adept at Romberg operetta or the jazzy musical comedies of the day. On the Romberg side of the ledger, his charts are lush and without that filmy coat of Muzak heard in later operetta scores. For this first-ever complete recording of *The Student Prince*, the Philharmonia Orchestra and conductor John Owen Edwards reached back to Gerstenberger's arrangements as much as they could—and they're a revelation. From the seven-minute overture to the bittersweet finale, the strings are full but not oppressive, the harp prominent but not obnoxious, and the brass thrillingly alive. It's also a treat to hear a lot of incidental music not available elsewhere: an attractive waltz intermezzo, a couple of choral numbers, and some near-recitative linking passages. Edwards might have brought a little more urgency to the tempi, especially in the ballads, but his musical direction is otherwise expressive. As for the lead singers, Marilyn Hill Smith and Norman Bailey: If her Kathie seems to have arrived in Old Heidelberg by way of Mayfair, and if there's a bit too much Dudley Do-Right to his attack, it doesn't compromise the material. David Rendall and Rosemary Ashe offer expert support and a young Maria Friedman turns up as a "serving wench." A single-disc highlights version is also available, but the double-CD set offers an authentic, one-hundred-minute operetta experience. —MARC MILLER

SUBWAYS ARE FOR SLEEPING
Original Broadway Cast, 1961 (Columbia/Fynsworth Alley) ★★★★

A legendary title, if for no other reason than David Merrick's scandalous marketing of the show: He found seven people in the phone book with the same names as New York critics and coaxed "rave reviews" from them, which he then had printed in an ad. This Jule Styne-Betty Comden-Adolph Green flop may have been a washout onstage, but it made for a cheerful, lively cast album that opens with a spectacular Styne overture, complete with subway effects and big, sassy orchestrations by Phil Lang. From there, it's one urban delight after another. The score is heavy on comedy songs written with inimitable Comden-Green élan: Second lead Phyllis Newman won a Tony Award largely on the basis of her hilarious "I Was a Shoo-In." Her vis-à-vis, Orson Bean, was nominated largely for his performance of "I Just Can't Wait (Till I See You With Clothes On)." You have to endure leading man Sydney Chaplin's braying in "I'm Just Taking My Time," but Chaplin nearly redeems himself in "Swing Your Projects," a commentary on over-leveraged Gotham real estate that's still topical. As Chaplin's love interest, Carol Lawrence makes pretty noises in "Girls Like Me" and "I Said It and I'm Glad," the latter a song with an arresting melody that was dropped during the run; another appealing number is "Comes Once in a Lifetime." The original LP album of *Subways Are for Sleeping* was packaged in a gatefold jacket, but reissues squeezed the notes onto one page. The CD edition offers intriguing bonuses: Comden and Green do a couple of cut songs; demo-album regulars Rose Marie Jun and Jack Haskell are heard from; and Comden's pensive rendition of "Life's Not That Simple," a soulful casualty from *Do Re Mi,* is a joy. —MARC MILLER

SUGAR
Original Broadway Cast, 1972 (United Artists/MGM) ★★

Sugar was a shocker, the first indication that the great David Merrick production machine of the 1950s-'60s was breaking down. Gower Champion, one of the most dazzling director-choreographers of the period, reconstructed the show on the road, replacing Johnny Desmond in the role of a singing gangster with hoofer Steve Condos, who was much more menacing because he said nothing, but threateningly tap-danced everything. Merrick threw out the entire set and paid for a new one, but still Champion came a cropper. Even the prolific and reliable composer Jule Styne was simply helpless when given lyrics as disgraceful as those provided by Bob Merrill. Perhaps the musical's source material, *Some Like It Hot*—one of the funniest movies ever made—simply resisted adaptation. Elaine Joyce had the impossible task of following Marilyn Monroe in what was easily her most appealing performance; even so, Joyce was cold and hard, though she wasn't given any musical material that might have helped. Cyril Ritchard does nicely with his two numbers, which are among the better items in the score, but Tony Roberts (in the Tony Curtis part) has the dullest of the songs. This show was in Robert Morse's pocket:

As Daphne (the Jack Lemmon role), he kept *Sugar* running for over a year, giving an old-fashioned clown performance and making the most of every opportunity he was handed. Elliott Lawrence's musical direction and Philip J. Lang's orchestrations are so strong and confident that, as you listen, you may think this material is better than it is.   —DAVID WOLF

SUGAR BABIES
Original Broadway Cast, 1983 (B∗way Entertainment/Varèse Sarabande) ★★

Lavishly produced, beautifully designed, lovingly directed, *Sugar Babies* was a burlesque show featuring very funny old sketches performed by the unleashed Mickey Rooney, with Ann Miller as his partner and Jack Fletcher as his straight man. The production had a dog act, a candy butcher, a fan dancer—and you never knew what was going to come at you next. Unfortunately, this recording preserves almost none of what made the show so entertaining: a bunch of low-comedy sketches, resurrected and dusted off by Ralph G. Allen. Instead, the album highlights the songs—mostly a lackluster bunch, even though nearly all of the music is by the great Jimmy McHugh. Some of the numbers have new lyrics by comedy writer Arthur Malvin; some are standards that McHugh wrote with Dorothy Fields, Ted Koehler, Harold Adamson, and others. They are well performed and orchestrated, but songs are not what we remember most about *Sugar Babies*.   —DAVID WOLF

SUNDAY IN THE PARK WITH GEORGE
Original Broadway Cast, 1984 (RCA) ★★★★

Few Broadway composers could successfully make a painting into a musical, but Stephen Sondheim turned Georges Seurat's *A Sunday Afternoon on the Island of la Grande Jatte* into one of his most unforgettable and distinctive works. In essence, *Sunday in the Park With George* is a meditation on the nature of art as viewed in the past (Seurat in the first act) and the present (his descendant, named George, in the second). Although the show has been criticized for the disparity between its two acts, each informs the other to create a cohesive musical, and the score has real depth and color. Sondheim reflects Seurat's unique painting style through the use of staccato notes, playing with the various hues of music much as the artist worked with pigments. Songs such as "Color and Light" and "Finishing the Hat" are particularly remarkable in sound and texture. A few of the compositions are slightly more conventional: "We Do Not Belong Together," the aching cry of Seurat's mistress, Dot; the beautiful "Beautiful" for Georges and his mother; and the rapturous "Sunday," during which the painting finally comes to life. The second act begins with the amusing "It's Hot Up Here," sung by the characters in the painting, followed by the brilliant musical scene "Putting It Together" (about George's fundraising attempts), "Children and Art" (about what we leave behind when we die), and "Lesson #8" (about the constantly mutating nature of art and life). As Georges/George and Dot, Mandy Patinkin and Bernadette Peters do some of the finest work of their careers, leading an excellent company through the score's intricacies. *Sunday* is one of Sondheim's finest achievements, though it may require several hearings to be fully appreciated.   —MATTHEW MURRAY

SUNSET
Original Off-Broadway Cast, 1990 (TER) Not recommended.

When it first appeared in 1978, *Sunset* was an unsuccessful Broadway musical titled *Platinum,* in which the stylish Alexis Smith played an aging movie star involved with a young rock singer. In 1983, a cut-down version of the show with four performers turned up Off-

Broadway but folded after one performance; that show is recorded here. With a libretto and lyrics by Will Holt and music by Gary William Friedman, *Sunset* concerns a straight male rock star named Danger Dan who wants to wear an old movie star's red-beaded evening gown on his upcoming TV special. The saddest part of the whole enterprise is the waste of a talented cast: Ronnie Blakely, Kim Milford, Walt Hunter, and most of all, Tammy Grimes in the central role.

—DAVID WOLF

SUNSET BOULEVARD
Original London Cast, 1993 (Polydor, 2CDs) ★★★★

Andrew Lloyd Webber wasn't wrong in hearing a semi-operatic, sung-through musical in Billy Wilder's 1950 melodrama *film noir.* He might, however, have made a mistake choosing Don Black and Christopher Hampton to write the prosaic lyrics, overrun as they are with tiresome exposition set to the same few melody lines. Whatever may be said about the composer's cribbing of tunes from Puccini and Rachmaninoff, when Lloyd Webber gets to the full-blown arias for Norma Desmond, he supplies steel-trap tunes: "With One Look," "The Perfect Year," and "As If We Never Said Goodbye" rank with his best. The London premiere production starred Patti LuPone, whose often-remarked-upon trouble with consonants is no problem here; on the contrary, her enunciation is impeccable, and her characterization fascinates. With her fluid reading of the songs and her delivery of what dialogue there is on the recording, LuPone presents the self-deluded Norma Desmond as someone who's surrendered spontaneity to a magnificent artificiality; her Norma is a defeated woman falling from a great height. Kevin Anderson sings and orates forcibly as Joe Gillis, the screenwriter supporting Desmond in her addled belief that she can make a return to film. Daniel Benzali is a sensitive Max, Madame's butler and former husband; and Meredith Braun is fine as Betty Schaefer, the would-be screenwriter who falls for Joe. The sumptuous orchestrations by David Cullen and Lloyd Webber himself possess 1950s-film-soundtrack fervor.

American Premiere Recording, 1994 (Polydor, 2CDs) ★★★

Whereas Patti LuPone's recorded performance as Norma Desmond may surpass what she accomplished onstage, Glenn Close, who played the role in the Broadway production of *Sunset Boulevard,* sounds crotchety and almost laughably desperate on disc. When speaking, Close comes across as an aging Ophelia; the effect worked better live. When singing the hothouse solos "With One Look" and "As If We Never Said Goodbye," the star sometimes strides confidently into a note and disports herself much more vigorously than one might have expected, yet she does have range and volume problems. Too often, her shifting from chest voice to head voice and back again is the aural equivalent of watching a hurdler clear obstacles. Also, more than seems appropriate, much of her delivery sounds like whispering. Alan Campbell plays Joe Gillis and he is more than adequate, although not entirely convincing. Judy Kuhn as Betty is, as always, lovely and real; what a lustrous voice she has. As Max, George Hearn adds another oddball performance to his list of Broadway oddballs. Musical director Paul Bogaev brings out all the overheated drama of Lloyd Webber's melodies, which include a sweeping opening theme.

Original Canadian Cast, 1995 (Polydor) ★★

Diahann Carroll fans are the likeliest targets for this recording, which cuts out a good deal of material that may be heard on the two previous *Sunset Boulevard* albums. But what's cut away isn't missed, since the heavy-handed satire of Hollywood's eat-'em-alive attitudes that's contained in the show is tedious. Carroll, an unexpected choice to play silent-screen-vamp Norma Desmond, gives a viable performance. Her Norma is full-bodied and commanding, and she brings interesting nuance particularly to "New Ways to Dream." Rex Smith has an engaging way about him as Joe Gillis; Walter Charles lends depth to the loyal Max; Anita Louise Combe is a sweet Betty Schaefer; and Jeffrey Huard's conducting is stately.

Betty Buckley: New Ways to Dream: Songs from *Sunset Boulevard*, 1995 (Polygram) ★★★★

When Betty Buckley replaced Glenn Close in the Broadway production of *Sunset Boulevard*, the show finally acquired its ideal Norma Desmond. From the first words that Buckley spoke—"You there! Why are you so late?"—the iron-butterfly quality of Desmond was suddenly, blazingly present in the dark musical's speeches and songs. That opening comment is the only bit of dialogue Buckley speaks on this CD, which includes four of the character's arias: "Surrender," "With One Look," "New Ways to Dream," and "As If We Never Said Goodbye." Still, they are enough to confirm Buckley's mastery of the role. Alan Campbell makes a guest appearance as Joe Gillis, Paul Bogaev conducts—and, somehow, their contributions here are superior to their previous recorded outings. Buckley, it would seem, causes them to rise to her vaunted level.

—DAVID FINKLE

SWEENEY TODD

Original Broadway Cast, 1978 (RCA, 2CDs) ★★★★★

Leave it to Stephen Sondheim to write a musical about a cannibalizing serial killer. When *Sweeney Todd* opened on Broadway, the great composer-lyricist had already tackled such unlikely topics as ancient Roman slavery and the Japanese-American cultural clash. So naturally, when he saw Christopher Bond's play *Sweeney Todd*—about a murderous barber and his pie-baking female accomplice—he thought in musical theater terms. The result is grand and terrifying: a blunt exposé of human venality set to a virtuosic, soaringly expansive score that encompasses Brechtian ballads, catalogue songs, Latin requiem mass, Victorian parlor ditties, lyrical outpourings of full-throated song, a riotous Rossini parody, and lush trios and quartets. All this is not merely for display; rather, it's in service of the tale, the setting, the racing pace of Hugh Wheeler's libretto. Because of its scale, *Sweeney Todd* has not been recorded often, but even if there were dozens of recordings out there, the original Broadway album would be definitive. Len Cariou as the alternately brooding and enraged barber, Angela Lansbury as the warmhearted yet cold-blooded Mrs. Lovett, Victor Garber and Sarah Rice as the young lovers, Edmund Lyndeck as the creepy, unjust Judge Turpin—they all leap off the disc and grab you by the throat. Capturing nearly the complete show, which was directed by Harold Prince, the recording includes some dialogue and several priceless line readings: Lansbury's "What about the Eye-talian?" is a classic of daffy charm until you realize that she's about to hack a cadaver into mincemeat. Jonathan Tunick's orchestrations are spectacular as always, and conductor Paul Gemignani is formidable in leading an orchestra that was enlarged for this essential recording.

New York Concert Cast, 2000 (N.Y. Philharmonic Special Editions, 2CDs) ★★★

With all due respect to those dedicated souls who toil in Broadway pits, hearing Stephen Sondheim's most ambitious score played by instrumentalists of this caliber—and by an orchestra of this size—is thrilling. Conductor Andrew Litton reveals himself to be a Broadway baby at heart, and the New York Philharmonic soars through the *Sweeney Todd* score with grandeur and drive. The cast of this concert performance ain't too shabby, either. George Hearn scored a personal triumph, having played the Demon Barber of Fleet Street some twenty years earlier on Broadway, and this recording demonstrates his timeless mastery of the role; the ovation that greets Hearn's wild rendition of Todd's "Epiphany" is tremendous. Patti LuPone as Mrs. Lovett is in classic form with laserlike comic timing, vibrant projection, and errant diction. Her startled entrance—"A customer!"—is a hoot. When LuPone and Hearn spar in the gruesomely hilarious "A Little Priest," you sense the mad fun and friendly one-upmanship of two prime performers evenly matched. Davis Gaines is an overwrought Anthony Hope with a voice that has no center; Heidi Grant Murphy sails through Joanna's trills with bright ease; Paul Plishka's basso is too profundo for Judge Turpin; John Aler nails the Beadle's falsetto flights; Stanford Olsen's Pirelli is wily and virtuosic; Neal Patrick Harris is a terrific Tobias, at once innocent and befuddled; and Audra McDonald, a star in every circumstance, makes the Beggar Woman both tragic and grotesque.

—ROBERT SANDLA

SWEET CHARITY

Original Broadway Cast, 1966 (Columbia) ★★★★★

This is a practically flawless recording of a Cy Coleman-Dorothy Fields score that ranks as one of the best of the 1960s. Bob Fosse's adaptation of Fellini's *Nights of Cabiria* starred Gwen Verdon in a beguiling, heartfelt performance as dance-hall girl Charity Hope Valentine, and she never sounded better than she does here. Verdon's every song is a pleasure, from the coy "You Should See Yourself" to the ecstatic "If My Friends Could See Me Now" and "I'm a Brass Band." Her performance of "Where Am I Going?" is heart-rending; listen to those final three words. Verdon finds all the warmth, humor, and vulnerability in Charity, selling the role from a vocal standpoint just as completely as she did with her world-class dancing onstage. The rest of the cast is also terrific: A full-voiced John McMartin sings the title song; Helen Gallagher and Thelma Oliver are equally effective in the big number "There's Gotta Be Something Better Than This" and the much more intimate "Baby, Dream Your Dream"; James Luisi soars in the gorgeous "Too Many Tomorrows"; and the chorus women sex it up in the classic "Big Spender." The musicians, playing Ralph Burns' dynamite orchestrations, sound like the ultimate Broadway orchestra under Fred Werner's musical direction; the overture and "The Rhythm of Life" will get your blood pumping and your feet tapping. The CD includes extended takes of "Rich Man's Frug" and "I Love to Cry at Weddings"; opening night interviews with Gallagher, Verdon, bookwriter Neil Simon, and celebrity guest Ethel Merman; and three great cuts of composer Coleman singing his songs with full accompaniment.

Film Soundtrack, 1969 (Decca) ★★

Shirley MacLaine lacks much of Verdon's conviction in the title role of *Sweet Charity;* she finds the character's basic mood but fails to offer distinctive vocal renditions of any of her numbers. The new songs written for the score by Cy Coleman and Dorothy Fields—"My Personal Property" and "It's a Nice Face"— are not the equals of those they replaced. The audio quality of many of the tracks is poor, and slipshod editing prevents the soundtrack album from being an accurate record of what's heard in the film. But some of the performances are excellent: Chita Rivera as a particularly tough-but-loving Nickie; Sammy Davis, Jr. as a thoroughly magnetic "Big Daddy" in "The Rhythm of Life"; and a jovial Stubby Kaye as Herman in "I Love to Cry at Weddings." John McMartin recreates his definitive Oscar but he gets only one song—a rewritten, less-exciting version of the title number. Joseph Gershenson supervises and conducts the music with verve and, audio quality aside, the orchestra sounds great.

Broadway Cast, 1986 (EMI) ★

What a step down, holy cow! You know you're in trouble from the first seconds of this recording when the musicians—playing Ralph Burns' orchestrations under Fred Werner's baton—lugubriously bleat out the opening salvos of the once-glorious *Sweet Charity* overture. Add in Debbie Allen's self-indulgent performance as Charity, complete with overwrought vocal stylings ("I'm the Bravest Individual" is particularly unlistenable), and the result is a misguided performance of the score with none of the thrills and charms to be found in other recordings. Only Michael Rupert as Oscar, Bebe Neuwirth as Nickie, and Mark Jacoby as Vittorio Vidal (offering the best "Too Many Tomorrows" on record) save the album from being a complete botch.

Studio Cast, 1995 (JAY, 2CDs) ★★★

The big benefit of this two-CD recording is its completeness: Every musical number from both the stage and film versions of *Sweet Charity* can be found here, plus all of the dance music. The downside: Conductor Martin Yates, leading the National Symphony Orchestra, slows down the tempi significantly. Jacqueline Dankworth is vocally the strongest Charity yet recorded, but she's rather "hard," failing to tap into the character's vulnerability and starry-eyed resilience. She leads a mostly fine cast: Gregg Edelman as a smoothly sung Oscar; Clive Rowe as a wild "Big Daddy"; and Josephine Blake and Shezwae Powell as Nicky and Helene. Only David Healey's Herman is surprisingly weak, making "I Love to Cry at Weddings" a skippable track. —MATTHEW MURRAY

SWEET SMELL OF SUCCESS
Original Broadway Cast, 2002 (Sony) ★★★

With a book by John Guare, this musical based on the dark film *Sweet Smell of Success* found few fans during its three-month Broadway run, but the cast recording is very good and only improves upon repeated listening. Composer Marvin Hamlisch and lyricist Craig Carnelia effusively capture the essence of 1952 New York's dark streets and smoky, neon-lit nightclubs; William David Brohn's orchestrations, liberally peppered with brass licks, and Jeffrey Huard's musical direction assist nicely. When Hamlisch drags Carnelia into the Broadway underworld, the results are estimable: "The Column," "Welcome to the Night," and "Dirt" are terrific songs. The more jazz and pop-influenced numbers—"One Track Mind," a solo tour-de-force number sung by Jack Noseworthy as a musician, and "Don't Know Where You Leave Off," Noseworthy's duet with power-voiced ingenue Kelli O'Hara as his girlfriend—are also great, though the score's more character-driven songs lack the daring of the other material. John Lithgow's Tony Award-winning performance as the powerful and ruthless gossip columnist J. J. Hunsecker is represented only occasionally in song, but his hard-edged acting in whatever of Guare's bitterly humorous book is heard here makes up for his vocal shortcomings. As the hungry press agent Sidney Falco, Brian d'Arcy James' enthusiasm and stamina keep him flying high throughout, particularly in his early vocal showcase "At the Fountain." At sixty minutes in length, the disc is missing a fair amount of musical material; this fractures and muddies some sequences, breaking up the show's continuity and making it sound more conventional than it was onstage. Even so, this is a fine preservation of an underrated score. —MATTHEW MURRAY

SWING!
Original Broadway Cast, 1999 (Sony) Not recommended.

On Broadway, this revue's main selling point was Lynne Taylor-Corbett's ultra-strenuous chore-ography; what's left on disc is a collection of mostly familiar swing tunes rendered with no par-ticular distinction. If you feel the need to own another anthology of songs like "It Don't Mean a Thing (If It Ain't Got That Swing)," "Boogie Woogie Bugle Boy," and "Blues in the Night," you might be interested, but be warned: Harold Wheeler's orchestrations are surprisingly sedate. The recording does provide a showcase for top nightclub chanteuse Ann Hampton Calloway and rising Broadway ingenue Laura Benanti, but the former is heard to much better effect on her solo albums and, except for an effective rendition of "Cry Me a River," the latter doesn't really stand out here.   —DAVID BARBOUR

SWINGING ON A STAR
Original Broadway Cast, 1996 (After 9) Not recommended.

Subtitled "The Johnny Burke Musical," this show tried to avoid being just another composer-tribute revue by placing the songs of lyricist Burke within seven short vignettes of American life, ranging in time from the 1930s through the 1950s: a speakeasy sequence, a radio broad-cast, a USO tour, and so on. Still, the net effect is that of an oldies songfest. Some items work better than others: Alvaleta Guess sings a sassy "Dr. Rhythm"; Lewis Cleale offers a heartfelt "Pennies From Heaven"; and three ladies—Kathy Fitzgerald, Denise Faye, Terry Burrell—deliver a peppy "Personality." But a lengthy tribute to the Hope-Crosby-Lamour *Road* pictures is thoroughly lame. Overall, the disc comes across as a negligible collection of new perfor-mances of songs from vintage films.   —DAVID BARBOUR

SWINGTIME CANTEEN
Studio Cast, 1997 (Performing Arts Preservation Assn.) ★★★

When producer William Repicci caught a performance of a work-in-progress by Linda Thorsen Bond that was being staged in Midland, Texas, he was so impressed with the material that he recruited playwright Charles Busch, and the two men set to work collaborating with Bond on the embryonic show. The result of their efforts is an all-female musical comedy set in London during World War II, when a company of American singers, headed by an aging movie star, embarks on a USO tour of the battlefront. The Off-Broadway production of *Swingtime Canteen,* featuring Alison Fraser and Emily Loesser, had a nine-month run that included replacement stints by Busch—in drag, of course—playing the movie star, and a surviving Andrews sister, Maxene, playing herself. This recording features original cast members plus others—Ruth Williamson, Amy Elizabeth Jones, Penny Ayn Maas, and Kelli Maguire—from subsequent regional productions of the show. The voice of Maxene Andrews opens the disc and sets the scene. Others billed as "guest artists" include Mary Cleere Haran, who blends classic and contemporary styles in "I'm Old Fashioned" (Jerome Kern-Johnny Mercer); and Alison Fraser, who delivers "A Nightingale Sang in Berkeley Square" (Eric Maschwitz-Manning Sherwin) with exquisite simplicity. The album reaches its apex when Emily Loesser caresses "How High the Moon" (Morgan Lewis-Nancy Hamilton) with bluesy inflections.   —CHARLES WRIGHT

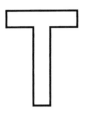

TABOO

Original London Cast, 2003 (First Night) ★★

Who would have imagined Boy George as a theater composer? Yet with this show—partly about George's rise to fame in the London club scene of the early 1980s—that's what the pop-rock star proves himself to be. As a bio-musical, what makes *Taboo* unusual is that its score does not consist exclusively of staples from a star's existing catalog. While one number—"Do You Really Want to Hurt Me?"—from George's Culture Club days is included, the rest of the songs are original and surprisingly attractive, written by George in collaboration with John Themis, Kevan Frost, Richie Stevens, and others. "Stranger in This World" is a fine song for the young George, given an impressive vocal imitation by Euan Morton; "Guttersnipe" is performed by Morton with Mark McGee as the transvestite Marilyn; and "Love Is a Question Mark" is an insightful duet sung by Luke Evans and Dianne Pilkington. Yet the show lacks focus: It covers not only George's ascent and subsequent fall from grace but so many other lives and stories that we can't latch onto any one of them for very long; even George seems to be a bit player at times. Among the people portrayed are performance artist Leigh Bowery (Matt Lewis and George himself share Bowery's songs); nightclub promoter Philip Sallon (Paul Baker); and photographer Billy (Evans) and his troubled family (Gemma Craven and Mark White).

Original Broadway Cast, 2004 (DRG) ★★★

Financed and promoted by an enthusiastic Rosie O'Donnell, *Taboo* moved to Broadway but lasted there only a few months. As heard on this recording, the musical still suffers from problems in terms of its dramaturgy, despite librettist Charles Busch's rewrite of Mark Davies' original book to help clarify the story line. Musical theater veterans Raúl Esparza and Liz McCartney narrate the show as a flashback and the peripheral characters are compressed into a central group, with the songs more skillfully divided among the principals. There are two holdovers from the London cast: Euan Morton, who sounds even better here as Boy George; and George himself, who is effective if a bit stilted as Leigh Bowery. The fine supporting cast includes Sarah Uriarte Berry, Jeffrey Carlson, and Cary Shields. Highlights of this recording are Esparza's songs, the decadent opening sequence "Freak"/"Ode to

ALL-TIME FAVORITES
OF PERFORMER

Harvey Evans

1. Show Boat
2. Guys and Dolls
3. A Funny Thing Happened on the Way to the Forum
4. My Fair Lady
5. South Pacific
6. Gypsy
7. West Side Story
8. A Little Night Music
9. Carousel
10. Follies

Attention Seekers" and the shattering "Petrified"; McCartney's searing "Talk Amongst Yourselves"; Berry's reflective "Il Adore"; Shields' tumultuous "I See Through You"; and "Love Is a Question Mark," a dueling quartet for Morton and Shields and George and Berry. There's also an effective new finale, "Come On in From the Outside," and gratuitous inclusions of the Culture Club standards "Church of the Poison Mind" and "Karma Chameleon." Intelligently produced by John McDaniel and Kevan Frost, this disc is a significant improvement over the London recording.   —MATTHEW MURRAY

TAKE ME ALONG
Original Broadway Cast, 1959 (RCA) ★★★★

Eugene O'Neill's uncharacteristic comedy *Ah, Wilderness!* seemed a natural candidate for stage musical treatment—even though the MGM musical *Summer Holiday,* based on the same play, hadn't been a big hit a decade earlier. Bob Merrill, who had skillfully turned O'Neill's *Anna Christie* into the Gwen Verdon vehicle *New Girl in Town,* wrote the music and lyrics for *Take Me Along,* which David Merrick presented with a ticket-selling cast: Jackie Gleason (a huge TV star) as Uncle Sid; Walter Pidgeon (a Hollywood star in his Broadway musical debut) as Nat Miller; the well-known British actress Eileen Herlie as Lily; and the former Hollywood soubrette Una Merkel as Essie Miller. Robert Morse, following up on his success in both *The Matchmaker* and *Say, Darling,* made a big splash in the juvenile role of Richard Miller. *Take Me Along* has all the elements of an old-fashioned, well-written score, and Lehman Engel's musical direction is excellent throughout. Highlights include "I Would Die," Morse's duet with Susan Luckey as his beloved Muriel; "Staying Young," Pidgeon's hearty song about "today's world" (1906); "I Get Embarrassed," Gleason's hilarious duet with Herlie, which is immediately followed by the latter's loving, anticipatory "We're Home"; and the vaudeville-inspired title song, with Gleason and Pidgeon stepping out in straw boaters and canes on their way to a Fourth of July picnic. One of the strongest numbers is the romantic ballad sung by young Richard, who can barely wait until "Nine O'Clock," when his beloved will meet him. Listen to Morse here and you'll get a very good idea of the innocence, charm, and heart that pervaded Broadway musicals of this era.   —JEFFREY DUNN

TAKING A CHANCE ON LOVE:
THE LYRICS & LIFE OF JOHN LATOUCHE
Original Off-Broadway Cast, 2000 (Original Cast) ★★★★★

This is a gilt-edged tribute to lyricist John Latouche, who wrote in a number of areas and had only occasional good fortune in any of them before dying at age forty-one. Latouche's collaborators for musical theater scores were composers Vernon Duke (*Cabin in the Sky*), Jerome Moross (*The Golden Apple*), and Leonard Bernstein (*Candide*); with Douglas Moore, he wrote the opera *The Ballad of Baby Doe.* "Take Love Easy," with music by Duke Ellington, is one of Latouche's best songs that was not part of a show score. Spreading himself around and then dying young worked against Latouche being widely remembered; but this revue, lovingly put together by Erik Haagensen, goes a comfy distance toward documenting the gifted lyricist's rightful place in musical theater history. Latouche's story, including his extensive homosexual experiences, is told between the songs, eighteen of which were previously unrecorded. His work is sophisticated—for example, he rhymes "Oscar Levant's room" with "Grant's Tomb" in a song called "I'll Take the City"—but can lean toward the rustic when appropriate, as in some songs from *Cabin in the Sky.* His biggest hit is surely "Taking a

Chance on Love," for which he collaborated with Ted Fetter on the lyrics; but some aficionados will point to "Lazy Afternoon" (from *The Golden Apple*), presented in the revue as a love song between Latouche and his late-in-life partner Kenward Elmslie, as the pinnacle of his achievement. The cast—all of them up to all challenges—includes Eddie Korbich, Terry Burrell, Donna English, and Jerry Dixon. —DAVID FINKLE

TAKING MY TURN
Original Off-Broadway Cast, 1983 (DRG) ★★★★

As was the case with *70, Girls, 70,* a flop Broadway musical by Kander and Ebb, *Taking My Turn* failed to become a hit not because there was anything wrong with the writing or the production but, rather, because the general public didn't think it wanted to see a musical about old people. Well, it was their loss: *Taking My Turn* is full of wonderful songs by composer Gary William Friedman and lyricist Will Holt. The show has no over-arching plot; it's really a revue about various facets of the lives of seniors, from retirement to sex after sixty, performed by an excellent cast. The famous 1940-'50s pop singer Margaret Whiting and film musical dubber extraordinaire Marni Nixon were still in terrific voice at the time of this recording: Nixon shines in "Vivaldi," about a nighttime concert in Central Park, while Whiting brings great depth of feeling to "In April," a mother's lament over the death of her son. The female company also includes Cissy Houston (mother of Whitney) and Sheila Smith (whose credits include *Follies* and *Sugar*). The men—Tiger Haynes, Victor Griffin, Mace Barrett, and Ted Thurston—are equally strong. Note that the CD is mislabeled as an "original soundtrack recording." (The show was taped for TV, but this is not the "soundtrack" of that performance.) —MICHAEL PORTANTIERE

TALLULAH
Original Off-Broadway Cast, 1983 (Painted Smiles) ★

One of the most colorful personalities in show business history, Tallulah Bankhead was so imitable that any impressionist worth his or her salt could evoke her with one growled "Dahhling!" Small wonder, then, that the musical *Tallulah* opens with a raft of male Bankheads going through the expected baritone-drawl motions. More surprising is the fact that the ambitious show, which ran briefly Off-Broadway, tried to be a full-scale biography of this magnetic and sometimes outrageous woman; instead, it comes across as a sort of scrapbook-cum-A&E Biography with songs that gaily (ahem!) skim the surface of Bankhead's life without providing anything of real insight or substance. Arthur Siegel wrote a hummable score and Mae Richard's lyrics are generally serviceable, but the prime asset here is Helen Gallagher in the title role. A true musical comedy pro, she manages to plow through everything, offering a decent imitation of Tallulah while singing far better than the real one ever could. (Oddly enough, Gallagher sings the curtain number "I'm the Woman You Wanted" in her own higher voice, not in Bankhead's way-down tones.) Russell Nype appears to adequate effect as Tallulah's senator father, and everyone works as hard as possible under the modest circumstances. But as Tallulah herself might have said, "There is less here than meets the eye." —RICHARD BARRIOS

THE TAP DANCE KID
Original Broadway Cast, 1984 (Polygram) ★★

Onstage, it was an entertaining, beautifully put together, old-fashioned show, but the cast album of *The Tap Dance Kid* reveals an uninteresting score. The musical's strongest component is its book, written by long-time Broadway stage manager Charles Blackwell. The story centers on an upper-middle-class black family ruled by a tyrannical father (Samuel E. Wright) whose ten-year-old son, Willie (Alfonso Ribeiro), wants to be a tap dancer, following in the footsteps of his uncle (Hinton Battle). The lawyer-father's adamant opposition to Willie's career choice, plus other conflicts within the family involving the boy's sympathetic mother and his outspoken older sister, drive the plot. The original cast members—Wright, Ribeiro, and Battle, plus Hattie Winston, Jackie Lowe, and Alan Weeks—give fine performances, and the songs, by composer Henry Krieger and lyricist Robert Lorick, help tell the story logically but without any particular inspiration. If ever there was a musical whose sum was greater than its individual parts, this is it.

—DAVID WOLF

TELL ME MORE
Studio Cast, 1998 (New World, 2CDs) ★★★

This was one of the Gershwins' middling, mid-1920s musicals, chockablock with mistaken identities, society marriages, and principal comics delivering numbers like "In Sardinia on the Delicatessen." The Ira Gershwin-Buddy DeSylva lyrics are lighthearted and expert. With Tommy Krasker producing, Rob Fisher conducting, and Russell Warner orchestrating, George Gershwin's melodies are in safe hands here even if the orchestra of seven can't capture the lush 1920s sound that's called for. But this is hardly the supreme achievement of the Gershwins in their Jazz Age phase; the outstanding numbers are "Kickin' the Clouds Away" and the lilting "Love Is in the Air," yet the hoped-for hit ballad "Why Do I Love You?" sank so quickly that two years later, Jerome Kern and Oscar Hammerstein could appropriate the title for one of their *Show Boat* songs with no fear of confusion. In a high-profile cast, comic-relief guy David Garrison is given more material than such roles usually command, and he's terrific throughout. But such stalwarts as Christine Ebersole and Patrick Cassidy are underutilized, and the delectable Sally Mayes is out of synch with the casual vocal demeanor of flapper soubrettes. The young lovers, Diane Fratantoni and Philip Chaffin, don't do much with the substandard Gershwin ballads, and even conductor Fisher seems to nod off a little in the ensembles. (Note: This two-CD set also includes the score of the Gershwins' *Tip-Toes*.)   —MARC MILLER

TENDERLOIN
Original Broadway Cast, 1960 (Capitol/Angel) ★★★★

It all starts with a marvelous *opéra bouffe* overture that sets the tone perfectly for this tale of the Tenderloin, New York's most notorious neighborhood during the final decade of the nineteenth century. The area's low-life denizens and a preacher determined to get rid of them are at the heart of the story, which unfolds excitingly through Jerry Bock's music and Sheldon Harnick's lyrics. From the rollicking "Little Old New York" and the wise "Reform," sung by the ladies of the evening, to the luscious art song "Artificial Flowers" to the ragtime "Picture of Happiness" to some brilliantly constructed musical scenes, *Tenderloin* is one of the team's top scores. The only problems are the two leading men: Maurice Evans as the preacher bent on banishing vice and corruption gives a one-note performance, and Ron Husmann as a scandal-sheet journalist has an arch singing style that displays no personality whatever.

Encores! Concert Cast, 2000 (DRG) ★★★★★

This is one of the rare revival cast albums that's better than the original, offering crisper performances and sound, as though the singers had been recorded closer to the microphones.

Patrick Wilson in the role of Tommy Howatt has a much more freewheeling style than Ron Husmann, especially in "Picture of Happiness," and a reprise of that terrific song adds to the fun of the disc. David Ogden Stiers comes across as a sincere preacher rather than the judgmental one portrayed by Maurice Evans of the Broadway cast. Another plus is the inclusion of introductory dialogue for many of the songs, none of which may be found on the original album.

—PETER FILICHIA

TEXAS, LI'L DARLIN'
Original Broadway Cast, 1949 (Decca) ★★★

Although it is now forgotten, this mild satire on Texas politics ran out the season and a near-hit song or two came out of its score, by composer Robert Emmett Dolan and lyricist Johnny Mercer. Originally released on 78s that preserved only about half of the score, the *Texas Li'l Darlin'* cast album is a delectable time warp, transporting listeners to a bustling Broadway that was the Hit Parade's primary source. "A Month of Sundays" is as typical as a 1949 ballad can get, with a pleasant melody and an all-purpose Mercer lyric; but "Hootin' Owl Trail" is a real rediscovery, an irresistible easy-listener. So is "Affable, Balding Me," a duet for Mary Hatcher, a spirited ingenue with a sweet soprano, and her suitor Fredd Wayne, who woos her with lyrics from Mercer's top drawer. The lyrics of "Politics" are just as wonderful, filled with infectious rhymes such as "sonnets," "bluebonnets," and "Kostelanetz." A no-name cast does very well with the material, which is paired with songs from the film soundtrack of *You Can't Run Away From It* on Decca's CD.

—MARC MILLER

THEY'RE PLAYING OUR SONG
Original Broadway Cast, 1979 (Casablanca) ★★

Neil Simon based his book for *They're Playing Our Song* on the real-life relationship of the show's composer and lyricist, Marvin Hamlisch and Carole Bayer Sager. The result was a hit musical with catchy, pop-oriented tunes for the leading characters, called Vernon and Sonia, and their alter egos—three boys for him, three girls for her. Robert Klein and Lucie Arnaz, who created the roles on Broadway, must have been better onstage than they are on this recording. Here, Klein is mannered and lacks a strong singing voice; his pseudo-pop sound doesn't put the songs across. Arnaz's vocals are scratchy and lack vulnerability. Still, the energy of this recording is unquestionable. Conductor Larry Blank and the back-up vocalists are first-rate. There is almost no dialogue to put the songs in context, but there are some solid numbers in the score. Both Vernon's and Sonia's versions of the title song are witty, and they also have their own separate versions of the introspective "If He Really Knew Me." "Fallin'" is presented as one of Vernon's hit compositions, while the strong ballad "I Still Believe in Love" is his collaboration with Sonia. Another nice song of Sonia's is "Just for Tonight."

Original London Cast, 1981 (JAY) ★★★★

It's hard to define just why this recording is so superior to the original Broadway album of *They're Playing Our Song*. Tom Conti is primarily a nonmusical actor and Gemma Craven is better known as a soprano than a belter, but the two use all of their acting and vocal abilities to create fully realized characters; so even though this recording contains no more dialogue than the Broadway album, it's far more theatrical. Conti immediately captures us with his touching performance of "Fallin'." He and Craven deliver their respective versions of the title song with wonderful abandon, and the fact that their sensitive performances of "If He/She Really Knew Me" are programmed on the CD as they are in the show only enhances their impact. Especially noteworthy is "I Still Believe in Love": This is supposedly the last song that Vernon and Sonia wrote before their breakup, and you can really hear that in Craven's voice. The six alter egos are fine and the orchestra sounds very good, but Craven and Conti are what make this disc spin.

Original Australian Cast (1996) (Festival Records) ★★

They're Playing Our Song became an international hit: Germany, Italy, Hungary, Austria, Mexico, Holland, and Australia all found the show to be a fine star vehicle. Down Under, Vernon and Sonia were played by John Waters (an Australian film actor, not the American film director) and Jacki Weaver (an Aussie TV star). Neither of them are accomplished vocalists but both are excellent actors, and their charms do come across on this recording. The alter egos here are very strong singers, perhaps to compensate for the fact that the leads are not. But overall, the performance is spirited and more than pleasant. —JEFFREY DUNN

THE THING ABOUT MEN
Original Off-Broadway Cast, 2004 (DRG) ★★★

A musical fairy tale for adults, *The Thing About Men* is based on Doris Dörrie's German film *Männer.* It shows us what happens when a philandering advertising executive (Marc Kudisch) becomes the roommate of the bohemian artist (Ron Bohmer) with whom his wife (Leah Hocking) is having an affair. With music by Jimmy Roberts and lyrics and book by Joe DiPietro, the show is an ingenious marriage of uptown and downtown sensibilities. The first-act finale, "Downtown bohemian Slum," brings a breathless theatrical excitement to the recording. The good date/bad date songs "Me, Too" and "One-Woman Man" are comic highlights, thanks to the performances of Jennifer Simard and Daniel Reichard, who function as an all-purpose ensemble. There are also some introspective songs, "Take Me Into You," "The Greatest Friend," and "The Better Man Won." The opening and closing numbers, with clever orchestrations by Bruce Coughlin, are good examples of the score's unique musical language; but Hocking gets the best song of all, "Because." —MATTHEW MURRAY

THIS IS THE ARMY
Original Broadway Cast, 1942 (Decca) ★★

Shortly after the start of World War II, Irving Berlin created a new version of his World War I revue *Yip! Yip! Yaphank.* The resulting show, *This Is the Army,* was incredibly successful: It played to turn-away business on Broadway before traveling the country, serving as the basis of a Hollywood film, and then touring cities and army bases all over the world for the duration of the war. All proceeds from ticket sales, music royalties, movie profits—about ten million dollars in all—were donated to the Army Emergency Relief Fund. But as acclaimed as the musical was onstage, it simply doesn't come across on disc. There are nine songs here and the best of them are the two that have become standards, "This Is the Army, Mr. Jones" and "Oh, How I Hate to Get Up in the Morning," the latter sung by Berlin himself. Others, including the attractive "I'm Getting Tired So I Can Sleep," are performed so squarely that they seem nearly comical. To fill out the CD, Decca has included the original cast recordings of songs from Harold Rome's returning-G.I. revue *Call Me Mister* (which are fun) and four choral selections from Moss Hart's Air Force drama *Winged Victory* (which are not). —DAVID WOLF

THOROUGHLY MODERN MILLIE
Film Soundtrack, 1967 (MCA) ★

There's no explanation for this bizarre camp exercise, which was designed to spoof the 1920s. Julie Andrews and Mary Tyler Moore play flappers seeking their fortunes in the big city, unaware that their hotel is a front for a kidnapping ring run by white-slavers led by Beatrice Lillie (absent on the disc). Carol Channing sings "Do It Again" while being shot out of a cannon, and Andrews performs something called the "Jewish Wedding Song." *Thoroughly Modern Millie* is barely a musical at all; it's just a mishmash of old and new numbers scattered about. The disc is padded with a lengthy overture, an intermission medley, exit music, and two cuts of the admittedly catchy title tune by James Van Heusen and Sammy Cahn. The ballad "Jimmy," by Jay Thompson, is also quite good. After that, you're on your own. Love interest James Fox can be heard talking but not singing (he was dubbed) in the Van Heusen-Cahn dance number "The Tapioca." Channing's rendition of "Jazz Baby" has probably been studied by drag queens around the globe; and that "Jewish Wedding Song" is beyond description; don't expect Andrews to turn up as Golde in a remake of *Fiddler on the Roof.*

Original Broadway Cast, 2002 (RCA) ★

This show is faux-'20s, faux-camp, faux-everything. The book by Richard Morris and Dick Scanlan focuses on the innocent Millie, played by Sutton Foster, whose steely belt and lack of warmth are major debits. Arriving in Manhattan from Kansas, Millie is determined to be "modern" and to find herself a rich husband. Instead, she's chased by the feckless Jimmy (Gavin Creel) and menaced by the faux-Oriental white-slaver Mrs. Meers (Harriet Harris). The score has about ten new songs (by Scanlan and composer Jeanine Tesori), "Jimmy" and the title song from the film, plus borrowings from other sources. Less-than-scintillating comedic turns include a rendition of "Mammy" in Chinese and lovers who burst into "Ah! Sweet Mystery of Life." Harris wrestles with "They Don't Know," one of the flattest comedy numbers in years. Creel gets better songs, including the jazzy "What Do I Need With Love?" and the enjoyable "I Turned the Corner." Sheryl Lee Ralph, playing a sort of adviser to Millie, sings the clinker "Only in New York" and the catchy "Long as I'm Here With You." The production number "Forget About the Boy," in which Millie renounces men, is toe-tapping fun; but Angela Christian and Marc Kudisch, as Millie's best friend and boss, have to contend with lackluster material. Doug Besterman and Ralph Burns' orchestrations often oversell the songs, particularly in the pumped-up eleven-o'clocker "Gimme Gimme." —DAVID BARBOUR

THOU SHALT NOT
Original Broadway Cast, 2001 (Swing Music) ★

In theory, it was an inspired idea to have Harry Connick, Jr. write the score for this Susan Stroman-David Thompson adaptation of *Thérèse Raquin,* Emile Zola's tale of love, crime, and guilt. Since the steamy French narrative was to be transplanted to New Orleans, Connick, who was born and raised there and has a command of its indigenous musical idioms, seemed the ideal choice for this project. In practice, however, that choice proved less than ideal. Almost none of the music on this hour-plus disc is spicy; most of it is pallid. But blame for the cast album's wan presence can't be pasted on Connick exclusively; he had to insert his dismal ditties into Thompson's inept libretto and also had to suffer two miscast leading players interpreting his work. As Thérèse and her illicit lover, Laurent, Kate Levering and Craig Bierko are as passionate as two glasses of tap water. Norbert Leo Butz, as Thérèse's doomed hubby,

Camille, delivers two songs that do have a little something extra: the reprise of "It's Good to Be Home" and "Tug Boat" (Levering duets on the latter). Debra Monk, as Camille's mother, gets to warble a couple of forgettable Connick tunes. No one who listens to *Thou Shalt Not* once will want to listen twice.

—DAVID FINKLE

3HREE

Original Cast, 2000 (DRG) ★★★★

If only more full-length musicals could be as melodic and charming as *3hree,* the triumvirate of one-act works that director Harold Prince put together to great acclaim in Philadelphia. Each mini-musical was penned by a different team of up-and-coming young talents. Composer Laurence O'Keefe, lyricist Nell Benjamin, and librettist Julia Jordan wrote the first and most satisfying piece, the darkly comic "The Mice." It features John Scherer as an exterminator who goes to extreme measures to escape his shrewish wife, played by the delightfully evil Jessica Molaskey. Less impressive overall is the show's middle section, the ghostly love story "Lavender Girl"; but songwriter John Bucchino's talent is evident here, notably in the pretty waltz "Dancing." *3hree's* showcase piece, "Flight of the Lawn Chair Man," is based on the true story of a man who soared into the sky on a lawn chair propelled by balloons. Songwriter Robert Lindsey Nassif and bookwriter Peter Ullian's fanciful work brings Leonardo DaVinci and Charles Lindbergh into the action for comic touches, but it's in the score's ballads that Nassif really shines. Christopher Fitzgerald and Donna Lynne Champlin perform "Tiny" and "The Air Is Free" with great sensitivity and great power, respectively.

—BROOKE PIERCE

3 GUYS NAKED FROM THE WAIST DOWN

Original Off-Broadway Cast, 1985 (Polygram/JAY) ★★

This three-character musical about the rise and ultimate dissolution of a gifted trio of young comedians has one main problem: It's never funny enough. Still, the story holds, supported by a peculiar and distinctive set of songs written in a jazz-rock fusion idiom. The music, by Michael Rupert, is always arresting if not terribly melodic, and it's bolstered considerably by Michael Starobin's orchestrations. The characters' introductory songs are the most satisfactory: "Promise of Greatness" (sung by Scott Bakula) and "Angry Guy" (sung by Jerry Colker). "Operator" sets up the third comic (played by John Kassir), who is the real genius of the group; he gets more unbalanced as the show unfolds and ultimately commits suicide. You may have comprehension problems with some of the lyrics, which often sound more like they were crafted for rock songs rather than theater songs.

—DAVID WOLF

THE THREEPENNY OPERA

Original Off-Broadway Cast, 1954 (MGM/Decca) ★★★★★

This is the Carmen Capalbo production that helped put Off-Broadway on the map. One of the most important musical theater works of the twentieth century, *The Threepenny Opera* is Marc Blitzstein's translation of *Die Dreigroschenoper,* as it was titled in Germany; the powerful score is sung here by Jo Sullivan, Scott Merrill, Beatrice Arthur, Charlotte Rae, Martin Wolfson, Paul Dooley, and the one-and-only Lotte Lenya. The story, lifted freely from John Gay's *The Beggar's Opera,* concerns the ruthless Mack the Knife, his doxies, and the Peachum family, headed by Mr. Peachum, who makes tattered costumes guaranteed to garner beggars a solid income. When Kurt Weill spewed the score, he hadn't yet begun to smooth the corners of his oom-pah-pah melodies; meanwhile, his collaborator Bertolt Brecht had honed his cynicism so that it cut as cleanly as Mack's signature weapon. Lenya doesn't sing much but what she does utter out of the corner of her mouth includes the vengefully triumphant "Pirate Jenny" and "The Solomon Song." She may also be heard with Merrill in the "Tango-Ballade" duet, and the Decca CD edition of this recording offers Lenya in a bonus track: her version of "Mack the Knife" with Blitzstein on the piano, taken from "an unidentified source." (Is any more reason needed to own this disc?) Beatrice Arthur knocks the "Barbara Song" around, Jo Sullivan is the innocent/tarnished Polly, and Charlotte Rae is the tough Mrs. Peachum.　　　—DAVID FINKLE

THREE WISHES FOR JAMIE
Original Broadway Cast, 1952 (Capitol/Angel) ★★
The singing in this Abe Burrows-Ralph Blane misfire is so gorgeous that you'll forgive Blane's score for being less than riveting. Based on a Charles O'Neal novel, *Three Wishes for Jamie* is a nouveau-operetta about a romantic Irishman who emigrates to 1896 Georgia, marries the girl of his dreams, and adopts a Gaelic-speaking son; those, after all, are his three wishes. Fortunately, the Irishman is John Raitt—and as soon as his voice soars above the staff in "The Girl That I Court in My Mind," you know that this disc will be listenable. Anne Jeffreys, in splendid voice, has even better chances: a lazy ballad titled "My Home's a Highway" and a sad soliloquy with intriguing harmonies, "What Do I Know?" Also on hand are Charlotte Rae as the frump, delicious in a showy piece of special material, and Bert Wheeler, who's rather tiresome. Working minus Hugh Martin, Blane produced pedestrian lyrics but often lilting music, especially as orchestrated by Robert Russell Bennett. The Irish blarney gets pretty thick, the story hasn't much fire, and songs like "It's a Wishing World" are time-passers; but as long as Raitt and Jeffreys are singing, it all passes pleasantly.　　　—MARC MILLER

THRILL ME
Original Cast, 2004 (Original Cast Records) ★★★★
In musicalizing the story of Nathan Leopold and Richard Loeb, who murdered a boy in 1924 Chicago, composer-lyricist-librettist Stephen Dolginoff didn't attempt to replicate the *Chicago* method of dealing with such a difficult and disturbing subject. Instead, he eschewed the splashy and comic and wrote a taut chamber-musical character study that became a sold-out hit in the 2003 Midtown International Theatre Festival. The cast recording omits a few songs and lots of dialogue but preserves the work's uncompromising intensity and perfectly integrated score. Christopher Totten handles Leopold's material very well: He gives the soul-searching "Way Too Far" a beautiful rendition, and his "Thrill Me" is provocative. Matthew S. Morris imbues Loeb with a desperate arrogance and is outstanding in the show's most memorable song, "Roadster," in which Loeb lures his victim into his clutches. Dolginoff depicts the murderers as sparring, codependent lovers, and Leopold's gradual transformation from victim to power player comes across well on the recording. Accompanied only by Gabriel Kahane on piano, Morris' and Totten's voices blend smoothly; just try listening to the climactic number "Life Plus 99 Years" without getting the chills.　　　—MATTHEW MURRAY

THROUGH THE YEARS
Studio Cast, 2001 (PS Classics) ★★
Hats off to PS Classics for issuing the premiere recording of this interesting curio, a Vincent Youmans 1931 flop—and hats back on for their having made such a muddle of it. Not that the

material, adapted from the old stage weepie *Smilin' Through,* isn't tricky, with its confusing multigenerational love story and subsidiary comic romance. Youmans seems to have written two scores for the two stories: one long-lined and elegant, one standard musical comedy, both melodically and harmonically beguiling. But, instead of the original orchestrations, the recording presents a soupy reduction by conductor Aaron Gandy, played by a twelve-piece group that sounds like the Mantovani Chamber Ensemble. Leading lady Heidi Grant Murphy, much admired in opera, is flat-out dull here, while leading man Philip Chaffin ably navigates Youmans' melodic leaps without sounding much engaged. Even the usually impeccable Brent Barrett is droopy, although he does come to life in "How Happy Is the Bride," a tricky Youmans melody saddled with awkward Edward Heyman lyrics. The best work comes from the real-life couple Hunter Thompson and Jennifer Cody; these two handle the lighter pieces with a fine understanding of 1930s style. Snatches of dialogue evoke what must have been a long evening of romantic entanglements punctuated by some pretty Youmans melodies. —MARC MILLER

TICK, TICK . . . BOOM!
Original Off-Broadway Cast, 2001 (RCA) ★★★

This minor but appealing Off-Broadway effort was adapted by playwright David Auburn from a semi-autobiographical one-person show that had been written and performed by the late songwriter Jonathan Larson; it also incorporates material from an unproduced Larson project titled *Superbia.* The show's main weakness is obvious: It's a little hard to care about the angst suffered by an unsuccessful musical theater songwriter as he approaches age thirty. But there are many mitigating factors, not the least of which is one's knowledge that Larson would die unexpectedly a few years later. The disc also provides an early showcase for Raúl Esparza, one of the best singing actors in musical theater today. Equally effective are Amy Spanger as Jonathan's increasingly fed-up lover and Jerry Dixon as his best friend, who has given up bohemia for business and who harbors a heartbreaking secret. And then there are the songs, which confirm Larson's thrilling talent. They include the touching trio "Johnny Can't Decide"; the witty "Sunday," a number about working in a diner that's also a parody of a certain Stephen Sondheim ballad; and the fervent "Come to Your Senses." The impassioned finale "Louder Than Words," with its wounded idealism, is excellent. A touching bonus track features Larson himself singing a cut number, "Boho Days." —DAVID BARBOUR

A TIME FOR SINGING
Original Broadway Cast, 1966 (Warner Bros./no CD) ★★★

Based on Richard Llewellyn's popular book *How Green Was My Valley,* which inspired the acclaimed 1941 movie of the same title, *A Time for Singing* deals with the grim lives of Welsh coal miners. The John Morris-Gerald Freedman score surely sings out their tale, right from the *a cappella* opening to the tragic finale. The choral work is ample and terrific throughout, and leading man Ivor Emmanuel's Welsh baritone is overpowering. Morris' harmonies are not standard-issue Broadway; they're wrapped up in evocative Don Walker orchestrations, and several ballads ("That's What Young Ladies Do," "There Is Beautiful You Are," "Let Me Love You") rate rediscovery. What kills the show more than anything is the casting. Shani Wallis is a simpering leading lady, while Tessie O'Shea and Laurence Naismith are far too old to be convincing as the parents of eight-year-old Huw (Frank Griso, an irritating child actor). Elizabeth Hubbard and an up-and-coming George Hearn are wasted in supporting roles. Also, the score goes conventional just when it needs to offer something special, as in Wallis' "When He Looks at Me" or the wimpy title tune. Still, this deeply felt neo-operetta doesn't deserve the obscurity it has suffered for decades, and its great ensemble work is all over the LP. — MARC MILLER

TINTYPES
Original Broadway Cast, 1980 (DRG) ★★★

Allegedly, this was the first-ever digitally recorded cast album. A cavalcade of early-twentieth-century Americana, *Tintypes* sounds splendid here as its five-member cast and small band run through several dozen period songs—some classic, some virtually forgotten—in witty arrangements by Mel Marvin. Unlike so many other revues, the show has a real arc and the songs comment wonderfully on themselves: "Toyland" becomes an anthem about America's lost innocence, for instance, and "I Want What I Want When I Want It" is sung by a bellicose Teddy Roosevelt. Hearing "The Stars and Stripes Forever" or "Meet Me in St. Louis" for the zillionth time isn't a thrill, but trivialities like "Electricity" and "Teddy Da Roose" are well worth a listen, especially as rendered by this talented quintet: The fine character actor Trey Wilson and the elegant soprano Carolyn Mignini play the elites; the funny Mary Catherine Wright and the predirectorial Jerry Zaks embody the downtrodden immigrant masses; and Lynne Thigpen is a marvel in everything she does. As Anna Held's maid (it's complicated, but the well-edited album supplies a context), Thigpen slowly builds the old Bert Williams favorite "Nobody" to a shattering finish. Wisely, this was the Act I finale; nobody in his right mind would have followed it. — MARC MILLER

TIP-TOES
New York Concert Cast, 1998 (New World, 2CDs) ★★★★

Enchanting piffle from 1925, *Tip-Toes* has a funny Fred Thompson-Guy Bolton book, a dancey Gershwin score, and an insuperable cast in this Carnegie Hall performance. The orchestral materials, as Rob Fisher relates in his liner notes, were in good shape except for the Arden and Ohlman dual-piano parts; Joseph Thalken and John Musto recreate these spectacularly. Fisher's orchestra sounds just a tad underpopulated, and Fisher might have picked up the pace of such songs as "When Do We Dance?" and "Sweet and Low-Down." The chorus is on the thin side, too, with just eight voices, but what a darling song collection this is—big on George Gershwin syncopation, blue-note harmonies, and lightly satirical Ira Gershwin lyrics. The cast members perform in perfect period style and with total conviction. Emily Loesser is an ideal Jazz Age heroine, her light soprano caressing "Looking for a Boy" with great affection, and Andy Taylor is a young hero right out of a John Held, Jr. cartoon. Principal comics Lewis J. Stadlen and Lee Wilkof winningly sock across the silly jokes and puns, and enough dialogue is included to give you an idea of the book. This is a lighter, simpler show than other Gershwin gems—so patently innocent that, at one point, the hero and heroine sing to each other, "Goody-goody-goodnight, sleep tight." But the charm never curdles; it just charms. (Note: Also included on this two-CD set is the score of the Gershwins' *Tell Me More*.) — MARC MILLER

TITANIC
Original Broadway Cast, 1997 (RCA) ★★★★★

You'll be hard-pressed to find more beautiful choral singing than you'll hear on the cast album of *Titanic,* the musical about the sinking of that famed "ship of dreams." Composer-lyricist

Maury Yeston's score is grand and sweeping, and more than forty voices are employed to represent the Irish peasants, middle-class professionals, and wealthy society types aboard the doomed vessel. For this clash of classes, Yeston offers a suitable variety of music, from the stunning, operatic opening sequence to some Celtic-tinged tunes. A rag number and Yeston's own lovely version of "Autumn"—supposedly one of the last songs played by the musicians on deck as the ship went down—give the score a sense of time and place, while Jonathan Tunick's lush orchestrations evoke the feelings of adventure, hope, and loss that the disaster still inspires; you can hear the growl of an angry ocean in the overture and see the black night described by a sailor in the haunting "No Moon." Yeston shows remarkable theatricality and innovation in his work here, notably in two sequences: "The Blame" (a heated colloquy sung by the ship's owner, builder, and captain) and "Mr. Andrews' Vision" (in which the horror-struck ship builder foretells the ship's chilling final moments). Yeston's lyrics are always strong, and he is fortunate that Michael Cerveris, Brian d'Arcy James, David Garrison, John Cunningham, Victoria Clark, and a superlative cast of actor/singers preserved his words and music on this disc.   — BROOKE PIERCE

TOMMY
Studio Recording, 1969 (MCA) ★★★★★
Originally conceived for presentation on record, this seminal "rock opera" is thrillingly melodic and dramatic; small wonder that it was subsequently adapted as a film and, later, a Broadway musical. *Tommy* was mostly composed for The Who by guitarist Pete Townshend but there is additional material by two other members of that legendary rock band, John Entwistle and Keith Moon. Oddly, the score also includes "Eyesight to the Blind," a preexisting song by Sonny Boy Williamson; Townshend presumably added the number because it fits well into this story of a deaf, dumb, and blind boy who becomes world famous as a "Pinball Wizard." Most of Tommy's songs are performed by Roger Daltrey, who sings beautifully and persuasively. Among the recording's many highlights are "Amazing Journey," "Go to the Mirror, Boy," "I'm Free," and "Sensation."

Studio Cast with Symphony Orchestra, 1972 (Ode) ★★
Realizing that the score of *Tommy* is filled with melodies that could benefit from symphonic treatment, Lou Reizner produced a complete recording of the score featuring the London Symphony Orchestra and Chambre Choir; soloists Pete Townshend, Roger Daltrey, and John Entwistle of The Who; Maggie Bell as the Mother; Steve Winwood as the Father; Ringo Starr as Uncle Ernie; Rod Stewart rasping out "Pinball Wizard"; and Richie Havens singing "Eyesight to the Blind." Unfortunately, arrangers Wil Malone and James Sullivan threw out the baby with the bathwater; rather than using violins, trumpets, and woodwinds to enhance these great songs, they largely obliterated the rock-band sound of the piece with symphonic orchestrations. On top of that, the veddy proper-sounding Chambre Choir creates an odd impression in numbers like "Pinball Wizard" and "We're Not Gonna Take It," as if they were recording Handel's *Messiah* rather than a seminal rock opera. Among the most successful cuts on the album are "It's a Boy" and "Amazing Journey," if only because they retain something of an authentic rock sound.

Film Soundtrack, 1975 (Polydor, 2CDs) ★
This recording has several things to recommend it: Roger Daltrey, at the peak of his vocal powers, is back again in the title role; The Who's drummer, Keith Moon, does a fine job in the role of Uncle Ernie; and the rest of the band members make cameo appearances in the "Pinball

Wizard" sequence and elsewhere. Ann-Margret sings quite well as Tommy's mother (here called Nora) even if she tends to overemote. The starry supporting cast includes Elton John singing "Pinball Wizard" and Eric Clapton doing "Eyesight to the Blind." On top of all this, the one-and-only Tina Turner is the definitive Acid Queen. But the album has two major strikes against it: The unrelenting deployment of synthesizers in the arrangements actually makes the score sound more dated than it does on The Who's original recording; and Oliver Reed sings very poorly in the role of Tommy's mother's lover. (Legend has it that Jack Nicholson, having been cast in the role of the Doctor, was nervous about his singing ability—but when he heard Reed's prerecordings, he relaxed.)

Original Broadway Cast, 1993 (RCA, 2CDs) ★★

It wasn't until almost a quarter-century after the release of The Who's original recording of *Tommy* that the piece was finally adapted as a full-fledged stage musical. The results were much better than might have been hoped for, and this recording—produced by the legendary George Martin—has a lot going for it. Michael Cerveris is persuasive in the title role, complete with a convincing if somewhat aggressive British accent. Also sounding credibly British are Marcia Mitzman and Jonathan Dokuchitz as Tommy's mother and father. The three leads sing spectacularly well, and sharply etched supporting performances are turned in by Paul Kandel as Uncle Ernie and Anthony Barrile as Cousin Kevin. The musical adaptation pays homage to the original album while adding a theatrical flair; the addition of conventional orchestrations to the basic rock-band sound is more successful here than on the 1972 symphonic recording. (Steve Margoshes is credited with the orchestrations, while Joseph Church is listed as musical supervisor and director.) Director Des McAnuff oversaw a production that's eminently praiseworthy in many respects. In fact, the only major flaw is that Pete Townshend rewrote two key sections of the opera for no good reason. First, although Cheryl Freeman as the Gypsy does a fine job with the "Acid Queen" number, the song has been strangely reconceived so that this drug-addicted prostitute sings about what she's going to do to Tommy but never actually does it. Much worse, Townshend futzed with the ending of the piece so that now it completely contradicts the original point. In all previous versions of *Tommy,* the title character becomes the leader of a quasi-religious cult and his followers turn against him when they realize that he's attempting to control their minds; in this version, Tommy's acolytes rebel because he tells them they should think for themselves! —MICHAEL PORTANTIERE

TOO MANY GIRLS
Studio Cast, 1977 (Painted Smiles) ★★

The world's oldest collection of co-eds bops to a lower-drawer score by Richard Rodgers and Lorenz Hart in this Ben Bagley recording of a 1939 hit that hasn't worn well. Although there are attractive songs sung on the campus of Pottawatomie College, including "I Didn't Know What Time It Was" and "You're Nearer" (written for the 1940 film version), they're undermined by Dennis Deal's blaring arrangements and one of Bagley's most indulgent exercises in camp interpretation. The vocal arrangements are subpar, too. As for the singers, undergrad Estelle Parsons croaks "My Prince"; Nancy Andrews injects some pizzazz into the glaringly un-P.C. "Spic and Spanish"; Johnny Desmond and Arthur Siegel sing well enough without ever coming anywhere near a character; and Tony Perkins, whose ringing baritenor had surprised everyone in *Greenwillow,* pretty much whispers his vocals here—not ineptly, but without any special insight. Some of the songs have the old Rodgers and Hart spirit; one example is the opening number, "Heroes in the Fall," with lyrics ghost-written by Rodgers for the off-on-a-binge Hart. But many of the others ("She Could Shake the Maracas," "'Cause We Got Cake," and "Sweethearts of the Team" in an excruciating rendition) sound like pale imitations of the team's better work.

—MARC MILLER

TOP BANANA
Original Broadway Cast, 1951 (Capitol/DRG) ★★★★

Nothing dates faster than comedy, and this zany musical expedition into the world of vaudeville comics is no exception. Still, it's a wonderful time capsule from the early 1950s, performed by many of the leading comedians of the day. Phil Silvers, Jack Albertson, and Rose-Marie joined forces to make *Top Banana* a solid hit in 1951; Silvers even won the 1952 Tony Award for Best Actor in a Musical. And while this star vehicle has faded into obscurity, the cast album is a spirited, buoyant tribute to showbiz of another era. The clever songs of the great Johnny Mercer are outstanding (the legendary lyricist also composed the music for this show). The recording is full of gems—"I Fought Every Step of the Way," "A Word a Day," and others—that can still elicit guffaws.

—GERARD ALESSANDRINI

TOUCH
Original Off-Broadway Cast, 1970 (Ampex/no CD) Not recommended.

This most ubiquitous of all show recordings turns up everywhere: at garage sales, school sales, library sales. Move into a new apartment and you'll find a copy of *Touch* in the closet. One has to wonder who on earth bought the thing, but somebody had to if it ended up in all those tag sales. For the record, this is a sweet-tempered, soft-rock musical, with a score by Jim Crozier and Kenn Long, that got decent notices and had a modest run. With its environmental and social concerns, the show was certainly well meaning, but its dramaturgy is primitive and its songs are flavorless. There's really nothing here to interest musical theater aficionados.

—DAVID WOLF

TOVARICH
Original Broadway Cast, 1963 (Capitol/Angel) ★★★

Those who purchase the CD after knowing this cast album in its original LP edition will think they've set their player on "Random" mode: Aside from the overture, no song is in the same position as it was on the original. Still, in either medium, *Tovarich* is a pleasant listen, with a score by composer Lee Pockriss and lyricist Anne Croswell. Film stars Vivien Leigh and Jean Pierre Aumont play the leads, Tatiana and Mikail, two Russian royals who flee to Paris after the revolution and hire themselves out as a butler and a maid. Most of the songs aren't terribly dramatic, as their titles indicate: "You Love Me," "The Only One," "I Know the Feeling," and "All for You." But they're all lovely and they do have the right feel. Margery Gray and Byron Mitchell, as the young adults in the household who fall in puppy love with their new servants, have two undistinguished but fun songs together. And Mitchell gets to do a Charleston with Leigh in the tuneful paean to "Wilkes-Barre, PA."

—PETER FILICHIA

A TREE GROWS IN BROOKLYN
Original Broadway Cast, 1951 (Columbia/Sony) ★★★★

With its high nostalgia quotient and dream ballet, this adaptation of Betty Smith's beloved novel (scripted by Smith herself, with George Abbott's help) may seem more like Rodgers and

Hammerstein than Arthur Schwartz and Dorothy Fields. Although *A Tree Grows in Brooklyn* didn't quite recoup its investment, the show felt like a hit at the time—and the cast album, produced by Goddard Lieberson with his usual finesse, captures the excitement of laying down the tracks just after the rave reviews came in. Schwartz's music shows his fine gift for evoking time, place, and mood in his songs, and Fields superbly captures the rough-and-tumble atmosphere of early-twentieth-century Brooklyn in her lyrics, which are poignant, salty, or hilarious by turns. As the tragic young Nolans, Johnny Johnston and Marcia Van Dyke are a bit on the dull side but are blessed with magnificent material, from his cocky "Mine 'Til Monday" and "I'm Like a New Broom" to her pensive "Make the Man Love Me" and joyous "Look Who's Dancing." As sassy Aunt Cissy, Shirley Booth is occasionally off-pitch but otherwise dead-on, wringing every drop of bawdiness and poignancy from "He Had Refinement" and "Is That My Prince?" Abrupt tonal shifts between comedy and tragedy betray the dramaturgical problems that brought the show down after eight months, and even with a hokey hit-song finale fashioned especially for the recording, the album lasts a mere fifty-two minutes. But it's an excellent preservation of an undersung, affecting score.   —MARC MILLER

TRIUMPH OF LOVE
Original Broadway Cast, 1997 (JAY) ★★★
Pierre Marivaux's 1722 farce *La Surprise de L'amour* gets a musical workout and an English title, *Triumph of Love,* thanks to librettist James Magruder, composer Jeffrey Stock, and lyricist Susan Birkenhead. Christoper Sieber is Agis, a young Prince of Sparta, raised by his rationalist Aunt Hesione (Betty Buckley) and Uncle Hermocrates (F. Murray Abraham) to hate emotions and the usurping Princess Leonide (Susan Egan). Naturally, the latter shows up, love blossoms, and complications multiply like rabbits. (This show sets a world's record for mistaken-identity plot twists.) The narrative is wearying at times—even reading the synopsis in the CD booklet can lead to fatigue—but the songs are accomplished and often enjoyable. Stock has a definite gift for soaring, exciting melodies, orchestrated here by Bruce Coughlin, and Birkenhead's lyrics are very witty. The best songs are the opener, "This Day of Days," "Serenity," and "Issue in Question," in which Hesione and Agis struggle with feelings of love. "Teach Me Not to Love You," is a notably pretty quartet. The score is less successful when trolling for Broadway laughs via the clown characters played by Nancy Opel, Roger Bart, and Kevin Chamberlin, whose songs include "Mr. Right" and "Henchmen Are Forgotten." The cast, however, is exemplary. Buckley's singing is nothing short of heroic, especially in "Serenity" and "If I Cannot Love," a number cut during previews but offered here as a bonus track. Sieber and Egan provide sterling vocals and Abraham is surprisingly effective in "Emotions." (Note that the melody of "Mr. Right" is by Van Dyke Parks and that of "Have a Little Faith" is by Michael Kosarin.)   —DAVID BARBOUR

TUSCALOOSA'S CALLING ME . . . BUT I'M NOT GOING!
Original Off-Broadway Cast, 1975 (Vanguard/no CD) Not recommended.
The dated humor of this revue makes the cast album more of a time capsule than a listening pleasure. Written as a love letter to New York, the score, by composer Hank Beebe and lyricist Bill Heyer, takes lightly satirical swipes at Big Apple attitude ("Everything You Hate Is Right Here," sung by "Sodom and the Gomorrahs"), nudity in the theater ("Things Were Out"), sex ("Fugue for a Ménage à Trois"), and the dating scene ("Singles Bar"). The archeologically minded will appreciate the two sketches included on the recording, especially the dialogue

between a cab driver and an out-of-towner who complains about Broadway theater tickets costing seventeen dollars. It's all very lacking in distinction, though the title tune is stirring. Of the three-person cast, only Patti Perkins stands out with her childlike belt. Seventies nostalgists may change the rating above to one star. —DAVID BARBOUR

TWO BY TWO
Original Broadway Cast, 1970 (Columbia/Sony) ★★★

With music by Richard Rodgers, lyrics by Martin Charnin, and a book by Peter Stone, *Two by Two* is an adaptation of Clifford Odets' play *The Flowering Peach.* The show became notorious for the onstage antics of its star, Danny Kaye, who turned the whole thing into an unruly vaudeville act when he resorted to performing the role of Noah in a wheelchair after tearing a ligament. None of his bad behavior need be suffered on disc, although showpieces like "Ninety Again!" and "You Have Got to Have a Rudder on the Ark" do reveal a self-indulgent star. Get past that and you'll hear mostly excellent, late-career Rodgers; the master infuses ballads like "I Do Not Know a Day I Did Not Love You" and "Something Doesn't Happen" with his trademark warmth and melodic surprises. Eddie Sauter's orchestrations have a comfy feel, and Charnin's lyrics are probably the best of his career, pitched midway between the sentiment of Hammerstein and the dexterity of Hart. The supporting cast is as youthful and exuberant as Kaye is old-school and steeped in shtick: Walter Willison sings out with real Broadway juvenile brio and Madeline Kahn nails a high C at the end of a vulgar piece of special material. The CD has a brief Act I finale track that's missing from the LP, and it's a much better sonic mix. —MARC MILLER

TWO GENTLEMEN OF VERONA
Original Broadway Cast, 1971 (Decca) ★★★

When you listen to the original cast recording of *Two Gentlemen of Verona,* you'll know why this show won the 1972 Tony Award for Best Musical but not for Best Score. Even though the score, by composer Galt MacDermot and lyricist John Guare, is hopelessly locked in the 1970s, the album is an enjoyable listen; it captures a show of tremendous youth, vivacity, and edge, a unique mixture of Shakespeare and rock. The result is a century-spanning musical party. Sure, there are some duds, such as "Thurio's Samba," in which swear words are rhymed with nonsense syllables. But the standouts—"Summer, Summer," "I Love My Father," "Night Letter," "Hot Lover," and the finale—are quite a bit of fun. A fine cast helps: the one-and-only Raul Julia, Clifton Davis, Diana Davila, and Jonelle Allen, all of whom sound as if they've having the time of their lives. —MATTHEW MURRAY

TWO ON THE AISLE
Original Broadway Cast, 1951 (Decca/MCA) ★★★★★

How does a recording of a second-rank show become an irreplaceable treasure? Here's how: By 1951, the big-star Broadway revue was beginning to gather up its stars and skits for a finale, largely due to competition from television variety shows. Nevertheless, Betty Comden and Adolph Green still had a few satirical tricks up their sleeves. In collaboration with composer Jule Styne, they came up with a smart throwback to the days of headliner-packed revues, and that's where *Two on the Aisle* shone most brightly: It starred Broadway's premier clown and one of the greatest singers ever to set foot on a stage. Nor were their tasks circumscribed, for Bert Lahr could sing (in an inimitable fashion) and Dolores Gray was an ace comedienne. There were also supporting actors, none of them too impressive, and a rather gruesome pair of singing lovers; fortunately, the cast album focuses on Lahr and Gray in both musical and comedic modes, without conveying their well-documented backstage feud. All here is golden, or close to it: Lahr's mock-Pagliacci ode to "The Clown"; the chorus's "Show Train," an amusing précis of then-current stage hits; and Lahr and Gray as a vaudeville team invading the Metropolitan Opera ("You'll be Lucia," he blusters, "and I'll be Sextet"). Gray is sensational, her songs perfectly tailored to her fabulous singing—intimate yet volcanic, funny, sexy, and so technically accomplished (with that precise diction) that lieder recitalists should study it. Gray's performance of "If (You Hadn't but You Did)" alone earns her a place in the Broadway pantheon.   —RICHARD BARRIOS

TWO'S COMPANY
Original Broadway Cast, 1952 (RCA) ★★★

Bette Davis always claimed that she knew exactly what she was doing when she decided to star in this revue. "Just turn me loose on Broadway as a musical comedy girl," she sings (?) here. *Two's Company* certainly had some prime talent behind it: composer Vernon Duke, lyricists Ogden Nash and Sammy Cahn, choreographer Jerome Robbins, and a strong cast that included David Burns, Ellen Hanley, and Nora Kaye. But the critics were bewildered, and Davis' illness forced the show to close after three sold-out months on Broadway. Without this particular star, *Two's Company* would have been just another late-entry collection of topical skits and so-so songs; with her, it has retained a status perched somewhere between legendary disaster and unparalleled curiosity. The cast album certainly makes for interesting listening. The material is adequate, the supporting cast and presentation are strong, and the opening "Theatre Is a Lady" is a worthy anthem to a still-sturdy 1950s institution. Onstage, Davis' authority may have masked some of her musical deficiencies; but on the recording, she sounds like a drag impersonator in a piano bar just before last call. Her pitch is uniquely her own and her phrasing is a harbinger of her odd line readings in her later films. In a hillbilly number, "Purple Rose," she's game but uneasy and not too funny, yet she's touching in the torchy "Just Like a Man." Since her only subsequent musical was the ill-fated, unrecorded *Miss Moffatt,* the *Two's Company* album is a fascinating footnote to a long, magnificently uneven career.   —RICHARD BARRIOS

THE UNSINKABLE MOLLY BROWN
Original Broadway Cast, 1960 (Capitol) ★★★★

"I Ain't Down Yet" shouts/sings the title character of this rowdy musical based on the real-life story of Molly Brown, and that might also be the motto of the show itself. Composer-lyricist Meredith Willson wrote this score right after his spectacular success with *The Music Man*. In a sense, *The Unsinkable Molly Brown* is the feisty younger sister of that great American musical; it's rough around the edges, not as suave or perfect, but just as appealing in its own way. One reason for its moderate initial success was the casting of the young Tammy Grimes and Harve Presnell, who were instantly recognized for their star quality in the show's leading roles. Grimes' inimitable voice is perfect for Molly, and her performance on the album is full of energy; especially rousing are "I Ain't Down Yet" and "Belly Up to the Bar, Boys." Presnell's gorgeous baritone is a joy; when he belts out "I'll Never Say No," goose bumps rise. The album is so well recorded that it makes you feel as if you're seated front-row-center for this joyous musical. (Note: Oddly, although Johnny Brown's "Colorado, My Home" is in the show's printed score and the melody is heard briefly in the overture, the song is not sung by Presnell on the album.)

Film Soundtrack, 1964
(MGM/Rhino-Turner) ★★★★

Debbie Reynolds wrapped this musical around her little finger when she made the movie version. Although the film is uneven, Reynolds propels it into the realm of a great MGM musical by shouting, grunting, and absolutely refusing to give less than 100 percent of herself to the role of Molly. Happily, Harve Presnell recreates his stunning Broadway performance as Johnny Brown; here, he sounds less baritonal and more tenorish than he does on the Broadway recording, but the effect is appropriate for the greater intimacy of the film medium. One of Presnell's best numbers is the majestic "Colorado, My Home" (absent on the Broadway album). "I Ain't Down Yet' and "Belly Up to the Bar Boys" are the highpoints for Reynolds. Robert Armbruster's musical direction is excellent and the thrilling orchestrations are just about up to par with the great MGM musical sound of earlier decades. The only unfortunate aspect of the film and the soundtrack album is that so many of the Broadway songs were excised; missed most

---

ALL-TIME FAVORITES

OF PERFORMER

Douglas Sills

1. The Music Man

2. Fiddler on the Roof

3. West Side Story

4. My Fair Lady

5. South Pacific

6. Dreamgirls

7. A Chorus Line

8. Les Misérables

9. Ragtime

10. Sunday in the Park
    With George

of all are "Beautiful People of Denver" and "Are You Sure?" Willson did write one new song for the film: "He's My Friend," a free-for-all dance number that helps keep the second half of the movie buoyant—at least until that scene where the *Titanic* sinks. Rhino's expanded soundtrack CD is a delight.

—GERARD ALESSANDRINI

URINETOWN
Original Broadway Cast, 2001 (RCA) ★★★★

Urinetown, which winks at Bertolt Brecht-Kurt Weill works and like-minded tuners, poses the musical question: Is it possible for a score to be too clever? The answer is probably yes. To complement a book about a Mahagonny-type burg where the citizens are oppressed by a corporation that controls all restrooms, composer-lyricist Mark Hollmann and lyricist-librettist Greg Kotis wrote a tuneful score that cannily mocks even as it pays homage. While hooting at musical clichés in song and dialogue, the creators walk a thin line with the agility of world-class aerialists. Spilling from this words-and-notes cornucopia are send-ups of such musical conventions as title tunes, double-edged ballads ("Follow Your Heart"), comedy turns ("Don't Be the Bunny"), and heart-lifters ("Run, Freedom, Run!"). The cast is led by staunch Hunter Foster, full-of-his-bad-self John Cullum, cute-as-a-frayed-button Spencer Kayden, sincere Jennifer Laura Thompson, and Jeff McCarthy, who places his tongue very firmly in his cheek in the role of Officer Lockstock. All have the required fervor. The problem is an embarrassment of riches that begins to tire the listener as the songs, delivered by a dynamic ensemble, start to sound alike. Of course, those who know *Urinetown* only on disc can't see the wonders worked by director John Rando and choreographer John Carrafa, who followed the tunesmiths' ribbing of various styles of musical theater writing by doing the same with direction and choreography. Still, the score is far above average for contemporary musicals and very well played by a sassy five-man band, with Edward Goldschneider at the piano.

—DAVID FINKLE

THE UTTER GLORY OF MORRISSEY HALL
Original Broadway Cast, 1979 (Original Cast Records) ★★

This was a good idea: a sort of unofficial musical version of the old "St. Trinian's" stories and movies about an English school filled with horrid little girls. The first ten minutes of the show are fun as authors Clark Gesner and Nagle Jackson (who also directed) set up various characters and story lines—and then simply abandon them. The rest of *The Utter Glory of Morrissey Hall* is plotless, filled with incidents that don't tie together. For example, one group of girls believe they're about to be sold into white slavery; a young boy in love mails himself to his girlfriend in a trunk; and there's a grown-up romance between a secretary and a salesman who must hide their passion. Presiding over all of this is the dotty headmistress, played amusingly by Celeste Holm. As events spin out of her control, the woman simply withdraws, locking herself in her office and happily pressing flowers. Gesner, the composer-lyricist of *You're a Good Man, Charlie Brown,* provides a score that's lightly mocking in a stiff-upper-lip sort of way—but, without anything substantial to hang these songs on, they don't add up to much.

—DAVID WOLF

VERY GOOD EDDIE
Broadway Cast, 1975 (DRG) ★★★

Very lively, very catchy, very melodic—but not *Very Good Eddie.* The Goodspeed Opera House's revival of the 1915 Jerome Kern musical—the first show in the famed Princess Theatre series— was such a hit in Connecticut that David Merrick picked it up and brought it intact to Broadway, where it ran for nearly a year. But, as is Goodspeed's bad habit, the production fiddled with perfectly fine original material. The result was a kind of hybrid, with several songs missing and others appropriated from various Kern shows—so much so that nine lyricists are credited! Russell Warner's lean orchestrations are probably reasonable reductions of Frank Saddler's originals but, as musical director, Warner sticks pretty much to one speed: "rollicking." Yes, the score is full of infectious ragtime, but even ragtime should have more variety than this. Worse, the performance style evinces much winking and borderline camping, especially among the women: Virginia Seidel's Minnie-Mouse-on-speed chirping just about kills the irresistible "Left All Alone Again Blues," and Travis Hudson stomps "Moon of Love" into the floorboards. But male leads Charles Repole and David Christmas are more sedate; and the chorus numbers, such as "I've Got to Dance" and "Hot Dog," are so ingratiating that you will, in fact, want to get up and dance.

— MARC MILLER

VICTOR/VICTORIA
Film Soundtrack, 1982 (MGM/Rhino) ★

The Blake Edwards film that served as the basis for Julie Andrews' last Broadway musical is really a comedy with a few incidental songs. Based on a 1933 German film, it stars Andrews as Victoria, a light opera soprano stranded in 1920s Paris; she's taken in by Toddy (Robert Preston), a gay nightclub performer who reinvents her as Victor, a Polish female impersonator. Trouble sets in when King Marchan, a Chicago gangster (James Garner), finds himself attracted to "Victor." The wildly padded soundtrack disc is filled with instrumental interludes from Henry Mancini's easy-listening score. The film's few actual songs, with lyrics by Leslie Bricusse, are heard repeatedly in different versions; for example, the silly specialty item "The Shady Dame From Seville." Andrews and Preston are never less than pros, but this recording is just barely worthwhile.

ALL-TIME FAVORITES
OF LYRICIST-LIBRETTIST

Bill Russell

1. Sweeney Todd
2. Gypsy
3. West Side Story
4. The King and I
5. Cabaret
6. Guys and Dolls
7. She Loves Me
8. The Music Man
9. Little Shop of Horrors
10. The Most Happy Fella

Original Broadway Cast, 1995 (Philips) ★

Julie Andrews' much-anticipated return to Broadway was upstaged to a certain extent by this show's many peripheral dramas, including Andrews' frequent absences, her Tony Awards boycott, and the notorious replacement runs of Liza Minnelli and Raquel Welch. Small wonder: *Victor/Victoria* was a long-run disappointment, a ham-fisted adaptation of a hit Andrews film put together by a mediocre creative team led by Andrews' husband, director-librettist Blake Edwards. As in the film—which was also written and directed by Edwards—Andrews' Victoria is transformed into Victor by Toddy, played here by Tony Roberts (see the review above for more of the plot). Even with her voice darkened by age and afflicted with mannerisms, Andrews is fun to hear on the album; but to get to the pleasant bits, you'll have to put up with some of the weakest songs ever written for a Broadway show. The main culprits are Henry Mancini and Leslie Bricusse, but additional music was written by Frank Wildhorn after Mancini's death. "If I Were a Man" sets up the plot in the most laborious fashion; even worse is "King's Lament," in which Victoria's love interest, King Marchan (Michael Nouri), wrestles with his masculinity. The rock-bottom songs go to Rachel York in the role of King's chorine girlfriend; they include "Chicago, Illinois" from the movie version ("Smack on the lake, this is a rare port / Someday they say we'll have an airport!") and the egregious "Paris Makes Me Horny," which rummages through the names of European cities for the sake of smutty jokes. (Sample: "Been to Munich, where every guy's a eunuch.") Andrews makes something out of generic ballads like "Crazy World" (again, from the film) and "Living in the Shadows," and she has fun with "Le Jazz Hot" (also from the film), but she and Nouri are defeated by the deadly "Almost a Love Song," which has almost a melody. An unintentional camp highlight is "Louis Says," one of Victor's onstage numbers, in which Andrews swans about the stage as Marie Antoinette. Just try to parse the impenetrable stream-of-consciousness lyrics of this song.   —DAVID BARBOUR

VIOLET
Original Off-Broadway Cast, 1998 (Resmiranda) ★★★

Dorris Betts' short story "The Ugliest Pilgrim"—about a young woman who, maimed by an axe blade as a child, goes on a journey of healing—was the basis for this gem with lyrics by Brian Crawley and music by Jeanine Tesori. Lauren Ward's Violet is a complex heroine; injured both inside and out, she's full of both bitterness and hope, and her lovely performance translates well onto the disc. It's when Violet's biting tongue turns sweet that she sings the highlight of the score, "Lay Down Your Head," with a melody that makes one's heart ache. The other songs don't quite reach that level of simple perfection, but the all-too-brief "Water in the Well," the thrilling "Let It Sing," and "On My Way"—a rousing ensemble number that sets Violet and her fellow passengers off on their bus trip—come close. Violet's trek takes her from North Carolina to Oklahoma, where she goes to meet the televangelist who she hopes will heal her. On the way, she becomes involved in a love triangle with two soldiers, one white (played by Michael Park) and one black (played by Michael McElroy). Crawley tells their story through colloquial lyrics that feel effortless and natural. Tesori comes up with a handful of fine countrified tunes; her gospel songs are less distinguished, but the Broadway Gospel Choir and the powerhouse singer-actor McElroy give this spirited musical some real soul.   —BROOKE PIERCE

WALKING HAPPY
Original Broadway Cast, 1966 (Capitol/Angel) ★★

One of the problems with *Walking Happy,* which is set in England, is that it seems too American. Still, the show has an entertaining score with some sprightly tunes and heartfelt ballads by the Academy Award-winning team of lyricist Sammy Cahn and composer James Van Heusen. The songs for the two leads—British star Norman Wisdom as Boot Black Will Mossop and American Louise Troy as Maggie Hobson, the eldest daughter of Will's employer—are very well integrated with the book. Troy touches the heart with Maggie's "Where Was I?" while Will ponders "What Makes It Happen?" in his love-seeking ballad. As their relationship turns romantic, Troy's Maggie does a beautiful "I'll Make a Man of the Man" and the pair sings the charming "I Don't Think I'm in Love." Throughout, Troy adds a reasonable British accent to her stylish Broadway belt. Wisdom brings a warm voice to the show's title song and comedic skill to his two duets with fellow bootblack Tubby (Gordon Dilworth), "How D'Ya Talk to a Girl" (inventively accompanied by the rhythmic sounds of men hammering nails into boot heels) and "It Might as Well Be Her." The rest of the score is less good. George Rose, as Maggie's father, participates in three weak songs dealing with the fellow's sobriety or lack thereof. "Use Your Noggin," sung by Maggie and her two sisters (Sharon Dierking and Gretchen Van Aken), features a sprightly melody but lyrics so generic that the song could be put into almost any musical. And one of Will's numbers is the unfortunate "If I Be Your Best Chance," a prickly "poor me" song. Missing from this disc are two dance numbers that were effective onstage: "Clog and Grog" and the "Box Dance." However, a good amount of dialogue is included, which makes it easy to follow the plot.   —JEFFREY DUNN

WATCH YOUR STEP
Off-Off-Broadway Cast, 2001
(Original Cast Records) ★

Irving Berlin's first hit was exhumed by the Off-Off-Broadway company Musicals Tonight! in 2001. According to the CD notes, the show is a fairly typical 1914 frolic with a thin-to-the-point-of-transparency plot about a will that requires its recipients never to have been in love. After that, you're on your own; there's no synopsis to indicate how the songs fit into the story. Furthermore, Berlin interpolated numerous songs into the show during its several months' run,

ALL-TIME FAVORITES OF
PLAYWRIGHT-LIBRETTIST

Arthur Laurents

1. Gypsy
2. West Side Story
3. Show Boat
4. As Thousands Cheer
5. My Fair Lady
6. Oh! What a Lovely War!
7. Carousel
8. Hello, Dolly!
9. Cabaret
10. Jelly's Last Jam

and all of them are included here. While the disc is unquestionably of archival importance, it comes off less as a show album than a collection of novelty tunes from the early World War I era. Songs like "Come to the Land of the Argentine," "Show Us How to Do the Fox Trot," and "Settle Down in a One-Horse Town" could come from virtually any musical of the same general provenance. For that matter, they all sound alike, set as they are to the same ragtime beat. The young cast sings with enthusiasm; the one semi-name, David Sabella, is amusing in numbers like "Lock Me in Your Harem." Berlin enthusiasts and those with an interest in the period should add a star or two to the rating above, but the CD has little to offer the general listener.   —DAVID BARBOUR

WEIRD ROMANCE
Original Off-Broadway Cast, 1993 (Columbia) ★★★★
Composer Alan Menken wrote some of his most dazzling and sophisticated music for this largely forgotten pair of one-act musicals. With librettist Alan Brennert, lyricist-librettist David Spencer, and director Barry Harman, Menken and his collaborators crafted a musical in that most neglected of stage genres: science fiction (also known as "speculative fiction"). The first piece, "The Girl Who Was Plugged In," is based on a James Tiptree, Jr. story; the second, "Her Pilgrim Soul," was adapted from an episode of *The New Twilight Zone* written by Brennert. The superlative cast includes Ellen Greene and Jonathan Hadary as both acts' leads, supported by Danny Burstein, Jessica Molaskey, Valerie Pettiford, Sal Viviano, Eric Riley, William Youmans, and Marguerite Macintyre. If the music isn't always at the level of Menken's best—"Amazing Penetration" will never be found on a greatest hits album—it's hard to think of better melodies than the first half's "Eyes That Never Lie" and the second's "Another Woman" and "Someone Else Is Waiting." As for Spencer's lyrics, they are solid and often clever. The only problem with the cast album is that, unfortunately, it's out of print.   —SETH CHRISTENFELD

WEST SIDE STORY
Original Broadway Cast, 1957 (Columbia/Sony) ★★★★★
With music by Leonard Bernstein, lyrics by Stephen Sondheim (and an uncredited Bernstein), and book by Arthur Laurents, *West Side Story* is a groundbreaking musical theater work that remains vital and is continually revived, both professionally and by schools and community theaters. The phenomenal score—including the songs "Tonight," "Maria," and "Somewhere"—deepens the audience's emotional involvement in an immortal story of star-crossed lovers, inspired by Shakespeare's *Romeo and Juliet* and reset among warring American and Puerto Rican gangs in Manhattan, circa 1957. Happily, the score is well represented by this recording, which has a theatrical snap and an emotional conviction that more than compensate for whatever it lacks in sheer musical values. Although Carol Lawrence's soprano thins out in the highest reaches of Maria's music and Larry Kert's tenor develops an unattractive, Jolsonesque quality when he pushes for volume, both performers sound fine in the more lyrical sections of the score and bring a youthful, unaffected style to their roles. Chita Rivera is a ball of fire as Anita, and Mickey Calin (later Michael Callan) sounds equally sexy as Riff. Reri Grist sings a lovely "Somewhere," and Marilyn Cooper makes a notable contribution to the "America" number. Nearly an hour's worth of material was laid down in the studio, making this one of the longest Broadway cast albums of its day—the better to document the superb score. (Among the few

significant sections missing are the "Blues" and "Promenade" sections of the Dance at the Gym.) The bravura playing of the orchestra, conducted by Max Goberman, is captured in excellent early stereo sound.

Film Soundtrack, 1961 (Columbia/Sony) ★★★★★

The ubiquitous movie vocal double Marni Nixon here sings Maria's music in lieu of the film's star, Natalie Wood, and her performance points up one of the problems in casting *West Side Story:* If you hire singers who can fulfill the musical requirements of this difficult score, they will probably not be convincing as New York street kids. Some listeners are put off by the operatic nature of Nixon's sound on the album, but her soprano is very beautiful in itself and the matching of her singing to Wood's speech is skillfully done in the film. Conversely, Jim Bryant—performing Tony's music for Richard Beymer—has a sound that is less "legit" and also less beautiful. Betty Wand does a terrific job singing most or all of Anita's role for Rita Moreno (depending on which source you believe). An intriguing fact of the recording is that, while Russ Tamblyn sings for himself in "Gee, Officer Krupke," he is dubbed by fellow cast member Tucker Smith for the "Jet Song." Since Smith does his own singing in "Cool," he's actually heard on the soundtrack as two different characters. (To make things even more interesting, Nixon sings Anita's part in the latter half of the "Quintet"—presumably because it was too high for Wand or Moreno.) Happily, this album features what are more or less the original theater orchestrations by Bernstein, Sid Ramin, and Irwin Kostal, souped-up for a much larger orchestra conducted by Johnny Green. The expanded CD includes dialogue and music taken directly from the film. Though it's great to have this extra material, including a thrilling recording of the "Mambo," the sound quality of the added sections does not exactly match that of the tracks taken from the soundtrack album master, and the switching from one to the other is disconcerting.

Studio Cast, 1985 (Deutsche Grammophon) Not recommended.

A complete disaster, preserved for posterity not only here but also in a gasp-inducing film documentary of the studio sessions. It was a great idea to have Leonard Bernstein conduct a full recording of the *West Side Story* score, but a horrendous idea to cast all of the major roles with opera singers. Although José Carreras' voice is impressive, it has nothing to do with the character of Tony, and the tenor's thick Latino accent makes him ridiculous in the role. The late Tatiana Troyanos was a great operatic artist but is an overripe Anita, while the equally talented baritone Kurt Ollman creates a sound more appropriate for Don Giovanni than for Riff. As Maria, Kiri Te Kanawa fares best among the principals but still sounds too mature and self-possessed to be credible as a young, unpolished Puerto Rican girl. Even Bernstein's conducting is a disappointment; there are wonderful moments but also some odd tempi. The saving grace of the project is Marilyn Horne's idiomatically gorgeous and moving rendition of "Somewhere."

London Studio Cast, 1993 (JAY, 2CDs) ★

According to a note in the accompanying booklet, "This recording is inspired by the Leicester Haymarket Theatre production which opened on November 20, 1992." It's a complete, two-disc recording of the score with some nice features. The tempi set by conductor John Owen Edwards are much closer to ideal than those usually found in a British performance of an American musical; one exception is the performance of "I Feel Pretty," which is far too slow,

Edwards here following the bad example set by composer Leonard Bernstein himself on the Deutsche Grammophon recording reviewed above. The brilliant *West Side Story* score, in its original orchestrations by Bernstein, Sid Ramin, and Irwin Kostal, is magnificently played by the National Symphony Orchestra under Edwards' leadership. Also, the sound quality of the recording is superb, its dynamic range allowing for many exciting musical moments. As for the singers, Tinuke Olafimihan is a lovely Maria, and Caroline O'Connor is very good as Anita despite her tendency to growl a little too often. Another plus is Sally Burgess' beautiful rendition of "Somewhere." But Paul Manuel's voice is so thin that it's hard to understand how he could ever have been cast as Tony. Another problem is Manuel's inability to disguise his English accent; the same thing can be said for all of the "Jets" on this recording, and it sure is disconcerting to hear New York street toughs sounding like Brits. (Note: An out-of-print LP of *West Side Story* that was billed as the original London cast album is mislabled; it's actually a London studio cast recording and is not recommended.)

London Studio Cast, 1993 (Pickwick/Warner Classics) Not recommended.

This recording stars Michael Ball and Barbara Bonney as Tony and Maria, LaVerne Williams as Anita, and Christopher Howard as Riff. (In a major oversight, the "Somewhere" soloist is not identified; it sounds like it could be Bonney, but your guess is as good as mine.) The principals are backed by the Royal Philharmonic Orchestra and Chorus as conducted by Barry Wordsworth—but if all of the above sounds good to you, please think twice. This is the most appalling recording of the *West Side Story* score that has ever been foisted on the public. The chief offender is Ball, who possesses an exceptional voice but apparently has no idea how to use it. When he sings "Tonight there will be no morning star," the last word sounds like "staah-uh-EHHHH." The tastelessness of Ball's vocalism is exacerbated by his attempt to sound like a New York teenager; instead, he sounds like a Brit affecting the mannerisms of a Las Vegas lounge singer. Williams, a mezzo with a cavernous register break, is just as bad; her performance as the earthy Anita sounds like something in a comedy sketch about opera singers ruining great musicals. Howard and the other Jets are less objectionable, though their attempts to hide their British accents are amusing. Bonney is the most successful of the vocalists by far. As for the orchestral cuts on this album, the prologue is lethargic and each section of the "Dance at the Gym" sequence is either a little too fast or a little too slow. This recording would be ready for landfill if the CD and its plastic jewel case weren't nonbiodegradable.

Studio Cast, 2001 (Naxos) ★★

This is billed as a recording of "the original score" of *West Side Story,* whatever that means. All sections of the "Dance at the Gym" are included but not the ethereally beautiful setting of "Maria" that accompanies Tony and Maria's love-at-first-sight scene. The version of "America" heard here is a hybrid; it's sung by the "Sharks" men and women, as in the 1961 film, but the lyrics are a mixture of those used in the stage show and the movie. Although the entire balcony scene is included, the dialogue is spoken so ineptly by Mike Eldred and Betsi Morrison that you'll wish it hadn't been. Eldred acquits himself best among the leads; in fact, his ardent, youthful tenor makes him the best Tony on records despite some intrusive pop mannerisms. Morrison is less consistent, coming through in the clutch (as in the "Tonight" quintet) but elsewhere sounding insipid. Similarly, Michelle Prentice calls to mind a breathy pop singer in the opening phrases of "Somewhere" but handles the song's climaxes well. Robert Dean offers a paradoxical Riff, his burly vocal tone undercut by sibilant esses. As captured in thrilling digital sound, the Nashville Symphony Orchestra sounds great playing the score, but some of Kenneth Schemerhorn's tempi are sluggish.   —MICHAEL PORTANTIERE

WHAT ABOUT LUV?
Studio Cast, 1990 (JAY) Not recommended.

The only reason to musicalize a play is to add something to it, to enrich the original material. But again and again in this show based on Murray Schisgal's unique, distinctive, and uproarious 1964 comedy *Luv,* moments from the play are flattened out by what can only be called by-the-numbers musical theater writing. For instance, one famous scene in the play has two men comparing their miserable childhoods, each trying to prove that he had a tougher upbringing; simply putting the scene into song form robs it of most of its surprise, and about half of the original material is missing entirely. In another scene, the wife of one of the men comes on with a graph illustrating their lack of a sex life, and the no-nonsense tone of her speech is immensely funny. But composer Howard Marren and lyricist Susan Birkenhead have set the sequence as a jazz waltz, which is not only emotionally inappropriate but also makes it very difficult to understand the words. The plot point is covered, but it's not the least bit funny anymore. Throughout, the thoroughly conventional songs sentimentalize the characters in a shocking betrayal of the loopy original material. The cast of this recording includes Judy Kaye (who starred in the original Off-Broadway production) along with her husband David Green and the unrelated Simon Green.   —DAVID WOLF

WHAT MAKES SAMMY RUN?
Original Broadway Cast, 1964 (Columbia/GL Music) ★

Longtime theatergoers will recall that, for a brief time decades ago, Steve Lawrence was touted as the next great Broadway leading man. Exhibit A is this now-forgotten hit (540 performances), adapted by Budd Schulberg and his brother Stuart from the former's scalding novel about Hollywood climbers. Lawrence is Sammy Glick, who rises from the position of copy boy for a New York newspaper to top Hollywood producer in record time, by any means needed. Sally Ann Howes plays a buttoned-up screenwriter with a yen for hustlers; she's loved from afar by fellow screenwriter and student of Glick Robert Alda. All three are fine, but they're let down by composer-lyricist Ervin Drake's score, which strains for ring-a-ding sophistication and doesn't achieve it. Every number sounds like the opener of a Vegas floor show. Lawrence and Howes do well in "A Room Without Windows" and Lawrence teams effectively with Bernice Massi, as a studio exec's predatory daughter, in the appropriately titled "You're No Good." Don Walker's generic orchestrations are no help; neither is the CD edition of the recording, released in mono by Lawrence. It was mediocre shows like this, with their derivative melodies and almost-clever lyrics, that helped bring down the curtain on Broadway's golden age.   —DAVID BARBOUR

WHAT'S A NICE COUNTRY LIKE YOU DOING IN A STATE LIKE THIS?
Original London Cast, 1976 (Galaxy/no CD) ★

This unlikely Off-Broadway success of 1972 (which had as its logo a drawing of an unhappily pregnant Statue of Liberty) did not yield a cast album until the revue crossed the Atlantic. The material, by lyricist-librettist Ira Gasman and composer Cary Hoffman, is not particularly distinguished and some of it is actually dispiriting. In the opening number, for example, the five performers sing a relentlessly cheerful song about how terrible everything in America is. ("How did Uncle Sam get in a jam like this?") The rest covers fairly shallow revue ground, which in the '70s meant songs about Nixon, Kissinger, the homeless, and man/woman relationships. Someone sings "The Liberation Tango," in which "the woman always leads." Someone else sings about her lover, killed in the war, and another woman delivers a series of brief, recurring torch songs about her tortured relationships: "I'm in love with a bisexual . . . when you're in love with a bisexual, you only stand half a chance." And: "When you're in love with a transvestite, your clothes wear out twice as fast." That's about as clever as it gets. The liner notes for this London recording don't identify who sings what, but all of the performers—Peter Blake, Billy Boyle, Neil McCaul, Jacquie Toye, and Leueen Willoughby—are fine.　　　　　　　　　　　　—DAVID WOLF

WHEN PIGS FLY
(aka Howard Crabtree's When Pigs Fly)
Original Off-Broadway Cast, 1997 (RCA) ★★

The second of two revues that showcased the talents of outré costume designer Howard Crabtree was an evening of bright, largely gay humor; though some of the songs by composer Dick Gallagher and lyricist-librettist Mark Waldrop are fun, the show's real strength was visual, matching sketches to outrageously elaborate costume designs. A number called "Light in the Loafers" loses something when you don't see dancers wearing electrified shoes; so does "Not All Man," which was delivered onstage by David Pevsner dressed as a centaur. A sketch featuring Stanley Bojarski as Carol Ann Knippel, the doyenne of a Midwest community theater, doesn't slay on disc the way it did live. Still, there are occasional pleasures—many of them courtesy of Jay Rogers, who delivers a series of torch songs aimed at the right-wing ideologues Newt Gingrich, Strom Thurmond, and Rush Limbaugh. Rogers also gets the show's best number: the sad, ruminative "Laughing Matters," which only gains in poignancy when one knows that Crabtree died of AIDS shortly after this show opened.　　　　　　　—DAVID BARBOUR

WHERE'S CHARLEY?
Original London Cast, 1958 (Columbia/Angel) ★★★★★
Based on *Charley's Aunt,* the reliable old farce by Brandon Thomas, *Where's Charley?* was a big hit on Broadway in 1948 with Ray Bolger in the lead but didn't yield an original cast album, apparently due to a musicians' strike; nor has there ever been a commercially released album drawn from the obscure 1952 film version, in which Bolger recreated his stage role of Charley Wykeham. Fortunately, the London production yielded an excellent recording of the delightful score by composer-lyricist Frank Loesser. British stage and film comedian Norman Wisdom may have lacked Bolger's high-wattage energy but he was much better suited to the part of Charley in terms of accent and singing ability, and his performance here is solid. The supporting cast is generally fine: Pip Hinton is adorable as Amy Spettigue, while Pamela Gale and Marion Grimaldi sing beautifully as (respectively) Kitty Verdun and Donna Lucia d'Alvadorez. Felix Felton is very funny as Mr. Spettigue, who has no idea that Charley's Aunt—the woman he's wooing for her money—is actually Charley in drag. Indeed, the one inadequate member of the company is Terence Cooper, who exhibits a throaty singing voice as Jack Chesney. "Once in Love With Amy" is the show's big hit, but the score is chocka-block with skillfully crafted comedy numbers ("Better Get Out of Here," "The Woman in

His Room") and sweepingly lyrical love songs ("My Darling, My Darling," "Lovelier Than Ever," "At the Red Rose Cotillion"). Disappointingly, only a fragment of the title song is included on the disc; a lengthy ensemble number, it's here reduced to one brief chorus introduced by Wisdom's quotation of the show's most famous line of dialogue: "I am Charley's aunt from Brazil—where the nuts come from!" The album would be essential if only because it's the sole recording of a fine Loesser score, so it's good news that the performance is so praiseworthy overall. The early stereo sound of the recording is excellent; it's too bad that the CD is out of print as of this writing.

—MICHAEL PORTANTIERE

WHISTLE DOWN THE WIND
Studio Cast, 1998 (Polydor) ★

Labeled *Songs from Whistle Down the Wind,* this collection of twelve numbers performed by a lineup of pop stars is easier to take than the subsequent London stage cast recording of the Andrew Lloyd Webber score. Divorced from the show's ludicrous story line (detailed below) and arranged as the disposable pop artifacts they really are, the songs actually provide some enjoyment. Tom Jones, aided by Sounds of Blackness, offers a soulful "Vaults of Heaven." The boy band Boyzone does right by the repetitive "No Matter What" and Donny Osmond proves to be the ideal interpreter of "When Children Rule the World." Also on hand are Elaine Paige, Meat Loaf, Boy George, Bonnie Tyler, and Michael Ball. It's a relatively painless way to enjoy the modest pleasures of a misbegotten show.

Original London Cast, 1999 (Really Useful Records) ★

This egregious Andrew Lloyd Webber musical is based on a novel by Mary Hayley Bell and a subsequent screenplay by Keith Waterhouse and Willis Hall; it's about poor children in rural England who mistake an escaped murderer for Jesus Christ. Told with restraint, it could have been a moving tale. But a committee of librettists—Patricia Knopf, director Gale Edwards, and Lloyd Webber himself—made the disastrous decision to reset the action in the American South in the 1950s. The show begins with one of the composer's finest songs, the gospel tune "Vaults of Heaven," but the score quickly turns into an unpalatable mixture of sticky sentiment and violent melodrama. Catchy tunes are often laughably unsuited to the onstage action, and matters aren't helped by Jim Steinman's clunky lyrics. The songwriters' try-anything approach includes a pair of faux Brecht-Weill items—"Annie Christmas" and "Charlie Christmas"—plus the unbearably cute "When Children Rule the World" and the ridiculous "A Kiss Is a Terrible Thing to Waste." The nadir is "Tire Tracks and Broken Hearts," assigned to a pair of interracial lovers, which recycles the melody of "English Girls" from *Song & Dance.* As the simple young waif Swallow and the escaped convict whom she believes is her Savior, Dottie Mayor and Marcus Lovett provide plenty of vocal emoting, but the songs are further sabotaged by the vulgar orchestrations of David Cullen and Lloyd Webber.

—DAVID BARBOUR

A WHITE HOUSE CANTATA (1600 PENNSYLVANIA AVENUE)
Studio Cast, 1998 (Deutsche Grammophon) ★

The recording of a heretofore unpreserved musical is usually a cause for celebration, but *A White House Cantata* is a maddening misfire. The 1976 Broadway flop *1600 Pennsylvania Avenue* deserves better than this, not least because its score was written by luminaries Leonard Bernstein and Alan Jay Lerner. Their compositions for the show, which concerns race relations in nineteenth-century America, are often of epic sweep, but here they're sabotaged by an inadequate presentation. Vocally, the cast is fine: Thomas Hampson and June Anderson sumptuously sing the music of all of the presidents and first ladies, while Barbara Hendricks and Kenneth Tarver are more than capable as their black servants. But the classical renditions of most of the songs are heavily overwrought and lacking in character and color; this is especially evident in "Duet for One," in which two first ladies duke it out in song. The choral numbers are rich and full, the orchestra (conducted by Kent Nagano) is beyond reproach, and a good amount of material that was lost during the show's tumultuous preview period has been restored. *A White House Cantata* is not a total loss, but the lack of theatrical verve makes this recording a poor representation of *1600 Pennsylvania Avenue* as a theater piece.   —MATTHEW MURRAY

WHOOP-UP
Original Broadway Cast, 1958 (MGM/Polydor) ★★
With a score by composer Moose Charlap and lyricist Norman Gimbel, *Whoop-Up* was a quick failure set in a Montana bar ("where you don't have to wear a tie to tie one on," goes one of the forced lyrics). You'll shake your head in amazement at such songs as "Nobody Throw That Bull," "'Caress Me, Possess Me' Perfume," "The Best of What This Country's Got (Was Taken From the Indians)," "I Wash My Hands," and "Montana," which will never become that state's official song. Susan Johnson has the strangest piece of material: "Men," in which she speak-sings nearly three minutes' worth of complaints about the male gender as a Dixieland melody plays underneath. The love songs, including the saccharine "Never Before," are no better. Particularly bizarre is "Love Eyes," sung by Ralph Young. (Sample lyric: "Your lipstick's wet and waitin' for my smear.") That there were cover versions of some of these songs would be hard to believe if the CD reissue didn't include quite a few of them. Particularly, jazz pianist Dick Hyman's two cuts are bewitching; they prove that composer Charlap did come up with some fetching melodies.   —PETER FILICHIA

WICKED
Original Broadway Cast, 2003 (Decca) ★★★★
Don't go to this recording for a perfectly accurate representation of what was heard in the theater; the songs have been somewhat edited to remove any hint of the twisty plot of *Wicked,* a musical based on Gregory Maguire's novel, which purports to tell the true story of the "good" and "bad" witches immortalized in L. Frank Baum's *The Wizard of Oz.* Still, this is Stephen Schwartz's best score—an unpopular opinion, admittedly!—and the excellent album boasts more than an hour of knockout songs, terrific high belting courtesy of stars Idina Menzel (Elphaba) and Kristin Chenoweth (Galinda/Glinda), and a fantastic orchestra conducted by Stephen Oremus. Listen particularly to Menzel's astounding performances of "The Wizard and I," "I'm Not That Girl," "No Good Deed," "Defying Gravity," and her two gorgeous duets, "As Long as You're Mine" (with Norbert Leo Butz as Fiyero) and "For Good" (with Chenoweth). Also pay special attention to William David Brohn's great orchestrations in a pop-rock idiom that's unusual for him. Unfortunately, very little of Winnie Holtzman's adept libretto is included on the disc; the absence of dialogue leaves the estimable supporting performers Carole Shelley, Joel Grey, Christopher Fitzgerald, and Michelle Federer in the lurch.   —SETH CHRISTENFELD

WILDCAT
Original Broadway Cast, 1960 (RCA) ★★

Why did *Wildcat* stray so far afield from its star's abilities? Lucille Ball had looks and charisma and great comic timing, but this was a musical, and its leading lady couldn't sing; all those *I Love Lucy* jokes about her tin-eared vocalizing were not exaggerations. The show itself is all right, sort of a female *Music Man* of the oil fields with a synthetic book by N. Richard Nash and a bouncy score by composer Cy Coleman and lyricist Carolyn Leigh. "Hey, Look Me Over" was the hit of the score, but "What Takes My Fancy" and some of the other tunes are also nice. The whole company sounds energetic on the disc, and the male lead, Keith Andes, handles his music very well. Although the recording can't convey the inventiveness of Michael Kidd's choreography, it does hint at the gusto with which Ball threw herself into her song-and-dance numbers. *Wildcat* would have run longer on Ball's name alone had she not become exhausted with the grind of eight performances a week, but the show is not compelling enough to have ever entered the arena of perennial showcase musicals.   —RICHARD BARRIOS

THE WILD PARTY (LaChiusa)
Original Broadway Cast, 2000 (Decca) ★★★★★

Composer-lyricist Michael John LaChiusa was not unknown when his adaptation of Joseph Moncure March's 1928 poem hit Broadway in 2000, but he truly laid his claim as a major force in the musical theater with this work, among the most dazzling of the "postmodern" school. The *Wild Party* CD is dynamic, a thrilling document of one of the most stirring theater scores of the late twentieth century. LaChiusa's songs—many of them pastiche on a par with Stephen Sondheim at his finest—are heavily steeped in period jazz and vaudeville styles (aided by Todd Ellison's flawless musical direction and Bruce Coughlin's searing orchestrations) while still sounding thoroughly modern and fresh. Beginning with a startlingly dissonant horn blast, the delights of the recording don't stop: Consider the raunchy "Queenie Was a Blonde"; the rip-roaring "Uptown Downtown"; the torchy "Lowdown-Down"; the bathtub-gin-infused "Wild"; the bluesy "Black Is a Moocher"; the lost-in-life lovers' duet "People Like Us"; and the eleven-o'clock showstopper, "When It Ends." That last number is delivered titanically by the legendary Eartha Kitt, but the whole cast is excellent. Leading the way are Toni Collette, sounding like a veteran in her Broadway debut as the bleached-blonde chorine Queenie, and Mandy Patinkin as her manic and violent lover Burrs. They receive top-notch support from Marc Kudisch, Tonya Pinkins, Norm Lewis, Brooke Sunny Moriber, Yancey Arias, and other distinctive performers. Although this is not a complete record of the score, there's a lot packed into the disc's seventy-eight minutes.   —MATTHEW MURRAY

THE WILD PARTY (Lippa)
Original Off-Broadway Cast, 2000 (RCA) ★★★★

This was the first of the entries in the 2000 race between two stage musical adaptations of Joseph Moncure March's epic poem. Although Andrew Lippa is a first-rate musical dramatist, his lyrics aren't always perfect (he employs a lot of metaphors that don't make any sense) and the pop-rock influence in Lippa's music is rarely accurate to the period. Still, the overall effect of the Manhattan Theatre Club production was dazzling. Unfortunately, the cast album doesn't fully indicate how brilliant the piece was onstage. For one thing, the nearly through-sung score was chopped down to seventy-three minutes of "highlights" for the recording, leaving out a great deal of interesting material. Also, the album was made shortly after the show closed, when its astounding leading lady—the previously unknown Julia Murney—wasn't in her best voice. Murney still belts the score to high heaven but not quite as high as she did in the theater. The other excellent leads are Brian d'Arcy James, Idina Menzel, and Taye Diggs, and there are terrific supporting performances by Alix Korey (who delivers the hilarious "Old-Fashioned Love Story"), Raymond Jaramillo McLeod, and Jennifer Cody. Even with the above caveats, this CD is still a fantastic listen: Among the highlights are "Raise the Roof," "A Wild, Wild Party," "Queenie Was a Blonde," "Poor Child," and "Make Me Happy." —SETH CHRISTENFELD

THE WILL ROGERS FOLLIES
Original Broadway Cast, 1991 (Sony) ★★★
Chameleonic composer Cy Coleman and stalwart Broadway lyricists Betty Comden and Adolph Green wrote the songs for *The Will Rogers Follies,* a completely original musical biography of the populist humorist as might have been concocted by Florenz Ziegfeld, in whose revues Rogers made numerous appearances. Coleman combines country twang and Broadway know-how in his music (evocatively orchestrated by Bill Byers), and the Comden-Green lyrics are bright and clever. If the score isn't of first-tier quality, it's better than just utilitarian; but it's hard to tell that from the cast recording, a lackluster audio presentation of a show that burst with life under Tommy Tune's direction. The cast certainly isn't to blame: Keith Carradine is ingratiating as Rogers, Dee Hoty's velvet voice brings Will's wife Betty to warm-hearted life, and future Tony winners Dick Latessa and Cady Huffman find great charm and humor in their supporting roles. But the score, separated from the energy of Tune's production and dances and Peter Stone's book, is less than wholly effective on its own. The dynamic production numbers "Will-a-Mania" and "Our Favorite Son" suffer the most, but even the major solo turns—Carradine's "Never Met a Man I Didn't Like" and Hoty's show-stopping "No Man Left for Me"—won't reach far beyond your sound system's speakers. Still, the music's attractiveness and the performers' abundant talents save the day, making a weak representation of the show still well worth a listen or three. —MATTHEW MURRAY

WINDY CITY
Original London Cast, 1982 (EMI/Angel) ★★★
Much of Tony Macaulay's music is too pop-rock-y for an adaptation of the classic 1920s Ben Hecht-Charles MacArthur farce *The Front Page,* but Macaulay and the gifted lyricist Dick Vosburgh created so many terrific songs for the *Windy City* that the show scores on disc in a way that it never did onstage. The story of ace newspaper reporter Hildy Johnson (played by Dennis Waterman) wanting to abandon his boss Walter Burns (played by Anton Rodgers) for marriage and a different career has some intoxicating songs ("Hey, Hallelujah," "I Can Just Imagine It," and the title song), some lovely ballads ("Wait Till I Get You on Your Own," "Long Night Again Tonight"), and only a couple of clunkers ("Waltz for Mollie," "Bensinger's Poem"). When the chorines sing "Saturday," which does sound like a 1920s tune, it reminds us how out-of-period the other songs are. Still, "Water Under the Bridge" is a terrific eleven-o'clock number and would be a great audition song for strong leading men. —PETER FILICHIA

WINGS

Original Off-Broadway Cast Members, 1995 (RCA) ★★★

Composer Jeffrey Lunden and lyricist-librettist Arthur Perlman deserve credit for tackling such difficult source material: Arthur Kopit's acclaimed play of the same title about a former aviatrix and stunt pilot recovering from a stroke. Their score for the musical *Wings* is a complex, multi-layered affair; if it doesn't quite reach the skies, it doesn't exactly crash, either. Much of the music is exquisite, but the style of the score is more like a chamber opera. There's very little in the way of "numbers," some of the vocal lines are curious, and the lyrics often eschew rhyme. However, there is one song that's likely to please those looking for an old-fashioned melody: "A Recipe for Cheesecake," here performed by Russ Thacker (the only cast member not from the stage production); it's as close to a "show tune" as *Wings* gets. The strange noises you'll hear at several points during the recording are part of a complex melding of sound design (Richard Woodbury) and orchestration (Lunden), designed to simulate the scary world inside the head of the central character, played by Linda Stephens. Recorded several years after *Wings* premiered at Chicago's Goodman Theatre and then moved to New York's Public Theater, this one-disc album contains nearly the entire show, dialogue and all. It was superbly produced by Thomas Z. Shepard; listen through headphones for the full effect.

— SETH CHRISTENFELD

WISH YOU WERE HERE

Original Broadway Cast, 1952 (RCA) ★★★

Eddie Fisher's megahit recording of the title tune helped turn this Catskills summer romance, based on Arthur Kober's play *Having Wonderful Time,* from an almost certain flop into the biggest success of a slow season. But there's much more to Harold Rome's score for his first book show to reach Broadway than that repetitive rumba. The other ballads are uncommonly fine, from the intense "They Won't Know Me" to the elegant melodic line of "Where Did the Night Go?" All of the above are lucky to be sung by Jack Cassidy; with his thrilling tenor and ardent delivery, he's the best thing on the album. His leading lady, Patricia Marand, is technically proficient but a little stolid; soubrette Sheila Bond hits some harsh, nasal notes; but Paul Valentine sings "Summer Afternoon" attractively. As befits a snappy musical of its period, *Wish You Were Here* has a steady stream of tangy comedy songs and a brassy set of Don Walker orchestrations, nicely matched by some excellent, uncredited vocal arrangements. Larry Blyden, Phyllis Newman, Florence Henderson, and Reid Shelton are in the chorus, though you probably won't be able to pick out their voices.

Original London Cast, 1953 (Philips/Sepia) ★★★★

London cast recordings of Broadway hits are often inferior to the originals, but this one bests its American cousin on several counts. The technical quality is superb once you get past an echo-y overture that seems like it was lifted directly from the Broadway album. Cyril Ornadel's musical direction is livelier than Jay Blackton's. The musical program is almost the same, though "Goodbye, Love" is replaced by "Nothing Nicer Than People" to make the heroine more sympathetic. It's fun to note the slight lyrical revisions that were made to suit West End audiences, such as changing "the BMT" to "the workmen's train." All of the Brit principals affect New York accents quite nicely, with Christopher Hewett outstanding as the unlikeliest wolf in the history of the Catskills. The rest of the London *Wish You Were Here* cast is inversely talented to the New York company: Where Jack Cassidy was the vocal muscle of the original, his London counterpart, Bruce Trent, is uninteresting (and requires a downward modulation in "They Won't Know Me"). But Shani Wallis is pert and more vocally secure than Sheila Bond as Fay, and Elizabeth Larner's Teddy has the edge on Patricia Marand's. They all sound like they're having a whale of a summer. — MARC MILLER

THE WIZ
Original Broadway Cast, 1975 (Atlantic) ★★★

L. Frank Baum hit theatrical pay dirt with *The Wonderful Wizard of Oz:* Two years after the novel's publication in 1900, Baum and partners launched a musical extravaganza based on the tale. The show was a sensation, racking up hundreds of performances in New York and around the country. After countless other variations, including an obscure 1939 film that starred some nobody named Judy Garland, Dorothy and her pals returned to Broadway in *The Wiz,* an African-American musical version of the story with a brisk book by William F. Brown and fun songs by composer-lyricist Charlie Smalls. Among the very few Broadway tunes to become mainstream hits since the 1960s, the score's infectious "Ease on Down the Road" got a lot of airplay, and Dorothy's yearning eleven-o'clock number, "Home," put Stephanie Mills (who played the heroine) on the pop map. *The Wiz* enjoyed a long run and nabbed a bunch of Tony Awards (including Best Musical). Heard on the recording are stellar turns in character roles: Clarice Taylor's Addaperle (think Good Witch of the North) is a daffy, knowing delight; Tiger Haynes' Tin Man is a smooth song-and-dance man; Hinton Battle's Scarecrow is sweet as pie; and Ted Ross' Lion is full of bravado. Mabel King sounds like a truly wicked witch, and her gospel-inflected "Don't Nobody Bring Me No Bad News" proves that, for Evillene, double negatives ain't the half of it. André De Shields is perhaps too campy as the Wiz; he sounds like a real friend of Dorothy. The arrangements are terrific, full of energy and *Soul Train* bounce. Geoffrey Holder's clever costumes and inventive direction helped turn the old tale into a fresh hit.

Film Soundtrack, 1978 (MCA, 2CDs) ★

What is it about Hollywood versions of Broadway musicals? Time and again, shows that worked onstage bomb big-time on screen. *The Wiz* seemed a natural for filming: It was a Tony-winning Broadway hit; the songs were climbing the pop charts; and the show's central concept of having the classic tale of *The Wizard of Oz* performed by a black cast was timely and hip. But what had been a brisk stage production was turned into a lumbering film; the soundtrack album is better only in that you don't have to watch the movie. The gifted Quincy Jones adapted and supervised the music, and he engaged A-list musicians: Toots Thielemans, Grady Tate, and Patti Austin, among others. But most everything is overblown here, lacking the drive and imagination that mark Jones' other work. Jones, Luther Vandross, and Ashford and Simpson contributed some negligible new material. Diana Ross was too old for the role of Dorothy, and although she sings well enough here, she begins every song as if she's just been on a weeklong crying jag. (A new ballad for Ross—"Is This What Feeling Gets?"—was cut from the movie but is on the soundtrack disc.) The nineteen-year-old Michael Jackson is irresistible as the Scarecrow, while Nipsy Russell has an affable vaudevillian flair as the Tin Man. Ted Ross repeats his Broadway role as the Lion, but his big moments are diminished. On the other hand, Mabel King reprises her show-stopping stage turn as Evillene to even more hilarious effect here; and the glamorous Lena Horne, in the role of Glinda, gives her all to "If You Believe." Richard Pryor plays the title role, and since he's not a singer, the propulsive "So You Wanted to Meet the Wizard" is reduced to bits of woeful dialogue.　　—ROBERT SANDLA

THE WIZARD OF OZ (1903, Various Composers)
Studio Recordings, Piano Rolls, Music-box Discs, 1902-08
(Hungry Tiger Press, 2CDs) ★★★

Shortly after L. Frank Baum published *The Wonderful Wizard of Oz,* a stage musical version became the biggest hit on Broadway. Finally, a century after the show opened, a masterful CD anthology reconstituted it. Great credit is due to producer David Maxine, for whom this daunting project was obviously a labor of love: There were no cast recordings, the sheet music survived only in fragments, and the show never had a set score. Originally, Baum worked on the book and lyrics, and Paul Tietjens wrote some music for the show, but those rather halting efforts soon gave way to a never-ending batch of interpolated songs. (The name A. Baldwin Sloane, frequently cited as the composer of the show, is nowhere in evidence here.) As Maxine's detailed notes make clear, *The Wizard of Oz* was topical and performer-driven, its material dropped in and removed incessantly. Among the more popular numbers were "Sammy," "Hurrah for Baffin's Bay," and the cheerfully sadistic "Football." If these titles don't sound like they should be found on the road to Oz, the plot synopsis indicates just how little of the Baum book remained; even the Cowardly Lion was reduced to the status of a bit player. The two CDs of this set are crammed with all manner of curiosities. The bulk of them are acoustical studio recordings of the songs, but a few numbers exist solely as piano rolls or as music-box tunes. Also included are some non-*Oz* songs recorded by members of the original cast. Obviously, the "score" is a patchwork, and very little of it is better than mediocre, but it's helpful that the lyrics are printed in the accompanying booklet.　　—RICHARD BARRIOS

THE WIZARD OF OZ (Arlen-Harburg-Stothart)
Film Soundtrack, 1939 (MGM/Rhino-Turner, 2CD- and 1CD-editions) ★★★★★

Is it an overstatement to call MGM's *The Wizard of Oz* the world's most beloved film? Happily, a superb job has been done with the soundtrack recording of this gem, and we owe thanks to Marilee Bradford and Bradley Flanagan for doing it so neatly and completely. Many of us have fond memories of an old MGM "highlights" LP, but on CD, we get the entire score by composer Harold Arlen and lyricist E. Y. Harburg and in the best possible sound. What's most impressive is all the musical detail that may be heard clearly for the first time. Yes, we know about "Over the Rainbow" and the other great songs performed by Judy Garland, Ray Bolger, Jack Haley, Bert Lahr, and Frank Morgan, but the background music by Herbert Stothart represents Hollywood scoring at its peak. Included on the two-CD version of the soundtrack are several other treats: multiple takes of many songs, including one of "Over the Rainbow" that comes to a premature stop with a big sneeze/cough from Garland; the song "Jitterbug," cut from the film, but tuneful and fun to hear; and the original Buddy Ebsen recording of "If I Only Had a Heart," made before Ebsen's reaction to the Tin Man's aluminum makeup forced his replacement by the far more suitable Haley. Another bonus with the two-disc set is a sumptuous booklet with rare photos and detailed notes.

Original London Cast, 1989 (JAY) ★★

What could have been more inevitable than a stage version of the great film *The Wizard of Oz*? By the 1960s, productions were cropping up on stages everywhere; one of them even had the wonderful Margaret Hamilton reprising her definitive performance as the Wicked Witch of the West. But the most determined effort to put *Oz* onstage came in the 1980s, by no less a force than London's Royal Shakespeare Company. The film's orchestrations were recreated, its special effects adapted, and variations of this production have been performed numerous times since. The cast recording is in no way comparable to the movie soundtrack, but it's passable. Conductor John Owen Edwards' tempi differ from those in the movie, and while the orchestra plays well, the results are somewhat jolting. The cast varies wildly, from a sweet Dorothy (Gillian Bevan) to an undistinguished Scarecrow-Tin Man-Lion trio to a geriatric Glinda (Joyce Grant, who doubles as Aunt Em) and on to a literal drag of a Miss Gulch/Wicked Witch (the coyly named Bille Brown). Of course, the score itself is imperishable.

New York Concert Cast, 1996 (Rhino-Turner) ★

Roger Daltrey as the Tin Man? Jackson Browne as the Scarecrow? Debra Winger as Miss Gulch and the Witch? Yes indeedy, that was the casting of a televised Lincoln Center concert version of *The Wizard of Oz,* performed only once for charity. But this disc also gives us Nathan Lane as quite a good Cowardly Lion. Of Browne and Daltrey, it might be said that they try hard. While Winger has some fun with her devilish doings, Natalie Cole's Glinda sounds extremely tentative. The Boys Choir of Harlem makes sweet sounds as the Munchkins, and the idea of casting Joel Grey as the Wizard was so good that it was carried forward to the Broadway musical "prequel" *Wicked.* Unfortunately, nothing that's good about this recording can overcome its terminal handicap: the horrific portrayal of Dorothy by Jewel, with her unending overlay of *American Idol*-style swoops and gulps. Those who revere "Over the Rainbow" are officially alerted: We're not in Kansas anymore!

Madison Square Garden Cast, 1998 (TVT) ★★★

This version of *The Wizard of Oz* was adapted from the Royal Shakespeare Company edition and an interim production by the Paper Mill Playhouse. The double role of Professor Marvel/ The Wizard was taken by Mickey Rooney, who at age seventy-eight was still a very game performer. As Miss Gulch and the Wicked Witch, Eartha Kitt has the time of her life, funneling her purring persona into this nasty pair. (Thank you, producers, for giving the bewitching Kitt the reinstated "Jitterbug" number, in which the prescient lyricist E. Y. Harburg supplied lots of Rs to rrrrroll!) While Jessica Grové is a pleasing Dorothy and Lara Teeter a good Scarecrow, Ken Page goes a bit over the top as the Lion. Another problem is the recorded sound, all reverbant and bass-ridden. This *Oz* may not cast the spell of the movie, but it has its own moments of magic.   —RICHARD BARRIOS

WOMAN OF THE YEAR
Original Broadway Cast, 1981 (Arista/Razor & Tie) ★★

This is a musicalized update of the famous Hepburn-Tracy movie, with the plot changed so that it now concerns a television anchorwoman and a cartoonist. The show is not one of composer John Kander and lyricist Fred Ebb's better efforts. In the title role, Lauren Bacall's foghorn voice sounds far worse than it did eleven years earlier in *Applause,* and the star also seems overwhelmed by having too much to do. On the recording, her limitations are clear in every number: such as "When You're Right, You're Right," her apology to the cartoonist (played by Harry Guardino); "One of the Boys," wherein she bonds with him and his colleagues; and "I Wrote the Book," which would be a pleasant ragtime number if Bacall weren't singing it. Guardino's big ballad, "Sometimes a Day Goes By," is a bit boring. Three other numbers delight in their negativity: "It Isn't Working," "I Told You So," and "Shut Up, Gerald." Just when the whole enterprise seems doomed, out comes Marilyn Cooper to duet with Bacall in "The Grass Is Always Greener," a wonderful eleven-o'clock showstopper and the only reason to buy this disc.   —PETER FILICHIA

WONDERFUL TOWN

Original Broadway Cast, 1953 (Decca/MCA) ★★★★

Nine years after their breakthrough show *On the Town,* composer Leonard Bernstein and lyricists Betty Comden and Adolph Green were hired on short notice to provide a replacement score for *Wonderful Town.* Their brilliant score was initially overshadowed by a dominant star, Rosalind Russell, who had headlined a 1942 nonmusical film version of Ruth Sherwood's comic memoir *My Sister Eileen* and agreed to become a song-and-dance gal for the Broadway musical adaptation. The show's success was immediate, with one critic chiming, "Roz for President." Russell's ace timing and rough-and-ready way with songs and dances were so beguiling that the merits of Bernstein's score weren't fully appreciated right away; filled with wit and sharp pastiche, it cleverly gives the more difficult parts to other characters in order to let Russell's Ruth thrive within a limited vocal range. The original cast album conveys most of the magic of the show: the complex comedy-and-music structure of "Conversation Piece"; the gentle parody "Ohio," in which Russell harmonizes with the sweet yet assertive Eileen of Edith (later Edie) Adams; and the wild "Conga!" with the Brazilian navy. No one would say that Russell was a singer of any polish, nor does her tone fall liltingly on the ear. Subsequent Ruths would have more voice, but Russell was unique and irresistible.

Television Cast, 1958 (Columbia) ★★★★

Wonderful Town was one of the glories of the age of the television musical spectacular. Repeating her stage role, Rosalind Russell was supported by a mostly new company, although Jordan Bentley (as the dumb jock) and Cris Alexander (as the drugstore guy) were retained from the original cast. Recorded in stereo, the performance stacks up quite well against the mono original. Jacqueline McKeever is nearly as good an Eileen as Edith (Edie) Adams, and Sydney Chaplin as Bob Baker outdoes the original's George Gaynes in "A Quiet Girl" and "It's Love." Nevertheless, the intervening five years (and countless performances of *Auntie Mame*) had taken a toll on Russell; the verve and humor are still there, albeit with an added soupçon of diva attitude, but her vocal decline exacerbates her tendency to bully her way through the music by hook or by crook. She's still Roz, however, and this is a fine recording of the score.

London Cast, 1986 (First Night) ★★★

Quality will out, at least some of the time, and *Wonderful Town* finally was appreciated on its own merits in the enthusiastically received London revival that yielded this recording. Even with a scaled-down orchestra including a synthesizer, this production soared. The quality of the show was more apparent than ever because its wagon wasn't hitched to a star. The wit of "One Hundred Easy Ways (to Lose a Man)," the daffy inventiveness of "Wrong Note Rag," the hilarious period charm of "My Darlin' Eileen," and all the rest became clear. Maureen Lipman has no difficulty with Ruth's character or music, and her American accent is fine; this expert performance is smart, deadpan-witty, hopeful, exuberant, and incisive. The Eileen of Emily Morgan is sweet if a shade thin-voiced, and Ray Lonnen is a bit weak as Bob Baker, but the rest of the cast is energetic and committed even as they struggle with various Noo Yawk accents. This is an enjoyable performance that makes a good case for the show as an ensemble piece.

Studio Cast, 1996 (JAY, 2CDs) ★★★★

A complete recording of *Wonderful Town*—including all of the music cues and dances—was inevitable and necessary. Karen Mason offers the best sung of all recorded Ruths so far, and she doesn't stint on the comedy in one of the highlights: the hilarious "Ruth's Stories" sequence, with its "literary" quick-changes and droll Bernstein interjections. Rebecca Luker is an outstanding Eileen, if perhaps just a shade too aware of her own charm, and Ron Raines is a better Baker than his predecessors. The supporting cast and chorus are fine, and the extended dialogue sections give a real sense of the show. Conductor John Owen Edwards does his customary efficient work.

Studio Cast, 1998 (EMI) ★★★★

Conductor Simon Rattle, a Leonard Bernstein partisan, decided to give the *Wonderful Town* score another big studio production. His Ruth, Kim Criswell, is a veteran of many show recordings, but the casting of the other leads was more adventurous: the much-loved Broadway singer-actress Audra McDonald as Eileen and the imposing operatic baritone Thomas Hampson as Baker. This time, the composer and conductor are the stars in what is orchestrally the best *Wonderful Town* ever. Under Sir Simon, the Birmingham Contemporary Music Group sounds like the finest pit orchestra of all time; every instrumental line is transparently clear and the whole of it a testament to Bernstein's wit, lyricism, and comedic savvy. The score's usual balance is further shifted with the ascension of Eileen; even though McDonald's voice might be a shade mature for the role, she's such an intelligent and intuitive artist that she dominates the proceedings vocally. Criswell tries hard, but her characterization is all on the surface, with externally applied shtick accessories. Hampson overwhelms and oversings his role, though he does add some good humor to the "Rigoletto" line in "What a Waste." Brent Barrett's "Pass the Football" is well sung, and operatic baritone Rodney Gilfry is excellent in two small roles.

Broadway Cast, 2003 (DRG) ★★★★

As the preceding roster of *Wonderful Town* recordings attests, this show has been especially fortunate in the studio. That certainly applies to the cast album of this revival, which was based on the 2000 Encores! presentation starring Donna Murphy. Not since Roz Russell has a star so completely dominated the proceedings—and this one can really sing! Murphy is a sensational Ruth, wry and funny and romantic by turns, all the while interacting fully with the other performers. Just listen to the spectrum of vocal colors she produces in "Swing" and you'll know that a true musical comedy expert is at work here. Jennifer Westfeldt is a charming Eileen, the rest of the cast (including Gregg Edelman and Michael McGrath) operates at a high level, and Rob Fisher conducts Bernstein's terrific score with his usual skill. As an appendix, DRG has included recordings of four songs from the show as performed by Betty Comden and Adolph Green, circa 1953.   —RICHARD BARRIOS

Original Broadway Cast, 2001 (Columbia/Fynsworth Alley) ★★★★

Studs Terkel's *Working,* the 1972 best-selling volume of interviews with Americans discussing the pros and cons of their occupations, struck Stephen Schwartz as a good idea for a musical; so he set about rounding up a group of songwriters, including himself, to musicalize Terkel's pungent, poignant chats. Craig Carnelia, Micki Grant, James Taylor, Mary Rodgers, and Susan Birkenhead turned out song vignettes on a wide spectrum of related subjects. Everyone from a newsboy to a retiree to a housewife to a cleaning lady showed up onstage to declare their highs and woes. A number of the songs—Carnelia's "Just a Housewife" and "The Mason" and Schwartz's "It's an Art"—became popular on the cabaret circuit. Grant's swinging "Cleanin' Women" is another catchy item, as is just about everything else on this resonant disc that features Kirk Nurock's tingling arrangements of the songs. To represent the hard-working multitudes, Schwartz tapped some stalwart Broadway singers and dancers: Lenora Nemetz, Joe Mantegna, Arny Freeman, Susan Bigelow, David Patrick Kelly, Bob Gunton, and others put elbow grease into their singing. The cast is so rich in talent that Patti LuPone appears in the ensemble, with no solo spot. Fynsworth Alley's disc includes six bonus tracks, four featuring Carnelia singing his own songs in his tremulous baritone.

Los Angeles Cast, 1999 (L.A. Theatre Works, 2CDs) ★★★

For this revival, Stephen Schwartz updated the Studs Terkel adaptation he'd overseen decades earlier and to which he had contributed along with Craig Carnelia, Micki Grant, Mary Rodgers, Susan Birkenhead, and James Taylor. That skilled group came up with a series of touching songs about the sense of accomplishment mingled with compromised self-esteem that's experienced by workers in many fields of endeavor. Along with adding more contemporary references, like chat about computers in the workplace, Schwartz used this recording opportunity to create a document of almost the entire show. The two-disc package includes not only the potent songs but also the pithy monologues that were lifted from Terkel's bestseller and then tweaked for dramatic effect. The result is that a much more rounded sense of the book's power is captured, as compared with the original Broadway cast album. The company rounded up by L.A. Theatre Works mover and shaker Susan Albert Loewenberg includes Orson Bean, Harry Groener, B. J. Ward, Michael Kostroff, Eileen Barnett, Kaitlin Hopkins, Vincent Tumeo, Kenna Ramsey, and Vickilyn Reynolds. Performing before a live audience only a few times, these singer-actors may not have had time to develop the flair of a cast who've refined the material during a Broadway run, but there is no featherbedding here. And it sure is a treat to hear the always lovable Bean, whose list of Broadway credits is surprisingly short, doing so well by Carnelia's "Joe."
— DAVID FINKLE

A YEAR WITH FROG AND TOAD
Original Cast, 2002 (PS Classics) ★★★

Although *A Year With Frog and Toad* played only a short time on Broadway in 2003, previous runs at the Children's Theatre Company of Minneapolis (where the show got started) and Off-Broadway were successful enough to yield this playful cast recording. The show is faithful to the Arnold Lobel books on which it was based, and the disc documents the witty songs by composer Robert Reale and lyricist-librettist Willie Reale that perfectly capture four seasons in the lives of two amphibian friends. These roles are nicely performed by Jay Goede and Mark Linn-Baker, with Danielle Ferland, Kate Reinders (who didn't follow the show to Broadway) and Frank Vlastnik rounding out the cast and getting plenty of opportunity to shine. Vlastnik's depiction of the Snail's determination to deliver the mail is almost as fall-down funny on disc, in the country-infused "The Letter" and its numerous reprises, as it was onstage; and his eleven-o'clock number, "I'm Coming Out of My Shell," is one of the score's treasures. There are warm moments such as Goede's touching "Alone" and the sweet "Merry Almost Christmas," but it's the score's willingness to embrace innocent fun shamelessly in songs such as "Cookies" (a tribute to yummy desserts) and "Getta Loada Toad" (a group number with a terrific comic and musical build) that sets it apart from the pack. A show that can truly be enjoyed by the whole family, *A Year With Frog and Toad* loses only a bit of dialogue in this recording but retains all of the qualities that made it one of the most charming new musicals in years. —MATTHEW MURRAY

YOU NEVER KNOW
World Premiere Cast, 2001
(Fynsworth Alley) ★★★

You never know, indeed. Although composer-lyricist Cole Porter supposedly considered this 1938 floppola the best show he'd written up to then, twenty years later he commented to one of his eventual biographers, George Eells: "Why anyone ever dug up *You Never Know* I shall never know. It was the worst show with which I was ever connected." It's a musical adaptation by Rowland Leigh of Siegfried Geyer's *By Candlelight*, which was in turn an adaptation of a Viennese operetta. In the 1980s, musical maven Paul Lazarus put together a new version of the tuner from bits of the original,

---

ALL-TIME FAVORITES OF
COMPOSER-LYRICISTS

*Robert Lopez
and Jeff Marx*

1. Avenue Q

2. A Chorus Line

3. Sweeney Todd

4. Gypsy

5. Cabaret

6. West Side Story

7. Hedwig and the
   Angry Inch

8. Company

9. Oliver!

10. Assassins

interpolated some songs from other Porter works, and then tried out the result at a couple of regional theaters. This CD is based on the 1991 Pasadena Playhouse treatment and is labeled as the "world premiere" recording. The big numbers from the original score were "From Alpha to Omega" and "At Long Last Love"—but, for some inexplicable reason, Lazarus doesn't include all the lyrics to either of those tunes. What is here is extremely well sung by Kristin Chenoweth, Harry Groener, Donna McKechnie, David Garrison, Angela Teek, and former Fynsworth Alley head Bruce Kimmel in his Guy Haines incarnation. —DAVID FINKLE

YOUR ARMS TOO SHORT TO BOX WITH GOD
Original Broadway Cast, 1976 (ABC/no CD) ★★

Just as *The Wiz* was the black rock musical version of *The Wizard of Oz,* this show might be considered the black rock musical version of *Jesus Christ Superstar.* That's because *Your Arms Too Short to Box With God* also deals with the last seven days in the life of Jesus, from Palm Sunday to Good Friday to Easter Sunday, but the profound difference between the two shows can be gleaned at a glance at the tune stack. While the entire score of *Superstar* is by Andrew Lloyd Webber and Tim Rice, the song list for this musical is littered with asterisks, plus signs, and minus signs before every item to indicate different authorship. Micki Grant wrote the eight asterisked songs; Alex Bradford penned the nine plus-signed songs; and H. B. Barnum wrote the one minus-signed song. They're all gospel tunes that attempt to be stirring, but none of them has any real power, passion, or distinction. To paraphrase the much better show on the same subject: You won't know how to love them. —PETER FILICHIA

YOU'RE A GOOD MAN, CHARLIE BROWN
Studio Cast, 1966 (MGM/no CD) ★★★

Out of print for decades, this recording was one of the first musical theater "concept albums." Few people seem to be aware that *You're a Good Man, Charlie Brown* began not as an Off-Broadway show but as a recording of ten songs by composer-lyricist Clark Gesner, inspired by Charles Schultz's extraordinarily popular "Peanuts" comic strip. Very difficult if not impossible to track down, the LP is noteworthy for several reasons aside from its historical value as the basis for one of the most successful Off-Broadway musicals ever. The four-member cast—Orson Bean as Charlie Brown, Barbara Minkus as Lucy, Bill Hinnant as Snoopy, and Gesner himself as Linus—is excellent. Although Bean is probably best known as a television game-show panelist, he was a fine actor, and his Charlie Brown is fully endearing even if Bean never really creates the impression of being a child. Minkus, on the other hand, does have a "little girl" voice that she puts to excellent use in Lucy's numbers, especially "Schroeder" and "The Doctor Is In." Gesner is charming in his one solo spot, Linus' "My Blanket and Me." Finally, Bill Hinnant is thoroughly delightful as Snoopy, a role that he owned for several years in various productions of the show. This is the only recording of the score to boast a full orchestra; those trumpets in the title song and those strings in "Snoopy" really add something to the music. Legendary conductor Jay Blackton leads the orchestra.

Original Off-Broadway Cast, 1967 (MGM/Decca) ★★★★

This recording of *You're a Good Man, Charlie Brown* is recommended for the excellent if not definitive performances of its cast. Gary Burghoff (later famous as Radar in the smash *M*A*S*H* television series) is perfect as Charlie Brown; it's a difficult assignment in that the character has to seem hapless as everyone (including himself) thinks he is, yet he must be entertaining and sympathetic to the audience in an Everyman sort of way. Burghoff walks that line beautifully and is persuasive in all of Charlie's vocal moments. Reva Rose is equally perfect in the role of Lucy; her semi-screaming of the high notes in "The Doctor Is In" (or "Dr. Lucy") is priceless, and she's a stitch when giving tons of wrong information to brother Linus in "Little Known Facts." Bob Balaban is an adorable Linus, and Bill Hinnant is even better as Snoopy here than he is on the concept album; he's also given more to do, thanks to the addition of the "Red Baron" scene and other juicy sections of dialogue taken directly from the "Peanuts" strip. Karen Johnson has virtually no solo moments in the thankless role of Patty, and Skip Hinnant (Bill's brother) has only slightly more to do as Schroeder. There are a few significant additions to the score for the show's stage debut. Among them are Charlie Brown's extended solo in "T-E-A-M" and "Book Report," a clever ensemble number in which Charlie, Lucy, Linus, and Schroeder each take different approaches to the same homework assignment. The title song has also been expanded considerably. The score's instrumentation is limited to piano and percussion, but the sound quality of the recording is exceptionally good and there's a palpable theatricality about it. Decca Broadway's CD reissue of the album contains four demo tracks performed by Gesner and Barbara Minkus, with Gesner at the piano.

Broadway Cast, 1999 (RCA) ★★

When the original production of *You're a Good Man, Charlie Brown* transferred uptown after a downtown, Off-Broadway run of more than fifteen hundred performances, it closed within a month. By 1999, the musical had received countless amateur and regional productions, which made it a hard sell at Broadway ticket prices. Perhaps the fear of overfamiliarity was what prompted the producers to have Andrew Lippa augment Clark Gesner's original score. Aside from aggressively rearranging Gesner's music, Lippa contributed a catchy new section of the title song, but two of his added numbers are questionable: Schroeder's "Beethoven Day" is a joyously rhythmic pop tune, but the problem is that this fussy, "serious-type" character would never express himself in such a way; and "My New Philosophy" simply isn't very funny, although the brilliant Kristin Chenoweth manages to mine comic gold from the number anyway. If nothing else, the recording is worthwhile for Chenoweth's hilarious performance in the newly created role of Sally Brown. There's also fine work from Anthony Rapp as her brother, Charlie; Ilana Levine as Lucy; B. D. Wong as a lisping Linus; and Roger Bart in a winning turn as Snoopy. As Schroeder, Stanley Wayne Mathis does a fine job with "Beethoven Day" even if the song is wildly inappropriate to the character. The largely superfluous role of Patty was eliminated for this production and replaced by Sally, who became an integral part of the show, thanks largely to Chenoweth's portrayal. —MICHAEL PORTANTIERE

YOUR OWN THING
Original Broadway Cast, 1968 (RCA) ★★

"'Tis wonder that enwraps me thus, yet 'tis not madness. What a groovy lady!" And there you have the central joke of this hit Off-Broadway musical, loosely adapted by librettist Donald Driver and songwriters Hal Hester and Danny Apolinar from Shakespeare's *Twelfth Night*. Set in a swinging Illyria that looks and sounds like the East Village (where the musical played for over two years), *Your Own Thing* has a mild subversiveness, an abundance of electric guitars and drums (Hayward Morris' orchestrations were beefed up for the album by Peter Matz), and a cheerful your-own-bag-is-where-it's-at philosophy. Some of the songs are undiluted

Shakespeare, others are closer to *Hullabaloo,* yet you'll be surprised at how well "Come Away, Death" and "Hunca Munca" complement each other. Unfortunately, the score also perpetuates the bogus philosophy of most rock musicals: pretty voices are, like, uncool, man. Leland Palmer's breathy Viola makes some unpleasant noises, even in the ballads, while Tom Ligon's Orson (read: Orsino) and Marcia Rodd's Olivia are just adequate from a vocal standpoint. (Rodd replaced Marian Mercer before the recording date.) Just about the only real musical comedy all-rounder on hand is Rusty (later Russ) Thacker, as Sebastian; it's a good thing that he gets some of the better material, such as "I'm on My Way to the Top" and a sweetly ironic reprise of "The Middle Years." Much of what made *Your Own Thing* such a groovy evening was visual: the Beatle haircuts, the Carnaby Street threads, rear-projection gags that poked fun at everyone from John Lindsay to John Wayne, and so on. Still, the score is energetic, ingratiating, and sometimes ingenious. If only it were better sung! —MARC MILLER

ZANNA, DON'T!
Original Off-Broadway Cast, 2003 (PS Classics) ★★

Like the show itself, the cast recording of composer-lyricist Tim Acito's "musical fairy tale" *Zanna, Don't!* will probably appeal mainly to teenagers or early-twentysomethings with limited interest in musical theater. Anyone with more sophisticated taste will find Acito's work unpolished and sometimes downright sloppy. His music is generally fine, a series of pop-influenced melodies well in keeping with the youthful, bouncy, otherworldly tone that helps sell this musical about a world where homosexuality is the dominant orientation. But Acito's lyrics may well cause fits among purists because they're inaccurately stressed throughout and very poorly rhymed, as in: love/enough, lover/another, clues/you, this/is, and town/around—all of these examples from the first song alone! Lyrical transgressions aside, Acito's songs often make for moderately enjoyable listening, with at least one—a high-school musical spoof about heterosexuals in the military titled "Don't Ask, Don't Tell"—demonstrating a cleverness that's worthy of notice. Jai Rodriguez gives an endearing performance as the title character who's determined to help his classmates find love, but it's Anika Larsen's high belting in "I Ain't Got Time (for Nothin' But Love)" that brings *Zanna, Don't!* as close as it ever gets to excitement. —MATTHEW MURRAY

ZIEGFELD FOLLIES OF 1919
Original Cast, 1919-20
(Smithsonian/no CD) ★★★

By the time of its thirteenth installment, Ziegfeld's legendary beauty-and-music revue was a Broadway institution. Some historians hold that this 1919 version was the greatest of all Follies, although others contend that the 1936 version, headlined by Bob Hope and Josephine Baker, brought the revue to a brilliant, posthumous apex four years after Ziegfeld's death. Fortunately, a large number of recordings exist to back up claims for the Ziegfeld Follies of 1919. This was probably the most star-laden of all the editions: Eddie Cantor, Bert Williams, Marilyn Miller, Van and Schenck, Eddie Dowling, and, in a cornerstone of Broadway mythology, tenor John Steel introducing Irving Berlin's "A Pretty Girl Is Like a Melody." Not all of the cast members left recordings of their contributions, but enough remained for The Smithsonian Collection to issue a fine compilation. Here is the trag-

ALL-TIME FAVORITES OF
THE VILLAGE VOICE
COLUMNIST

Michael Musto

1. A Chorus Line

2. Funny Girl

3. Gypsy

4. Chicago

5. Sweet Charity

6. Follies

7. A Little Night Music

8. Annie

9. Hairspray

10. Mame

ically short-lived Williams in "Somebody" and "Everybody Wants a Key to My Cellar"; Cantor having a ball with Berlin's "You'd Be Surprised"; and Van and Schenck's distinctive, close harmony in "Mandy." The sound quality of these acoustical recordings is variable and distinctly lo-fi, but this is history come to life. (One succulent item was dropped from the show during tryouts and not recorded: "Perfume of Opium.") Steel's "Pretty Girl" is alone worth having the whole album, the annotations are excellent—and Cantor and Williams are nothing to sneeze at, either.

—RICHARD BARRIOS

ZIEGFELD FOLLIES OF 1936
Encores! Concert Cast, 1999 (Decca) ★★★★★

You can always tell a Hans Spialek-orchestrated overture: The brass announces something important, the woodwinds flutter and swoop upward in anticipation, and the tension builds to a point where the only thing that can break it is a great song. Spialek's overture to Vernon Duke's score for *Ziegfeld Follies of 1936* takes in one standard ("I Can't Get Started") and several interesting not-quite-standards ("My Red-Letter Day," "Words Without Music," "Island in the West Indies"). As conducted superbly by Rob Fisher, it's the entry point to one of the most fully realized excursions into the past ever attempted by City Center Encores! With the series' repertoire growing steadily safer over the years, this title was a real anomaly: an ancient, not particularly well-regarded topical revue with forgotten Ira Gershwin lyrics and an all-star cast that could never be replicated. Well, are you in for a surprise! Nearly every number is a gem and nearly every member of the Encores! cast is up to the material. "Words Without Music" has one of the strangest, most sophisticated melodies written for Broadway in the 1930s, and Ruthie Henshall matches Gertrude Niesen, who introduced it, for individuality; throaty and idiosyncratic, Henshall is like Tammy Grimes with more musicality. Christine Ebersole, handling Eve Arden's songs, is insinuating in "Island in the West Indies" (which serves up another fabulous Spialek arrangement) and hilarious in "The Economic Situation," a fascinating Gershwin curiosity. Later, Ebersole shares "I Can't Get Started" with Peter Scolari, who emulates Bob Hope's comic-leading-man timing and light-but-secure voice perfectly. So luxurious is the casting that such Broadway stalwarts as Howard McGillin, Jim and Bob Walton, and Karen Ziemba are nearly crowded out, though all are exemplary in what they're given to do. Stephanie Pope lacks heat and Mary Testa is a slightly bland Fanny Brice—but when a time capsule is this beautifully engineered, the best thing to do is shut up, climb aboard, and enjoy the ride. Great cover art, too.

—MARC MILLER

ZOMBIE PROM
Original Off-Broadway Cast, 1996 (First Night) ★★★★

The talented team of librettist-lyricist John Dempsey and composer Dana P. Rowe mined the familiar terrain of *Little Shop/Rocky Horror* teen-nostalgia-science-fiction-horror, with a little *Bye Bye Birdie* and *Grease* thrown in, and came up with this short-running Off-Broadway lark. As the title suggests, it's about an undead senior in Eisenhower's America who comes back to attend his high school prom and reclaim the love of Toffee, his sweetheart. Sure, *Zombie Prom* is a goof—but it's a well-structured, modestly scaled goof with smart pastiche melodies and fun, intelligent lyrics that really rhyme. Listen to how smoothly the songs segue into dialogue and into other songs on this spiffily produced CD, which features an appreciative essay by musical theater historian Martin Gottfried. And the cast is among the best of the 1990s: Jessica-Snow Wilson is quite an adorable Toffee ("Where once that girl was effervescent / She's now a poster-child depressant / A problematic post-pubescent"), while Richard Roland is a sweet, supple-voiced zombie. As a scandal-sheet editor who gets mixed up with the denizens of Enrico Fermi High, Richard Muenz for once finds a role wherein his natural hamminess is an asset. And as Delilah Strict, the school's horrifying principal, Karen Murphy is a powerful-voiced camp diva with just the right sense of mockery. In the theater, her "Rules, Regulations, and Respect" stopped the show; we're lucky to have it preserved. —MARC MILLER

ZORBA
Original Broadway Cast, 1968 (Capitol) ★★★★★

Are you sitting down? When I saw *Zorba* in its original Broadway production (not the horrible Anthony Quinn revival), I thought it a better show than *Cabaret,* the previous Broadway outing of the team that put this show together: composer John Kander, lyricist Fred Ebb, and director Harold Prince. To me, *Zorba* is more emotional, deals with life more broadly, and is brilliantly theatrical. I find it a deeper show—not your typical, presentational, razzle-dazzle, Kander and Ebb musical. Many of their scores are made up of a succession of special-material songs, but *Zorba* has an honest, mature, character- and plot-driven score. The opening number, "Life Is," perfectly sets the theme of the evening. (The first line, "Life is what you do while you're waiting to die," was changed in subsequent productions to "Life is what you do till the moment you die.") "Happy Birthday" is a wonderfully touching number for the death scene of Madame Hortense, while "Why Can't I Speak" is an excruciatingly beautiful song that exemplifies the protagonist Niko's emotional problems. Although the events in this libretto may be tragic, the audience leaves the theater moved, enlightened, even uplifted—and the cast album has the same effect on the listener. Herschel Bernardi, Maria Karnilova, John Cunningham, Carmen Alvarez, and Lorraine Serabian drive this recording with their sincerity, energy, and abundant talent.

Broadway Cast, 1983 (RCA) ★★

Anthony Quinn and Lila Kedrova, who played the title character and Mme. Hortense in the 1964 nonmusical film *Zorba the Greek,* starred in this revival of the Kander and Ebb musical *Zorba.* Unfortunately, Quinn sings so poorly here that many people will find this recording unlistenable. The other performers, including Robert Westenberg as Niko and Debbie Shapiro (later Debbie Gravitte) as The Woman, fare much better. —KEN BLOOM

THE ZULU AND THE ZAYDA
Original Broadway Cast, 1965 (Columbia/no CD) ★

This was an odd little show, billed as "a play with music." Columbia probably decided to record *The Zulu and the Zayda* because the songs are by composer-lyricist Harold Rome. The fact that the cast included Menasha Skulnik, a Yiddish theater star in one of his final Broadway performances, plus Ossie Davis and Louis Gossett, perhaps enhanced the label's interest. The score combines South African folk-style music and Yiddish theater-style songs. Particularly catchy is the first-act closer: Skulnik gives his new-found African friends a lesson in Yiddish, teaching them the meaning of "Oisgetzaichnet" (translation: "Out of this world!") after they have sung "Like the Breeze Blows," an uplifting song of freedom. Skulnik's duet with Gossett ("It's Good to Be Alive") is charming, as is his solo "River of Tears." Most of the songs are attractive, but the show remains a play with music rather than a full-scale musical. The LP is a collector's item, alphabetically the last on many a musical theater buff's shelf. —JEFFREY DUNN

Index: ★ ★ ★ ★ ★
Five-Star Recordings

Please refer to the pages shown to find the top-rated recordings. Some shows have more than one five-star recording (on the same or different pages).

Index: Composers/Lyricists